Research Methods
for Business and Management

Research is a creative and scholarly endeavor.

L. R. Gay
Florida International University, Miami, Florida

P. L. Diehl
St. Thomas University, Miami, Florida

Research Methods for Business and Management

Macmillan Publishing Company
NEW YORK

Maxwell Macmillan Canada
TORONTO

Maxwell Macmillan International
NEW YORK   OXFORD   SINGAPORE   SIDNEY

Editor: Charles E. Stewart
Production Supervisor: Paul Smolenski
Production Manager: Helen Wallace
Text and Cover Design: Robert Freese

Photo Credits: **Frontispiece:** *My Gems* by William C. Harnett. Reproduced by permission of the National Gallery of Art; **Chapter 1:** Reprinted by permission of Putnam Publishing Group. Copyright © 1968 by Econ-Verlag GMBH. English translation copyright © 1969 by Micheal Heron and Souvenir Press. **Chapter 2:** The Kobal Collection/Superstock, Inc.; **Chapter 3:** "The Sundicates" by Rembrandt. Reproduced by permission of Rijksmuseum, Amsterdam; **Chapter 4:** From Gorgo. Reproduced by permission of King International Corporation; **Chapter 5:** From "The Picture of Dorian Gray," © 1945 by Loew's Inc. Reproduced by permission of Metro-Goldwyn-Mayer, Inc.; **Chapter 6:** Courtesy of Antioch Bookplate Company, Yellow Springs, Ohio; **Chapter 7:** The Kobal Collection/Superstock, Inc.; **Chapter 8:** © 1939 Turner Entertainment Co. All Rights Reserved; **Chapter 9:** Reproduced by permission of David Strickler. Monkmeyer Press Photo Service; **Chapter 10:** The Kobal Collection/ Superstock, Inc.; **Chapter 11:** The Kobal Collection/Superstock, Inc.; **Chapter 12:** From "The Wolf Man," 1941. Courtesy of Universal Pictures; **Chapter 13:** AP/Wide World Photos; **Chapter 14:** "Study of Erasmus of Rotterdam by Holbein." Courtesy of the Louvre Museum; **Chapter 15:** The Kobal Collection/Superstock, Inc.

This book was set in Souvenir Light by The Clarinda Company
and was printed and bound by R. R. Donnelley & Sons Company—Harrisonburg.
The cover was printed by R. R. Donnelley & Sons Company—Harrisonburg.

Copyright © 1992 by Macmillan Publishing Company, a division of Macmillan, Inc.

PRINTED IN THE UNITED STATES OF AMERICA

Macmillan Publishing Company
866 Third Avenue, New York, New York 10022

Macmillan Publishing Company is part of
The Maxwell Communication Group of Companies

Collier Macmillan Canada, Inc.
1200 Eglinton Avenue East
Suite 200
Don Mills, Ontario M3C 3N1

LIBRARY OF CONGRESS CATALOGING IN PUBLICATION DATA
Gay, L. R.
    Research methods for business and management/L. R. Gay,
P. L. Diehl.
        p.   cm.
    Includes bibliographical references and indexes.
    ISBN 0-02-340810-3
    1. Management—Research—Methodology. 2. Business—Research—
—Methodology. I. Diehl, P. L. II. Title.
HD30.4.G39 1992
650'.072—dc20   91-18761
                                                            CIP

Printing: 1 2 3 4 5 6 7 8   Year: 2 3 4 5 6 7 8 9 0 1

To Cristina and Lori—May you "Have it all!"

Acknowledgments

We would like to thank the following individuals for their review of the text and for their helpful suggestions: Richard S. Blackburn, University of North Carolina–Chapel Hill; Bill Brooks, Friends University; Michael P. Dumler, Illinois State University; Ricky W. Griffin, Texas A&M University; Michael Segalla, Baruch College.

We express our sincere appreciation to our research students. Their efforts, struggles, questions, and suggestions add immeasurably to our understanding of the learning process.

Our colleagues, including Drs. Laura Melvin, Barbara Graham, Paul Wieser, and Professor Peter Diehl, are always appreciated for their insight and suggestions.

The librarians at our universities, most especially Philip Browning of St. Thomas University and Steve Morris at Florida International University, were of great assistance to us.

We are grateful to the Literary Executor of the late Sir Ronald A. Fisher, F.R.S., to Dr. Frank Yates, F.R.S., and the Longman Group Ltd., London, for permission to reprint Tables VII, III, V, and IV from their book *Statistical Tables for Biological, Agricultural and Medical Research* (6th Edition, 1974).

Last but not least, our families provided support and encouragement that allowed us to complete this task, and we thank them for it.

Student Preface

Like employers, colleges and schools of business are increasingly concerned over the ability of their graduates to collect and present data for decision making in a thorough and professional manner. Increasingly the business climate emphasizes efforts at improving productivity, handling extraordinary technological change, and managing with a shortage of resources, including humans. As business schools and employers are realizing, these conditions tend to favor the manager who is able to support his or her ideas with concrete evidence. As a small example, an issue of *Psychology Today* ran an article ("Work or Perk," 11/88) lamenting the lack of quantitative evaluation of the effectiveness of expensive management training programs. Concrete evidence and quantitative evaluation do not come from those who rely on intuition and authority but from persons who possess the necessary skill, knowledge, and ability to evaluate and conduct research in areas previously closed to the more quantitatively trained business major. As change becomes even more rapid, and accountability and competition increase, the need for training in business-and-management research is very likely to increase, thus expanding the market demand for graduates skilled in business-and-management research. The underlying need for these skills has been expressed in the following way:

> The behavioral sciences have enormous potential to add to organizational effectiveness. Carefully managed interventions like quality circles have the potential to aid managers as they attempt to compete in both domestic and international arenas. The key to effectiveness may be to avoid a faddish, bandwagon approach and, instead, to develop an appropriate menu of interventions that we have some basis for recommending and some understanding of how to manage. (Griffin. June, 1988. *Academy of Management Journal,* p. 356.)

The research course you are beginning is intended to help you become competent in finding, evaluating, and applying research findings to a wide variety of problems you will encounter both as a student and also as a working professional.

INSTRUCTIONAL PHILOSOPHY

The philosophy guiding the development of this text is the conviction that an introductory research course should be skill- rather than knowledge-oriented, and application- rather than theory-oriented. It is not our intention to have you, as a student, become confused and turned off by excessive theory and statistical jargon.

Neither is it our intention to have you gain complete mastery in your understanding of theory as it relates to research. Rather, our intention is to provide a book that will enable you to acquire the skills, knowledge, and ability to be a competent consumer and producer of research in management. The emphasis is not on what you know but rather on what you are able to do with your knowledge. We recognize that expertise involves more than the acquisition of skills and knowledge; through experience one acquires insights, intuitions, and strategies related to business-and-management research. Further, we make a basic assumption that there is considerable overlap between the competencies required of a competent consumer and those of a competent producer of research. We have found that individuals are better at evaluating the work of others when they have experienced the major tasks involved in the process. Finally, we have selected a point of view that emphasizes research aimed at hypothesis testing in support of decision making. It is our belief that you are better served by understanding classical research design and methodology first before learning to accept the shortcuts and threats to validity imposed by the real world.

INSTRUCTIONAL STRATEGY

The overall strategy of this text is to develop expertise through acquisition of knowledge and involvement in the processes related to management research. This book is designed to allow you (a) to read about research problems, designs, and reports, (b) to become familiar with good examples of reports that have been published by professionals in the business and management field, and finally (c) to create your own mock study and report.

Chapter 1, which comprises *Part One* of the text, provides an overview of the book as well as an introduction to research for managers. It emphasizes the application of scientific method to an area too often characterized, because of the emphasis on managing people, as an "art rather than a science." Thus it provides a bridge between the behavioral sciences and quantitative analysis. By applying the knowledge, skills, and ability provided by research in the behavioral sciences to management decisions, you will be able to justify decisions on a rational basis rather than by primarily intuitive input. In addition, you will find also that decision making can be supported by factoring in the human element rather than by simply emphasizing the bottom-line approach of the more quantitative decision bases. In Chapter 1 you will become familiar with the approaches to research as classified by purpose and also as classified by method. Following the first chapter, there is an example of an excellent professional research article for you to read. At the beginning, you probably won't understand much of what you read, but as you continue through the textbook, we will refer back to that article so that you can gain greater understanding about what the author was doing. Also, as a part of Chapter 1, you will be introduced to your first project. Project I requires you to find a research article on your own and evaluate it using the categories presented in Chapter 1. The information that follows may also give you some insight not only into understanding the research article in Chapter 1, but also into the way the rest of this textbook is organized.

The basic research report is divided into several main sections and subsections. Generally the format is as follows:

Introduction

Statement of the Problem
Review of the Related Literature
Statement of the Hypothesis

Method

Subjects/Samples
Instruments
Design
Procedures

Results

Discussion and Conclusions

In this outline, Introduction, Method, Results, and Discussion and Conclusions are all main sections. The *Statement of the Problem, Review of the Related Literature,* and *Statement of the Hypothesis* are subsections under the main section Introduction; similarly, *Subjects/Samples, Instruments, Design,* and *Procedures* are subsections under the main section Method. The Results and Discussion and Conclusions main sections seldom have subsections. Sometimes Discussion and Conclusions are presented as separate main sections.

Beginning with *Part Two,* the text is designed to reflect the organization just discussed. At the beginning of the part, you will be given some guidelines for the project to be completed in that part. Part Two, which is chapter 2, then covers all the material included under the main section Introduction. Reading this chapter will help you in selecting your research topic, carrying out a review of the literature, and formulating a research hypothesis. The chapter and part close with an example of a student project much like the one you will be expected to produce after you have completed Part Two.

Chapter 2 continues the emphasis on becoming a competent consumer of research as you carry out a preliminary evaluation of existing research. In this chapter, we have included practical suggestions for the use of computers for word processing, outlining, and literature searches.

Part Three covers all the material included under the main section Method. Just as in Part Two, Part Three begins with the guidelines for Project III, which is to be completed when you have finished Part Three. Due to the amount of material to be covered, this part has been divided into chapters that cover the subsections under Method.

Chapter 3 gives an overview of the methods used in carrying out research. We have discussed various types of research plans and proposals. In addition, there is an emphasis on the ethical and legal issues related to research. **Chapter 4** covers the subsection regarding Subjects/Samples, **Chapter 5** covers the subsection regarding Instruments, and **Chapters 6** through **10** cover the wide variety of Designs and Procedures which may be included in a research study and report. At the beginning of Chapter 4, there are guidelines for completing the Subjects subsection of your project. At the beginning of Chapter 5, you will find guidelines for completing the Instrument subsection, and at the beginning of Chapter 6, there are guidelines for completing the Design and Procedures subsections. To give you more experience reading professional research articles, examples of published research have been included after Chapters 6 through 9 that reflect the particular type of research covered in each chapter. For instance, an example of Historical Research follows Chapter 6, an example of Descriptive Research follows Chapter 7, and so on. We did not include an example of Experimental Research after Chapter 10 because the one you're already familiar with that followed Chapter 1 is an excellent example of Experimental Research. What *is* printed after Chapter 10, however, is another example of a student project, such as you saw at the end of Part Two. By this time, the student who wrote the project example had covered the Method section; his paper should provide you with a model of the project you will be expected to complete when you have finished studying Part Three. We are extremely grateful to the authors, both student and professional, and the publishers of these materials for allowing us to share them with you.

Just as Parts Two and Three covered main sections of a research report, Part Four covers the Results main section, and Part Five covers the Discussion and Conclusions main section. Again, at the beginning of Part Four you will find the guidelines for the Results section of your project, and at the beginning of Part Five are the guidelines for the Discussion and Conclusions section of your project. Following each of these parts, a student example is provided to give you a model for your own projects.

Chapters 11 through **13,** which comprise *Part Four,* cover the procedures and statistical analyses required for interpretation of the data generated in the research process. Descriptive and inferential statistics are covered, as are the preparation for data collection and provision for acceptable data storage. Here, as in all other parts of the book, we placed an emphasis on the practical use of computer software, including statistical packages for mainframes and micros, data base management, and word processing capabilities. A computer disk, *Statpak,* suitable for personal computers, accompanies the text and provides you with the capability of computing the basic statistics covered in the text.

Chapter 14, also designated as *Part Five,* covers the preparation of the research report, either for publication or presentation in the form of an executive summary. Again, we placed an emphasis on the use of computers in both written and oral presentations.

Chapter 15, or *Part Six,* provides you with a summary of all you have covered so far. By this time, you should have met the major purpose of the course: you should be a competent user of research articles. To evaluate this result, you will be given another professionally done research article that is printed following Part Six, accompanied by guidelines for evaluating it.

As you will see, this book represents more than just a textbook to supplement classroom instruction; it is actually a total instructional system which includes stated objectives, instruction, and procedures for evaluation of each objective. The instructional strategy of the system emphasizes demonstration of skills and individualization within structure.

The projects require you to demonstrate that you can perform particular research functions. Since each of you works with a different research problem, each student is able to demonstrate the competency required by a project as it applies to her or his problem. The objectives entail both the knowledge and skills that facilitate your ability to perform a project.

The discussion in the text is intended to be as simple and straightforward as possible. Whenever feasible, procedures are presented as a series of steps, and concepts are explained in terms of illustrative examples. In a number of cases, relatively complex topics, or topics beyond the scope of the text, are presented at a very elementary level, and you are directed to other sources for additional in-depth discussion. There is also a degree of intentional repetition: A number of concepts are discussed in different contexts and from different perspectives. Also, at the risk of eliciting more than a few groans, an attempt has been made to sprinkle the text with touches of humor.

Each chapter includes a rather lengthy summary with headings and subheadings that directly parallel those in the chapter. The summaries are designed to facilitate both review and location of related textual discussion. Finally, where relevant, chapters conclude with suggested procedures for evaluation of projects and objectives. The chapter objectives may be evaluated either as written exercises submitted by you or by criterion-referenced tests, whichever your instructor prefers. Self-tests are also provided to assist you in checking your understanding and preparing for tests.

The entire instructional system is intended to provide you with a palatable approach enabling you to generalize the concepts of research beyond the classroom setting. We hope that it is basically "user friendly." We also hope that the competency-based approach proves useful for you. In our experience, most students respond favorably to the clarity of an approach based on specified competencies. Experience with several other management courses that were revised to conform with this model leads us to believe that business and management students in particular appreciate an approach that specifies the task to be completed, the standards of evaluation, and concrete suggestions for completing the task. Such specificity in no way denigrates your work to the level of busywork; it simply reduces the nonsense. Thus, you are freed to concentrate your work on a research product rather than trying to decipher the meaning of textual material and determine the levels of importance of the information provided.

We hope you will be pleased when you compare your skills at the end of the course to your ability to evaluate research at the beginning of the course. Students often tell us they can't believe how much more knowledgeable and sophisticated they have become. At the beginning of the course, they had difficulty identifying even the most basic information asked for in Project I, the Review of a Research Article; at the end they are able to form judgments regarding the appropriateness of specific research issues from design problems to data analysis and conclusions. It is our firm belief that the skills you learn in this course will help you not only as a student but will prove to be critically important to your success as a professional businessperson.

L. R. Gay
P. L. Diehl

Contents

Lists of Illustrations

FIGURES

TABLES

Research Methods
for Business and Management

PART ONE
Introduction

If you are taking a research course because it is required in your program of studies, raise your right hand. If you are taking a research course because it seemed as if it would be a real fun elective, raise your left hand. When you have stopped laughing, read on. No, you are not the innocent victim of one or more sadists. There are several legitimate reasons why decision makers believe a research course is an essential component of your education.

First, research findings in business and management contribute significantly to both business and management theory and practice. The effectiveness of behavior modification techniques, such as behavior modeling in supervisory training, for example, has repeatedly been demonstrated; similarly, collection and analysis of data to support decision making will be critical to your success as a manager. Therefore, it is important that you, as a professional, know how to obtain, understand, and evaluate research findings.

Second, you are constantly exposed to research findings, whether you seek them out or not, which are presented in professional publications and, increasingly, by the media. Factors leading to increased productivity and effective leadership, for example, are recurrent themes. As a professional, you have a responsibility to be able to distinguish between legitimate claims or conclusions and ill-founded ones.

And third, believe it or not, research courses are a fruitful source of future researchers. A number of our students have become sufficiently intrigued with the research process to pursue further education and careers in the field. Researchers work not only in business and industry but also in such diverse settings as research and development centers, federal and state agencies, and universities.

For most of you, research is probably a relatively unfamiliar discipline. In order for you to learn about and perform components of the research process in a meaningful way, you need to develop a framework of understanding into which such experiences can be integrated. Therefore, the goal of Part One is for you to acquire an understanding of the research process and methodology that will facilitate your acquisition of specific research knowledge and skills. In succeeding parts of the book, you will systematically study and execute specific components of the research process. After you have read Part One, you should be able to complete the following project:

Project I Guidelines

Find a research study in your field of interest. Then:

1. Identify and state the problem or purpose of the study.
2. Identify and state the procedures.
3. Identify and state the statistical method of analysis.
4. State the major conclusions.
5. Classify the study as historical, descriptive, correlational, causal-comparative, or experimental research.
6. List the characteristics of the study that support your classification.

(See Project I Performance Criteria, p. 23)

A cave drawing of a strange being, which is an ancient astronaut to Von Däniken, may be simply an imaginary god to an archaeologist. (page 14)

1

Introduction to Business and Management Research

Objectives

After reading Chapter 1, you should be able to do the following:

1. List and briefly describe the major steps involved in conducting a research study.

2. Select one article published within the last year in *Academy of Management Journal*, *Administrative Science Quarterly*, *The Journal of Applied Behavioral Science*, *The Journal of Business*, or *Management Science*. After reading your article, identify and briefly state:
   a. the problem.
   b. the procedures.
   c. the method of analysis.
   d. the major conclusions.

3. Briefly define, and state the major characteristics of, each of the five methods of research.

4. For each of the five methods of research, briefly describe three possible research studies.

> **Example:** Experimental—A study to determine the effect of positive reinforcement on the productivity of customer service representatives.

THE SCIENTIFIC METHOD

The goal of all scientific endeavors is to explain, predict, and/or control phenomena. This goal is based on the assumption that all behaviors and events are orderly and that they are effects that have discoverable causes. Progress toward this goal involves acquisition of knowledge and the development and testing of theories. The existence of a viable theory greatly facilitates scientific progress by simultaneously explaining many phenomena. Compared to other sources of knowledge, such as experience and authority, application of the scientific method is undoubtedly the most efficient and reliable. Some of the problems associated with experience and authority as sources of knowledge are graphically illustrated by a story told about Aristotle. According to the story, one day Aristotle caught a fly and carefully counted and recounted its legs. He then announced that flies have five legs. No one questioned the word of Aristotle. For years his finding was uncritically accepted. Of course, the fly that Aristotle caught just happened to be missing a leg! Whether or not you believe the story, it does illustrate the limitations of relying on personal experience and authority as sources of knowledge.

Both inductive and deductive reasoning are of limited value when used exclusively. Inductive reasoning involves formulation of generalizations based on observation of a limited number of specific events.

> **Example:** Every research textbook examined contains a chapter on sampling. Therefore, all research textbooks contain a chapter on sampling.

Deductive reasoning involves essentially the reverse process, arriving at specific conclusions based on generalizations.

> **Example:** All research textbooks contain a chapter on sampling. This book is a research text. Therefore, this book contains a chapter on sampling. (Does it?)

Although neither approach alone is entirely satisfactory, when used together as integral components of the scientific method, they are very effective. Basically, the scientific method involves induction of hypotheses based on observation, deduction of implications of the hypotheses, testing of the implications, and confirmation or disconfirmation of the hypotheses.

The scientific method is a very orderly process entailing a number of sequential steps:

1. Recognition and definition of the problem.
2. Formulation of hypotheses.
3. Collection of data.
4. Analysis of data.
5. Statement of conclusions regarding confirmation or disconfirmation of the hypotheses.

These steps can be applied informally in the solution of everyday problems such as the most efficient route to take from home to work or school, the best time to go to the drive-in window at the bank, or the best kind of electronic calculator to purchase. The more formal application of the scientific method to the solution of problems is what research is all about.

APPLICATION OF THE SCIENTIFIC METHOD IN BUSINESS AND MANAGEMENT

Research is the formal, systematic application of the scientific method to the study of problems; business-and-management research is the formal, systematic application of the scientific method to the study of business-and-management problems. The goal of this research follows from the goal of all science, namely, to explain, predict, and/or control phenomena occurring in a work setting. The major difference between research in business and management and other scientific research is the nature of the phenomena studied. It is considerably more difficult to explain, predict, and control situations involving human beings, who are by far the most complex of all organisms, than it is to control inanimate objects. There are so many variables, known and unknown, operating in a work environment that it is extremely difficult to generalize or replicate findings. The kinds of rigid controls that can be established and maintained in a biochemistry laboratory are virtually impossible in a work setting. Observation is also more difficult in business-and-management research. Observers may be subjective in recording behaviors, and persons observed may behave atypically just because they are being observed; chemical reactions, however, tend to be oblivious to the fact that they are being observed! Precise measurement is also considerably more difficult in management research. Most measurement must be indirect; there are no instruments comparable to a barometer for measuring morale, leadership, or even productivity. Difficult as it is for beginning researchers to believe, the purpose of research is not to make a case in favor of a belief—that is what position papers are for—or to prove a point. Research is an objective, unbiased quest for replicable findings.

Perhaps it is precisely the difficulty and complexity of business-and-management research that makes it such a challenging and exciting field. Despite a popular stereotype that depicts researchers as spectacled, stoop-shouldered, elderly gentlemen who endlessly add chemicals to test tubes, every day thousands of men and women of all ages, shapes, and sizes conduct research in a wide variety of settings. Every year many millions of dollars are spent in the quest for knowledge related to business questions and the management process. Research has contributed many findings concerning principles of motivation, leadership, and productivity. In addition, significant contributions have been made related to work design, direct and indirect compensation administration, training effectiveness, and the efficiency and effectiveness of adoption of technological innovations. Both the quantity and quality of research are increasing. Senior managers, reflecting the current business climate, demand more concrete information to support management decisions; increasing quality is also the result of better trained researchers and research methodologies. In fact, a great many graduate programs in business and management, in such diverse areas as human resources, health-care management, and sports administration, now include a course in research for all students.

The steps involved in conducting research should look familiar since they directly parallel those of the scientific method.

1. *Selection and definition of a problem.* A problem is a hypothesis or question of interest to business people and managers that can be tested or answered through the collection and analysis of data.

2. *Execution of research procedures.* Procedures typically include selection of subjects and selection or development of measurement methodologies. The design

of the study will dictate to a great extent the specific procedures involved in the study.

3. *Analysis of data.* Data analysis usually involves application of one or more statistical techniques. Data are analyzed in a way that permits the researcher to test the research hypothesis or answer the research question.

4. *Drawing and stating conclusions.* The conclusions are based on the results of data analysis. They should be stated in terms of the original hypothesis or question. Conclusions should indicate, for example, whether the research hypothesis was supported or not supported.

In a research report, such as an article published in a journal, these steps should be readily evident if the report is well written. The problem will generally be presented in statements that begin with phrases such as, "the purpose of this study was to . . ." and "it was hypothesized that . . ." The procedures, or methods, section of a report may be quite lengthy and detailed, but there are certain major steps that can be identified, such as the number and characteristics of the subjects (the sample), a description of the measuring instruments including when they were administered (e.g., whether there was a pretest before management training was begun), and a description of treatment groups, if appropriate. Data analysis techniques are usually easy to identify; they will generally be presented in statements that include phrases like "data were analyzed using . . ." or "an analysis of covariance was used . . ." Conclusions are usually labeled as such. While many conclusions may be presented, at least one of them should relate directly to the original hypothesis or question. Statements such as "it was concluded that more research is needed in this area" are fine but certainly do not represent the most important conclusion of the study. More research is always needed!

Research studies can be classified in a number of ways. Two major approaches are to classify by purpose or by method. When purpose is the classification criterion, all research studies fall into one of two categories, either basic or applied research. Further, applied research may include evaluation research, research and development (R & D), or action research. Research method refers to the overall strategy followed in collecting and analyzing data; this strategy is referred to as the research design. Even using research method as the criterion can lead to several different classification schemes. There are, however, five distinct types, kinds, or methods of research: (a) historical, (b) descriptive, (c) correlational, (d) causal-comparative, and (e) experimental.

CLASSIFICATION OF RESEARCH BY PURPOSE

Classification of research by purpose is based primarily on the degree to which findings have direct application and the degree to which they are generalizable to other situations. Both of these criteria are functions of the research control exercised while the study is being conducted. In general, the following distinctions may be made:

Basic research involves the development of theory. *Applied research* is concerned with the application of theory to the solution of problems, including the following:

1. *Evaluation research,* which is intended to support decision making regarding the relative worth of two or more alternative actions.
2. *Research and development,* which is directed at the development of effective products that can be used in the marketplace.
3. *Action research,* which is concerned with immediate solutions to local problems.

Basic Versus Applied Research

It is difficult to discuss basic and applied research separately because they are actually on a continuum. Most business-and-management research probably would be classified at the applied end of the continuum; however, examples of basic research in management do exist. In its purest form, basic research is conducted solely for the purpose of theory development and refinement. It is not concerned with practical applicability, and it most closely resembles the laboratory conditions and controls usually associated with scientific research. Applied research, as the name implies, is conducted for the purpose of applying, or testing, theory and evaluating its usefulness in solving business problems. Rightly or wrongly, the emphasis on the bottom line tends to encourage more applied research; these studies emphasize *what* works best more than *why* it works. Basic research is concerned with establishing general principles of human behavior; applied research is concerned with their utility in the workplace. For example, much basic research has been conducted with animals to determine the basic principles of reinforcement and their effect on animal behavior. Applied research has tested these principles to determine their effectiveness in improving training (e.g., behavior modeling in supervisory training) and behavior (e.g., use of praise as a motivator for employees). Some studies, those located in the middle of the continuum, try to integrate both approaches by conducting controlled research in special or simulated settings, using employees or undergraduate or graduate business students and involving work-relevant topics and materials.

Evaluation Research

Evaluation is the systematic process of collecting and analyzing data in order to make decisions. For example, many of us accept the concept that removal of asbestos from our buildings is an important environmental and health concern. At least one writer, however, has suggested that the expenditure of possibly $100 billion over 25 years to remove this asbestos is not only unnecessary but could actually cost more lives than it saves (Richman, 1988). A substantial evaluation study could support decision making on this important topic. On a more common level, evaluation involves questions such as the following:

1. Is the new, state-of-the-art system of processing orders better than the former system?

2. Is this new ATM (automatic teller machine) worth what it costs?

3. Should Fenster's graduate program in management be covered by the employee tuition-reimbursement program?

Answers to these questions require the collection and analysis of data and interpretation of that data with respect to one or more criteria. The more objective the criteria, the better, although some degree of subjectivity is unavoidable since people determine the criteria. For example, whether a new order-processing system is "better" depends upon the criteria for success. One obvious criterion would be speed. Other criteria might include accuracy and employee attitudes. Examination of processing speed for orders might reveal that employees processed 2% more orders using the new system. Objectively, and strictly speaking, the new system was "better" with respect to speed. The operations manager, however, may have decided that an increase of at least 10% would be necessary in order to justify the time, effort, and cost required to change over to the new system. Similarly, determining whether Fenster meets the criteria for receiving tuition reimbursement (e.g., has been employed a sufficient amount of time, is maintaining an acceptable grade point average [GPA], and is enrolled in a job-related program) would be an objective process; setting the criteria themselves would be a more subjective process.

Deciding whether a new ATM is "worth" what it costs may be even more complex and typically may involve some value judgments. If the ATM cost the bank $100,000 per year but reduced the need for tellers' salaries by $150,000, there would not be much disagreement concerning whether the ATM was worth what it cost. But what if the ATM cost $100,000 per year and caused dissatisfaction among 25% of the bank's elderly customers? How much is customer satisfaction worth? To what extent does a business have an obligation to provide service to special segments of the population? Opinion on these issues varies greatly. The philosophy of the bank's senior management would probably determine whether or not the new technology was continued or an accommodation was made for the dissatisfied customers.

Notice that in none of the examples was the purpose of the evaluation to determine whether something was "good," or worthwhile, as opposed to "bad," or worthless, per se. That is not the function of evaluation. The purpose of evaluation is to select an alternative in order to make a decision. There may be only two alternatives (e.g., adopt the new order-processing system or continue with the old method, invest in the new ATMs or not) or there may be several alternatives (e.g., Fenster may be reimbursed for all, a percentage, or none of his educational costs).

A major point of disagreement among researchers is the issue of whether evaluation is a type of research or a separate discipline. A related issue is whether evaluations should be based on research designs, particularly when group comparisons are involved such as deciding whether training method A is more effective than training method B. Some argue that research and evaluation have distinctly different purposes, that research seeks control while evaluation assesses what is, and that the natural settings characteristic of evaluation essentially preclude that control. In reality, however, there is a fine line between research and evaluation, and an evaluation may very easily utilize a research design. Both research and evaluation involve decision making, and both involve steps that parallel those of the scientific method. Further, many research studies are conducted in real-world settings and are subject to the same control problems involved in many evaluations. Thus, while the issue has not yet been resolved, the case seems stronger for classifying evaluation as a type of research whose purpose is to facilitate decision making. In the business setting, however, "evaluation" may be a more popular term than "research" because of certain stereotypes regarding research and researchers.

Research and Development (R & D)

The major purpose of R & D efforts is not to formulate or test theory but to develop new products or processes. R & D efforts aimed at specific-product development are generally quite extensive in terms of objectives, personnel, and time to completion. The process involves meeting specific needs in accord with detailed specifications. Once completed, products are field-tested and revised until a specified level of effectiveness is achieved. Although the R & D cycle is an expensive one, it results in products designed to meet the overall business plan of the company and provides for future growth and development. During 1988, 25% of 3M's worldwide sales were from products developed within the preceding five years. Johnson & Johnson had similar results with their U.S. sales; their expenditures for R & D were about 8% of sales. At the same time, Corning Glass Works was spending about 5% of sales on R & D (Labich, 1988). Although all these were above average for U.S. industrial companies, the expenditures and results reflect a commitment to R & D that permeates all levels of employees at these innovative companies. In order to share expenses of R & D, some industries are experimenting with a horizontal sharing among three or more companies of research capacity (Inman cited in Weintraub, 1991; Ouchi & Bolton, 1988; Smith, 1989). The emphasis on new-product development has led to some inadvertent discoveries. For example, the first commercial microwave oven was the ultimate result of an observation by a Raytheon engineer that the chocolate bar in his shirt pocket had melted while he was working on experimental radar equipment in the lab. Aspartame was initially discovered by a G. D. Searle chemist who absentmindedly licked his fingers after cleaning up a spill of an experimental fluid. Similarly, Scotchgard was developed after a 3M researcher noticed her sneaker stayed clean for several days after she dropped an industrial compound that splashed onto it (Labich, 1988).

Action Research

The purpose of action research is to solve business-and-management problems through the application of the scientific method. It is concerned with a local problem and is conducted in a local setting. In most instances, action research is not concerned with whether the results are generalizable to any other setting and is not characterized by the same kind of control evident in other categories of research. The primary goal of action research is the solution of a given problem, not a contribution to science. In some cases, action research has pointed in a direction that may be followed up with a research effort that is characterized by greater control and therefore more generalizability. Whether the action research is conducted in one department of a company or in many companies, the manager is very much a part of the process. The more research training the managers involved have had, the more likely it is that the research will produce valid, if not generalizable, results.

The value of action research is normally confined to those conducting it, although reports of action research may be of assistance to others facing similar situations. The use of the case study in management education is an example of a utilization of a product that might come from action research. Despite its shortcomings, action research does represent a scientific approach to problem solving that is considerably better than change based on the alleged effectiveness of untried procedures. For this reason, action research is advocated by organizational development (OD) specialists who are concerned with bringing about planned change intended to increase the effectiveness of an organization (Huse & Cummings, 1985). Thus action research becomes a means by which concerned managers can attempt to improve a variety of situations, at least within their environment. Often this becomes an organized and informed trial-and-error process, which calls for periodic evaluation and adjustment during the change process. As mentioned before, the value of action research for true scientific progress is limited. True progress requires the development of sound theories having implications for many businesses, not just one or two local situations. One sound theory that includes 10 principles of motivation may eliminate the need for hundreds of would-be action research studies. Given the current status of business-and-management theory, however, action research provides immediate answers to problems that cannot wait for theoretical solutions.

CLASSIFICATION OF RESEARCH BY METHOD

Although there is sometimes a degree of overlap, most research studies represent a readily identifiable method, or strategy. All studies have certain procedures in common such as the statement of a problem, collection of data, and drawing of conclusions. Beyond these, however, specific procedures are to a high degree determined by the research method. Each of the methods is designed to answer a different type of question. Knowledge of the various methods and of the procedures involved in each is important both for researchers and consumers of research. Even when method is used as a criterion, there are several different ways in which research studies can be classified, for example, experimental versus nonexperimental, or historical versus descriptive versus experimental. These alternatives, however, tend to lump together studies entailing distinctly different research strategies. A classification scheme that appears to be the most efficient, in that it minimizes categories and maximizes differentiation, places all research studies into one of five categories: (a) historical, (b) descriptive, (c) correlational, (d) causal-comparative, or (e) experimental. The purpose of the following explanations is to provide you with an overview so that you will at least be able to read a research report and, based on its procedures, determine which of the five methods it represents. This competency is one that will aid you in reviewing the literature for the problem you select in Chapter 2. The methods of research will be discussed further in Chapters 6 through 10.

Historical Research

Historical research involves studying, understanding, and explaining past events. The purpose of historical research is to arrive at conclusions concerning causes, effects, or trends of past occurrences that may help to explain present events and anticipate future events. While historical studies are less frequently conducted than other types, there are certain problems and issues (such as hiring policies) that can be better understood in the light of past experience. The steps involved in conducting a historical study are generally the same as for other types of research; a historical study should be guided by a hypothesis, just as an experimental study should, lest it degenerate into an aimless "treasure hunt."

Historical researchers do not typically gather data by administering instruments to individuals. They must seek out data that are already available. Sources of data are referred to as primary or secondary. Primary sources constitute firsthand knowledge, such as eyewitness reports and original documents; secondary sources constitute secondhand information, such as a description of an event by someone other than an eyewitness. If you interview someone who witnessed an accident, that someone is a primary source; if you interview that someone's husband or wife, who did not witness the accident but heard an account of what happened from his or her spouse, that person is a secondary source. Primary sources are admittedly harder to acquire but are generally more accurate and are to be preferred. Management consultant George Labovitz uses the building of the pyramids in an amusing and useful way to illustrate management principles; trying to find an eyewitness to verify his account, however, would be quite a feat! A major problem with much historical research is excessive reliance on secondary sources.

Evaluation of historical data involves external criticism and internal criticism. External criticism assesses the authenticity of the data; internal criticism evaluates their worth. The worth of the data, the degree to which data are accurate and reliable and do indeed support the hypothesis, is judgmental and sometimes a matter of opinion. For example, a researcher investigating trends in productivity might use an article attributed to Carl Rogers containing an assertion that a supervisor's effective use of listening skills will probably improve productivity of the overall work group (Rogers & Farson, 1979). The results of external criticism might verify that the article was indeed written by Carl Rogers. Internal criticism would be involved with whether he could be considered a reliable source concerning management practices of the day. As another example, in his book *Chariots of the Gods?* E. von Däniken (1972) hypothesizes that thousands of years ago our ancestors were visited by intelligent beings from other worlds who, among other things, presented early humanity with advanced technology. Von Däniken points to such remains as cave drawings, ancient maps, and relics of advanced, early civilizations as evidence in support of his theory. In general, the authenticity of his evidence is without question; it is his interpretation of its meaning that is debatable. A cave drawing of a strange being, which is an ancient astronaut to Von Däniken, may be simply an imaginary god to an archaeologist. In any event, his work represents a fascinating example of historical research.

The following are examples of typical historical research studies:

1. Factors leading to the development and growth of trade unions.
2. Effects of civil rights legislation on American hiring practices.
3. Trends in employee performance appraisal, 1965–1990.

Descriptive Research

Descriptive research involves collecting data in order to test hypotheses or answer questions concerning the current status of the subject of the study. A descriptive study determines and reports the way things are. One common type of descriptive research involves assessing attitudes or opinions toward individuals, organizations, events, or procedures; pre-election political polls and market research surveys are examples of this type of descriptive research. Descriptive data are typically collected through a questionnaire survey, interviews, or observation(s).

Descriptive research sounds very simple; there is considerably more to it, however, than just asking questions and reporting answers. Since one is generally asking questions that have not been asked before, instruments usually have to be developed for specific studies; instrument development requires time and skill and is not a casual enterprise. A major problem further complicating descriptive research is lack of response—the failure of subjects to return questionnaires or attend scheduled interviews. If the response rate is low, valid conclusions cannot be drawn. For example, suppose you are doing a study to determine attitudes of managers toward research. You send a questionnaire to 100 managers and ask the question, "Do you usually cooperate if asked to participate in a research study?" Suppose 40 managers respond and they all answer yes. Could you then conclude that managers cooperate? No! Even though all those who responded said yes, those 60 who did not respond may never cooperate with research efforts. After all, they did not cooperate with you! A third problem with descriptive research is the credibility of the researcher. Can you be trusted to maintain confidentiality to an employee responding to questions about her or his boss? Observational research, another form of descriptive research, also involves complexities that are not readily apparent. Observers must be trained and forms must be developed so that data can be collected objectively and reliably.

The following are examples of typical questions investigated by descriptive research studies:

1. *How do general managers spend their time?* General managers would be observed for a period of time and results would probably be presented as percentages. In an

actual study of this type (Kotter, 1982), it was found that almost 90% of the time of general managers was spent in communicating with others.

2. *How will the employees of Dissatisfaction, Inc., vote in the upcoming union election?* A survey of the employees would be taken (questionnaire or interview), and results would probably be presented as percentages; e.g., 70% indicate they will vote for the union, 20% against, and 10% undecided.

3. *How do employees feel about flex-time scheduling?* Employees would be surveyed, and results would probably be presented in terms of percentages for, against, or undecided.

Correlational Research

Correlational research attempts to determine whether, and to what degree, a relationship exists between two or more quantifiable variables. (Note: A variable is a concept that can assume any one of a range of values. Examples of variables include income, age, educational level, motivation, and success.) The purpose of a correlational study may be to establish a relationship, or the lack of it, or to use relationships in making predictions. Correlational studies typically assess a number of variables believed to be related to a major, complex variable, such as leadership. Variables found not to be highly related are eliminated from further consideration; variables that are highly related may suggest causal-comparative or experimental studies to determine if the relationships are causal.

For example, a study indicating that there is a relationship between high consideration by the leader and higher levels of employee satisfaction does not imply that high consideration for people "causes" higher satisfaction or that higher satisfaction "causes" high consideration (Goodson, McGee, & Cashman, 1988). Such a relationship only indicates that managers with high consideration have employees with higher levels of satisfaction and that managers with low consideration have employees with lower levels of satisfaction. From the fact that two variables are highly related, a researcher cannot conclude that one is the cause of the other; there may be a third factor that "causes" both of the related variables.

As a second example, suppose you read an article indicating that there is a high degree of relationship between number of years of schooling and lifetime income (two quantifiable variables). The temptation might be to conclude that if you stay in school longer, you will make more money; this conclusion would not necessarily be justified. There might be a third variable, such as motivation, which "causes" people to stay in school and also to do well in their jobs. The important point to remember is that correlational research never establishes a cause-effect relationship, only a relationship.

Regardless of whether a relationship is a cause-effect relationship, the existence of a strong relationship permits prediction. As a prospective student you were undoubtedly expected to submit a record of your previous grades as a part of your application process. The reason for this expectation is that college and university admissions people have found that high school grades and college grades are highly related; students who have high grade point averages (GPAs) in high school tend to have high GPAs in college, and students who have low GPAs in high school tend to have low GPAs in college. Therefore, high school GPAs can be, and are, used to predict GPA in college. The same relationship is usually true for undergraduate and graduate school GPAs. (The fact that you happen to know an exception to the rule does not mean the relationship does not exist!) The degree of relationship between two variables is generally expressed as a correlation coefficient, which is a number between .00 and 1.00. Two variables that are not related will produce a coefficient near .00; two variables that are strongly related will produce a coefficient near 1.00. Two variables can be inversely related. When this occurs the coefficient is a negative number; in this case, a strong relationship is near -1.00. A negative relationship occurs when two variables are related in such a way that a high score on one is accompanied by a low score on the other and vice versa. This will be discussed further in Chapter 8. Since very few relationships are perfect (as you may have noticed), prediction is rarely perfect. For many decisions, however, predictions based on known relationships are very useful.

The following are examples of typical correlational studies:

1. *The relationship between productivity and task structure.* Productivity figures and a quantitative measure of task structure would be obtained from several work situations. These figures would be correlated and the resulting coefficient would indicate the degree of relationship.
2. *The relationship between anxiety and accuracy.* Scores on an anxiety scale and accuracy rates on a specific task would be acquired from each member of a group. The two sets of scores would be correlated and the resulting coefficient would indicate the degree of relationship.
3. *Use of an aptitude test to predict success in a job.* Scores on an aptitude test would be correlated with ultimate success in the job as measured by the supervisors' quantitative appraisals, for example. If the resulting coefficient were high, the aptitude test would be considered a good predictor.

Causal-Comparative and Experimental Research

While causal-comparative and experimental research represent distinctly different methods, they can best be understood through comparison and contrast. Both attempt to establish cause-effect relationships; both involve group comparisons. The major difference between them is that in experimental research the alleged "cause" is manipulated, and in causal-comparative research it is not. In experimental research, the alleged "cause," the activity or characteristic believed to make a difference, is referred to as a treatment; the more general term for "cause" is independent variable (I.V.). The difference, or "effect," which is determined to occur or not occur is referred to as the dependent variable (D.V.). Dependent on what? Dependent on the independent variable. Thus, a study that investigates a cause-effect relationship investigates the effect of an independent variable on a dependent variable.

In an experimental study the researcher manipulates at least one independent variable and observes the effect on one or more dependent variables. In other words, the researcher determines "who gets what," which group of subjects will get which treatment. The groups are generally referred to as the experimental and control groups. Manipulation of the independent variable is the one single characteristic that differentiates experimental research from other methods. Ideally, in experimental research the groups to be studied are randomly formed before the experiment, a procedure not involved in the other methods of research. The essence of experimentation is control. The researcher strives to insure that the experiences of the groups are as equal as possible on all important variables except, of course, the independent variable. If, at the end of some period of time, groups differ in performance on the dependent variable, the difference can be attributed to the independent variable. It is important to understand that because of the direct manipulation and control of variables, experimental research is the only type of research that can truly establish cause-effect relationships.

The following are examples of typical experimental studies:

1. *The comparative effectiveness of interactive-video versus standard classroom instruction on customer service training.* The independent variable, or cause, is the type of instruction (interactive-video versus classroom); the dependent variable, or effect, is the efficiency and effectiveness of customer-service training as was done at Federal Express (Yakal, 1989). In this type of a study, at least two groups (preferably randomly formed) would be exposed to essentially the same experiences, except for the method of instruction. After some period of time, their customer-service knowledge would be compared.

2. *The effect of self-appraisal on employee morale.* The independent variable, or cause, is appraisal (self-appraisal versus supervisor appraisal); the dependent variable, or effect, is morale. Two groups (preferably randomly formed) would be exposed to essentially the same experiences, except for the method of appraisal. After some period of time, their morale would be measured.

3. *The effect of positive reinforcement on job performance.* The independent variable, or cause, is the type of reinforcement (e.g., positive reinforcement versus correction, or positive reinforcement versus no reinforcement); the dependent variable, or effect, is job performance. Two groups (preferably randomly formed) would be exposed to essentially the same experiences, except for the type of reinforcement received. After some period of time, their job performance would be compared.

In a causal-comparative study the independent variable, or "cause," is not manipulated; it has already occurred. Independent variables in causal-comparative studies are variables that cannot be manipulated (e.g., sex, male-female), should not be manipulated (e.g., physical impairment), or simply are not manipulated but could be (e.g., method of training). In causal-comparative research, groups are also compared on some dependent variable; these groups, however, are different on some variable before the study begins. Perhaps members of one group possess a characteristic and members of the other group do not. In any event, the difference between the groups (the independent variable) is not, was not, or could not be determined (controlled) by the researcher. Further, since the independent variable has already occurred, the same kinds of controls cannot be exercised as in an experimental study. Owing to the lack of manipulation and control, cause-effect relationships that are established are at best tenuous and tentative. On the positive side, causal-comparative studies are less expensive and take much less time to conduct. Further, apparent cause-effect relationships identified in causal-comparative studies may lead to experimental studies designed to confirm or disconfirm the findings. Also, there are a number of important variables that simply cannot be manipulated. Studies designed to investigate the effects of socioeconomic status, intelligence, or sex on success must be causal-comparative, as none of these variables can be manipulated.

The following are examples of typical causal-comparative studies:

1. *The effect of presupervisory training on job performance at the end of the first six months as a supervisor.* The independent variable, or cause, is involvement in presupervisory training (employees attended training or did not attend); the dependent variable, or effect, is job performance at the end of six months. Two groups of new supervisors would be identified—one group who had attended presupervisory training and one group who had not. The job performance of the two groups would be compared.

2. *The effect of having elderly parents on employee absenteeism.* The independent variable, or cause, is elderly parents (the employee has elderly parents or has not); the dependent variable, or effect, is absenteeism, or number of days absent. Two groups of employees would be identified—one group who have elderly parents and one group who have not. The absenteeism of the two groups would be compared.

3. *The effect of sex on job success of MBA graduates.* The independent variable, or cause, is gender; the dependent variable, or effect, is job success. The job success of males with MBAs would be compared to the job success of females with MBAs.

Guidelines for Classification

Which of the five methods is most appropriate for a given study depends on the way in which the problem is defined. The same general problem can often be investigated using several of the methods. Research in a given area is often sequential; preliminary descriptive and/or correlational studies may be conducted followed by causal-comparative and/or experimental studies, if such seem warranted. As an example, let us look at motivation and job performance.

The following studies might be conducted:

1. *Historical.* A review of management theory from 1960 to 1980 to determine what relationships management authors saw between motivation and job performance.

2. *Descriptive.* A survey of supervisors to determine how and to what degree they believe employee motivation affects job performance.

3. *Correlational.* A study to determine the relationship between scores on a motivational scale and results of employee performance appraisals.

4. *Causal-comparative.* A study to compare the job performance of a group of employees classified as highly motivated and a group classified as minimally motivated.

5. *Experimental.* A study to compare the achievement of two groups—one group working in a highly motivating environment and the other group working in an environment with relatively few motivating factors.

When analyzing a study in order to determine the method represented, one approach is to use the decision tree in Figure 1.1. In using the decision tree, ask yourself the following questions:

1. Was the researcher attempting to establish a cause-effect relationship? If yes, the research is either causal-comparative or experimental. If no, skip to question 3.

2. Was the alleged cause, or independent variable, manipulated by the researcher? Did the researcher control who got what and what they got? If yes, the research is experimental; if no, the research is causal-comparative.

3. If you answered question 1 no, the next question should be, Was the researcher attempting to establish a relationship or use a relationship for prediction? If yes, the research is correlational. If no, the research is either descriptive or historical.

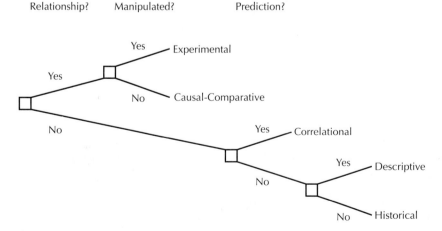

Figure 1.1. Decision tree for determining methods of research.

4. If the researcher is describing current conditions (at the time of the research), the study is probably descriptive; if no, it's probably historical.

The following examples should further clarify the differences among the methods:

1. *Employee attitudes toward working conditions.* Probably descriptive. The study is determining the current attitudes of employees. Data are probably collected through use of a questionnaire or interviews.
2. *Effect of physical impairment on absenteeism.* Probably causal-comparative. The effect of physical impairment on absenteeism is being investigated. The independent variable, physical impairment, cannot be manipulated.
3. *Effects of merit raises versus regular increments on job performance.* Might be experimental or causal-comparative. The effect of different raises on job performance is being investigated. The independent variable, merit raises or regular increments, must be controlled by the researcher if this example is to qualify as experimental.
4. *Prediction of success in graduate school based on Graduate Management Aptitude Test (GMAT) scores.* Probably correlational. A cause-effect relationship is not involved, but a relationship is involved, namely the relationship between GMAT scores and success in graduate school (e.g., GPA).
5. *Participation of women in senior management, 1945–1990.* Probably historical. The study is investigating a trend, probably increased participation by women.

Of course, as implied in example 3, you cannot usually identify method simply by reading the title of a research report. However, by reading the report, looking for identifying characteristics, and asking appropriate questions, you should have no trouble classifying most studies. Classifying a study by method is the first step in both conducting and reviewing a study, since each method entails different specific procedures and analyses.

Summary/Chapter 1

THE SCIENTIFIC METHOD

1. The goal of all scientific endeavors is to explain, predict, and/or control phenomena.
2. Compared to other sources of knowledge, such as experience and authority, application of the scientific method is undoubtedly the most efficient and reliable.
3. Basically, the scientific method involves induction of hypotheses based on observations, deduction of implications of the hypotheses, testing of the implications, and confirmation or disconfirmation of the hypotheses.

APPLICATION OF THE SCIENTIFIC METHOD IN BUSINESS AND MANAGEMENT

4. Research is the formal, systematic application of the scientific method to the study of problems; business-and-management research is the formal, systematic application of the scientific method to the study of business-and-management problems.

5. The major difference between research in business and management and other scientific research is the nature of the phenomena studied. It is considerably more difficult to explain, predict, and control situations involving human beings, by far the most complex of all organisms.

6. The steps involved in conducting research directly parallel those of the scientific method: (a) selection and definition of a problem, (b) execution of research procedures (collection of data), (c) analysis of data, and (d) drawing and stating conclusions.

CLASSIFICATION OF RESEARCH BY PURPOSE

7. Classification of research by purpose is based primarily on the degree to which findings have direct business application and the degree to which they are generalizable. Both of these criteria are a function of the research control exercised throughout the study.

Basic Versus Applied Research

8. In its purest form, basic research is conducted solely for the purpose of theory development and refinement.

9. Applied research, as the name implies, is conducted for the purpose of applying, or testing, theory and evaluating its usefulness in solving business-and-management problems.

Evaluation Research

10. The purpose of evaluation research is to facilitate decision making regarding the relative worth of two or more alternative actions.

Research and Development (R & D)

11. The major purpose of R & D efforts is not to formulate or test theory but to develop effective products.

Action Research

12. The purpose of action research is to solve business-and-management problems through the application of the scientific method.

CLASSIFICATION OF RESEARCH BY METHOD

13. While there is sometimes a degree of overlap, most research studies represent a readily identifiable method, or strategy.

14. All studies have certain procedures in common such as the statement of a problem, collection of data, analysis of data, and drawing of conclusions; beyond these, specific procedures are to a high degree determined by the research method.

Historical Research

15. Historical research involves studying, understanding, and explaining past events.

16. The purpose of historical research is to arrive at conclusions concerning causes, effects, or trends of past occurrences that may help to explain present events and anticipate future events.

17. Primary sources of data constitute firsthand knowledge; secondary sources constitute secondhand information.

18. External criticism assesses the authenticity of the data; internal criticism evaluates their worth.

Descriptive Research

19. Descriptive research involves collecting data in order to test hypotheses or answer questions concerning the current status of the subject of the study.

20. Descriptive data are typically collected through a questionnaire survey, interviews, or observations.

21. Since one is generally asking questions that have not been asked before, instruments usually have to be developed for specific studies.

22. A major problem further complicating descriptive research is lack of response—the failure of subjects to return questionnaires or attend scheduled interviews.

Correlational Research

23. Correlational research attempts to determine whether, and to what degree, a relationship exists between two or more quantifiable variables.

24. The purpose of a correlational study may be to establish a relationship (or lack of it) or to use relationships in making predictions.

25. From the fact that two variables are strongly related, one cannot conclude that one is the cause of the other; there may be a third factor that "causes" both of the related variables.

26. Regardless of whether a relationship is a cause-effect relationship, the existence of a strong relationship permits prediction.

27. The degree of relationship between two variables is generally expressed as a correlation coefficient, which is a number between .00 and 1.00; inverse correlations result in a number between .00 and -1.00.

Causal-Comparative and Experimental Research

28. The activity or characteristic believed to make a difference is referred to as the "cause," or treatment, and, more generally, as the independent variable.

29. The difference, or "effect," which is determined to occur or not occur is referred to as the dependent variable.

30. In an experimental study the researcher manipulates at least one independent variable and observes the effect on one or more dependent variable.

31. Ideally, in experimental research the groups to be studied are randomly formed before the experiment, a procedure not involved in the other methods of research.

32. The essence of experimentation is control.

33. Only experimental research can truly establish cause-effect relationships.

34. In a causal-comparative study the independent variable, or "cause," is not manipulated; it has already occurred.

35. In causal-comparative research, the difference between the groups (the independent variable) is not, was not, or could not be, controlled by the researcher.

36. Owing to the lack of manipulation and control, cause-effect relationships established through causal-comparative research are at best tenuous and tentative.

Guidelines for Classification

37. Which of the five methods is most appropriate for a given study depends upon the way in which the problem is defined. The same general problem can often be investigated using several of the methods.

38. When analyzing a study in order to determine the method represented, one approach is to ask the following questions: (a) was the researcher attempting to establish a cause-effect relationship? (b) was the alleged cause, or independent variable, manipulated by the researcher? (c) was the researcher attempting to establish a relationship or use a relationship for prediction?

Project I Performance Criteria

The first step in this project was to find a research study. Then, if the study that you located was designed to investigate one major problem, one sentence should be sufficient to describe the problem. If several problems were investigated, one sentence per problem should be sufficient.

Three to six sentences or less will adequately describe the major procedures of most studies. Do not copy the procedures section of the study or describe each and every step. Briefly describe the subjects, instrument(s), and major steps.

As with the problem, one or two sentences will usually be sufficient to state the major analyses. You are not expected to understand the analyses, only identify them. By the time you get to statistics you will be at least somewhat desensitized and will not be unnerved by terms such as t-test and analysis of variance (ANOVA).

The major conclusions that you identify and state (one or two sentences should be sufficient) should directly relate to the original problem or problems. Remember, statements like "more research is needed in this area" do not represent major conclusions.

The characteristics of the study that you describe should be characteristics that are unique to the research method represented by the study. The following are illustrative examples of responses you might give for studies representing each of the methods of research:

1. This study was historical because trends in hiring practices of minorities during the past 20 years were investigated.

2. This study was descriptive because a questionnaire was used in order to determine how employees feel about the company's benefits package.
3. This study was correlational because the predictive validity of a new aptitude test for data-processing personnel was investigated.
4. This study was causal-comparative because a cause-effect relationship was investigated, but the independent variable was not manipulated; the researcher could not and did not determine "who got what," that is, which employee subjects were high school dropouts and which had completed high school.
5. This study was experimental because subjects were randomly assigned to treatments and the independent variable (cause) was manipulated; the researcher determined "who got what," that is, which employee subjects received career counseling from their supervisor and which subjects received career counseling as part of a session conducted by the training department.

On the following pages a research report is reprinted. In the Practice Self-Test following the report, spaces are provided for listing the components required and for classifying the research by method as specified by Project I. After you have studied Part One, see if you can correctly identify the components and method. If your responses differ greatly from the Suggested Responses in Appendix C, study the article again until you see why you were in error. When you select your article for Project I, be sure it looks similar to the "practice" article in your text. Not all the articles in the journals you are to use are research reports; some are based on research but do not use the format of a research report. In general, however, you will be looking for an article that has an abstract, at least one hypothesis, some statistical analysis of data, and one or more tables presenting the analysis.

Consequences of Quality Circles in an Industrial Setting: A Longitudinal Assessment

Ricky W. Griffin

Texas A&M University

The purpose of this study was to test the consequences of implementing quality circles in an industrial setting. Using a longitudinal and experimental research design, the study tracked 73 employees organized into eight circles over a

© *Academy of Management Journal* 1988, Vol. 31, No. 2, 338-358.

three-year period. A matched-pairs comparison group was drawn from another plant within the same company. Results indicated that attitudes, behaviors, and effectiveness all improved initially for the experimental group but then dropped back to previous levels. Implications for future research and practice are discussed.

In recent years, the topics of Japanese management practices in general and quality circles in particular have been frequently discussed in the popular press and managerial literature. Unfortunately, however, there is a paucity of scientific research into the true value and usefulness of quality circles. In particular, much of the research concerned with quality circles in the United States is anecdotal or cross-sectional. The research reported here was undertaken as a first step toward developing an empirical basis for assessing the consequences of quality circles for both the participants in the circles and the sponsoring organization. The study was a longitudinal and experimental investigation into the effects of quality circles on participants' attitudes and job performance. In addition, it assessed managerial opinion as to the value of the quality circles for enhancing organizational performance.

RESEARCH ON QUALITY CIRCLES

Quality circles, or QCs, are generally defined as "small groups of volunteers from the same work area who meet regularly to identify, analyze, and solve quality and related problems in their area of responsibility" (Munchus, 1983: 255). They usually consist of eight to ten members and meet once a week during normal working hours. Moreover, members of QCs usually receive some form of training in problem-solving techniques.

Keys and Miller (1984) noted that QCs are rooted historically in the humanistic tradition represented by human relationists like Argyris, McGregor, and Likert. Previous research has also clearly documented that QCs are not as much a Japanese invention as an American invention of which the Japanese were the first adopters (Cole, 1980). Japanese managers have historically been more receptive and committed to employee participation in the workplace than have American managers. Since QCs are basically a formal mechanism for channeling and directing employee participation, it follows logically that QCs would be more widely adopted in Japan than in the United States.

QCs first came into vogue in U.S. companies around the beginning of this decade. The strengths of the Japanese approach to management were being formally acknowledged, and American managers were looking for ways to compete more effectively. One source of tactics was the Japanese themselves. Ouchi's work (1981a, 1981b) on Japanese management practices, for example, was very well received in the United States by managers looking for ways to enhance organizational effectiveness. So, too, was the concept of QCs.

Meyer and Stott (1985) recently estimated that at least 500 U.S. firms are currently using QCs. They also noted the lack of evaluative research undertaken to assess the effectiveness of the circles. Indeed, most of the evidence pertaining to their effectiveness is anecdotal or based on cross-sectional survey research (Weiss, 1984).

The sparse scholarly research that is available also provides inconclusive or noncomparable evidence. Lawler and Mohrman (1985), for example, reported on the experiences that many organizations have had with QCs. Their observations are apparently based on the popular literature and their own consulting observations. They noted that some firms report considerable success with QCs and others report less success. They also noted that although QCs have certain advantages, they are poor vehicles for institutionalizing participation in general and that if an organization wants to adopt a more participative culture, a broader, more institutionalized strategy is needed.

In the most rigorous assessment published to date, Marks, Mirvis, Hackett, and Grady (1986) surveyed 46 participants and 46 nonparticipants before and after the implementation of a quality circle program in a single plant. Their results suggested that the QC program tended to buffer participants from negative contextual factors but did little to enhance the quality of work life. They did find, however, that both productivity and absenteeism improved modestly but significantly for participants over a 24-month period following the implementation of the QC program.

In summary, then, much has been written, but little learned, about the use of quality circles in organizations. There are several apparent reasons for that state of affairs. First, no consistent theoretical framework has guided the use of QCs—there is no theory of quality circles. Such a framework could serve to guide implementation, clarify expectations, and explain consequences. Second, since the widespread use of QCs in this country is a fairly recent development, perhaps researchers have simply not yet had sufficient time to undertake rigorous assessments. Finally, the empirical evaluation of QCs brings the same difficulties confronted in research in other organizational areas. Namely, it is often difficult to find sponsoring organizations and to then elicit the requisite cooperation for rigorous evaluation. Thus, researchers may gain entrée only after a QC program is already underway, be asked to analyze flawed data collected by the organization, or not be allowed to design a truly rigorous study to begin with.

RELEVANT THEORY

Although the development of a theory of quality circles is beyond the scope of this study, it is possible to draw several clear inferences about QCs from existing theory and previous research as well as from organizational practice. The implicit theoretical foundation for the use of QCs is participation. QCs are seen as a formalized avenue for eliciting and managing employee participation in relevant operational areas (Marks et al., 1986; Munchus, 1983).

Historically, participation has been seen as an avenue for achieving a variety of outcomes. First, researchers have often cited participation as a method for enhancing employee attitudes and behaviors. For example, participation has commonly been studied in conjunction with satisfaction (Griffin & Bateman, 1986). Research has linked organizational commitment, another important attitude, to both satisfaction (Griffin & Bateman, 1986) and participation (Munchus, 1983). Intentions to quit have also been tied both descriptively (Munchus, 1983) and empirically (Marks et al. 1986) to participation in QCs. Finally, there is empirical support for a relationship between participation in a quality circle and individual performance (Marks et al., 1986).

The broader literature on participation, however, is inconsistent regarding the effects of participation on various outcome measures. At one time, it was generally believed that participation caused employees to feel more satisfied, be more productive, and so forth. Later investigation has seen much of the research on which those beliefs were based as deficient in one or more ways. For example, two recent meta-analyses (Miller & Monge, 1986; Wagner & Gooding, 1987) have suggested that methodological artifacts explain many of the positive relationships found between participation and its presumed outcomes. Nevertheless, the relationships have not been refuted but simply called into question. Thus, there is still a reasonable basis for expecting positive consequences to result from increased employee participation.

The second set of outcomes that organizations evidently hope to achieve with QCs relates to overall organizational performance. First, the individual outcomes are presumed to aggregate to the benefit of an organization. Second, and more specifically, management expects the circles to provide tangible and objective suggestions and methods that will lead to such direct benefits as lower costs, improved quality, and more efficient work procedures.

HYPOTHESES

In summary, then, QCs are presumed to have positive effects at two levels of analysis. First, they may result in improved attitudes and behaviors for individual employees. Second, they may result in improved financial performance for an organization as a whole. Accordingly, the following hypotheses were tested in this research.

Hypothesis 1: Participants in quality circles will report higher levels of job satisfaction than will nonparticipants.

Hypothesis 2: Participants in quality circles will report higher levels of organizational commitment than will nonparticipants.

Hypothesis 3: Participants in quality circles will perform at higher levels than will nonparticipants.

Hypothesis 4: Participants in quality circles will report fewer intentions to quit than will nonparticipants.

Hypothesis 5: Managers will report positive assessments of the contributions of quality circles to organizational effectiveness.

Hypothesis 6: Quality circles will provide measurable financial returns to the sponsoring organization.

Each of the hypotheses is consistent with the implicit theory underlying the use of quality circles and with the sparse evidence available to date. The first four pertain to outcomes that are reasonably expected to accrue to individuals, and the last two underscore the organizational benefits that should follow from the use of QCs.

METHODS

Overview of the Study

To test the hypotheses summarized above, a field experiment with a pretest-posttest, nonequivalent control group design employing repeated measures was conducted. One plant provided an experimental group of individuals who had volunteered to participate in QCs, and another plant within the same company provided a matched comparison group. I measured affective and behavioral variables immediately before initiation of the QC intervention (time 1) and again 6 months (time 2), 18 months (time 3), and 36 months (time 4) later. Limited interview data were also collected from both participants and managers at the 18-month mark and again 48 months after initiation.

Research Sites and Participants

The study was conducted in two manufacturing plants of a moderate-sized electronics company. The company has a total of six assembly plants located in five states. The two plants located in the same state were used for this study.

Plant managers within the company enjoy considerable autonomy over local issues like the management of turnover, the establishment of wages appropriate for local labor conditions, and so forth. During the time of this study, the company was doing fairly well financially but was also quite sensitive to the inroads foreign manufacturers were making in the electronics industry. In response to that threat, the company was quite actively keeping abreast of new management techniques and practices, especially those associated with the Japanese. Quality circles were one technique that attracted the attention of top managers.

In early 1982, the six plant managers attended a presentation sponsored by corporate management on the advantages and disadvantages of quality circles. They were then offered the option of choosing to implement a QC program in their plant or to postpone a decision until more facts were available on the effectiveness of QCs. Four managers decided to implement circles, and the other two decided to wait.

During the planning stages of the program, in mid-1982, the human resources manager at one of the plants about to adopt QCs contacted me and requested that I monitor the effectiveness of the effort. I decided to restrict the study to the one plant, with one other plant not using QCs providing comparative data. The manager of the experimental plant contacted his counterpart at the other plant, in another major city in the same state, and enlisted his cooperation in providing a comparison group. That manager had decided to not implement the QC effort and had indicated in the initial meeting that he did not foresee wanting to use QCs in the foreseeable future. His reasoning was that he had always followed a participative approach to management, and he saw QCs as doing little more to enhance participation than he was already doing.[1]

The experimental plant, hereafter referred to as plant A, had a workforce of 496 employees at the time the study was planned. The plant was located in a city of approximately 1.2 million in the Midwest. The comparison plant, called plant B, was located in a city of around 900,000 across the state. This plant employed 427 employees at the beginning of the study. The two plants produced a variety of electronic measuring and control devices such as metering instruments, gauges, and control panels. Both plants produced the same set of products, employed the same technologies and operating systems, and had highly similar layouts.

In-depth interviews with both plant managers and human resources managers at the two plants suggested that there were several minor differences in organizational practices between the plants. For example, plant A used a time clock, and plant B had employees manually complete time sheets. Likewise, plant A required all employees to take their breaks and lunch time according to a fixed schedule, and plant B allowed employees to take their breaks and lunch time whenever they chose. At the time the study was designed, I did not consider those differences to be particularly meaningful, at least in terms of their potential impact on QCs. Hence, the differences were not controlled for or measured. There remains the possibility, therefore, that between-plant differences influenced the pattern of results obtained.

Procedures

All employees at the two plants responded to a baseline (time 1) questionnaire administered on-site by their plant's human resources manager. I was present for about half the sessions at each plant. Employees were told that the survey was part of a company-sponsored study of employee attitudes being conducted by a

---

1. Conversations with corporate officials suggested that, in reality, his practices were no more participative than those of his counterparts in other plants. He simply saw himself as being more open.

university researcher. They were assured of confidentiality. In particular, it was explained that I would be summarizing the data for company management but that no one else would have access to their individual questionnaires.

Employees completed the questionnaires in small groups in a conference room during normal working hours. Those who completed it while I was not present were asked to put their questionnaire in a large metered envelope addressed to me. Before each group was dismissed, its envelope was sealed and a volunteer solicited to place the envelope in the mail. Follow-up analyses revealed no significant differences between employees whose questionnaires were collected directly and those who mailed them. Employees who were absent were surveyed on their first day back at work. Employees were asked to identify themselves with their payroll number. I tabulated performance data for the six months immediately preceding the administration of the questionnaires at each time point, including time 1.

Quality Circle Implementation

In early 1983, the QC program was implemented in plant A. Volunteers were solicited through the plant newsletter and through several informational sessions that were scheduled during lunch hours and after work. The company offered no direct financial incentives for participating. Instead, management explained that all employees would benefit through the existing profit-sharing plan if the QC program was able to cut costs and thereby increase profits. A total of 73 operating employees committed themselves to participating in the program. The 73 volunteers were organized into eight quality circles on the basis of general work locations and areas of responsibility. Members of three of the circles were from the same departments and therefore had the same supervisors. Four of the circles included employees from very similar but not identical work units and consequently had multiple employee-supervisor dyads. For example, the members of one circle came from three different departments; their work was quite similar across departments, but they reported to three different supervisors. The remaining circle was more heterogeneous than the others and was specifically charged to address fairly general problems germane to all employees.

At the first meeting of each QC I explained that, to follow up the earlier survey, I was interested in assessing their attitudes and behaviors as they participated in the QC program and asked that they agree to respond to identical questionnaires three more times. The same assurances of confidentiality were made, and all members agreed to participate.

Selection of the Comparison Group

To truly assess change, of course, it is necessary to have a control or comparison group. One alternative was to use others in the same plant as a control. That idea was rejected, however, because those individuals had specifically been given the opportunity to participate and had declined. Thus, there were reasons to believe that there may have been differences between participants and nonparticipants in the same plant.[2] Moreover, interaction between participants and nonpartici- pants could have affected the data.

Another alternative was to use employees who might be similar to the experimental group but who would be unaware of the treatment and had not specifically rejected an opportunity to participate. This option seemed to have more strengths and fewer weaknesses than the other. Thus, I decided to use a matched-pairs nonequivalent control-group design. The goal was to identify a group of employees in the same company that was as similar as possible to the experimental group. Such a design overcomes all basic threats to validity except the effects of selection-maturation, scaling, and local history (Campbell & Stanley, 1966). Scaling effects are negligible in this form of research (Kaplan, 1964). Local history effects can be partially assessed through the monitoring and assessment of organizational activities. Finally, selection-maturation effects can be determined through the use of treatment-effect correlations (Cook & Campbell, 1976; Joyce, 1986).

The matched group was to consist of 73 employees in plant B whose responses to the questionnaire were as similar as possible to those of the QC participants. I used an iterative comparison process to identify the group. The four individual-level measures used in this study (and discussed in a later section) were first transformed to a common metric of 100 each both for the 73 QC participants and for all employees at plant B. I then used a computer program to match a plant B individual to each QC participant. The procedure was as follows: from the questionnaire scores of a given QC participant, the scores of each employee in plant B were subtracted and the absolute values of the differences summed. The employee at plant B with the smallest total difference was identified as the given QC participant's match.

The 73 people so selected and I met at plant B in small groups. I asked them to participate in a study of employee attitudes the company was conducting, made the same assurances of confidentiality as with the plant A employees, and outlined the same procedures for data collection. It was explained that the study would be comparing data across plants and that they had been randomly selected to participate; the QC program at plant A was not discussed.[3] Three of the original 73 employees declined to participate. Three other employees who provided the next-best match were then chosen; each agreed to participate.

The QC members participated in a two-day off-site training program in problem solving and then began following standard QC procedures. They met

2. For example, Brockner and Hess (1986) found self-esteem to be a factor contributing to QC success.

3. The rationale for this mild deception was that if plant B employees were told of the QC program at the other plant, they might question why they were not given an opportunity to participate in such a program themselves. At the very least, it would raise questions in their minds. At the other extreme, it might have made them angry, hostile, or resentful.

once a week for the duration of this study, except for a few weeks when several members were absent from work, such as around Christmas and during peak summer vacation periods. Meetings typically lasted one to two hours, although they occasionally lasted a little longer. Members chose the problems to address and communicated their activities and suggestions to plant management about once a month, reporting on forms prepared specifically for that purpose.

Each group chose its own leader, typically a volunteer from among the members but in a few cases an individual nominated and voted on by the membership. The leaders handled the reporting duties. The QCs tackled a variety of problems. For example, one group recognized that at one stage of assembly, work-in-process was allowed to sit in a high-traffic, open area for several hours and sometimes even for days. When it next entered the work system, it was not uncommon for some of the work to have been damaged. The group developed a plan to rearrange work stations so that the waiting station was close to an unused storage closet. The work-in-process was then stored in the closet. Consequently, waste and damage at this stage were greatly decreased.

Follow-up Measures

The baseline measures described earlier served as time 1 assessments. All individual-level variables were subsequently measured again at 6 months (time 2), 18 months (time 3), and 36 months (time 4). The plants' respective human resources managers administered each follow-up questionnaire on-site during normal working hours.[4]

If an employee from either group had left the company or been transferred during the period of the study, data from his or her counterpart in the other group were not used in the remaining statistical analyses. The size of each group declined to 72 at the 6-month mark, to 70 at the 18-month mark, and to 64 at the 36-month mark.[5]

The executive committee of plant A and the plant controller also provided assessments of the effectiveness of the QC effort at each of the follow-up measurement periods, using 3-item assessment scales developed specifically for this study. Twelve months beyond time 4 (at the 48-month mark), the plant controller also provided an assessment of the financial impact of the QC program.

At the time 3 mark, I visited plant A and met with each QC individually. These meetings were unstructured, at the request of the plant manager, and very informal. The purpose of the interviews was to get general impressions as to how the QC program was going, if there were problems, and so forth. More

4. I was not present for these sessions; the same sealed envelope procedure described earlier was used.

5. Follow-up analyses using only the 64 participants across all time points did not reveal any differences in results.

systematic interviews with participants and managers were conducted approximately 12 months after time 4.

Measures

Job Satisfaction

Overall job satisfaction was measured with the short form of the Minnesota Satisfaction Questionnaire (MSQ) (Weiss, Davis, England, & Lofquist, 1967). The MSQ is a 20-item instrument that has been shown to have acceptable levels of reliability and validity across a variety of settings (Cook, Hepworth, Wall, & Warr, 1981). Responses are on 5-point scales ranging from strongly agree to strongly disagree. At time 1, the coefficient alpha for this study was .86 at plant A and .90 at plant B.

Organizational Commitment

Organizational commitment was measured with the 15-item scale developed by Porter, Steers, Mowday, and Boulian (1974). Responses are on 7-point scales anchored by strongly agree and strongly disagree. Again, this scale has well-documented psychometric properties (Griffin & Bateman, 1986). The coefficient alpha was .78 at plant A and .83 at plant B at the baseline.

Performance Rating

Performance was based on supervisory ratings. Each employee in the two plants received an evaluation every six months. The evaluation involved the supervisor rating the employee on performance quantity (40 points possible), performance quality (40 points), attendance (10 points), and other contributions, such as cooperativeness and willingness to help others (10 points). The four separate indices were summed to provide an overall index of performance with a maximum value of 100. The evaluations, which have been used by the organization for several years, provided the basis for all merit wage increases in the plant.[6] Supervisors had been explicitly told that employee participation in the QC program was not to be considered in the normal evaluations. There were two reasons for this. First, the company wanted the performance data for participants and nonparticipants to be as comparable as possible. Second, the popular literature on QCs argues that no additional compensation should be given to participants. Of course, there was no way to ensure that contamination did not, in fact, occur.

---

6. The company also occasionally provides cost-of-living and seniority-based increases for all employees.

Intentions to Quit

Intentions to quit were assessed with the 3-item scale developed by Seashore, Lawler, Mirvis, and Cammann (1982). Responses are on 7-point scales anchored by not at all likely and extremely likely. The baseline alpha was .93 for plant A and .92 for plant B.

Managerial Assessment

Managers at plant A also assessed the effectiveness of each QC relative to its costs at each of the three follow-up measurement points. Four members of the plant executive committee, the plant manager, the operations manager, the human resources manager, and the distribution manager, responded to a 3-item scale summarized in the Appendix. The plant controller provided independent assessments of the effectiveness of the QCs. Although he was also a member of the executive committee, he was perhaps better attuned than its other members to the financial costs and benefits of the QCs within their plant. The three items on the controller's scale paralleled those on the other managers' but were related more specifically to the dollar value of the QC program. The Appendix also lists these items.

After time 4, the controller also provided an estimate of the actual financial costs and benefits of the program. The data were generated as part of a report to corporate management on the cost effectiveness of the program. Because of the proprietary nature of the data, I only received summary figures. Moreover, although there is no reason to question the validity of the data, there is also no evidence of their accuracy beyond the fact that confidence can be placed in generally accepted accounting and reporting procedures.

RESULTS

Table 1 presents the baseline (time 1) means and standard deviations for all variables for both plants and for each group within the plants. I performed MANOVAs to assess mean differences between (1) plant populations, (2) participant groups, and (3) participant groups and plant populations minus participant groups. No significant F-values were obtained. Thus, there were no apparent differences between the two plants or between volunteers and nonvolunteers for the QC program before the QC program was introduced, at least in terms of the four dependent variables under investigation.

Table 2 shows the correlation matrix for the four variables for the experimental and control groups at time 1. The values in upper triangle are within-experimental-group intercorrelations; those in the lower right triangle are within-comparison-group intercorrelations; and those in the lower left square of the matrix are between-group intercorrelations. The strong positive correlations in the diagonal of the square provide support for the validity of the matching procedure. As might be expected, there were also moderate to large

TABLE 1
Baseline Means and Standard Deviations[a,b]

	Plant A		Plant B		Experimental Group		Comparison Group	
Variables	Means	s.d.	Means	s.d	Means	s.d.	Means	s.d.
Job satisfaction	3.23	1.02	3.17	1.10	3.18	0.99	3.12	1.04
Organizational commitment	4.31	1.46	4.49	1.61	4.40	1.42	4.47	1.56
Performance ratings	82.78	12.94	80.44	11.55	80.17	11.64	81.92	12.13
Intentions to quit	3.49	1.26	3.54	1.17	3.31	1.09	3.47	0.98

[a]The results of multivariate F-tests between plant populations, between participant groups, and between participant groups and plant populations minus participant groups were not significant at $p < .05$.
[b]Ns for the four groupings were 496, 427, 73, and 73.

correlations among the measures of organizational commitment, job satisfaction, and intentions to quit both within and between groups. Performance ratings were not correlated with any of the other three variables, although performance ratings between the two groups were correlated.

Quantitative Results

A MANOVA was performed on the three individual-level questionnaire-derived dependent variables across time points to assess between-and within-group changes over time. The resultant F-value, 18.13, was significant beyond the .001 level. I then conducted univariate F-tests across time periods for each variable. Table 3 presents results. There were significant differences over time for each variable for the experimental group but not for the comparison group. For example, there was a significant difference between the mean values for job satisfaction within the experimental group across the four time points. There were also significant differences at time 3 between the two groups in mean values for job satisfaction, organizational commitment, and performance ratings, and at time 2 there were significant differences between means for commitment.

Duncan's multiple range tests were then conducted to determine which pairs of means within groups and across time points were significantly different. Table 4 summarizes the results, which show a very clear pattern of changes in the means. The greatest and most consistent changes were between time 1 and time 3, when all four variables in the experimental group increased significantly. By time 4, however, all variables had decreased back to a level not significantly different from time 1 levels.

As noted earlier, treatment-effect correlations were also calculated to assess the possible effects of selection and maturation. As explained by Joyce (1986), this procedure involves correlating measures of a treatment, coded with a dummy variable, with measures of the criterion before and after the treatment. If exposure to the treatment affects the criterion, the treatment-effect

TABLE 2
Time 1 Baseline Correlation Matrix for the Two Groups[a]

Variables	Experimental Group				Comparison Group			
	1	2	3	4	5	6	7	8
Experimental group								
1. Job satisfaction	(86)							
2. Organizational commitment	38**	(78)						
3. Performance rating	06	−04	N.A.					
4. Intentions to quit	−24*	−57***	−09	(93)				
Comparison group								
5. Job satisfaction	88***	21	01	−26*	(90)			
6. Organizational commitment	17	84***	07	−29*	38***	(83)		
7. Performance rating	06	08	72***	04	−03	10	N.A.	
8. Intentions to quit	−22	−31**	06	90***	−37***	−51***	07	(92)

[a]Numbers in parentheses are reliability estimates. For each group, $N = 73$. Decimal points have been omitted.
* $p < .05$
** $p < .01$
*** $p < .001$

TABLE 3
Results of Univariate F-tests for Differences Between Experimental and Comparison Groups[a]

Dependent Variables	Time 1 (N = 73)	Time 2 (N = 72)	Time 3 (N = 70)	Time 4 (N = 64)	Time 4-Time 1 (N = 64)	F
Job satisfaction						
Experimental group	3.18	3.72	**3.96**	3.34	0.16	5.37*
Comparison group	3.12	3.21	**3.08**	3.27	0.15	1.06
Organizational commitment						
Experimental group	4.40	**5.21**	**6.04**	4.92	0.52	6.72**
Comparison group	4.47	**4.20**	**4.75**	4.81	0.34	2.19
Performance rating						
Experimental group	80.17	82.24	**86.82**	78.04	−2.13	4.82*
Comparison group	81.92	82.02	**80.26**	81.16	−0.76	1.42
Intentions to quit						
Experimental group	3.31	3.04	2.72	3.44	0.13	4.94*
Comparison group	3.47	3.51	3.14	3.37	−0.10	1.36

[a]Pairs of means in boldface are significantly different at $p < .05$.
* $p < .05$
** $p < .01$

TABLE 4
Results of Duncan's Multiple Range Tests[a]

Dependent Variables	Time 1-Time 2	Time 1-Time 3	Time 1-Time 4	Time 2-Time 3	Time 2-Time 4	Time 3-Time 4
Job satisfaction						
Experimental group	.05	.05	n.s.	n.s.	n.s.	.05
Comparison group	n.s.	n.s.	n.s.	n.s.	n.s.	n.s.
Organizational commitment						
Experimental group	.05	.01	n.s.	.05	n.s.	.05
Comparison group	n.s.	n.s.	n.s.	n.s.	.05	n.s.
Performance rating						
Experimental group	n.s.	.05	n.s.	n.s.	n.s.	.05
Comparison group	n.s.	n.s.	n.s.	n.s.	n.s.	n.s.
Intentions to quit						
Experimental group	n.s.	.05	n.s.	n.s.	n.s.	.05
Comparison group	n.s.	n.s.	n.s.	n.s.	n.s.	n.s.

[a]Significance levels indicate within-group differences across corresponding time intervals for the variable noted.

correlation between the dummy and criterion should be significant. Since this design was somewhat complex, with multiple criterion variables and three posttreatment measures, it was necessary to employ a multivariate analog. My approach was to conduct a one-way analysis of variance among groups before the treatment and a three-way analysis of variance after the treatment and to compare the results. This approach simulates a pure treatment-effect design (Cook & Campbell, 1976) and controls for both selection and maturation. The pretreatment F-value (1.92) was not significant, but the posttreatment F-value (9.46) was significant at the .01 level. The F-values were also significantly different from each other at the .01 level. Thus, neither selection nor maturation appears to have had a detectable influence on the results.

Finally, Table 5 summarizes the results of the executive committee's and controller's ratings of QC effectiveness. Given the sizes of the data sets, no statistical tests could be conducted. The ratings, however, followed the same pattern as the mean values for the experimental group on the four dependent variables. In particular, the ratings increased from time 2 to time 3 but declined between time 3 and time 4.

Qualitative Results

Considering the qualitative data gleaned through the interviews helps to bring out the meaning and pattern of the empirical results. As noted earlier, the time 3 interviews were very informal and unstructured. I visited the site and met with each individual QC for about 30 minutes, asking general questions about how things were going for the circle, whether the members thought their time was being used wisely, and similar issues. This format was followed because the plant manager did not want the members to feel they were being examined too critically or systematically. Essentially, each group felt that it was doing a good job and making a positive contribution to the organization and that the organization appreciated and valued it. Members of one group expressed some frustration that the organization had not adopted two recommendations they felt very good about. This unhappiness, however, seemed to be relatively minor.

Twelve months after time 4 (about 48 months after the program began) the QC program was still operational. At that point, I again interviewed each of the circles as a group, as well as the plant manager and the controller. The results

TABLE 5
Managerial Assessments of QC Effectiveness

Variables	Time 2	Time 3	Time 4	Time 4−Time 2
Executive committee composite rating	4.40	5.62	4.55	0.15
Controller's rating	3.33	4.67	3.00	−0.33

this time were much different. Few members of the QCs were actually negative, but most had become somewhat indifferent about their participation. Several, for example, noted that the company had started taking them for granted. They felt that their efforts were no longer appreciated as much, that management was becoming less interested in their recommendations, and that they were simply not contributing as much as they had earlier in the program. Each group provided a few anecdotes to support its feelings, and the anecdotes were quite similar across groups. Members generally noted, for example, that managers asked fewer questions about how the group was functioning, displayed less enthusiasm when suggestions were made, and did not evaluate the suggestions as thoroughly as they had earlier in the program.

Some members also speculated that perhaps the QC program had reached a point at which it might be best to discontinue it. One group, for example, recalled that it had initially been easily able to identify problems and solutions. After the obvious problems had been solved, though, the work became harder. Finding problems was difficult, and solving them was even more so.

Only one group really felt that it was making the same level of contributions that it had originally made. Its members seemed to believe that there were plenty of problems to be tackled and that their work was far from done. Even they, however, agreed that they were not as valued by management as they had been earlier.

The tenor of the discussion with the plant manager was consistent with the feelings of the QC members. He too agreed that the QCs were contributing less and less. He thought, for example, that their value to the company had peaked around the 24-month mark and had then started to decline. Interestingly, however, he made no reference to taking the QCs for granted, nor did he think that the list of problems had been exhausted. Instead, he formulated a quite different explanation for the drop in effectiveness. His feeling was that the members of the QCs had simply lost interest in what they were doing. The manager felt that there were many more problems they could choose to address but that they had simply lost their motivation to do so. For example, he observed that they were not as enthusiastic when they met as they had been earlier and that the write-ups of their suggestions were increasingly superficial.

Finally, the feelings of the controller mirrored those of the plant manager, although he took a more balanced approach to understanding why things had deteriorated. At the time of the interview, he had just completed a report requested by corporate management on the effectiveness of the program. He was willing to share important but limited data from that report. In particular, he reported that the QCs had made a total of 122 formal recommendations during the 48 months the program had been in effect. Of those, the company had adopted 81 as proposed, adopted another 10 in a modified form, and rejected the remainder.

He estimated that the total cost of the program to that point was about $142,520—$107,520 in wages, $15,000 for the original training, and $20,000 to implement several of the recommendations. He also estimated that over the 48-month period, the company had realized $65,000 in one-time savings. For example, one QC planned how to best install several new machines; the controller noted that their plan saved the company $8,000 over its standard procedures for installing new equipment. The company was also realizing approximately $20,000 per year in continued cost savings from recommendations about operating systems. For example, the storage of work-in-process in a convenient closet, as described earlier, was estimated to be saving around $1,500 per year in damage costs.

The bottom line for the controller, then, was that the QC program was fairly effective to date. The costs were greater than the benefits, but those benefits would continue to accrue for the foreseeable future. However, he also indicated that many of the benefits had come between the two- and the three-year mark. He noted in particular that the financial impact of the QCs during their fourth year had been minimal. He attributed that pattern to three things: fewer problems to tackle, loss of enthusiasm by the participants, and loss of interest by the management team.

DISCUSSION

The purpose of this study was to assess the consequences of quality circles for both participants and a sponsoring organization. The study employed a longitudinal and experimental design. The results were fairly unambiguous. Scores for the four primary individual-level dependent variables, job satisfaction, organizational commitment, performance, and intentions to quit, improved gradually up to the 18-month mark and then decreased back to their initial levels. During the same periods, management's perceptions of the effectiveness of the QC program followed the same pattern.

On the basis of the organization's own analysis of the effectiveness of its QC program and the findings of this study, the company undertook several changes in the program. For example, about 42 months into the program, the manager of plant B was reassigned to open a new plant for the company. His successor decided to implement a QC program in plant B. At plant A, the manager planned an attempt to revitalize the program. In particular, he decided to meet with each group and express his renewed enthusiasm and commitment to the QC concept. He also decided to implement a new reward system: QC members would share in the cost savings they generated through direct payments. He also decided to solicit volunteers for up to four new circles.

Each of the plant managers at the other four plants also spoke briefly with me. Three who had adopted QCs reported experiences remarkably similar to those at plant A: impressive initial results, with a decline after anywhere from 12 to 36 months. However, their responses to that pattern differed. One manager had already dropped the QC program, and another was planning to drop his program in the near future. The third was still optimistic and, after discussing things with the plant A manager, had decided to follow the latter's strategy for attempting to revitalize the program.

Thus, the evidence is fairly straightforward and consistent: in this organization, QCs were successful from the standpoints of both the participants and the organization for around two years but then began to decline. Before that conclusion is accepted at face value, however, rival hypotheses and alternative explanations should be considered.

As noted earlier, the design used in this study entails three basic threats to validity: scaling, local history, and selection-maturation effects. Possible selection-maturation effects were controlled statistically through the treatment-effect correlations comparison, and scaling effects do not play a major role in social experiments. Thus, local history effects would be the remaining threat to consider. The follow-up interview with the plant manager explored the extent to which layoffs, changes in top management, major conflicts at the plant, and labor opposition could have intervened. He said that no such events had occurred during the period of the study and that things had been pretty much "business as usual." Of course, his view may well have been biased, and there were no objective measures or controls available to cross-validate his assessment. Thus, there is no way to assure that local history did not intervene.

Other limitations and issues also constrain the findings. For one thing, it is always possible in research on change that nothing more than a Hawthorne effect has occurred—that employee perceptions and attitudes have altered because of increased attention, measurement, or other factors rather than because of the specific intervention studied. In addition, there is no meaningful way to determine the representativeness of the QC program. There is a general feeling, for example, that in Japanese organizations a very high percentage of the workforce is involved in QC activities (cf., Cole, 1980). However, there are no published statistics available as to what the exact percentage is. Likewise, there are no statistics available regarding the extent of QC participation in American companies that have adopted the approach. In all likelihood, there are some companies with only a small percentage of their workers involved in QCs, and others with a much higher level of participation. The fact remains, however, that a reasonable number of people in the organization studied did participate in what appears to be a representative QC program.

Beyond those considerations, it can only be noted that as much care as possible was taken to ensure the strongest and most thorough assessment of the QC program. The multiple measures, for example, provided at least reasonable additional support for the validity of the findings.

Given the inherent strengths and weaknesses of the design, then, there are several possible implications that can be drawn from this study both for theory and research and for practice. Lawler and Mohrman (1987) recently described a so-called honeymoon effect in quality circle programs. They noted that "during this phase a small number of groups is formed; these groups are strongly motivated to produce good ideas and improvements, and as a result the organization often realizes significant gains" (1987: 43). Most organizations consequently add many more groups, which have to compete for management attention and are established more mechanistically than the original groups. The overall program is subject to declining interest, nonproductive groups, and extra costs. They concluded that QCs are best viewed as transitional techniques for implementing a more participative culture in an organization. For example, they suggested that QCs be transformed into task forces and then workteams and also advocated adding a reward component to QC participation after a program is institutionalized.

Taken together with the results of this study, Lawler and Mohrman's suggestions seem quite plausible. The honeymoon effect is quite likely what occurred at plant A. Although the organization did not add new circles right away, there was clear evidence of an increasingly mechanistic approach and declining interest and enthusiasm. The organization's later decision to add more circles and implement a reward component also fits Lawler and Mohrman's conclusions.

An alternate approach might also call for the use of QCs as an organic short-term strategy for enhancing organizational effectiveness. In particular, in some settings it might be possible to develop a QC program, monitor the results, and disband groups as their effectiveness begins to diminish. Of course, the organization that takes such an approach runs the risk of resentment or hostility from its workers if they do not share management's perceptions of diminishing effectiveness.

The organization studied has apparently achieved some value from its QC program. It incurred considerable costs but is likely to realize long-term gains. It also seems quite likely that QC programs will remain in vogue for at least the near future. In all likelihood, QCs will become another in a set of organizational change interventions (like job enrichment, MBO, and modified workgroups) that are appropriate and effective in some settings but less appropriate and effective in others. Thus, there is a clear need for additional research into the effects of QCs. In particular, we need to develop additional insights into all of the following questions: When are QCs most effective? Who chooses to participate in QCs? How should QCs be managed? Can the extent of their effectiveness cycle be increased? Can their costs and benefits be more accurately measured? Are they best viewed as a self-contained intervention or as a transitional technique?

To approach such questions, it will be necessary to develop research programs that span a variety of organizations, rely on both participant-level and organizational measures and data, and take a long-term, experimental view. In addition, careful consideration should be given to the organizational context of QCs.

Finally, as noted earlier, the use of QCs is implicitly grounded in the theory of participation in workplaces. The literature on participation strongly argues for its positive effects on a variety of outcomes, although the empirical research on such effects is less than convincing. The present study, then, can also be seen as making a valuable contribution to that literature. Although the effects of other participative strategies may have differed, the approach studied here yielded fairly clear and unambiguous patterns over time. It seems reasonable to speculate that other approaches to participation might well have resulted in the same pattern. That is, perhaps the context and general nature of participation, not a given participative technique, cause change effects to first increase and then diminish.

The behavioral sciences have enormous potential to add to organizational effectiveness. Carefully managed interventions like quality circles have the potential to aid managers as they attempt to compete in both domestic and international arenas. The key to effectiveness may be to avoid a faddish, bandwagon approach and, instead, to develop an appropriate menu of interventions that we have some basis for recommending and some understanding of how to manage.

REFERENCES

Brockner, J., & Hess., T. 1986. Self-esteem and task performance in quality circles. *Academy of Management Journal*, 29: 617–623.

Campbell, D. T., & Stanley, J. 1966. *Experimental designs and quasi-experimental designs for research.* Chicago: Rand McNally & Co.

Cole, R. E. 1980. *Work, mobility, and participation: A comparative study of American and Japanese industry.* Berkeley, Calif.: University of California Press.

Cook, J. D., Hepworth, S. J., Wall, T. D., & Warr, P. B. 1981. *The experience of work.* London: Academic Press.

Cook, T. D., & Campbell, D. T. 1976. The design and control of quasi-experiments in field settings. In M. D. Dunnette (Ed.), *Handbook of industrial and organizational psychology:* 223–326. Chicago: Rand McNally & Co.

Griffin, R. W., & Bateman, T. 1986. Job satisfaction and organizational commitment. In C. L. Cooper and I. Robertson (Eds.), *International review of industrial and organizational psychology:* 157–188. London: John Wiley & Sons.

Joyce, W. F. 1986. Matrix organization: A social experiment. *Academy of Management Journal*, 29: 536–561.

Kaplan, A. 1964. *The conduct of inquiry.* New York: Chandler.

Keys, J. B., & Miller, T. R. 1984. The Japanese management theory jungle. *Academy of Management Review*, 9: 342–353.

Lawler, E. E. III, & Mohrman, S. A. 1985. Quality circles after the fad. *Harvard Business Review*, 63(1): 65–71.

Lawler, E. E. III, & Mohrman, S. A. 1987. Quality circles: After the honeymoon. *Organizational Dynamics*, 15(4): 42–54.

Marks, M. L., Mirvis, P. H., Hackett, E. J., & Grady, J. F., Jr. 1986. Employee participation in a quality circle program: Impact on quality of work life, productivity, and absenteeism. *Journal of Applied Psychology*, 71: 61–69.

Meyer, G. W., & Stott, R. G. 1985. Quality circles: Panacea or Pandora's box? *Organizational Dynamics*, 13(4): 34–50.

Miller, K. I., & Monge, P. R. 1986. Participation, satisfaction, and productivity: A meta-analytic review. *Academy of Management Journal,* 29: 727–753.

Munchus, G. III. 1983. Employer-employee based quality circles in Japan: Human resource policy implications for American firms. *Academy of Management Review,* 8: 255–261.

Ouchi, W. 1981a. Organizational paradigms: A commentary on Japanese management and Theory Z organizations. *Organizational Dynamics,* 9(4): 36–43.

Ouchi, W. 1981b. *Theory Z.* Reading, Mass.: Addison-Wesley.

Porter, L. W., Steers, R. M., Mowday, R. T., & Boulian, P. V. 1974. Organizational commitment, job satisfaction, and turnover among psychiatric technicians. *Journal of Applied Psychology,* 69: 603–609.

Seashore, S. E., Lawler, E. E. III, Mirvis, P., & Cammann, C. 1982. *Observing and measuring organizational change: A guide to field practice.* New York: Wiley.

Wagner, J. A. III, & Gooding, R. Z. 1987. Shared influence and organizational behavior: A meta-analysis of situational variables expected to moderate participation-outcome relationships. *Academy of Management Journal,* 30: 524–541.

Weiss, A. 1984. Simple truths of Japanese manufacturing. *Harvard Business Review,* 62(4): 119–125.

Weiss, D. J., Davis, R. V., England, G. W., & Lofquist, L. H. 1967. *Manual for the Minnesota Satisfaction Questionnaire.* Minneapolis: University of Minnesota.

Appendix

Managerial Assessment Items

All responses were on 7-point scales ranging from strongly agree (7) to strongly disagree (1). The three items for the managers ($\alpha = .96$) were:

1. Relative to the costs of the program, the QCs in the plant are making a great contribution to plant effectiveness.
2. The QC program in this plant has been quite successful.
3. All things considered, the QC program in this plant has done all it was expected to do.

The three items for the controller were:

1. The dollar savings generated by the QCs in our plant are greater than the costs of running those QCs.
2. The suggestions made by the QCs have saved the company money.
3. The financial impact of the QC program in this plant has been more positive than negative.

Ricky W. Griffin is an associate professor of management at Texas A&M University. He obtained his doctorate from the University of Houston in 1978. His current research interests include quality circles, task design, and the determinants of managerial success.

Practice Self-Test

The Problem(s)

_____

_____

_____

The Procedures

_____

_____

_____

The Method(s) of Analysis

_____

_____

_____

The Major Conclusion(s)

_____

_____

_____

Method

_____

_____

_____

Reasons

_____

_____

_____

REFERENCES

Goodson, J. R., McGee, G. W., & Cashman, J. F. (1988). Situational leadership theory. *Group & Organization Studies, 14*(4), 446–461.

Huse, E. F., & Cummings, T. G. (1985). *Organization development and change* (3rd ed.). St. Paul, MN: West Publishing Co.

Kotter, J. P. (1982). *The general managers.* New York: The Free Press.

Labich, K. (1988, June 6). The innovators. *Fortune,* pp. 49–64.

Ouchi, W. G., & Bolton, M. K. (1988). The logic of joint research and development. *California Management Review.* 30(3), 9–33.

Richman, L. S. (1988, June 6). Why throw money at asbestos? *Fortune,* pp. 155–170.

Rogers, C. R., & Farson, R. E. (1979). Active listening. In Kolb, D. A., Rubin, I. M., & McIntyre, J. M. (Eds.), *Organizational psychology: A book of readings* (3rd ed., pp. 168–180). Englewood Cliffs, NJ: Prentice-Hall.

Smith, L. (1989, June 5). Can consortiums defeat Japan? *Fortune,* pp. 245–254.

Von Daniken, E. (1972). *Chariots of the gods?* New York: Bantam Books.

Weintraub, P. (1991, January). Challenge and response: Business management in the 21st century. *Omni,* pp. 35–37, 54.

Yakal, K. (1989, June). Express training at Federal Express. *Training,* pp. 12, 14.

PART TWO
Research Problems

Selection and definition of a research problem is a refinement process that begins with the identification of a problem area and terminates with one or more testable hypotheses or answerable questions. The refinement process is based primarily upon a thorough review and critical analysis of related literature. Once a problem area is identified and a specific problem within it selected, a tentative hypothesis is formulated; this tentative hypothesis guides the literature review, which in turn forms the basis for the final statement of the research hypothesis. Selection and definition of a problem is a very important component of the research process and entails much time and thought. The statement of the problem, the review of related literature, and the statement of the hypothesis comprise the introduction section of both research plans and research reports on completed research. The only difference may be the tense in which the introduction is written; research plans are usually written in the future tense ("The subjects will be selected . . ."), but research reports are always written in the past tense ("The subjects were selected . . .").

The problem that you ultimately select in this part of the book is the problem with which you will work in succeeding parts. Therefore, it is important that you select a problem that is relevant to your area of study (e.g., management in multinational companies), of particular interest to you, and researchable using an experimental design. Also, since you will be responsible for a comprehensive literature search, it will be to your benefit to select a manageable, well-defined problem. For example, "the use of reinforcement in management" is not manageable and well defined; "the effect of specific and timely praise on the weekly productivity of customer-service representatives" is manageable and well defined.

The goal of Part Two is for you to acquire the ability to identify and define a meaningful problem, conduct an adequate review of related literature, and state the problem in terms of a testable hypothesis. After you have read Part II, you should be able to perform the following project.

Project II Guidelines

Write an introduction for a research study including:

1. statement of the specific problem to be investigated in the study.
2. background concerning the significance of the problem.
3. review of related literature including a summary statement.
4. testable hypothesis.

Include definitions of terms where appropriate.

(See Project II Performance Criteria, p. 82)

Some students spend many anxiety-ridden days and sleepless nights worrying about where they are going to find the problem they need for their research paper, thesis, or dissertation. (page 51)

2

Selection and Definition of a Problem

Objectives

After reading Chapter 2, you should be able to do the following:

1. Make a list of at least three management problems for which you would be interested in conducting a research study.

2. Select one of the problems; identify at least 15 complete references that directly relate to the selected problem. The sources of the references should include at least the following:

   Readers' Guide to Periodical Literature
   Business Periodicals Index
   Wall Street Journal Index
   Dissertation Abstracts International
   Psychological Abstracts

   (At least one of your references should come from each of the above sources as you need to learn to access all of them.)

3. Read and abstract the references you have listed.

4. Formulate at least one testable hypothesis for your problem

SELECTION AND STATEMENT OF THE PROBLEM

After a problem area of interest is identified, a specific problem is selected for investigation. Theory and experience are two major sources of problems. A good problem has a number of identifiable characteristics. A good statement of a problem also conforms to a set of important criteria.

Selection of a Research Topic

For beginning researchers, selection of a problem is the most difficult step in the research process. Some students spend many anxiety-ridden days and sleepless nights worrying about where they are going to find the problem they need for their research paper, thesis, or dissertation. To the poor student it seems as if every problem she or he identifies is dismissed by his or her professor as being trivial or "already done." The problem is not a lack of problems; there is almost an unlimited supply of problems that need to be researched. The problem is a lack of familiarity with the literature on the student's part. Learning how and where to locate problems and systematically attacking this phase of the research process are much better for your mental health than worrying yourself into a nervous collapse!

The first step in selecting a problem is to identify a general problem area that is related to your area of expertise and is of particular interest to you. Examples of problem areas might be the use of computers in training and development of employees, increasing productivity among specific worker groups, issues related to American managers working in foreign countries, union-management issues, ethical issues for whistle blowers, the impact of technology on workers' health, substance abuse in the workplace, and the effect of various kinds of restructuring on profitability. Since you will be doing a great deal of reading in the area you select, and devoting many hours to the planning and implementation of the ultimate study, choosing a topic of interest that will increase your knowledge and understanding in your particular professional area makes good sense. If you can view this as the chance to read widely in the subject in which you want to develop special expertise, it will help with this process.

The next step is to narrow down the general problem area to a specific, researchable problem. One of us recently overheard an undergraduate student approach the university librarian with the statement, "I need information on leveraged buyouts." "What do you want to know about them?" the librarian asked. "Everything," the student replied. A problem that is too general can only cause you grief. In the first place, the scope of the review of related literature that you must inevitably conduct will be unnecessarily increased, possibly resulting in your spending many more hours in the library. This will in turn complicate the organization of the results in the review and subsequent hypothesis development. Even more important than the practicalities, a problem that is too general tends to result in a study that is too general, includes too many variables, and produces results that are too difficult to interpret. Conversely, a well-defined, manageable problem results in a well-defined, manageable study. One major way to narrow your problem is to read sources giving overviews or summaries of the current status of research in your area. Academic and professional journals can be useful in this respect.

In narrowing the problem area you will want to select an aspect of the general problem area that is related to your area of expertise. For example, the general problem area "the use of performance reviews to increase productivity" could generate many specific problems such as "the effect of monthly versus semiannual performance reviews on the productivity of bank tellers" or "the effect of narrative versus checklist performance reviews on the productivity of first line supervisors." In your efforts to delineate a problem sufficiently, however, be careful not to get carried away; a problem that is too narrow is just as bad as a problem that is too broad. A study on the effect of daily reminders in reducing personal phone calls during work hours would probably contribute little, if anything, to the science of management! Remember, you must always be ready to answer the dreaded question: So what?

In summary, selecting a good problem is well worth the time and effort. As mentioned previously, there is no shortage of significant problems that need research; there is really no excuse for selecting a trite problem. Besides, it is generally to your advantage to select a worthwhile problem; you will certainly get a great deal more out of it professionally and academically. If the subsequent study is well conducted and reported, besides making a contribution to knowledge, it also has a good probability of being published in a professional journal. The potential personal benefits to be derived from publication include increased professional status and job opportunities, not to mention tremendous self-satisfaction.

Sources of Problems

You may be asking yourself, "So where do I find one of those numerous significant problems that need research?" While there are several major sources of problems, the most meaningful ones are generally those derived from theory. Many of us will casually comment that we have a theory about something, meaning that we have a hunch or belief about something. As Kerlinger (1973) states, "A theory is a set of interrelated constructs (concepts), definitions, and propositions that represent a systematic view of phenomena by specifying relations among variables, with the purpose of explaining and predicting phenomena (p. 9)."

There are many relevant theories in management, such as theories of motivation and leadership, from which problems can be drawn. The fact that a theory is a theory and not a body of facts means that it contains generalizations and hypothesized principles that must be subjected to rigorous scientific investigation. Problems derived from a theoretical problem area are not only preferable in terms of contribution to true scientific progress in management, they also facilitate the formulation of hypotheses based on a sound rationale; these hypotheses in turn facilitate ultimate interpretation of study results. The results of a study based on a theoretical problem contribute to their related theory by confirming or disconfirming some aspect of the theory and also by suggesting additional studies that need to be done.

To be perfectly honest, however, the selection of a problem based on theory may be too complicated for many beginning researchers. There are a great number of problems that need research that are not theoretical in nature. An obvious source of such problems is the researcher's personal experiences. Many management students who are beginning researchers come from the ranks of the employed. It is hard to imagine an employee who has never had a idea concerning a better way to do something (a way to increase efficiency or improve morale) or been a participant in a program or consumer of a product whose effectiveness was untested. Thus practical experience may be a source of researchable problems. This is not to say that an idea based on these experiences will never lead to a theoretical problem, it is just more likely that the problem will result in an applied research study that may be easier for the beginning researcher to manage.

As mentioned previously, the literature is also a good source of problems. In addition to overviews and summaries, which are more helpful in narrowing down a problem area, specific studies often indicate next-step studies that need to be conducted. The suggested next step may involve a logical extension of the described study or simply replication of the study in a different setting in order to establish the generalizability of its findings. For example, in the study reprinted at the end of Chapter 1 investigating the consequences of quality circles (QCs), suggestions for further study include: (a) When are QCs most effective? (b) Who should choose the participants in QCs?, and (c) How should QCs be managed? It is generally not a good idea, however, simply to replicate a study as it was originally conducted; there is much to be learned from developing and executing your own study. Replication of certain studies, however, is highly desirable, especially those whose results conflict with previous research or do not support some aspect of an established theory.

Characteristics of Research Problems

Since a research problem by definition involves an issue in need of investigation, it follows that a basic characteristic of a research problem is that it is "researchable." A researchable problem is first one that can be investigated through the collection and analysis of data. Some problems dealing with philosophical or ethical issues are not researchable. Research can assess how people feel or what they think about some of these issues, but research cannot resolve them. Whether or not there is reward and punishment in the hereafter may be an important problem to many people, but it is not researchable; there is no way to resolve it through the collection and analysis of data (at least at the present time!). Similarly, in management there are a number of issues that make great topics for debates (such as "Should drug testing be implemented for all employees?") but are not researchable problems when stated in that way.

A second major characteristic of a good problem is that it has theoretical or practical significance. Of course the most significant problems are those derived from theory; even if the problem is not theoretical, however, its solution should contribute in some way to improvement of the management process. If the typical reaction to your problem is, "Who cares?" it probably is not of sufficient significance to warrant a study!

A third major characteristic of a good problem is that it is a good problem for you. The fact that you have chosen a problem of interest to you, in an area in which you have expertise is not sufficient. It must be a problem that you can adequately investigate given: (a) your current level of research skill, (b) available resources, and (c) time and other restrictions. A study similar to the one reported at the end of Chapter 1, for example, would not be a good choice if you intend to finish the course this semester! As a beginning researcher, you more than likely have access to one or more faculty members in addition to your instructor who can help you to assess the feasibility of your proposed study.

Statement of the Problem

A first characteristic of a well-written statement of a problem is that it generally indicates the variables of interest to the researcher and the specific relationship between those variables that is to be investigated. A possible exception to this might be a descriptive study in which the problem is simply stated as a question to be answered; even with descriptive studies, however, the more meaningful studies are concerned with relationships between variables.

A second characteristic of a well-written problem statement is that it defines all relevant variables, either directly or operationally; operational definitions define concepts quite specifically in terms of operations, or processes. Two good sources of definitions are the *Dictionary of Business and Management* (Rosenberg, 1982) and the *Macmillan Dictionary of Business and Management* (Lamming & Bessant, 1988). For example, a problem statement might state, "The problem to be investigated in this study is (or "The purpose of this study is to investigate . . . ") the effect of positive reinforcement on the productivity of customer-service representatives." The variables to be defined are "positive reinforcement" and "productivity"; you probably will also want to define "customer-service representatives." Positive reinforcement might be defined in terms of positive verbal comments such as, "You handled the customer's anger very well" or "Your follow-up on that problem was very thorough." Productivity might be defined in terms such as number of calls handled, average time-per-call, or thoroughness in terms of the customer being satisfied with the response. Customer-service representatives might be operationally defined by specifying the industry, type of calls normally received, nature of the calls, and general expectations by management of employees having this job title. In this example, the relationship to be investigated between the variables is cause-effect; the purpose of the study is to see if positive reinforcement (the cause, or independent variable) influences the productivity of the worker (the effect, or dependent variable).

A statement of the problem is invariably the first component of the introduction section of both a research plan and a research report on a completed study. Since the problem statement gives direction to the rest of the plan or report, it should be stated as soon as possible. The statement of the problem should be accompanied by a presentation of the background of the problem. The background of the problem means information required for an understanding of the problem. The problem is usually justified in terms of its contribution to management theory or practice. For example, an introduction might begin with a problem statement such as, "The purpose of this study is to compare the productivity of teenagers versus retirees as workers in fast food restaurants." This statement might be followed by a discussion concerning: (a) the role of the fast food restaurant worker, (b) the general utilization of teenagers as restaurant employees, (c) factors such as availability, reliability, and turnover, and (d) the search for alternatives, such as retirees. The significance of the problem would be that if retirees are equally or more productive, they can be used as substitutes for the traditional teenage work force. Business is therefore provided with a new employee pool from which to draw, while retirees are able to supplement their retirement income and/or find new outlets for their time and energy. Any practice that solves more than one problem at a time is certainly worthy of investigation!

After a problem has been carefully selected, delineated, and clearly stated, the researcher is ready to attack the review of related literature. Typically he or she has a tentative hypothesis that guides that review. In the above example, the tentative hypothesis would be that retirees are equally effective as teenage workers. It is not unlikely that the tentative hypothesis will be modified, even changed radically, as a result of the review. It does, however, give direction to the literature search and narrows its scope to include only relevant topics.

REVIEW OF RELATED LITERATURE

Having happily found a suitable problem, the beginning researcher is usually "raring to go." Too often the review of related literature is seen as a necessary evil to be completed as fast as possible so that one can get on with the study. This feeling is due to a lack of understanding concerning the purpose and importance of the review and to a feeling of uneasiness on the part of students who are not too sure exactly how to go about it. The review of related literature, however, is as important as any other component of the research process, and it can be conducted quite painlessly if it is approached in an orderly manner. If, however, it is conducted in an disorderly manner, it can lead into many fascinating byroads and tangents! However it is approached, some researchers even find the process quite enjoyable! One former student used his newly honed library skills to find out the procedure for harvesting and selling a timber crop that was on land he had recently purchased for personal recreation use; his instructor never did find out if the profit covered the student's tuition costs!

Definition, Purpose, and Scope

The review of related literature involves the systematic identification, location, and analysis of documents containing information related to the research problem. These documents include periodicals, abstracts, reviews, books, statistical material, and other research reports. The review has several important functions that make it well worth the time and effort. The major purpose of reviewing the literature is to determine what has already been done that relates to your problem. This knowledge not only avoids unintentional duplication, but it also provides the understandings and insights necessary for the development of a logical framework into which your problem fits. In other words, the review tells you what has been done and what needs to be done. Studies that have been done will provide the rationale for your research hypothesis; indications of what needs to be done will form the basis for the justification for your study.

Another important function of the literature review is that it points out research strategies and specific procedures and measuring instruments that have and have not been found to be productive in investigating your problem. This information will help you to avoid other researchers' mistakes and to profit from their experiences. It may suggest approaches and procedures previously not considered. For example, suppose your problem involves the comparative effectiveness of a training program for new managers versus on-the-job training on the performance of middle managers. The review of the literature reveals several studies already conducted that found no differences in performance. In each study a pretest and posttest was done with the supervisors to measure their ability according to self-report in tasks such as conducting performance appraisals, counseling employees, and interviewing prospective employees; no significant difference was found between the pretests and posttests. In one of the studies, however, the employees supervised by the managers were also surveyed before and after the managers were trained. Although there was no significant difference in the managers' self-reported ability, there was a significant difference in the employees' ratings of the managers. The researcher suggests that this apparent discrepancy might be based on the managers' perceptions before training that they were doing a good job; after training, they realized how much they didn't know before but still rated themselves as doing a good job. The researcher suggests that there may be a problem using self-reports of the managers to evaluate the training and that employee reports are probably more accurate. Thus, you might reformulate your procedure to avoid having problems with inaccurate or biased self-reporting on the part of the managers in your treatment group.

Being familiar with previous research also facilitates interpretation of the results of your study. The results can be discussed in terms of whether they agree with, and support, previous findings or not; if the results contradict previous findings, differences between your study and the others can be described, providing a rationale for the discrepancy. If your results are consistent with other findings, your report should include suggestions for the next step; if they are not consistent, your report should include suggestions for studies that will resolve the conflict.

Beginning researchers seem to have difficulty in determining how broad their literature review should be. Experienced faculty often complain that students either don't know when to quit or don't produce enough work to be taken seriously. Understanding that all literature directly related to the problem should be reviewed, students sometimes have difficulty determining which articles are "related enough" to their problem to be included. Unfortunately, there are no quantitative criteria; the decision must be based on judgment. These judgments become easier as one acquires experience, but there are three guidelines for the beginner:

1. Bigger doesn't mean better (or small can be beautiful). A smaller, well-organized review is definitely to be preferred to a review containing many studies that are more or less, but mostly less, related to the problem.

2. Heavily researched areas require a smaller focus than newer areas. Because of the extent of research in a given area, you will need to concentrate your review efforts on a narrower area. Although the literature on behavior modification may be the theoretical basis for your study on the use of praise in training new managers, there's no good reason for going clear back to animal research and including a reference to Pavlov's dog in your review.

3. Conversely, new areas of research need to include wider research reviews. These broader reviews help to develop a logical framework for the more exploratory study and provide a sound rationale for the research hypothesis. A study of provisions by employers for care of employees' elderly parents, for example, might

include reviews of studies on child-care provisions and stress-management programs on employee absenteeism and productivity.

A common misconception among beginning researchers is the idea that the worth of their problem is a function of the amount of literature available on the topic. This is not true. There are many new, important areas of research for which there is comparatively little available literature; as indicated above, time off or other provisions for employees to care for elderly parents is one such area. On the one hand, the very lack of such research, especially given the predictions that we will have far greater numbers of elderly citizens in the future, increases the worth of the study. On the other hand, the fact that 1,000 studies have already been done in a given problem area does not mean there is no further need for research in that area. Often the needed research will be readily identifiable in these well-developed areas. One example is the area of leadership, where research has been conducted steadily over at least the past 50 years; yet, one of the hottest research topics among experienced researchers toward the end of the 1980s focused on transformational and visionary leaders.

Preparation

Since it will be a second home to you, at least for a while, you should become completely familiar with the library before beginning your review. Many libraries offer guided tours of the facilities; although tours are often scheduled for groups, some libraries have audiotape-led tours for individuals. Written guides may also be available covering both general offerings and, for those of you who are fortunate, specific areas such as business and management. In addition, some libraries have videotape presentations covering the process for finding references and reviewing the literature. Some of the things you'll probably want to check out in your own library include the following:

1. What are the rules and regulations regarding the use of library materials? Hours of operation, especially on weekends and at night, privileges for checking materials out, and access to the stacks are some matters you may want to investigate. The stacks is an area of the library where most of the books and periodicals are stored; in some libraries, users may freely browse through the stacks, whereas in others only librarians have access to this area and provide library materials to users upon written request.

2. What general references and services are available? While many references are standard and can be found in any library, you may have to rely on interlibrary loan to obtain more specific information. Also find out what information-retrieval services, such as computer searches, are available. Does your library have DIALOG or BRS? The technological advances in libraries over the past five years are significant and likely to continue. As more and more data bases become available not only in print format but also via microform, compact disk (CD-ROM), and on-line, the researcher's task becomes easier and easier—but the researcher also needs to keep up on the latest technological advances. Throughout this chapter we will discuss the literature review from the standpoint of print format, since this media should be

available to all students. It will be important for you, however, to determine the labor-saving devices your own library has available. On a very mundane level, it may even help you to know that the copy machines in your library really prefer exact change.

3. What specific business-and-management references and services are housed in your library? While browsing may seem inefficient, a half hour or so spent wandering with your eyes open in the business-and-management sections now can provide you with needed information later when you wonder, "How could I find out . . . ?" Finally, your library may have a librarian dedicated to business and management. While librarians usually are very willing to help, their enthusiasm may deteriorate the tenth time you approach them with the same question. Although it takes more time at the beginning to familiarize yourself with your library, your own efficiency will be tremendously increased over time if you are able to find things yourself rather than waiting for a librarian to help you.

Having formulated your problem and acquainted yourself with the library, you have one final task before you take the plunge—make a list of key words or phrases for your literature search. Most of the sources you will consult will have an alphabetical subject or descriptor index (a thesaurus) to help you locate specific references. You will look in these indexes under the subjects or descriptors you have selected. It is to be hoped that your subject or descriptor words or phrases will be obvious, but you may have to play detective. Suppose, for example, that your problem concerned the effects of training in creative problem solving on the productivity of middle managers. If you looked under "training techniques," you would be referred to "employee training methodology"; using "managers" as a subject/descriptor would lead you to "executives" and then to "management development programs" before you found usable references. Better subjects/descriptors might be "creative ability" and "problem solving." You might find references under "brain hemisphere dominance," since right-brain-hemisphere-dominant individuals are thought to be more creative than the more logical and sequential left-brained types. A librarian skilled in computer searches, particularly in the business indexes, can be a big help here. Persistence will pay off, however. Some years ago, a student of one of the authors was interested in the effect of artificial turf on knee injuries in football. He looked under every descriptor he could think of, such as "surface, playing," "surface, turf," and "artificial turf." He could find nothing. Both he and the professor knew that studies had been done, so he kept trying. When he finally did find a reference, it was listed under, of all things, "lawns"! Identifying descriptors is usually not such a problem. In looking at initial sources you will usually find additional descriptors that will help you in locating succeeding sources. Giving some thought to subjects/descriptors initially will help you organize what may appear to be an overwhelming task.

Sources

There are usually many sources of literature that might be related to a given problem. In general, however, there are several major sources commonly used by researchers in business and management. Some of these sources are primary and some are secondary; as you recall from Chapter 1, primary sources are definitely preferable. In historical research, a primary source is an eyewitness or an original document or relic; while this is also true in management, a primary source in a literature search is also a description of a study written by the person who conducted it. A secondary source in the literature is generally a much more brief description of a study written by someone other than the original researcher. In the article concerning quality circles (QCs) at the end of Chapter 1, for example, the author briefly describes a study involving 46 QC participants and 46 QC nonparticipants in a single plant (Marks, Mirvis, Hackett, & Grady cited in Griffin, 1988). Since primary sources usually give complete information on the references cited, they direct the researcher to other relevant primary sources. You should not be satisfied with the information contained only in secondary sources; the corresponding primary sources will be considerably more detailed and should give you the sort of specific information you need to understand exactly what was done and how. In the quality circles example, you would want to look up the other study and see exactly what was done, with whom, and what the results were; information that was not important in the article where you found the reference may be critically important to your study.

The number of individual references that could be consulted for a given problem is staggering; fortunately there are indexes, abstracts, and other retrieval mechanisms including computer searches that facilitate identification of relevant references. In this section we will discuss the ones most often used in business-and-management research. As indicated before, you should check your own library for other sources in your specific area of specialization.

Books

Let's start with something relatively easy. It is hard to imagine a graduate student who has never used the library to find books related to a given problem. Although libraries usually maintain their old card catalogs, most have converted to a computer-based catalog, which alphabetically indexes (by author, subject, and title) all the publications in the library except the periodicals. Some of these computer programs will inform you whether the book is on the shelf or checked out at the moment. Although problems in business and management tend to change rather rapidly, it is worthwhile checking to see if there may be books on the subject. You may also find a comprehensive description of research in a given field that has been compiled and published in book form. If such a book exists for your problem, it can be an invaluable reference. Another general resource in book form that may be useful is *Business Information Sources* (Daniels, 1985). This book could be useful in helping you locate other sources of information since it catalogs a wide variety of sources.

Encyclopedias may also be useful, especially those in specialized areas such as business and management. As you probably remember from grade school, generalized encyclopedias contain articles on a wide range of topics written by experts. Encyclopedias in specialized areas contain more detailed information on a restricted number of topics. A good example is *The Encyclopedia of Management* (Heyel, 1982) which summarizes the major topics of management and also provides a number of references for further reading. Remember, however, that any encyclopedia is a secondary source.

Indexes to Periodicals

Most of you probably have also used general indexes such as the *Readers' Guide to Periodical Literature.* Articles from more than 200 widely read magazines are indexed here. Although these will generally be nontechnical, opinion-type references, they can be very useful in documenting the significance of your problem. For example, many articles have been written in popular magazines expressing concern on the part of the American public over substance abuse and AIDS in the workplace. Articles are listed alphabetically in the *Readers' Guide* by subject and author, and the procedures for its use are essentially straightforward; in most libraries general indexes are accessible in both bound and computer-based formats. In addition to the *Readers' Guide,* there are some other sources of popular literature such as *The New York Times Index* and *The Wall Street Journal Index.* Published monthly, *The Wall Street Journal Index* has one section arranged by name of firm, which gives corporate news. A second section is arranged by subject and covers general business news.

More important to you than the general indexes will be the specialized business-and-management indexes. Probably the most important of these is the *Business Periodicals Index* (BPI). Arranged by subject, this index covers articles in more than 250 periodicals in business and economics. For more technical information, you should probably check the *Applied Science and Technology Index* (ASTI). This index focuses on industries such as aeronautical, chemical, and environmental; although it emphasizes technical subjects such as engineering, some management information is included. *PAIS Bulletin* surveys 1,400 periodicals, books, and government documents with a focus on public policy decisions affecting business and societal interactions with business rather than more detailed reports. For specific information on companies, including acquisitions, mergers, new products, and technology, *Predicasts F&S Index* could prove useful. This index covers 750 financial publications, business magazines, papers, and special reports. Finally, you may find even more specific indexes in your area of interest such as *Personnel Literature,* which is put out by the Office of Personnel Management in Washington.

Are you wondering which of the journals and periodicals are considered most valuable or prestigious? Two recent studies (Coe & Weinstock, 1984; Sharpin & Mabry, 1985) have addressed this question. Journals identified by both the original studies included the following:

Academy of Management Journal
Academy of Management Review
Administrative Science Quarterly
California Management Review
Harvard Business Review
Management Science
Organizational Behavior and Human Performance

Other journals that were mentioned in one or the other study included *Academy of Management Proceedings, Administrative Management, Decision Sciences, Human Relations, Industrial and Labor Relations Review, Journal of Applied Psychology, Journal of Business, Journal of Management Studies, Journal of Operations Management, Journal of Purchasing and Materials Management, Journal of Systems Management, Long Range Planning, Operations Research, Organizational Dynamics, Personnel, Personnel Psychology, Sloan Management Review, Supervisory Management.*

The procedure for using most indexes is the same, so it will be described in detail:

1. Start with the most recent issue of the index and look under key words you have already identified.

2. Under the key words you will find a list of references presented alphabetically by title, or you will be directed to other key words. If you were researching the study mentioned earlier regarding elderly workers at fast food restaurants, you might look under "elderly employment" in *Business Periodicals Index.* Under this heading you would find "See Age and Employment" (1986–87, p. 746), and when you looked at Age and Employment, you would find, "See Retired Workers—Employment." (1986–87, p. 59).

3. Decide whether each reference is related to your problem or not. With the same problem identified above, you would find the following references in Business Periodicals Index (1986–87, p. 59):

Older persons good resource for corporations (Aging in America/Projects with Industries) *Adm Manage* 47:8–9 O '86.

Employment problem of older chemical scientists. A. Cairncross. *Chem Eng News* 64:44–5 S 8 '86.

Obviously the first reference would be worth looking up while the second would appear not to apply in this study.

4. If the reference is probably related or might be related, copy the complete reference. To avoid having to switch entries around later, you may want to use the format your school requires for references, such as American Psychological Association (APA), Turabian, or *Chicago Manual of Style.* Some students, however, find that listing the periodical first will facilitate finding the references later. That way you can look up all the articles in *Academy of Management Journal* at one time. Either way, it's advisable to use separate 4 × 6 index cards to copy each complete reference; this way you can sort and organize your material efficiently as you go along. If you are using a small laptop computer, depending on what software you're using, you may be able to record the reference either way and have the computer sort it for you later in the order in which you want to access your references. A third alternative, especially if your library does not allow you access to the stacks, would be to complete a request form for each reference at this point. If you are not familiar with the abbreviations used by the index, look in the front of the volume. Use of these abbreviations past this point in your search may send you back to the library at a very inconvenient time to discover

what on earth "Adm Sci Q" meant. (*Administrative Science Quarterly,* in case you're curious.)

5. Repeat steps 1 to 4 for previous issues of the index. Continue until you reach a logical stopping point. As discussed earlier, this will be determined to some extent by your problem. There isn't much point in looking for articles on AIDS before about 1980, for example.

Abstracts

Dissertation Abstracts International contains abstracts of doctoral dissertations conducted at hundreds of academic institutions. Abstracts are brief summaries of the most important facets of the dissertation. *Dissertation Abstracts International* summarizes the main components of dissertation studies. The advantage of having an abstract is that it usually allows you to classify all references as related to your problem or not related, and it greatly reduces time spent looking up unrelated references with fuzzy titles. *Dissertation Abstracts* classifies entries by subject, author, and institution. It is divided into two parts: Part A covers humanities and social sciences, and Part B covers sciences and engineering. Since management is partially art and partially science, you'll have to check both sections. Seriously, psychological aspects of management may be covered in Part A; more technical aspects are referenced in Part B.

The procedure for using the Abstracts is similar to the procedure for using indexes; the major difference is that once a related dissertation title is located, the next step is not to locate the dissertation but to locate an abstract of the dissertation using the entry number given with the reference. For example, if the entry number were 27/03B/ 3720, the abstract would be located in volume 27, issue number 3B, page number 3720. If, after reading an abstract, you wish to obtain a copy of the complete dissertation, check and see if it is available on microfiche in your library. Although the chances are slim, your librarian can check to see if it is available through interlibrary loan. If not, it can be obtained from University Microfilms International on microfilm for a small fee or in print for a larger fee. Complete and specific directions for ordering by phone or mail are printed in the front of each *Dissertation Abstracts* volume. You probably will not be able to order more than about five dissertations in a single phone call; payment by credit card is possible for phone orders.

University Microfilms International also provides a computer retrieval service called DATRIX. By filling out a request form available at most libraries and indicating appropriate key words, you can receive a bibliography of related dissertations for a nominal fee. DIALOG, which is a popular computer data base service, also includes dissertation references back to 1861 and most of the abstracts from 1980 to the present. You should be aware that using abstracts alone as a source of information in your literature review is not acceptable; the entire dissertation must be reviewed.

Psychological Abstracts presents summaries of completed psychological studies. Each issue contains 12 sections corresponding to 12 areas of psychology. The section on applied psychology is generally the most useful to management researchers. The December issue contains an annual cumulative author index and subject index. In addition, cumulative subject indexes and cumulative author indexes, which cover approximately 30 years, are available. The procedure for using *Psychological Abstracts* is similar to the procedures for other indexes. You will want to consult the *Thesaurus of Psychological Index Terms* (APA, 1988) initially to identify the descriptors of interest before you begin to search the index itself. The major difference between *Psychological Abstracts* and *Dissertation Abstracts* is that the *Psychological Abstracts* index does not give reference information; for a given topic, abstract numbers of related references are given. These numbers are located in *Psychological Abstracts,* which provides the complete reference as well as an abstract of the reference. If the abstract indicates that the study is related to the problem of interest, the original reference can then be located. In addition to the key words identified for a given problem, the word *bibliography* should also be checked. A bibliography related to your problem may exist, which might lead you to important references that might otherwise be missed.

How fruitful *Psychological Abstracts* will be for you will depend upon the nature of your problem. If it is a nontheoretical problem, such as the previously mentioned study concerning the effect of daily reminders in reducing the number of personal phone calls during work hours, you probably will not find anything in *Psychological Abstracts*. If the problem does relate to some theory, such as a study on leadership, you will probably find some useful references.

Finally, you may be able to find specific abstracts in your area of interest. For example, *Personnel Management Abstracts* covers approximately 100 references and is indexed by subject and by author. This publication also includes abstracts of selected books in the field.

Other References

When you have reviewed the appropriate books, periodicals, and materials found through abstracts, you may still need more specific information. A considerable amount of statistical information relative to business may be found in sources ranging from government census data to a company's annual report. Don't overlook the possibility of calling a company and asking questions, but be sure you record the name of the individual you spoke to and the date of the interview. The closer you get to specific and potentially sensitive company information, however, the more difficult it may be to collect data. In a review of a book that purported to be an exposé of a prominent investment banking firm, the review's author concluded that the company in question probably would not pursue its objections to the book in court; to do so would have opened the company's records to the probing of discovery proceedings (Sherman, 1988).

Computer Searches

In addition to using the print references mentioned earlier, you can also use a computer to identify related references for you. Searching that would take you days to do, a computer can do in a matter of minutes. No, a computer will not find most articles or review related literature for you. In addition to most of the indexes already mentioned, the computer can also search data bases such as *Management Contents, Business and Industry News,* and *Industry Data Sources.* It will provide you with a list of references and, if provided by the data base, abstracts.

Computer searches are made possible by the fact that various data bases are available on computer tapes. Information-retrieval systems, such as the DIALOG or BRS system, provide institutions with access to the tapes in their system. Some institutions have some tapes themselves. In addition many popular data bases are available in the library through CD-ROMs. Again, you need to check with your library to see what's available. A useful source of information on computer-based literature searches in business is *Business Online* (Scanlon, de Stricker, & Fernald, 1989). It is also possible to do computer-based literature searches from your home using your personal computer, a modem (phone hookup), and one of several data bases. At least one software program (*EndNote,* Niles, 1988) will allow you to download references, abstracts, and articles; then it puts your reference list into proper APA format. As one student said, "That almost seems like cheating!" If you want to get this involved, check with your instructor, the librarian, and/or your computer software dealer for options.

To initiate a computer search, you will need a specific statement of your problem. From this, you can select the key words, or descriptors, as discussed in relation to indexes. The key words you have been using in your search of periodicals should work very nicely for your computer search, but you will probably want to discuss this with the librarian. Before you initiate the search, it makes sense to use the descriptors you have selected and ask the person helping you with your search to find out how many references you can expect. If you have too many, you may want to limit your search by adding the connector *and.* For example, key descriptors such as "productivity" and "positive reinforcement" might bring you hundreds of references. Stating the descriptors as "productivity" *and* "positive reinforcement" would limit the search to those references including both. Conversely, if you will receive too few references, the connector *or* might be used. In this instance you would use "positive reinforcement" *or* "praise" and expand your references. You will also be asked to provide delimitors; these help weed out references you won't need. In the example above, you would probably want to specify in some way that you were interested in work-related references; otherwise you might get references relating to education or some other area that is not of specific interest to you.

In any event, you will also be asked which of the data bases you want to search. They are usually listed by area so that you can specify categories, thereby limiting your search. The category of "business" in the DIALOG system, for example, gives subcategories such as "company directories," "business news," and "business statistics." Probably the largest and most useful business data base on DIALOG is ABI/INFORM, but using it can be very expensive. Other possible data base programs your librarian may suggest include WILSONLINE, which includes the *Business Periodicals Index* (BPI) and *Readers' Guide,* among many others, or, in some cases, NEXIS or LEXIS. The possibilities are already extensive and growing very rapidly. The days of librarians worrying primarily about keeping patrons quiet and avoiding dust and insect damage are gone as librarians scramble to stay ahead of the available technology in our information age. These days one of the most exciting places on campus may once again be the library! Anyway, after you have identified your descriptors and data bases, the computer will search the data bases you have selected for references having those descriptors. As a result of the computer search that is done for you, you will receive a computer printout listing the identified references and abstracts. In a few cases you may receive the entire article, but usually it's up to you now to find the references and continue with your review.

In addition to computer searches done by the library, many students use on-line and CD-ROM searches very effectively. If the search is done on-line, the student uses a computer terminal in the library or at home to search some of the data bases mentioned previously. A problem with on-line computer searches, however, is that they can get very expensive very quickly if you haven't limited your search effectively both with regard to appropriate descriptors and the amount of time you want covered. They are very useful, however, in ensuring that you have the most up-to-date information available because the on-line data bases are constantly updated, whereas both print and CD-ROM data bases are updated on a monthly, quarterly, or annual basis.

A less expensive alternative is the CD-ROM search. CD-ROMs are essentially compact disks that store information rather than music or video. They are read by a laser player and the contents displayed on a computer terminal. As a first-time CD-ROM user, you probably should ask the librarian or a library technician for some training in the use of the CD-ROMs, but after about twenty minutes, you'll feel comfortable enough to use the CD-ROMs to try out possible descriptors that relate to your topic. When you find something useful, you can usually print the reference out immediately. A possible disadvantage to CD-ROM technology is that it is so expensive that your library may have limited facilities and will need to monitor the use of the equipment so that many users can access it. In this situation, you may be limited to 20 minutes or so or have to sign up to use the equipment at a specific time.

To summarize, you will probably want to begin your literature search by using a thesaurus to identify key words, or descriptors, for your topic. Check some of the print media indexes to see whether these terms seem to be turning up appropriate references. Then meet with the librarian for some suggestions of appropriate data bases that you can search yourself, using CD-ROM or some other inexpensive methodology. Finally, have a limited on-line search done to pick up the very recent sources or others that you were unable to access inexpensively.

If all of this has you totally panicked, do not despair! Thousands of other students have handled this, and you wouldn't have come this far if you weren't capable of it too. Before requesting a computer search done by the library or one you plan to do on-line, schedule a heart-to-heart talk with your librarian; at least until you are an accomplished researcher, you can avoid a lot of headaches and expense by seeking assistance from someone who works with the system on a daily basis. An important limitation you need to discuss is how far back you want to search (last six months? last two years?) and how much you are willing to spend (an unanticipated bill of $50 or so can put a real crimp in your weekend!). The real benefit to your career, of course, is that you will have acquired information-gathering skills that may be as useful to you as reading and writing in the future. On-line data bases provide information useful in business enterprises as diverse as advertising, marketing, planning, and accounting, and you can expect to see on-line data base access increasingly available in individual offices and businesses in the future (Scanlon, de Stricker, & Fernald, 1989).

Abstracting

After you have identified the primary references related to your problem, using the appropriate indexes, abstracts, and reviews, you are ready to move on to the next phase of a review of related literature—abstracting the references. Basically, this involves locating, reviewing, summarizing, and classifying your references. Make sure the references you identified in each source are listed in reverse chronological order, starting with the most recent, because the abstracting process will be conducted in the same order. The main advantage of beginning with the latest references on a given problem is that in terms of research strategy the most recent research is likely to have profited from previous research. Also, recent references may contain references to preceding studies you may not have identified. For each reference, a suggested procedure for abstracting is as follows:

1. If the article has an abstract or a summary, which most research articles do, read it to determine the article's relevancy to your problem.

2. Skim the entire article, making a mental note of the main points of the study. (Remember the article reviews you did in Chapter 1?)

3. If you used separate cards to find each reference, check the reference at the top of the card to be sure it's complete. If you did not use separate cards before, on the top of an index card (4×6 is a convenient size) write the complete reference, including the library call number if it is a book. If you know that your final report must follow a particular style, put your reference in that form. If not, use the format of the American Psychological Association (APA). The APA format is becoming increasingly popular, primarily because it eliminates the need for formal footnotes; it is also the format you see throughout this book. For a journal article, the APA formatted reference would be:

Snurd, B. J. (1992). The use of brown versus black type in business résumés. *Journal of Useless Findings, 22* (3), 1–99.

In the above example, 1992 refers to the date of publication, *22* to the volume, (3) to the issue number, and 1–99 to the page numbers. If this reference were cited in a paper (perhaps published by Senator Proxmire in an article on funding for useless research), then its description would be followed by (Snurd, 1992), and no other footnote beyond the reference would be required. In the case of a direct quotation, however, you will need to include the page number as in (Snurd, 1992, p. 45). Whatever format you use, be certain the reference you copy is accurate; you never know when you might have to go back and get additional information from an article. Besides, even if you do not have to find it again, it is very sloppy to have an incorrect or incomplete reference in a research report. Put only one reference on each index card. The purpose of using index cards is that they allow easy sorting and facilitate organization of the articles prior to writing the review of the literature.

An alternative to this step is to use a laptop computer for your note taking. If you use this option, you still need to record the correct and complete reference citation. Software programs, such as *EndNote* (Niles, 1988), *Manuscript Manager* (Elwork, Hall, & Stone, 1988), *Publish or Perish* (Kearsley, 1987), and *ProCite* (Personal Bibliographic Systems, 1986), are available that use APA format, but they may not all run on a laptop computer. If you are buying a software program that will assist you with your references and you use a laptop computer frequently, you may want to ask about this.

4. Classify and code the article according to some system and place the code on the index card in a conspicuous place, such as the upper right-hand or left-hand corner. If you are a laptop computer user, create a code that can be easily accessed when you want to have the computer sort your notes for you into the categories you devise. In either case, you might want to use a three-part coding system to describe each article. Remember the study about elderly employees versus teenage employees in a fast-food restaurant? In this case the first part of your code might indicate whether the study was concerned with elderly employees (EE), teenage employees (TE), or both (B). The second part of the code would tell you whether it was an opinion article (O) or a study (S), and the third part of the code shows the degree of its relevance to your study (say 1, 2, or 3, with 3 meaning very relevant). Thus, EE/O/2 might be the code for an article expressing concern for elderly persons who are forced to work to supplement their inadequate Social Security payments. Any coding system that makes sense to you, given your problem, will facilitate your task later when you have to sort, organize, analyze, synthesize, and write your review of the literature.

5. On the same index card (under the reference) abstract, or summarize, the reference. As neatly as you can (you're going to have to read them later!), write the essential points of the reference. If it is an opinion article, write the main points of the author's position; for example, "Jones believes that elderly workers should be used because . . . . " and list the reasons. If it is a study, write the same kind of information you wrote for Project I, Chapter 1: (a) the problem, (b) the procedures (including the sample and instruments), and (c) the major conclusions. Make special note of any particularly interesting or unique aspect of the study, such as a new measuring instrument that was used. Double-check the reference to make sure you have not omitted any pertinent information.

6. Indicate on the index card any thoughts that come to your mind, such as points on which you disagree (make an X, for example) or components that you do not understand (put a "?" next to them). For example, if the author stated that he or she used a double-blind procedure, and you were unfamiliar with that technique, you could indicate that with a "?." Later you can look it up or seek out a knowledgeable person, such as your instructor, and quickly obtain clarification or explanation.

7. Indicate on the index card any statements that are direct quotations (plagiarism is absolutely forbidden) or personal reactions; if you do not put quotation marks

around direct quotations on your index card, for example, you may not remember later which statements are and which are not direct quotations. Also, jot down the exact page of the quotation in case you use the quotation later in your paper. Incidentally, direct quotations should be kept to a minimum in your research plan and report; both should be in your words, not other researchers'. Occasionally, however, a direct quotation may be quite appropriate.

An alternate strategy to making notes on index cards is to photocopy references whenever possible (you wouldn't want to copy a book, and if you did, you'd probably get nasty treatment from those behind you in the copy line). If you copy the articles, you can take them home with you and make your notes in the comfort of your home. The advantages of this approach are reduced time in the library and elimination of the possibility that you might have to go back and find a reference because you inadvertently left something out of your notes. Be sure, however, that you record the exact reference on your photocopy; not all journals list everything you need on each page. Another alternative for the truly technological among us, is to use a portable, hand-held scanner—a computer accessory similar to those used in offices to scan documents. The main disadvantage of photocopying or scanning documents, of course, is the cost. Some researchers think that the approach is well worth it in terms of convenience. Probably some sort of compromise makes sense, such as using index cards for minor references and photocopying the articles that apply very directly to your study and provide lots of information or use very complicated procedures.

Whichever approach you use, guard your notes with your life. When you have completed your reviewing task, those notes will represent many hours of work. Students have been known to be literally in tears because they left their notes "on the bus" or "on a table in the cafeteria." Beyond being sympathetic, your instructor can do little more than tell you to start over. When the research report is completed, your notes can be filed and saved for future reference and future studies (research studies are like potato chips—nobody can do just one!)

Analyzing, Organizing, and Reporting

For beginning researchers, the hardest part of writing the review of related literature is thinking about how hard it is going to be to write the review of related literature. Many students tend to dread this step so much that more time is spent worrying about doing it than actually doing it. If you have efficiently abstracted the literature related to your problem and approach the task in an equally systematic manner, then analyzing, organizing, and reporting can be relatively painless. Begin by reading through your notes to refresh your memory. More than likely you will see some references that no longer seem sufficiently related. Do not force references that do not really fit into your review. Many students think that if they spent the time looking it up and writing it down, they deserve to get it into the report. Your review forms the background and rationale for your hypothesis and should contain only those references that serve this purpose well. Editing your own work is tough and occasionally painful, but your end results will be better for it. The following suggestions are based on experience gained the hard way and may be helpful to you:

1. Make an outline. Don't groan; your eighth-grade teacher was right about the virtues of an outline. For those of you who are working on small computers, there are several software programs such as *Think Tank* (Winer & Winer, 1984), *Acta* (Summetry, 1986), and *More* (Symantec, 1986) that can help you outline; in addition, the word processing program you are using may also have an outlining program as one of its features. However you do it, the time and thought you put into the outline will save you time in the long run and will increase your probability of having an organized review. The outline does not have to be excessively detailed. First, identify the main topics and the order in which they should be presented. For example, the outline that was used for this chapter started out as three main headings— "Selection and Statement," "Review of Related Literature," and "Formulation and Statement of a Hypothesis." As another example, the outline for the review for the problem concerning the effectiveness of teenagers versus elderly employees might begin with the headings "Literature on Elderly Employees," "Literature on Teenage Employees," and "Literature Comparing the Two." The next step is to differentiate each major heading into logical subheadings. In the outline for this book, "Review of Related Literature" was subdivided into the following:

Review of Related Literature

Definition, purpose, and scope

Preparation

Sources

Computer searches

Abstracting

Analyzing, organizing, and reporting

The need for further differentiation will be determined by your problem; the more complex it is, the more subheadings will be required. When you have completed your outline you will invariably see topics that need rearranging. It is much easier, however, to reorganize an outline on paper or on your computer than it is to reorganize a document written in paragraph form.

2. Analyze each reference in terms of your outline; in other words, determine under which subheading each one fits. Then sort your references into appropriate piles or sections. If you end up with one or more references without a home, there are three logical possibilities:

a. There is something wrong with your outline.

b. The references do not belong in your review and should be discarded.

c. The references do not belong in your review but do belong somewhere else in your introduction.

For example, a reference concerned with problems of the elderly might state that many have difficulty making ends meet on Social Security alone. Such a reference would belong in the significance section of the problem statement in the study on elderly employees. Opinion articles, or reports of descriptive research, will usually be more useful in the problem statement portion of an introduction, whereas formal studies will almost always be included in the review of related literature portion.

3. Take all the references identified for a given subheading and analyze the relationships or differences between them. If three references say essentially the same thing, there is no need to describe each one; it is much better to make one summary statement followed by three references. For example:

> Several studies have found black type to be more effective than brown type in résumés (Snurd, 1986; Trivia, 1989; Ziggy, 1992).

Do not present your references as a series of abstracts or annotations (Jones found X, Smith found Y, and Brown found Z). Your task is to organize and summarize the references in a meaningful way. Do not ignore studies that are contradictory to most other studies or your personal bias. Analyze and evaluate contradictory studies and try to determine a possible explanation. For example:

> Contrary to these studies is the work of Rottenstudee (1984), who found brown type to be more effective than black type in résumés . However, the size of the treatment group (two applicants per group) and the breadth of the study (one company) may have seriously affected the results.

4. The review should flow in such a way that the references least related to the problem are discussed first, and the most related references discussed last, just prior to the statement of the hypothesis. Think in terms of a big *V*. At the bottom of the *V* is your hypothesis; directly above your hypothesis are the studies most directly related to it, and so forth. For example, if your hypothesis stated that black type would be more effective than brown type in résumés, immediately preceding it would be the studies indicating the effectiveness of black type in business letters. Preceding these studies might be studies indicating that people prefer reading black type to other colors, such as brown. At the top of the *V* (the beginning of the review), several references might be cited, written by well-known authors, expressing the belief that variables such as type and color of paper in business communications are important ones in determining the effectiveness of these communications. These might be followed by similar references indicating that these variables might be even more critical in specific areas such as résumé writing, and so forth. The idea is to organize and present your literature in such a way that it leads logically to a tentative, testable conclusion, namely your hypothesis. If your problem has more than one major aspect, you may have two *V*s or one *V* that logically leads to two tentative, testable conclusions.

5. The review should conclude with a brief summary of the literature and its implications. How lengthy this summary needs to be depends upon the length of the review. It should be detailed enough to show clearly the logic chain you have followed in arriving at your implications and tentative conclusion. Having systematically developed and presented your rationale, you will now be ready to state your hypothesis.

FORMULATION AND STATEMENT OF A HYPOTHESIS

Before you review the related literature, you have a tentative hypothesis that guides your search. Following the review, and preceding the actual implementation of the study, the hypothesis is refined and finalized.

Definition and Purpose

A hypothesis is a tentative explanation for certain behaviors, phenomena, or events that have occurred or will occur. A hypothesis states the researcher's expectations concerning the relationship between the variables in the research problem; a hypothesis is the most specific statement of the problem. It states what the researcher thinks the outcome of the study will be. The researcher does not then set out to "prove" his or her hypothesis but rather collects data that either support the hypothesis or do not support it; research studies do not "prove" anything. Hypotheses are essential to all research studies with the possible exception of some descriptive studies whose purpose is to answer certain specific questions.

The hypothesis is formulated following the review of related literature and prior to the execution of the study. It logically follows the review since it is based on the implications of previous research. The related literature leads one to expect a certain relationship. For example, studies finding black type to be more effective than brown type in business letters would lead a researcher to expect it to be more effective in résumés, if there were no findings to the contrary. Hypotheses precede the study proper because the entire study is determined by the hypothesis. Every aspect of the research is affected by the hypothesis, including subjects (the sample), measuring instruments, design, procedures, data-analysis techniques, and conclusions. Although all hypotheses are based on previous knowledge and aimed at extending knowledge, they are not all of equal worth. There are a number of criteria that can be, and should be, applied to a given hypothesis to determine its value.

Characteristics of the Hypothesis

By now it should be clear that a hypothesis should be based on a sound rationale. It should follow from previous research and lead to future research; its confirmation or disconfirmation should contribute to management theory or practice. Therefore, a major characteristic of a good hypothesis is that it is consistent with previous research. The chances of your being a Christopher Columbus of management research who is going to show that something believed to be square is really round are slim. Of course, in areas of research where there are conflicting results, you will not be able to be consistent with all of them, but your hypothesis should follow from the rule, not the exception.

The previously stated definition of a hypothesis indicated that it is a tentative explanation for the occurrence of certain behaviors, phenomena, or events. A good hypothesis provides a reasonable explanation. If your telephone is out of order, you might hypothesize that it is because there are butterflies sitting on your telephone wires; such a hypothesis would not be a reasonable explanation. A reasonable hypothesis might be that you forgot to pay your bill or that a repair crew is working outside. In a research study, on the one hand, a hypothesis suggesting that employees with freckles are more effective salespeople than employees without freckles would not be a reasonable explanation for effective salesmanship, unless the product they were selling was a cosmetic cover-up. On the other hand, a hypothesis suggesting that employees with high motivation are able to sell more might be a good hypothesis.

A good hypothesis states as clearly and concisely as possible the expected relationship (or difference) between two variables and defines those variables in operational, measurable terms. A simply but clearly stated hypothesis makes it easier for consumers of research to understand, simplifies the testing, and facilitates formulation of conclusions following data analysis. The relationship expressed between two variables may or may not be a causal one. For example, the variables of high motivation and effective salesmanship might be hypothesized to be significantly related, or it might be hypothesized that salespeople with high motivation perform better on low-volume, high-cost sales than they do on high-volume, low-cost sales. The above example also illustrates the need for operational definitions. What is high motivation? What does "perform better" mean? What are low-volume, high-cost sales as opposed to high-volume, low-cost sales? What type of sales are we talking about? Cosmetics? Electronics? Cars? The dependent variable in a hypothesis will often be operationally defined in terms of scores on a given test. For example, high motivation may be defined as a score of 40+ on the Sales Motivation Inventory, Revised (Bruce, 1977). You may have already defined your terms in your problem statement; the general rule of thumb is to define terms the first time they are used. If the appropriate terms can be operationally defined again within the actual hypothesis statement without making it unwieldy, this should be done. If you didn't define your terms in the problem statement or the hypothesis, then you should place your definitions immediately following the hypothesis.

If it is well formulated, defined, and stated, a hypothesis will also be testable. It should be possible to support or not support the hypothesis by collecting and analyzing data. It would not be possible to test a hypothesis that indicated that some employees are more honest than others because some have an invisible little angel on their right shoulder and some have an invisible little devil on their left shoulder. There would be no way to collect data to support or not support the hypothesis. In addition to being testable, a good hypothesis should normally be testable within some reasonable period of time. For example, the hypothesis that requiring new employees to participate in preretirement planning as part of their orientation will result in happier retirees would obviously take a very long time to test. The researcher would very likely be long gone before the study was completed, not to mention the negligible significance of the hypothesis to managers. A more manageable hypothesis with the same theme might be that requiring new employees to participate in preretirement planning as part of their orientation will result in more employee participation in voluntary retirement benefit programs.

Types of Hypotheses

Hypotheses can be classified in terms of how they are derived (inductive verses deductive hypotheses) or how they are stated (declarative versus null hypotheses). An inductive hypothesis is a generalization based on observation. Certain variables are noted to be related in a number of situations, and a tentative explanation, or hypothesis, is formulated. Such inductively derived hypotheses can be very useful but are of limited scientific value in that they produce results that are not meaningfully related to any larger body of research. Deductive hypotheses derived from theory do contribute to the science of management by providing evidence that supports, expands, or contradicts a given theory and by suggesting future studies. Remember the suggestions that were contained in the quality circles article? In deriving a hypothesis from a theory, you should be sure that your V does not have any holes in it (you do remember the big V, don't you?). In other words, your hypothesis should be a logical extension of previous efforts, not an inferential leap.

Hypotheses are classified as research hypotheses or statistical hypotheses; research hypotheses are stated in declarative form, and statistical hypotheses are stated in null form. A research hypothesis states an expected relationship or difference between two variables; in other words, the relationship the researcher expects to verify through the collection and analysis of data is specified. Research, or declarative, hypotheses are nondirectional or directional. A nondirectional hypothesis simply indicates that a relationship or difference exists; a directional hypothesis indicates the nature of the relationship or difference. For example, a nondirectional hypothesis might state:

> There is a significant difference in amount of data input by data entry personnel who are evaluated on a weekly basis and those who are evaluated on a six months basis only.

The corresponding directional hypothesis might state:

> Data entry personnel who are evaluated on a weekly basis input more data than personnel who receive evaluations on a six months basis.

A directional hypothesis should not be stated if you have any reason whatsoever to believe that the results may occur in the opposite direction. Nondirectional and directional hypotheses involve different types of statistical tests of significance which will be discussed in detail in Part IV.

A statistical, or null, hypothesis states that there is no relationship (or difference) between variables and that any relationship found will be a chance relationship, not a true one. For example, a null hypothesis might state:

> There is no difference in the data entry input of personnel who are evaluated on a weekly basis and those who are evaluated on a six months basis.

While a research hypothesis may be a null hypothesis, this is not very often the case. Statistical, or null, hypotheses are usually used because they suit statistical techniques that determine whether an observed relationship is probably a chance relationship or probably a true relationship. The disadvantage of null hypotheses is that they rarely express the researcher's true expectations based on insight and logic regarding the results of a study. One solution is to state two hypotheses, a declarative research hypothesis that communicates your true expectation and a statistical null hypothesis that permits precise statistical testing. Another solution is to state a research hypothesis, analyze your data assuming a null hypothesis, and then make inferences concerning your research hypothesis based on your testing of a null hypothesis. Given that few studies are really designed to verify the nonexistence of a relationship, it seems logical that most studies should be based on a nonnull research hypothesis.

Stating the Hypothesis

As previously discussed, a good hypothesis is stated clearly and concisely, expresses the relationship between two variables, and defines those variables in operational measurable terms. A general paradigm, or model, for stating hypotheses for experimental studies which you may find useful is as follows:

> Ss who get X do better on Y than
> Ss who do not get X (or get some other X)

If this model appears to be an oversimplication, it is, and it may not always be appropriate. However, this model should help you to understand the nature of a hypothesis statement. Further, this model, or a variation of it, will be applicable in a surprising number of situations. In the model,

> S = the subjects,
> X = the treatment, the independent variable (IV), and
> Y = the observed outcome, the dependent variable (DV).

Study the following example and see if you can identify S, X, and Y:

> New employees who have assigned mentors have higher first year performance evaluations than new employees who do not have assigned mentors.

In this example,

> S = new employees
> X = mentoring (assigned versus not assigned), IV, and
> Y = performance (higher first year ratings), DV.

OK? Try one more:

> Management students, who have not had previous training in research or statistics, who successfully complete a research course during their first semester in graduate school, have higher overall GPAs (grade point averages) than management students . . . who successfully complete a research course at the end of their graduate studies.

In this example,

> S = management students who have not had previous training in research or statistics,
> X = timing of successful completion of a research course (first semester versus end of graduate studies), IV, and
> Y = overall GPAs, DV.

For a null hypothesis, the paradigm is

> There is no difference on Y between Ss who get X and Ss who do not get X (or get some other X).

See if you can think of an example that illustrates the model for null hypotheses.

Testing the Hypothesis

Hypothesis testing is really what scientific research is all about. In order to test a hypothesis, the researcher determines the sample, measuring instruments, design, and procedure that will enable her or him to collect the necessary data. Collected data are then analyzed in a manner that permits the researcher to determine the validity of the hypothesis. Analysis of collected data does not result in a hypothesis being proven or not proven, only supported or not supported. You may find as a result of taking this course that your language is changed; you may forever be less likely to assert what is proven or not, and, it is to be hoped, you will be better able to evaluate others' results rather than accepting them on face value. The results of a study only indicate whether a hypothesis was "true" for the particular subjects involved in the study. Many beginning researchers have the misconception that if their hypothesis is not supported by their data, then their study is a failure, and, conversely, if it is supported then their study is a success. Neither of these beliefs is true. It is just as important, for example, to know what variables are not related as it is to know what variables are related. If a hypothesis is not supported, a valuable contribution may be made in the form of a revision of some aspect of a theory; such revision will generate new or revised hypotheses. Thus, hypothesis testing contributes to the science of management, as well as business effectiveness, primarily by expanding, refining, or revising theory.

Summary/Chapter 2

SELECTION AND STATEMENT OF THE PROBLEM

Selection of a Research Topic

1. The first step in selecting a problem is to identify a general problem area that is related to your area of expertise and of particular interest to you.

2. The next step is to narrow down the general problem area to a specific, researchable problem.

Sources of Problems

3. The most meaningful problems are generally derived from theory.

4. A major source of nontheoretical problems is the researcher's personal experiences.

5. The literature is also a good source of problems; in addition to overviews and summaries, specific studies often indicate next-step studies that need to be conducted.

6. It is generally not a good idea simply to replicate a study as it was originally conducted; there is much to be learned from developing and executing your own study.

Characteristics of Research Problems

7. A basic characteristic of a research problem is that it is "researchable"; that is, it can be investigated through the collection and analysis of data.

8. A good problem has theoretical or practical significance; its solution should contribute in some way to improvement of business or management processes.

9. A good problem must be a good problem for you. It must be a problem that you can adequately investigate given: (a) your current level of research skill, (b) available resources, and (c) time and other restrictions.

Statement of the Problem

10. A well-written statement of a problem generally indicates the variables of interest to the researcher and the specific relationship between those variables that is to be investigated.

11. A well-written problem statement also defines all relevant variables, either directly or operationally; operational definitions define concepts in terms of operations, or processes.

12. Since the problem statement gives direction to the rest of the plan or report, it should be stated as soon as possible.

13. The statement of the problem should be accompanied by a presentation of the background of the problem, including a justification for the study in terms of the significance of the problem.

REVIEW OF RELATED LITERATURE

Definition, Purpose, and Scope

14. The review of related literature involves the systematic identification, location, and analysis of documents containing information related to the research problem.

15. The major purpose of reviewing the literature is to determine what has already been done that relates to your problem.

16. Another important function of the literature review is that it points out research strategies and specific procedures and measuring instruments that have and have not been found to be productive in investigating your problem.

17. Familiarity with previous research also facilitates interpretation of the results of the study.

18. A small, well-organized review is definitely to be preferred to a review containing many studies that are more or less related to the problem.

19. Heavily researched areas usually provide enough references directly related to a specific problem to eliminate the need for relying on less related studies.

20. New or little-researched problem areas usually require review of any study related in some meaningful way to the problem in order to develop a logical framework for the study and a sound rationale for the research hypothesis.

21. A common misconception among beginning researchers is the idea that the worth of their problem is a function of the amount of literature available on the topic.

Preparation

22. Time spent initially will save time in the long run; you should find out what references are available and where they are located, especially the periodicals.

23. You should also be familiar with services offered by the library as well as rules and regulations.

24. Many libraries provide written guides detailing what the library has to offer and the procedures for utilizing references and services; others may also have videotape presentations on the process of reviewing the literature.

25. One important service offered by most libraries is interlibrary loan; another is computer search.

26. Specialized resources, such as a business-and-management librarian, may also be available.

27. Before beginning the review, make a list of key words related to your problem to guide your literature search.

Sources

28. A primary source is a description of a study written by the person who conducted it; a secondary source is generally a much more brief description of a study written by someone other than the original researcher.

29. You should not be satisfied with only the information contained in secondary sources; the corresponding primary sources will be considerably more detailed and may be more accurate.

30. The number of individual references that could be consulted for a given problem is staggering; fortunately, there are indexes, abstracts, and other retrieval mechanisms that facilitate identification of relevant references.

Books

31. Books may be found, using either the card catalog or a computer-based catalog, alphabetically indexed by author, subject, and title.

32. In addition to content information on your subject, books may also contain valuable references and identify additional sources of information; *Business Information Sources* is an example of this kind of resource in book form.

33. Encyclopedias in special areas contain detailed discussions, written by experts, on a restricted number of topics. *The Encyclopedia of Management,* for example, summarizes major topics and provides additional references.

Indexes to Periodicals

34. The *Readers' Guide to Periodical Literature* indexes articles in widely read magazines; it is indexed by subject and author.

35. Newspaper materials may be found by using *The New York Times Index* and *The Wall Street Journal Index.*

36. More specific business-and-management information, indexed by subject, is to be found in the *Business Periodicals Index;* this is probably the best general source of business-and-management references.

37. For more technical information, you should check the *Applied Science and Technology Index;* this is indexed by industry.

38. For references relating to public-policy decisions and societal interactions with business, use the *PAIS Bulletin.*

39. Information relating to acquisitions, mergers, new products, and technology is included in *Predicasts F&S Index.*

40. Your own area may include a specialized index; an example is *Personnel Literature.*

41. Some journals and periodicals are considered more valuable and prestigious than others as sources of information.

42. The procedure for using indexes is as follows: Start with the most recent index and look under your key words. Under the key words you will find a list of references presented alphabetically by title; decide whether each reference is related to your problem or not. If the reference is related, copy the complete reference. Look up unfamiliar abbreviations in the front of the volume. Repeat these steps for previous issues; locate each of the references.

Abstracts

43. *Dissertation Abstracts International* contains abstracts (usually brief summaries) of doctoral dissertations written at hundreds of academic institutions.

44. The procedure for using *Dissertation Abstracts* is similar to the procedure for using indexes with the exception that the reference also gives an entry number with which one locates an abstract.

45. Directions for ordering copies of dissertations are included in each volume of *Dissertation Abstracts.*

46. *Psychological Abstracts* presents summaries of completed psychological research studies.

47. The procedure for using *Psychological Abstracts* is similar to that for using indexes; the major difference is that the *Psychological Abstracts* index gives numbers that are used to locate both references and accompanying abstracts.

48. In addition to the key words identified for a given problem, the word *bibliographies* should also be checked.

49. *Psychological Abstracts* will be more useful for theoretical problems.

50. Specialized abstracts may be available in your particular area; an example is *Personnel Management Abstracts.*

Other References

51. Statistical information related to your study may be found in a variety of sources ranging from government census reports to annual reports from specific companies.

52. Very specific information may be obtained by calling the company in question; be sure to record the name and position of the person you talk to as well as the date of the interview.

Computer Searches

53. The computer can also be used to locate related references; the printout will provide you with a list of references and, if provided by the data base, abstracts.

54. To initiate a computer search, you provide key words, or descriptors; if multiple data bases are available, you will also have to specify those you want searched.

55. Schedule a meeting with the librarian skilled in this area to help you with your search; be ready to specify how far back you want to search and how much you're willing to spend.

Abstracting

56. Abstracting references involves locating, reviewing, summarizing, and classifying your references.

57. The main advantage of beginning with the latest references on a given problem is that in terms of strategy, the most recent research is likely to have profited from previous research; also, recent references may contain references to preceding studies you may not have identified.

58. A suggested procedure for abstracting is as follows: If available, read the article abstract or summary first to determine the relevancy of the article to your problem. Skim the entire article, making mental note of main points. Write the complete reference, using either a required format or the APA format. Classify and code the article according to some system. Abstract, or summarize, the reference. Write down any thoughts that come to your mind concerning the reference. Identify direct quotations.

59. An alternate strategy to taking notes on index cards or your laptop computer is to photocopy references when appropriate; be sure to include the complete reference on your photocopy.

60. Save your notes for future reference and future studies.

Analyzing, Organizing, and Reporting

61. All notes should be reread; this will first of all refresh your memory, and also, you will more than likely identify some references that no longer seem sufficiently related.

62. The following guidelines should be helpful: Make an outline. Analyze each reference in terms of your outline and sort your references into appropriate piles. Take all the references identified for a given subheading and analyze the relationships and differences between them (do not present your references as a series of abstracts or annotations). Arrange your review from references least related to the problem to those most related to the problem coming just prior to the statement of the hypothesis (think in terms of the big V). Conclude the review with a brief summary of the literature and its implications.

FORMULATION AND STATEMENT OF A HYPOTHESIS

Definition and Purpose

63. A hypothesis is a tentative explanation for certain behaviors, phenomena, or events that have occurred or will occur.

64. The researcher does not set out to "prove" his or her hypothesis but rather collects data that either support the hypothesis or do not support it.

65. The hypothesis is formulated following the review of related literature and prior to the execution of the study. The hypothesis logically follows the review, and it is based on the implications of previous research. It precedes the study proper because the entire study is determined by the hypothesis (including subjects, instruments, design, procedures, analysis, and conclusions).

Characteristics of the Hypothesis

66. A major characteristic of a good hypothesis is that it is consistent with previous research.

67. A good hypothesis is a tentative, reasonable explanation for the occurrence of certain behaviors, phenomena, or events.

68. A good hypothesis states as clearly and concisely as possible the expected relationship (or difference) between two variables and defines those variables in operational, measurable terms.

69. A well-stated and defined hypothesis must be testable.

Types of Hypotheses

70. An inductive hypothesis is a generalization based on observation.

71. Deductive hypotheses derived from theory contribute to the science of business and management by providing evidence that supports, expands, or contradicts a given theory.

72. Research hypotheses are stated in declarative form, and statistical hypotheses are stated in null form.

73. A research hypothesis states the expected relationship (or difference) between two variables, in other words, what relationship the researcher expects to verify through the collection and analysis of data.

74. A nondirectional hypothesis simply indicates that a relationship or difference exists; a directional hypothesis indicates the nature of the relationship or difference.

75. A statistical, or null, hypothesis states that there will be no relationship (or difference) between variables and that any relationship found will be a chance relationship, not a true one.

Stating the Hypothesis

76. A general paradigm, or model, for stating hypotheses for experimental studies is as follows:
Ss who get X do better on Y than Ss who do not get X (or get some other X).
In the model, Ss are the subjects, X is the treatment (or independent variable), and Y is the observed outcome (or dependent variable).

Testing the Hypothesis

77. In order to test a hypothesis, the researcher determines the sample, measuring instruments, design, and procedure that will enable her or him to collect the necessary data. Collected data are then analyzed in a manner that permits the researcher to determine the validity of the hypothesis.

78. It is just as important to know what variables are not related as it is to know which ones are related.

Project II Performance Criteria

The introduction that you develop for Project II will be the first part of the research report required for Project V. Therefore, it may save you some revision time later if, when appropriate, statements are expressed in the past tense ("it was hypothesized," rather than "it is hypothesized," for example). We all understand, however, that this is the *one and only* time we'll ever take this shortcut; it would look pretty peculiar in a real research proposal or prospectus to use the past tense!

Your introduction should include the following subheadings and contain the following types of information:

> Introduction
> (Background and significance of the problem)
> Statement of the problem
> (Problem statement and necessary definitions)
> Review of related literature
> (Don't forget the big *V* and the summary)
> Statement of the hypothesis(es)

As a guideline, three to five typed pages will generally be a sufficient length for Project II. As indicated throughout Chapter 2, you are strongly urged to develop your introduction using computer-based word processing. The necessary revisions combined with the capacity of word processing programs for checking spelling and other details makes time spent learning word processing invaluable for any student.

Because of feedback from your instructor on objective 4, and insight gained through developing your review of related literature, the hypothesis you state in Project II may very well be somewhat different from the one you stated for objective 4.

One final note. The hypothesis you formulate now will influence all further projects, i.e., who will be your subjects, what they will do, and so forth. In this connection, the following is an informal observation based on the behavior of thousands of students; it is not a research-based finding! All beginning research students fall somewhere on a continuum of realism. At one extreme are the Cecil B. DeMille-type research students, who want to design a study involving a cast of thousands, over an extended period of time, and so forth. At the other extreme are the Mr. Magoo-type students, who will not even consider a procedure unless they know *for sure* that they could actually execute it in their work setting, with their associates, and so forth. If your instructor requires that you complete your study by collecting data, be careful to design a feasible study to be completed with subjects who are accessible and during the time frame you have available. If you do not actually have to execute the study you design, feel free to operate in the manner most comfortable for you. There is a middle ground, however, between Cecil B. DeMille and Mr. Magoo; you may become so intrigued with your study that you will actually want to execute it after you get your grade (yes, it happens!).

At the end of Chapter 1, a research article was reprinted that illustrates the format and content of an introduction that meets the criteria described above. It would probably be useful to review this part of the article at this time so you have a clear example in mind before beginning your own review. The final chapter in the book also has several checklists for evaluating and critiquing research articles; you may want to use these as a way of making sure you've covered everything.

In addition, below and on the following pages a student example is presented that illustrates the format and content of an introduction that also meets the criteria described above. This project example is based on a project submitted by a former student in an introductory management research course This example reflects the performance which is expected of you at your present level of expertise.

Note: In your paper, the material below would be the first page of your report, typed on a separate sheet of paper.

Effects of Involvement in a Participatory
Budget Planning Team on Employee Attitudes
Toward Their Job and Company

Richard D. Prentiss
St. Thomas University

Submitted in partial fulfillment of
the requirements of MAN 503
September, 1989

Policy development and decision making traditionally have been handled at the highest levels of management. In areas such as budget planning, most employees have had little or no opportunity to participate in decision making; the extent of their involvement has been to implement the decisions made by senior managers. Over time, however, some managers have become aware that employee involvement is beneficial to the operation of the organization, and that, in order for businesses to excel, managers must solicit employee participation at all levels (Bookman, 1987). In the management literature, the terms participatory management and teamwork have come into common use. Webster (1984) defines participate as ''to have or take a share with others,'' (p. 436) and teamwork as ''joint action by a group of people'' (p. 613). In a business context, these definitions can be further refined to suggest a process involving multidisciplinary, collaborative sharing of information and coordination and goal setting by a group (Fiorelli, 1983). In organizations that have implemented the teamwork process, reactions have been favorable, and a number of benefits have been experienced (Barmore, 1987; Hoerr, 1988). Indeed, in the minds of many, team-work is a process whose application proves beneficial to any organization, regardless of the product or service provided. Thus the concept of employee involvement has now become as complex as the formation of participatory management teams (Hoerr, 1989a; Reynolds, 1988).

Statement of the Problem

The purpose of this study was to compare the attitudes toward job and company of employees involved in participatory budget-planning teams with those of employees who experienced traditional, nonparticipatory budget-planning. Participatory budget planning was defined as the use of employee teams in the planning, implementing, and reviewing of the annual budget. Traditional, nonparticipatory budget planning was defined as the use of senior management in the planning, implementing, and reviewing of the annual budget.

Review of Related Literature

In the past, businesses have been primarily concerned with the distribution of goods and services, with the primary emphasis being on low cost and high-profit margin. Employees have had little input regarding the operation of these organizations. Management felt that as long as employees remained somewhat motivated, the production and distribution of goods and services would be accomplished (Steers & Porter, 1975). Occasionally, however, management would solicit suggestions from employees regarding policies and procedures, and at some point it began to be recognized that employee suggestions often proved to be beneficial to the organization. Managers in some organizations began to capitalize on this by

1

incorporating employee participation into their businesses. Over time, the process became more formalized and came to be referred to as participatory management. Eventually, team formation was found to be an effective strategy for implementation of the participatory management concept, and it was realized that the responsibilities of such teams could range from specific problem solving to overall operation of the company (Bunting, 1988; Gallagher, 1987).

As the incidence of participatory management teams has increased, the need for careful planning and monitoring has become evident (Vogt & Hunt, 1988). For successful implementation, it is imperative that key employees and managers who can assist in facilitating teamwork be identified (Booth, 1988; Reynolds, 1988). Further, after teams have been formed, both the role of the employees and the role of management must be clearly defined, group identity established, and plans developed (Belzer, 1989; Porco, 1985). And, in order to be effective, it is critical that the team concept be a continuous process that facilitates open communication and trust between employees and management (Bookman, 1987).

Overall, it appears that implementation of participatory management teams has proven to be beneficial both to employees and to the organizations that have used them. Employees and managers are experiencing a new form of enhanced communication. Employees have demonstrated a feeling of ownership of their workplace and a willingness to participate (Hardaker & Ward, 1987). For the organizations involved, the outcome has been increased productivity and cost—effective distribution of goods and services resulting from the development and application of more effective procedures (Barmore, 1987; Hoerr, 1988; Hoerr, 1989b).

As participatory management teams have evolved and become more proficient, their scope of responsibility has increased. Currently, such teams are becoming increasingly involved in budgetary matters, and there is some research evidence that such participation benefits both employees and organizations. Brownell and Hirst (1986), for example, found an inverse relationship between employee participation in budget processes and job—related tension; high budgetary participation was associated with low job—related tension. In addition, Mia (1988) reported a direct relationship between employee participation and the effectiveness of the budgetary process; if employees are motivated and effective, communication improved, and an improved budgetary process was demonstrated.

Despite its apparent effectiveness, however, the participatory management team concept currently has only a superficial acceptance in the majority of business organizations. The reasons for this remain unclear, although some feel that management and/or organized labor are the major

2

adversaries of this concept (Hardaker & Ward, 1987). It is likely, however, that as the research base supporting its effectiveness grows, so will its implementation.

Statement of the Hypothesis

Implementation of participatory management teams in an organization has reportedly resulted in a variety of benefits, including enhanced employee-management communication and improved institutional efficiency and productivity. No research has been done related to the effects on employees' attitudes toward their jobs and company. This variable is critical, however, as it affects both employees, in terms of job satisfaction, for example, and organizations, in terms of factors such as absenteeism. Based on the research reporting feelings of employee ownership and decreased tension, it was hypothesized that employees at companies using participatory budget-planning teams have more positive attitudes toward their jobs and company than employees of companies using traditional, nonparticipatory budget planning.

References

Barmore, G. T. (1987). Teamwork: Charting a course for success. Mortgage Banking, 47(11), 90—96.

Belzer, E. J. (1989, August). 12 ways to better team building. Working Woman, pp. 12—14.

Bookman, B. (1987). Year round teamwork: Cooperation is not for Christmas only. Management World, 16, 37.

Booth, P. (1988). Employee involvement and corporate performance. Canadian Business Review, 15, 14.

Brownell, P., & Hirst, M. (1986). Reliance on accounting information, budgetary participation, and task uncertainty: Tests of a three-way interaction. Journal of Accounting Research, 24, 241—249.

Bunting, C. (1988, February). 'Group initiatives' make a game out of problem-solving. Camping Magazine, pp. 26—29.

Fiorelli, J. S. (1983). Power, decision making, and participation in interdisciplinary treatment teams. Dissertation Abstracts International, 44, 351B. (University Microfilms No. DA8311597).

Gallagher, M. (1987). Productive problem solving. Chilton's Distribution, 86(11), 70.

Guralnik, D. B. (Ed.) (1984). Webster's new world dictionary. New York: Warner.

Hardaker, M., & Ward, B. K. (1987). How to make a team work. Harvard Business Review, 65, 112—120.

Hoerr, J. P. (1988, November 28). Work teams can rev up paper-pushers, too. Business Week, pp. 64—72.

Hoerr, J. P. (1989, February 20). Is teamwork a management plot? Mostly not. Business Week, p. 70.

Hoerr, J. P. (1989, July 10). The payoff from teamwork. Business Week, pp. 56—62.

Mia, L. (1988). Managerial attitude, motivation and the effectiveness of budget participation. Accounting Organizations and Society, 13, 465—475.

Milani, K. (1975). The relationship of participation in budget-setting to industrial supervisor performance and attitudes: A field study. The Accounting Review, 50, 274—284.

Porco, C. (1985). Developing a proactive communication style in employees. Supervisory Management, 30(4), 23—28.

Reynolds, M. (1988, Spring). Building teams that work. Electric Perspectives, pp. 28—35.

4

Steers, R., & Porter, L. (1975). *Motivation and work behavior.*
    New York: McGraw-Hill.
Vogt, J. F., & Hunt, B. D. (1988). What *really* goes wrong with
    participatory work groups? *Training & Development Journal, 42*(5),
    96–100.

REFERENCES

AMERICAN PSYCHOLOGICAL ASSOCIATION. (1985). *Thesaurus of psychological index terms* (5th ed.). Washington, DC: Author.

AMERICAN PSYCHOLOGICAL ASSOCIATION. (1927 to date). *Psychological abstracts.* Washington, DC: Author.

AMERICAN PSYCHOLOGICAL ASSOCIATION. (1983). *Publication manual of the American Psychological Association* (3rd ed.). Washington, DC: Author.

Applied Science and Technology Index. (1958 to date). New York: H. W. Wilson.

BRUCE, M. M. (1977). *Sales motivation inventory (rev.)* Larchmont, NY: Martin M. Bruce, Publisher.

Business Periodicals Index. (1958 to date). New York: H. W. Wilson.

COE, R. K., & WEINSTOCK, I. (1984). Evaluating the management journals: A second look. *Academy of Management Journal, 27:* 660–666.

DANIELS, L. M. (1985). *Business information sources* (Rev. ed.). Berkeley, CA: University of California Press.

Dissertation Abstracts International (1969 to date). Ann Arbor, MI: University Microfilms International. (Prior to 1969, the title was *Dissertation abstracts.*)

ELWORK, A., HALL, P., & STONE, B. (Co-designers). (1988). *Manuscript Manager* [computer program]. Elmsford, NY: Pergamon.

GRIFFIN, R. W. (1988). Consequences of Quality Circles in an industrial setting: A longitudinal assessment. *Academy of Management Journal, 31*(2): 338–358.

HEYEL, C. (Ed.). (1982). *The encyclopedia of management.* (3rd ed.). New York: Van Nostrand Reinhold.

KERLINGER, F. N. (1973). *Foundations of behavioral research.* (2nd ed.). New York: Holt, Rinehart and Winston.

LAMMING, R. & BESSANT, J. (1988). *Macmillan dictionary of business and management.* London: Macmillan.

NILES & ASSOCIATES. (1988). *EndNote* [computer program]. Emeryville, CA: Author.

PAIS bulletin (1914 to date). New York: Public Affairs Information Services, Inc.

KEARSLEY, G. (1987). *Publish or Perish* [computer program]. La Jolla, CA: Park Row

PERSONAL BIBLIOGRAPHIC SYSTEMS (1986). *ProCite* [computer program]. Ann Arbor, MI: Author.

Personnel literature (1972 to date). Washington, DC: Office of Personnel Management.

Personnel management abstracts (1972 to date). Cleveland, OH: Author.

READERS' GUIDE TO PERIODICAL LITERATURE (1900 to date). New York: H.W. Wilson.

ROSENBERG, J. M (1982). *Dictionary of business and management.* New York: John Wiley & Sons.

SCANLON, J. M., DE STRICKER, U., & FERNALD, A. C. (1989). *Business online.* New York, NY: John Wiley & Sons.

SHARPEN, A. D., & MABRY, R. H. (1985). The relative importance of journals used in management research: An alternative ranking. *Human Relations, 38*(2): 139–148.

SHERMAN, S. P. (1988, June 20). Fast stepping at the predators' ball. *Fortune,* pp.107–108.

SUMMETRY (1986). *Acta* [computer program]. Mesa, AZ: Author.

SYMANTEC (1986). *More* [computer program]. Mountain View, CA: Author.

The New York Times Index. (1851 to date). New York, NY:The New York Times Co.

The Wall Street Journal Index. (1957 to date). Princeton, NJ: Dow Jones Books.

WINER, P., & WINER, D. (1984). *ThinkTank* [computer program]. Mountain View, CA: Living Videotext, Inc.

PART THREE
Method

Once specific hypotheses have been formulated, it is necessary to delineate the method and procedure to be followed in testing them. This part discusses *method*.

Beginning with a sound research plan as described in Chapter 3, you will identify the subjects and instruments you need to use to test your hypothesis (Chapters 4 and 5), and the design of the study and the specific procedures needed to implement the plan (Chapters 6 to 10). Chapter 4 will provide you with information regarding the selection of subjects; Chapter 5 covers the instruments you will be using in your study. Chapters 6 through 10 review the various types of research designs and procedures as they relate to historical, descriptive, correlational, causal-comparative, and experimental studies.

After you have read Part Three, you should be able to complete the following project, which starts in Chapter 4.

Project III Guidelines

For the hypothesis you have formulated, develop a method section for the study you would conduct in order to test your hypothesis. You should include the following:

Method

> *Subjects/Samples*
> *Instruments*
> *Design*
> *Procedure*

Your assumptions, limitations, and definitions should be included where appropriate. If you are using American Psychological Association (APA) Publication Manual (1983) format, your headings will probably appear as they do above; if not, check your style manual for headings.

(See Project III Performance Criteria, p. 446)

Having a written plan also allows others not only to identify flaws but also to make suggestions as to ways the study might be improved. (page 95)

3

Preparation and Evaluation of a Research Plan

Objectives

After reading Chapter 3, you should be able to do the following:

1. Briefly describe three ethical considerations involved in conducting and reporting research involving human subjects.

2. Briefly describe one major piece of legislation affecting research involving human subjects, a second area of legislation affecting research involving personnel and educational records, and a third piece of legislation affecting the selection of research subjects.

3. Briefly describe each of the components of a research plan.

4. Briefly describe two major ways in which a research plan can be evaluated.

INTRODUCTION

Development of a research plan is a critical step in conducting research. Occasionally it will become apparent in formulating a plan that the proposed study is not feasible in its present form. That decision is best made before you have expended considerable time and energy on a study that cannot be adequately executed. While very few research plans are executed exactly as planned, the existence of a plan permits the researcher to assess the overall impact of any changes on the study as a whole.

You, of course, are not yet in a position to develop a complete plan. A research plan, for example, generally states the statistical technique that will be used to analyze the data; this ensures that data will be collected that are analyzable. By now, however, you have read enough research reports to be aware of some of the possibilities. It will be interesting for you to compare the plan you begin to develop now with the research report you will finally develop after you have acquired competencies related to the research process.

The goal of Chapter 3 is for you to understand the importance of developing a research plan and to become familiar with the components of such a plan. A complete research plan should include at least the following:

Introduction
Statement of the Problem
Review of Related Literature
Statement of the Hypothesis
Method
Subjects
Instruments
Design
Procedure
Data Analysis
Time Schedule

DEFINITION AND PURPOSE

A research plan is a detailed description of a proposed study designed to investigate a given problem. It includes justification for the hypothesis to be tested, a detailed presentation of the research steps that will be followed in collecting and analyzing required data, and a projected time schedule for each major step. A research plan may be brief and formal, such as a proposal or prospectus submitted for review by senior management of a company or agency, or very lengthy and formal, such as a proposal that is submitted to governmental and private funding agencies. Graduate schools typically require that a proposal, or prospectus, be submitted for approval before thesis or dissertation studies are begun; these proposals differ from those used in industry in both length and terminology. For example, academic proposals should emphasize in a great deal more detail the review of previous studies and the technicalities of the analysis methods to be used; business-and-management proposals will place greater emphasis on the practical information to be gained from the study.

Whatever you call it, the research plan must be completed before a study is begun. Playing it by ear is all right for piano playing but not for conducting research. After you have completed the review of related literature and formulated your hypothesis, you are ready to develop the rest of the plan. Since your study will be designed to test a hypothesis, the hypothesis must be developed first. The nature of your hypothesis will determine to a high degree the sample group, measuring instruments, design, procedures, and statistical techniques used in your study. A research plan serves several important purposes:

1. It makes you think through every aspect of the study. The very process of getting it down on paper usually makes you think of something you might otherwise have overlooked.

2. It facilitates evaluation of the proposed study by yourself and others. Sometimes great ideas don't look so great after all when they're written down. Certain problems may become apparent or some aspect may not be feasible. Having a written plan also allows others not only to identify flaws but also to make suggestions as to ways the study might be improved. This is as true for experienced researchers as it is for beginners.

3. It provides a guide for conducting the study. Detailed procedures need only be thought through once and then followed, not remembered. Also, if something unexpected occurs that alters some phase of the study, the overall impact on the rest of the study can be assessed. For example, suppose you ordered 60 copies of a test that was to be administered on May 1. If on April 15, you received a letter saying that because of a shortage of available tests your order could not be filled until May 15, your study might be seriously affected. At the very least it would be delayed several weeks. Reworking of the time schedule in your research plan might indicate that given your deadlines you could not afford to wait. Therefore, you might decide to use an alternate measuring instrument.

4. It may give you protection from "meddling" while you're conducting the study. Having all the appropriate sign-offs on a detailed level ahead of time provides you with some backup if someone else has a bright idea during the study and says, "Gee, while you're at it, why don't you just find out . . . ." Another example of "meddling" you may encounter is a request by a supervisor for information about an employee(s); it helps to be able to back up your polite, but firm, refusal to provide this information by indicating that this was never a part of the original proposal.

A well-developed plan saves time, reduces the probability of costly mistakes, and generally results in higher-quality research. If your study is a disaster because of poor planning, *you* lose. The research plan really is not written for your boss's or even your professor's benefit; it is written for you. If something goes wrong, which could have been avoided with a little foresight, you may have to redo the whole study, at worst, or somehow salvage the remnants of a less-than-ideal study, at best. "Oops!" would look terrible on your final report!

Murphy's law states approximately that "If anything can go wrong, it will." Gay's law states that "If anything can go wrong, it will—unless you make sure that it doesn't!" Diehl's law suggests that "When something goes wrong, you'd better have a handle ahead of time on containing the damages." Most of the minor tragedies that occur during studies could have been avoided with proper planning, good coordination, and careful monitoring. Part of good planning is anticipation. You don't want to wait until something happens before you figure out how to deal with it. Try to anticipate potential problems that might arise and then do what you can to prevent them. Plan your strategies for dealing with them if they do occur. For example, you might anticipate resistance on the part of some supervisors to giving you permission and support in using their employees as subjects in your study. To deal with this contingency you should work up the best sales pitch possible. Do not ask, "Hey, can I use your people for my study?" Instead, tell them how wonderful the study is and how it will benefit them, their employees, and the company. Be prepared to reassure them about confidentiality, if appropriate, and also be sensitive to overall business timing. Asking for help from certain employees in certain businesses on Monday mornings, Friday afternoons, or at the end of the quarter or year simply demonstrates your lack of business sense. Of course you'll want to let the supervisor know senior management's position on the study and exactly what the procedures and requirements will be.

You may tend to get frustrated at times because you cannot do everything the way you would like to because of real or bureaucratic constraints. Don't let such obstacles exasperate you. Just relax and do your best. On the positive side, a sound plan critiqued by others is likely to result in a sound study conducted with a minimum of grief. You cannot guarantee that your study will be executed exactly as planned, but you can guarantee that things will go as smoothly as possible.

GENERAL CONSIDERATIONS

In planning the actual procedures of your study, there are a number of factors you should consider. Two of these factors, the ethics of conducting research and legal restrictions, are relevant to all research studies. Any potential subject in your study, for example, has the right to refuse to be involved and the right to stop being involved at any time. A third factor to consider is strategies for achieving and maintaining necessary cooperation from those concerned. A fourth factor is the need for training if others will be assisting you in conducting your study. Your research plan may not specifically address any of these factors, but the plan's chances of being properly executed will be increased if you are aware of them.

The Ethics of Research

There are ethical considerations involved in all research studies. Ethical concerns are, of course, more acute in experimental studies, which, by definition, manipulate and control subjects. The ends do not justify the means, and perhaps the foremost rule of ethics is that subjects should not be harmed in any way (physically or mentally) in the name of science. If an experiment involves any risk to subjects, they should be completely informed concerning the nature of the risk, and permission for participation in the experiment should be acquired in writing from the subjects themselves. The researcher should take every precaution and make every effort to minimize potential risk to subjects. Even if there is no risk to subjects, they should be completely informed concerning the nature of the study. Frequently, for control purposes, subjects are not aware of their participation in a study or, if aware, do not know the exact nature of the experiment. Such subjects should be informed as soon as the study is completed. An appropriate level of concern for this issue is demonstrated in an award-winning article by Sutton and Rafaeli (1988) regarding employee behavior in convenience stores:

> In closing, we would like to return to the methods used in this study. The observational methods used here are not widely employed in organizational research. Thus, questions may arise about whether it is ethical to secretly observe employees. Procedures used in the present research were, however, consistent with ethical guidelines on the conduct of nonreactive research and contrived observations (Salancik, 1979; Sechrest & Phillips, 1979; Webb et al., 1981). The American Psychological Association discourages "covert investigations in private places" (American Psychological Association, 1973: 13). The convenience stores used in the present research are, however, public places. Moreover, the corporation's use of incognito observers and our own use of that method during the qualitative phase were only partly covert. Although specific, informed consent was not obtained from each clerk observed, all clerks had been informed that encounters with mystery shoppers were part of the job: the corporate training program explained the use of mystery shoppers and the expected expressive behaviors. Furthermore, the names of individual clerks were not recorded in either the quantitative research conducted by the corporation or in our own qualitative research. Thus, in terms of a harms-benefit analysis, such data were not, and could not, be used to harm any individual clerk.

In addition, there is some question regarding the ethics of withholding a potentially beneficial treatment from subjects in the control group. Suppose, for example, that a study was concerned with the benefits of a particular training program in furthering the career development of potential managers. If you were part of the control group that didn't get the training or something of equal value to your career, you would probably feel that you hadn't been given fair and equal treatment.

The subject's right to privacy is of equal importance to the right to be free of undue risk. Employees need to be reassured that their personal opinions, practices, and behaviors not directly related to the workplace are not going to become part of company records or even known to the company. It is perfectly legitimate to hold certain political opinions that differ from those of your employer; it is equally legitimate to make a choice not to inform your employer of these opinions. As indicated in the Sutton and Rafaeli study (1988), collecting information on subjects or observing them without their knowledge or without appropriate permission is not ethical. Secret monitoring of employee phone calls and computer use, hidden camera observations, and psychological and physical testing have prompted the American Civil Liberties Union (ACLU) to mount a major campaign to protect employee rights in the workplace (Rankin, 1990). Furthermore, any information that is collected, either from or about a subject, should be strictly confidential, especially if it is at all personal. Individual scores should never be reported or made public even for an innocuous measure such as a typing test. This is especially important when you are dealing with psychological measures or personality inventories. Employees especially have a right to psychological privacy. It is usually sufficient to present data in terms of group statistics; if individual scores, or raw data, need to be presented, they should be coded and should not be associated with subjects' names or other identifying information. In addition to applying to individuals, usually this means that the name(s) of companies involved in studies are not reported; rather they are described in general terms such as "a medium-size bank in southeastern United States." Access to raw data must be limited to persons directly involved in conducting the research. Frequently this means that individuals within companies are not given access to individual scores, for example, although they certainly are informed concerning overall findings. For a more complete discussion of ethics in business, you may want to refer to a book such as *Business Ethics* (Velasquez, 1988) or to one of the journals specializing in business ethics. More specific information may be available through your own professional organization, such as the American Marketing Association, or through such organizations as the American Psychological Association (Ad Hoc Committee, 1973).

Above all, the researcher must have personal integrity. The reader of a research report must be able to believe that what the researcher says happened, really happened; otherwise it is all for nothing. Falsifying data in order to make findings agree with a hypothesis is unprofessional, unethical, and unforgivable. Conversely, changing your hypothesis to make it agree with your findings is also unforgivable, although it does occur (Sutton & Rafaeli, 1988).

Legal Restrictions

The year 1974 marked the beginning of an era in which ethical standards in research increasingly are given the force of law. The need for legal restrictions is graphically illustrated by a study on the effects of group pressure that was conducted some years ago (Milgram, 1964). The purpose of the study was to answer the question Can a group induce a person to deliver punishment of increasing severity to a protesting individual? Basically, the study involved one person (A) testing another person (B) on a paired-associate learning task. Person A was instructed to administer an electric shock to person B each time person B gave an incorrect response. In the experimental group, each A subject was pressured by two confederates (persons working with the experimenter but pretending to be part of the experiment) to increase voltage levels for succeeding wrong answers given by the corresponding B subject. In the control group, each A subject made independent, unpressured decisions concerning voltage levels throughout the experiment.

For both groups, B subjects were also confederates; in other words, no one actually received shocks, but A subjects did not know this. Prerecorded tapes provided pain responses from B subjects, which ranged from mild protests at lower voltage levels to agonized screams at higher levels. The results were very clear: the two pressuring confederates strongly influenced the level of shock administered to B subject confederates. In the experimental group, mean (average) shock levels steadily increased as the experiment progressed, whereas mean shock levels remained relatively stable in the control group. It is more than likely that at least some of the subjects in the experimental group suffered mental stress for some time following the experiment, even though they were told in the debriefing that they had not really hurt anyone. The point was that they knew what they were capable of, regardless of what they had actually done (Milgram, 1964; 1975).

The major provisions of legislation passed to date have been designed to protect subjects who participate in research and ensure the confidentiality of their records. The National Research Act of 1974 established a commission to make recommendations regarding ethical guidelines for research to a National Advisory Council for the Protection of Subjects of Biomedical and Behavioral Research. Generally speaking, proposed research activities involving human subjects must be reviewed and approved by an authorized group in an institution, prior to the execution of the research, to ensure protection of subjects. Protection of subjects is broadly defined and requires that subjects not be harmed in any way, physically or mentally, and that they participate only if they freely agree to do so. The latter provision is known as *informed consent.* If you obtain funding for your research from the federal government or you are associated with an institution, such as a university, that receives federal funds, you must comply with these guidelines; even though you may not be forced to comply, you will probably want to follow the guidelines because they represent good practice in research.

Most colleges and universities have either formed such a review group or assign the review function to an already constituted group such as a university research committee. Typically, the researcher submits a proposal to the chair of the review group, who in turn distributes copies to all members. They in turn review the proposal in terms of proposed treatment of subjects. If there is any question as to whether subjects might be harmed in any way, the researcher is usually asked to meet with the review group to answer questions and to clarify proposed procedures. In rare cases the researcher is asked to rewrite the questionable or unclear areas in the research plan. When the review group is satisfied that the subjects will not be placed at risk (or that potential risk is minimal compared to the potential benefits of the study), the committee members sign the appropriate approval forms. Members' signatures on the approval forms indicate that the proposal is acceptable with respect to subject protection and that the actual execution of the research will be periodically reviewed to insure that subjects are being properly treated. Most companies will probably not have as elaborate procedures for reviewing proposed research, but it's wise to check with the Human Resources Department before proceeding. In some rare cases, senior management may want to obtain legal counsel before proceeding, but most research in business and management does not require this sort of caution. If you want more complete information on the provisions of the National Research Act, you can use your library research skills to look it up, or write to the National Commission for the Protection of Human Subjects, 5333 Westbard Avenue, Bethesda, Maryland 20016.

A second area of legislation that may affect your study includes the Privacy Act of 1974, the Freedom of Information Act, and the Family Educational Rights and Privacy Act of 1974, more commonly referred to as the Buckley Amendment. Although the first two acts apply only to federal employees, they have generated voluntary compliance on the part of employers as well as state laws protecting the privacy of individual employees. The general guidelines for employers were proposed by the report of the Privacy Protection Study Commission to the President in July 1977; the guidelines suggest that employers agree to

1. "limit the employer's collection of information about applicants and employees to matters that are relevant to the particular decisions to be made and to avoid items of information that tend to stigmatize an individual unfairly;

2. "inform all applicants, employees, and former employees with whom it maintains a continuing relationship (such as retirees) of all uses that may be made of the records the employer keeps on them;

3. "notify employees of each type of record that may be maintained on them, including records that are not available to them for review and correction;

4. "institute and publicize procedures for assuring that individually identifiable employment records are (a) created, used, and disclosed according to consistently followed procedures; (b) kept as accurate, timely, and complete as is necessary to assure that they are not the cause of unfairness in decision making, . . . and (c) disclosed within and outside the employing organization only according to stated policy;

5. "institute and publicize a broadly applicable policy of letting employees see, copy, correct or amend, and if necessary, dispute individually identifiable information about themselves in the employer's records;

6. "monitor the internal flow of individually identifiable employee record information;

7. "regulate external disclosures of individually identifiable employee-record information in accordance with an established policy of which employees are made aware;

8. "assess its employee record-keeping policies and practices, at regular intervals, with a view to possibilities for improving them." (Privacy Protection Study Commission, 1977, pp. 236–237).

In addition, if your study requires information such as GPAs or some other educational records, for example, you will need to understand the provisions of the Buckley Amendment. Among these provisions is the specification that data that actually identify students may not be made available unless written permission is acquired from the students (if of age), their parents, or legal guardians. The consent must indicate what data may be disclosed, for what purposes, and to whom (Michael & Weinberger, 1977; Weinberger & Michael, 1976). For complete information on the provisions of the Buckley Amendment, again, you can look it up or write to the Family Educational Rights and Privacy Office, 200 Independence Avenue, S.W., Washington DC 20201.

The final area of legislation with potential impact for researchers in business settings is Title VII of the 1964 Civil Rights Act and Equal Employment Opportunities Commission (EEOC) regulations and guidelines. Essentially this act and the commission promote a policy of fairness so that individuals are not treated differently and that the ultimate impact of the way they are treated is not disparate. You can readily see the implications here for the design of research. It would be clearly unfair, for example, to give one group some training that you believe will ultimately improve their career opportunities while withholding comparable opportunities from a control group.

Cooperation

Very rarely is it possible to conduct business-and-management research without the cooperation of a number of people, typically senior management. The first step in acquiring the needed cooperation is to follow required procedures, if these have been established. Certainly, approval for the proposed research must be granted by the highest-level manager involved or some other high-level manager such as the senior vice president for human resource management. The approval process should begin with a specific written request in which the nature of the research, potential benefits to be derived by the company or agency, and exact requirements in terms of number of employees involved and employee time are specifically identified. Although you will want a written proposal that is both specific and concise, your face-to-face meeting with your company contact person will be critical to your obtaining full cooperation. If you are associated with a college or university at the time of your study, it may help if you already have written approval from the university to indicate the study is legitimate and has been reviewed. The reason for all this caution is that companies are extremely careful regarding any information that might be concerned with employee personnel records or construed as proprietary (i.e., company secrets affecting competition). Many companies have inculcated their employees with the absolute necessity of never discussing their work with anyone, including family members. Observe, for example, the following statement from an article concerning corporate spying:

> Warn your workers about companies that hire headhunting firms to grill unwitting job candidates on business plans and R & D secrets. Assume that any consulting firm or organization that calls and says it is doing an industry study is digging up nuggets for the competition. Ben Zour, a senior analyst for business research at Eastman Kodak, says, "You have to make employees sensitive to the fact that if they leak, they will lose their jobs." Or worse—if the breach is serious enough, an employee could face criminal prosecution. (Dumaine, 1988).

In some cases, companies will ask to review your findings before you use them; you will have to decide how much this may compromise your study and whether the risk of interference is great enough to cause you to revise your plans. In addition to formal company approval, approval may also be required from the manager(s) whose employees are involved. Even if such approval is not required, it should be sought, both out of courtesy and for the sake of a smoothly executed study.

The key to gaining approval and cooperation is good planning. The key to good planning is a well-designed, carefully thought-out study. Managers and supervisors who are hesitant or hostile about people doing research in their departments have probably had a bad experience. They don't want anyone else running around their department disrupting work and administering useless, poorly constructed question-naires. Unfortunately, there are instances in which improperly trained, though well-intentioned, persons go into a company and become a source of bad feelings regarding research. It is up to you to convince management that what you are proposing is of value, that your study is carefully designed, and that you will work with managers and supervisors to minimize inconvenience and loss of productive time.

Achieving full cooperation, and not just approval on paper, requires that you invest as much time as is necessary to discuss your study with managers, supervisors, employees, and perhaps even unions. These groups have varying levels of knowledge and understanding regarding the research process. Their concerns will focus mainly on the perceived value of the study, its potential affective impact, the actual logistics of carrying it out, and the safeguards for employees and the company. Senior managers, for example, will probably be more concerned with the potential impact on the bottom line and with legalities than with your specific design and procedures. All groups will be interested in what you might be able to do for them as a separate constituency. Potential benefits to be derived by the managers, supervisors, or employees as a result of your study should be explained fully. Your study, for example, might involve group and individual interviews with employees regarding ideas they have for improving their working conditions, which will be provided to management in the form of suggestions after the study has ended. Even if all parties are favorably impressed, however, the spirit of cooperation will quickly dwindle if your study will involve considerable extra work on their part or will inconvenience them in any major way. Thus if changes can be made in the planned study to accommodate the normal routine, they should be made unless the study will suffer as a consequence. No change should be made solely for the sake of compromise without considering its impact on the study as a whole.

Clearly, human relations is an important factor in conducting research in applied settings. That you must be your usual charming self goes without saying, but you should keep in mind that you are dealing with sincere, concerned managers and workers who probably do not have your level of research expertise. Therefore, you must make a special effort to discuss your study in plain English (it *is* possible—and if it isn't, maybe you'd better review your study until you can talk about it in ways that anyone can understand). If you aren't able to talk about your study in plain English, you'll probably give the impression that you're talking down to your listeners. Alas, your task is not over once the study begins. The feelings of involved persons must be monitored and responded to throughout the duration of the study if the initial level of cooperation is to be maintained.

Training Research Assistants

In addition to determining *what* will be done, you must also decide *who* will do it. Anyone who is going to assist you in any way in actually conducting your study, whether a colleague or a manager, should be considered a research assistant.

Regardless of who they are or what role they will play, all assistants should participate in some type of orientation that explains the nature of the study and the part they will play in it. They should understand exactly *what* they are going to do and *how* they are to do it. Their responsibilities should be described both orally and in writing, and, if necessary, they should receive training related to their assigned task and be given opportunities for supervised practice. Simulations, in which assistants go through the entire task (e.g., conducting an interview) with one another or with you, are an especially effective training strategy.

Before any data are actually collected, anyone involved in any way with data-collection procedures should become thoroughly familiar with all relevant restrictions, legal or otherwise, related to collecting, storing, and sharing obtained information. All necessary permissions from participants, managers, agencies, and the like should be obtained *in writing*. Finally, all data collection activities should be carefully and systematically monitored to ensure that correct procedures are being followed.

COMPONENTS

Although they may go by other names, research plans typically include an introduction, a method section, a description of proposed data analysis, and a time schedule. Each component will be discussed in detail, but basically the format, using appropriate levels of headings as specified by the APA manual (1983), for a typical research plan is as follows:

Introduction

Statement of the Problem

Review of Related Literature

Statement of the Hypothesis

Method

Subjects/Samples

Instrument(s)

Design

Procedure

Data Analysis

Time Schedule

Budget

Other headings may also be included, as needed. For example, if special materials are being developed for the study or special equipment is being used (such as computer terminals), then headings such as "Materials" or "Apparatus" might be included under "Method," between "Instruments" and "Design."

Introduction

If you have completed Project II, you are familiar with the content of the introduction: (a) statement of the problem, (b) review of related literature, and (c) statement of the hypothesis. In a business setting, you probably will want your introduction to start with a one-page summary of the key elements of the entire research plan. This may be in the form of an executive summary or a formal memo to management; it should specify that detailed information regarding the plan is attached and that you will be readily available to answer questions. (See Figure 3.1 for an example of a hypothetical executive summary.)

Statement of the Problem

Since the problem sets the stage for the rest of the plan, it should be stated as early as possible. The statement should be accompanied by a description of the background of the problem and a rationale for its significance.

Review of Related Literature

The review of related literature should present the least related references first and most related references last, just prior to the statement of the hypothesis (do not forget the big V described in Chapter 2). The literature review should lead logically to a tentative, testable conclusion, which is your hypothesis. The review should conclude with a brief summary of the literature and its implications.

Statement of the Hypothesis

Each hypothesis should represent a reasonable explanation for some behavior, phenomenon, or event. It should clearly and concisely state the expected relationship (or difference) between the variables in your study, and it should define those variables in operational, measurable terms. Finally, each hypothesis should be clearly testable within some reasonable period of time. Be certain that all terms in the introduction are either common-usage terms or are operationally defined. The persons reading your plan (and especially persons reading your final report, of which this introduction will be a part) may not be as familiar with your terminology as you are.

Method

The specific method of research your study represents will affect the format and content of your method section. The method section for an experimental study, for example, typically includes a description of the experimental design, whereas a descriptive study may combine the design and procedures sections into one. In general, however, the method section includes a description of the subjects, measuring instruments, design, and procedures. Each of these subsections will be described in detail later in the book; this merely provides you an overview of the method section.

MEMORANDUM

Date: April 15, 1990
To: Medical Education Committee
From: Ruthie Researcher, Chair, Stress Management Subcommittee
Subject: Stress Management Research Project

As we discussed at the March meeting, a Stress Management Research Project for our interns is being developed by the Stress Management Subcommittee. For many years, the interns have lost considerable work time due to disorders, such as colds, headaches, and accidents, that are possibly stress related; in addition, their effectiveness and efficiency are somewhat diminished by excessive fatigue and anxiety. The Stress Management Research Project is designed to test whether a Stress Management Program, using biofeedback or exercise-and-diet training, will alleviate these problems.

Subject to the approval by the Medical Education Committee, the Stress Management Research Project is scheduled to begin when the new group of interns arrive on July 1. The attached packet of materials outlines the details of the research project for your review. Briefly, the proposed plan involves the following steps:

1. Random selection of 60 interns to participate in the experimental groups and 40 in the control group in the study. The experimental group interns will be randomly assigned to biofeedback training or the exercise-and-diet training program. All interns will be tested using the Maslach Burnout Inventory (Maslach & Jackson, 1981) to determine their initial stress level; in addition, their resting pulse rates and blood pressures will be measured as part of their initial physical examination. This will provide baseline data for the 60 interns who will be receiving training as well as the other 40 who will comprise the control group.

2. Training will be conducted three times a week; each training session will be one hour in duration. The total amount of time devoted to the training will be three months.

3. At the conclusion of the training, all interns will be tested again using the Maslach Burnout Inventory; their resting pulse rates and blood pressures will again be taken. Attendance records, visits to the medical office, and interviews of resident supervisors will be reviewed to determine absences, incidence of minor illness, and relative effectiveness and efficiency. At this time, the control group of interns will be invited to participate in stress-management training so that no charges of favoritism may be made.

We have received enthusiastic responses from all the hospital personnel we've asked to assist with the project, and we are looking forward to the review of the Medical Education Committee at the May 1 meeting. If you have questions I can answer before or after that time, please feel free to call me at extension 245.

Figure 3.1. Hypothetical example of an executive summary.

Subjects

The description of subjects should clearly define the population, the larger group, from which the sample will be selected. The description should indicate the size and major characteristics of the population. In other words, where are the subjects for your study going to come from? What are they like? How many do you have to choose from? For example,a description of the subjects might include the following:

> Subjects will be selected from a population of 2,053 customer-service representatives employed by an electric utility company based in Miami, Florida. The population is multicultural, being composed almost equally of Caucasian, Hispanic, and Afro-Americans. Seventy-five percent of the customer-service representatives are female; the ages of the representatives range from 20 to 45, with over 50% under the age of 30.

The technique for selecting the sample or samples to be included in the study may be described here, but usually the selection procedure is described in the overall procedure section of the plan.

Instruments

Since measurement in business and management is frequently indirect, the measuring instrument you select or develop really represents an operational definition of whatever construct you are trying to measure. There is no physical yardstick for measuring motivation, for example, although many studies involving motivation rely on the Job Diagnostic Survey (JDS) or its short form (JDSSF) (Hackman & Oldhan, 1980). Similarly, intelligence or general cognitive ability may be defined as scores on the Wonderlic Personnel Test (Wonderlic, 1930–1983). Therefore, it is important to provide a rationale for the selection of the instrument to be used as well as a description of the instrument. Validity and reliability data should also be presented; the degree to which the instrument for collecting data is valid is directly related to the degree to which the study is valid. If you are going to develop your own instrument, you should describe how the instrument will be developed, what it will measure, and how you plan to evaluate its validity and reliability before its utilization in the actual study. For example, a description of the instrument might include the following:

> The Maslach Burnout Inventory (Maslach & Jackson, 1981) will be used as the data-gathering instrument. The Inventory provides three scales: Emotional Exhaustion, Depersonalization, and Personal Accomplishment. Test-retest reliability coefficients range from .53 to .82; alpha coefficients range from .71 to .90. Construct and concurrent validity data are provided; although small, these coefficients are statistically significant (Bodden, 1985; Dowd, 1985).

Of course, if more than one instrument is to be used, which is not uncommon, each should be described separately and in detail. You are probably not yet able to identify and describe the instrument you would use in your study, although you may have noticed some common ones in addition to the JDS in your textbooks or literature review such as the Leader Behavior Description Questionnaire (LBDQ-12) (Bureau of Business Research, 1963) or the Management Style Questionnaire (MSQ) (McBer, 1980). The latter instrument, however, raises some interesting questions regarding instrumentation, as there are at least two major instruments known as the MSQ; the McBer instrument should not be confused with the Management Styles Questionnaire (Michalak, 1983), and the researcher needs to be sure that the selected instrument suits both the hypothesis and the subjects. Chapter 5 will give you a great deal more information about this topic. The instrument section of a research plan, however, may include a description of when each instrument will be administered and for what purpose (as a pretest, for example), but such a description is usually included in the procedure section. In writing this section of a research plan, a researcher may discover that an appropriate instrument for collecting data to test the hypothesis is not available. If this occurs, a decision needs to be made, probably either to alter the hypothesis and change the dependent variable or to develop an instrument. Again, it is better to be aware of the unavailability of an appropriate instrument *before* a study has begun than *while* you're conducting it.

Materials/Apparatus

As mentioned previously, if special materials (such as handouts, training manuals, or computer programs) are going to be developed, they should be described in some detail in the research plan. Also, if special apparatus (such as simulation apparatus or computer terminals) are going to be used, they should be described also. If your study involves using biofeedback equipment in a stress-management program, for example, the description might include the following:

> Biofeedback training will be provided using the MedAC instrument (Davicon, Inc., Boston); this equipment records heart rate, galvanic skin response (GSR), electromyogram (EMG), and skin temperature.

Design

The description of the design indicates the basic structure of the study. The nature of the hypothesis, the variables involved, and the constraints of the real world all contribute to the design to be used. For example, if the hypothesis involved comparing the effectiveness of biofeedback training versus diet and exercise in reducing stress, the study would involve comparing the stress level of two groups after some period of time, one group having engaged in biofeedback training and one group in improving their diet-and-exercise programs. Therefore, a design involving two groups would be needed. The real world might determine whether those groups could be randomly formed or whether existing groups would have to be used; these two alternatives dictate distinctly different designs. If the dependent variable involves measurement of employee attitudes, for example, use of a design involving a pretest may be precluded. Administration of a pretest of attitudes may alert employees to what is coming, to what the study is all about—the "I know what you're up to" phenomenon. Subjects may then react differently to a treatment intended to change attitudes, for example, from the way they would have had they not been pretested. Thus, the design typically indicates the number of groups to be included in the study, whether the groups will be randomly formed, and whether there will be a pretest. Other factors may also be discussed, such as particular arrangements of groups and time intervals between components of the design. In the quality circles study at the end of Chapter 1, for example, several different types of measurement were used at different times over the course of the study. This entire discussion, it should be pointed out, is appropriate primarily for experimental studies. The choice of designs is greatly reduced for a causal-comparative study; research plans and reports for historical, descriptive, and correlational studies usually do not include a separate design section.

There are a number of basic designs to select from as well as an almost endless number of variations on those designs that can be used. While the design can become very complex, especially if multiple independent and/or dependent variables are involved, such complex designs are really sophisticated variations of the basic designs. By the time you develop Project III, you will be familiar with the basic designs and will be able to identify them by name and apply them to your study. At this point you do not have this knowledge. You should be able, however, to begin to describe the kinds of information that a given design conveys. In regard to your own study, you should be thinking about the number and arrangement of groups, whether they will be randomly formed or existing groups, and whether there will be a pretest.

Procedure

The procedure section describes all the steps that will be followed in conducting the study, from beginning to end, in the order in which they will occur; in other words, your plan will explain how the design selected for testing the hypothesis will be operationalized. The procedure section typically begins with a description of the technique to be used in selecting the sample, or samples, for the study. A description might be as follows:

> In June of 1990, before the arrival of the new group of interns, a list of the 100 interns scheduled to report to the hospital on July 1 will be obtained. From this list, 60 interns will be randomly selected to participate in the experimental groups in the study. These 60 interns will be randomly assigned to biofeedback training or diet-and-exercise training in the stress-management program.

Occasionally an entire population is used and simply randomly assigned to two or more groups. This situation might be described as follows:

> The entire population of 120 new flight attendants will participate in the study. All flight attendants will be randomly assigned to one of six groups; three of those groups will be randomly designated as experimental groups and three as control groups.

In both examples, the population would already have been described under subjects at the beginning of the method section.

If the design includes a pretest, the procedure for its administration—when it will be administered and how—will usually be described next. Any other measure to be administered at the beginning of the study will also be discussed; for example, in addition to a pretest on the current level of stress, a general physical examination might be administered in order to check for initial equivalence of groups. For the study involving the interns in the stress-management program, this portion of the procedure section might include a statement such as the following:

> On July 1, the Maslach Burnout Inventory (Maslach & Jackson, 1981) will be administered to all experimental and control groups. In addition, blood pressures and pulse rates, at rest and following 20 minutes of strenuous exercise, will be recorded.

In research plans that do not include a separate section for a description of the instrument, relevant information concerning the measure will be presented here.

From this point on, the procedure section will describe exactly what is going to occur in the study. In an experimental study, this will basically involve a description of how the groups will be the same and how they will be different. How they will be different should be a function of the independent variable only; in other words, major differences between groups should be intentional treatment differences. How they will be the same will be a function of control procedures. Since the essence of experimentation is groups equivalent on all relevant variables except the experimental variable, all procedures designed to insure equivalence should be described; if two groups are equivalent to begin with, are treated the same for some period of time except for the independent variable, and are different at the end on some dependent variable, that difference can be attributed to the independent variable. Variables that typically need to be controlled include supervisor or trainer skill and experience, materials, work environment, and testing conditions. For example, if an experimental group was supervised by Carmel Kandee (a Pollyanna type), and a control group was supervised by Horatio Hartless (charter member of the Lizzie Borden fan club), then the final differences between groups might be attributable to supervisor differences, not treatment differences. In order to control for the supervisor variable, you might have both groups supervised by the same person, or you might have several experimental groups and several control groups and randomly assign supervisors to groups. The following are examples of the kinds of statements which typically appear in the procedure section:

The types of insurance claims for both groups will be the same.

All experimental and control groups will use the Word software program on the IBM PS2 computer.

All eight supervisors have more than 5 years' experience.

All flight attendants will meet for the same amount of time each day.

The procedure section will generally conclude with a discussion concerning administration of the posttest similar to the discussion for the pretest. As an example:

> On September 1, the Maslach Burnout Inventory (Maslach & Jackson, 1981) will be administered to all experimental and control groups of interns. Blood pressure and pulse rates, at rest and following 20 minutes of strenuous exercise, will be recorded.

The procedure section should also include any identified assumptions and limitations. An assumption is an important "fact" presumed to be true but not actually verified. For example, in the study involving stress management for interns, it might be assumed that, given the age of the population, many of the interns may have subsisted primarily on junk food before the study began. Such assumptions are probabilistic in nature; the reader of the research plan (and ultimately the research report) can determine whether he or she is willing to accept the researcher's assumption. For example, if the population included many interns from medical schools that emphasized the role of diet in maintaining good health, the assumption just discussed might be questionable. In the quality circles article at the end of Chapter 1, an assumption is made that a fixed schedule for breaks and lunch at plant A and a flexible schedule for breaks and lunch at plant B would not affect the outcome of the study; therefore the researcher chose not to control for or measure these differences. A limitation is some aspect of the study that the researcher knows may negatively affect the results or generalizability of the results but over which she or he probably has no control. In other words, something is not as good for the study as it should be, but the researcher can't do anything about it. Two common limitations are sample size and length of the study. A research plan might state, for example:

> Only one group of 30 trainees will be available for participation.
>
> *or*
>
> While ideally subjects should be exposed to the experimental treatment for a longer period of time in order to assess its effectiveness more accurately, permission has been granted to the researcher to have access to the interns for a maximum of two months.

In the quality circles article, the author indicates in his discussion that there were several possible limitations; one such limitation was the effect of local history, or events that happened within the area where the study was conducted. It may be helpful to review the discussion section in the article to see the way other limitations can be stated. When such limitations are openly and honestly stated, the readers can judge for themselves how seriously the study may be affected.

Assumptions and limitations are generally stated within context; for example, a time limitation would be stated within the procedures section, probably at the same time administration of the posttest was discussed. Some colleges and universities require that assumptions and limitations be presented in a separate section. This forces the student to give some thought to where they occur in his or her study.

The procedure section needs to be as detailed as possible and have any new terms defined at the time they are introduced. The key to writing this section is replicability. It will be successful if it is precise to the point where someone else could read your plan and execute your study exactly as you intended it to be conducted. This way it will be detailed enough to permit *you* to execute it exactly as planned.

Data Analysis

The research plan must include a description of the statistical technique or techniques that will be used to analyze study data. For certain descriptive studies, data analysis may involve little more than simple tabulation and presentation of results. For most studies, however, one or more statistical methods will be required. Identification of appropriate analysis techniques is *extremely* important; very few situations cause as much weeping and gnashing of teeth as collecting data only to find that there is no appropriate analysis or that the analysis that is appropriate requires sophistication beyond the researcher's level of statistical competence. Once the data are collected, it is too late. Settling for a less appropriate technique in order to salvage the study is definitely prohibited, although it is done on occasion by poor planners. The hypothesis of the study determines the design, which in turn determines the statistical analysis; an inappropriate analysis, therefore, does not permit a valid test of the research hypothesis. Which available analysis technique should be selected depends on a number of factors, such as how the groups will be formed (for example, by random assignment, by matching, or by using existing groups), how many different treatment groups will be involved, how many independent variables will be involved, and the kind of data to be collected (interval data, for example, will require different techniques from those required by ordinal data). In a correlational study, similar factors will determine the appropriate correlational analysis.

Although you may not understand some of the terms mentioned above, don't worry about it; you're not supposed to, *yet!* They will be discussed in succeeding chapters. The important thing to understand is the relationship between the hypothesis, the design, and the statistical analysis. At this point, even though you probably are not familiar with any specific statistical analyses, you should be able to describe in your research plan the *kind* of analysis you would need. You might say, for example:

> An analysis will be used appropriate for comparing the effect of stress management, on pulse rates and blood pressures, of two randomly formed groups of interns.

By the time you get to Project IV, you *will* know exactly what you need.

Time Schedule

A realistic time schedule is equally important for both beginning researchers working on a thesis or dissertation and for experienced researchers working under the deadlines of a research grant, a contract, or a request from management for information. It is an infrequent event when a researcher has as long as she or he pleases to conduct a study. The existence of deadlines typically necessitates careful budgeting of time. Basically, a time schedule includes a listing of major activities or phases of the proposed study and a corresponding expected completion time for each activity. Such a schedule in a research plan enables the researcher to assess the feasibility of conducting a study within existing time limitations. It also helps him or her to stay on schedule while conducting the study. In developing a time frame, do not make the mistake of allowing only a minimum amount of time for each activity. Allow yourself enough time so that if an unforeseen minor delay occurs, you can still meet your final deadline. A wise precaution might be to set a completion date for your final activity sometime earlier than your actual deadline. Your schedule will not necessarily be a series of sequential steps such that one activity must be completed before another begins. For example, while you are conducting the study, you may also be working on the first part of the final research report.

One approach to use in constructing a time schedule is the Gantt chart (Carlisle, 1979). Developed in 1910 by H. L. Gantt, one of the pioneers in management, the chart is useful in planning and controlling nonrepetitive operations such as research studies. To construct a Gantt chart for your study, list the steps to be completed down the left-hand side of your paper and the time to be covered by the entire project across the top of the page. An open bar graph format can be used to indicate the beginning and ending date for each activity. The chart permits the researcher easily to visualize the entire project and identify concurrent activities. As the study progresses, you can fill in the open bar graphs to provide a constant reminder of the status of each activity (see Figure 3.2).

Several obvious problems exist with Gantt charts. The use of bar graphs doesn't allow you to identify interdependencies of activities, for example, nor are you able to indicate clear milestones as you complete parts of projects. In Figure 3.2, you see that you may be working on the report preparation at the same time that the experiment is going on; what you are not able to see is the exact part of the report you expect to be able to complete during that time. A more elaborate planning and control device is a network known as the Program Evaluation and Review Technique (PERT) and Critical Path Methodology (CPM). As with the Gantt chart, you will have to list each step to be completed, but this time you indicate specific events, or *milestones,* that will occur. Each of these milestones is designated by an oval, while the tasks leading up to the event are indicated by a rectangle; lines show the connection between milestones and tasks (see Figure 3.3). In this example, following approval by the Medical Education Committee (a milestone), the pretests are ordered and the exercise-and-diet training materials are developed (both are tasks). The connections between approval by the medical education committee (milestone), development of training materials (task), approval of training materials (milestone), printing of training materials (task), and, finally, the beginning of treatment (milestone) are indicated by a line. The numerals over the milestones and tasks indicate the target date for completion.

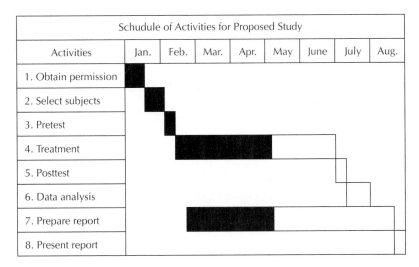

Figure 3.2. Hypothetical, simplified example of a Gantt chart for a proposed research study.

An important advantage of the PERT network is the connection of interdependent milestones and tasks indicated by the lines that connect them. For example, suppose you have made all the arrangements for your experimental group to begin their training on July 2, as indicated on the example. On June 28, you discover that the pretests you need to have completed on July 1 before the groups begin their training are delayed in shipping. A quick review of your PERT/CPM network will indicate that you'd better require overnight delivery of your pretest; no such emergency exists for delivery of the posttests so you can avoid extra expense by agreeing to normal shipment. An additional advantage of the PERT/CPM network is that you will be able to identify and visualize the longest operation necessary in your study; this is known as the *critical path*. It is usually highlighted in bold print or a different color. Identification of the critical path enables you to speed up only those operations that are indicated on the critical path. The critical path in Figure 3.3 is (1) approval by medical education committee, (2) subject selection and group assignment, (3) pretest, and (4) beginning of treatment. For example, suppose you planned to send a letter to the interns explaining the study (this would be indicated by a *task* between subject selection and pretest). If you needed to move things along more quickly, you could cut time out of the critical-path activities by substituting a meeting for the letter. If all of this sounds complicated, it may be. It may not make sense to go into this much detailed planning if your study is relatively straightforward. For the Steven Spielbergs among you, however, the extra planning time can be extremely beneficial and will produce a much less harried researcher. A PERT/CPM chart for an entire project would, of course, run into considerable more length than the example in Figure 3.3; only the beginning portions have been displayed here to give you the general idea.

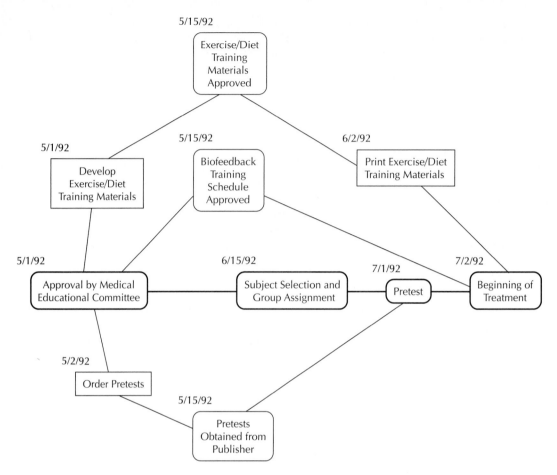

Figure 3.3. Hypothetical example of a portion of a PERT/CPM network for a research project.

Fortunately, there are computer programs that can be used to develop charts and plans appropriate to your study. The relatively simple example in Figure 3.3 was developed using a project management program called MacProject II (Young & Willrett, 1987). This program not only allows you to identify milestones, tasks, target dates, and interconnections, but it also allows you to identify responsibilities, budget, and many other factors. The program is designed not only as a planning tool but also as a way of tracking progress. When a conflict between dates occurs within a path, the program will highlight the conflict to draw it to your attention. Gantt charts, PERT/CPM networks, and other visual displays can be selected to present the information in your project management program. In addition to MacProject II, other project management programs include Harvard Project Manager (Software Publishing), SuperProject Plus (Computer Associates International), and Time Line (Symantec).

Budget

A formal research plan is referred to as either a proposal or a prospectus. Proposals are generally submitted to governmental or private funding agencies in the hope of receiving financial assistance to conduct a study. Proposals almost always require the inclusion of a tentative budget. Depending upon the amount requested and the agency to which the proposal is submitted, items included in the budget will vary. With the exception of some very small grants, however, budgets typically include such items as personnel such as clerical assistance, expenses such as travel and postage, equipment, and overhead (see Figure 3.4). Assistance in developing budgets is usually available at most colleges and universities, provided either formally by a research or grants office or informally by colleagues who have had experience in developing proposals. Similarly, the prospectus used in business will require a budget. The budget items will be essentially the same as those required for a proposal. Assistance for researchers developing plans for research within a company will probably be available from departments such as human resources, purchasing, accounting, and the like.

Stress Management Research Project
Proposed Budget

Personnel salaries[1]

Research director	40% × 8 months
Registered dietician	20% × 6 months
Exercise physiologist	20% × 6 months
Biofeedback engineer	30% × 6 months
Part-time secretary	20% × 8 months

Equipment and supplies

200 copies Maslach Burnout Inventory	$ 500.00
Exercise/diet training manuals	1000.00
MedAc biofeedback instrument	4000.00
Computer time	1000.00
General office supplies @ $50 per month	400.00
Total expenses other than salaries	$6900.00

1. As confidential information, salary figures are not available. Time requirements have been provided as a general guideline on expenses.

Figure 3.4. Hypothetical, simplified example of a budget for a proposed research study.

Salary and benefit information for existing employees usually is not required; close estimates of any time away from regular duties will certainly be required, however (a clear example of the old adage that "Time is money").

EVALUATION OF A RESEARCH PLAN

Evaluation of a research plan can involve both informal and formal procedures. Informally, it should be reviewed and critiqued; formally, it may be field-tested in a preliminary pilot study. Having a research plan permits it to be carefully scrutinized by yourself and others. Rereading a plan several days after having written it often results in suddenly discovering flaws and weaknesses. Having a written plan also allows others not only to identify problems but also to make suggestions as to how the study might be improved. A research plan should be reviewed by at least one skilled researcher and at least one expert in the study's area of investigation (for example, employee training). There is no researcher, no matter how long he or she has been in the business, whose plan cannot benefit from the insight of others.

Formal evaluation of a research plan involves a pilot study, which is sort of a dress rehearsal. In a pilot study the entire study is conducted, each and every procedure is followed, and the resulting data are analyzed—all according to the research plan. If you are evaluating the effectiveness of a presupervisory training program, for example, you will want to use subjects who are the same as those you plan to use in your actual study; it would not make sense to use middle managers instead of potential supervisors as your subjects in the pilot study "because it will build enthusiasm for the program." Beginning researchers gain valuable experience from conducting a pilot study; the quality of one's final product may be considerably improved as a result. Even a small-scale pilot study, based on a small number of subjects, can help in refining procedures, such as instrument administration and scoring routines, and in trying out analysis techniques. The larger the scope of the pilot study, the more like the full-scale study it is, the more likely it is that potential problems such as uncontrolled variables and inefficient data processing routines will be identified. You may discover, for example, that scoring the instruments takes twice as much time as you originally estimated. The research plan will almost always be modified as a result of a pilot study, and in some cases it may be completely overhauled. Besides time constraints, a major reason more large-scale pilot studies are not conducted is lack of available subjects. It is usually difficult enough to locate a sufficient number of subjects for the actual study, let alone a like number for a pilot study. Whenever feasible, however, a pilot study should be considered a very worthwhile use of your time. If a great deal of money will be involved with the study or major methods of production may be changed as a result of your study, a pilot study becomes more of a necessity than a luxury item.

Summary/Chapter 3

DEFINITION AND PURPOSE

1. A research plan is a detailed description of a proposed study designed to investigate a given problem; it includes justification for the hypothesis to be tested, a detailed presentation of the research steps that will be followed in collecting and analyzing required data, and a projected time schedule for each major step.

2. A research plan may be relatively brief and informal or very lengthy and formal, such as the proposals which are submitted to governmental and private funding agencies. Proposals in business and management tend to be brief and formal.

3. The research plan must be completed before a study is begun.

4. Since your study will be designed to test a hypothesis, this hypothesis must be developed first; the nature of your hypothesis will determine to a high degree the sample group, measuring instruments, design, procedures, and statistical techniques used in your study.

5. The research plan makes you think through every aspect of the study.

6. A written plan facilitates evaluation of the proposed study by yourself and by others.

7. A research plan provides a guide for conducting the study.

8. A written research plan, which has been approved, may protect you from undue interference while the study is being conducted.

9. A well-thought-out plan saves time, reduces the probability of costly mistakes, and generally results in higher quality research.

10. Part of good planning is anticipation. Try to anticipate potential problems which might arise, do what you can to prevent them, and plan your strategies for dealing with them if they do occur.

GENERAL CONSIDERATIONS

The Ethics of Research

11. There are ethical considerations involved in all research studies. Ethical concerns are, of course, more acute in experimental studies which, by definition, manipulate and control subjects.

12. Perhaps the foremost rule of research ethics is that subjects should not be harmed in any way (physically or mentally) in the name of science.

13. An equally important consideration is the subject's right to privacy.

14. Above all, the researcher must have personal integrity.

Legal Restrictions

15. The major provisions of legislation passed to date have been designed to protect subjects who participate in research and to ensure the confidentiality of records.

16. The National Research Act of 1974 established a commission to recommend ethical guidelines for research. Primarily, this means that proposed research activities involving human subjects be reviewed and approved by an authorized group in an institution, prior to the execution of the research, to ensure protection of the subjects.

17. The Privacy Act of 1974 and the Freedom of Information Act provide protection for federal employees' personnel records; the provisions of these acts have been extended by voluntary compliance by employers and by state laws and provide the basis for guidelines made by the report of the Privacy Protection Study Commission to the President in July 1977.

18. The Family Educational Rights and Privacy Act of 1974, more commonly referred to as the Buckley Amendment, basically protects the privacy of the educational records of students.

19. Title VII of the 1964 Civil Rights Act and Equal Employment Opportunities Commission (EEOC) guidelines require fairness both in treatment and in the impact of treatment.

20. Companies involved in research activities may want to review the legal ramifications of proposed research before granting approval.

Cooperation

21. The first step in acquiring needed cooperation is to follow required procedures, if these have been established.

22. The approval process involves providing complete, written information specifying the nature of the research, the specific steps and requirements needed, as well as a face-to-face meeting with approval-granting management.

23. The key to gaining approval and cooperation is good planning. The key to good planning is a well-designed, carefully thought-out study.

24. Achieving full cooperation, and not just approval on paper, requires that you invest as much time as is necessary to discuss your study with managers, supervisors, employees, and perhaps even unions. Potential benefits to be derived by each of these groups as a result of your study should be explained fully.

25. If changes can be made in the planned study to better accommodate the normal routine of participating personnel, these changes should be made *unless* the study will suffer as a consequence.

26. The feelings of involved persons must be monitored and responded to throughout the duration of the study if the initial level of cooperation is to be maintained.

Training Research Assistants

27. Regardless of who they are or what role they will play, all assistants should participate in some type of orientation that explains the nature of the study and the part they will play in it.

28. Responsibilities should be described both orally and in writing, and, if necessary, assistants should receive training related to their assigned task and be given opportunities for supervised practice.

29. Before any data are actually collected, anyone involved in any way with data collection procedures should become thoroughly familiar with all relevant restrictions, legal or otherwise, related to the collection, storing, and sharing of obtained information.

COMPONENTS

30. Although they may go by other names, research plans typically include an introduction, a methods section, a description of proposed data analysis, a time schedule, and a budget.

31. A business proposal for research should include an executive summary in the form of a one-page statement with references to attached details.

Introduction

32. The introduction includes a statement of the problem, a review of related literature, and a statement of the hypothesis.

33. Be certain that all terms are either common-usage terms or are operationally defined.

Method

34. The specific method of research your study represents will affect the format and contents of your method section.

Subjects

35. The description of subjects should clearly define the population, the larger group from which the sample will be selected.

36. The description should indicate the size and major characteristics of the population.

Instruments

37. Since measurement in business and management is frequently indirect, the measuring instrument you select or develop really represents an operational definition of whatever construct you are trying to measure.

38. It is important to provide a rationale for the selection of the instrument to be used as well as a description of the instrument.

39. If you are going to develop your own instrument, you should describe how the instrument will be developed, what it will measure, and how you plan to evaluate its validity and reliability.

Materials/Apparatus

40. If special materials (such as handouts, training manuals, or computer programs) are going to be developed, they should be described in some detail.

41. If special apparatus (such as simulation apparatus or computer terminals) are going to be used, they should be described.

Design

42. The description of the design indicates the basic structure of the study.

43. The nature of the hypothesis, the variables involved, and the constraints of the real world—all contribute to the design to be used.

44. The design typically indicates the number of groups to be included in the study, whether the groups will be randomly formed, and whether there will be a pretest.

45. There are a number of basic designs to select from as well as an almost endless number of variations on those designs which can be used.

Procedure

46. The procedure section describes all the steps that will be followed in conducting the study, from beginning to end, in the order in which they will occur.

47. The procedure section typically begins with a description of the technique to be used in selecting the sample, or samples, for the study.

48. If the design includes a pretest, the procedure for its administration, when it will be administered, and how will usually be described next.

49. From this point on, the procedure section will describe exactly what is going to occur in the study. In an experimental study, this will basically involve a description of how the groups will be the same (control procedures) and how they will be different (the independent variable, or treatment).

50. The procedure section will generally conclude with a discussion concerning the administration of the posttest similar to the discussion for the pretest.

51. The procedure section should also include any identified assumptions and limitations. An assumption is any important fact presumed to be true but not actually verified; a limitation is some aspect of the study that the researcher knows may negatively affect the results or generalizability of the results but over which he or she probably has no control.

52. The procedure section should be as detailed as possible and any new terms introduced should of course be defined; it should be precise to the point where someone else could read your plan and execute your study exactly as you intended it to be conducted.

Data Analysis

53. The research plan must include a description of the statistical technique or techniques that will be used to analyze study data.

54. The hypothesis of the study determines the design, which in turn determines the statistical analysis; an inappropriate analysis, therefore, does not permit a valid test of the research hypothesis.

55. Which available analysis technique should be selected depends on a number of factors, such as how the groups will be formed (for example, by random assignment, by matching, or by using existing groups), how many different treatment groups will be involved, how

many independent variables will be involved, and the kind of data to be collected. (Interval data, for example, will require different techniques than ordinal data.) In a correlational study, similar factors will determine the appropriate correlational analysis.

Time Schedule

56. Basically, a time schedule includes a listing of major activities or phases of the proposed study and a corresponding expected completion time for each activity.

57. A useful approach for constructing and controlling a time schedule is the Gantt chart method, which uses a bar-graph format.

58. A more detailed and specialized approach for constructing and controlling a time schedule is the PERT network and critical path method; this allows the researcher to see interdependencies of events and activities and make time corrections as necessary.

59. Computer software programs are available to assist in developing both Gantt charts and PERT networks with identification of the critical path.

Budget

60. A formal research plan is referred to as a proposal or a prospectus; it almost always requires the inclusion of a tentative budget.

61. Budgets typically include such items as personnel, clerical assistance, expenses, equipment, and overhead; a budget within a company may require time estimates for personnel rather than actual salary figures.

EVALUATION OF A RESEARCH PLAN

62. Having a research plan permits it to be carefully scrutinized, by yourself and by others.

63. Having a plan also allows others not only to identify problems but also to make suggestions as to how the study might be improved.

64. A research plan should be reviewed by at least one skilled researcher and at least one expert in the study's area of investigation.

65. Formal evaluation of a research plan involves a pilot study; in a pilot study the entire study is conducted, each and every procedure is followed, and the resulting data are analyzed—all according to the research plan.

66. Even a small-scale pilot study based on a small number of subjects can help in refining procedures, such as instrument administration and scoring routines, and in trying out analysis techniques.

67. The research plan will almost always be modified as a result of a pilot study, and in some cases it may be completely overhauled.

68. If the amount of money to be spent on the study is great or the production changes to be made as a result of the study are extensive, a pilot study should be considered a necessity.

REFERENCES

AD HOC COMMITTEE ON ETHICAL STANDARDS IN PSYCHOLOGICAL RESEARCH. (1973). *Ethical principles in conducting of research with human subjects.* Washington, DC: American Psychological Association.

AMERICAN PSYCHOLOGICAL ASSOCIATION. (1983). *Publication manual of the American Psychological Association* (3rd ed.). Washington, DC: Author.

BODDEN, J. L. (1985). Review of Maslach Burnout Inventory in J. V. Mitchell, Jr. (Ed.), *The ninth mental measurements yearbook,* Vol. I., Lincoln, NB: University of Nebraska Press.

BUREAU OF BUSINESS RESEARCH. (1963). *Leader Behavior Description Questionnaire.* Columbus, OH: Ohio State University.

CARLISLE, H. M. (1979). *Management essentials: Concepts and applications.* Chicago: Science Research Associates.

COMPUTER ASSOCIATES INTERNATIONAL. (1988). *SuperProject Plus* (computer program). San Jose, CA: Computer Associates International.

DOWD, T. (1985). Review of Maslach Burnout Inventory in J. V. Mitchell, Jr. (Ed.). *The Ninth Mental Measurements Yearbook,* Vol. I., Lincoln, NB: University of Nebraska Press.

DUMAINE, B. (1988, November 7). Corporate spies snoop to conquer. *Fortune,* pp. 68–76.

HACKMAN, J. R., & OLDHAM, G. R. (1980). *Work redesign.* Reading, MA: Addison-Wesley.

MCBER, INC. (1980). *Management Style Questionnaire.* Boston, MA: Author.

MASLACH, C., & JACKSON, S.E. (1981). *Maslach Burnout Inventory.* Palo Alto, CA: Consulting Psychologists Press.

MICHALAK, D. (1983). *Management Styles Questionnaire.* New York: Harper & Row.

MICHAEL, J. A., & WEINBERGER, J. A. (1977). Federal restrictions on educational research: Protection for research participants. *Educational Researcher, 6*(1), 3–7.

MILGRAM, S. (1964). Group pressure and action against a person. *Journal of Abnormal and Social Psychology, 69,* 137–143.

MILGRAM, S. (1975). *Obedience to authority: An experimental view.* New York: Harper & Row.

PRIVACY PROTECTION STUDY COMMISSION. (1977). Personal privacy in an information society. *The final report of the privacy study commission.* Washington, DC: U.S. Government Printing Office.

RANKIN, R. (1990, December 19). ACLU takes up issue of workers' rights. *The Miami Herald,* pp. 1B, 7B.

SALANCIK, G. R. (1979). Field simulations for organizational behavior research. *Administrative Science Quarterly, 25,* 252–260.

SHERMAN, A. W., BOHLANDER, G. W., & CHRUDEN, H. J. (1988). *Managing human resources* (8th ed.). Cincinnati, OH: South-Western.

SOFTWARE PUBLISHING CORPORATION. (1988). *Harvard Project Manager* (computer program). Mountain View, CA: Software Publishing.

SUTTON, R. I., & RAFAELI, A. (1988). Untangling the relationship between displayed emotions and organizational sales: The case of convenience stores. *Academy of Management Journal, 31*(3), 461–487.

SYMANTEC. (1988). *Time Line* (computer program). Cupertino, CA: Symantec.

VELASQUEZ, M. G. (1988). *Business ethics: Concepts and cases* (2nd ed.). Englewood Cliffs, NJ: Prentice-Hall.

WEBB, E. J., CAMPBELL, D. T., SCHWARTZ, D. W., SECHREST, L., & GROVE, G. B. (1981). *Nonreactive measures in the social sciences.* Boston: Houghton-Mifflin.

WEINBERGER, J. A., & MICHAEL, J. A. (1976). Federal restrictions on educational research. *Educational Researcher, 5*(11), 3–8.

WONDERLIC, E. F. (1930–1983). *Wonderlic Personnel Test.* Northfield, IL: Wonderlic & Associates.

YOUNG, S. D., & WILLRETT, D. (1987). *MacProject II* (computer program). Mountain View, CA: CLARIS.

. . . every individual has the same probability of being selected and selection of one individual in no way affects selection of another individual.
(page 147)

4

Selection of a Sample

Objectives

After reading Chapter 4, you should be able to:

1. Identify and define, or briefly describe, four sampling techniques.

2. List the procedures for using a table of random numbers to select a random sample.

3. Identify three variables on which you could stratify.

4. List the procedures for selecting a stratified random sample.

5. Identify three possible clusters.

6. List the procedures for selecting a cluster sample.

7. List the procedures for selecting a systematic sample.

Project III Guidelines

As discussed at the beginning of Part Three, you will be developing the *Method* portion of your research report as Project III. When it is complete, it will include:

Method

Subjects/Samples
Instruments
Design
Procedure

You may want to glance ahead to the end of Chapter 10 to see an example of a completed Project III; also, if you review the quality circle article at the end of Chapter 1, you can see how this section looks in a published research article.

We recommend that you complete each subsection of Project III as you study the appropriate chapter in your text.

Project III Subsection 1: Subjects/Samples Guidelines

Having selected a problem and formulated one or more testable hypotheses or answerable questions, describe a sample appropriate for evaluating your hypotheses or answering your questions. This description will include the following:

1. A definition of the population from which the sample would be drawn.
2. The procedural technique for selecting the sample and forming the groups.
3. Sample sizes.
4. Possible sources of sampling bias.

(See Project III Subsection I Performance Criteria, p. 147.)

SAMPLING: DEFINITION AND PURPOSE

Sampling is the process of selecting a number of units for a study in such a way that the units represent the larger group from which they were selected. The same procedures are used when the units are items from an inventory, an order, or a production run and also when the units are individuals such as employees, trainees, applicants, customers, or some other group of people. For the purpose of the discussion in this chapter, however, we will assume that the sample involves human beings, not inanimate objects.

The purpose of sampling is to gain information about a population. The individuals who are selected comprise a sample; the larger group is referred to as a population. Rarely is a study conducted that includes the total population of interest as subjects. Generally it isn't feasible to use the total group; usually it isn't even necessary. If the group of interest is unmanageably large or geographically scattered, study of this group can result in considerable expenditure of time, money, and effort. If a sample is well selected, however, research results based on the sample will be generalizable to the population. The degree to which the sample represents the population is the degree to which results for one are applicable to the other.

As an example, suppose a police chief wants us to find out how the 5,000 police officers in the department feel about gun control, whether they will support a proposed local law requiring a cooling-off period, and, if so, for what reasons. If we decide an interview is the best way to collect the desired data, it will take a very long time to interview each and every police officer; even if one interview takes only 15 minutes, it will take a minimum of 1,250 hours, which is equivalent to 156 work days (without breaks), or approximately 31 work weeks to collect the desired information! If, however, we interview 10%, or 500, of the police officers, it will take only 125 hours, or approximately 3 weeks. Assuming the police chief needs the information "now, not next year," as the saying goes, the latter approach is definitely preferable, assuming the same information can be acquired.

As it happens, the conclusions based on the interviews of the sample of police officers will in all probability be the same as the conclusions based on interviews of all police officers if the sample is correctly selected. We can't select just any 500 police officers. Interviewing 500 traffic-patrol officers, for example, is not satisfactory. In the first place, a highly disproportionate number of young officers are in that position, and older officers might feel differently about gun control. In the second place, opinions of traffic-patrol officers might not be the same as those of homicide detectives or school-resource officers. How about interviewing 500 police officers who are members of the Police Benevolent Association (PBA)? While they will probably be more representative of all 5,000 police officers than the traffic-patrol officers, they still won't do. Police officers who are members of a professional association may be more likely to support political action than police officers who don't belong to the professional association. If neither of these approaches is acceptable, how can a representative sample be selected?

Give up? Don't! As you will see shortly, there are several relatively simple sampling techniques that can be used to select an acceptable sample of police officers. The sampling techniques will not guarantee a sample that is perfectly representative of the population, but the odds of obtaining a good sample definitely will increase. Using these techniques should also increase the degree of confidence that the police chief can have regarding the generalizability of findings for the 500 police officers to all 5,000 police officers.

DEFINITION OF A POPULATION

Regardless of the technique to be used in selecting a sample, the first step in sampling is definition of the population. The population is the group of interest to the researcher, the group to which she or he would like to generalize the results of the study. A *defined population* has at least one characteristic that differentiates it from other groups. Examples of defined populations that might be used in research include all holders of graduate degrees in management in the United States, all first-line supervisors in the banking industry in the state of Florida, and all recently hired economically disadvantaged employees in Washington, D.C., who have participated in government-funded training programs. These examples illustrate two important points about populations:

1. Populations may be virtually any size and may cover almost any geographical area.
2. The group the researcher would really like to generalize to is rarely available.

The population that the researcher ideally would like to generalize to is referred to as the *target population;* the population that the researcher realistically can select from is referred to as the available population, or *accessible population*. In practice, the definition of a population is generally a realistic choice, not an idealistic one.

As an example, suppose we want to investigate the computer skills of individuals with graduate degrees in management. Idealistically, our study would involve measurement of the computer skills of all such individuals. Of course, this is not feasible. By the time we measure the last individual, the first subject may be ready to retire! By now it may have occurred to you that the solution is to select a representative sample and test all the members of the sample. A little more thought will reveal that this procedure is also highly impractical. If we identify all the appropriate graduates, our population will be located from coast to coast; to complete the study adequately, a staff of qualified researchers and a healthy bank account will be required. Clearly, we will have to bring your idealistic research plan into line with cold, hard reality. In the end, we might settle for a more manageable population, such as all defined graduates in a given geographic area, and select our sample from this group. By selecting from a more narrowly defined population we can save time and money, but we will also lose generalizability. Assuming we select an adequate sample, the results of our study will be directly generalizable to all appropriate graduates in the area but not to all appropriate graduates in the United States. The degree to which the graduates in the area are similar to graduates in other cities will be the degree to which our results have implications for other settings. The key is to define the population in sufficient detail so that others may determine how applicable the findings are to their situation.

METHODS OF SELECTING A SAMPLE

Selection of a sample is a very important step in conducting a research study because the quality of the sample determines the generalizability of the results. Conducting a study generally requires a great deal of time and energy, so results that are not generalizable are extremely wasteful. If the results are true only for the group on which they were based, every study would have to be replicated an almost infinite number of times, and managers would never benefit from anyone else's work. Imagine how slow the progress of science would be if every scientist had to reconfirm Newton's laws!

A primary characteristic of a good sample is the degree to which it is representative of the population from which it was selected. As we saw with our police chief who wants us to assess police officers' attitudes, selecting a representative sample is not a haphazard process. There are, however, several valid techniques for selecting a sample. While certain techniques are more appropriate for certain situations, not all of the techniques give the same level of assurance concerning representativeness. As with populations, however, we sometimes have to compromise the ideal for the feasible. This is true in many areas of scientific research and is not a situation peculiar to business research. Much medical research aimed at relieving human suffering, for example, must be conducted on animals such as rats; researchers in this field encounter similar problems to those faced by business researchers with respect to the generalizability of their findings.

Regardless of the specific technique that is used, the steps in sampling are essentially the same:

1. Identify the population.
2. Determine the required sample size.
3. Select the sample.

The degree to which the selected sample represents the population is the degree to which results may be generalized. There are four basic sampling techniques or procedures:

1. Random sampling.
2. Stratified random sampling.
3. Cluster sampling.
4. Systematic sampling.

Random Sampling

Random sampling is the process of selecting a sample in such a way that all individuals in the defined population have an equal and independent chance of being selected for the sample. In other words, every individual has the same probability of being selected, and selection of one individual in no way affects selection of another individual. You may recall in physical education class the teacher occasionally formed teams by having the class line up and count off by twos. With this method, you could never be on the same team as the person next to you, but you had an equal chance of being assigned to a particular team. Selection was not independent; whether you were on one team or another was determined by where you were in line and the team for which the person next to you was selected. If selection of teams had been random, you would have had a 50-50 chance of being on either team regardless of which team the person next to you was on.

Random sampling is the best single way to obtain a representative sample. No technique, not even random sampling, guarantees a representative sample, but the probability is higher for this procedure than for any other. Differences between the sample and the population should be small and unsystematic. For example, you would not expect exactly the same ratio of males and females in a sample as in a population; random sampling, however, assures that the ratio will be close and that the probability of having too many males is the same as the probability of having too many females. In any event, the differences are a function of chance and are not the result of any conscious or unconscious bias on the part of the researcher.

Another point in favor of random sampling is that it is required by inferential statistics, about which we will say more later. This is very important since inferential statistics permit the researcher to make inferences about populations based on the behavior of samples. If samples are not selected randomly, then one of the major assumptions of inferential statistics is violated, and inferences are correspondingly tenuous. In Part IV, you will learn how to select and apply several commonly used inferential statistics. (If you haven't had statistics before, don't groan and say you're going to hate statistics; you'll be amazed at how easy statistics really is!)

Steps in Random Sampling

In general, random sampling involves defining the population, identifying each member of the population, and selecting individuals for the sample on a completely chance basis. Probably the simplest way to do this is the technique used in a lottery: Write each individual's name on a separate slip of paper, place all the slips in a container, shake the container, and select slips from the container until the desired number of individuals is selected. Usually this procedure is unsatisfactory; for example, if the population is 5,000 police officers, the police chief will need a large container and lots of little pieces of paper. A more satisfactory approach is to use a table of random numbers. In essence, a table of random numbers selects the sample for you, each member of the sample being selected on a purely random, or chance, basis. Such tables are included in the appendix of most statistics books and some research books; they usually consist of columns of five-digit numbers that have been randomly generated by a computer (see Table A.1 in the Appendix). To select a sample using a table of random numbers use the following steps:

1. Define the population.
2. Determine the desired sample size.
3. List all the members of the population.
4. Assign each of the individuals on the list a consecutive number from zero to the required number, for example, 00-89, or 000-249.
5. Select an arbitrary number in the table of random numbers. (Close your eyes and point!)
6. For the selected number, look at only the appropriate number of digits. For example, if a population has 90 members, you use the last 2 digits of the number; if a population has 300 members, you use the last 3 digits.
7. If the selected number corresponds to the number assigned to any individual in the population, then that individual is in the sample. For example, if a population has 500 members and the number selected is 375, the individual numbered 375 is in the sample; if a population has only 300 members, then 375 is ignored.
8. Go to the next number in the column and repeat step 7.
9. Repeat step 8 until the desired sample size is reached.

Once the sample has been selected, members may then be randomly assigned to two or more treatment groups in an experimental study. This can be done by flipping a coin, for example, or by randomly selecting half the group and assigning these members to the treatment group and the others to the control group.

Actually, the random-selection process is not as complicated as the above explanation may have made it sound. The following example should make the procedure clear.

An Example of Random Sampling

Now it is time to help our police chief who wants us to select a sample of police officers so we can determine their attitudes toward gun control. We will apply each of the nine steps just described to the solution of this problem:

1. The population is all 5,000 police officers in the chief's department.
2. The desired sample size is 10% of the 5,000 officers, or 500 officers.
3. The chief gives us a computer printout of all the officers in the department.
4. Using the printout, we assign each officer a number from 0000 to 4999.
5. We enter a table of random numbers at an arbitrarily selected number such as the one underlined here:

   59058
   11859
   53634
   48708
   71710
   83942
   30000
   and so on.

6. Since the population has 5,000 members, we are concerned with only the last four digits of the underlined number, 3634.
7. There is a police officer assigned the number 3634, so that officer is in the sample.
8. The next number in the column is 48708. The last four digits are 8708. Since there are only 5,000 officers, there is no officer assigned the number 8708. Therefore, number 48708 is skipped.
9. Applying the above steps to the remaining numbers shown in the above column, we include the officers numbered 1710, 3942, and 0000. (*Now* you know why the numbering began with 0000!) We apply this procedure to the numbers following 30000 in that column and succeeding columns until we have selected 500 officers.

At the completion of this process in all probability we will have a representative sample of all the police officers in the system. We can expect the 500 selected officers to represent appropriately all relevant subgroups of officers such as traffic patrol, school resource officers, detectives, and PBA members. With random sampling, however, such representation of subgroups is probable but not guaranteed. The probable does not always occur, however; if you flip a quarter 100 times, the probable outcome is 50 heads and 50 tails. (You may want to try this on your next study break!) You may get 53 heads and 47 tails, or 45 heads and 55 tails, but most of the time you can expect to get close to a 50-50 split. Although other outcomes are possible, they are less probable. In tossing a quarter 100 times, 85 heads and 15 tails is a possible, low-probability outcome. Similarly, it is possible, although less probable, that the sample of police officers will not represent the total group of officers on one or more dimensions. For example, if 60% of the 5,000 officers are male and 40% female, we expect to find roughly the same percentages in the sample of 500. Just by chance, however, the sample may contain 30% males and 70% females.

If the chief believes that one or more variables might be highly related to attitudes on gun control, he might not be willing to leave accurate representation on those variables to chance. For example, if the chief thinks that age is a significant variable because veteran officers might feel differently about gun control than do mid-career and younger officers, he will want us to sample in such a way that appropriate representation on the variable of age is guaranteed. In this case we will probably use stratified random sampling rather than simple random sampling.

Stratified Random Sampling

Stratified random sampling is the process of selecting a sample in such a way that identified subgroups in the population are represented in the sample in the same proportion that they exist in the population. It can also be used to select equal-size samples from each of a number of subgroups if subgroup comparisons are desired. In a survey taken prior to a national election in order to predict the probable winner, for example, proportional stratified sampling would be appropriate. To represent the voting population the sample should have the same proportion of Democrats and Republicans as exist in the population. In a survey taken to compare attitudes toward the death penalty, however, the researcher might select equal-size groups of people representing different parts of the country, different employment statuses, and different educational levels. Then the researcher could compare the attitudes of college-educated Southerners to the attitudes of high school-educated Westerners, or the attitudes of employed Midwesterners to the attitudes of unemployed New Englanders, for example. Other likely variables for stratification include such things as age, race, sex, socioeconomic status, and so on.

Suppose, for example, that we are interested in comparing the satisfaction of workers following two different conditions of child care (on-site company-provided child care versus child-care allowances). We know that our workers include several different parenting statuses, i.e., some are raising children alone (single parents), some are part of a couple in which both work (dual-career-couple parents), and some are part of a couple in which only one works outside the home (single-career-couple parents). Simply randomly selecting a sample and assigning one half of the sample to each of the methods would not guarantee equal representation of each of the parenting statuses in each of the methods. In fact, just by chance, one of the methods might not have any single-career-couple parents. However, listing the workers by parenting status, randomly selecting workers from each parenting status, and then assigning half of each selected group to each of the methods, would guarantee equal representation of each parenting status in each method of child care. That is the purpose of stratified sampling, to guarantee desired representation of relevant subgroups.

Steps in Stratified Random Sampling

The steps in stratified random sampling are very similar to those in random sampling except that selection is from subgroups in the population rather than from the population as a whole. Stratified random sampling involves the following steps:

1. Define the population.
2. Determine the desired sample size.
3. Identify the variable and subgroups (strata) for which you want to guarantee appropriate representation (either proportional or equal).
4. Classify all members of the population as members of one of the identified subgroups.
5. Randomly select (using a table of random numbers) an appropriate number of individuals from each of the subgroups, "appropriate" meaning either a proportional number of individuals or an equal number of individuals.

As with simple random sampling, once the samples from each of the subgroups have been randomly selected, each may be randomly assigned to two or more treatment groups. If we are interested in the comparative effectiveness of two methods of child care for three different types of parenting, the steps in sampling might be as follows:

1. The population is all 300 parents employed at Innovation, Inc.
2. The desired sample size is 45 parents in each of the two methods.
3. The desired subgroups are three types of parenting—single parent, dual-career-couple parent, and single-career-couple parent.
4. Classification of the 300 parents indicates that there are 175 single parents, 75 dual-career-couple parents, and 50 single-career-couple parents.
5. Using a table of random numbers, we randomly select 30 parents from each of the parenting subgroups, that is, 30 single parents, 30 dual-career-couple parents, and 30 single-career-couple parents.
6. The 30 parents in each sample subgroup are randomly assigned to one of two methods, that is, 15 of each 30 are randomly assigned to one of the two methods.

Therefore, each method group contains 45 parents—15 single, 15 dual-career-couple parents, and 15 single-career-couple parents. Figure 4.1, based on the child-care and different-parenting statuses example, should help to further clarify the process of stratified random sampling and assignment to groups.

As you may have guessed, stratification can be done on more than one variable. In the previous example, we could have stratified not only on parenting status but also on level of employment (exempt and nonexempt positions, for example). It is important, however, not to stratify on "every little thing"; this procedure should be limited to one or two key variables that we have good reason to believe will make a difference. Otherwise, our sampling process becomes unnecessarily complex; there are easier, statistically based procedures for handling some of the differences that may or may not be important. The procedure we used in the parenting example made it possible for us to select equal-size groups using stratified random sampling. It is also possible to use this technique to select proportional samples, as we shall see.

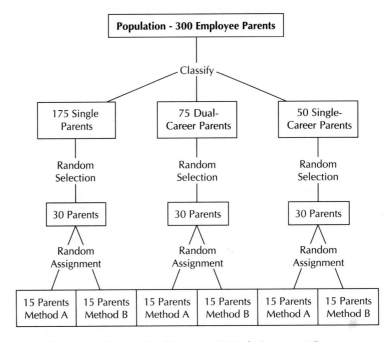

Method A = 15 Single + 15 Dual Career + 15 Single Career= 45 Parents
Method B = 15 Single + 15 Dual Career + 15 Single Career= 45 Parents

Figure 4.1. Procedure for selecting a stratified sample based on parenting condition for a study designed to compare two methods (A and B) of child-care provisions.

An Example of Stratified Random Sampling

Let us suppose that the police chief wants to guarantee appropriate representation of age groups in the sample of police officers in his study. We will apply each of the five steps previously described for selecting a stratified sample.

1. The population is all 5,000 police officers in the chief's department.
2. The desired sample size is 500 officers.
3. The variable of interest is age, and there are three subgroups—under 30, 30 to 45, and over 45.
4. We classify the officers into the subgroups. Of the 5,000 officers,
   20% or 1,000, are under age 30
   65% or 3,250, are age 30 to 45
   15% or 750, are over age 45

5. We want 500 officers. Since we want proportional representation,
    20% of the sample (100 officers) should be under age 30
    65% (325 officers) should be age 30 to 45
        15% (75 officers) should be over age 45

Therefore, using a table of random numbers,
    100 of the 1,000 under age 30 officers are selected
    325 of the 3,250 age 30 to 45 officers are selected
    75 of the 750 over age 45 officers are selected
At the completion of this process, we will have a sample of 500 officers (100 + 325 + 75 = 500), or 10% of the 5,000, and each age group will be proportionally represented.

So far we have discovered two ways in which we can get a sample of officers, random sampling and stratified random sampling. Both of these techniques, however, will result in a sample scattered over the entire city. The interviewer will have to visit many, many police stations and officers during three shifts; any one location may contain only one officer in the sample. (It's very unlikely the officers will be asked to come to the interviewer.) In the event that the chief wants the information quickly, a more expedient method of sampling is needed. For the sake of convenience, cluster sampling may be used.

Cluster Sampling

Cluster sampling is sampling in which groups, not individuals, are randomly selected. To be part of a cluster, all the members of selected groups must have similar characteristics. Instead of randomly selecting individual bank tellers, for example, we can randomly select bank branches (clusters) and use all the tellers in each branch. Cluster sampling is more convenient when the population is very large or spread out over a wide geographic area. Sometimes it is the only feasible method of selecting a sample. It is not always possible, for example, to obtain or compile a list of all members of the population; in such cases, it is not possible to use random sampling. On other occasions, researchers do not have the control over subjects that they would like. For example, if our population is graduate students in management, it is unlikely that we will be able to obtain approval from the administration or the professors to randomly select students and remove a few from each of many classrooms for a study. We will have a much better chance of securing permission to use several intact classes.

Any intact group of similar characteristics is a cluster. Most often these intact groups are found in one physical location. In addition to bank branches, examples of clusters also include classes, departments, hospitals, businesses, local chapters of professional associations, or even city blocks. Cluster sampling usually involves less time and less expense and is generally more convenient. Let us look at a few examples that illustrate this point. As the example concerning bank tellers illustrated, it is easier to use all the tellers in several branches than several tellers in many branches. Similarly, in taking a survey, it is easier to use all the people in a limited number of city blocks than a few people in many city blocks. You can apply this logic to the examples of clusters just mentioned. In each case you can see that cluster sampling would be easier, although not necessarily as good, as we shall see later, than either random sampling or stratified random sampling.

Steps in Cluster Sampling

The steps in cluster sampling are not very different from those involved in random sampling. The major difference, of course, is that random selection of groups (clusters) is involved, not individuals. Cluster sampling involves the following steps:

1. Define the population.
2. Determine the desired sample size.
3. Identify and define a logical cluster.
4. Obtain, or make, a list of all the clusters in the population.
5. Estimate the average number of population members per cluster.
6. Determine the number of clusters needed by dividing the sample size by the estimated size of the cluster.
7. Randomly select the needed number of clusters (using a table of random numbers).
8. Include in the sample all population members in each selected cluster.

Cluster sampling also can be done in stages, involving selection of clusters within clusters. This process is called *multistage sampling*. For example, first businesses can be randomly selected, and then departments within each selected business can be randomly selected.

One common misconception that seems to exist among beginning researchers is the belief that it is all right to randomly select just one cluster. It is not uncommon, for example, for the beginning researcher to define a population as all the accountants in Downtown, U.S.A., a cluster as an accounting firm, and then indicate random selection of one accounting firm. However, the same researcher would not dream of randomly selecting one accountant! The principle is the same. In as much as a good sample is representative of the population from which it is selected, it is highly unlikely that one randomly selected accountant—even if she is your sister-in-law—could ever be representative of an entire population. Similarly, it is unlikely that one randomly selected accounting firm could be representative of all the accounting firms in a population. Thus, one would normally have to select a number of clusters in order for the results of a study to be generalized to the population. The following example should make the procedures involved in cluster sampling clear.

An Example of Cluster Sampling

Let us see how our police chief can get a sample of police officers if cluster sampling is used. We will follow the steps previously listed:

1. The population is all 5,000 police officers in the chief's department.
2. The desired sample size is 500.
3. A logical cluster is a precinct.
4. The chief gives us a list of all the precincts in the county; there are 50 precincts.
5. Although the precincts vary in the number of officers per precinct, there is an average of 100 officers per precinct.
6. The number of clusters (precincts) needed equals the desired sample size, 500, divided by the average size of a cluster, 100. Thus, the number of precincts needed is $500 \div 100 = 5$.
7. Therefore, we randomly select 5 of the 50 precincts.
8. All the officers in each of the 5 selected precincts are in the sample (5 precincts with 100 officers per precinct equals the desired sample size of 500). Thus, the interviewer can conduct interviews at 5 precincts and interview many officers at one time instead of traveling to 50 possible precincts.

The advantages of cluster sampling are evident. As with most things, however, nothing is all good. Cluster sampling has several drawbacks. For one thing, there is a greater chance of selecting a sample that is not representative in some way of the population; the officers in the example are all from a limited number of precincts, for example, not from a high percentage of the precincts. Thus the possibility exists that the 5 precincts selected are somehow different from the other 45 in the county (say the racial/ethnic composition of the precinct's officer force, suburban or urban nature of the community served, types of crime most frequently seen, and so forth). One way to compensate for this problem is to select a larger sample, one including more precincts for example, thus increasing the likelihood that the precincts selected adequately represent all the precincts.

Another solution would be to use multistage cluster sampling. In this instance we would consider each of the three shifts within each precinct to be a cluster. If there are approximately 34 officers assigned to each of three shifts, we could select 15 precincts and then randomly select 1 shift from each precinct. What? you ask. Originally we had selected 5 precincts each having 3 shifts ($5 \times 3 = 15$), so we know we need a total of 15 shifts. Instead of drawing all our shifts from 5 precincts, we can randomly select 15 precincts and then randomly select 1 shift from each. Another alternative would be to select 15 precincts and then randomly select 34 ($15 \times 34 = 510$, so our sample actually would be slightly more than we needed) officers from the entire group of officers assigned at that station. Although this would probably give us a better sample in terms of being representative of all the officers, it also means that the interviewer would be running around from precinct to precinct at all hours of the day and night. As in other decisions made regarding a study, the method of sampling selected is not just a matter of desirability but also of feasibility. In certain large market-survey research problems, cluster sampling can become very complex; in general, however, researchers in other areas of business and management probably will not deal with populations of such size that cluster sampling makes much sense.

In addition to the problem of representation, another problem is that commonly used inferential statistics are not appropriate for analyzing data resulting from a study using cluster sampling. Such statistics generally require random sampling. Randomly assigning treatments to existing groups (clusters) is not enough; the groups must be randomly formed. The statistics that are available and appropriate for cluster samples are generally less sensitive to differences that may exist among groups. Thus, researchers need to weigh the advantages and disadvantages of cluster sampling carefully before choosing this method; similarly, readers of research reports need to be aware of the problems associated with it.

Finally, there is one more type of sampling with which you will want to be familiar. Systematic sampling, although not used very often, is appropriate in certain situations and in some instances is the only feasible way to select a sample.

Systematic Sampling

Systematic sampling is sampling in which individuals are selected from a list by taking every Kth name. What's a "Kth" name? It really goes back to the old system of counting off (one-two-one-two, and so on). Using this system we determine what K will be so that if K = 4, selection involves taking every 4th name, if K = 10, every 10th name, and so forth. What K actually equals depends on the size of the list and the desired sample size. The major difference between systematic sampling and the other types of sampling so far discussed is the fact that all members of the population do not have an independent chance of being selected for the sample. Once the first name is selected, all the rest of the individuals to be included in the sample are automatically determined.

Even though choices are not independent, a systematic sample can be considered a random sample *if* the list of the population is randomly ordered. One or the other has to be random—either the selection process or the list. Since randomly ordered lists are rarely available, systematic sampling is rarely as good as random sampling. While some researchers argue this point, the major objection to systematic sampling of a list that is not in random order is the possibility that certain subgroups of the population may be systematically excluded from the sample. The classic example usually given to support this contention is the fact that certain nationalities have distinctive last names that tend to group together under certain letters of the alphabet (if your last name begins with Q or Z, you already know this). When taking every Kth name, if K is at all large, it is possible that certain nationalities can be skipped over completely.

Steps in Systematic Sampling

Systematic sampling involves the following steps:

1. Define the population.
2. Determine the desired sample size.
3. Obtain a list (preferably randomized) of the population.

4. Determine what K is equal to by dividing the size of the population by the desired sample size.

5. Select some random place at the top of the population list.

6. Starting at that point, take every Kth name on the list until the desired sample size is reached.

7. If the end of the list is reached before the desired sample is reached, go back to the top of the list.

Now let's see how our police chief would use systematic sampling.

An Example of Systematic Sampling

If our chief wants to use systematic sampling, the process will be as follows:

1. The population is all 5,000 police officers in the chief's department.

2. The desired sample size is 500.

3. The chief gives us a computer printout of all the officers in the system listed by date of hire. The list is not randomly ordered, but it is the best available.

4. K is equal to the size of the population, 5,000, divided by the sample size, 500. Thus, $K = 5,000 \div 500 = 10$.

5. Some random name at the top of the list of officers is selected.

6. From that point, every following 10th name is automatically in the sample. For example, if the officer selected in step 5 is the 3rd name on the list, then the sample will include the 13th name, the 23rd, the 33rd, the 43rd, and so forth.

In this instance, owing to the fact that the list is not in random order, the sample used will not be as likely to be representative as the samples resulting from application of the other techniques. For example, if for many years the chief's department discriminated in hiring so that minorities were underrepresented and only recently instituted affirmative action goals to ensure appropriate minority representation, using a date-of-hire list might result in a badly skewed sample from the standpoint of minority representation.

Conclusion

In most studies, either simple or stratified random sampling will usually be the most appropriate sampling technique. Sometimes cluster sampling will be most expedient, and, in a very few situations, systematic sampling will be appropriate. Depending upon the type of study, a sample may be used intact or may be randomly assigned to two or more treatments. If the entire population is used in the study, none of these sampling techniques may be used. A study may not, however, involve any of the four major techniques discussed so far, or a combination of more than one technique may be used. In the quality circles study, for example, the experimental sample was made up of 73 volunteers in one of the four plants interested in initiating a quality circles program; the control group included 73 employees in similar jobs in a work situation as nearly like that of the experimental plant's employees as possible. Each of the experimental subjects was specifically matched to a control subject in what is called a matched-pairs nonequivalent control-group design (more about this in Chapter 10).

As you have worked through this discussion of sampling, you have undoubtedly noticed that many of the steps in the sampling techniques are very similar. In addition to identification and definition of the population, determination of the desired sample size is another step common to all sampling techniques.

DETERMINATION OF SAMPLE SIZE

The question about sampling most frequently asked by beginning researchers is probably, "How do you know how large a sample should be?" And the answer is "large enough!" While that answer is not very comforting, the question is a difficult one. If the sample is too small, the results of the study may not be generalizable to the population. The results may hold only for the sample and may not be the same results that would have been obtained if the entire population had been used. Another way of looking at it is in terms of the hypothesis of the study. If the sample is not large enough, the wrong decision may be made concerning the validity of the hypothesis.

A sample that is too small can affect the generalizability of the study regardless of how well it is selected. Suppose, for example, the population is 300 members of a local professional association. If on the one hand, we randomly select only one member, clearly that member can't represent all the members. Nor could two, three, or four members, even if randomly selected, adequately represent the population. On the other hand, we would all agree that a sample of 299, 298, or 297 members would represent the population. How about 10? Too small, you say. How about 30? 75? 100? At what point does the sample size stop being "too small" and become "big enough?" That is a question without an easy answer. Knowing that the sample should be as large as possible helps some but still does not give guidance as to what size sample is "big enough." In most situations, the researcher does not have access to many subjects. In fact, obtaining permission to involve employees in a study, or finding adults willing to participate in a study is generally not an easy task. Usually the problem is too few subjects rather than too many. In any event, there are some guidelines that can be applied in order to determine what size sample is "big enough."

In general, the minimum number of subjects believed to be acceptable for a study depends upon the type of research involved. For descriptive research, a sample of 10% of the population is considered a bare minimum. For a smaller population, 20% or more may be required. For correlational studies at least 30 subjects are needed to establish the existence or nonexistence of a relationship. For causal-comparative studies and many experimental studies, a minimum of 30 subjects per group is generally recommended. Experimental studies with tight experimental controls may be valid with as few as 15 subjects per group (Roscoe, 1975), however, some authorities believe that 30 subjects per group should always be considered the minimum. Considering the difficulty involved in securing subjects, and the number of studies that are reported with less than 15 in a group, requiring 30 seems to be a little on the idealistic side. Further, while we would not be superconfident about the results of a single study based on small samples, if a number of such studies obtained similar results, our confidence in the findings would generally be as high as, if not higher than, for a single study based on very large samples. There is a lot to be said for replication of findings.

The minimums discussed are just that, minimums. If it is at all possible to use more subjects, you should do so. Using samples larger than the minimums is especially important in certain situations. For example, in an experimental study if the expected difference between groups is small, this difference might not show up if the samples are too small. Also, it should be noted that there are relatively precise statistical techniques that can be used to estimate required sample sizes for experimental studies; use of such techniques requires knowledge of certain facts about the population such as the difference expected between groups (for further discussion of these techniques, see Cohen, 1988). Although larger samples are better than smaller samples in general, even very large samples can lead to erroneous conclusions. There are many sources of sampling bias that can affect a study, regardless of sample size.

AVOIDANCE OF SAMPLING BIAS

Selecting samples using the very best technique does not guarantee that they will be representative of the population. *Sampling error,* beyond the control of the researcher, can exist. Of course no sample will have a composition precisely like that of the population. The sample may have, for example, fewer males proportionally, or a higher average IQ. If the sample is well selected and sufficiently large, the chances are that the sample will be highly similar on such variables. Occasionally, however, just by chance, a sample will differ significantly from the population on some major variable. Usually this will not make a significant difference. If there is a variable for which a lack of representation might really affect the outcome of the study, the researcher should stratify on that variable rather than leaving all to chance.

Sampling bias is another story. Sampling bias does not result from chance differences between samples and populations. Sampling bias is systematic and is generally the fault of the researcher. If aware of sources of bias, a researcher must try to avoid bias if at all possible. The fact that size alone does not guarantee representativeness was graphically illustrated by the presidential election of 1936. The *Literary Digest* poll predicted that Roosevelt would be defeated by Landon. It based its prediction on a poll of several million people. Unfortunately for the *Literary Digest,* the prediction was wrong because it was based on a biased sample. The sample of people polled was selected primarily from automobile registration lists and telephone directories. In 1936, however, a sizable portion of the voting population did not own a car or have a telephone. Thus, the sample did not adequately represent the voting population. And guess what—people without cars and telephones voted anyway! Modern pollsters are more knowledgeable and take great care to insure that samples are representative of the voting population on relevant variables.

A major source of bias is the use of *nonprobability sampling* techniques. When such techniques are used, it is not possible to specify the probability, or chance, that each member of a population has of being selected for the sample. In fact, it is usually difficult, if not impossible, even to describe the population from which a sample was drawn and to whom results can be generalized. These techniques, which include convenience sampling, judgment sampling, and quota sampling, are used mainly for reasons of cost and expediency. Of these sampling methods, convenience sampling is the most used in business research and is therefore the major source of sampling bias in business research studies.

1. *Convenience sampling,* also referred to as accidental sampling and haphazard sampling, basically involves using as the sample whoever happens to be available. Two major examples of convenience sampling are the use of volunteers and the use of existing groups just because "they are there." Volunteers are bound to be different from nonvolunteers. For example, they may be more motivated in general or more interested in a particular study. Since a population is composed of volunteers and nonvolunteers, the results of a study based on volunteers may not be generalized to the entire population, only to other volunteers. Two examples should help to make this point clear. Suppose you send a questionnaire to 100 randomly selected people and ask the question, "How do you feel about questionnaires?" Suppose that 40 people respond and all 40 indicate that they love questionnaires. Should you then conclude that the group from which the sample was selected loves questionnaires? Certainly not. The 60 who didn't respond may not have done so simply because they hate questionnaires!

As a second example, suppose we want to do a study on the effectiveness of networking on the career development of management trainees. We ask for volunteers from a new group of management trainees, and 60 trainees volunteer. Of course, right off the bat, they are not representative of all trainees. For example, they may be trainees who are bored with their work assignments and willing to volunteer for anything that is different. In any event, suppose we then randomly assign the volunteers to two groups of 30, an experimental group to have training in, and opportunities for, networking, and the other group to serve as a control. Both groups receive one hour of training in networking, and then the experimental group receives invitations to social and professional gatherings once a week for six weeks; the control group does nothing special. Since they are all volunteers, the subjects feel free to drop out of the study. Members of the control group have no need to drop out since no demands are made on their time. Members of the experimental group, however, may drop out after one or two events, not wishing to "waste" any more of their time. Suppose at the end of the study, only 15 of the original 30 trainees in the experimental group remain while all 30 members of the control group remain. Suppose further that a comparison of their subsequent career achievement indicates that the group that received the invitations achieved significantly more rapid career advancement. Could we then conclude that the networking was effective? Certainly not! In essence, we would be comparing the achievement of those in the control group with those members of the experimental group who chose to remain. Thus, they might very well be more motivated to achieve, as a group, than the control group; the less motivated trainees dropped out of the study. It would be very difficult to determine how much of their achievement was due to the treatment (networking) and how much was due to motivation. As noted previously, the quality circles study used volunteers from the plant whose manager was willing to institute quality circles. To compensate for the use of volunteers, workers "most like" the volunteers from another plant were identified and asked to serve as part of the study; when 3 of the 73 control-group employees didn't want to participate, they were replaced by 3 others who agreed to participate. The researcher identified the validity problems with this selection and stated his methods for handling the problems. When employees from either group dropped out, for example, the researcher deleted the data collected from his or her counterpart (matched-pair) in the other group.

The problem with using available groups just because "they are there" is illustrated in the following example. Suppose we want to do a study on the effectiveness of frequently scheduled, short work breaks on the accuracy of order-processing clerks. We happen to have a friend who supervises a large order-processing department with several different groups of clerks. We ask our friend if we may conduct a study using those groups and our friend says yes. We then tell our friend to continue the normal work conditions in one group and to begin scheduling 5 minute breaks every 45 minutes for another group. At the end of two weeks, the accuracy of the two groups is compared and the short-break group has achieved significantly more than the nonbreak group. Can we conclude that short breaks are effective? Not necessarily. In our study we found that breaks were effective for one group. Since the group was not selected from any larger unit, we have no assurance that the group is representative of any other groups. Therefore, we have no assurance that our results are generalizable to any other order processing groups.

2. *Judgment sampling,* also referred to as purposive sampling, basically involves selecting a sample that is believed to be representative of a given population. In other words, the researcher uses expert judgment to select a representative sample. For example, a number of work groups in a given corporation may be selected to obtain a representative cross section of all work groups in the corporation. The problem, however, as Kalton (1983, p. 91) points out, is that in practice different researchers would likely disagree on what constitutes a "representative" sample and, in any event, a judgment sample is "subject to a risk of bias of unknown magnitude."

3. *Quota sampling* is most often used in survey research involving interviews, usually when it is not possible to list all members of the population of interest. When quota sampling is involved, interviewers are given exact numbers, or quotas, of persons of varying characteristics who are to be interviewed, e.g., 35 working women with children under the age of 16 and 20 working women with no children under 16. The most widely known survey of this type is probably the Gallop Poll. Obviously, when quota sampling is used, interviews are obtained from easily accessible

individuals. Thus, people who are less accessible (more difficult to reach, more reluctant to participate, and so forth) are underrepresented (Badia & Runyon, 1982).

As mentioned before, securing management approval to involve employees in a study generally is not easy. Researchers often use what subjects they can get or, in other words, whatever is most convenient for management. This may amount to a researcher receiving permission to use several groups of employees of management's choice. Cooperating with management is of course advisable but not at the expense of good research. If the study can't be conducted properly, the researcher should try hard to convince management to allow the study to be conducted the way the researcher wants. If this fails, the researcher needs to look elsewhere for subjects. If suitable subjects can't be found or selected properly, the study probably should be abandoned temporarily. This may sound harsh, but conducting a study requires considerable time and energy, if not expense. To expend time and energy on a study with little generalizability is a waste of both. If, however, it is the researcher's intention to conduct an action research project, some modifications may be made. As you may recall from Chapter 1, action research is intended to answer specific questions under conditions that are unique to a local situation. Suppose, for example, that a needs assessment was completed for a specific company, and, based on the assessment a management-development program was designed. If a researcher is asked to design an evaluation study to determine the effectiveness of the management-development program, the researcher should try to follow the guidelines for good research as closely as possible. Given the circumstances, however, in order to provide management with answers for further decision making, some rules may need to be bent. To refuse to conduct a study under these conditions simply deprives management of a needed, and probably beneficial, measure of effectiveness. To assume that the study could be generalized, however, would indicate a lack of understanding of the requirements for good research.

The researcher should be aware of sources of sampling bias and do his or her best to avoid it. If this is not possible, the researcher must decide whether the bias is so severe that the results will be seriously affected. If a decision is made to continue with the study, with full awareness of the existing bias, such bias should be completely reported in the final research report. The consumers of the research findings may then decide for themselves how serious they believe the bias to be; as noted, an example of this may be found in the quality circle article at the end of Chapter 1.

Summary/Chapter 4

SAMPLING: DEFINITION AND PURPOSE

1. Sampling is the process of selecting a number of items or individuals for a study in such a way that the items or individuals represent the larger group from which they were selected.

2. The purpose of sampling is to use a sample to gain information about a population.

DEFINITION OF A POPULATION

3. A population is the group to which a researcher would like the results of the study to be generalizable.

4. A *defined population* has at least one characteristic that differentiates it from other groups.

5. The population that the researcher would ideally like to generalize results to is referred to as the *target population;* the population that the researcher realistically selects from is referred to as the *accessible population.*

METHODS OF SELECTING A SAMPLE

6. Regardless of the specific technique used, the steps in sampling are to define the population, determine the required sample size, and select the sample.

7. The degree to which the selected sample represents the population is the degree to which results are generalizable.

Random Sampling

8. Random sampling is the process of selecting a sample in such a way that all individuals in the defined population have an equal and independent chance of being selected for the sample.

9. Random sampling is the best single way to obtain a representative sample.

10. Random sampling involves defining the population, identifying each member of the population, and selecting individuals for the sample on a completely chance basis.

11. A random sample is generally selected using a table of random numbers.

Stratified Random Sampling

12. Stratified random sampling is the process of selecting a sample in such a way that identified subgroups in the population are represented in the sample in the same proportion that they exist in the population.

13. Stratified random sampling can also be used to select equal-size samples from each of a number of subgroups if subgroup comparisons are desired.

14. The steps in stratified random sampling are very similar to those in random sampling except that selection is from subgroups in the population rather than from the population as a whole.

Cluster Sampling

15. Cluster sampling is sampling in which groups, not individuals, are randomly selected.

16. Any intact group with similar characteristics is a cluster.

17. The steps in cluster sampling are similar to those in random sampling except that the random selection of groups (clusters) is involved, not individuals.

Systematic Sampling

18. Systematic sampling is sampling in which individuals are selected from a list by taking every Kth name, where K equals the number of individuals on the list divided by the number of subjects desired for the sample.

19. Even though choices are not independent, a systematic sample can be considered a random sample *if* the list of the population is randomly ordered (a relatively infrequent event).

DETERMINATION OF SAMPLE SIZE

20. Samples should be as large as possible; in general, the larger the sample, the more representative it is likely to be, and the more generalizable the results of the study are likely to be.

21. Minimum, acceptable sample sizes depending on the type of research are:

    a. descriptive research—10% of the population

    b. correlational research—30 subjects

    c. causal-comparative research—30 subjects per group

    d. experimental research—15 subjects per group.

22. Even large samples can lead to erroneous conclusions if they are not well selected.

AVOIDANCE OF SAMPLING BIAS

23. Sampling bias does not result from random, chance differences between samples and populations; sampling bias is systematic and is generally the fault of the researcher.

24. A major source of bias is the use of *nonprobability sampling* techniques. When such techniques are used, it is not possible to specify the probability, or chance, that each member of a population has of being selected for the sample.

25. *Convenience sampling,* also referred to as accidental sampling and haphazard sampling, basically involves using as the sample whoever happens to be available. Two major examples of convenience sampling are the use of volunteers and the use of existing groups just because "they are there."

26. *Judgment sampling,* also referred to as purposive sampling, basically involves selecting a sample that is believed to be representative of a given population.

27. *Quota sampling* is most often used in survey research involving interviews, usually when it is not possible to list all members of the population of interest. When quota sampling is involved, interviewers are given exact numbers, or quotas, of persons of varying characteristics who are to be interviewed,

28. Researchers should avoid being talked into using a seriously biased sample for the sake of management convenience.

29. Any sampling bias present in a study should be fully described in the final research report.

Project III Subsection 1 Performance Criteria

The definition of the population should describe its size and relevant characteristics (such as age, sex, educational level, and so on).

The procedural technique for selecting subjects should be described in detail. For example, do not just say that stratified sampling was used; indicate on what basis population members were stratified and how (and how many) subjects were selected from each subgroup. Also describe how selected subjects were placed into treatment groups, by random assignment, for example. If the entire population was used in the study, say so and simply describe how population members were assigned to groups. Include a summary statement that indicates resulting sample size for each group. For example:

> There were 2 groups of 30 subjects each; each group included 15 subjects with more than 3 months' experience and 15 subjects with less than 3 months' experience.

Any identifiable source of sampling bias should also be discussed. Small sample sizes, unavoidable use of volunteers, or use of intact groups are examples that should be included.

You may want to review the entire quality circles article to see the way the population was described and how the sample was selected. You will also want to see the specific way sources of sampling bias were described and handled. Also, review the Project III Student Example at the end of Chapter 10 to see the level of expertise expected of you at this point. Your instructor may have given you a checklist for this project, or you may want to look at the checklists for evaluating studies in the last chapter of this book as a way of reviewing your work.

REFERENCES

Badia, P., & Runyon, R. P. (1982). *Fundamentals of behavioral research*. Hightstown, NJ: McGraw-Hill.

Cohen, J. (1988). *Statistical power analysis for the behavioral sciences* (2nd ed.). Hillsdale, NJ: Lawrence Erlbaum.

Kalton, G. (1983). *Introduction to survey sampling*. Newbury Park, CA: Sage.

Roscoe, J. T. (1975). *Fundamental research statistics for the behavioral sciences* (2nd ed.). New York: Holt, Rinehart and Winston.

The Thematic Apperception Test presents the individual with a series of pictures; the respondent is then asked to tell a story, about each picture. (page 178)

5

Selection of Measuring Instruments

Objectives

After reading Chapter 5, you should be able to do the following:

1. Identify and describe the four scales of measurement.

2. Discuss validity by:
   a. defining or describing content validity.
   b. defining or describing construct validity.
   c. defining or describing concurrent validity.
   d. listing the procedures for determining concurrent validity by establishing relation-ship.
   e. defining or describing predictive validity.
   f. listing the procedures for determining predictive validity.

3. Discuss reliability by:
   a. defining or describing reliability.
   b. listing the procedures for determining test-retest reliability.
   c. listing the procedures for determining equivalent-forms reliability.
   d. listing the procedures for determining split-half reliability.
   e. defining or describing rationale equivalence reliability.
   f. defining or describing standard error of measurement.
   g. explaining the difference between interjudge and intrajudge reliability.

4. Discuss types of measuring instruments by:
   a. describing the purpose of a vocational test.
   b. describing the purpose of an achievement (performance) test.
   c. describing the purpose of projective and nonprojective tests including personality inventories, attitude scales, tests of creativity, and interest inventories.
   d. describing the purpose of aptitude tests.

5. Discuss the selection of a test by:
   a. stating the two most important guidelines, or rules, for test selection.
   b. identifying and briefly describing three sources of test information.
   c. listing, in order of importance, the factors that should be considered in selecting one test from a number of alternatives.

6. Discuss test administration by listing three guidelines for test administration.

7. List the steps involved in scoring standardized tests and self-developed tests.

Project III Subsection 2: Instrument Selection Guidelines

Having stated a problem, formulated one or more hypotheses or questions, and described a sample, describe the instrument(s) appropriate for collection of data pertinent to the hypothesis or question. For each instrument selected, the description will include the following:

1. name of the instrument.
2. description of the instrument.
3. validity and reliability data.
4. type of subjects for whom the instrument is appropriate.
5. instrument administration requirements.
6. training requirements for scoring and interpretation of resulting data.
7. synopsis of critical reviews.

Note: You will also need to include the name of the author and publisher in your reference list.

(See Project III Subsection 2 Performance Criteria, p. 198.)

PURPOSE AND PROCESS

Since all research studies are designed either to test hypotheses or answer questions, they all require data with which to do so. Most studies use some sort of data-collection instrument or methodology. Essentially, there are three major ways to collect data:

1. Administer a standardized instrument.
2. Administer a self-developed instrument.
3. Record naturally available data (such as production, sales, or absenteeism rates).

For several good reasons, this chapter will be concerned primarily with the selection of published, standardized tests. Collection of naturally available data, requiring a minimum of effort, sounds very attractive. Unfortunately, there are problems inherent in this type of data even if the researcher has determined that available data is appropriate, meaning that it can be employed to test the intended hypothesis or answer the desired question. Suppose, for example, that you were collecting information regarding salary ranges. Using the job title "administrative assistant to the president," you might discover a very wide range of salaries; not only would this range be based upon the size of the companies involved, but the duties required of the administrative assistant in one company would probably be very complex and highly responsible whereas another administrative assistant might be in a clerical position. Although you could collect the salary information, owing to the wide variability of company size and the duties and responsibilities of the job incumbent involved, your information would be essentially useless. Developing an instrument for a particular study also has several major drawbacks. The development of an effective instrument requires considerable time, effort, and skill. The total time for execution of a study will be greatly increased if instrument development is involved. Also, training at least equivalent to a course in measurement is necessary in order to acquire the skills needed for good instrument development. When we come to Chapter 7 dealing with descriptive research, you will find guidelines for the development of certain types of instruments, such as questionnaires. The very nature of descriptive research often necessitates the development of instruments for particular studies, but it's a lot more complicated than a casual let's-just-send-out-a-little-questionnaire kind of attitude sometimes seen in business. The reason for this casual attitude is probably lack of training and information in testing and research rather than a desire to cut corners in time and money. Many business people are simply unaware of the availability of excellent instruments for measuring and evaluating a number of different skills, levels of knowledge, and situations. Regardless of whether the researcher uses a standardized instrument, uses a self-developed instrument, or collects naturally available data, the data can be classified as representing one of the four types of measurement scales.

TYPES OF MEASUREMENT SCALES

Data for analysis result from the measurement of one or more variables. Depending upon the variables, and the way in which they are measured, different kinds of data result, representing different scales of measurement. It is important to know which type of scale is represented by your data since each type adds special characteristics to your study, and also different statistics are appropriate for the different scales of measurement. There are four types of measurement scales.

Nominal Scales

Nominal scales represent the lowest level of measurement. Such a scale classifies persons or objects into two or more categories. Whatever the basis for classification, a person can only be in one category, and members of a given category have a common set of characteristics. Classifying subjects as tall versus short, male versus female, or salaried versus hourly pay are all examples of nominal scales. When a nominal scale is used, the data simply indicate how many subjects are in each category. For 100 new employees, for example, it might be determined that 40 are college graduates and 60 are not. The problem with these sorts of data, of course, is that employees who haven't completed high school would be lumped together with employees who are only one course short of graduating from college. The same principles apply when the samples are objects: widgets may be brown or green, large or small, heavy or light.

For identification purposes, categories are sometimes numbered from 1 to however many categories there are. It is important to realize, however, that a category labeled 4 is only different from the category labeled 3; 4 is not more, or higher, than 3, only different from 3. To avoid confusion, it is sometimes a good idea to label categories with letters instead of numbers, in other words, A, B, C, D instead of 1, 2, 3, 4. While nominal scales are not very precise, as just indicated, occasionally their use is not only necessary but even desirable when simple categories such as "yes," "no," or "not applicable" will suffice.

Ordinal Scales

Ordinal scales not only classify subjects but also rank them in terms of the degree to which they possess a characteristic of interest. In other words, an ordinal scale puts the subjects in order from highest to lowest, from most to least. Probably the best known ordinal scale in business is the *Fortune* 500, which ranks firms from largest to smallest based on a number of different factors. For the 500 companies that "make the cut," each is assigned a number, with 1 being the largest and the company ranked 500 the smallest of the group. Class rank and percentile rank are other familiar measures of relative standing that represent ordinal scales.

Although ordinal scales do indicate that some subjects are higher, or better, than others, they do not indicate how much higher or how much better. In other words, the intervals between ranks are not equal; the difference between rank 2 and rank 3 is not necessarily the same as the difference between rank 3 and rank 4, as the *Fortune* 500 example below illustrates (see Table 5.1). The difference in sales between Ford and Exxon is $10,276.6 million; the difference between Exxon and IBM is $23,218 million. In this example, the difference in sales represented by the differences in rank range from approximately $10,000 million to nearly $25,000 million. Thus, while an ordinal scale results in more precise measurement than a nominal scale, it still does not allow the level of precision usually desired in a research study.

Interval Scales

Interval scales have all the characteristics of nominal and ordinal scales, but in addition, they are based upon predetermined equal intervals. Most of the standardized tests used in management research, such as personality and aptitude tests, represent interval scales. Therefore, you will often be working with statistics appropriate for interval data. When we talk about "scores," we are usually referring to interval data.

Table 5.1

Ranks and Sales Figures for Fortune 500 Companies Ranked 1 Through 5

Rank 1989	Company	Sales $ millions
1	General Motors	126,974.3
2	Ford Motor	96,932.6
3	Exxon	86,656.0[1]
4	International Business Machines	63,438.0
5	General Electric	55,264.0

Note: From "The Fortune 500," 1990, April, *Fortune*, 346. © 1990 Time Inc. Magazine Company. All rights reserved.

1. Does not include excise taxes

When scores have equal intervals, it is assumed, for example, that the difference between a score of 30 and a score of 40 is essentially the same as the difference between a score of 50 and a score of 60. Similarly, the difference between 81 and 82 is approximately the same as the difference between 82 and 83. Interval scales resulting from tests such as aptitude tests, however, do not have a true zero point. Such scales typically have an arbitrary maximum score and an arbitrary minimum score, or zero point. If the Graduate Management Admission Test (GMAT) produces scores ranging from 200 to 800, a score of 200 does not indicate the absence of aptitude for graduate study in business, nor does a score of 800 indicate possession of the ultimate aptitude for graduate study. A score of 200 only indicates the lowest level of performance possible on that particular test, and a score of 800 represents the highest level. Thus, scores resulting from administration of an interval scale can be added and subtracted but not multiplied or divided. We can say that a typing test score of 90 is 45 points higher than a score of 45, but we cannot say that a person scoring 90 is twice as good a typist as a person scoring 45. Similarly, a person with a measured IQ of 140 is not necessarily twice as intelligent as a person with a measured IQ of 70. For most management research, however, such generalizations are not needed.

Ratio Scales

Ratio scales represent the highest, most precise, level of measurement. A ratio scale has all the advantages of the other types of scales and, in addition, has a meaningful true zero point. Dollars, units produced, number of employees, and time are all examples of interval scales occuring in business-and-management research. If money is considered as a ratio scale, then clearly the difference between $5.50 and $6.50 ($1) is the same as the difference between $6.50 and $7.50. Thus, with a ratio scale we can say not just that in 1989 General Motors' sales were greater than Ford's, but we can also say that General Motors generated $126,974.3 million and Ford generated $96,932.6 million in sales (*Fortune* 500, 1990, p. 346). As another example, the concept of "no time" is a meaningful one. Because of the true zero point, not only can we say that the difference between sales of $30 million and sales of $40 million is the same as the difference between sales of $40 million and $50 million, but we can also say that $60 million in sales is twice as much as $30 million in sales. Similarly, 60 minutes is 3 times as long as 20 minutes, and 40 pounds is 4 times as heavy as 10 pounds. Thus, with a ratio scale we can say that General Motors is over $100,000 million in sales and Ford is under $100,000 million (nominal scale), General Motors has greater sales than Ford (ordinal scale), General Motors is $126,974.3 million in sales and Ford is $96,932.6 million (interval scale), *and* Ford's sales are 0.76, or 76% of General Motor's sales (ratio scale).

The important concept to remember in using different scales is that a statistic appropriate for a lower level of measurement may be applied to data representing a higher level of measurement. A statistic appropriate for ordinal data, for example, may be used with interval data, since interval data possess all the characteristics of ordinal data and more. The reverse, however, is not true. A statistic appropriate for interval data cannot be applied to ordinal data since such a statistic requires equal intervals. In general, data should not be converted to a lower-level scale because precision will be lost. Therefore in selecting a methodology for collecting data, you should try to use the most precise measure (interval rather than ordinal scale, for example) possible. If, however, the only way to obtain one aspect of your needed data is in ordinal scale, for example, then you may have to convert interval data to an ordinal scale in order to apply a particular statistical technique to your data. The type of measurement scale that is used by an instrument is only one consideration in selection. Again, although we will focus primarily on standardized instruments, the concepts that will be discussed can be applied to both self-developed instruments and methodologies for collecting naturally available data.

CHARACTERISTICS OF STANDARDIZED INSTRUMENTS

With regard to standardized instruments, the time it takes to select an appropriate standardized instrument is invariably less than the time it takes to develop an instrument that measures the same thing. Standardized instruments typically are developed by experts, both in subject matter and testing, who possess the necessary skills to develop good instruments. From a research point of view, an additional advantage of using a standardized instrument is that results from different studies using the same instrument can be compared.

Suppose, for example, that two separate studies were conducted to determine whether method A or method B of training managers in leadership results in better final performance. Suppose further that study 1 used a local self-developed test of leadership behavior and study 2 used the highly respected Leader Behavior Description Questionnaire (LBDQ-12, 1957). Now if study 1 found no difference between methods A and B, but study 2 found method B to be superior, interpretation of these conflicting results would be difficult. It might be that the two tests were measuring different variables, for example, memorization of leadership principles versus actual leader behavior. It might also be that the test used in study 1 was inadequately constructed. In any event, it would be difficult to distinguish differences due to the training method and differences due to the test used. If you, as a consumer of research, found these studies, would you be more likely to rely on the results of study 1 or study 2? In addition to allowing for comparisons, the use of a standardized instrument facilitates replication of a study by an independent researcher. The researcher—and the consumer of research reports—must be extremely careful in comparing results using well-known instruments to be sure that the same instruments were actually used; as mentioned in Chapter 3, for example, there are at least two tests that are known as the MSQ—the Management Styles Questionnaire (Michalak, 1983) and the Management Style Questionnaire (McBer, 1980).

There are thousands of standardized instruments available that yield a great variety of data for a wide variety of purposes. Major areas for which numerous measuring instruments have been developed include personality, achievement or performance, intelligence or general aptitude, and specific aptitude. Each of these can in turn be further divided into many subcategories. Personality instruments, for example, can be classified as nonprojective or projective. Selection of an instrument for a particular research purpose involves identification and selection of the most appropriate one from among alternatives; a researcher does not find an instrument suited for his or her study but rather selects the best one of those that are available. The selection process involves determination of the most appropriate type of instrument, for example, clerical aptitude, and then a comparative analysis of available instruments of that type. Therefore, in order to select an instrument intelligently, a researcher must be familiar with the wide variety of types of instruments that exist and must also be knowledgeable concerning the criteria that should be applied in selecting one from among alternatives.

Standardized Tests

As you may have noticed, the word *test* has thus far been carefully avoided. This is because "test" has a very narrow connotation for many people. A test is not necessarily a written set of questions to which an individual responds in order to determine whether he or she passes. A more inclusive definition of a test is a means of measuring the knowledge, skills, feelings, intelligence, or aptitude of an individual or group. Tests produce numerical scores that can be used to identify, classify, or evaluate test takers. In addition, there are a number of characteristics shared by standardized tests. While these characteristics are desirable for all tests, they are more likely to be in evidence for a standardized test. Regardless of the type of test being sought, there are certain kinds of information that should be available about any standardized test. This information, or lack of it, forms the basis for test selection.

Standardized tests are typically developed by experts and therefore should be well constructed. Individual test items are analyzed and revised until they meet given standards of quality. Directions for administering, scoring, and interpreting standardized tests are carefully specified. One resulting characteristic of a standardized test is referred to as *objectivity*. In essence, test objectivity means that an individual's score is the same, or essentially the same, regardless of who is doing the scoring. Another major characteristic of standardized tests is the existence of *validity* and *reliability* data. Validity is the most important quality of any test. Validity is concerned with what a test measures and for whom it is appropriate; reliability refers to the consistency with which a test measures whatever it measures. Because of their importance and the fact that they must also be considered in developing instruments or specifying methodologies for collecting naturally available data, these two concepts will be discussed in considerable detail later in this section.

Specification of the conditions of administration is a very important characteristic of a standardized test. This insures that if directions are carefully followed, the test will always be administered the same way and will always yield the same kind of data. If directions are carefully spelled out, even a beginning researcher should be able to administer most tests properly. The directions usually include instructions to be read to the test takers, restrictions on time, if any, and guidelines concerning the amount and nature of communication permitted between the test administrator and the test takers. Last, but not least, standardized tests generally include directions for scoring and guidelines for interpretation of scores. Directions for scoring include specifications such as the criteria for acceptable responses, when such are appropriate, the number of points to be assigned to various responses, and the procedure for computing total scores. Guidelines for test-score interpretation generally include a table of norms. Typically a test is administered to a large number of appropriately defined individuals, and resulting test scores are analyzed. A table of norms presents raw scores and one or more equivalent transformations, such as corresponding percentile ranks, which facilitate interpretation of an individual's score with respect to the performance of the group. Since researchers generally work with raw scores, this type of information is generally of more interest to other consumer groups such as licensing and accrediting agencies or company human resources or personnel officers. If data collection instruments are self-developed, or naturally occuring data are used, the researcher must carefully specify the conditions for both the data collection and scoring.

As stated previously, the most important characteristic of a standardized test, or any test for that matter, is validity. Validity is indispensable; there is no quality or virtue of a test—cost, ease of administration, or time required—that can compensate for inadequate validity.

Validity

The simplest definition of validity is that it is the degree to which a test measures what it is supposed to measure. A common misconception is that a test is, or is not, valid. A test is not valid per se; it is valid for a particular purpose and for a particular group. The question is not "valid or invalid?" but rather "valid for what and for whom?" A valid test of clerical aptitude is not very likely to be a valid personality test. It would be obvious to almost anyone looking at a test of clerical aptitude that the test did not measure any aspect of personality. It would probably not be quite as evident whether the test was a valid measure of clerical skills or clerical principles, if either. With respect to the "for whom" aspect of validity, a test that is a valid measure of computer proficiency for data analysts is certainly not a valid measure for clothing sales personnel. It might not be as evident whether the test was valid for both entry-level and experienced data analysts, if either. To clarify the concept of valid "for what and for whom," further let us apply the concept of validity to sales. In general, a valid salesperson is one who sells whatever he or she is supposed to sell (or, if you prefer, whose customers buy what is being sold). But a salesperson, no matter how outstanding, is not valid per se. A salesperson is valid for a particular purpose, such as a specific product, and a particular market. A "valid" car salesperson is not very likely also to be a "valid" children's clothing sales associate, and a "valid" salesperson on TV is not very likely also to be a "valid" stockbroker. While the above analogy is admittedly loose, the concept it illustrates is important.

It is the "valid for whom" concern that makes the description of the *norm group* so important. Only to the degree that persons in the norm group are like the persons to whom we wish to administer the test can proper interpretation of results be made. One criticism of the LBDQ-12 mentioned previously, by the way, is that the original norm group was 395 aircraft commanders and 64 educational administrators who were tested in 1957 (Dipboye, 1978). Thirty-year-old norms are not likely to be appropriate for employees in the 1990s, and, to be fair, an enormous amount of research using the instrument has taken place which provides a great deal of useful validity and reliability information for the instrument.

As a second example, the usefulness of norms based on a sample of 50,000 upper-middle-class managers in New York City is certainly questionable if the test is to be administered to beginning factory workers in the Midwest and so forth. Of course even an "ideal" norm group with a cast of thousands is not going to be entirely appropriate in any situation. There are just too many variables and individual characteristics that might affect results. Thus care must always be taken in selecting a test and interpreting results. But if information concerning the norm group is insufficient or if the information given indicates any major way in which the norm group is inappropriate, then every effort must be made to locate a more suitable test. If none is available, then the shortcomings must be seriously considered when results are interpreted.

Since tests are designed for a variety of purposes, and since validity can be evaluated only in terms of purpose, it is not surprising that there are several different types of validity: (a) content, (b) construct, (c) concurrent, and (d) predictive. Because of the different ways in which they are determined, they are classified as either logical or criterion-related validity. Logical validity includes content validity and is so named because validity is determined primarily through judgment. *Criterion-related validity,* or *empirical validity,* includes concurrent and predictive validity and is so named because in each case validity is determined by relating performance on a test to performance on another criterion. Criterion-related validity is determined in a more objective manner than content validity. Assessment of construct validity involves both judgment and external criteria. For any test it is important to seek evidence concerning the appropriate type of validity, given the intended purpose or purposes of the test.

Content Validity

Content validity is the degree to which a test measures an intended content area. Content validity requires both item validity and sampling validity. *Item validity* is concerned with whether the test items represent measurement in the intended content area, and *sampling validity* is concerned with how well the test samples the total content area. A test designed to measure knowledge of facts concerning Human Resource Management might have good item validity because all the items do indeed deal with facts in Human Resource Management, but it might have poor sampling validity, for example, if all the items deal only with interviewing skills and not with compensation administration or training. A test with good content validity adequately samples the appropriate content area. This is important because we cannot possibly measure each and every aspect of a certain content area; the required test would be ridiculously long. And yet we do wish to make inferences about performance in the entire content area based on performance on the items included in the test. Such inferences are only possible if the test items adequately sample the domain of possible items. This sampling is, of course, easier for well-defined areas such as accounting than for less quantitative content areas such as organizational behavior.

The term *face validity* is sometimes used in describing tests. While its meaning is somewhat ambiguous, basically "face validity" refers to the degree to which a test appears to measure what it purports to measure. While determining face validity is not a psychometrically sound way of estimating validity, the process is sometimes used as an initial screening procedure in test selection.

Content validity is of prime importance for achievement or information tests. A test score cannot accurately reflect a trainee's achievement if it does not measure what the trainee was supposed to learn. While this seems obvious, content validity has been a problem in a number of research studies. Many studies, for example, are designed to compare the effectiveness of two or more different ways of doing the same thing. Effectiveness is often defined in terms of final achievement of the treatment groups as measured by a test. It sometimes happens that the test used is more content valid for one of the groups than for the other. When this happens, final achievement differences may be at least partially attributable to the test used and not just the methods that were involved.

Suppose, for example, that a service company for many years trained its customer-service representatives in a fairly routine way to handle customer calls and complaints. In a burst of innovation and an attempt to involve employees more completely in the work, however, a new training program is devised, which gives the trainees much more background about the company and the procedures used and emphasizes the importance of excellent customer relations in maintaining market share. A test used previously in the older training program is used with the new and innovative program, and the results are the same: Customer-service representatives trained under both methods provide essentially the same information in response to routine questions. Does this mean the new program was not worth the effort? Or does it mean that the test does not reflect the depth of understanding and worker motivation the new program intends to instill? The moral of the story is that in a study that compares treatments and measures achievement, take care that the test measures what the trainees learned in the treatments and is, therefore, valid for your study and for your subjects.

Content validity is determined by expert judgment. There is no formula by which it can be computed, and there is no way to express it quantitatively. Usually experts in the area covered by the test are asked to assess its content validity. These experts carefully review the process used in developing the test as well as the test itself and make a judgment concerning how well the test items represent the intended content area. This judgment is based on whether all subareas have been included and are in the correct proportions. In other words, a comparison is made between what ought to be included in the test, given its intended purpose, and what is actually included. When selecting a test for a research study, the researcher assumes the role of expert and determines whether the test is content valid for her or his study. The researcher compares what will be covered in the study with what is measured by the test.

Construct Validity

Construct validity is the degree to which a test measures an intended hypothetical construct. A *construct* is a nonobservable trait, such as intelligence, leadership, or honesty, which explains behavior. You cannot see a construct; you can only observe its effect. In fact, constructs were invented to explain behavior. We cannot prove they exist; we cannot perform brain surgery on a person and "see" his or her honesty. Constructs, however, do an amazingly good job of explaining certain differences between individuals. For example, it was always observed that some individuals learn faster than others, learn more, and retain information longer. To explain these differences, a theory of intelligence was developed, and it was hypothesized that there is something called intelligence that is related to learning and that everyone possesses to a greater or lesser degree. Tests were developed to measure how much of it a person has. As it happens, individuals whose scores indicate that they have a lot of it, that is, they have high IQs, tend to do better in school and other learning environments such as training. Other constructs that have been hypothesized to exist, and for which tests have been developed, include anxiety, creativity, curiosity, interpersonal relations, leadership, and motivation, to cite only a few. The LBDQ-12 mentioned before is frequently used in studies involving leadership, whereas the Job Diagnostic Survey (JDS) (Hackman & Oldham, 1980) is often seen in studies involving motivation.

Research studies that involve a construct, either as an independent or a dependent variable, are only valid to the extent that the measure of the construct involved is valid. Honesty, for example, can be an independent or a dependent variable. A study might be designed to determine whether extremely honest employees perform better in an auditing function than somewhat honest employees. A test of honesty would need to be administered to the employees in the study in order to classify them as "extremely honest" or "somewhat honest." Another study might be designed to determine whether training in business ethics results in more honest behavior by employees than threats and punishments do. A test of honesty would need to be administered to both groups at the conclusion of the study. In both situations, the validity of the findings would be a direct function of the validity of the honesty test used. If the test did not really measure honesty (employees are able to "lie" successfully when taking the test, for example), conclusions based on a study that used it would be meaningless. During the late 1980s, the American Civil Liberties Union (ACLU), American Psychological Association (APA), and the House Education and Labor Committee all expressed concern regarding the validity of honesty tests used in employment situations. Lest you think this an insignificant concern, it was estimated that by 1990, 5.5 million honesty tests would be administered annually by American business (Caprino,1989). When selecting a test of a given construct, the researcher, like the employer, must look for and critically evaluate evidence presented related to the construct validity of the instrument.

The process of validating a test of a construct is by no means an easy task. Basically, it involves testing hypotheses deduced from a theory concerning the construct. If, for example, a theory of honesty hypothesized that extremely honest individuals will be whistle-blowers even if it means losing their jobs, and the individuals who scored high on the test under consideration did indeed identify subsequent questionable practices, this would be evidence to support the construct validity of the test. Of course, if the "extremely honest" persons did not, as hypothesized, identify questionable practices, then it would not necessarily mean that the test did not measure honesty; the hypotheses related to the behavior of extremely honest persons might be incorrect. Generally a number of independent studies are required to establish the credibility of a test of a construct.

Concurrent Validity

Concurrent validity is the degree to which the scores on a test are related to the scores on another, already established, test administered at the same time or to some other valid criterion available at the same time. Often, a test is developed that claims to do the same job as some other test, but it measures the content more easily or faster. If this is shown to be the case, that is, the concurrent validity of the new test is established, in most situations the new test will be used instead of the other tests. A paper-and-pencil test that does the same job as a performance or observation test, or a short test that measures the same behaviors as a longer test, would certainly be preferred, especially in a research study.

Concurrent validity is determined by establishing relationship or discrimination. The relationship method involves determining the relationship between scores on the test and scores on some other established test or criterion (e.g., sales or some other quantifiable measure). In this case, the steps involved in determining concurrent validity are as follows:

1. Administer the new test to a defined group of individuals.
2. Administer a previously established, valid test (or acquire such scores if already available) to the same group, at the same time, or shortly thereafter.
3. Correlate the two sets of scores.
4. Evaluate the results.

The resulting number, or validity coefficient, indicates the concurrent validity of the new test; if the coefficient is high, the test has good concurrent validity. Suppose, for example, that Professor Jeenyus developed a group test for certified public accountants (CPAs) that took only 5 minutes to administer. If scores on this test did indeed correlate highly with scores on the national CPA exam (which is normally given to a large group at a time and takes many hours to complete), then Professor Jeenyus' test would definitely be preferable in a great many situations. The discrimination method of establishing concurrent validity involves determining whether test scores can be used to discriminate between persons who possess a certain characteristic and those who do not or between those who possess it and those who possess it to a greater degree. For example, the tests of honesty discussed previously would have concurrent validity if scores resulting from them could be used correctly to classify thieves and honest people.

When selecting a test for a given research purpose, you will usually be seeking a test that measures what you wish in the most efficient manner. If you select a shorter or more convenient test that allegedly measures the desired behavior, be careful that concurrent validity has been established using a valid criterion.

Predictive Validity

Predictive validity is the degree to which a test can predict how well an individual will do in a future situation. A clerical aptitude test that has high predictive validity will fairly accurately predict which employees will do well in clerical tasks and which employees will not. Predictive validity is extremely important for tests that are used to classify or select individuals, particularly for employment situations. Before the 1960s, employers frequently used general IQ tests as a part of the employment practice, but these were found not to be specifically related to the requirements of most jobs. Now it is important for an employer to be able to demonstrate the predictive validity of a test that is given in the employment process. The U.S. Employment Service, for example, sometimes uses the General Aptitude Test Battery (GATB) as a means of predicting future job performance. Claims have been made that this test battery is a better predictor of performance than the applicant's credentials, experience, and education. Charges have also been made, however, that the GATB is biased against minorities (Seligman, 1989). Another example with which you may be all too familiar is the use of the GMAT or the Graduate Record Examination (GRE) scores to select students for admission to graduate schools. Many graduate schools require a certain minimum score for admission in the belief that students who achieve at least the minimum score have a higher probability of succeeding in graduate school. The predictive validity of these tests has been the subject of many research studies with results seeming to indicate that they have higher predictive validity for certain areas of graduate study than others as well as better predictive ability for American-born, Caucasian students than for other applicants (Ledvinka & Boulton, 1985). As another example, the MacQuarrie Test for Mechanical Ability, which measures skills such as tracing, tapping, dotting, copying, locating, arranging blocks, and pursuing, seems to be a valid predictor for aviation mechanics and stenographers. Another psychomotor test, the O'Connor Finger and Tweezer Dexterity Tests, appears to be a valid test for power sewing machine operators and dental students (Schuler, 1987).

As the GMAT example illustrates, the predictive validity of a given instrument varies with a number of factors such as the training program involved, manuals used, and even geographic location. The Mindboggling Finance Aptitude Test, for example, may predict achievement better in courses using the Brainscrambling Finance text than in courses using other texts. Thus, if a test is to be used for prediction, it is important to compare the description of the manner in which it was validated with the situation in which it is to be used. In a study of organizational culture, for example, the authors commented that new organizations or those undergoing rapid change may not appear to have strong organizational cultures as measured by a particular instrument, the Organizational Culture Inventory (OCI). Therefore comparisons between these organizations and more stable organizations based on the findings from the OCI must be cautiously interpreted, and norms from more stable organizations may not apply to newer or more rapidly changing organizations (Cooke & Rousseau, 1988).

No test, of course, has perfect predictive validity. Therefore, predictions based on the scores of any test will be imperfect. As the Educational Testing Service (ETS) points out, GRE and GMAT scores should not be used as the sole determining factor for admission to a particular school; ETS even offers a Validity Study Service for schools using or considering the GMAT (Crosby, 1985; Ledvinka & Boulton, 1985). However, predictions based on a combination of several test scores or measures will invariably be more accurate than predictions based on the scores of any one test. Therefore, when important classification or selection decisions are to be made, they must be based on data from more than one indicator. An example of this is found in studies related to the GMAT:

> Figures for 1982–83 indicate a median correlation of .30 between Total GMAT (quantitative & verbal) and first-year grades in MBA or equivalent programs. The multiple correlation of GMAT and undergraduate GPA with first-year grades is slightly higher at .38, although multiple correlations in the mid .40s have been noted previously (Crosby, 1985, p. 621).

Similarly, in a job situation, a combination of interviews, references checks, and employment tests will probably give us a better prediction than interviews or tests alone.

The predictive validity of a test is determined by establishing the relationship between scores on the test and some measure of success in the situation of interest. The test used to predict success is referred to as the *predictor,* and the behavior predicted is referred to as the *criterion.* In establishing the predictive validity of a test, the first step is to identify and carefully define the criterion. The criterion selected must be a valid measure of the behavior to be predicted. For example, if we wished to establish the predictive validity of a clerical aptitude test, accuracy in filing and completing simple reports after several months on the job might be considered a valid criterion, but number of days absent from the job during the same number of months probably would not. Do you think a formal performance appraisal would be a valid criterion? It would depend upon the validity of the performance appraisal in measuring actual job performance, wouldn't it?

Another caution in dealing with predictive validity is related to the concept of base rate. *Base rate* is the proportion of individuals who can be expected to meet a given criterion. You should avoid trying to predict a criterion for which the base rate is very high or very low. For example, suppose we wished to establish the predictive validity of a test designed to predict who will eventually become a chief executive officer (CEO). Since a very, very small percentage of employees do so, all we would have to do is predict that no one would, and we would be correct in almost every case! A test could hardly do better—but it would, therefore, be of very limited value.

Once the criterion has been identified and defined, the procedure for determining predictive validity is as follows:

1. Administer the test, the predictor variable, to a group.
2. Wait until the behavior to be predicted, the criterion variable, occurs.
3. Obtain measures of the criterion *for the same group.*
4. Correlate the two sets of scores.
5. Evaluate the results.

The resulting number, or validity coefficient, indicates the predictive validity of the test; if the coefficient is high, the test has good predictive validity. For example, suppose we wished to determine the predictive validity of an aptitude test for airline pilots. First we would administer the test to a large group of potential pilots. Then we would wait until the prospective pilots had completed their training and would obtain a measure of their success, for example, flight simulator results. The correlation between the two sets of scores would determine the predictive validity of the test; if the resulting correlation coefficient was high, the test would have high predictive validity.

As mentioned previously, often a combination of predictors is used to predict a criterion. A prediction equation is developed from this combination of predictors. In the case of our airline pilot, we might use a test of mechanical and electrical knowledge, eye-and-hand coordination, physical condition (including hearing and eyesight), interview ratings by experienced pilots, and a test to determine the ability of the candidate to perform mathematical problems while listening to and acting upon information from the air traffic controller. Our future airline pilot's scores on each of these tests would be inserted into the prediction equation and her or his future performance predicted. In this case the validity of the equation should be reestablished through cross-validation. Cross-validation involves administering the predictor tests to a different sample from the same population and developing a new equation. Of course, even if only one predictor test is used, it is a good idea to determine predictive validity for more than just one sample of individuals. In other words, the predictive validity of a test should be reconfirmed.

You may have noticed (if you had a high score on the GMAT or GRE) that the procedures for determining concurrent validity and predictive validity are very similar. The major difference is in terms of when the criterion measure is administered. In establishing concurrent validity, it is administered at the same time as the predictor or within a relatively short period of time; in establishing predictive validity, one usually has to wait for a much longer period of time to pass before criterion data can be collected. Occasionally, concurrent validity is substituted for predictive validity in order to save time and to eliminate the problems of keeping track of subjects. For example, with our pilots, we might administer the tests listed to a group of airline pilots and correlate scores on the test with some measure of their skill. The problem with this approach is that we would be dealing only with those who passed. Persons for whom the test would have predicted a low probability of success would not become airline pilots. In other words, most of the persons in the sample would be persons for whom the test would have predicted success. Therefore, the resulting validity coefficient would probably be an underestimate of the predictive validity of the test. This approach also presents the possibility that the group of successful pilots share some other characteristic (such as good judgment?) that we may have failed to measure but that is really responsible for their success. (By the way, during the 1950s and 1960s, some airlines used employment tests for pilots that measured their knowledge of fine wines and perfumes, among other things; application of the concept of predictive validity has at least done away with those "measures.")

In the discussion of both concurrent and predictive validity there was a statement to the effect that if the resulting coefficient is high, the test has good validity. You may have wondered, "How high is high?" The question of how high the coefficient must be in order to be considered "good" is not easy to answer. There is no magic number that a coefficient should reach. In general, it is a comparative matter. The coefficents presented previously regarding GMATs ranged from .30 to .40, which may seem low when the decision being made is very important. A coefficient of .50 might be acceptable if there is only one test available designed to predict a given criterion; on the other hand, a coefficient of .50 might be inadequate if there are other tests available with higher coefficients. This really involves judgment on the part of the researcher or test administrator. What coefficient would you prefer for the pilot on your next flight?

All of this discussion is meaningless, however, without the closely related concept of reliability. Simply stated, reliability deals with the question of score consistency.

Reliability

In everyday English, *reliability* means consistency, dependability, or trustworthiness. The term means essentially the same thing with respect to measurement. Basically, reliability is the degree to which a test consistently measures whatever it measures. The more reliable a test is, the more confidence we can have that the scores obtained from the administration of the test are essentially the same scores that would be obtained if the test were readministered. An unreliable test is essentially useless; if a test is unreliable, then scores for a given sample would be expected to be different every time the test was administered. If an intelligence test was unreliable, for example, then a person scoring an IQ of 120 today might score an IQ of 140 tomorrow and 95 the day after tomorrow. If the test was reliable, and if the person's IQ was 110, then we would not expect his or her score to fluctuate too greatly from testing to testing; a score of 105 would not be unusual, but a score of 145 would be very unlikely.

Reliability is expressed numerically, usually as a coefficient; a high coefficient indicates high reliability. If a test were perfectly reliable, the coefficient would be 1.00; this would mean that a person's score perfectly reflected her or his true status with respect to the variable being measured. Alas and alack, however, no test is perfectly reliable. Scores are invariably affected by errors of measurement resulting from a variety of causes. High reliability indicates minimum error variance; if a test has high reliability, then the effect of errors of measurement has been reduced. Errors of measurement affect scores in a random fashion; some scores may be increased while others are decreased. Errors of measurement can be caused by characteristics of the test itself (ambiguous test items, for example, that some test takers just happen to interpret correctly), by conditions of administration (directions not properly followed, for example), by the current status of the persons taking the test (some are tired, others unmotivated or in a hurry), or by a combination of these factors. High reliability indicates that these sources of error have been eliminated as much as possible.

Errors of measurement that affect reliability are random errors; systematic or constant errors affect validity. If an achievement test was too difficult for a given group of trainees, all scores would be systematically lowered; the test would have low validity for that group (remember "valid for whom?"). The test might, however, yield consistent scores; in other words, it might be reliable because the scores are systematically lowered in the same way every time. A particular trainee whose "true" achievement score was 80 and who scored 60 on the test (invalidity) might score 60 every time the trainee took the test (reliability). This illustrates an interesting relationship between validity and reliability: a valid test is always reliable but a reliable test is not necessarily valid. If, for example, you determined that the reliability of a particular test was .32, would that test be valid? No, because the reliability is too low. If the reliability is .92, would it be valid? Certainly it is reliable; however, we still don't know if it is valid regardless of how reliable it may be. In other words, if a test is measuring what it is supposed to be measuring, it will be reliable and do so every time, but a reliable test can consistently measure the wrong thing and be invalid! Suppose a test purporting to measure management-information-systems concepts really measured facts. It would not be a valid measure of concepts, but it could certainly measure the facts very consistently.

All this talk about error might lead you to believe that measurement in research (and practice) is pretty sloppy and imprecise to say the least. Certainly we would encourage you to inquire of people administering a test or questionnaire in a work environment regarding the validity and reliability of the instrument. If they don't know what you're talking about or try to reassure you that it's "not important," you have more cause for concern. Although a good bit of caution is certainly warranted, the situation regarding measurement is not as bleak as it may sound. There are many tests that measure intended traits quite accurately, and we have a right and an obligation to insist that materials used as a basis for important decision making be as sound as possible. Nevertheless, as Nunnally (1978) has pointed out, measurement in other areas of science often involves as much, if not more, random error. To use his example, the measurement of blood pressure, a physiological trait, is far less reliable than many psychological measures. There are any number of "conditions of the moment," which may temporarily affect blood pressure—joy, anger, fear, and anxiety, to name a few. Thus a person's blood pressure reading is also the result of a combination of "true" blood pressure and error.

With the possible exception of content validity, reliability is much easier to assess than validity. There are a number of different types of reliability; each is determined in a different manner and each deals with a different kind of consistency. Test-retest, equivalent-forms, and split-half reliability are all determined through correlation; rationale equivalence reliability is established by determining how each item on a test relates to all other items on the test and to the total test. Split-half reliability and rationale equivalence reliability are types of *internal-consistency reliability,* which, as the name implies, is based on the internal consistency of the test. Whereas test-retest reliability and equivalent-forms reliability require a group to take two tests (either the same test twice or two forms of the same test), internal-consistency reliability can be estimated based on one administration of a test to a group.

Test-Retest Reliability

Test-retest reliability is the degree to which scores are consistent over time. It indicates score variation that occurs from testing session to testing session as a result of errors of measurement. In other words, we are interested in evidence that the score a person obtains on a test at some moment in time is the same score, or close to the same score, that the person would get if the test were administered at some other time. We want to know how consistently the test measures whatever it measures. This type of reliability is especially important for predictor tests that serve as the basis for important decisions such as employment or entrance into graduate programs. If an aptitude test of any kind indicated a different level of aptitude each time it was administered, it would obviously not be very helpful.

Determination of test-retest reliability is appropriate when alternate (equivalent) forms of a test are not available and when it is unlikely that persons taking the test the second time will remember responses made on the test the first time. Although test takers are less likely to remember items from a test involving math problems than tests involving procedures or facts about companies, some test takers do remember even math problems—and do so over a fairly long period of time. With these caveats in mind, the procedure for determining test-retest reliability is basically quite simple:

1. Administer the test to an appropriate group.
2. After some time (perhaps a week) has passed, administer the *same* test to the *same* group.
3. Correlate the two sets of scores.
4. Evaluate the results.

If the resulting coefficient, referred to as the *coefficient of stability,* is high, the test has good test-retest reliability. A major problem with this type of reliability, as indicated earlier, is knowing how much time should elapse between the two testing sessions. If the interval is too short, the chances of the test takers remembering responses made on the test the first time are increased, and the estimate of reliability tends to be artificially high. If the interval is too long, the test takers' ability to do well on the test may increase due to intervening experiences, and the estimate of reliability tends to be artificially low. Thus, when test-retest information is given concerning a test, the time interval between testings should be given as well as the actual coefficient. Essentially this is a matter of expert judgment, but, depending upon the type of test involved, one day will generally be too short and much more than a month too long. At least one study (Ho, 1988) cited test-retest reliabilities for an instrument measuring cognitive processing styles that were appropriately based on elapsed times of up to three years! Since the instrument in question purports to measure brain hemisphere information-processing differences, both the instrument and the material being tested (since it is based on physiology) should have a very high level of stability and should not be affected by intervening experience. These problems associated with test-retest reliability are, however, taken care of by equivalent-forms reliability.

Equivalent-Forms Reliability

Equivalent forms of a test are actually two tests that are identical in every way except for the actual items included. The two forms measure the same variable and have the same number of items, the same structure, the same difficulty level, and the same directions for administration, scoring, and interpretation. In fact, if the same group takes both tests, the average score as well as the degree of score variability should be essentially the same on both tests. Only the specific items are not the same, although they do measure the same traits or objectives. In essence, we are selecting, or sampling, different items from the same group of behaviors. Just as a well-selected sample should be similar to any other well-selected sample drawn from a population of subjects, both sets of test items on equivalent forms of tests should represent the body of information or skills we are trying to assess. What we are interested in is whether obtained scores depend upon the particular set of items selected or whether performance on one set of items is generalizable to other sets. If items are well selected, and if each set adequately represents the area of interest, the latter should be true.

Equivalent-forms reliability, also referred to as alternate-forms reliability, indicates score variation that occurs from form to form. It is appropriate when it is likely that test takers will recall responses made during the first session and, of course, when two different forms of the test are available. When alternate forms are available, it is important to know the equivalent-forms reliability; it is reassuring to know that a person's score will not be greatly affected by which form is administered. Also, sometimes in research studies two forms of a test are administered to the same group, one as a pretest and the other as a posttest. It is crucial, if the effects of the intervening activities are to be validly assessed, that the two tests be measuring essentially the same things.

The procedure for determining equivalent-forms reliability is very similar to that for determining test-retest reliability:

1. Administer one form of the test to an appropriate group.
2. At the same session, or shortly thereafter, administer the *second* form of the test to the *same group.*
3. Correlate the two sets of scores.
4. Evaluate the results.

If the resulting coefficient, referred to as the *coefficient of equivalence,* is high, the test has good equivalent-forms reliability. If the two forms of the test are administered at two different times (the best of all possible worlds—at least for researchers) the resulting coefficient is referred to as the *coefficient of stability and equivalence* (try dropping *that* during your coffee break tomorrow!). In essence this approach represents a combination of test-retest and equivalent-forms reliability and thus assesses stability of scores over time as well as the generalizability of the sets of items. Since more sources of measurement error are possible than with either method alone, the resulting coefficient is likely to be somewhat lower. Thus the coefficient of stability and equivalence represents a conservative estimate of reliability.

Equivalent-forms reliability is the single most acceptable and most commonly used estimate of reliability for most tests used in research. The major problem involved with this method of estimating reliability is the difficulty of constructing two forms that are essentially equivalent. Lack of equivalence is a source of measurement error. Even though equivalent-forms reliability is considered to be the best estimate of reliability, it is not always feasible to administer two different forms of the same test or even the same test twice. Imagine your reaction if your instructor told you that you would be taking the final exam in this course twice! Or imagine the reaction of a senior manager if you told her or him that you'd be testing employees twice "in order to determine the coefficient of stability and equivalence of the instrument!" Fortunately, there are other methods of estimating reliability that require administering the test only once.

Split-Half Reliability

A common type of internal consistency reliability is referred to as *split-half reliability.* Since split-half-reliability procedures require only one administration of a test, certain sources of errors of measurement are eliminated, such as differences in testing conditions, which can occur in establishing test-retest reliability. Split-half reliability is especially appropriate when a test is very long.

The procedure for determining split-half reliability is as follows:

1. Administer the *total* test to *one* group.
2. Divide the test into two comparable halves, or subtests; the most common approach is to include all odd items in one half and all even items in the other half.
3. Compute each subject's score on the two halves—each subject will consequently have two scores, a score for the odd items and a score for the even items.

4. Correlate the two sets of scores.

5. Apply the Spearman-Brown correction formula.

6. Evaluate the results.

If the coefficient is high, the test has good split-half reliability. A number of logical and statistical methods can be used to divide a test in half. Random selection of half the items, for example, will work, but the odd-even strategy is most often used. Actually, this approach works out rather well regardless of how a test is organized. Suppose, for example, that a test consists of true-false and multiple-choice items. Chances are the true-false items are grouped together and the multiple-choice items are in a different section. Using the odd-even strategy, each of your halves will have about half the true-false items and half of the multiple-choice items. If the test is arranged by topic, however, so that the first half of a test on procedures for bank tellers deals with topics related to ensuring that a check presented for deposit is good and the second part of the test relates to customer relations, the odd-even strategy will allow you to measure how teller trainees perform in relation to both topics. Thus, regardless of how the test is organized, an odd-even split should produce essentially equivalent halves. In fact, what we are doing in essence, is artificially creating two equivalent forms of a test and computing equivalent-forms reliability; the two equivalent forms just happen to be in the same test. Thus the label "internal consistency reliability" is used with this kind of procedure.

Since longer tests tend to be more reliable, and since split-half reliability represents the reliability of a test only half as long as the actual test, a correction formula must be applied to the coefficient. The correction formula that is used is the Spearman-Brown prophecy formula. An example of this formula and the way it is used is provided in Part IV. One problem with the correction formula that you need to keep in mind is that it tends to give a higher estimate of reliability than would be obtained using other procedures; the correction formula overcorrects, in other words.

Rationale Equivalence Reliability

Another approach to determining internal consistency is *rationale equivalence reliability*. This is not determined through correlation but rather by the way all items on a test relate to all other items and to the total test. Rationale equivalence reliability is usually determined through application of one of the Kuder-Richardson formulas (KR-20 or KR-21) explained in Part IV. Application of these formulas provides an estimate of reliability that is essentially equivalent to the average of the split-half reliabilities computed for all possible halves. Kuder-Richardson formula 21 (KR-21) is one of the quickest ways to determine reliability and provides a conservative estimate, especially if more than one trait is being measured.

Figure 5.1 summarizes the methods for estimating test reliability. The horizontal axis, "number of different tests," indicates either that only one (1) test is administered (split-half, KR-21, and test-retest reliabilities) or that two (2) tests are administered (equivalent-forms). The vertical axis, "number of administration times," indicates that the test is administered at essentially the same (1) time (split-half, KR-21, equivalent-

		Number of Different Tests	
		1	2
Number of Administration Times	1	Split-half KR-21	Equivalent Forms
	2	Test-retest	Stability and Equivalence

Figure 5.1. Summary of methods for estimating reliability.

forms), or that a time interval (2) of at least a week exists between the administrations (test-retest). In reviewing test information, the reliability coefficient is of prime importance, but the method used to calculate it is also a consideration.

Reliability Coefficients

What constitutes an acceptable level of reliability is to some degree determined by the type of test. A coefficient over .90 would, of course, be acceptable for any test. The question really is concerned with what constitutes a minimum level of acceptability. For achievement and aptitude tests, there is generally no good reason for selecting a test whose reliability is not at least .90 for the population in your study. There are a number of achievement and aptitude tests available that report such reliabilities, and usually it is not necessary to settle for less, particularly considering the importance of the decisions that are based on such tests. Although some do, personality measures typically do not report such high reliabilities, and one would therefore be very satisfied with a reliability in the .80s and might even accept a reliability in the .70s. When tests are developed in new areas, one usually has to settle for lower reliability, at least initially. A new area of testing such as curiosity would not provide high reliabilities at this stage of development. If you are using a fairly new test or using an old test with a slightly different group than the test norm group, you will want to report the reliabilities for your group; publishing reliability figures for relatively new tests or for tests used under slightly unusual circumstances will help all the researchers who follow you.

If a test is composed of several subtests, then the reliability of each subtest must also be evaluated in addition to the reliability of the total test. Since reliability is partially a function of test length, the reliability of a given subtest is typically lower than the total test reliability ("the whole is greater than the sum of its parts"). Examination of subtest reliability is especially important if one or more of the subtests are going to be used in the research rather than the total test. You, as a researcher, will want to be a good consumer of test information. If a test manual states that "the total test reliability is .90, and all subtest reliabilities are "satisfactory," you will certainly want to know exactly how "satisfactory" they are. Similarly, if the manual states that "average subtest reliabilities are . . . ," then what is the lowest reliability (and highest) of the subtests?

After all, the average of .95, .95, .95, and .10 is .74; this may be an acceptable reliability unless the subtest you want to use is the .10 one! Most of the major, well-established tests report subtest reliabilities. Test publishers are in the business of selling tests, and if they omit pertinent information, you will want to be aware of such omissions and request additional data.

Standard Error of Measurement

In addition to reliability coefficients, reliability can also be expressed in terms of the *standard error of measurement,* usually abbreviated as SE_m. Test information sources often report these data for tests; basically, it is an estimate of how often you can expect errors of a given size. Thus, a small SE_m indicates high reliability, and a large SE_m indicates low reliability. If a test were perfectly reliable—you already know no test is—a person's obtained score would be his or her true score. As it is, an obtained score is really an estimate of a true score. If you administered the same test over and over to the same group, the score of each individual would vary. How much variability would be present in individual scores would be a function of the test's reliability. The variability would be small for a highly reliable test (zero if the test were perfectly reliable) and large for a test with low reliability. If we could administer the test many times, we could see how much variation actually occurred. Of course, realistically we can't do this; administering the same test twice to the same group is tough enough. Fortunately, it is possible to estimate this degree of variation, the SE_m, using the data from the administration of a test once to a group. In other words, the SE_m allows us to estimate how much difference there probably is between a person's obtained score and true score, the size of the difference being a function of the reliability of the test.

To determine the SE_m, you need to know both the reliability coefficient and the standard deviation of the test scores. In Part IV we'll discuss the ways these are determined and then discuss the specifics of determining the SE_m. For now, however, suffice it to say that we prefer the SE_m to be small, indicating less error. It is impossible, however, to say how small is "good." This is because SE_m is expressed in the same units as the test; how small is "small" is relative to the size of the test. Thus on the other hand, $SE_m = 5$ would be large for a 20-item test because it would mean that an obtained score of 15 might mean the person's true score was anywhere from 10 to 20 (15 plus or minus 5). On the other hand, a $SE_m = 5$ would be small for a 200-item test because a score of 150 might be anywhere from 145 to 155 (no big difference unless the cut-off score for passing is somewhere in that range). To facilitate better interpretation of scores, some test publishers present not only the SE_m for the total group but also give a separate SE_m for each of a number of identified subgroups.

Interjudge/Intrajudge Reliability

In addition to reliabilities directly related to the test itself, there is at least one other area of concern with regard to reliability. When judgment in evaluation is concerned, as with rating scales, observation instruments, or tests such as essays and answers of more than one-word responses, we need to be concerned with interjudge and/or intrajudge reliability. *Interjudge reliability,* also known as interscorer, interrater, or interobserver reliability, refers to the reliability of two or more independent scorers. *Intrajudge reliability,* also known as intrascorer, intrarater, or intraobserver reliability, refers to the reliability of the scoring of individual scorers. Scoring and rating are sources of errors of measurement, and it is important to estimate the consistency of scorers' assessments. Estimates of interjudge reliability are obtained by having the scorers independently score the measure and then correlating the results. With intrajudge reliability, one scorer scores and then rescores the measure after a period of time, and the two sets of results are correlated. If, for some reason, correlations are not appropriate, interjudge and intrajudge reliabilities can also be expressed as percent of agreement. While such reliabilities are usually not very good, a number of standardized instruments have been developed to the point where interjudge and intrajudge reliabilities in the mid .80s to low .90s have been reported when trained raters were used.

TYPES OF TESTS

There are many different kinds of tests available and many different ways to classify them. The *Mental Measurements Yearbooks* (Buros, 1938–1978; Conoley & Kramer, 1989; Mitchell, 1985) are the major source of test information for researchers. The *Yearbooks* include major headings such as "Vocations," "Personality," "Intelligence," and more specific subsections. Table 5.2 presents a complete listing of the

Table 5.2
Number and Percentage of Tests, by Major Classifications, in the
Tenth Mental Measurements Yearbook

Classification	Number	Percentage
Vocations	100	25.3
Personality	72	18.2
Miscellaneous	43	10.9
Developmental	31	7.8
Intelligence/Scholastic Aptitude	28	7.1
English	24	6.1
Reading	24	6.1
Speech and Hearing	22	5.6
Education	20	5.1
Achievement	12	3.0
Social Studies	3	.8
Fine Arts	2	.5
Foreign Languages	2	.5
Sensory-Motor	2	.5
Neuropsychological	2	.5
Total	396	100.0

major classifications, as well as the number and percentage of test entries related to each.

Vocations

The tests covered by the "vocations" section of the *Yearbooks* will be of particular interest to researchers in business and management. There are essentially three major types of tests classified in this section: (a) Aptitude, (b) Skills, and (c) Management topics. You will find a number of interest inventories and aptitude tests described that will be helpful in career-development activities that might take place either within a company or in a school or college setting. The skills tests cover specific skills and knowledge in jobs ranging from "business analyst" to "certified picture framer." In addition to the aptitude and skills tests, a number of other areas of interest to business researchers are covered under "vocations." These areas are as wide-ranging as tests of communications, conflict assessment, management appraisal, management style, and productivity assessment. Before you "reinvent the wheel," do some investigation here!

Personality

Tests of personality are designed to measure characteristics of individuals along a number of dimensions and to assess feelings and attitudes toward self, others, and a variety of other activities, institutions, and situations. They may well be the most-used tests in behavioral research. Coming in many different varieties, such as performance versus paper-and-pencil or individual versus group, there are tests to measure almost any aspect of personality you can think of. Although they can be classified in many ways, a logical initial differentiation, which is used by the *Yearbooks* (prior to the *Tenth*) is to categorize such tests as nonprojective or projective.

Nonprojective Tests

Most tests of character and personality are nonprojective, or self-report, measures. These tests ask an individual to respond to a series of questions or statements and are frequently used in descriptive studies (to describe corporate climate, for example), correlational studies (to determine relationships between various personality traits and other variables such as success, for example), and experimental studies (to investigate the comparative effectiveness of different motivational techniques for different kinds of employees, for example).

Personality Inventories.   Personality inventories present lists of questions or statements describing behaviors characteristic of certain personality traits, and the individual is asked to indicate (yes, no, undecided) whether the statement describes her or him. Some inventories are presented as checklists in which the individual simply checks items that characterize her or him, while others ask the individual to rate herself or himself on a scale from "very characteristic" to "very uncharacteristic," for example. An individual's score is based on the number or strength of the responses characteristic of the trait being measured. An introvert, for example, would be expected to check the statement "Reading is one of my favorite pastimes" and not to check the statement "I love large parties," while the extrovert would be expected to do just the opposite. Inventories may be specific and measure only one trait, such as introversion-extroversion, or may be general and measure a number of traits. Since general inventories measure more than one trait at the same time, they are typically relatively long and may take an hour or more to complete. Many of the longer inventories require professional training in measurement, psychology, or the specific test to interpret the results.

General inventories frequently used in research include the following: Adjective Check List, California Psychological Inventory, Edwards Personal Preference Schedule, Job Description Inventory (JDI), Job Diagnostic Survey (JDS), Leader Behavior Description Questionnaire (LBDQ-12), Management Style Questionnaire (MSQ), Minnesota Multiphasic Personality Inventory (MMPI), Mooney Problem Check List, Myers-Briggs Type Indicator, FIRO-B, Performax, and the Sixteen Personality Factor Questionnaire. The MMPI alone has been used in hundreds of research studies and the Myers-Briggs is gaining in popularity.

One serious problem involved with the use of self-report inventories is the problem of accurate responses. Personality scores are valid only to the degree that the respondent is self-aware and honest and therefore selects responses that truly are characteristic of him or her. A common phenomenon is the concept of a *response set,* or the tendency of an individual continually to respond in a given way. A common response set is the tendency of an individual to select the responses that he or she believes are the most socially acceptable. This is particularly true in a work environment. Whether response sets result from conscious or unconscious motivations, they can seriously distort an appraisal of the individual's personality structure. If a large proportion of a research sample is not responding accurately, results of the study may be essentially meaningless. Therefore, in studies using these tests, every effort, such as guarantees of confidentiality, must be made to increase the likelihood that valid test results are obtained.

Attitude Scales.   Attitude scales attempt to determine what an individual believes, perceives, or feels. Attitudes can be measured toward self, others, and a variety of other activities, institutions, and situations, such as the corporate climate studies described in the article following Chapter 7. The most common scales are Likert scales and semantic differential scales; you will likely see many varieties of these scales and occasionally will hear them called "forced-choice" scales.

A *Likert scale* (Likert, 1932) asks an individual to respond to a series of statements by indicating whether she or he strongly agrees (SA), agrees (A), is undecided (U), disagrees (D), or strongly disagrees (SD) with each statement. Each response is associated with a point value, and an individual's score is determined by summing the point values for each statement. For example, the following point values might be assigned to responses to positive statements: SA = 5, A = 4, U = 3, D = 2, and SD = 1. For negative statements, the point values would be reversed so that SA = 1, A = 2, and so on. An example of a positive statement might be, "Short people are entitled to the same job opportunities as tall people." A high point value on a positively stated item would indicate a positive attitude, and a high total score on the test would be indicative of a positive attitude. An obvious limitation of the Likert scale is that all the items on the instrument that are to be summed must relate to a single concept or trait; otherwise, you will be measuring apples and oranges.

A *semantic-differential scale* asks an individual to give a quantitative rating to the subject of the attitude scale on a number of bipolar adjectives such as good-bad, friendly-unfriendly, positive-negative. The respondent indicates the point on the continuum between the extremes that represents her or his attitude. Based on their research (Osgood, Suci, & Tannenbaum, 1957), the original developers of this approach reported that most adjective pairs represent one of three dimensions, which they labeled evaluation (good-bad), potency (strong-weak), and activity (active-passive). This type of scale is used, for example, to assess leadership characteristics by Fiedler and Chemers (1974) in the Least Preferred Co-Worker (LPC) instrument. In this instrument, the following items are included:

Pleasant ____ ____ ____ ____ ____ ____ ____ ____ Unpleasant
            8   7   6   5   4   3   2   1

Rejecting ____ ____ ____ ____ ____ ____ ____ ____ Accepting
            1   2   3   4   5   6   7   8

As you can see, each position on the continuum has an associated score value; by totaling score values for all items, it can be determined whether the responder's attitude is positive or negative. Although it would appear that the individual who is rated by this instrument is someone else, the score is used to determine characteristics of the individual doing the rating, thus making this a projective test (which will be discussed shortly) rather than a nonprojective test. It does, however, provide an example of a semantic-differential scale. Semantic-differential scales usually have five to seven intervals and, unlike the example given above, indicate a neutral attitude in the center with a value of zero. In this case the above item might appear as follows:

Pleasant ____ ____ ____ ____ ____ ____ ____ Unpleasant
            3   2   1   0   -1   -2   -3

Rejecting ____ ____ ____ ____ ____ ____ ____ Accepting
           -3   -2   -1   0   1   2   3

A further discussion of the semantic differential scales can be found in Snider and Osgood (1969).

Some of the forced-choice scales ask the individual to assess himself or herself in terms of agreement or disagreement with a particular statement. Thus the individual might be given a total of five points to distribute between two statements. In Burke's Leadership Questionnaire (1988), for example, individuals are asked to divide five points between the options on the following item:

I enjoy:
        _____ (A) rewarding followers for a job well done
        _____ (B) stimulating followers to want to do more

Measures of "attitude toward self" are referred to as measures of self-concept. Measures of self-concept are used in many research studies, especially studies designed to investigate

1. the relationship between self-concept and other variables, such as advancement
2. the effects of self-concept on other variables, such as motivation
3. the effects of various environments or methods of supervision on self-concept

Rating scales, which are frequently derived from the scales previously described, are also used to measure attitudes toward others. Such scales ask an individual to rate another individual on a number of behavioral dimensions. There are two basic types of rating scales; these are frequently found in quantitatively oriented performance-appraisal situations. One type is composed of items that ask an individual to rate another on a continuum (good to bad, excellent to poor), much as is done in the semantic-differential example, the LPC, shown previously. The second type asks the individual to rate another person on a number of items by selecting the most appropriate response category (for example, excellent, above average, average, below average, or poor). Attitude scales are also used in rating situations and organizations. The study at the end of Chapter 7, which will be discussed in more detail in that chapter, illustrates the use of attitude scales in large research efforts. Two problems associated with rating scales are referred to as the "halo effect" and the "generosity error." The halo effect is the tendency of a rater to let overall feelings toward a person or an organization affect responses to individual items. A supervisor might rate a good employee as "loyal," for example, even though the supervisor has no real basis for making any judgment regarding the employee's loyalty. The generosity error is the tendency of a rater to give the person or organization being rated the benefit of the doubt whenever the rater does not have enough knowledge to make an objective rating. Both the halo effect and the generosity error can also work in reverse, of course. When rating scales are involved in a study, every effort should be made to reduce these problems by giving appropriate instructions to the raters.

Attitude scales, like other personality inventories, present problems for the researcher in that he or she can never be sure whether the individual is expressing his or her true attitude or a "socially acceptable" attitude. Again, the validity of a study is directly related to the validity of the responses made by individuals in the sample. Every effort needs to be made, therefore, to increase accuracy and honesty by guaranteeing confidentiality and giving appropriate directions to those completing the instruments.

Creativity Tests. Tests of creativity are really tests designed to measure those personality characteristics that are related to creative behavior. One such trait is referred to as divergent thinking. Unlike convergent thinkers, who tend to look for the right answer, divergent thinkers tend to seek alternatives. Guilford (1967, 1959), probably the best-known researcher in this area, has developed a number of widely used tests of divergent thinking. One such test asks the individual to list as many uses as he or she can think of for an ordinary brick. Think about it and list a few. If you listed uses such as build an office complex, build a house, or build a library, then you are not very creative; all of those uses are really the same, namely, you can use a brick to build something. Now, if you are creative, you listed different uses such as break a window, drown a rat, and hit a robber on the head.

Another test asks individuals to compose plot titles for brief stories. The titles are then rated for their originality. One of the stories concerns a missionary who is captured by cannibals. He is given a choice of being boiled alive or marrying a princess of the tribe. He chooses death. Take a few minutes and think of some possible titles. Perhaps you came up with a title like "Missionary in Trouble," "The Cannibal and the Missionary," or "Boiled Alive!" If you are especially clever, you may have come up with a title like "Better Boil Than Goil" (a favorite of one of the authors), "A Mate Worse Than Death," or "He Left a Dish for a Pot." The more clever titles a person comes up with, the higher the score on originality, which is one aspect of divergent thinking.

Another well-known researcher in this area is Torrance. The Torrance Tests of Creativity (Torrance, 1984) include graphic, or pictorial, items as well as verbal items. Tests are scored in terms of four factors: fluency, flexibility, originality, and elaboration. Like the Guilford test, the Torrance tests also involve tasks such as listing as many uses as possible for an object and coming up with titles for pictures.

Interest Inventories.   An interest inventory asks an individual to indicate personal likes and dislikes, such as the kinds of activities he or she prefers to engage in. Responses are generally compared to known interest patterns. Vocational-interest inventories are the most widely used type of interest measure. Such inventories typically ask the individual to indicate preferences with respect to leisure-time activities, such as hobbies. The individual's pattern of interest is then compared to the patterns of interest typical of successful persons in various occupational fields. The individual can then be counseled as to the fields in which she or he is more likely to be happy and successful. Two frequently used inventories are the Strong-Campbell Interest Inventory, which measures interest in professional and business fields, and the Kuder Preference Record—Vocational, which measures interest in broad occupational areas such as mechanical, scientific, persuasive, and social science.

Projective Tests

Projective tests were developed in an attempt to eliminate some of the major problems inherent in the use of self-report measures, such as the tendency of some respondents to give "socially acceptable" responses. The purposes of such tests are usually not obvious to respondents; the individual is typically asked to respond to ambiguous items. Since the purpose of the test is not clear, conscious dishonesty of response is reduced, and the respondent "projects" his or her true feelings. Projective tests are used mainly by clinical psychologists and very infrequently by other researchers. This is partly because of their questionable validity and partly because administration, scoring, and interpretation of projective tests require very specialized training. If it is necessary to use a projective device in your research study, be sure to have it administered and scored by qualified personnel.

The most commonly used projective technique is the method of association. This technique asks the respondent to react to a stimulus such as a picture, inkblot, or word. Word-association tests are probably the most well known of the association techniques (tell me the first thing that comes into your mind). Two of the most commonly used association tests are the Rorschach Inkblot Test and the Thematic Apperception Test; thousands of studies using the Rorschach test have been conducted. The Rorschach test presents the respondent with a series of inkblots, and the respondent is asked to tell what he or she sees. The Thematic Apperception Test presents the individual with a series of pictures; the respondent is then asked to tell a story about each picture. A version of this test has been used, for example, to assess types of motivation using McClelland's categories of need for achievement, need for power, or need for affiliation (McClelland, 1961).

Until recently, all projective tests had to be administered individually. There have been some recent efforts, however, to develop group projective tests. One such test is the Holtzman Inkblot Technique, which is intended to measure the same variables as the Rorschach Inkblot Test. Group projective instruments, including the Holtzman, are still in relatively early stages of development. They do, however, offer great promise of becoming more objective projective devices.

Aptitude

Aptitude tests are measures of potential. They are used to predict how well someone is likely to perform in a future situation. Tests of general aptitude are variously referred to as tests of general mental ability, intelligence tests, and scholastic aptitude tests. Since intelligence tests have developed a bad reputation in recent years, the term *general aptitude* or even "personnel" test is frequently used in business. The intents of all such tests, however, are basically the same. Aptitude tests are also available to predict a person's likely level of performance following some specific future instruction or training. Aptitude tests are available in the form of individual tests in specific areas, such as computer-systems analysis, and in the form of batteries that measure aptitude in several related areas, such as clerical skills. Virtually all aptitude tests are standardized, but extreme caution must be used in selection of aptitude tests in the workplace. Not only must they be thoroughly reliable, but the employer must be able to demonstrate that any tests used are valid not only for the position in question but also that they do not adversely affect applicants on account of the applicant's age, sex, level of education, or racial background. Information from the review of one such test, the Wonderlic Personnel Test (WPT) is informative regarding this concern:

> The WPT was introduced in 1938, and flowered after WW II, at a time when testing job applicants on general intelligence, or anything else for that matter, was commonplace. The popularity of this test prompted a previous reviewer to note that "it is probably a rare applicant who is not exposed to the Wonderlic test several times during any given job search;

the promotional literature on the test claims that over 6,500 organizations are using it for selection and placement procedures." All of this changed in 1971, when the U.S. Supreme Court, in the case of Griggs v. Duke Power, ruled that the tests used by the defendant, Duke Power, which included the WPT, were inappropriate in that they: (a) failed to measure the applicant for the job (i.e., show appropriate validity), and (b) adversely impacted protected groups. In the present environment, it is probably a rare applicant who is exposed to the WPT during any given job search. (Schoenfeldt, 1985, p. 1757)

The reviewer goes on to point out another case *(Cormier v. PPG Industries)* in which use of the WPT was upheld, but he still cautions potential users regarding potential Equal Employment Opportunity (EEO) issues, while another reviewer (Schmidt, 1985) sees an increase in testing and recommends this test.

General Aptitude

There are a variety of tests, like the WPT, that fall into this category representing a variety of different definitions of general aptitude (or scholastic aptitude, or intelligence, or what have you). While the basic purpose of all such tests is to predict future performance, primarily in an academic area, there is disagreement as to the factors that are being measured and are serving as the predictors. The term aptitude is variously defined to include variables such as abstract reasoning, problem solving, and verbal fluency. Such tests generally yield three scores—an overall score, a verbal score, and a quantitative score—representing, for example, a total IQ, a verbal IQ, and a quantitative IQ. While general-aptitude tests are intended to be measures of innate ability, or potential, they appear actually to measure current ability; there is also some evidence to suggest that scores are to some degree affected by an individual's past and present environment.

General-aptitude tests may be group tests or individually administered tests. Each type has its relative advantages and disadvantages. Group tests are more convenient to administer, save considerable time, and provide an estimate of potential that is often adequate for research studies. Batteries of some tests are also available that comprise a number of tests suitable for different age levels. A commonly used group-administered battery is the California Test of Mental Maturity (CTMM). The CTMM has six levels and can be administered to adults and college students as well as school-age children. The previously mentioned WPT was originally a revision of the Otis Self-Administering Tests of Mental Ability; the 50-item, 12-minute test uses a variety of problem types including analogies, analysis of geometric figures, disarranged sentences, and definitions (Schoenfeldt, 1985).

Unlike the WPT, many group tests have the disadvantage that they require a great deal of reading. Thus, individuals with poor reading ability are at a disadvantage and may receive scores reflecting, for example, an IQ level lower than their true level. Individual tests require much less reading. Another advantage of individual tests is that since they are administered one-on-one, the examiner is aware of factors such as illness or anxiety that might be adversely affecting the individual's ability to respond. From a research point of view, the main disadvantages of individual tests are that they are more time-consuming and difficult to administer and score; individuals with specific training ranging from workshops for simple tests to graduate degrees in tests and measurement for the more complex tests are required to administer the tests and score them. If, however, there is any reason to question the validity of group tests for a particular sample, physically challenged individuals, for example, an individual test should be used, even if this requires a reduction of sample size. Probably the best-known of the individually administered tests is the Stanford-Binet Intelligence Scale, which has been extensively used in research projects; there is considerable information concerning its validity. More and more, however, the Wechsler scales are being used. Both the Stanford-Binet and the Wechsler Adult Intelligence Scale-Revised (WAIS-R) are appropriate for use with older adolescents and adults. While the Stanford-Binet yields one IQ score, the Wechsler scales also yield a number of subscores.

As mentioned previously, there is evidence to indicate that IQ scores are affected by the individual's past and present environment. As was indicated, the validity of IQ tests for certain minorities has been questioned, and such tests have been accused of being culturally biased. This criticism has prompted the development of "culture-fair" IQ tests. Culture-fair tests attempt to exclude culturally related items, such as items that include words that might not be familiar to certain groups of individuals. In fact, most of these tests do not require the use of language. Interestingly, however, evidence suggests that such tests may not be as culture-fair as originally believed; nonverbal tests may in fact be less culture-fair than verbal tests. The Culture-Fair Intelligence Test (ages 4 to adult) is probably the most frequently used culture-fair test. Other test publishers, such as Wonderlic, have addressed this problem by providing interpretation tables for different ages, sexes, educational levels, and racial groups.

Specific Aptitude

As the term is generally used, specific-aptitude tests attempt to predict the level of performance that can be expected of an individual following future instruction or training in a specific area or areas. As mentioned in the previous discussion of vocational tests, aptitude tests are available for a wide variety of areas ranging from clerical to mechanical skills. As with tests of general aptitude, they are used by career-development specialists and human resources personnel. Specific aptitude tests are also frequently used in research studies. Their most common use in this regard is probably to equate groups that are going to be compared on achievement after receiving different treatments. If groups are different in aptitude to begin with, then final achievement differences might be attributable to this initial difference rather than to the differences in treatment. Aptitude scores can be used to equate groups either by using stratified sampling or through a statistical procedure called analysis of covariance. While most aptitude tests are written standardized tests, some are performance tests. The latter are appropriate when the subjects taking the tests have an English-language difficulty or when the skill areas being tested involve psychomotor rather than cognitive skills. In job interviews, pilots, for example, are often expected to do well in performance tests in flight simulators in addition to completing written tests of information.

In addition to specific-area tests, multi-aptitude batteries measuring aptitudes in several related areas are also available. The Differential Aptitude Tests (DAT), for example, include tests on spatial relations, mechanical reasoning, and clerical speed and accuracy, among other things, and are designed to predict success in various job areas.

Achievement Tests

A final type of test is the achievement, or proficiency, test, which measures the current status of individuals with respect to knowledge or skill in given areas. You undoubtedly remember the standardized achievement tests used in most school systems, which measured knowledge of facts, concepts, and principles. In these, the student's level of achievement is compared to the norm, or average score, for his or her grade or age level. They include subtests, which measure achievement in areas such as reading, math, spelling, and so on. Work-related, standardized achievement tests are commonly used in situations involving licensing for occupations such as pilots, accountants, nurses, lawyers, and cosmeticians. In addition, other occupations, such as human resources personnel and financial planners, have established standardized achievement tests for certification of individuals within the profession. In the previous discussion of vocational tests, some additional achievement and skills tests were also mentioned.

In addition to standardized achievement tests, locally developed achievement, or proficiency, tests are used in some companies to measure competency at the completion of a training experience. Development of such a test should not be a haphazard affair if any sort of decision making is be based on the test results, whether that decision be one involving future advancement for the individuals involved or retention and/or revision of the training experience and materials. Occasionally such a test is developed when a perfectly acceptable test with an established track record is available, so it is wise to check out the possibilities before deciding to develop your own test.

Achievement tests may also be used to diagnose training needs or deficiencies. Although instruments intended specifically for diagnosis are available, on occasion a standard achievement test for a job or specific skills may be used to pinpoint areas in need of remediation or additional training. When training money is scarce and the emphasis on accountability is heavy, application of these tests will aid planners in allocating resources in a focused manner. For the researcher, diagnostic tests may serve both as a means of equating groups and also as a source of ideas for future research needs. Achievement tests, of course, may well be used as measures of the level of success in a variety of experimental situations, so long as the tests have acceptable reliability and validity for the situation in question.

SELECTION OF A TEST

The most important guidelines for test selection are the following related rules:

1. *Do not,* repeat, do not stop with the first test you find that appears to measure what you want, say "Eureka, I have found it!" and blithely use it in your study!

2. *Do* identify those tests that are appropriate for your study, compare them on relevant factors, and select the best one.

If you are knowledgeable concerning the qualities a test should possess and familiar with the various types of tests that are available (which you are, of course, by now), then the selection of an instrument is an orderly process. Assuming you have defined the specific purpose of your study and defined your population, the first step is to determine precisely what type of test you need. The next step is to identify and locate appropriate tests. Finally, you must do a comparative analysis of the tests and select the best one. In order to locate appropriate tests, you need to be familiar with sources of test information.

Sources of Test Information

A vast amount of test information is available to researchers, if they know where to look. Collectively, the various sources of information help the researcher to identify the possibilities, narrow the list of candidates, and made a final selection. Some of the possible sources include the following:

Mental Measurements Yearbooks.

Once you have determined the type of test you need, for example, a test of management for first-line supervisors, a logical place to start looking for tests is in the *Mental Measurements Yearbooks*, otherwise known as the *MMY*s. The *MMY*s, which are updated by supplements, have been published periodically since 1938 and represent the most comprehensive source of test information available to behavioral science researchers. *The Tenth Mental Measurements Yearbook* (Conoley & Kramer, 1989) is the latest publication in a series that includes the *MMY*s, *Tests in Print,* and other related works such as *Vocational Tests and Reviews.* The *MMY*s are expressly designed to assist test users in making informed selection decisions. The stated purposes of the *MMY* are to provide (1) factual information on all known new or revised tests in the English-speaking world, (2) objective test reviews written specifically for the MMY, and (3) comprehensive bibliographies, for specific tests, of related references from published literature. Each volume contains information on tests that have been published or revised since the previous MMY or have generated 20 or more references since the last MMY.

As Mitchell (1985), the editor of the *Ninth MMY,* suggests, getting maximum benefit from the MMYs requires becoming knowledgeable concerning their contents and the various ways of using them. At the very least, you should familiarize yourself with the organization and with the indexes provided. The basic organization of the most recent *MMY*s is encyclopedic in that all the test descriptions and reviews are presented alphabetically by test title. Thus, if you are looking for a particular test, you can go right to it without using any index. Perhaps the most important thing you need to know in order to use the *MMY*s is that the numbers given in the indexes are test numbers, not page numbers. For example, in the classified subject index, under "Specific Vocations," you will find the following entry (among others):

Situational Leadership, managers, leaders, administrators,
supervisors, and staff, see 1133.

The 1133 means that the description of the situational leadership test is entry 1133 in the main body of the volume; it does not mean that it is on page 1133 (actually, it's on page 1384). Page numbers are used only for table of contents purposes.

The *MMY* provides six indexes. The index of titles is simply an alphabetical listing of test titles. The index of acronyms gives full titles for commonly used abbreviations. Not everyone who has heard of the GMAT, for example, knows that GMAT stands for Graduate Management Admissions Test. The classified subject index lists tests alphabetically under each classification heading, e.g., "Specific Vocations." As previously illustrated, each entry also gives the population for which the test is intended. A feature new with the *Ninth MMY* is that, when appropriate, a test is listed under more than one classification. The publishers' directory and index gives the names and addresses of the publishers of all the tests included in the *MMY,* as well as a list of test numbers for each publisher. The index of names includes the names of test developers and test reviewers, as well as authors of related references. So, for example, if you heard that Professor Jeenyus had developed a new general-aptitude test, but you did not know its name, you would look under "Jeenyus"; there you would be given test numbers for all tests developed by Professor Jeenyus that were included in the volume. Lastly, the score index, a new addition to the MMYs, directs you to information concerning the scores obtained from tests in the MMY. Because of the need for updated information, a *Supplement* (Conoley, Kramer, & Mitchell, 1988) to the *Ninth MMY* was published; the practice of providing supplemental information is continuing in the future, so users of test materials need to be aware of this information.

As mentioned previously, if you are looking for information on a particular test, you can find it easily because of the alphabetical organization of the *MMY.* If you have no specific test in mind, but know generally what kind of test you need, you may use the following procedure:

1. Go to the back of the *MMY* to the classified subject index and find the appropriate classification (and subclassification, if appropriate), e.g., "Specific Vocations."

2. Identify promising titles from among those listed and their corresponding entry numbers.

3. Using the entry numbers, locate the test descriptions in the tests and reviews section of the *MMY* (the main body of the volume).

Entries for new tests in the tests and reviews section typically include the following information: title, author (developer), publisher, cost, brief description, description of the groups for whom the test is intended, norming information, validity and reliability data, group or individual test, time requirements, test references, and critical reviews by qualified reviewers. Among other things, the reviews generally cite any special requirements or problems involved in test administration, scoring, or interpretation. MMYs prior to the ninth edition, while differing organizationally, provide essentially the same information.

Tests in Print.

A very useful supplemental source of test information is *Tests in Print* or *(TIP)* (Mitchell, 1983). *TIP* is a comprehensive bibliography of all tests that have appeared in preceding MMYs. It also serves as a master index of tests that directs the reader to all original reviews that have appeared in the MMYs to date. The structure of *TIP* is very similar to that of the classified subject index of the MMYs, but considerably more information is given for each entry; for all commercially available tests, descriptions and references are given.

The criteria for inclusion of a test in *TIP* are very different from the criteria for inclusion in a MMY. As previously discussed, to be included in a new edition of the MMYs, a test must have been published or revised or have generated 20 or more references since publication of the last MMY. To be included in *TIP*, a test must simply be in print and available for purchase or use.

The main body of *TIP III*, the latest edition, is organized alphabetically, like the latest MMY. *TIP* also provides an index of titles, a classified subject index, a publishers' directory and index, and an index of names, all of which are used in the same way as they are in the MMYs. Also, as with the MMYs, it is beneficial to familiarize yourself with the format and content of *TIP* before attempting to use it. And if you are seeking a particular test, you can find it easily since entries are listed alphabetically. If not, the following procedure may be used:

1. Go to the classified subject index and find the appropriate classification.
2. Identify promising titles from among those listed and their corresponding entry numbers.
3. Using the entry numbers, locate the test descriptions in the main body of the volume.
4. If you are referred to additional information in MMYs, as you often will be, go to the suggested MMYs.

Thus, *TIP* provides information on many more tests than the MMYs, but is less comprehensive in terms of information given for each test. Both *TIP* and the MMYs are virtually indispensable tools for behavioral science researchers. As Mitchell, the editor of both *TIP III* and the *Ninth MMY,* has stated, the two publications are "interlocking volumes with extensive cross-referencing requiring their coordinated use as a system" (1985, p. 143).

Test Corporation of America Publications.

Other sources of information regarding tests include the publications of the Test Corporation of American. *Tests* (Keyser & Sweetland, 1986) lists a number of tests intended for assessment in psychology, education, and business. Although no reviews are printed, complete information is given regarding the test publisher so you can call or write for additional information. In addition, lists of tests appropriate for individuals with physical, visual, and hearing impairments are listed as well as those tests that are available in a variety of languages other than English. The *Test Critiques Compendium* (Keyser & Sweetland, 1987) includes reviews of 60 "major" tests, while the multi-volumed *Test Critiques* (Keyser & Sweetland, 1984) reviews a substantial number of tests.

Educational Testing Service Test Collection.

Sometimes you may be aware of a new test that sounds exactly like what you need but for which you can find no information. Although it sounds as if it were only intended for educational situations, an excellent source of test information, especially for recently developed tests, is the Educational Testing Service (ETS) Test Collection. The ETS Collection is an extensive, ever growing library containing, to date, more than 13,000 tests. Like the *MMY*, the library's stated purpose is to make test information available to behavioral science researchers and other interested professionals. In contrast to the *MMYs*, the ETS Collection includes unpublished as well as published tests but provides much less information per test.

The collection provides several publications and services. Probably the most valuable of these for researchers is the availability of annotated bibliographies for a wide variety of testing areas. For each test included in a bibliography, the following information is given: title, author, publication date, target population, publisher or source, and purpose of the instrument. There are currently more than 200 annotated bibliographies available, representing eight major categories: (1) achievement, (2) aptitude, (3) attitudes and interests, (4) personality, (5) sensory-motor, (6) special populations, (7) vocational/occupational, and (8) miscellaneous.

The collection publishes two sources of test-related information, one on an ongoing basis. Upon request, anyone may receive, at no charge, a pamphlet that gives the names, addresses, and telephone numbers of major U.S. publishers of standardized tests. Ten times a year the collection produces *News on Tests*, which includes announcements of new tests, citations of test reviews, new reference materials, and other related items. Because of its frequency of publication, it provides more current information on tests than the *MMYs*. A typical entry in *News on Tests* is the following:

Multidimensional Self-Esteem Inventory by Edward J. O'Brien and Seymore Epstein, 1988
Ages: Adults

Available from: Psychological Assessment Resources, P.O. Box 998, Odessa, FL 33556
A 116-item, objective, self-report inventory that provides measures of the components of
self-esteem. Theory underlying the scale is based on belief that the elements of
self-evaluation are organized in a hierarchical fashion. There are 11 subscales: global
self-esteem, competence, lovability, likability, self-control, personal power, moral self
approval, body appearance, body functioning, identity integration, and defensive self
enhancement.

Data on norms, validity, and reliability are available. (Halpern, 1989, p. 5)

The ETS Collection also provides two services to test users, Tests in Microfiche and the
Test Collection Database. Tests in Microfiche provides copies of tests that are not
available commercially. Buyers of Tests in Microfiche are given permission to make
copies for their own use. Test Collection Database makes the Test Collection library
a publicly searchable data base through Bibliographic Retrieval Services (BRS).

For further information and current prices, write ETS Test Collection, Princeton, NJ
08541, or call (609) 734-5737. Also, check your library for the availability of collection
materials and services.

Professional Journals.

There are a number of journals that regularly publish information of interest to test
users. Since a number of these journals are American Psychological Association
publications, *Psychological Abstracts* is a potential source of desired information.
Using the monthly or annual index, you can quickly determine if the *Abstracts* contain
any information on a given test. Journals of interest to test users include *Journal of
Applied Measurement, Journal of Consulting Psychology, Journal of Educational
Measurement, Journal of Personnel Psychology,* and *Educational and Psychological
Measurement.* The article reprinted at the end of Chapter 7 is an example of test
information that might be found in a professional journal.

Test Publishers and Distributors.

An additional source of information regarding tests is the publisher's test manual.
Manuals typically include detailed validity and reliability data, a description of the
population for whom the test is intended, a detailed description of the norming
procedures, the acceptable conditions of administration, scoring instructions, and
requirements for score interpretation.

As mentioned previously, however, you must be a good consumer. Relevant data
omitted from the manual are probably unfavorable to the test. Thus, if information on
subtest reliabilities is missing, they probably are not very good; if they were, they
would be reported! As the Romans used to say, *caveat emptor* ("let the buyer
beware!").

If no information can be found, or if available information is inadequate, you can
generally obtain additional data by writing to the test developer, if known. Test
developers will usually comply with such requests, especially if you agree to supply the
results of your study in return. Some test developers will respond that their data is in
Dr. Obscure's file, so allow yourself lots of time to obtain needed information!

Final selection of a test usually requires examination of the actual tests. A test that appears from all descriptions to be exactly what you need may have one or more problems detectable only by inspection of the test itself. The test may not be content valid for your study; for example, it may contain many items measuring content not covered by your treatment groups. An initial inspection copy of a test, as well as additional required copies if you select that test for your study, should be acquired from the test publisher if it is commercially available. Check to see if there is a "research version" available, which may be lower in cost than other versions. For many tests, the publisher's name and address are given in the *MMY*. If the test is not commercially available, you may be able to obtain it either in microfiche form from the ETS Collection or directly from the test developer.

Selecting from Alternatives

Eventually a decision must be reached. Once you have narrowed the number of candidates and acquired all relevant information, a comparative analysis of the tests must be made. While there are a number of factors to be considered, for example, validity data and cost, these factors are not of equal importance; the least expensive test is not necessarily the best test!

As you undoubtedly know by now, the most important factor to be considered in test selection is validity. Is one of the tests more appropriate for your sample? If you are interested in prediction, does one of the tests have a significantly higher validity coefficient? If content validity is of prime importance, are the items of one test based on the same materials that will be used in your study? These are typical questions that might be raised. If after the validity comparison there are still several tests that seem appropriate, the next factor for consideration is reliability.

Assuming all coefficients were acceptable, you would presumably select the test with the highest reliability, but there are other considerations. A factor to be considered in relation to reliability, for example, is the length of the test and the time it takes to administer it. Shorter tests are, in general, to be preferred. A test that can be administered in an hour, for example, would be considerably more convenient than a 2-hour test; shorter tests are also preferable in terms of test-taker fatigue and motivation. Since reliability is related to length, however, a shorter test will tend to be less reliable. For example, for many tests a short form is also available; the reliability of the short form is invariably lower. Thus, if a long form and a short form of a test (or two different tests of different lengths) are both valid for your study, the questions to be considered are: How much shorter? How much less reliable? If one test takes half as long to administer and is only slightly less reliable, the shorter test is probably better. For example, suppose Test A (or Form A) has a KR-20 reliability of .94 and takes 90 minutes to administer, and Test B (or Form B) has a KR-20 reliability of .90 and takes 50 minutes to administer; which would you choose? Most probably Test B. If after comparing validity and reliability data, you still have more than one candidate, you should consider administration, scoring, and interpretation requirements.

By the time you get to this point, you have probably already made a decision concerning whether you need an individually administered test. If not, and if there is no essential reason for using an individually administered test, now is the time to eliminate them from contention. Most of the time individually administered tests will not even be a consideration since they are used primarily for certain IQ and personality testing situations. When they are, however, you should keep in mind the potential disadvantages associated with their use: (1) additional cost, (2) additional time, (3) need for trained administrators, (4) complicated scoring procedures, and (5) need for trained interpreters. Of course, if the nature of your subjects or the research variable of interest requires it, by all means use an individually administered test. Either way, you should consider the administration, scoring, and interpretation requirements. In addition to the time consideration mentioned previously, you should consider factors such as unusual administration conditions, difficult scoring procedures, and sophisticated interpretation. Are you qualified to execute the requirements of the test as specified? If not, can you afford to acquire the necessary personnel? If after all this soul-searching, by some miracle you still have more than one test in the running, by all means pick the cheapest one!

There are two additional considerations in test selection that have nothing to do with the psychometric qualities of a test. Both are related to the use of tests in the workplace. First, if you are planning to use employees in your study, you should check to see what tests they have already been given. You would not want to use a leadership test with individuals who have just completed a training course involving this same leadership test! Second, you should be sensitive to the fact that both employees and managers might object to a test that contains "touchy" items. Certain personality inventories, for example, ask questions related to the sexual behavior of the responders. If there is any possibility that the test contains potentially objectionable items, either choose another test or acquire appropriate permissions before administering the test. There have been instances where researchers have been ordered to destroy (as in burn!) test results. As the old saying goes, an ounce of prevention. . .

Occasionally, you will find yourself in the position of not being able to locate a suitable test. The solution is *not* to use an inadequate test with the rationale, "Oh well, I'll do the best I can!" One logical solution is to develop your own test. Good test construction requires a variety of skills. As mentioned previously, training at least equivalent to a course in measurement is needed. If you do develop your own test, you must collect validation data; a self-developed test should not be used in a research study unless it has been pretested first with a group very similar to the group to be used in the actual study. In addition to collecting validity and reliability data, you will need to try out the administration and scoring procedures. In some cases, the results of pretesting will indicate the need for revisions and further pretesting. Sometimes this procedure may also be followed for an existing test. You may find a test that seems very appropriate but for which certain relevant types of validation data are not available. In this case you may decide to try to validate this test with your population rather than develop a test from scratch.

TEST ADMINISTRATION

There are several general guidelines for test administration of which you should be aware. First, if the testing is to be conducted in a work setting, arrangements must be made beforehand with the appropriate person, usually a human resources manager. Consultation with this individual should result in agreement as to when the testing will take place, under what conditions, and with what assistance from company personnel. The human resources manager can be very helpful in supplying such information as dates for which testing is inadvisable (e.g., beginning or ending of a quarter or fiscal year, Mondays and Fridays, and days immediately preceding or following holidays). Second, whether you are testing in a company or elsewhere, you should do everything you can to insure ideal testing conditions; a comfortable, quiet environment is more conducive to subject cooperation. Also, if testing is to take place in more than one session, the conditions of the sessions should be as identical as possible. Third, follow the Boy Scout motto and be prepared. Be thoroughly familiar with the administration procedures presented in the test manual and follow the directions precisely. If they are at all complicated, practice beforehand. Administer the test to some friends or your family; if this is not feasible, stand in front of a mirror and give it to yourself!

As with everything in life, good planning and preparation usually pay off. If you have made all necessary arrangements, secured good cooperation, and are completely familiar and comfortable with the administration procedures, the actual testing situation should go well. If some unforeseen catastrophe occurs during testing, such as an earthquake or a power failure, make careful note of the incident. If it is serious enough to invalidate the testing, you may have to try again another day with another group. If in your judgment the effects of the incident are not serious, at least mention its occurrence in your final research report. Despite the possibility of unforeseen difficulties, it is certain that the probability of all going well will be greatly increased if you adequately plan and prepare for the big day.

PREPARING DATA FOR ANALYSIS

Execution of a research study usually produces a mass of raw data resulting from the administration of one or more standardized or self-developed instruments or from the collection of naturally available data (such as number of absences from work). Collected data must be accurately scored or tallied, if appropriate, and systematically organized in a manner that facilitates analysis.

Scoring Procedures

All instruments or measures used to collect data should be scored accurately and consistently; each subject's data should be recorded using the same procedures and criteria (remember objectivity?). If absences from work is the measure used, for example, you must decide in advance how to handle an absence of four hours or less; does it count as a full absence? a half-day? or will you count by hours? Additionally, does the reason for the absence make a difference? If a standardized instrument is used, the scoring process is greatly facilitated. A test manual, for example, usually spells out the steps to be followed in scoring each test (or answer sheet), and a scoring key is often provided. If the manual is followed conscientiously and each instrument is scored carefully, scoring errors are minimized. As an extra check, it is usually a good idea to recheck all measures or tests, or at least some percentage of them. Twenty-five percent or every fourth measure or test is sufficient.

Scoring self-developed instruments, such as questionnaires and surveys, is more complex, especially if open-ended items are involved. There is no manual to follow, and the researcher has to develop and refine a scoring procedure. Steps for scoring each item and for arriving at a total score must be delineated and carefully followed. If other than objective-type test items (multiple-choice, true-false, short-answer) are to be scored, it is advisable to have another person score the tests again as a reliability check. Tentative scoring procedures should always be tried out beforehand by administering the instruments to a group of subjects from the same or a similar population as the one from which the subjects will be selected for the actual study. Problems with the instruments or with scoring procedures can be identified and corrected before it is too late to do anything about them. The procedure ultimately used to score study data should be described in detail in the final research report.

If a test-scoring service is available on your campus, and if your instrument or survey questions can be responded to on a standard, machine-scorable answer sheet, you can save yourself a lot of time and increase the accuracy of the scoring process if you take advantage of the service. If instruments are to be machine scored, answer or data sheets should be checked carefully for stray pencil marks and a percentage of them rescored by hand just to make sure that the key is correct and that the machine is scoring properly. The fact that your instruments are being scored by a machine does not relieve you of the responsibility of carefully checking your data before and after processing.

In the unlikely event that you are using a projective test, you are probably aware that these tests involve complex scoring procedures generally beyond the capabilities of beginning researchers. If such an instrument is used, however, you will want to describe the scoring procedures and qualifications of the scorers in your final report.

MEASUREMENT CONCEPTS AND NATURALLY AVAILABLE DATA

As mentioned earlier in this chapter, a great deal of attention has been given to finding and using standardized tests. Although university and professional research people are probably familiar with appropriate tests in their areas of interest, this is generally an area of unfamiliarity for business people and students. In addition, the concepts discussed here—validity, reliability, objectivity, standardization of administration, and scoring—are all important to researchers using any methodology of collecting data. Whether you need to collect data using standardized tests and human subjects or using production rates and objects, the principles are the same. If your study is to have internal validity, you will need to be confident that your data are a valid measure of whatever you are studying and that they have been collected in a reliable way.

Summary/Chapter 5

PURPOSE AND PROCESS
TYPES OF MEASUREMENT SCALES

1. Data for analysis result from the measurement of one or more variables. Depending upon the variables and the way in which they are measured, different kinds of data result, representing different scales of measurement.

2. It is important to know which type of scale is represented by your data, since different statistics are appropriate for different scales of measurement.

   A. *Nominal scales* represent the lowest level of measurement. Such a scale classifies persons or objects into two or more categories. Whatever the basis for classification, a person can only be in one category, and members of a given category have a common set of characteristics.

   B. *Ordinal scales* not only classify subjects but also rank them in terms of the degree to which they possess a characteristic of interest. Intervals between ranks are not equal.

   C. *Interval scales* have all the characteristics of nominal and ordinal scales, but in addition, they are based upon predetermined equal intervals. Most of the standardized tests used in management research, such as aptitude tests, represent interval scales. Interval scales do not have a true zero point.

   D. *Ratio scales* represent the highest, most precise, level of measurement. A ratio scale has all the advantages of the other types of scales and, in addition, has a meaningful true zero point. Because of the true zero point, not only can we say that the difference between sales of $30 million and sales of $40 million is the same as the difference between sales of $40 million and sales of $50 million, but we can also say that $60 million in sales is twice as much as $30 million in sales.

3. A statistic appropriate for a lower level of measurement may be applied to data representing a higher level of measurement; the reverse is not true.

CHARACTERISTICS OF
STANDARDIZED INSTRUMENTS

4. The time it takes to select an appropriate standardized instrument is invariably less than the time it takes to develop an instrument that measures the same thing.

5. There are thousands of standardized instruments available that yield a wide variety of data for a wide variety of purposes.

6. Selection of an instrument for a particular research purpose involves identification and selection of the most appropriate one from among alternatives.

Standardized Tests

7. A test is a means of measuring the knowledge, skill, feeling, intelligence, or aptitude of an individual or group.

8. Test *objectivity* means that an individual's score is not affected by the person scoring the test.

9. Validity is the most important quality of any test. *Validity* is concerned with what a test measures and for whom it is appropriate; *reliability* refers to the consistency with which a test measures whatever it measures.

10. Specification of conditions of administration, directions for scoring, and guidelines for interpretation are important characteristics of standardized tests.

11. A table of norms presents raw scores and one or more equivalent transformations, such as corresponding percentile ranks.

Validity

12. *Validity* is the degree to which a test measures what it is supposed to measure.

13. A test is not valid per se; it is valid for a particular purpose and for a particular group.

Content Validity

14. *Content validity* is the degree to which a test measures an intended content area.

15. *Item validity* is concerned with whether the test items represent measurement in the intended content area, and *sampling validity* is concerned with how well the test samples the total content area.

16. Content validity is of prime importance for achievement tests. Content validity is determined by expert judgment. When selecting a test for a research study the researcher assumes the role of "expert" and determines whether the test is content valid for her or his study.

Construct Validity

17. *Construct validity* is the degree to which a test measures an intended hypothetical construct. A *construct* is a nonobservable trait, such as intelligence, which explains behavior.

18. Validating a test of a construct involves testing hypotheses deduced from a theory concerning the construct.

Concurrent Validity

19. *Concurrent validity* is the degree to which the scores on a test are related to the scores on another, already established, test administered at the same time, or to some other valid criterion available at the same time.

20. The relationship method involves determining the relationship between scores on the test and scores on some other established test or criterion (e.g., GPA or some other quantifiable measure).

21. The discrimination method of establishing concurrent validity involves determining whether test scores can be used to discriminate between persons who possess a certain characteristic and those who do not or between those who possess it and those who possess it to a greater degree.

Predictive Validity

22. *Predictive validity* is the degree to which a test can predict how well an individual will do in a future situation.

23. The predictive validity of a test is determined by establishing the relationship between scores on the test and some measure of success in the situation of interest.

24. The test used to predict success is referred to as the *predictor,* and the behavior predicted is referred to as the *criterion.*

Reliability

25. *Reliability* is the degree to which a test consistently measures whatever it measures.

26. Reliability is expressed numerically, usually as a coefficient; a high coefficient indicates high reliability.

27. A valid test is always reliable but a reliable test is not necessarily valid.

Test-Retest Reliability

28. *Test-retest reliability* is the degree to which scores are consistent over time.

29. Test-retest reliability is established by determining the relationship between scores resulting from administering the same test, to the same group, on different occasions.

30. A major problem with test-retest reliability is knowing how much time should elapse between the two testing sessions.

Equivalent-Forms Reliability

31. *Equivalent forms* of a test are two tests that are identical in every way except for the actual items included.

32. Equivalent-forms reliability is determined by establishing the relationship between scores resulting from administering two different forms of the same test, to the same group, at the same time.

33. Equivalent-forms reliability is the most acceptable estimate of reliability for most tests used in research and is the most commonly used.

34. The major problems associated with equivalent-forms reliability are the difficulty of constructing two forms that are essentially equivalent and the feasibility of administering two different forms of the same test.

Split-Half Reliability

35. *Split-half reliability* is determined by establishing the relationship between the scores on two equivalent halves of a test administered to a total group at one time.

36. Since longer tests tend to be more reliable, and since split-half reliability represents the reliability of a test only half as long as the actual test, a correction known as the Spearman-Brown prophecy formula must be applied to the coefficient.

Rationale Equivalence Reliability

37. *Rationale equivalence reliability* is not established through correlation but rather estimates internal consistency by determining how all items on a test relate to all other items and to the total test.

38. Rationale equivalence reliability is usually determined through application of the Kuder-Richardson (KR-20 or KR-21) formulas.

Reliability Coefficients

39. What constitutes an acceptable level of reliability is to some degree determined by the type of test, although, of course, a coefficient over .90 would be acceptable for any test.

40. If a test is composed of several subtests, then the reliability of each subtest must be evaluated, not just the reliability of the total test.

Standard Error of Measurement

41. The *standard error of measurement (SE$_m$)* is an estimate of how often you can expect errors of a given size.

42. A small SE_m indicates high reliability; a large SE_m, low reliability.

43. The SE_m allows us to measure how much difference there probably is between a person's obtained score and true score, the size of this difference being a function of the reliability of the test.

Interjudge/Intrajudge Reliability

44. When judgment in evaluation is concerned, as with rating scales, observation instruments, or tests such as essays and answers of more than one-word responses, we need to be concerned with interjudge and/or intrajudge reliability.

45. *Interjudge reliability* refers to the reliability of two or more independent scorers; *intrajudge reliability* refers to the reliability of the scoring of individual scorers.

46. Estimates of interjudge or intrajudge reliability are usually obtained using correlational techniques but can also be expressed simply as percent agreement.

TYPES OF TESTS

Personality

47. Tests of personality are designed to measure characteristics of individuals along a number of dimensions and to assess feelings and attitudes toward self, others, and a variety of other activities, institutions, and situations.

48. They may well be the most used tests in research.

Nonprojective Tests

Personality Inventories

49. Personality inventories present lists of questions or statements describing behaviors characteristic of certain personality traits, and the individual is asked to indicate (yes, no, undecided) whether the statement describes him or her.

50. Personality inventories may be specific and measure only one trait, such as introversion versus extroversion, or may be general and measure a number of traits.

Attitude Scales

51. Attitude scales attempt to determine what an individual believes, perceives, or feels.

52. Attitudes can be measured toward self, others, and a variety of other activities, institutions, or situations.

53. The most common scales used to measure attitudes are Likert scales and semantic differential scales.

54. Measures of "attitude toward self" are referred to as measures of self-concept.

55. Rating scales are also used to measure attitudes toward others and toward situations and organizations.

Creativity Tests

56. Tests of creativity are really tests designed to measure those personality characteristics that are related to creative behavior.

57. One such trait is referred to as divergent thinking; unlike convergent thinkers, who tend to look for the right answer, divergent thinkers tend to seek alternatives.

Interest Inventories

58. An interest inventory asks an individual to indicate personal likes and dislikes, such as kinds of activities he or she likes to engage in.

59. The most widely used type of interest measure is the vocational interest inventory.

Projective Tests

60. Projective tests were developed in an attempt to eliminate some of the major problems inherent in the use of self-report measures. Such tets are used mainly by clinical psychologists and infrequently by other researchers.

Aptitude

61. Aptitude tests are measures of potential used to predict how well someone is likely to perform in a future situation.

62. Tests of general aptitude are variously referred to as tests of general mental ability, intelligence tests, scholastic aptitude tests or personnel tests.

63. Virtually all aptitude tests are standardized, but extreme caution must be used in selection of aptitude tests in the workplace.

General Aptitude

64. General aptitude tests typically ask the individual to perform a variety of verbal and/or nonverbal tasks that measure the individual's ability to apply knowledge and solve problems.

65. While general aptitude tests are intended to be measures of innate ability or potential, they appear actually to measure current ability.

66. Culture-fair tests attempt to exclude culturally related items, such as items that include words that might not be familiar to certain groups of individuals.

Specific Aptitude

67. Specific aptitude tests attempt to predict the level of performance that can be expected of an individual following future instruction or training in a specific area or areas.

68. Aptitude tests are available for a wide variety of areas ranging from clerical to mechanical skills.

69. In addition to specific area tests, multi-aptitude batteries measure aptitudes in several related areas are also available.

Achievement Tests

70. Achievement tests measure the current status of individuals with respect to proficiency in given areas of knowledge or skill.

71. Work-related, standardized achievement tests are commonly used in situations involving licensing for occupations such as pilots, accountants, nurses, lawyers, and cosmeticians. In addition, other occupations such as human resources personnel and financial planners have established standardized achievement tests for certification of individuals within the profession.

SELECTION OF A TEST

72. *Do not* use the first test you find that appears to measure what you want.

73. *Do* identify those tests that are appropriate for your study, compare them on relevant factors, and select the best one.

Sources of Test Information

Mental Measurements Yearbooks

74. The *Mental Measurements Yearbooks* (*MMY*s) represent the most comprehensive source of test information available to educational researchers.

75. The stated purposes of the latest *MMY* are to provide: (a) factual information on all known new or revised tests, (b) objective test reviews, and (c) comprehensive bibliographies.

76. Perhaps the most important thing you need to know in order to use the *MMY*s is that all the numbers given by the indexes are test numbers, not page numbers.

Tests in Print

77. *Tests in Print (TIP)* is a comprehensive bibliography of all tests that have appeared in preceding *MMY*s.

78. *TIP* also serves as a master index of tests, which directs the reader to all original reviews that have appeared in the *MMY*s to date.

79. *TIP* provides information on many more tests than the *MMY*s but is less comprehensive in terms of information given for each test.

Test Corporation of America Publications

80. Other sources of test information include *Tests, Test Critiques,* and the *Test Critiques Compendium.*

Educational Testing Service Test Collection

81. The ETS Test Collection is an extensive, ever growing library containing, to date, more than 13,000 tests.

82. Like the *MMY*s, its stated purpose is to make test information available to researchers and other interested professionals.

83. In contrast to the *MMY*s, it includes unpublished tests but provides much less information per test.

84. The collection provides several publications and services; probably the most valuable of these for researchers is the availability of annotated test bibliographies for a wide variety of testing areas.

Professional Journals

85. There are a number of journals that regularly publish information of interest to test users.

86. Since a number of these journals are American Psychological Association publications, *Psychological Abstracts* is a potential source of desired test information.

Test Publishers and Distributors

87. A good source of information on tests is publishers' test manuals.

88. If no information can be found or if available information is inadequate, you can generally obtain additional data by writing to the test developer, if known.

89. Final selection of a test usually requires examination of the actual tests.

Selecting from Alternatives

90. Final selection of a test requires a comparative analysis of the alternatives.

91. The most important factor to be considered is validity.

92. The next factor for consideration is reliability.

93. Other important factors include administration, scoring, and interpretation requirements.

94. A self-developed test should not be used in a research study unless it has been pretested first with a group very similar to the group to be used in the actual study.

TEST ADMINISTRATION

95. If testing is to be conducted in a work setting, arrangements should be made beforehand with the appropriate person, usually a human resources manager.

96. Every effort should be made to insure ideal testing conditions.

97. Be thoroughly familiar with the administration procedures presented in the test manual and follow the directions precisely.

PREPARING DATA FOR ANALYSIS

Scoring Procedures

98. All instruments administered should be scored accurately and consistently; each subject's instrument should be scored using the same procedures and criteria.

99. When a standardized instrument is used, the scoring process is greatly facilitated. The test manual usually spells out the steps to be followed in scoring each test (or answer sheet), and a scoring key is often provided.

100. Scoring self-developed instruments, such as questionnaires and surveys, is more complex, especially if open-ended items are involved. There is no manual to follow, and the researcher has to develop and refine a scoring procedure. Steps for scoring each item and for arriving at a total score must be delineated and carefully followed. If other than objective-type test items (multiple-choice, true-false) are to be scored, it is advisable to have another person score the tests again as a reliability check. Tentative scoring procedures should always be tried out beforehand by administering the instruments to a group of subjects from the same or a similar population as the one from which the subjects will be selected for the actual study.

101. If a test scoring service is available on your campus, and if your test or survey questions can be responded to on a standard, machine-scorable answer sheet, you can save yourself a lot of time and increase the accuracy of the scoring process if you take advantage of the service.

MEASUREMENT CONCEPTS AND NATURALLY AVAILABLE DATA

102. The concepts of validity, reliability, objectivity, standardization of administration, and scoring are all important to researchers using any methodology of collecting data.

103. Whether you need to collect data using standardized tests and human subjects or using production rates and objects, the principles are the same.

104. If your study is to have internal validity, you will need to be confident that your data are a valid measure of whatever you are studying and that they have been collected in a reliable way.

Project III: Subsection 2 Performance Criteria

All the information required for your instrument(s) will be found in *Mental Measurements Yearbooks* or one of the other resources listed. Following the description of the tests, you should present a comparative analysis that forms a rationale for your selection of the "most acceptable" test for your study. As an example, you might indicate that several tests have similar reliability coefficients reported but that one of the tests is more appropriate for your subjects.

In addition to reviewing the article following Chapter 7, you will probably find it useful to review the Instrument section of the student example following Chapter 10 to see the level of proficiency required for this task.

REFERENCES

BURKE, W. W. (1988). *Leadership report* (2nd ed.). King of Prussia, PA: Organization Design and Development.

BUROS, O. K. (ED.). (1938–1978). *Mental measurements yearbooks.* Lincoln, NB: University of Nebraska Press.

CAPRINO, M. (1989, May 7). Honesty testing replacing lie detector. *The Miami Herald,* pp. 1–2F.

CONOLEY, J. C., & KRAMER, J. J. (1989). *The tenth mental measurements yearbook.* Lincoln, NB: University of Nebraska Press.

CONOLEY, J. C., KRAMER, J. J., & MITCHELL, J. V., JR. (EDS.). (1988). *Supplement to the ninth mental measurements yearbook.* Lincoln, NB: University of Nebraska Press.

COOKE, R. A., & ROUSSEAU, D. M. (1988). Behavioral norms and expectations. *Group & Organization Studies,* 13(3), 245–273.

CROSBY, L. A. (1985). Review of Graduate Management Admission Test. In J. V. Mitchell, Jr. (Ed.), *The ninth mental measurements yearbook: Vol. 2* (pp. 620–621). Lincoln, NB: University of Nebraska Press.

DIPBOYE, R. L. (1978). Review of Leader Behavior Description Questionnaire. In O. K. Buros (Ed.), *The eighth mental measurements yearbook* (pp. 1745–1747). Lincoln, NB: University of Nebraska Press.

FIEDLER, F. E., & CHEMERS, M. (1974). *Leadership and effective management.* New York: Scott, Foresman.

FORTUNE 500. (1990, April). *Fortune,* p. 346.

GUILFORD, J. P. (1959). Three faces of intellect. *American Psychologist, 14,* 469–479.

GUILFORD, J. P. (1967). *The nature of human intelligence.* New York: McGraw-Hill.

HACKMAN, J. R., & OLDHAM, G. R. (1980). *Work redesign.* Reading, MA: Addison-Wesley.

HALPERN, M. (ED.). (1989, September.) *News on tests.* Princeton, NJ: Educational Testing Service Test Collection.

HO, K. (1988). The dimensionality and occupational discriminating power of the Herrmann Brain Dominance Instrument. *Dissertation Abstracts International, 49,* 6B. (University Microfilms No. 8811716).

KEYSER, D. J., & SWEETLAND, R. C. (EDS.). (1984). *Test critiques.* Kansas City: Test Corporation of America.

KEYSER, D. J., & SWEETLAND, R. C. (EDS.). (1986). *Tests: A comprehensive reference for assessments in psychology, education, and business* (2nd ed.). Kansas City: Test Corporation of America.

KEYSER, D. J., & SWEETLAND, R. C. (EDS.). (1987). *Test critiques compendium.* Kansas City: Test Corporation of America.

LEADER BEHAVIOR DESCRIPTION QUESTIONNAIRE (LBDQ-12). (1957). Columbus, OH: Ohio State University.

LEDVINKA, J., & BOULTON, W. R. (1985). Review of Graduate Management Admission Test. In J. V. Mitchell, Jr. (Ed.), *The ninth mental measurements yearbook:* Vol. 2 (pp. 621–622). Lincoln, NB: University of Nebraska Press.

LIKERT, R. (1932). A technique for the measurement of attitudes. *Archives of Psychology,* No. 140.

MCBER AND COMPANY. (1980). *Management Style Questionnaire.* Boston: Author.

MCCLELLAND, D. C. (1961). *The achieving society.* Princeton, NJ: Van Nostrand.

MICHALAK, D. (1983). *Management Styles Questionnaire.* New York: Harper & Row.

MITCHELL, J. V., JR. (ED.). (1983). *Tests in print III: An index to tests, test reviews, and the literature on specific tests.* Lincoln, NB: The University of Nebraska Press.

MITCHELL, J. V., JR. (ED.). (1985). *The ninth mental measurements yearbook.* Lincoln, NB: University of Nebraska Press.

NUNNALLY, J. C. (1978). *Psychometric theory* (2nd ed.). New York: McGraw-Hill.

OSGOOD, C. E., SUCI, G. J., & TANNENBAUM, P. H. (1957). *The measurement of meaning.* Urbana, IL: University of Illinois Press.

SCHMIDT, F. L. (1985). Review of Wonderlic Personnel Test. In J. V. Mitchell, Jr. (Ed.), *The ninth mental measurements yearbook: Vol. 2* (pp. 1755–1756). Lincoln, NB: University of Nebraska Press.

SCHOENFELDT, L. F. (1985). Review of Wonderlic Personnel Test. In J. V. Mitchell, Jr. (Ed.), *The ninth mental measurements yearbook: Vol. 2* (pp. 1757–1758). Lincoln, NB: University of Nebraska Press.

SCHULER, R. S. (1987). *Personnel and human resource management* (3rd ed.). St. Paul, MN: West.

SELIGMAN, D. (1989, July 17). More Normal Nonsense. *Fortune,* p. 118.

SNIDER, J. G., & OSGOOD, C. E. (1969). *Semantic differential technique: A sourcebook.* Chicago: Aldine Press.

TORRANCE, E. P. (1984). *Torrance Tests of Creative Thinking.* Bensenville, IL: Scholastic Testing Service.

The historical researcher's task is to evaluate and weigh objectively all evidence in arriving at the most tenable conclusion. (page 203)

6

The Historical Method

Objectives
After reading Chapter 6, you should be able to do the following:

1. Briefly state the purpose of historical research.

2. List and briefly describe the major steps involved in designing and conducting a historical research study.

3. Explain why primary sources of data are preferable to secondary sources.

4. Briefly describe external and internal criticism of data.

5. Briefly describe four factors that should be considered in determining the accuracy of documents.

Project III Subsection 3: Design and Procedures Guidelines

Having stated a problem, formulated one or more hypotheses, described a sample, and selected one or more measuring instruments you are now ready to develop the last subsection of the *method* section of a research report. This should include a description of the research design and specific procedures. Chapters 6 through 10 will help you determine the appropriate design for your study and clarify some of the procedures you need to include in your method section.

In these chapters, you will be working with different types of research. These include the historical method (this chapter), the descriptive method (Chapter 7), the correlational method (Chapter 8), the causal–comparative method (Chapter 9), and the experimental method (Chapter 10). Design and research procedures will be illustrated with each of these methods. Examples of published research in each of these methods are given in the readings following Chapters 6, 7, 8, and 9 to serve as helps in illustrating what you are learning to do. Experimental research is illustrated in the Chapter 1 reading.

(See Performance Criteria, p. 446)

DEFINITION AND PURPOSE

While research studies have a number of similar components, such as a defined problem and a set of conclusions, specific procedures in a study are to a great extent determined by the particular method of research involved. As each of the five methods of research (historical, descriptive, correlational, causal-comparative, and experimental) has a unique purpose, application of each method entails a unique set of procedures and concerns. Chapters 6 through 10 will give you a more detailed oversight of each of these specific research methods. As previously suggested, however, there are procedural steps common to all research studies; all studies, for example, involve some type of data collection and analysis.

Historical research is the systematic collection and objective evaluation of data related to past occurrences in order to test hypotheses concerning causes, effects, or trends of those events that may help to explain present events and anticipate future events. Many beginning researchers tend to think of historical research as a rather unscientific method of investigation. This is only true, however, of poorly designed and conducted historical research. Admittedly, the nature of historical research precludes exercise of many of the control procedures characteristic of other methods; if well done, however, historical research also involves systematic, objective data collection and analysis and the confirmation or disconfirmation of hypotheses.

Many current business-and-management practices, theories, and issues can be better understood in light of past experiences. The ethics issue, for example, is not a new one in business, nor is participatory management an innovation of the 1980s. A knowledge of the history of business and management can yield insight into the circumstances involved in the evolution of the current business system as well as practices and approaches that have been found to be ineffective or infeasible. As Griffin (1988) so eloquently states at the end of the quality circles study in Chapter 1:

> The behavioral sciences have enormous potential to add to organizational effectiveness. Carefully managed interventions like quality circles have the potential to aid managers as they attempt to compete in both domestic and international arenas. The key to effectiveness may be to avoid a faddish, bandwagon approach and, instead, to develop an appropriate menu of interventions that we have some basis for recommending and some understanding of how to manage (pp. 356–357).

Ohio historians Loveday, Blackford, and Kerr have written a book intended to assist amateurs and company insiders in preparing historical studies of their own companies (Schechter, 1990). They see the study of an individual company's history as providing insight into corporate culture, structure, values, and decision making, as well as being a potential marketing and training methodology. In discussing the value of company history to current employees, Blackford commented that newcomers without an understanding of the past history of the company may not understand how a decision made 5 to 10 years ago affects the present functioning of the company.

Studying the history of business and management might lead one to believe that not only is there not much that is new under the business sun but also that business people never learn; some practices seem to appear and disappear with regularity. Most students of Japanese management know, for example, that Edward Deming, an American government statistician, is credited with introducing Japanese business to the quality-control methods that later became the basis for quality circles. Drucker (1973) has pointed out, however, that group problem solving was used at least as far back as 1890 at Zeiss, the famous German optical company; in addition, AT&T began using group problem solving as far back as 1925, and Disney, IBM, and others had established the techniques well before World War II (Ingle, 1982).

THE HISTORICAL RESEARCH PROCESS

The steps involved in conducting a historical research study are essentially the same as for other types of research:

1. Definition of a problem
2. Formulation of hypotheses (or questions to be answered)
3. Systematic collection of data
4. Objective evaluation of data
5. Confirmation or disconfirmation of hypotheses

In conducting a historical study, on the one hand, the researcher can neither manipulate nor control any of the variables. On the other hand, there is no way the researcher can affect events of the past; what has happened has happened. The researcher can, however, apply scientific objectivity in attempting to determine exactly what did happen.

Definition of a Problem

The purpose of a historical research study should not be to find out what is already known about a topic and to retell it. Recall that the goal of all scientific research in general, and business-and-management research in particular, is to explain, predict, and/or control phenomena. The nature of historical research, of course, eliminates control of phenomena; therefore, the purpose of a historical research study should be to explain or predict, not to rehash. The purpose of a historical research study is not to prove a point or to support a pet position of the researcher. One can easily verify almost any point of view by consciously or unconsciously "overlooking" evidence to the contrary. There are probably data available to support almost any position; the historical researcher's task is to evaluate and weigh objectively all evidence in arriving at the most tenable conclusion. For example, a number of articles in popular business magazines during the middle to late 1980s blamed the education of business people holding a master's degree in business administration (MBA) for causing a very short-term focus on the quarterly bottom line. One could do a historical study describing how the number of MBAs has increased in the last decade and how emphasis on profitability in companies has correspondingly increased. Of course such a study would indicate very poor critical analysis, since two separate, independent sets of factors are probably responsible for each of these trends rather than one being the cause or effect of the other. To avoid this sort of biased data collection and analysis, one probably should avoid topics about which one has strong feelings; it's a lot easier to be objective when you aren't emotionally involved.

As with the other methods of research, the purpose of a historical research study should be to discover new knowledge or to clarify, correct, or expand existing knowledge. For example, the article at the end of this chapter involves a study about the impact the deaths of chief executive officers (CEOs) have on investor wealth. In the introduction, the authors point out the extensive amount of research that already exists in the general area of management turnover and state that additional research on the determinants of turnover will probably yield low results. Little research was found on the impact of the deaths of key executives on company stock—certainly a matter of interest not only to investors but also to employees!

Worthwhile historical research problems are identified in much the same way as are problems for other types of research. The researchers in the article on investor wealth just mentioned, for example, point out a number of studies suggesting that research on turnover be redirected from looking at antecedents to looking at consequences. It is just as important in historical research as in any other method to formulate a manageable, well-defined problem; otherwise it is likely that an overwhelming amount of data will be collected, considerably complicating analysis and synthesis of the data and the drawing of adequately documented conclusions. As a way to define the problem specifically, the article limited its study to officers' deaths reported in the *Wall Street Journal* between 1967 and 1981; in the interest of being able to obtain usable data, the sample was further reduced to include only those firms that were traded on the New York or American stock exchanges.

Rather than having to limit the data that will be used, an opposite concern of historical researchers is the possibility that a problem will be selected for which insufficient data are available. Unlike researchers utilizing the other methods of research, the historical researcher cannot "create" data by administering instruments such as attitude surveys or opinion questionnaires to subjects. It is sometimes possible, however, to interview participants or observers of an event. Even in these situations, however, the number of persons who can be interviewed and the kinds of questions that can be asked are usually limited. The historical researcher is normally limited to whatever data are already available. Thus, if insufficient data are available, the problem will be inadequately investigated, and the hypothesis will be inadequately tested; conclusions concerning the confirmation or disconfirmation of such hypotheses will be extremely tentative at best.

It is better to conduct an in-depth study of a well-defined problem with one or more specific, well-stated hypotheses than to investigate either a too broadly stated problem with a fuzzy hypothesis or a problem for which insufficient data are available with a virtually untestable hypothesis. As with other methods of research, the hypothesis guides the data collection. If the hypothesis is well stated, and if sufficient data are available, the collection and logical analysis of that data will confirm or disconfirm the hypothesis.

Data Collection

In a historical research study, the review of related literature and the study procedures are part of the same process (remember, there are no measuring instruments). The review of the literature does not take place before data collection; this does not mean, of course, that the literature is not consulted to identify a problem initially and estimate whether sufficient data will be available to conduct the study. The term *literature* takes on a much broader meaning in a historical study and refers to all sorts of written communication; in addition, identification, acquisition, and review of the literature is considerably more complex. Written communication may be in the form of legal documents, records, minutes of meetings, letters, and other documents, which will not normally be indexed alphabetically by subject, author, and title in a library. Thus, identification of such data requires considerably more detective work on the part of the researcher. Further, unless the problem deals with a local event or issue, it is not uncommon for identified relevant documents to be available only at distant locations, in a special library collection, for example. In such cases, proper examination of the data requires either considerable travel or, when feasible, extensive reproduction of materials. Both of these alternatives present the researcher with problems. Travel requires that the researcher have a healthy bank account (which few do, as pointed out in Chapter 4), unless, of course, the effort is supported by a funding agency or company. Reproduction (for example, acquiring photocopies of documents in a private collection) can also become costly and often wasteful; a 50-page document may turn out to contain only one paragraph directly related to the problem under investigation. A useful analogy for the potential historical researcher to keep in mind is that many legal cases involve extensive historical research. In the pretrial investigation of the Iran-Contra affair, Marine Lt. Col. Oliver North's attorneys asked for approximately 40,000 pages of classified documents by December of 1988 ("Reagan for the Defense?" 1988).

A historical research study in business may also involve interviews with persons who participated in the event or process under investigation, if it occurred in the recent past, or an examination of "relics and remains," such as annual reports. Similar problems apply in these situations as when only written documents are involved; they are more difficult to identify, they may be located some distance from the researcher, and they may be unproductive sources after all. An interview with a person believed to have been involved in an incident, for example, may reveal that she or he was only peripherally involved or recollects only partially the details of the events. Again, the analogy of the legal case applies. How often have we read accounts or seen TV coverage of witnesses stating that they simply "don't remember" conversations or meetings?

Sources of data in a historical research study are classified as primary sources or secondary sources. *Primary sources* constitute firsthand information, such as original documents and reports by actual participants or direct observers; *secondary sources* constitute secondhand information, such as reference books (encyclopedias, for example) or reports by relatives or friends of actual participants or observers. A worker who participated in the strike at Safety Last Airlines would be a primary source of data concerning the event; her or his spouse would be a secondary source. Primary sources are definitely to be preferred; the further removed the evidence is, the less comprehensive and accurate the resulting data are likely to be. For many years one of the authors of this book has used an exercise in an organizational behavior class to make this point. Using a sentence from a book (Hampton, Summer, & Webber, 1982, pp. 207–208), the professor asks a student to read it and then whisper the statement to the student behind him or her; the sentence is as follows:

> One academic experiment suggests that at any given instant in a college lecture hall, 20 percent of both men and women are thinking about sex, 60 percent are off on some mental trip of their own, and the remaining 20 percent are concentrating on the professor (Cameron, 1968).

Very seldom does the citation, "Cameron, 1968," make it to the second student; by the time the message has been passed up and down the rows of the classroom, the only thing the last student usually hears is that the original message involves something about a professor, students, a classroom, and sex! Obviously there is a considerable discrepancy between the first version and the last one.

Because primary sources are admittedly more difficult to acquire, a common criticism of historical research is excessive reliance on secondary sources. It is better to select a less pretentious problem for which primary sources are available and accessible than inadequately to investigate the problem of the year. Of course, the further back in time the event under study occurred, the more likely it is that secondary sources may also have to be used. As a general rule, however, the more primary sources, the better.

The process of reviewing and abstracting pertinent data from primary and secondary sources is essentially the one described in Chapter 2:

1. Assess the source's relevancy to your problem.
2. Record complete bibliographic information.
3. Code the data from each source with respect to the hypothesis (or aspect of a hypothesis) to which it relates.
4. Summarize the pertinent information.
5. Note questions, comments, and quotations.

One slight difference is that owing to the nature of historical sources, several different note cards may be required for any one source. Minutes of an annual meeting, for example, might include information relating to two hypotheses; to facilitate later analysis and organization of data, they are best recorded separately. A major difference is that historical sources must also be subjected to a careful analysis to determine both their authenticity and their accuracy.

Data Analysis: External and Internal Criticism

When you read a report of a completed study in a professional journal, written by the person who conducted the research, you can generally assume that the report is accurate; the reported procedures and results can be assumed to be the procedure and results that actually occurred. This is not true with historical sources. Historical sources exist independently of your study; they were not written or developed for use in a research project. Thus, while they may very well serve the purpose for which they were created, they may not serve your purpose. As an example, a researcher who relied on annual reports to provide definitive data would be running counter to the widespread belief that such documents, with their glossy illustrations and extravagant prose, are essentially corporate advertising. In an article on evaluating annual reports, however, John Kaweske, a mutual fund group vice president suggests: "I would be wary of a company whose chairman didn't acknowledge *any* problems" (Micheli, 1988). The article goes on to suggest what students have long known: Footnotes may contain the most important information available.

All sources of historical data must be subjected to rigorous scientific analysis to determine both their authenticity (external criticism) and their accuracy (internal criticism). As with the story of Aristotle and his fly with five legs mentioned in Chapter 1, too often statements are uncritically accepted as factual statements if they are made by well-known persons. An authority in one area may have opinions concerning other areas, but they are not necessarily based on facts. Similarly, the fact that records are "official" does not necessarily mean that all information contained in those records is accurate. A newspaper story might quote a company representative, for example, stating that his company would not tolerate sexual harassment of its employees. This would probably be an opinion, however, and would not be objective evidence. Thus, for each source, first it must be determined whether it is authentic (was this statement really made by the company representative?), and second, a judgment must be made concerning the accuracy of its contents.

External criticism, or the establishment of authenticity, is generally not the problem in business research. The researcher does not usually have to worry about possible hoaxes or forgeries; in the case just cited, a simple phone call to the company representative's office could confirm or deny the authenticity of the quotation. If the researcher is dealing with a problem for which sources are relatively old and for which authenticity is not necessarily a given, there are a number of scientific techniques available. The age of a document or relic, for example, can be fairly accurately estimated by applying various physical and chemical tests. It's difficult to image a business research problem, however, where this would be an issue.

Internal criticism, establishment of accuracy, is considerably more difficult. It might appear to the casual observer that at least the financial records in an annual reports would include fairly straightforward accounting of the financial state of a particular firm. There exists, however, a governmental agency that is an offspring of the Securities and Exchange Commission called the Financial Accounting Standards Board (FASB); this board is charged with "narrowing accounting alternatives" (Loomis, 1988, p. 93). During 1988, FASB instituted changes in cash-flow statements that appeared for the first time in 1988 annual reports; other changes in reporting standards required in 1988 would have changed General Motors' 1987 revenues from the reported $102 billion to $114 under the new guidelines. Many other similar changes were made at that same time. Imagine the problems of a researcher trying to compare 1987 figures with those from 1988. In determining the accuracy of documents there are at least four factors that must be considered:

1. *Knowledge and competence of the author.* It must be determined whether the person who wrote the document is, or was, a competent person and a person in a position to be knowledgeable concerning what actually occurred. The company representative in the previous example concerning sexual harassment might be an employee of a public relations firm that has a contract with the company in question; such a person might have no knowledge of actual working conditions in the company.

2. *Time delay.* An important consideration is how much time is likely to have elapsed between the event's occurrence and the recording of the facts. Reports written while an event is occurring (such as minutes of meetings) or shortly after (such as entries in a diary or log—as the IRS suggests for business expenses) are more likely to be accurate than reports written some time after, such as an anecdote in an autobiography. It was interesting to compare, for example, the "recollections" of government officials during the Nixon era with the audiotapes made in the Oval Office!

3. *Bias and motives of the author(s).* People often report or record incorrect information. Such distortion of the truth may be intentional or unintentional. People, for example, tend to remember what they want to remember. People also tend to amplify and add little details, in order to make a story more interesting. A more serious problem occurs when the recorder has motives for consciously or unconsciously misinterpreting the facts. An account of working conditions prior to a strike given by management and one given by a union official would probably differ considerably. Similarly, the accounts of practices at various companies recorded by consultants in the "popular management" books may ultimately prove to be an unconscious attempt on the part of the author to tout his or her own expertise. Similarly, published recollections by well-known business leaders may provide a biased view of activities and practices.

4. *Consistency of data.* Each piece of evidence must be compared with all other pieces to determine the degree of agreement. If one observer's account disagrees with those of most other observers, his or her testimony may be suspect. Thus, in a sense, by the very fact that they agree, sources may validate their accuracy.

Having reviewed, abstracted, and evaluated the data, the researcher then organizes and synthesizes the findings. The final research report is prepared after this important step.

Data Synthesis

As with a review of related literature, historical data should be organized and synthesized, and conclusions and generalizations should be formulated. Just as a review of literature should not be a series of annotations, the results of a historical study should not be a chronological listing of events. Critics of historical research question the validity of generalizations based on events that can never be exactly duplicated. On the one hand, this concern has some merit and supports the need for extreme caution in forming generalizations. On the other hand, historical research may serve the useful purpose of refuting commonly held misconceptions. Using common sense, most of us would probably assume that the death of a CEO would certainly send a company's stock into a downward trend; the article at the end of this chapter suggests, "It ain't necessarily so!" At any rate, the problem of generalization is not unique to historical research. It is virtually impossible to duplicate exactly any business research study involving human beings, even highly controlled experimental studies. With historical research, as with other research methods, the more similar a new situation is to a former situation, the more applicable generalizations based on the past situation will be. The rationale for using the case study method in business education is based on the premise that one can gain from the past experiences of others.

Since summarization of historical research data usually involves logical analysis rather than statistical analysis, the researcher must take care to be as objective as possible. It is very easy to "overlook" or discard evidence that does not support, or contradicts, the research hypothesis. One may, for example, subconsciously apply stricter criteria when engaged in internal criticism of unwanted data. You may want to adopt a caveat from the medical field: if in doubt, get a second opinion. From time to time even the most experienced experts in any field feel uncomfortable with a particular situation and find it helpful to find an unbiased and respected colleague and ask, "Take a look at this and tell me what you think."

You probably realize by now that there is a lot more to historical research than you originally thought. Even a "simple" request for a historical account of a company's background can become fairly difficult when you begin to discover important company myths that just aren't so, or the existence of a skeleton in the file room. Although the complex demands of data collection and analysis generally require skill, experience, and resources beyond those of the beginning researcher (Berlinger, 1978; Block, 1971), interested students may want to ask the Ohio Historical Society for information regarding procedures for writing company histories (Schechter, 1990).

Summary/Chapter 6

DEFINITION AND PURPOSE

1. Historical research is the systematic collection and objective evaluation of data related to past occurrences in order to test hypotheses concerning causes, effects, or trends of these events that may help to explain present events and anticipate future events.

2. The steps involved in conducting a historical research study are essentially the same as for other types of research: (a) definition of a problem; (b) formulation of hypotheses (or

questions to be answered); (c) systematic collection of data; (d) objective evaluation of data; and (e) confirmation or disconfirmation of hypotheses.

THE HISTORICAL RESEARCH PROCESS

Definition of a Problem

3. The purpose of a historical research study should be to explain or predict, not to rehash.

4. The historical researcher is basically limited to whatever data are already available.

5. It is much better to study in depth a well-defined problem with one or more specific, well-stated hypotheses, than to investigate either a too-broadly stated problem with a fuzzy hypothesis or a problem for which insufficient data are available.

Data Collection

6. In a historical research study, the review of related literature and study procedures are part of the same process.

7. The term *literature* takes on a much broader meaning in a historical study and refers to all sorts of written communication; in addition, identification, acquisition, and review of the literature is considerably more complex.

8. Written communication may be in the form of legal documents, records, minutes of meetings, letters, and other documents that will not normally be indexed alphabetically by subject, author, and title in a library.

9. A historical research study in business may also involve interviews with persons who participated in the event or process under investigation, if it occurred in the recent past.

10. *Primary sources* constitute firsthand information, such as original documents and reports by actual participants or direct observers; *secondary sources* constitute secondhand information, such as reference books (encyclopedias, for example) or reports by relatives or friends of actual participants or observers.

11. A common criticism of historical research is excessive reliance on secondary sources.

Data Analysis: External and Internal Criticism

12. All sources of historical data must be subjected to rigorous scientific analysis to determine both their authenticity *(external criticism)* and their accuracy *(internal criticism)*.

13. In determining the accuracy of documents, at least four factors must be considered: (a) knowledge and competence of the author; (b) time delay between the occurrence and recording of events; (c) biased motives of the author; and (d) consistency of the data.

Data Synthesis

14. As with a review of related literature, historical data should be organized and synthesized, and conclusions and generalizations should be formulated.

15. Since summarization of historical research data involves logical analysis rather than statistical analysis, the researcher must take care to be as objective as possible.

An example of a research study using historical material is reprinted on the following pages (Project III Reading 1). This example differs from the description given in the text of this chapter in that quantitative data are available to support statistical analysis, so the study might also be classified as causal-comparative research. As you read the article, try to decide how you would classify it; you may want to refer back to the decision tree in Chapter 1 to assist you in determining a proper classification.

Following the article, a Practice Self-Test for reviewing the article is provided for you so that you can practice your review skills; Appendix C contains "Suggested Responses" so that you can check your responses from the self-test. Questions are also provided to allow you to evaluate the article from the standpoint of historical research.

Management Turnover Through Deaths of Key Executives: Effects on Investor Wealth

Dan L. Worrell
Appalachian State University

Wallace N. Davidson III
P.R. Chandy
North Texas State University

Sharon L. Garrison
East Tennessee State University

As an initial step in redirecting research on turnover to focus on its consequences, this study examined the reaction of the securities' market to the deaths of certain key executives. Although death had little influence on the market for the population studied as a whole, when key executives were differentiated by position, significant differences did occur. Negative abnormal returns were also found to be associated with name recognition and suddenness of executives' deaths.

Turnover has been one of the most examined topics in the literature on organizations. As Bluedorn (1982) reported, over 1,500 studies of turnover have

We would like to thank the three anonymous reviewers for their helpful comments and suggestions.
©*Academy of Management Journal* 1986, Vol. 29. No. 4. 674–694.

appeared in this century. The major focus of this literature has been on the determinants of turnover. Empirical research has primarily focused on its demographic, psychological, and economic antecedents, and theoreticians have developed models of turnover behavior based on these findings (e.g., Bluedorn, 1982; Mobley, Griffeth, Hand, & Meglino, 1979; Muchinsky & Tuttle, 1979; Porter & Steers, 1973; Price, 1977).

Staw (1980) argued that, given the voluminous empirical data and the detailed theoretical models already available, the yield of additional studies on the determinants of turnover will likely be rather low. Others have made a case for redirecting research on turnover, suggesting that scholars examine the consequences of individuals' leaving organizations rather than antecedents alone (Dalton & Todor, 1979; Staw, 1980; Staw & Oldham, 1978).

Recently, there also has been a call for closer working relationships between researchers in management and financial researchers on problems that lie at the interface of the two disciplines (Bettis, 1983; Peavy, 1984). This study, a first effort in that direction, tested the reaction of the securities' market to the deaths of certain key executives.

FINDINGS ON TURNOVER AND SUCCESSION

Most prior research on the consequences of turnover focuses on managerial succession. Although there is much overlap, studies of succession tend to center more on the effects of replacement than on the effects of employee separations, or turnover. The results of such studies have been mixed. Christensen (1953) found that changes in top management threatened profits in small manufacturing firms. Gouldner (1954), in a case study of managerial succession in a gypsum plant, observed that a change of managers disrupted the operations of the plant. However, in a case study of an automobile assembly line, Guest (1962) reported that a change in managers resulted in improved plant performance.

Grusky (1963) conducted the first of a series of empirical examinations (Allen, Panian, & Lotz, 1979; Brown, 1982; Eitzen & Yetman, 1972; Gamson & Scotch, 1964; Grusky, 1964; Pfeffer & Davis-Blake, 1986) focusing on managerial succession and organizational performance in sport teams. Pfeffer and Davis-Blake, for example, recently reported in a study of 22 National Basketball Association teams for the 1977 through 1981 seasons that succession had no effect on subsequent team performance when prior performance was controlled. However, when coaching competence was included in the analysis, succession was found to affect subsequent performance. Sport teams have been chosen in these studies largely because they have clear measures of both succession and performance. Although these studies have yielded insights, the applicability of their results to other types of complex organizations is uncertain (Neale, 1964).

Lieberson and O'Connor (1972) found support for scapegoating (Gamson & Scotch, 1964) in their study of changes in top management in 167 large corporations over 20 years. They reported that little variance in sales, earnings, and profit margins could be attributed to changes in chief executives. Salancik and Pfeffer (1977), in a study of the influence of mayors in 30 U.S. cities on city budgets over the period 1951–68, reached a similar conclusion; of three possible factors, year, city, or mayor, the city was consistently the most important factor accounting for variance in budget expenditures and income. Staw (1980) asserted that the apparent moderator of the effects of turnover in both these studies was the extent of the external constraints facing key executives. Weiner and Mahoney (1981), in a reanalysis of Lieberson and O'Connor's data, as well as in an examination of 193 manufacturing companies over a 19-year period, found that top leadership did account for more variance in organizational performance than did many organizational or environmental factors. They attributed differences between their findings and Lieberson and O'Connor's largely to the levels of specificity of criterion measures and the statistical procedures used. Smith, Carson, and Alexander (1984), in a study of the effects of 50 ministers on organizational performance between 1961 and 1980, reported that changes in leadership did not disrupt organizational performance or lead to immediate improvements in the group as a whole. However, when effective leaders were differentiated, churches led by these superior performers repeatedly experienced greater giving, membership growth, and property development than did other churches.

Although there has been relatively little research on the consequences of turnover,[1] it appears evident that its effects on organizational functioning are extremely complex. Moderating variables condition outcomes, and there are benefits as well as costs of turnover in organizations (Dalton, Krackhardt, & Porter, 1981; Dalton & Todor, 1979; Mobley, 1982; Staw, 1980; Staw & Oldham, 1978). Because of this complexity, this study was necessarily a preliminary one.

RESEARCH ISSUES

To date, there has been no empirical examinations of the specific variables the current analysis uses to measure the impact of executive death on investors' wealth,[2] so formulation of hypotheses must be largely speculative. However, as

---

1. In a recent study on the effects of executive succession on stock returns, Reinganum (1985) reported positive returns around the time of the announcement of a change for external appointments in small firms that announced the departure of the former office holder concurrently with the successor's appointment. Reinganum's study dealt with succession in general; this study examined returns from turnover caused by key executives' deaths.

2. However, in a recently published exception from the accounting literature, Johnson, Magee, Nagarajan, and Newman (1985), using similar methodology and a shorter sampling period, examined the reaction of stock returns to only sudden deaths of key executives. Sudden deaths were reported to have little systematic effect on stock returns, but founder status was found to be associated with positive returns. This contrasts with the current study, which reports both sudden deaths of CEOs and founder status to be associated with negative returns. Both studies obtained negative abnormal returns for top leadership positions, with Johnson and colleagues defining position by compensation and the current study defining position by title.

Price observed, "The conventional wisdom is probably correct in its belief that turnover generally has a basically negative impact on effectiveness" (1977: 119). Pfeffer notes, "If leadership has any impact, it should be more evident at higher organizational levels or where there is more discretion in decisions and activities" (1977: 108). Further, Staw (1980: 267) proposed that the higher the level of the positions to be filled, the greater the potential for disruption, and the greater the costs of recruitment, selection, and training, particularly if outside succession occurs. Thus, it seems reasonable to hypothesize that the deaths of key executives will be negatively associated with investors' wealth.

Financial theory suggests that a firm's value is affected positively when its expected cashflows increase or its systematic risk decreases (Fama & Miller, 1972). If involuntary turnover occurs through the death of a key executive, the price of shares will go down if expected cashflows are reduced or if systematic risk increases. This study tested the reaction of the securities' market to turnover among key executives through the deaths of CEOs and corporate chairmen.

As discussed in the introductory section, this study differs from most of the existing empirical literature on turnover in focusing on consequences rather than determinants. A second important difference is that it centers on involuntary turnover, and most of the existing empirical literature concentrates on voluntary turnover. Price (1977) stated three reasons for this concentration: most turnover is voluntary, the formation of theory is easier when the phenomenon to be explained is homogeneous, and voluntary turnover is more subject to control by managers.

It is important to study involuntary turnover in order to improve understanding of the overall process of turnover. Voluntary and involuntary turnover probably have quite different antecedents and consequences; separating the two phenomena should make it easier to develop viable theory. However, we suggest that further refining this traditional dichotomy might yield an even more realistic portrayal of the effects of turnover on organizations (Dalton, Krackhardt, & Porter, 1981).

Incidents of involuntary turnover, such as layoffs, dismissals, and retirements, tend to be initiated by organizations rather than by individuals. For key executives, however, involuntary, organization-initiated turnover is often difficult to distinguish from voluntary turnover. As James and Soref noted, "chief executives and companies usually prefer to treat the matter delicately; hence, generally, 'resignations' are accepted, or 'early retirements' are taken, but firings do not occur" (1981:4). When turnover and succession are anticipated, as in the case of retirement, the stock market may not respond because the event has been expected. Examining deaths of key executives largely avoids such methodological problems because death is typically involuntary and not initiated by a company, and in many cases it is completely unanticipated.

The present study differs from most previous empirical literature on turnover in two additional ways. First, it focuses on turnover among key executives. Although a small sociological literature on executive succession exists, most research on turnover has focused on lower-level employees in organizations (Staw, 1980). This study concentrates on key executives at the very top levels of organizations (CEOs and chairmen) rather than on general managerial succession and turnover.

Second, this study employs a methodology new to the study of turnover in organizations. We describe the specific features of event methodology in the next section and present them more fully in the Appendix. This methodology seemed especially appropriate because death is a relatively unanticipated and clear-cut event. The procedure provides a dramatic test of the effects of involuntary turnover on firms' stock market values.

METHODS

Data Analysis

The purpose of this study was to determine the securities' market's reaction to the deaths of certain key executives by measuring abnormal returns. We used the standard event methodology first developed by Fama, Fisher, Jensen, and Roll (1969). Others have used this procedure, with minor variations, to test events such as the release of earnings information (Ball & Brown, 1968), secondary stock sales (Scholes, 1972), changes in accounting procedures (Cassidy, 1976; Kaplan & Roll, 1972), dividend changes (Charest, 1978), public utility rate cases (Davidson, 1984), and corporate divestiture (Montgomery, Thomas, & Kamath, 1984). Because the complete explanation of the procedure appears in the Appendix, we only briefly summarize it here.

Regressing the returns on each security against the return on a market index provided a predictive model. We used this market model to predict the normal returns for a period of 90 days prior to an event—an announcement of the death of a key executive—and 30 days afterward. The actual returns on the stock were compared to the predicted returns, and the difference called an abnormal return. We then summed and averaged the abnormal returns across companies for each day relative to an event and cumulated them over various intervals relative to the date of the event. These computations provided the average abnormal returns and cumulative abnormal returns. If investors have received information that causes stock prices to rise relative to the market, the average abnormal returns and cumulative abnormal returns will be positive. If the information causes stock prices to decline relative to the market, then these same statistics will be negative. We conducted t-tests on these statistics to determine significance; the Appendix fully explains these tests.

Such predictive models have been criticized (Scholes & Williams, 1977). Although research suggests that many of these criticisms are unfounded (Brenner, 1979; Brown & Warner, 1980, 1983; Davidson, 1984), we also used a second model, the average return model, which is similar except that the regression parameters for the intercept and slope are replaced with 0 and 1. All other computations are the same.

Study Population

We defined key executives as corporate presidents or chief executive officers, both referred to as CEOs hereafter, or as chairmen of boards of directors. We further restricted the population studied to only those officers who were CEOs, chairmen, or both, of parent corporations; officers of subsidiaries were excluded. An officer's death had to have been announced in the *Wall Street Journal* during the 15-year period from 1967 to 1981.

After finding an initial 220 deaths, we excluded officers of any firms that were not traded on the New York or American Stock Exchange. This restriction biased the group to large companies, but served two purposes. It permitted the use of the CRSP tapes from the University of Chicago's Center for Research in Security Prices, which contain data on returns for all stocks listed on these exchanges. It also ensured that the securities were traded frequently enough to permit good estimates of the market model's parameters. Finally, we further restricted the study population by excluding firms in which the death of a second key executive occurred during the parameter estimation period following the death of one key executive. The final population included 127 key executives, 61 had the title of Chairman of the Board, 23 were CEOs, and 43 both CEOs and chairmen. We present results for the total population and for each of the three subgroups separately.

RESULTS

Total Population

Table 1 and Figure 1 present results for the population as a whole. Table 1 shows the abnormal returns and cumulative abnormal returns for various subintervals. The *t*-tests on the abnormal returns are all insignificant at conventional levels of significance; the market did not react significantly to the news of the death of a key executive on a single day. For days on which deaths were reported in the *Wall Street Journal,* represented by 0 in the first column, the abnormal return is positive, but insignificant. Results from both the market model and the average return model are qualitatively the same. Second, it is important to note that the cumulative abnormal return for the interval 0 to 30 is .0156, indicating that the reaction of the market in the 30 days following reports of deaths was positive.[3] Figure 1 depicts this upward movement. Prior to day 0, the cumulative abnormal returns hover below 0, but become positive during the 30 days after the reports.

---

3. Initially, we computed cumulative abnormal returns for up to +90 days. To minimize the overlap between the turnover and subsequent succession events, this study reports *CAR*s only to +30 days. For the total group studies, the positive reaction continued beyond 30 days (day 60, .0171; day 90, .0335). However, the reactions during these periods may result from the succession following a key executive's death is necessary to isolate recations. For CEO's deaths, the cumulative abnormal return stabilizes after day 6 and remains negative even through +90 days.

TABLE 1
Cumulative Abnormal Returns for Deaths in Total Population and
Deaths of CEOs

Intervals[a]		Market Model[b]		Average Return Model[b]	
T_1 to T_2	CARs	Test Statistics		CARs	Test Statistics

Intervals[a] T_1 to T_2	CARs	Test Statistics	CARs	Test Statistics
(a) Total population (N = 127)				
−90 to 0	−.0061	−0.09	.0103	0.32
−10 to 0	.0008	0.11	.0026	0.37
− 7 to 0	−.0025	0.41	−.0018	−0.30
− 7 to −3	−.0040	−0.81	−.0025	−0.51
−7	−.0003	−0.10	.0004	0.13
−6	−.0004	−0.13	.0002	0.07
−5	.0003	0.10	.0003	0.09
−4	−.0024	−0.79	−.0023	−0.75
−3	−.0015	−0.49	−.0008	−0.26
−2	−.0002	−0.06	−.0004	−0.13
−1	.0004	0.13	−.0001	−0.03
0	.0013	0.43	.0013	0.43
1	−.0005	−0.16	−.0008	−0.26
2	.0042	1.38	.0046	1.51
0 to 30	.0156	0.71	.0198	0.91
(b) CEOs (N = 23)				
−90 to 0	−.0930	−1.42	−.0623	−0.93
−10 to 0	−.0182	−1.09	−.0147	−0.90
− 7 to 0	−.0196	−1.38	−.0214	−1.50
− 7 to −3	−.0162	−3.29***	−.0138	−2.80***
−7	.0047	1.41	.0049	1.45
−6	−.0029	−0.87	−.0027	−0.80
−5	−.0008	−0.24	−0010	−0.30
−4	−.0065	−1.95*	−.0056	−1.66
−3	−.0060	−1.79*	−.0044	−1.30
−2	−.0021	−0.63	−.0021	−0.62
−1	−.0050	−1.50	−.0052	−1.54
0	−.0009	−0.27	−.0003	−0.09
1	.0002	0.66	.0015	0.44
2	.0065	1.95*	.0063	1.86*
0 to 30	−.0006	−0.03	.0093	0.43

[a]Announcement days (day 0) generally follow the actual dates of deaths by 3 to 7 days. Hence, these days are highlighted along with day 0.

[b]CARs = cumulative abnormal returns. The test statistics are described in the Appendix. When an interval of more than one day is used, the test statistic is of the form reported in Brenner (1979). When the interval includes only one day, the test statistic is the time series t-test as reported in Davidson (1984).

*$p < .10$
***$p < .01$

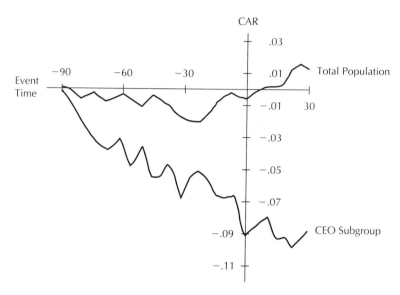

Figure 1. Cumulative abnormal returns surrounding the deaths of key executives for total population and CEO subgroup.

For days −10 to 0, −7 to 0, and −7 to −3, the cumulative abnormal returns are insignificant. We tested the subinterval between days −7 and −3 because, in most instances, firms reported key executives' deaths from three to seven days after the actual date of death. By testing this specific subinterval, we tested the market's reaction to the actual dates of deaths as well as to the public announcements. We did not use the actual dates of deaths as the event dates because they were not as consistently available as the dates of announcements, and the population's size would have been further restricted. Therefore, by accumulating the abnormal returns over these pre-event subintervals, we could test for the market's reaction between dates of death and dates that the news reached the market. As the table shows, the cumulative abnormal returns for the total population over these subintervals are insignificantly different from 0.

Subgroups

The roles of CEOs and chairmen may be quite different. In the past, except in times of crisis, boards of directors customarily had little true authority and rubber-stamped management's decisions (Mace, 1971). Although the recent increase in outsiders on many boards, coupled with increased legal challenges by stockholders and various social reform movements, have led to more active roles for board members (Boulton, 1978), the actual strategic operation of most organizations remains primarily in the hands of CEOs. Because of these potential differences, we subdivided key executives into three groups: (1) CEO only, (2) chairman only, and (3) both CEO and chairman.

The bottom half of Table 1 presents the reaction of the market to the deaths of 23 CEOs. In contrast to results based on the total population, the deaths of CEOs appear to be associated with a negative reaction by the securities' market. From days -7 to -3, the cumulative abnormal return is negative and statistically different from 0 ($p < .01$). On days -4 and -3, the abnormal returns are significantly negative, and all of the abnormal returns from days -6 to -1 are negative. These negative abnormal returns may be results of the news of the CEOs' deaths reaching the market on the dates of deaths or on subsequent days, before announcements appeared in the *Wall Street Journal*. The frequent three-to-seven-day time lag in reporting deaths is the period over which there are statistically significant abnormal returns. From day -6 to day 0. there is a large drop in the cumulative abnormal return, which generally remains at this lower level for the next 30 days (Figure 1).

The market's reaction to the deaths of the 61 corporate chairmen in our population appears in the top half of Table 2. No evidence of significantly negative abnormal returns appears on, or around, day 0. On the contrary, a significantly positive abnormal return on day 0 suggests that the market reacted favorably to the news of the deaths of corporate chairmen. As with any statistical tests, it is possible that chance accounts for these results. However, both return-generating models confirm these results, and the significant reactions are notably right on the announcement date. In Figure 2, the upward drift in the cumulative abnormal return is evident. Results for the subintervals from -10 to 0 and 0 to 30 are insignificant, but positive (Table 2). This evidence also supports the idea that the market reacted positively to the deaths of the chairmen.

The bottom half of Table 2 presents the abnormal returns for the deaths of executives who served both as CEO and chairman. For this group, significantly negative abnormal returns on days -7 and 0 indicate that the death of a CEO/chairman is associated with negative market returns on and before the date of announcement. Figure 2 shows an apparent upward movement in the cumulative abnormal return over the period -30 to $+30$, but on the days immediately around day 0, the movement is downward.

Other Results

In an attempt to determine whether other circumstances determine how the market reacts to the deaths of key executives, we created two additional subgroups and recomputed results. The first subgroup included CEOs who died suddenly, and the second was executives whose names might be easily recognizable.

Any CEO, regardless of other titles, who died of a heart attack, an accident, or violence was included in the first regrouping. Results for this subgroup, which included 41 firms, appear in the top half of Table 3. Over the intervals between days -7 and 0, and -7 and -3, there are statistically significant ($p < .05$), negative cumulative abnormal returns of .0269 and .0134. In addition, the abnormal returns on day -7 and 0 are statistically significant ($p < .10$ and $p <$

TABLE 2
Cumulative Abnormal Returns for Deaths of Chairmen and
CEO/Chairmen

Intervals[a] T_1 to T_2	Market Model[b]		Average Return Model[b]	
	Test CARs	Statistics	Test CARs	Statistics
(a) Chairmen (N = 61)				
−90 to 0	.0043	0.05	.0225	0.24
−10 to 0	.0136	1.33	.0151	1.50
− 7 to 0	.0065	0.74	.0056	0.64
− 7 to −3	−.0018	−0.37	−.0013	−0.26
−7	.0020	0.61	.0034	1.02
−6	.0009	0.27	.0016	0.48
−5	−.0001	−0.03	−.0006	−0.18
−4	.0001	0.03	−.0002	−0.06
−3	−.0025	−0.76	−.0020	−0.60
−2	.0010	0.30	.0016	0.48
−1	−.0005	−0.15	−.0009	−0.27
0	.0078	2.36**	.0077	2.31**
1	−.0020	−0.61	−.0023	−0.69
2	.0034	1.03	.0041	1.22
0 to 30	.0219	0.71	.0242	0.81
(b) CEO/Chairmen (N = 43)				
−90 to 0	.0269	0.27	.0327	0.30
−10 to 0	−.0049	−0.40	−.0051	−0.43
− 7 to 0	−.0031	−0.30	−.0034	−0.32
− 7 to −3	−.0004	−0.08	.0018	0.37
−7	−.0062	−2.17**	−.0063	−2.18**
−6	−.0006	−0.21	−.0001	−0.03
−5	.0014	0.49	.0024	0.83
−4	−.0034	−1.19	−.0033	−1.14
−3	.0022	0.77	.0028	0.97
−2	−.0007	−0.24	−.0023	−0.79
−1	.0045	0.16	.0037	1.18
0	−.0065	−2.27**	−.0066	−2.88***
1	.0002	0.07	.0001	0.03
2	.0039	1.36	.0043	1.38
0 to 30	.0114	0.39	.0152	0.41

[a]Announcement days (day 0) generally follow the actual dates of deaths by 3 to 7 days. Hence, these days are highlighted along with day 0.

[b]CARs = cumulative abnormal returns. The test statistics are described in the Appendix. When an interval of more than one day is used, the test statistic is of the form reported in Brenner (1979). When the interval includes only one day, the test statistic is the time series t-test as reported in Davidson (1984).

*p < .10
**p < .05
***p < .01

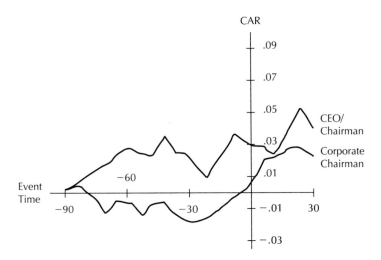

Figure 2. Cumulative abnormal returns surrounding the deaths of corporate chairmen.

.01, respectively) and are negative. The sudden-death subgroup is associated with very strong negative abnormal returns—it appears that the market reacted very strongly to the deaths of these executives.

The second regrouping, based on name recognition, includes only those key executives whose names are incorporated in their companies' names, because it is very difficult to determine whether a name was easily recognized, particularly when considerable time has passed since a death. Generally, these executives were founders, or relatives of the founders, of the companies. The bottom half of Table 3 shows results for this subgroup of 18. The abnormal return on day −6 is statistically significant and negative, but although it is negative for the interval between days −7 and −3, it is insignificant. The deaths of these executives seem to be associated with negative returns, but the results are not as strong as some of the findings reported earlier in this section.

Discussion

Our hypothesis was that key executives' deaths would be negatively associated with investors' wealth. An examination of the results for the total group studied, however, reveals that such deaths do not significantly affect the market. This finding supports the position that studies of sports teams have put forth— namely, that succession has a null effect (Brown, 1982; Eitzen & Yetman, 1972; Gamson & Scotch, 1964)—and it is consistent with the findings of Lieberson and O'Connor (1972), Salancik and Pfeffer (1977), and Smith, Carson, and Alexander (1984).

There are a number of possible reasons why the market did not significantly react to the deaths of key executives in the full population. One possibility is that

TABLE 3
Cumulative Abnormal Returns for Other Subgroups

Intervals[a]		Market Model[b]		Average Return Model[b]	
T_1 to T_2	CARs	Test Statistics	CARs	Test Statistics

Intervals[a]		Market Model[b]		Average Return Model[b]	
T_1 to T_2		CARs	Test Statistics	CARs	Test Statistics
(a) CEOs—Sudden Death Subgroup (N = 41)					
−90 to	0	−.0358	0.36	−.0356	−0.34
−10 to	0	−.0222	−1.72	−.0227	−1.73
− 7 to	0	−.0269	−2.45**	−.0308	−2.50**
− 7 to	−3	−.0134	−2.68**	−.0142	−2.73**
	−7	−.0060	−1.75*	−.0059	−1.69
	−6	−.0035	−1.02	−.0034	−0.99
	−5	.0023	0.67	.0022	0.64
	−4	−.0021	−0.61	−.0021	−0.61
	−3	−.0041	−1.19	−.0050	−1.23
	−2	−.0035	−1.02	−.0043	−1.29
	−1	−.0003	−0.09	−.0004	−0.09
	0	−.0097	−2.84***	−.0119	−3.06***
	1	.0005	0.15	.0004	0.14
	2	.0054	1.58	.0055	1.49
0 to 30		.0035	0.12	.0036	0.15
(b) Name Recognition Subgroup (N = 18)					
−90 to	0	.0062	0.09	.0829	1.20
−10 to	0	−.0121	−0.73	−.0100	−0.60
− 7 to	0	−.0042	−0.30	−.0032	−0.23
− 7 to	−3	−.0060	−1.22	−.0042	−0.85
	−7	−.0049	−1.03	−.0041	−0.85
	−6	−.0132	−2.78**	−.0129	−2.69**
	−5	.0062	1.31	.0061	1.27
	−4	.0010	0.21	.0003	0.06
	−3	.0000	0.00	.0022	0.46
	−2	−.0041	−0.86	−.0036	−0.75
	−1	−.0004	−0.08	.0005	0.10
	0	.0062	1.30	.0041	0.85
	1	.0046	0.97	.0022	0.46
	2	.0006	0.13	.0027	0.56
0 to 30		−.0015	−0.08	−.0113	0.60

[a]Announcement days (day 0) generally follow the actual dates of deaths by 3 to 7 days. Hence, these days are highlighted along with day 0.

[b]CARs = cumulative abnormal returns. The test statistics are described in the Appendix. When an interval of more than one day is used, the test statistic is of the form reported in Brenner (1979). When the interval includes only one day, the test statistic is the time series t-test as reported in Davidson (1984).

*$p < .10$
**$p < .05$
***$p < .01$

some firms experienced significant positive abnormal returns during trading days around the event date, but other firms experienced significant negative abnormal returns. Offsetting positive and negative abnormal returns may have averaged out to an overall zero effect.

A second possibility is that the variation in the number of trading days between dates of the publication of the obituary notices by the *Wall Street Journal* and the actual dates of deaths may have inhibited accurate measurement. The daily average abnormal returns may not provide an adequately precise representation of the effects of key executives' deaths on abnormal returns.

The results may also be sample-specific. The effects of key executives' deaths on investors' returns may well vary with organizational size, and this population was restricted to firms large enough to be listed on the major exchanges. In smaller organizations, management may rest in the hands of a few dominating figures. In addition, no highly refined management training program to provide back-up management support may be in place.

A final potential explanation is that the market may have anticipated the deaths before they happened. This scenario seems particularly likely where the deaths were not sudden. If the market has an indication of a key executive's impending departure (for example, a terminal illness), the prices of securities may embody evaluative implications of the event prior to its occurrence.

Table 4 summarizes the results for the various subgroups. The results indicate that if key executives are viewed as a homogeneous group, their deaths appear to have little influence on the market. However, although we found no systematic reaction in stock prices for the full group, we observed important adjustments in stock prices for subgroups. Many of these significant adjustments appear in the columns for the intervals between days -7 and -3, -7 and 0, and for day 0. The results indicate that if key executives are differentiated by position into chairman-only, CEO-only, and CEO-and-chairman subgroups, their deaths seem to make a difference. In addition, negative abnormal returns are also associated with suddenness of death and executive name recognition.

For the chairman-only subgroup, the results suggest that the market reacted positively to the deaths. Any possible explanations for this occurrence must be largely speculative, but it is interesting to note that the chairmen in our population were often in their 70s, 80s, and even 90s. The positive reaction may imply that the market viewed such turnover as a positive sign and a chance for innovation and adaptation (Staw, 1980). It should be stressed that in order for a price reaction to take place, expected cash flows would have to change.

Another similar explanation comes under the general heading of "settling up" (Fama, 1980: 304–306), a notion we can illustrate with an example. Suppose an executive is doing an adequate job, but is overpaid relative to ability. When this executive dies, the market settles up by treating this news as positive. These results may represent such an effort; the marginal benefits many chairmen bring may be perceived to be less than their marginal compensation.

The market's reaction to the deaths of CEOs appears to be negative, at least in the short run. In addition, the market reacted on or around the actual dates of

TABLE 4

A Comparison of Cumulative Abnormal Returns and Test Statistics[a]
for the Various Groupings, Market Model

Groupings	−7 to 0	−7 to −3	−7	−6	−5	−4	−3	−2	−1	0
					Intervals[a]					
Total population	−.0025	−.0040	−.0003	−.0004	.0003	−.0024	−.0015	−.0002	.0004	.0013
(N = 127)	(0.41)	(−0.81)	(−0.10)	(−0.13)	(0.10)	(−0.79)	(−0.49)	(−0.06)	(0.13)	(0.43)
CEOs	−.0196	−.0162	.0047	−.0029	−.0008	−.0065	−.0060	−.0021	−.0050	−.0009
(N = 23)	(−1.38)	(−3.29)***	(1.41)	(−0.87)	(−0.24)	(−1.95)*	(−1.79)*	(−0.63)	(−1.50)	(−0.27)
Chairmen	.0065	−.0018	.0020	.0009	−.0001	.0001	−.0025	.0010	−.0005	.0078
(N = 61)	(0.74)	(−0.37)	(0.61)	(0.27)	(−0.03)	(0.03)	(−0.76)	(0.30)	(−0.15)	(2.36)**
CEOs and chairmen	−.0031	−.0004	−.0062	−.0006	.0014	−.0034	.0022	−.0007	.0045	−.0065
(N = 43)	(−0.30)	(−0.08)	(−2.17)**	(−0.21)	(0.49)	(−1.19)	(0.77)	(−0.24)	(0.16)	(−2.27)**
CEOs, sudden death	−.0269	−.0134	−.0060	−.0035	.0023	−.0021	−.0041	−.0035	−.0003	−.0097
(N = 41)	(−2.45)**	(−2.68)**	(−1.75)*	(−1.02)	(0.67)	(−0.61)	(−1.19)	(−1.02)	(−0.09)	(−2.84)***
Name recognition	−.0042	−.0060	−.0049	−.0132	.0062	.0010	.0000	−.0041	−.0004	.0062
(N = 18)	(−0.30)	(−1.22)	(−1.03)	(−2.78)**	(1.31)	(0.21)	(0.00)	(−0.86)	(−0.08)	(1.30)

[a]The test statistics are described in the Appendix. When an interval of more than one day is used, the test statistic is of the form reported in Brenner (1979). When the interval includes only one day, the test statistic is the time series t-test reported in Davidson (1984).

*p < .10
**p < .05
***p < .01

deaths and not necessarily at the time of announcements in the financial press. It seems that the market reacts more negatively toward the deaths of hands-on key executives than it does toward the deaths of chairmen.

An individual who is both CEO and chairman is likely to have much power within an organization, and the death of such an individual is likely to create uncertainty, since two key positions become vacant. The results show statistically significant, negative returns on the dates that the deaths of such individuals were reported, indicating that the market reacted negatively. In terms of settling up theory, if the market views CEOs' deaths as negative, it perceived their productivity as outweighing their compensation. The market settles up to the loss of their productivity by reacting negatively.

It is important to note that the market often reacted strongly prior to the dates deaths were announced. These pre-event reactions are not uncommon in other studies applying event methodology; in fact, it was evident in the study in which the methodology was pioneered (Fama, Fisher, Jensen, & Roll, 1969). There are at least two explanations. The first implies super efficiency on the part of securities' analysts, who keep in touch with companies regularly. Although a death may not be public information for a few days, they may obtain the information sooner and adjust even before the announcement.

A second, related explanation centers around the event date used in this research, the date of announcement in the *Wall Street Journal*. Local news media may report the deaths of executives from their vicinities days before the national press picks up on these stories.

In an effort to sort out differences in the full population that were not due to differences in executives' positions, we examined two additional groups: CEOs who died suddenly and executives with name recognition. The results indicate that reactions to sudden deaths tend to be negative. We found very negative abnormal returns between the dates of deaths and the dates the deaths were reported, and the reaction on the dates of announcements in the *Wall Street Journal* (day 0) was particularly large and negative. For this subgroup, the market was unable to anticipate CEOs' deaths, and the reaction upon receipt of the news was particularly negative. Unexpected deaths minimize the probability that the securities' market can anticipate the event.

Likewise, although the results for the name-recognition subgroup were not as strong as for the sudden-death subgroup, they also indicate a possible negative impact on the market. A key executive who is highly publicized or who has the status of a founder may be seen as the personality of a company, and the death of such an individual could have an especially negative effect on the market. For example, in 1966, when the market learned Walt Disney was facing a lingering death from cancer, a substantial drop in Disney stock prices occurred. Stockholders in that firm have since spent many years mourning the loss of the founder's magic touch. Indeed, a recent article (*Wall Street Journal,* 1982) observed, "There is not as yet any firm evidence that the company's motion picture division has climbed out of the black hole it stumbled into after Mr. Disney's death" (1982: 1).

Although some significant differences in the effects of the deaths of key executives emerged when we took executive position, predictability of death, and name recognition into account, several caveats should be kept in mind. First, the nature of the population and the many nonsignificant findings restrict the generalizability of results. Although this study was a step toward redirecting research to focus on the consequences of turnover, it was itself very narrowly focused on the short-run effects of the deaths of key executives from large companies on investor wealth. Second, although we used two predictive models (McDonald & Nichols, 1984), the results may have been dependent on the model for generating normal returns. Additionally, the influence of outside factors and chance cannot be ignored. Leaders, even key executives, seldom have unilateral control over resources and policies.

These limitations, and others discussed previously in this paper, suggest directions for future research. Strongly indicated are additional investigations into how the positions of CEO and chairman differ. Organizational size and the extent to which key executives are aggressively managing organizations prior to death might also be included in future research. Additional control variables, such as age, length of tenure, and percentage of compensation in the form of profit sharing or stock options, may also affect how the market perceives an executive's death. Better ways of determining how the market recognizes an executive's name could also be developed to determine how it would react to deaths of executives perceived very favorably or unfavorably.

Finally, a follow-up is needed that would build on Reinganum's (1985) research exploring the effects of executive succession on stock prices in 1978 and 1979, and that would specifically examine the effects of succession among key executives following a death. Such research would indicate how long the cumulative abnormal returns attributable to deaths are sustained following successions, and what additional effects successions themselves have on investors' wealth. Results could be compared with the financial consequences of the more general phenomena of turnover and succession among key executives.

The lack of prior data on the relationships between the deaths of key executives and investors' wealth and the limitations of the present study permit few strong generalizations. However, we can identify a few implications for both investors and managers. First, for investors, significant results from analyses of subgroups give further credence to the need for diversification of portfolios. In addition, investors faced with a CEO's death, or an executive's sudden death, or the death of an executive who had name recognition, might consider going short on the stocks of the affected firms. On the other hand, the death of a corporate chairman appears to present an opportunity for investors to go long. However, an investor would have to have insider information about an actual date of death and would have to act before the date of announcement in the *Wall Street Journal*. An investor would also generally have to invest in affected firms one at a time, since it is unlikely that deaths of key executive officers would occur in groups.

Since death is an unplanned event, implications for managers are difficult to develop. However, with the aging of the baby-boom generation and the extension of mandatory retirement, understanding the consequences of executives' deaths is more important than ever. We made no attempt in this study to determine differences in reactions for companies that were prepared for CEO turnover and those that were not, but preparedness may well lessen the potential negative effects on shareholders' returns. Firms should identify potential successors and groom them to assume key leadership positions. Furthermore, some top executives may need to carry life insurance with their companies named as the beneficiaries. Although few companies will release information about such insurance coverage, its presence may lessen effects on investors' returns and provide a firm with the liquidity necessary to overcome a tragedy.

In conclusion, it is evident that the effective management of turnover presupposes a fuller understanding of its consequences. We hope this study encourages further interdisciplinary investigations that reorient turnover research from primarily examining the antecedents of individuals' leaving organizations. The consequences of turnover deserve fuller research attention than they have been accorded.

REFERENCES

Allen, M. P., Panian, S. K., & Lotz, R. E. 1979. Managerial succession and organizational performance: A recalcitrant problem revisisted. *Administrative Science Quarterly,* 24: 167–180.

Ball, R., & Brown, P. 1968. An empirical evaluation of accounting income numbers. *Journal of Accounting Research,* 6: 159–178.

Bettis, R. A. 1983. Modern financial theory, corporate strategy, and public policy: Three countdowns. *Academy of Management Review,* 8: 406–415.

Bluedorn, A. C. 1982. The theories of turnover: Causes, effects, and meanings. In S. B. Bacharach (Ed.), *Research in the sociology of organization:* 75–128. Greenwich, Conn.: JAI Press.

Boulton, W. 1978. The evolving board: A look at the board's changing roles and information needs. *Academy of Management Review,* 3: 827–836.

Brenner, M. 1979. The sensitivity of the efficient market hypothesis to alternative specifications of the market model. *Journal of Finance,* 34: 915–929.

Brown, M. C. 1982. Administrative succession and organizational performance: The succession effect. *Administrative Science Quarterly,* 27: 1–16.

Brown, S. J., & Warner, J. B. 1980. Measuring security price performance. *Journal of Financial Economics,* 8: 205–258.

Brown, S. J., & Warner, J. B. 1983. *Using daily stock returns in event studies.* Unpublished manuscript.

Cassidy, D. B. 1976. Investor evaluation of accounting information: Some additional empirical evidence. *Journal of Accounting Research,* 14: 212–229.

Charest, G. 1978. Dividend information, stock returns, and market efficiency—II. *Journal of Financial Economics,* 6: 297–330.

Christensen, R. C. 1953. *Management succession in small and growing enterprises.* Boston: Division of Research, Graduate School of Business, Harvard University.

Dalton, D. R., Krackhardt, D. M., & Porter, L. W. 1981. Functional turnover: An empirical assessment. *Journal of Applied Psychology,* 66: 716–721.

Dalton, D. R., & Todor, W. D. 1979. Turnover turned over: An expanded and positive perspective. *Academy of Management Review*, 4: 225–235.

Davidson, W. N. 1984. The effect of rate cases on public utility stock returns. *Journal of Financial Research*, 7: 81–93.

Eitzen, D. S., & Yetman, N. R. 1972. Managerial change, longevity, and organizational effectiveness. *Administrative Science Quarterly*, 17: 110–116.

Fama, E. F. 1980. Agency problems and the theory of the firm. *Journal of Political Economy*, 88: 288–307.

Fama, E. F., Fisher, L., Jensen, M. C., & Roll, R. 1969. The adjustment of stock prices to new information. *International Economic Review*. 10: 1–21.

Fama, E. F., & Miller, M. H. 1972. *The theory of finance*. Hindsdale, Ill.: Holt, Rinehart & Winston.

Gamson, W. A., & Scotch, N. A., 1964. Scapegoating in baseball. *American Journal of Sociology*, 70: 69–72.

Gouldner, A. W. 1954. *Patterns of industrial bureaucracy*. New York: Free Press.

Grusky, O. 1963. Managerial succession and organizational effectiveness. *American Journal of Sociology*, 69: 21–31.

Grusky, O. 1964. Reply to scapegoating in baseball. *American Journal of Sociology*, 70: 72–76.

Guest, R. H. 1962. Managerial succession in complex organizations. *American Journal of Sociology*, 68: 47–54.

Jain, P. C. 1985. The effect of voluntary sell-off announcements on shareholder wealth. *Journal of Finance*, 40: 209–224.

James, D. R., & Soref, M. 1981. Profit constraints on managerial autonomy: Managerial theory and the unmaking of the corporation president. *American Sociological Review*, 46: 1–18.

Johnson, W. B., Magee, R. P., Nagarajan, N. J., & Newman, H. A. 1985. An analysis of the stock price reaction to sudden executive deaths. *Journal of Accounting and Economics*, 7: 151–174.

Kaplan, R. S., & Roll, R. 1972. Investor evaluation of accounting information: Some empirical evidence. *Journal of Business*, 45: 225–357.

Lieberson, S., & O'Connor, J. F. 1972. Leadership and organizational performance: A study of large corporations. *American Sociological Review*, 37: 117–130.

Mace, M. L. 1971. *Directions: Myth and reality*. Cambridge, Mass.: Harvard University Press.

McDonald, B., & Nichols, W. D. 1984. Nonstationarity of beta and tests of market efficiency. *Journal of Financial Research*, 8: 315–322.

Mobley, W. H. 1982. *Employee turnover: Causes, consequences, and control*. Reading, Mass.: Addison-Wesley.

Mobley, W. H., Griffeth, R. W., Hand, H. H., & Meglino, B. M. 1979. Review and conceptual analysis of the employee turnover process. *Psychological Bulletin*. 86: 493–522.

Montgomery, C. A., Thomas, A. R., & Kamath, R. 1984. Divestiture, market valuation, and strategy. *Academy of Management Journal*, 27: 830–840.

Muchinsky, P. M., & Tuttle, M. L. 1979. Employee turnover: An empirical and methodological assessment. *Journal of Vocational Behavior*, 14: 43–77.

Neale, W. C. 1964. The peculiar economics of professional sports. *Quarterly Journal of Economics*, 78: 1–14.

Peavy, J. W. 1984. Modern financial theory, corporate strategy, and public policy: Another perspective. *Academy of Management Review,* 9: 152–157.

Pfeffer, J. 1977. The ambiguity of leadership. *Academy of Management Review,* 2: 104–112.

Pfeffer, J., & Davis-Blake, A. 1986. Administrative succession and organizational performance. How administrator experience mediates the succession effect. *Academy of Management Journal,* 29: 72–83.

Porter, L. W., & Steers, R. M. 1973. Organizational, work, and personal factors in employee turnover and absenteeism. *Psychological Bulletin,* 80: 151–176.

Price, J. L. 1977. *The study of turnover.* Ames: Iowa State University Press.

Reinganum, M. R. 1985. The effect of executive succession on stockholder wealth. *Administrative Science Quarterly,* 30: 46–60.

Salancik, G. R., & Pfeffer, J. 1977. Constraints on administrative discretion: The limited influence of mayors on city budgets. *Urban Affairs Quarterly,* 12: 475–498.

Scholes, M. S. 1972. The market for securities: Substitution versus price pressure and the effects of information on share prices. *Journal of Business,* 45: 179–211.

Scholes, M. S., & Williams, J. 1977. Estimating betas from nonsynchronous data. *Journal of Financial Economics,* 5: 309–327.

Smith, J. E., Carson, K. P., & Alexander, R. A. 1984. Leadership: It can make a difference. *Academy of Management Journal,* 27: 765–776.

Staw, B. M. 1980. The consequences of turnover. *Journal of Occupational Behavior,* 1: 253–273.

Staw, B. M., & Oldham, G. R. 1978. Reconsidering our dependent variables. A critique and empirical study. *Academy of Management Journal,* 21: 539–559.

Wall Street Journal. 1982. Disney's Epcot Center, big $1 billion gamble opens in Florida Oct. 1. September 16: 1, 21.

Weiner, N., & Mahoney, T. A. 1981. A model of corporate performance as a function of environmental, organizational, and leadership influences. *Academy of Management Journal,* 24: 452–470.

Appendix

The purpose of this study was to determine the securities' market's reaction to the deaths of certain key executives. We computed and analyzed abnormal returns. The measurement of abnormal returns implies that a model can be specified that generates normal returns; we used the following market model:

$$R_{it} = \alpha_1 + \beta_i R_{mt} + e_{it}, \tag{1}$$

where R_{it} is the return on security i at time t, α_i is a regression intercept, β_i is the beta coefficient of the regression, R_{mt} is the return on the market index at time t_1, and e_{it} is the disturbance term.

Day 0 is defined as the day that news of an executive's death appeared in the *Wall Street Journal.* A first-pass regression of each security's returns against the returns on the market (Equation 1) is run over days −291 to −91 to obtain estimates for the parameters of the market model, α_i and β_i.

The market model parameters for each of the i company's securities are applied to the actual market returns for days −90 to +30, which provide the predicted returns for company i. These predicted returns are compared to the actual returns for each of the i companies from -90 to $+30$. We limited the days after an event to 30 to minimize the effect of succession. In this population, it took an average of 20.8 days to replace a key executive; in addition, it is not unreasonable to expect a further time delay before a replacement gains effective control. The difference between the actual returns and the predicted returns for security i at time t is called the abnormal return, AR_{it}:

$$AR_{it} = R_{it} - (\alpha_i + \beta_i R_{mt}), \tag{2}$$

where R_{it} represents the actual return on security i at time t, and the term in parentheses is the normal return. The other variables are as previously defined.

The average abnormal return is computed by summing the abnormal returns across all N firms for each relative event time, t, as follows:

$$AR_t = \sum_{i=1}^{N} \frac{AR_{it}}{N}. \tag{3}$$

The cumulative abnormal return (CAR) is also computed over various intervals, T_1 to T_2:

$$CAR_{T_1, T_2} = \sum_{t=T_1}^{T_2} AR_t. \tag{4}$$

In an efficient market, the return on a security will react immediately to an event that affects its intrinsic value. Under these conditions, the AR_t and CAR will be random except upon receipt of the news of an event. When information that affects the value of firms reaches the market for each firm at the same time relative to day 0, then the AR_t should not be 0. If the information flow is not uniform with respect to event times, the CAR will not be 0. We used test statistics to determine when an AR_t or CAR was significantly different from 0.

The test statistic for the AR_t is a time series t-test as reported in Davidson (1984), and is similar to the one in Jain (1985). The statistic T_t can be computed in the following manner:

$$T_t = \frac{AR_t}{SD_{ar}}, \tag{5}$$

where SD_{at} is the standard deviation of the AR_t across time from -90 to $+30$. Using this method assumes that the AR_ts are independent and identically, normally distributed across time. Since the event dates are not uniform with respect to calendar time, the assumption of independence should not be violated. If the assumption is violated, and the AR_ts are not independent, the statistic will be overstated. Brown and Warner's (1980) simulation study concluded the t-test was superior to other tests in event studies.

A test statistic is computed for the cumulative abnormal returns over various intervals T_1 to T_2. This statistic is the one originally reported in Brenner (1979) and is computed as follows:

$$T = \frac{CAR_{T_1, T_2}}{CSD_{T_1, T_2}}. \tag{6}$$

The CAR_{T_1, T_2} is the change in CAR over the interval. CSD is the cumulative standard deviation. It is found by summing the cross-sectional variances of the AR_t at each time t during the specified interval and dividing by N. The square root is taken to provide the standard deviation.

For this study, if the securities' market viewed the death of a key executive as negative information, the test statistics for the AR_ts and CARs around the time of the announcement will be statistically negative. However, if a key executive's death was considered irrelevant, the test statistics will show the AR_ts and CARs to be insignificantly different from 0.

The single-index market model has been criticized particularly for the nonsynchronous data problem described by Scholes and Williams (1977). However, Brown and Warner (1983) concluded that procedures for correcting nonsynchronous data are unnecessary. Furthermore, Brown and Warner (1980) and Brenner (1979) concluded that the market model reaches correct conclusions at least as often as more complex models. In addition, Davidson (1984) found that alternate specifications of the predictive model, even including an industry factor, did not qualitatively change the conclusions obtained with the market model.

To confirm the results obtained with the market model, we also used the average return model to generate the normal returns. The procedure is similar to that for the market model, except that instead of using first-pass regressions to estimate the model's parameters, α_i (the regression intercept) is defined as 0, and the slope, β_1, is defined as 1. The use of the average return model permits the computation of the abnormal returns and the cumulative abnormal returns without relying on potentially unstable market parameters.

One final potential problem with this methodology is the possible presence of heuristic noise in the data. For example, other major announcements that affect value may affect the return series of the firms studied. If these announcements are unrelated to the deaths of the key executives and are therefore random with respect to the event time, they generally have little effect on reported events. This is especially true with large sample sizes, because of the averaging process shown in Equation 3.

Dan L. Worrell earned his Ph.D. degree from Louisiana State University; he is an associate professor and Chairperson of the Management Department at the John A. Walker College of Business, Appalachian State University. His current research interests include turnover and ethical decision making.

Wallace N. Davidson III is an associate professor of finance at North Texas State University. He received his Ph.D. degree from The Ohio State University. His current research interests include stock market efficiency and public utilities.

P. R. Chandy earned his D.B.A. degree from Texas Tech University. He is an associate professor of finance at North Texas State University. His current research interests focus on investments and utilities.

Sharon L. Garrison is an assistant professor of finance at East Tennessee State University. She received her D.B.A. degree from the University of Texas, Arlington. Her current research interests include corporate finance and investments.

Practice Self-Test

The Problem

_____

_____

_____

The Procedures

_____

_____

_____

The Method of Analysis

_____

_____

_____

The Major Conclusion(s)

_____

_____

_____

Reasons for Classification as Historical Research

_____

_____

_____

Method-Specific Evaluation Criteria

1. Were the sources of data related to the problem mostly primary or mostly secondary?

2. Was each piece of data subjected to external criticism?

3. Was each piece of data subjected to internal criticism?

REFERENCES

BERLINGER, R. E. (1978). *Historical analysis: Contemporary approaches to Clio's craft.* New York: John Wiley & Sons.

BLOCK, J. (1971). *Understanding historical research: A search for truth.* Glen Rock, NJ: Research Publications.

DRUCKER, P. F. (1973). *Management: Tasks, responsibilities, practices.* New York: Harper & Row.

GRIFFIN, R. W. (1988). Consequences of quality circles in an industrial setting: A longitudinal assessment. *Academy of Management Journal, 31*(2), 338–358.

HAMPTON, D. R., SUMMER, C. E., & WEBBER, R. A. (1982). *Organizational behavior and the practice of management* (4th ed.). Glenview, IL: Scott, Foresman.

INGLE, S. (1982). *Quality circles master guide: Increasing productivity with people power.* Englewood Cliffs, NJ: Prentice-Hall.

LOOMIS, C. J. (1988, December 19). Will 'Fasbee' pinch your bottom line? *Fortune,* pp. 93–108.

MICHELI, R. (1988, March). A few key items in an annual report can tell you a lot. *Money,* p. 181.

REAGAN FOR THE DEFENSE? (1988, December 6). *The Miami Herald,* p. 26A.

SCHECHTER, B. (1990, July 5). Past can enrich a company. *The Columbus Dispatch,* p. 6D.

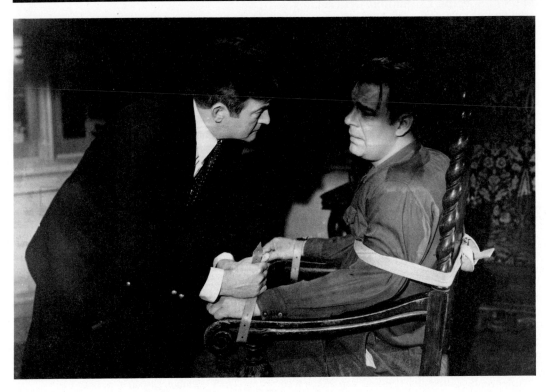

The responses given by a subject may be affected by her or his reaction to the interviewer . . . (page 252)

7

The Descriptive Method

Objectives

After reading Chapter 7, you should be able to do the following:

1. State briefly the purpose of descriptive research.
2. List the major steps involved in designing and conducting a descriptive research study.
3. State the major difference between self-report and observational research.
4. Describe briefly four types of self-report research.
5. List and briefly describe the steps involved in conducting a questionnaire study.
6. Identify and briefly describe four major differences between an interview study and a questionnaire study.
7. Describe briefly three types of observational research.
8. Describe briefly the steps involved in conducting an observational study.

DEFINITION, PURPOSE, AND PROCESS

Descriptive research involves collecting data in order to test hypotheses or to answer questions concerning the current status of the subject of the study. A descriptive study determines and reports the way things are. The descriptive method in general, and specific types of descriptive research in particular, will be discussed in some detail for two major reasons. First, a high percentage of reported research studies are descriptive. Second, the descriptive method is useful for investigating a variety of business-and-management problems. Typical descriptive studies are concerned with the assessment of attitudes, opinions, demographic information, conditions, and procedures. Descriptive data are usually collected through a questionnaire survey, interviews, observation, or some combination of these methods. Just as the historical researcher has no control over what *was*, the descriptive researcher has no control over what *is* and can only measure what already exists.

Descriptive research sounds very simple; many of you have probably heard someone say, "Well, let's just use a little questionnaire to find out what people think about that." There is considerably more to it, however, than just asking questions and reporting answers. The same basic process is involved as for the other methods of research, and each component must be just as conscientiously executed; for example, samples must be carefully selected, and appropriate relationships and conclusions must be derived from the data. In addition, descriptive studies involve a number of unique problems. For example, self-report studies, such as those utilizing questionnaires or interviews, often suffer from lack of response; many subjects do not return mailed questionnaires or attend scheduled interviews. In these situations, it is very difficult to interpret findings, since people who do not respond may feel very differently from those who do. Twenty percent of a sample, for example, might feel very negatively about tiered pay systems and might avail themselves of every opportunity to express their unhappiness, such as on your questionnaire. The other 80%, who are neutral or even positively inclined to the subject, might not be as motivated to respond. Thus, if conclusions were based only on those who responded, wrong conclusions might be drawn concerning feelings toward tiered pay systems.

In a recent study on customer satisfaction, 5,400 senior executives in service companies were asked to define customer satisfaction (Gerber, 1989). The survey results were based on 686 questionnaires that were returned—a 13% response rate! Also, uncontrolled variables may interfere with the best-planned study involving interviews if some significant event occurs halfway through the interviewing time so that those interviewed before the event feel one way and those interviewed after the event feel very differently about the same subject. In a similar way, descriptive studies using observational techniques to collect data also involve complexities that are not readily apparent. Observers, for example, must be trained and recording forms developed so that data will be collected objectively and reliably.

Once a descriptive problem has been defined, related literature reviewed, and hypotheses or questions stated, the researcher must give careful thought to sample selection and data collection. Which population has the desired information, for example, is not always readily apparent; this point is often not sufficiently thought through ahead of time. Also, alternative methods frequently are available for collecting desired data, one of which is generally more appropriate. Suppose, for example, that your boss appears at your desk one morning waving an article from the local newspaper; the article states that the average worker wastes over half his or her time at work. Your boss wants you to find out how much time is wasted in your company. As you think about the problem, you identify some activities that you think of as wasted time. These include taking breaks, socializing, making personal phone calls, trying to find materials, waiting for meetings to begin, and so on, and you hypothesize that the average worker in your company probably spends one third of her or his time doing these things. Your first thought might be to send a questionnaire to a sample of department heads. This procedure, however, would be based on the assumption that department heads know how workers spend their time. On the one hand, while it is hoped that department heads would be familiar with the duties and responsibilities of the workers in their departments, it is likely that worker reports concerning time devoted to each activity would differ, perhaps significantly, from department head reports. Thus, directly asking the workers themselves might result in more accurate information. On the other hand, it is just possible that workers might subconsciously tend to underestimate the amount of time they spend on activities they consider to be interesting, such as socializing or making personal phone calls, while exaggerating the amount of time they spend on activities they consider to be distasteful, such as waiting for meetings to begin. Thus, further thought might indicate that direct observation would probably yield the most objective, accurate data.

Once you have decided on a target population and a data-collection strategy, the next steps are to identify your accessible population, determine the needed sample size, select an appropriate sampling technique, and select or develop a data-collection instrument. Since one frequently is asking questions that have not been asked before or seeking information that is not already available, a descriptive study requires the development of an instrument appropriate for obtaining the desired information. Of course, if there is a valid, reliable instrument available, it can be used, but using an instrument just "because it is there" is not a good idea. If you want the correct answers, you have to ask the correct questions. If instrument development is necessary, the instrument should be tried out and revised where necessary before it is used in the actual study. Once you have identified an appropriate sample and selected or developed a valid data-collection instrument, your next step is to plan and execute the specific procedures of the study (when the instrument will be administered, to whom, and how) and the data-analysis procedures. Of course, the basic steps in conducting a descriptive study will vary, depending upon the nature of the research. In a content-analysis study, for example, human subjects are not involved. If you were concerned about the completeness and clarity of your company's performance-appraisal forms, you would conduct a content-analysis study in which you would review actual forms and might not talk to the individuals who filled them out.

There are many different types of descriptive studies, and classifying them is not easy. However, a logical way to categorize them initially is in terms of how data are collected, through self-report or observation. In a self-report study, information may be solicited from individuals using questionnaires, interviews, or standardized attitude scales. In an observation study, individuals are not asked for information; rather, the researcher obtains the desired data through other means, such as direct observation. These two categories are not, of course, mutually exclusive; a self-report study may involve observation and vice versa. A case study, for example, is primarily observational in that information is collected *about* an individual or group. One or more instruments may be administered, however, in order to describe more fully the characteristics of the individual or group under study.

SELF-REPORT RESEARCH

There are several major types of self-report research studies. The most well known and most often used is probably survey research, which generally uses questionnaires or interviews to collect data.

Types of Self-report Research

While survey research is the most frequently encountered type of self-report research, there are several other types of self-report research that you may encounter. Although seldom used in business settings, these include follow-up and sociometric studies.

Survey Research

A survey is an attempt to collect data from members of a population in order to determine the current status of that population with respect to one or more variables. Although people generally use the terms *survey* and *questionnaire* interchangeably, the term *survey* is used here as a general category with *questionnaire* and *interview* as specific methodologies used to conduct survey research. Populations used in survey research may be broadly defined, such as the American buying public, or more narrowly defined, such as all working mothers in Typicalville, U.S.A. Determining "current status . . . with respect to some variable" may involve assessment of a variety of types of information such as attitudes, opinions, characteristics, and demographic information. Surveys are often viewed with some disdain because many people have encountered poorly planned, poorly executed survey studies using poorly developed instruments. An additional reason for disliking surveys is that we often feel we have been surveyed too often on too many issues—particularly at dinner time on the telephone. Condemning survey research because it has often been misused, however, is similar to disliking telephones because people use them to make obscene calls.

Although we often hear political candidates claiming that they "don't pay attention to the polls," descriptive research at its best can provide very valuable data. It represents considerably more than asking questions and reporting answers. Successful survey research involves careful design and execution of each of the components of the research process, including the formulation of hypotheses; it may also describe variables and relationships among variables. Surveys are used in many fields, including political science, sociology, economics, education, and, of course, business. In business a common use is in the area of market research; within companies, the most common use of surveys is to determine employee attitudes and opinions. Although you may be called upon to understand and use the results of market research in your work, you are more likely to be the recipient of, or the originator of, internal surveys intended to assess needs, determine trends, ascertain opinions, or evaluate employee morale and the overall corporate climate.

Surveys may be either sample surveys or census surveys; usually they are sample surveys. In a *sample survey,* as the name suggests, the researcher infers information about a population of interest based on the responses of a sample drawn from that population; preferably, the sample is either a simple-random sample or a stratified-random sample. In a *census survey,* an attempt is made to acquire data from each and every member of a population; a census survey is usually conducted when a population is relatively small and readily accessible, such as when a manager collects data from each first-line supervisor in her or his department. Sample surveys are sometimes referred to as cross-sectional; this means that information is collected at a specific point in time from a sample that is supposed to represent all the relevant subgroups in the population. Another term sometimes used for a cross-sectional sample in an organization is a *vertical slice;* in a vertical slice, all levels of management or all levels of employees are sampled. Surveys concerned with the current status of construct variables (such as attitude or morale), as distinguished from concrete variables (such as the number of business journals managers read or the number of absences due to illness in a month), not only involve careful selection from, and definition of, a population but also require care in selection or development of the data-gathering instrument. It is considerably easier to develop a valid, reliable instrument for determining the percentage of managers holding advanced degrees than it is to develop an instrument for assessing managers' attitudes toward required management-training programs, for example.

There are a variety of types of surveys, many of which are familiar to most people. The results of various public opinion polls, as mentioned previously, are frequently reported by the media. Such polls represent an attempt to determine how all the members of a population (be it the American public in general or the citizens of Skunk Hollow) think about a political, social, educational, or economic issue, and not just the opinion of vocal, special-interest groups within the population. Public opinion polls are almost always sample surveys. You may even have complained, "How do they know what I think—they never ask me!" Samples are selected to represent properly relevant subgroups (in terms of such variables as socioeconomic status, sex, and geographic location) and results are often reported separately for each of those subgroups as well as for the total group.

One type of survey that has gained popularity in business recently is the employee-attitude, or morale, survey. Generally it is conducted for the purpose of identifying problem areas and strengths within a company. Many employee-attitude surveys are developed within a particular company. In addition, some surveys may be used for multiple purposes such as job evaluation, training-needs assessment, and development of performance appraisals and compensation; examples of these include the Management Position Description Questionnaire (Tornow & Pinto, 1976) or the Job Diagnostic Survey (Hackman & Oldham, 1980). A more complex purpose of survey research is to assess parts of the overall corporate culture. As Schein (1985) has pointed out, corporate culture is a subject of increasing concern, whether it is perceived as simply the "felt" differences between companies or as the most essential values and assumptions that define an organization. Research might be done, for example, by using the Organizational Culture Inventory (Cooke & Lafferty, 1983, 1986), an instrument that attempts to measure the behavioral norms and expectations of an organization and its subunits. Comparisons of similarities and differences within and between different organizations may be made by using survey research to ascertain at least some of the elements comprising corporate culture.

Follow-up Studies

A follow-up study is conducted to determine the status of a group of interest after some period of time. Like attitude or morale surveys, follow-up studies are often conducted by businesses for the purpose of determining the current state of affairs as contrasted to affairs at some previous date. In a large organizational development program intended to improve employee morale and overall effectiveness, follow-up studies should be built into the basic design of the program. Without these studies, organizational development specialists and senior management will never be able to ascertain whether improvement has been made. Some portions of the quality circles article at the end of Chapter 1 illustrate the use of follow-up studies regarding employee morale.

Follow-up studies may also be conducted solely for research purposes. A researcher may be interested, for example, in assessing the degree to which initial treatment effects have been maintained over time. If you have been involved in training within a company, you probably have been exposed to the sort of survey training professionals call "happiness surveys"; in these you are asked at the end of the training what you liked and didn't like about the program. A more appropriate assessment of training, however, would be to determine whether or not employees actually use the knowledge or skills from the training program back on the job. To determine this, a follow-up study would be conducted in which the former trainees are asked whether they use the new skills, how effective they think they are, and what additional training they might want. A follow-up study might be used to determine whether training that was perceived to be highly effective immediately after it was conducted is still effective six months to a year later. Given the amount of money spent annually on training, it's unfortunate that more follow-up studies aren't done to provide information for revision or continuance of specific training programs (Rice, 1988). Many treatments that have an initial impact do not have a lasting effect; initial differences "wash out," or disappear, after some period of time. A treatment may temporarily change attitudes, for example, but when the subjects are removed from the experimental setting they may gradually regress to their original point of view. As you may recall in the quality circle study, initially productivity and morale were improved; however, after 18 months there was no significant change from the level before the study. Conversely, some treatments do not result in initial differences but may produce long-range effects. Delayed feedback concerning the adequacy of job performance, for example, may not necessarily improve initial job performance, but it may facilitate employee satisfaction. If follow-up data were not collected in this example, it would be erroneous to conclude that delayed feedback has no effect. Thus, in many areas of research, a follow-up study is essential to a more complete understanding of the effects of a given approach or technique.

Sociometric Studies

Sociometry is the assessment and analysis of the interpersonal relationships within a group of individuals. By analyzing the expressed choices or preferences of group members for other members of the group, degree of acceptance or rejection for members of the group can be determined. The basic sociometric process involves asking each member to indicate with which other members she or he would most like to engage in a particular activity. For example, you might ask subjects to list in order of preference the three individuals they would most like to work with on a cooperative project. As you well know, choices will vary depending upon the activity; the person you would most enjoy going with to a party is not necessarily the same person with whom you would like to work on the management team—or vice versa. The choices made by the group members are graphically depicted in a diagram called a sociogram. A sociogram may take many forms and use a variety of symbols, but basically it shows who chose whom. A sociogram will clearly identify "stars"—members chosen quite frequently, "isolates"—members not chosen, and "cliques"—small subgroups of individuals who mutually select each other.

Sociometric techniques are used by both researchers and practitioners. A number of studies, for example, have been concerned with the relationship between group status and other variables such as personality characteristics. Another type of research study involves assessment of initial interpersonal relationship patterns, introduction of a treatment designed to change the existing pattern, and posttreatment assessment to determine pattern changes. The increasing popularity of project management and the use of team building to create good working teams suggests that sociometric studies will increasingly be used in business settings. In a traditional business setting, for example, the boss may communicate with each of the workers, but they may not communicate with one another. A sociometry-based representation of this hierarchical communication pattern is shown in Figure 7.1. If the communication pattern is found to be a traditional chain of command in which each individual communicates only with the person next higher or lower in the organization, the communication can be represented as it is in Figure 7.2. For good communications within a working group such as a project team, the communication should flow freely between and among all members of the group, as shown in Figure 7.3.

In addition to displaying existing communication patterns between and among group members in a project team, the sociometric technique also may be used by managers in an attempt, for example, to bring isolates into the group. If Sally Shy were identified as being an isolate, her manager could make a concerted effort to provide

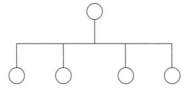

Figure 7.1. Hierarchical communication pattern.

Note: Adapted from "Communication Networks" by M. Shaw, 1964, In L. Berkowitz (Ed.), *Advances in experimental social psychology, 1,* pp. 111–147.

Figure 7.2. Chain-of-command communication pattern.

Note: Adapted from "Communication Networks" by M. Shaw, 1964, In L. Berkowitz (Ed.), *Advances in experimental social psychology, 1,* pp. 111–147.

opportunities for Sally to interact with other members of the work group. It is hoped that sociometric data will be used ethically and not to the detriment of workers who may have valuable skills but need some assistance in interpersonal relations. The introduction of a minority worker into an established work group suggests some opportunities for effective uses of sociometrics on the part of the manager who wants this to be a smooth and comfortable transition for everyone. Thus, the sociometric process is one that is relatively simple to apply and can provide data useful for the solution of immediate social problems and for the development of theories concerning interpersonal relationships within a group.

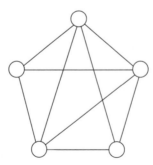

Figure 7.3. Open communication pattern.

Note: Adapted from "Communication Networks" by M. Shaw, 1964, In L. Berkowitz (Ed.), *Advances in experimental social psychology, 1,* pp. 111–147.

Conducting Self-Report Research

Self-report research requires the collection of standardized, quantifiable information from all members of a population or sample. In other words, in order to obtain comparable data from all subjects, the same questions must be asked. Many of the types of tests described in Chapter 5 can be used in a self-report research study. Two commonly used procedures for collecting self-report data are the questionnaire study and the interview study.

Conducting a Questionnaire Study

Unfavorable criticisms of questionnaires are related not to their use but to their misuse. Too many carelessly and incompetently constructed questionnaires have unfortunately been administered and distributed. Development of a sound questionnaire requires both skill and time. The use of a questionnaire, however, has some definite advantages over other methods of collecting data that are not available through other sources. In comparison to use of an interview procedure, for example, a questionnaire is much more efficient in that it requires less time, is less expensive, and permits collection of data from a much larger sample. Questionnaires may be administered directly to subjects but are usually mailed. Although a personally administered questionnaire has some of the same advantages inherent in the use of an interview, such as the opportunity to establish rapport with responders, explain the purposes of the study, and clarify individual items, it is not usual that the members of a sample of interest are conveniently found together in one location. Attempting to travel to each responder in order to administer the questionnaire is generally impractical and eliminates the advantage of being able to reach a large sample.

A strategy that may be used for administering a questionnaire study is via a computer terminal. If individuals frequently are near a central location, such as the company cafeteria or employee entrance, a terminal might display the questionnaire for their completion. If office computers are linked by a phone mail or networking system, the questionnaire may be made available in this fashion. IBM, for example, uses such a system to determine employee training needs (J. Cheatham, personal communication, May 16, 1989). The advantage of this system is that the computer can also handle the compilation of questionnaire data; a disadvantage for the researcher is the need to devise ways to prevent individuals from responding to the questionnaire more than once and also to protect the confidentiality of those who respond. Fax machines provide another means for distributing and receiving questionnaire results.

The steps in conducting a questionnaire study are essentially the same as for other types of research, although data collecting involves some unique considerations. The steps are as follows:

1. *Statement of the problem.* The problem under investigation, and the topic of the questionnaire, must be of sufficient significance to motivate subjects to respond; questionnaires dealing with trivial issues usually end up in the circular file of potential

subjects. The problem must be defined in terms of specific objectives concerning the kind of information needed; specific hypotheses or questions must be formulated, and every item on the questionnaire should directly relate to them.

2. *Selection of subjects.* Subjects should be selected using an appropriate sampling technique (or an entire population may be used), and identified subjects must be persons who not only have the desired information but who also are likely to be willing to give it. Individuals who possess the desired information but are not sufficiently interested, or for whom the topic under study has little meaning, are not likely to respond. It is sometimes worth the effort to do a preliminary check of potential subjects to determine their receptivity. In some situations it is more productive to send the questionnaire to a person of authority rather than directly to the person with the desired information; if a person's boss passes along a questionnaire and asks the person to complete and return it, that person is more likely to do so than if you ask him or her. Of course in some instances, you'll need to be careful to maintain the confidentiality of the subject; having your boss hand you a questionnaire regarding her or his effectiveness with the suggestion that the boss will review it before returning it to the researcher will get you pretty predictable results!

3. *Construction of the questionnaire.* As a general guideline, the questionnaire should be as attractive and brief, and as easy to respond to, as possible. Sloppy-looking questionnaires turn people off, lengthy questionnaires turn people off, and questionnaires requiring lengthy responses *really* turn people off! Turning people off is not the way to get them to respond. To meet this guideline you must carefully plan both the content and the format of the questionnaire. No item should be included that does not directly relate to the objectives of the study, and structured, or closed-form, items should be used if at all possible. A structured item consists of a question and a list of alternative responses from which the responder selects. The list of alternatives should include all possible responses, and each possible response should be distinctly different from the rest. The difference between "often" and "frequently" as responses is not clear to many of us! In some situations, a very short written response may be required, but generally a structured item is multiple-choice in nature (yes or no; A, B, C, D, or E). In addition to facilitating responses, structured items also facilitate data analysis; scoring is very objective and efficient. A potential disadvantage is the possibility that a subject's true response is not listed among the alternatives. Therefore, questionnaires should include an "other" category for each item, except something such as male or female, and a space for a subject to write in a response not anticipated by the researcher.

An unstructured-item format, in which the responder has complete freedom of response (questions are asked with no possible responses indicated), is sometimes defended on the grounds that it permits greater depth of response and may give insight into the reasons for responses. While this may be true, and unstructured items may be simpler to construct, the disadvantages of this approach generally outweigh the advantages; subjects often provide information extraneous to the objectives of the study, responses frequently are difficult to score and analyze, and subjects usually are not happy with an instrument that requires written responses. For certain topics or purposes unstructured items may be necessary, and some questionnaires contain both structured and unstructured items. In general, however, structured items are to be preferred.

Individual items should also be constructed according to a set of guidelines. The number one rule is that each question should deal with a single concept and be worded as clearly as possible; any term or concept that might mean different things to different people should be defined. You wouldn't want to ask, for example, "Do you spend a lot of time each week copying materials for your boss?"; one secretary might consider one hour per day "a lot," while another might consider one hour per week "a lot." Instead, ask "How much time do you spend per week copying materials for your boss—(A) less than 30 minutes, (B) between 30 minutes and a hour, (C) between 1 and 3 hours, (D) between 3 and 5 hours, (E) more than 5 hours?" Also, when necessary, questions should indicate a point of reference. In the example just given, rather than asking just "how much time" was spent, the question specified "per week." As another example, if you were interested not only in how many hours were actually spent in copying materials but also in secretaries' perceptions concerning that time, you would not ask, "Do you think you spend a lot of time copying materials?" Instead, you would ask, "Do you think you spend a lot of time *compared to other secretaries* (or compared to whatever you wished) copying materials for your boss?" as several of the previous examples illustrate, underlining (in a typed questionnaire) or italicizing (in a printed one) key phrases may also help to clarify questions.

There are also a number of "don'ts" to keep in mind when constructing items. First, avoid leading questions that suggest that one response may be more appropriate than another. Second, avoid touchy questions to which the responder might not reply honestly. Asking a manager, for example, if he or she sets high standards for performance is like asking a mother if she loves her children; the answer in both cases most likely is going to be "of course!" Asking a question that assumes a fact not necessarily in evidence is another major "don't"; such questions present alternatives that are all unacceptable. The classic question of this nature is, "Have you stopped beating your spouse?" The question calls for a simple yes or no response, but how does a person respond who has never beaten his or her spouse? If the answer is yes, it suggests that person *used* to beat his or her spouse but has stopped; if the answer is no, it suggests that the person is *still* beating his or her spouse!

Typically, unwarranted assumptions are more subtle and more difficult to spot. Several years ago, one of the authors received a questionnaire on which appeared the question, "Were you satisfied with the salary increase you received last year?" It so happened that the previous year had been a financially tough one; no faculty member had received a salary increase. Thus, there was no way to answer the question. A yes answer would have indicated satisfaction with no salary increase; a no response would have indicated dissatisfaction with whatever salary increase was received. The problem could have been avoided by the addition of a qualifying question such as, "Did you receive a salary increase last year?"

Finally, don't include a series of questions that will allow anyone to identify a specific responder. Most likely you will want to include demographic data (sex, age, years in current position, and so on) in your questionnaire so that you are able to discuss subgroups within your overall population. In some instances, however, the series of questions will be such that only one member of the population could answer the questions in a particular way. For example, if only one person received a doctoral degree from a specific university in 1986, alumni questionnaires asking the responder to specify which degree was received and the year in which it was received would certainly identify the responder very clearly.

When you are developing items for a questionnaire, it helps to place each item on a separate index card. This facilitates arrangement of the items so that they will be presented in a logical order; it is much easier to reorder index cards than to redo a questionnaire once it is developed. Of course, if you are using a computer to develop your questionnaire, you can easily rearrange your items, adding, subtracting, and editing at will. After the items have been developed, and their order determined, directions to responders must be written. Standardized directions promote standardized, comparable responses. Directions should specify how the subject is to respond and where. When determining how subjects should respond, you will want to consider how the results will be tabulated. If the results are to be machine-scored, for example, you may need to have subjects use a separate answer sheet and a number two pencil instead of having them circle responses on the questionnaire. If you are using a telephone-linked computer response system in which your responders will touch a specific telephone key to indicate their response, you will need different instructions. Whatever method is used, the directions need to be clear.

4. *Validation of the questionnaire.* A too-often-neglected procedure is validation of the questionnaire in order to determine if it measures what it was developed to measure. Researchers probably avoid validation because it is not easy and requires much additional time and effort. If, however, you are going to expend considerable time and effort on the project, you probably will want to remember the old axiom that anything worth doing is worth doing well. The appropriate validation procedure for a given questionnaire will depend upon the nature of the instrument. A questionnaire developed to determine work behavior of secretaries, for example, might be validated by observing a sample of responders to determine the degree to which their actual behavior is consistent with their self-reported behavior.

5. *Preparation of a cover letter.* Every mailed questionnaire must be accompanied by a cover letter that explains what is being asked of the responder and why and, one hopes, motivates the responder to fulfill the request. The letter should be brief, neat, and addressed specifically to the potential responder (Dear Mr. Magoo, not Dear Sir). Luckily, data base-management computer programs can assist you with the chore of personalizing your letters. The letter should also explain the purpose of the study, emphasize its importance and significance, and give the subject a good reason for cooperating; the fact that you need the data for your thesis or dissertation is not a good reason (to anyone other than you). If at all possible, you will probably want to offer to share the results of the study when completed. It also helps if you can obtain the endorsement of a professional organization, institution, group, or manager with whom the subject is associated or whom the subject views with respect. If the group is too

heterogeneous or has no identifiable affiliation in common, a general appeal to professionalism can be made. Sometimes even humor and a little psychology are used. For example, a professional association sent out a questionnaire concerning program ideas for the coming year to its members. A dollar bill was enclosed along with a note indicating that the board of directors was aware that the recipient of the questionnaire was quite busy and that the dollar was a gesture of appreciation for the anticipated cooperation. Not only did the association receive a high rate of return on the questionnaire, most of the responders also returned the dollar! Another strategy that sometimes works is having the letter signed by a respected, well-known person.

If the questions to be asked are at all threatening (such as items dealing with sexual harassment on the job or attitudes toward management), anonymity or confidentiality of responses must be assured. Complete anonymity, on the one hand, probably increases the truthfulness of responses as well as the percentage of returns. On the other hand, anonymity makes follow-up efforts extremely difficult, since you do not know who responded and who did not. It also makes subgroup comparisons impossible (for example, first-line supervisors versus middle managers) unless specific classification items are included in the questionnaire itself (for example, what is your job classification?). As noted previously, these demographic questions, if not carefully constructed, may serve to identify unusual subjects. If identification is deemed necessary, complete confidentiality of responses must be guaranteed. You might say, for example, "All responses will be retained by Olde Ivie University;" or "Information provided to the management of Curious Corporation will be in the form of generalized, statistical reports designed to protect the confidentiality of your response."

A specific deadline by which the completed questionnaire is to be returned should be given. This date should give subjects enough time to respond but discourage them from placing your questionnaire on the bottom of the "To do" list. Usually 2 to 3 weeks is sufficient. Each letter to be sent should be individually signed; admittedly this takes considerably more time than making copies of one signed letter, but it adds a personal touch that might make the difference in the potential subject's decision to comply or not. Again, some computer programs have the capacity to include signatures that appear to be individually done under all but the closest scrutiny. Finally, the act of responding should be made as painless as possible. A stamped, addressed, return envelope should be included; if not, your letter and questionnaire will very likely be placed into the circular file along with the mail addressed to "occupant"! (See Figure 7.4 for an example of a properly written cover letter and questionnaire.)

6. *Pretesting the questionnaire.* The questionnaire should be tried out in a field test just as a research plan should be executed first as a pilot study, and for essentially the same reasons. Nothing is more disconcerting than sending out a questionnaire that was not pretested only to discover that the subjects didn't understand the directions or the questions. Pretesting the questionnaire yields data concerning instrument deficiencies as well as suggestions for improvement. Having two or three available people complete the questionnaire first will result in the identification of major

David Peters
7475 W. 18th Ave.
Hialeah FL 33014

Dear David Peters:

On behalf of everyone at AT&T, I'd like to take this opportunity to wish you and those
close to you the best this holiday season and to extend my sincere thanks to you for using
AT&T as your long distance company.

All of us at AT&T appreciate your business. And we intend to keep working hard to provide
you with the highest quality of long distance service.

As a valued AT&T customer, your opinion leads our efforts to improve our service to meet
your changing communications needs. To help us meet those needs, please take a moment to
complete the enclosed questionnaire. In return, we'll send you an AT&T Long Distance Gift
Certificate which may be redeemed for AT&T Long Distance Service.

Once again, our best wishes for a joyous holiday and a happy healthy year ahead.

Sincerely,

Kevin Hanft
AT&T
Consumer Program Manager

Figure 7.4. Example of a cover letter and questionnaire. Reprinted with
permission of AT&T.

problems. The subsequently revised instrument and the cover letter should then be
sent to a small sample from your intended population or a highly similar population.
Pretest subjects should be encouraged to make comments and suggestions concerning
directions, recording procedures, and specific items. If the percentage of returns is very
low, then both the letter and the instrument should be carefully reexamined. The
feedback from those who do respond should be carefully studied and considered.
Lastly, proposed data-tabulation and analysis procedures should be applied to the
pretest data. The end product of the pretest will be a revised instrument ready to be
mailed to the already selected subjects.

   7. *Follow-up activities.* Not everyone to whom you send a questionnaire is going to
return it (what an understatement!). Some recipients have no intention of completing
it, others mean to but put it off so long that they either forget it or lose it. It is for this
latter group that follow-up activities are primarily conducted. The higher your

So we can better meet your future communications needs,
please take a moment to answer a few questions.

1. To me, AT&T's most valuable benefit is its:
   (Please check only one)
   a ☐ Customer Service
   b ☐ Network Technology
   c ☐ International Capability
   d ☐ Price Value

2. To meet my future needs, AT&T should increase the value of its:
   (Please check as many as apply)
   a ☐ Customer Service
   b ☐ Network Technology
   c ☐ Public Phone Service
   d ☐ Price Value

3. In the future I would recommend AT&T Long Distance Service to a friend.
   a ☐ Yes
   b ☐ No

In appreciation for your time and effort in completing and returning this survey by January 15, 1990, we wi ll send you an AT&T Long Distance Gift Certificate.

Thank you from everyone at AT&T.

---

(307) 821-7102 NT-0481267
David Peters
7475 W. 18th Ave.
Hialeah FL 33014

Figure 7.4. continued

percentage of returns, the better. Although you won't expect 100%, you should not be satisfied with whatever you get after your first mailing. If your percentage of returns is not 70 or so, the validity of your conclusions will be weak. Given all the work you have already done, it makes little sense to end up with shaky findings and a study of limited value when some additional effort on your part may make a big difference.

An initial follow-up strategy is simply to send out a reminder postcard. This will prompt those who meant to fill out the questionnaire but put it off and have not yet lost it. If responses are not anonymous, you can mail a card only to those who have not responded. If they are anonymous, and you do not know who has and who has not responded, send a card to everyone; include a statement like the ones used by magazine subscription companies— "If you have already responded, please disregard this reminder and thank you for your cooperation." Follow-up activities are usually begun shortly after the deadline for responding has passed. A second set of questionnaires is sent to subjects but with a new cover letter and, of course, another stamped envelope. The new letter should suggest that you know they meant to respond but that they may have misplaced the questionnaire or maybe they never even received it. In other words, do not scold them; provide them with an acceptable reason for their nonresponse. The significance and purpose of the study should be repeated and the importance of their input reemphasized. You may want to suggest subtly that many others are responding; this implies that their peers have found the study to be important and so should they.

If the second mailing does not result in an overall acceptable percentage of return, be creative. Magazine-subscription agencies have developed follow-up procedures to a science and have become very creative. One of the authors once let a subscription to a popular weekly magazine lapse and received several gentle reminders and "sensational one-time-only offers." As the incident was described later: "One afternoon I received a long-distance call from several thousand miles away, and the sweet voice at the other end suggested that my mail was apparently not getting through, and wouldn't I like to renew my subscription? I bit!" The point is that phone calls, if feasible, may be used, or any other method of written, verbal, or personal communication that might induce additional subjects to respond. They may grow to admire your persistence!

If your questionnaire is well constructed and your cover letter well written, you should get at least an adequate response rate. First mailings will typically produce at least a 40% return. A second mailing should bring your percentage up to around 70%; mailings beyond a second are generally not too cost effective. After a second mailing, use other approaches until an acceptable percentage of returns is achieved.

8. *Dealing with nonresponse.* Despite your initial and follow-up efforts, you may find yourself with an unacceptably low response rate of perhaps 60%. The problem is one of generalizability of results since you do not know if the 60% represents the population from which the sample was originally selected as well as the total original sample. If you knew that the responding subjects were essentially a random sample of the total sample, there would be no problem, but you do not know that. The subjects who responded may be different in some systematic way from subjects who did not respond (the old "volunteer syndrome"); they may be better educated, feel more strongly about the issue (one of the authors responded promptly to at least five follow-up surveys intended to measure satisfaction over a new car purchase; in this case, the response was based on *loving* the car!), or be more successful.

The usual approach to dealing with excessive nonresponse is to try to determine if subjects who do not respond are different from subjects who do respond in some systematic way by randomly selecting a small subsample of nonresponding subjects and interviewing them, either in person or by phone. Through an interview, the researcher may be able to obtain responses to questionnaire items as well as determine any distinguishing characteristics. If responses are essentially the same for the interviewed subjects as for the original responding subjects, it may be assumed that the response group is representative and the results generalizable. If they are significantly different, such differences as well as resulting limitations to generalizability must be discussed in the research report. For example, instead of concluding that all new Mazda owners have few problems with new cars, you might conclude that at least those who love their cars have few problems (naturally!).

9. *Analysis of results.* When presenting the results of a questionnaire study, the response rate for each item should be given as well as the total sample size and the overall percentage of returns, since all responders may not answer all questions. The simplest way to present the results is to indicate the percentage of responding subjects who selected each alternative for each item. For example, "On item 4 dealing with possession of an MBA, 30% said yes, 40% said no, 20% said they were working on one, and 10% did not respond to this item." This sort of calculation is frequently built into the computer programs available for analyzing your data. In addition to simply determining choices, relationships between variables can be investigated by comparing responses on one item with responses on other items. For example, it might be determined that 80% of those who have an MBA use desktop computers frequently, while only 40% of those without degrees use desktop computers. Thus, possible explanations for certain attitudes and behaviors can be explored by identifying factors that seem to be related to certain responses. This type of relationship analysis can also be used to test hypotheses. For example, it might be hypothesized that managers with MBAs are more receptive to use of personal computers. The previous findings concerning MBAs and desktop computers would be data in support of the hypothesis. Establishment of a direct cause-effect relationship between possession of degrees and use of computers would not, however, be warranted. Owing to lack of manipulation of the variables, it would not be possible to determine whether (a) increased education results in use of computers, (b) companies employing MBAs expect them to use computers, or (c) managers who are interested in computers also seek out advanced degrees. Resolution of such issues would require the researcher to conduct a study using another method of research.

Conducting an Interview Study

An interview is essentially the oral, in-person, administration of a questionnaire to each member of a sample. The interview has a number of unique advantages and disadvantages. When well conducted it can produce in-depth data not possible with a questionnaire; it is expensive and time consuming, however, and generally involves smaller samples. The interview study may also be combined with a questionnaire study. In an organizational analysis, for example, a researcher may want to interview top management first and use a questionnaire to sample opinions from a more general group of employees. Another way to use the interview survey is to do preliminary interviews with a small sample of employees to determine the kinds of issues or problems that exist and then use a follow-up questionnaire to verify the results of the interview survey. An example of a large interview study is described in the popular management book *In Search of Excellence* (Peters & Waterman, 1982). In this study, a total of 33 companies were selected for in-depth interviewing, while an additional 22 companies were interviewed in less depth.

The interview is most appropriate for asking questions that cannot effectively be structured into a multiple-choice format, such as questions of a personal nature. In contrast to the questionnaire, the interview is flexible; the interviewer can adapt the situation to each subject. By establishing rapport and a trust relationship, the interviewer can often obtain data that subjects would not give on a questionnaire. The interview may also result in more accurate and honest responses since the interviewer can explain and clarify both the purpose of the research and individual questions. However, computer-based questionnaires sometimes give an impression of anonymity, which encourages very honest responses! Another advantage of the interview is that the interviewer can follow up on incomplete or unclear responses by asking additional probing questions. Reasons for particular responses can also be determined.

Direct interviewer-interviewee contact also has its disadvantages. The responses given by a subject may be affected by her or his reaction to the interviewer, either positive or negative. For example, a subject may become hostile or uncooperative if the interviewer reminds him of his first wife's father. In a work environment, of course, the credibility of the interviewer is important in interview surveys; employees are often concerned that their confidentiality will not be preserved, thereby jeopardizing their employment. Another disadvantage is that it is very time consuming and expensive, and the number of subjects who can be handled is generally considerably less than the number to whom you can send a questionnaire; as we discussed in Chapter 4, interviewing 500 people would be a monumental task compared to mailing 500 questionnaires. In addition, the interview requires a level of skill usually beyond that of the beginning researcher. Not only are research skills such as knowledge of sampling and instrument development required, but also a variety of communication and interpersonal relations skills are needed.

The steps in conducting an interview study are basically the same as for a questionnaire study, with some unique differences. The process of selecting and defining a problem and formulating hypotheses is essentially the same. Samples of subjects who possess the desired information are selected in the usual manner except that the sample is typically smaller. An effort must be made to get a commitment of cooperation from selected subjects. Subjects who do not keep their interview appointments present the same problems as subjects who do not return questionnaires. The problem is more serious for interviews, however, since the sample size is already smaller. If at all possible, it is best to schedule the interview in the subject's office rather than expecting interviewees to find the researcher; at the time the appointment is made, the researcher will probably want to specify what amount of time will be needed to complete the interview. The major differences between an interview study and a questionnaire study are the nature of the instrument involved (an interview guide as distinguished from a questionnaire), the need for good human relations and communications skills, methods for recording responses, and the nature of the pretest activities. Some concerns specific to interviews include the following:

1. *Construction of the interview guide.* The interviewer must have a written guide that indicates what questions are to be asked and in what order and what additional prompting or probing is permitted. It's extremely frustrating to have incomplete, and therefore relatively useless, answers when a lot of effort has been expended to obtain the interview in the first place. For example, a student recently conducted interviews with a small group of extremely busy people in widely dispersed sections of the city. One of her questions was, "How do you decide what kind of management training to offer?" The response she received in 80% of her interviews was, "A needs analysis." Because the student didn't use follow-up questions to find out *what kind* of needs analysis—written, interview, informal, and so on—her information was essentially useless.

In order to obtain useful, standardized, comparable data from each subject, each question in the interview should relate to a specific study objective. Also, as with a questionnaire, questions may be structured or unstructured. Since an interview is used when a questionnaire is not really appropriate, it usually involves unstructured or semi-structured questions. Structured questions, which require the interviewee to select from alternatives, are, of course, easier to analyze but tend to defeat the purpose of the interview. By contrast, completely unstructured questions, which allow absolute freedom of response, can yield in-depth responses and provide otherwise unobtainable insights but produce data that are very difficult to quantify and tabulate. Therefore, most interviews use a semi-structured approach involving the asking of structured questions followed by clarifying unstructured, or open-ended questions. The unstructured questions facilitate explanation and understanding of the responses to the structured questions. Thus, a combination of objectivity and depth can be obtained, and results can be tabulated as well as explained.

Many of the guidelines for constructing questionnaires apply to the construction of interview guides. The interview should be as brief as possible, and questions should be worded as clearly as possible. Terms should be defined when necessary and a point of reference given when appropriate. Also, leading questions should be avoided, as should questions based on the assumption of a fact not in evidence (for example, "Have you stopped beating your spouse?").

2. *Communication during the interview.* Effective communication during the interview is critical, and interviewers should be well trained before the study begins. Since first impressions can make a big difference, getting the interview off on the right foot is important. Before the first formal question is asked, some time should be spent in establishing rapport and putting the interviewee at ease. The purpose of the study should be explained and strict confidentiality of responses assured. As the interview proceeds, the interviewer should make full use of the advantages of the interview situation. He or she can, for example, explain the purpose of any question whose relevance to the purpose of the study is unclear to the subject. The interviewer should also be sensitive to the reactions of the subject and proceed accordingly. If a subject appears to be threatened by a particular line of questioning, for example, the interviewer may want to move on to other questions and return to the threatening questions later, when perhaps the interviewee is more relaxed. Or, if the subject is

carried away with a question and runs off the track, the interviewer can gently bring him or her back on target. Above all, the interviewer needs to avoid words or actions that may make the subject feel threatened or unhappy. Frowns and disapproving looks have no place in an interview!

3. *Recording responses.* Responses made during an interview can be recorded manually by the interviewer or mechanically by audio or video tape recording. If the interviewer records the responses manually, space is provided in the interview guide after each question; the responses are recorded either during the interview as it progresses or immediately after it is completed. If responses are recorded during the interview, it may tend to slow things down, especially if responses are at all lengthy; it also may make some subjects nervous to have someone writing down every word they say. If responses are recorded after the interview, the interviewer is not likely to recall every response exactly as given, especially if many questions are asked. If, however, a recording device such as an audio cassette recorder or video camcorder is used, the interview moves more quickly, and responses are recorded exactly as given. If responses need clarifying, several persons can listen to or watch the recordings independently, and classifications can be compared. A recorder, of course, may initially make subjects nervous, but usually they tend to forget even the presence of a camcorder as the interview progresses; when the interview is manually recorded, however, the interviewee is constantly aware that someone is recording his or her responses. A mechanical recording is generally more objective unless the subject never overcomes the nervousness; recorded interviews, however, require the interviewer to go back through the tapes coding interview responses into a meaningful format for analysis. If mechanical recording devices are used, it is important to be sure the subject knows that he or she is being recorded and agrees to the procedure. The decision of a recording method is not an easy one; it needs to be made in the light of a number of issues, as have been discussed.

4. *Pretesting the interview procedure.* The interview guide, interview procedures, and analysis procedures should be tried out before the main study begins, using a small sample from the same or a very similar population to the one being used in the study. Feedback from a small pilot study can be used to revise questions in the guide that are apparently unclear, do not solicit the desired information, or produce negative reactions in subjects. Insights into better ways to handle certain questions can also be acquired. Finally, the pilot study will determine whether the resulting data can be quantified and analyzed in the manner intended. As with the pretesting of a questionnaire, feedback should be sought from pilot subjects as well as from the interviewers. A pretest of procedures is also a good use of the researcher's time.

OBSERVATIONAL RESEARCH

In an observational study, the current status of a phenomenon is determined not by asking but by observing. In fact, some marketing firms consider this the latest trend in consumer research (Foltz, 1990). For certain research questions, observation is clearly the most appropriate approach. For example, you could ask telephone order processors how they handle telephone orders, but, you could probably obtain more objective information by actually observing several order processors at work. Observational techniques may also be used to collect data in nondescriptive studies. In an experimental study designed to determine the effect of courtesy training on grocery store personnel, for example, employees could be observed prior to and following the introduction of courtesy training in order to determine if instances of courtesy were increased in number. Observational data can be collected on inanimate objects such as files as well as on human beings. In either category an observational study must be planned and executed just as carefully as any other type of research study.

Types of Observational Research

The major types of observational research are nonparticipant observation, participant observation, and ethnography. Nonparticipant observation includes naturalistic observation, simulation observation, case studies, and content analysis. The article at the end of this chapter provides an interesting contrast between nonparticipant and participant research strategies. Although you may encounter other applications of the observational approach, those just mentioned are the ones most commonly used in business research.

Nonparticipant Observation

In nonparticipant observation, the observer is not directly involved in the situation to be observed. In other words, the observer is on the outside looking in and does not intentionally interact with, or affect, the object of the observation. The different types of nonparticipant observation include the following:

1. *Naturalistic observation*. Certain kinds of behavior can only be (or best be) observed as they occur naturally. In such situations the observer purposely controls or manipulates nothing, and in fact works very hard at not affecting the observed situation in any way (Agnew & Pyke, 1978). The intent is to record and study behavior as it normally occurs. As an example, workplace behavior—behavior of the supervisor, behavior of the employees, and the interaction between supervisor and employees—can best be studied through naturalistic observation. Observation studies have been a basic part of business research since the turn of the century with the time-and-motion studies that characterized Frederick Taylor's *scientific management* approach (Taylor, 1911). Today, the value of naturalistic observation on an informal basis is attested to by companies such as United Airlines and Hewlett Packard that urge their supervisors to "Manage by Walking Around" (Peters & Waterman, 1982). In other settings it is common practice to monitor employee-customer telephone interactions on a routine basis. A newer, and often controversial, version of naturalistic observation is the use of computer-based programs to record employee productivity. The U.S. Postal Service, for example, uses a computer-based system to monitor the time that approximately 300,000 employees spend at specific work

assignments (Smalheiser, 1989); the workers' advocacy group, 9 to 5, estimates that 10 million American workers are monitored for phone calls, number of keystrokes, and time spent on transactions, with increased fear, stress, and illness resulting from the monitoring (Associated Press Washington 1990). Assuming that ethical concerns are handled well, however, insights gained as a result of naturalistic observation may form the foundation for later, more controlled research in an area of interest.

2. *Simulation observation.* In simulation observation the researcher creates the situation to be observed and tells subjects the activities in which they are to engage. The technique is frequently used in business training and is the basis for many appraisal centers. You'll be glad to know that the IRS used simulation observation to discover what problems taxpayers had in completing the federal income tax forms (Russakoff, 1989). Simulation observation allows the researcher to observe behavior that occurs infrequently in a natural situation or not at all (for example, having a potential supervisor role play a performance-appraisal situation). The major disadvantage of this type of observation is, of course, that it is not natural, and the behavior exhibited by subjects may not be the behavior that would occur in a natural setting. Subjects may behave the way they think they should behave rather than the way they really would or do behave. In reality, this potential problem is not as serious as it may sound. Subjects tend to get carried away with their roles and often exhibit very true-to-life emotions. Besides, even if subjects fake it, at least they show that they are aware of the correct way to behave. A potential supervisor who demonstrates the correct way to conduct a performance appraisal at least knows what should be done!

The three major types of simulation are individual role playing, group role playing, and gaming. In individual role playing, the researcher is interested in the behavior of one person, although other "players" may be involved. The individual is given a role, a situation, and a problem to solve. The observer then records and evaluates the subject's solution to the problem and the way she or he executes it. As an example, a management trainee might be told:

> Yesterday Bill Bungle was caught sleeping at his work station. You made him stay after his regular shift and complete all the work. Your boss has just informed you that a very angry union steward is on her way to see you. The role will begin when the union steward arrives at your desk.

In this situation, a trained individual will act as the union steward and will attempt to say the same thing to each trainee involved in the simulation. Another strategy that does not involve other individuals is the "in-basket" exercise; in this situation, the trainee is presented with a pile of simulated phone messages, memos, and letters and asked to write responses or describe the actions he or she would take to each.

In a group role-playing situation, a small group is presented with a situation and a problem, and solutions are recorded and evaluated. Qualities such as leadership ability may be studied using this methodology. As an example, a group might be told:

> The boss has alloted you a task force of six. Your charge is to evaluate the candidates for the position of employee ombudsman.

In this situation the researcher might be looking at individual behavior or the interaction of the small group in problem solving.

The final type of simulation is gaming. Again the focus of observation may be an individual or a group, but in this situation the "work" that is to be performed is the solution to a problem usually involving the manipulation of materials. These materials may range from paper supplies to tinker toys; while the subjects become absorbed in trying to win or beat the game, the researcher is able to observe behavior that simulates actual behavior in problem solving, leadership, communication, or other concepts of interest. In another type of gaming simulation, individuals or groups may be involved with a computer-based simulation of a company's business and economic decision making; again, researchers are able to observe behavior related to problem solving or other variables of interest.

An important consideration in simulations, particularly those used in assessment centers, is to demonstrate the reliability and validity of the simulations. When hiring or promotional decisions are based on information gained through evaluation by an assessment center, validation and periodic revalidation are required; certainly the same standards apply to simulations used in research.

3. *The case study.* Probably the most famous (or infamous) methodology in business education is the case study. As you undoubtedly know, a case study is the in-depth investigation of an individual, group, or institution. In business, case studies are typically conducted to determine the background, environment, and characteristics of employees or businesses with problems. The primary purpose of the case study is to determine the factors, and relationships among the factors, that have resulted in the current behavior or status of the subject of the study. In other words, the purpose of a case study is to determine *why,* not just what. Kanter (1983) used a variety of methodologies such as interviews, observations, and quantitative research to develop the case studies that form the basis of her book on organizational change. The major problems with case studies are possible observer bias (the observers sees what he or she wants to see) and lack of generalizability. The insights that may be acquired concerning a particular case may not apply to any other case. Therefore, the major use of case studies is in training individuals in the analysis of problems, not the solution of research problems. Case studies may, however, suggest hypotheses that can be tested using another method of research.

4. *Content analysis.* Content analysis is the systematic, quantitative description of the composition of the object of the study. Naisbitt (1982), for example, used content analysis of the news sections of daily papers as the basis for his projections of societal and business trends. Typical subjects for content analysis include reports, documents, and files. Annual reports are frequently analyzed to determine such things as the financial health of companies or industrial trends. Content analysis, for example, can be used to determine whether a company's affirmative-action plan is actually being followed by analyzing such variables as frequency of minority applications and patterns of promotion and retention. Content-analysis studies may be quite simple, involving primarily frequency counts, or very sophisticated and complex, involving investigation of the existence of bias or prejudice in an industry or profession.

Participant Observation

In participant observation, the observer actually becomes a part of, a participant in, the situation to be observed. The rationale for participant observation is that in many situations the view from the inside is somewhat different from the view from the outside looking in. There are, of course, degrees of participation, and observation may be overt or covert. For example, if a researcher obtains permission to attend union meetings at the local Teamsters affiliate in order to study member-leader interactions, the observation is more overt. If the researcher manages to be hired in a union job, the intent being to study member-leader interactions without anyone being aware that such observation is occurring, the degree of participation is greater and the observation is covert. It is very likely that the conclusions drawn from the two approaches would differ. Although the covert observations might provide more valid findings, this type of observation has some obvious drawbacks. This issue was discussed in Chapter 3, when the topic of research ethics was raised; you may recall, for example, the use of a "mystery shopper" in the convenience store research (Sutton & Rafaeli, 1988). As you will recall from that discussion, first and foremost is the highly questionable ethics involved in observing people without their knowledge and, more than likely, recording conversations with concealed recording devices. Another major problem is the issue of the impact of the observer's participation on the situation observed. In other words, the situation is somewhat different from what it would have been if the observer did not participate. Also, there is the possibility that the greater the participation, the greater the bias. Generally, observers strive to be totally objective. But in the previous example, it is possible that the observer would tend to identify with the role of the union member, and observations and/or interpretations of member-leader interactions would be affected by this role identification.

Participant observation studies also vary in the degree of structure involved in the inquiry. Participant observation studies may be designed to test hypotheses, to derive hypotheses, or both. Those that are oriented toward hypothesis testing are more structured and more focused in terms of the behaviors to be observed and recorded. More typically, however, such studies are hypothesis generating. Thus, participant observation research is characterized by the collection of large amounts of data that are difficult to analyze. This problem is illustrated and described in the following statement made by a participant observer:

> Our files contain approximately five thousand single-space pages of such material. Faced with such a quantity of "rich" but varied data, the researcher faces the problem of how to analyze it systematically and then to present . . . conclusions so as to convince other scientists of their validity (Becker, 1958).

Thus, the good news is that participant observation typically yields an abundance of potentially useful data. The bad news is that analyzing such data and drawing defensible conclusions is not an easy task.

Ethnography

Although most business people have probably never heard the term, a relatively recent trend in business research is a growing interest in ethnographic methods of research (Slipy, 1990; Zemke, 1989). The main reason for enthusiasm over this kind of research is probably the dissatisfaction with more traditional approaches for investigating certain kinds of business problems such as studies of corporate culture (Schein, 1985). While application of ethnographic methodology may be new to business, it is not a new research strategy. It has been used extensively by anthropologists for years and is, in fact, frequently referred to as the anthropological approach.

Definition. Ethnography involves data collection on many variables over an extended period of time in a naturalistic setting. As you will recall from the previous discussion of nonparticipant observations, the term *naturalistic setting* refers to the fact that the variables being investigated are studied where they naturally occur and as they naturally occur, not in researcher-controlled environments under researcher-controlled conditions. Because of the naturalistic settings characteristic of ethnographic research, it is also referred to as naturalistic research or field research. Other researchers prefer the term *qualitative research,* primarily because participant observation and in-depth interviewing are the methodologies most frequently involved. As you may have guessed, a major issue in business research is the validity and preferability of qualitative versus quantitative approaches to inquiry, especially with respect to their potential for meaningfully investigating business phenomena. While each position has its advocates, and, predictably, some researchers advocate a combination approach, a reasonable position would appear to be that the choice of type of inquiry and corresponding methodologies depends upon the nature of the phenomena being studied. It must be noted, however, that at the present time more researchers favor the quantitative methodologies to the qualitative ones.

In any event, as stated previously, ethnographic research takes place in naturalistic settings. The unit of observation in an ethnographic study in business is typically a particular business or even an industry. Rather than, for example, studying the training process by collecting questionnaires before and after some treatment, the ethnographer works more inductively by observing many aspects of the work environment and attempting to identify factors associated with effective and ineffective environments (Schein, 1985). The Peters and Waterman study (1982) is an example of this kind of work. The rationale behind the use of ethnography is the research-based belief that behavior is significantly influenced by the environment in which it occurs. In other words, behavior occurs in a context, and accurate understanding of the behavior requires understanding of the context in which it occurs. Organizations such as a business, for example, definitely influence the behavior of persons in them. Relatedly, ethnographers point out that if we wish to generalize our findings to real-world settings, the findings should be derived from research conducted in real-world settings.

Method. Ethnographic research may involve nonparticipant observation, participant observation, or both. Typically, ethnographic studies are characterized by some type of participant observation at an overt level. Ethnography, however, represents multi-instrument research, and the ethnographer uses a variety of data-collection strategies in conjunction with observation. Preliminary participant observation provides data that guide the researcher in selecting other appropriate approaches. Schein (1985), in assessing corporate cultures, calls this level of observation "Artifacts and Creations." As he says,

> One can look at physical space, the technological output of the group, its written and spoken language, artistic productions, and the overt behavior of its members. Since the insiders of the culture are not necessarily aware of their own artifacts, one cannot always ask them, but one can always observe them for oneself (Schein, 1985, p. 14).

In a more general context, Pelto and Pelto (1978) classify the possibilities as verbal and nonverbal. Verbal techniques involve interactions between the researcher and persons in the research environment and include tools such as questionnaires, interviews, attitude scales, and other psychological instruments. Nonverbal techniques are less obtrusive, that is, less likely to affect behaviors being studied, and include such strategies as the use of recording devices and examination of written records.

The fact that ethnographic research is characterized by participant observation and a more inductive approach does not mean that it is unsystematic or haphazard. Ethnographers plan their research studies just as carefully as researchers conducting other types of research. Having refined the research problem of interest, the ethnographic researcher makes informed decisions concerning the most appropriate environment, or setting, to study and the most effective level of participation. As one practitioner describes it,

> The ethnographer obtains concrete data in order to understand the culture he is interested in, presumably for intellectual and scientific reasons. Though the ethnographer must be faithful to the observed and experienced data, he brings to the situation a set of concepts or models that motivated the research in the first place. The group members studied are often willing to participate but usually have no stake in the intellectual issues that may have motivated the study (Schein, 1985, p. 21).

Having selected an environment and specified a level of participation, the researcher then makes related decisions such as which persons in the environment should be interacted with and what should be the nature of the interaction, what kinds of questions should be asked, which records should be reviewed, and so on. These decisions are guided by tentative, preliminary hypotheses. As you will recall from Chapter 2, a tentative hypothesis, derived, one hopes, from concepts or theories, guides the review of related literature, which in turn guides the formulation of a specific, testable hypothesis. The same basic process is involved in ethnography. The tentative hypothesis or hypotheses guide the initial data-collection strategies. Initial data-collection efforts suggest other appropriate strategies, and so forth. Following completion of the study, which may last for months, the researcher analyzes the mass of data collected and attempts to derive specific, testable hypotheses that explain the observed behavior. These hypotheses can then be tested in other studies.

A major difference between ethnographic and traditional approaches is that the review of related literature, the study of previous research and theory, does not result in testable hypotheses to be supported or not supported by the results of the study. Instead, the study of previous work results in tentative, working hypotheses and strategies only. The ethnographer does not want to be overly influenced by findings produced by the application of other methods of research; such studies probably did not involve careful study of the environment in which the results were obtained, or, more likely, the results were obtained in an environment different from the one to which the results were intended to be generalizable.

The application of ethnographic methodologies to the study of business represents a synthesis of parallel approaches that have been used over the last four decades. As Schein describes it,

> This shift takes me back full circle to my graduate work in Harvard's Department of Social Relations in the late 1940s and early 1950s, a time when anthropology, sociology, social psychology, and clinical psychology were making a concentrated effort to enhance each other through . . . joint educational efforts. In many respects this book is a journey of "integration" for me, in that it attempts to bring together many intellectual strands that have occupied me for many years (Schein, 1985, p. xi).

An Example.   The application of ethnography to the investigation of organizational climate is illustrated by an example provided by Schein. He describes a consulting experience in which he was called in to assist a management group in improving communication, decision making, and interpersonal relationships. After observing the group for several months, he made a series of suggestions intended to decrease the high level of interrupting, emotional confrontation, extensive debate, and a general feeling of frustration on the part of the managers over the competitive interactions that characterized all their interchanges. Schein's efforts at improving the situation were met with polite appreciation but effected no change in the interactions. Only after an intensive study of the corporate culture was he able to determine that in this particular company, "Truth is discovered through conflict and debate, . . . conflict is valued, and the individual is expected to take initiative and fight for ideas in every arena" (Schein, 1985, pp. 12–13). With this deeper understanding, he was able to shift his consulting efforts to more productive approaches.

Ethnography in Summary.   By now you should have a reasonably good understanding of the ethnographic method. Its drawbacks are obvious, although not necessarily unique. Proper application of the approach requires accurate recording of large amounts of data, over long periods of time, by persons thoroughly trained in observational methods. Results are difficult to analyze, and given the length of the typical study, findings are difficult to replicate. At a practical level, ethnographic research tends to be more costly than other approaches. A more serious problem is the fact that the researcher is usually dealing with an N of one. In other words, since the unit under study is typically a business or an industry, the number of "subjects" is one. Thus, findings may be unique to the unit studied (Schein, 1985).

A current problem with ethnography is not a fault of the method but rather the way in which it is being used. As more and more people are aware of important, but extremely complex, business concepts such as the study of corporate culture, there has been an increase in the number of poorly conducted studies, some by individuals with little or no related training. When properly used, however, ethnography has the potential for providing insights not obtainable with other methods. The hypotheses generated by ethnographic studies are in many cases more valid than those based on theory alone. It is, of course, unrealistic to believe that a method that has been used successfully in another field, that is, anthropology, can be adopted and used effectively in business without some change. The approach needs to undergo constant refinement and adaptation in the direction of a more-structured ethnography. This adaptation can be a positive one with the potential result being a research method incorporating the best features of the integrated approaches.

Conducting Observational Research

The steps in conducting observational research are essentially the same as for other types of descriptive research. Selection and definition of the problem are essentially the same, as is selection of subjects. Like the interview technique, observation is time-consuming and typically involves smaller samples. While nonparticipant observation, participant observation, and ethnography involve some unique procedures, all observation involves definition of the variables to be observed, recording of observations, and training and monitoring of observers.

Definition of Observational Variables

There is no way that an observer can observe and record everything that goes on during a session, especially in a natural setting such as a business meeting. What will be observed is determined by the research hypothesis or question. For example, if the study is concerned with the use of behavior modification in increasing instances of courteous treatment of customers, attention would be focused only on courteous treatment. The phrase *courteous treatment,* however, does not have universal meaning. For one customer, being addressed by her or his first name is courteous, while a second customer may be highly insulted by this "overly familiar" practice. The researcher must clearly define what specific behaviors do and do not match the intended behavior. In this example, "courteous treatment" might include greeting the customer by his or her full name, smiling, maintaining good eye contact, and saying "please," "excuse me," and "thank you." Pausing to handle a phone call quickly would probably not be considered a breach of courtesy.

Once a behavioral unit is defined, observations must be quantified so that all observers count the same way. If Gorgo chews gum *and* belches at the same time, that could be considered as one instance of rude behavior or as two instances. Researchers typically divide observation sessions into a number of specific observation periods, that is, they define a time unit. Thus, for a 1-hour session, a time unit of 30 seconds might be agreed upon, resulting in a total of 120 observations per hour. The length of the time unit will usually be a function of both the behavior to be observed and the frequency with which it normally occurs. If it is simply a matter of observing and recording a high-frequency behavior, the time unit may be 10 seconds. If any judgments or inferences are required on the part of the observer or if the behavior is a low-frequency behavior, the time unit is typically longer, perhaps 30 seconds or 1 minute. There should be correspondence between actual frequency and recorded frequency. Once the time unit has been established, the observer then records what occurred during the observation period. If during a 15-second interval an employee exhibits courteous behavior, this would be indicated, regardless of how often the courteous behavior occurred.

After the variables have been defined and the time unit established, a decision must be made as to when observations will be made. For example, if behavior varies with factors such as day of the week and time of day, it would be unwise to observe every Monday morning only. One solution is to select observation times randomly so that different days and different times of day are reflected in the observations. A second solution is to avoid selecting observation times and simply to observe all the possibilities (i.e., all day every day). The latter approach, of course, is only feasible for short periods of time and for a limited number of subjects. You could observe one employee for a week, but observing a group of employees for a month would be a unreasonable (Webb, Campbell, Schwartz, & Sechrest, 1966).

Recording of Observations

One point, which at first reading may seem obvious, is that observers should have to observe and record only one behavior at a time. Even if you are interested in two types of behavior, for example supervisor behavior and employee behavior, the observer should only have to make one decision at a time. Thus, if two types of behavior are to be observed, they should probably be observed alternately. In other words, for the supervisor-employee observation example, supervisor behavior might be observed during the first, third, fifth, seventh (and so forth) observation periods, and employee behavior during the second, fourth, sixth, and eighth. Such a procedure would present a fairly accurate picture concerning what occurred in the observed workplace. It is also a good idea to alternate observation periods and recording periods, especially if any inference is required on the part of the observers. Thus the observer might observe for 15 seconds, record for 5 seconds, observe for 15 seconds, record for 5 seconds, and so forth. This approach controls for the fact that the observer is not paying complete attention while recording, and it tends to increase the reliability of observations.

While the point is debatable, as a general rule it is probably better to record observations as the behavior occurs. Since each observation must be made within a set period of time, for example 15 seconds, the recording process should be as simplified as possible. Most observation studies facilitate recording by using an agreed-upon code, or set of symbols, and a recording instrument. Often the task is not just to determine whether a behavior occurred or not but to record *what* occurred. For example, Benne and Sheats (1948) have developed a list of "group roles" or behaviors that individuals tend to exhibit when working in groups. These roles are categorized as task, maintenance, or self-oriented. The observation recording instrument, using only the task roles, shown in Figure 7.5 can be used to record behavior in any type of meeting or group activity; the observer can simply make a mark in the square provided each time one of the group members exhibits one of the task roles. This form can be modified in a number of ways to allow the observer to concentrate on one individual or the entire group or to record brief verbatim comments to allow the observer to recall more specifically the comment or behavior that caused the observer to record as she or he did.

There are a number of different types of forms that are used to record observations. Some very good coding and recording systems, for example, have been developed by behavior-modification practitioners; these are typically designed for recording the behavior of just one individual. Quality circles practitioners have also developed workable observation-recording instruments for data collection in specific applications. Probably the most often used, and the most efficient, recording forms are checklists that list all the behaviors to be observed so the observer can simply check each behavior as it occurs. The checklist usually allows the observer to spend his or her time thinking about what is occurring rather than how to record it. If you are familiar with performance-appraisal systems using checklists, you understand the basic format— and you are also aware of the importance of recording information very soon after the behavior being recorded occurs!

Another common recording device, also familiar to users of performance appraisals, is the rating scale. It requires the observer to evaluate the behavior and give it a rating from, for instance, 1 to 3. For example, an observer might rate a supervisor's explanation as 1, not very clear, 2, clear, or 3, very clear. Although as many as five categories (infrequently more than five) are used, three is probably the ideal number. The more categories, the more difficult it becomes to classify correctly. An observer could probably discriminate between "not very clear" and "clear" fairly easily; deciding between "very unclear" and "not very clear" would not be as simple. For an example of a rating scale that is used for airline flight engineers, see Figure 7.6.

Before developing your own observation form, you will want to check to see if there is a standardized observation form that is appropriate for your study. Using a standardized observation form has the same advantages as using a standardized test in terms of time saved, validity, and reliability. An additional advantage in using a standardized form is that the results of your study can be compared with the results of other studies that have used the same form. In addition to the periodicals reporting research studies that you used in your literature review, journals such as the *Journal of Applied Behavior Analysis* may be a source for observation systems that have been used in other studies. The human resource department of a company may also have task analysis, job analysis, or performance appraisal forms that will meet your needs.

	Group Members			
Task Roles	Mary	Sue	Jose	Gorgo
Initiating				
Information seeking				
Information giving				
Opinion seeking				
Opinion giving				
Clarifying				
Coordination				
Energizing				
Procedure developing				
Recording				

Recording Key for Task Roles:

Initiating—Suggests methods, goals, and procedures; starts the group moving in different directions by proposing a plan.

Information seeking—Asks for ideas, data, personal experiences, and reports.

Information giving—Offers ideas, data, personal experiences, and factual statements.

Opinion seeking—Asks for statements of belief, convictions, values, or expressions of feeling.

Opinion giving—States own beliefs, convictions, values, and feelings.

Clarifying—Interprets issues, elaborates on ideas expressed by others, gives examples or illustrations.

Coordinating—Demonstrates relationships between ideas, restates ideas, summarizes, and offers integrated statements for consideration.

Energizing—Prods group to greater activity, stimulates others to action.

Procedure developing—Handles such tasks as seating arrangements, setting up flipchart, running the projector, providing note pads.

Recording—Keeps written record of meeting on paper, records ideas on flipchart or overhead projector transparency.

Figure 7.5. Observation recording chart for group meetings based on Benne & Sheats (1948)..

TWA ═══ **FLIGHT ENGINEER or INT. RELIEF OFFICER** ═══

LINE TRAINING and LINE CHECK

ADDITIONAL LINE
CHECK PROGRAM
PARAMETERS

COMPUTER INPUT

JXTFP [ ] REGNUM

name / domicile

JXCQ [ ] REGNUM

LTC [ ] EQUIPMENT

home city / state / zip

airman certificate no. (rating_____)

SLP [ ] EQUIPMENT

[ ] POSITION

FAA physical _____ class _____ date

[ ] POSITION

limitations / waivers

┌ CODES* ┐
[ ] TYPE TRAINING/CHECK

FLIGHT ENGINEER

AAE - Operating Experience - F/E
ILC - Initial Line Check-
    Additional Equipment
ALC - Annual Line Check
SLC - Special Line Check

INTERNATIONAL RELIEF OFFICER
    Same as Flight Engineer

┌ PARAMETER C ┐

0 = Cancels Special Line Check

3 = 3 and 11 Months

7 = * Check due only on Specific
    month and year.

* When using Parameter 7, enter
   month and year of the next
   specific check desired.

[ ] NEXT LINE CHECK DUE

[ ] mo yr LAST LINE CK

[ ] damoyr END TNG/CK

[ ] TOTAL TIME

* All codes must be preceded by either
  D - If given on domestic segment; or,
  I - If given on international segment.

[ ] damoyr START TNG/CK

[ ] LAST FLT NO.

PREVIOUS FLIGHT TIME [ ]

[ ] LAST ACFT NO.

FLIGHT/TIME RECORD

[ ] FROM STATION

[ ] TO STATION

[ ] TOTAL TRIP LDGS.

[ ] regnum CHECK AIRMAN

[ ] ADNL QUAL

[ ] ADNL QUAL

[ ] ADNL QUAL

FLT NO/DATE	ACFT. NO.	FROM-TO	INTERMEDIATE STOPS	FLIGHT TIME

☐ QUALIFIED ☐ NOT QUALIFIED On _____ Date _____

TOTAL
GRAND TOTAL [ ]

[ ] FAA OBSERVER'S NAME

CHECK AIRMAN _____
June. 1985   print name   signature   T3081

Figure 7.6. Example of observation form courtesy of Trans World Airlines, Inc.

DATE [ ][ ][ ][ ]   DATE [ ][ ][ ][ ]

A. PREPARATION FOR FLIGHT	*LINE CHECK* [ ]
1. Navigation kit, manuals, licenses	[ ][ ][ ][ ]
2. Preliminary flight information	[ ][ ][ ][ ]
3. Bulletins/messages review	[ ][ ][ ][ ]
4. Appearance	[ ][ ][ ][ ]

B. PRE-FLIGHT	*LINE CHECK* [ ]
1. Exterior inspection	[ ][ ][ ][ ]
2. Fuel/oil servicing	[ ][ ][ ][ ]
3. Water/hydraulic servicing	[ ][ ][ ][ ]
4. Cabin interior	[ ][ ][ ][ ]
5. Logbook check/MEL	[ ][ ][ ][ ]
6. Cockpit general	[ ][ ][ ][ ]
7. Cockpit F/E panel	[ ][ ][ ][ ]

C. PRE-TAKEOFF	*LINE CHECK* [ ]
1. Computation of T/O data/ radio closeout	[ ][ ][ ][ ]
2. Load reduction - monitors start	[ ][ ][ ][ ]
3. Electrical changeover	[ ][ ][ ][ ]
4. Stabilizer trim check	[ ][ ][ ][ ]
5. After start/taxi checks	[ ][ ][ ][ ]
6. Ramp radio procedures	[ ][ ][ ][ ]

D. TAKEOFF AND DEPARTURE	*LINE CHECK* [ ]
1. Monitors takeoff (engine limitations)	[ ][ ][ ][ ]
2. Traffic watch	[ ][ ][ ][ ]

E. CLIMB/EN ROUTE/DESCENT	*LINE CHECK* [ ]
1. Setting climb/cruise thrust	[ ][ ][ ][ ]
2. Fuel system management-fuel log	[ ][ ][ ][ ]
3. Use of logbook	[ ][ ][ ][ ]
4. Landing data	[ ][ ][ ][ ]
5. Traffic watch	[ ][ ][ ][ ]

F. APPROACH AND LANDING	*LINE CHECK* [ ]
1. Crew coordination	[ ][ ][ ][ ]
2. Monitor bug settings, position indicators, instruments, altimeter settings, and back up all required call-outs	[ ][ ][ ][ ]
3. Monitor landing roll-out brake pressure, anti-skid, thrust reversers, engine parameters, etc.	[ ][ ][ ][ ]

G. POST LANDING	*LINE CHECK* [ ]
1. Taxi/radio procedures	[ ][ ][ ][ ]
2. Load reduction	[ ][ ][ ][ ]
3. Electrical changeover	[ ][ ][ ][ ]

H. GENERAL	*LINE CHECK* [ ]
1. Check list handling	[ ][ ][ ][ ]
2. Logbook write-ups/fault isolation procedures and codes	[ ][ ][ ][ ]
3. Attitude	[ ][ ][ ][ ]
4. Crew coordination	[ ][ ][ ][ ]
5. Takeoff +3 landing -8	[ ][ ][ ][ ]
6. FAR restrictions below 10,000 feet	[ ][ ][ ][ ]
7. Radio usage/ACARS	[ ][ ][ ][ ]
8. Air conditioning and pressurization	[ ][ ][ ][ ]
9. Maintenance coordination	[ ][ ][ ][ ]
10. Analytical ability	[ ][ ][ ][ ]
11. Ability to keep ahead of operation	[ ][ ][ ][ ]

I. DISCUSSION ITEMS	*LINE CHECK* [ ]
1. A/C system knowledge	[ ][ ][ ][ ]
2. Operating limits	[ ][ ][ ][ ]
3. Emergency procedures	[ ][ ][ ][ ]
4. RTB review	[ ][ ][ ][ ]

J. INT. RELIEF OFFICER - CRUISE	*LINE CHECK* [ ]
1. Use of autopilot	[ ][ ][ ][ ]
2. Turbulence procedures	[ ][ ][ ][ ]
3. En route planning/ATC clearance compliance	[ ][ ][ ][ ]
4. Use of INS	[ ][ ][ ][ ]

ADDITIONAL COMMENTS/ RECOMMENDATIONS:

QUALIFIED AS:_____ ON: _____ _____
                                            (Type of Equipment/Route)   *(Date)*

Approved by: _____ Title: _____

T3081   June, 1985   Page 2

Figure 7.6. continued

Assessing Observer Reliability

Unreliable observations are as useless as data based on an unreliable test. Determining observer reliability generally requires that at least two observers independently make observations; their recorded judgments as to what occurred can then be compared to see how well they agree. If we wanted to estimate the reliability of scoring for a short-answer test, we could correlate the scores resulting from two independent scorings of the same answers. In other words, all of the tests would be scored twice, and the correlation between the two sets of scores would be our estimate of the reliability of scoring. When we observe behavior, however, we are not typically dealing with scores but rather with frequencies, that is, how frequently certain behaviors occurred. In this case, reliability is generally calculated based on percentage of agreement. For example, we might have two independent observers in a service industry recording the number of courteous behaviors exhibited by a selected employee during a 1-hour period. If one observer recorded 20 incidents and the other observer recorded 25 incidents, we could compute interobserver reliability by dividing the smaller total (20) by the larger total (25) to obtain a percentage of agreement score of 80.

As Barlow and Hersen (1984) point out, however, while 80% agreement may be considered satisfactory in most situations, if many frequencies are involved over a long period of time, the possibility exists that the two observers are not recording the same behaviors at the same time. One observer, for example, may have underrecorded during the first half of the session and overrecorded during the second half; the other observer may have done just the opposite. Thus, their totals might agree very well even though their observations did not. One reasonable solution to this potential problem, as suggested by Bijou, Peterson, Harris, Allen, and Johnston (1969), is to use shorter observation periods and to base reliability calculations on both agreements and disagreements on occurrences and nonoccurrences of behavior. Bijou and associates argue that with shorter observation periods it is easier to determine whether observers are recording the same events at the same time. To calculate reliability using both observer agreement and disagreement, we divide the number of agreements by the total number of agreements and disagreements. To use our courtesy example, suppose that during the first 30 minutes of the observation period the two observers agreed on the occurrence of nine instances of courteous behavior but disagreed on the occurrence of three instances. To calculate interobserver reliability we would divide the number of agreements by the total of the agreements and the disagreements (9 + 3 = 12), and the resulting reliability estimate would be 9/12, or 75%. There are a number of different situations for which slightly different approaches for calculating reliability are recommended. Barlow and Hersen discuss a number of these situations and refer the reader to appropriate references.

Sometimes it is not possible to have several observers observe the same situation at the same time. One solution is to record the to-be-observed situation with a camcorder or tape recorder, for example. This allows each observer to play back tapes at a convenient time. Another advantage to recording a situation is that you can replay it as often as you like. If behaviors to be observed are at all complex or occur at a fairly rapid rate, for example, it may be difficult to obtain reliable observations. If you record the behavior, you can play it back to your heart's content, as can other observers. This is especially useful if judgment and evaluation are required on the part of the observer. Of course, taping may raise some interesting questions on the part of the individuals being recorded; historically, the labor movement has been suspicious of observations of employees since the days of the early time-and-motion studies (Howell & Dipboye, 1986). These considerations will have to be a part of your decision making in regard to your research design. Regardless of whether observations are recorded as they occur or while viewing or listening to a tape, and assuming usage of a valid, reliable observation system, the best way to increase observer reliability is by thoroughly training and monitoring observers.

Training Observers

In order to determine agreement between observers, at least two observers are required. That means that there will be at least one other person besides yourself (or two, if you are not going to observe) who needs to be familiar with the observational procedures. Additional observers need to be trained in order to have some assurance that all observers are observing and recording the same behaviors in the same way. Thus, they must be instructed as to what behaviors to observe, how behaviors are to be coded, how behaviors are to be recorded, and how often (time unit). Observers should participate in numerous practice sessions at which they observe situations similar to those to be involved in the study and compare their recordings. Each point of disagreement should be discussed so that the observer who is incorrect understands why. Practice sessions using recordings of behavior are most effective since segments with which observers have difficulty can be replayed for discussion and feedback purposes. The individuals using the flight engineer observation form shown earlier (Figure 7.6) practice with the form and discuss their differences before actually using it on the job, for example. If recordings are used, however, the researcher needs to allow for the fact that the real-life situation may be far more confusing to the observer because of distracting sights or sounds; observer nervousness may also become a factor in the real situation. Estimates of observer reliability should be calculated periodically to determine the effectiveness of the training and practice; observer reliability should increase with each session. Training may be terminated when a satisfactory level of agreement, say 80%, is achieved.

Monitoring Observers

Training of observers only guarantees that the initial level of reliability is satisfactory. It does not guarantee that this level will be maintained throughout the study. Also, as we have noted, observers may be exhibiting acceptable levels of reliability and yet not be observing the same behaviors in the same way at the same time. As Barlow and Hersen (1984) point out, the major way to insure continued satisfactory levels of reliability is to monitor all observers. This technique is usually not feasible, however. At the very least, spot checks should be made (Reid & DeMaster, 1972). As a general rule, the more monitoring that can reasonably be managed, the better.

Reducing Observation Bias

Observers should be made aware of two factors that may serious affect the validity of observations—observer bias and observee bias. Observer bias refers to invalid observations that result from the way in which the observer observes. Observee bias refers to invalid observations that result from the fact that those being observed may behave differently simply because they are being observed. Each observer brings to the observation session a unique background that may affect the way she or he perceives the situation. Having observers record independently helps to detect the presence of bias but does not eliminate it. Training and practice sessions should help to reduce it by making observers aware of its existence and by providing feedback when it appears to be occurring. Other types of observer bias are similar to those discussed in Chapter 5 concerning rating scales and are referred to as response sets. A *response set* is the tendency of an observer to rate the majority of observees as above average, average, or below average regardless of the observees' actual behavior. A related problem is the *halo effect* whereby initial impressions concerning an observee (positive or negative) affect subsequent observations. A final major source of observer bias occurs when the observer's knowledge concerning observees or the purposes of the study affect observations. In the previously discussed study of the effectiveness of behavior modification in increasing courteous behavior, the observer might tend to see what was expected, namely an increase in courteous behavior. In this instance, having observers view recordings rather than live behavior would help, since they would not have to be told which recordings were made *before* the introduction of behavior modification and which were made *after*. The above discussion should have made obvious the problems associated with using data recorded by untrained observers such as incident reports or performance appraisals on employees made by supervisors. Such data tend to be subjective and biased and not useful for research purposes unless, of course, the purpose of the study is to compare perceptions of different groups.

The other side of the problem, observee bias, refers to the phenomenon whereby persons being observed behave atypically simply because they are being observed. Solutions to this problem such as those depicted on television crime shows (one-way mirrors, for example) may seem intriguing but are hardly ever practical, to say nothing of ethical, in observational settings. Offices and plants, for example, rarely are equipped with such devices. The best way to handle the problem is to make observers aware of it so they can attempt to be as inconspicuous or unobtrusive as possible. Observees apparently tend to ignore the presence of an observer after a few sessions. Thus, simply observing a few sessions prior to recording any data is an effective technique. Observers should also be instructed not to discuss the purpose of the observations with the observees. The fact that they may be behaving differently is bad enough; having them behave the way they think you want them to behave is worse! Another approach to the problem of observee bias is to eliminate observees. If the same information can be determined by observing inanimate objects (referred to as unobtrusive measures), use them. Records of customer complaints, for example, have never been known to act differently because they were being observed; such records might be one unobtrusive measure of courteous behavior on the part of employees. The following newspaper article by Krebs (1974), although not necessarily sufficient to withstand the scrutiny of economics professors, does illustrate the concept of unobtrusive measures:

> Maury Graham—known in the world of freight train hoboes as "Steamtrain Maury"—reports that the current U.S. economy is in frightful shape.
>
> The former "King of the Hoboes" says that hoboes can guage the seriousness of inflation by the length of the cigar and cigarette butts found along the streets.
>
> Says Steamtrain Maury, "The longer they are, the better times are. And right now the butts are awfully short. People are smoking them right down to the end." (Copyright © 1974 by The New York Times Company. Reprinted by permission.)

Another amusing example is found in the statement of a police officer to the effect that one way to identify car thieves is by examining license plates. Police officers look for clean cars with dirty plates and dirty cars with clean license plates, because thieves usually switch plates (Reddy, 1965).

Summary/Chapter 7

DEFINITION, PURPOSE, AND PROCESS

1. Descriptive research involves collecting data in order to test hypotheses or to answer questions concerning the current status of the subject of the study.

2. The researcher must give careful thought to sample selection and date collection; which population has the desired information is not always readily apparent.

3. Frequently, since one is generally asking questions that have not been asked before or seeking information that is not already available, a descriptive study requires the development of an instrument appropriate for obtaining the desired information.

4. A logical way to categorize descriptive studies initially is in terms of how data are collected, through self-report or observation. In a self-report study, information is solicited from individuals using questionnaires, interviews, or standardized attitude scales. In an observation study, individuals are not asked for information; rather, the researcher obtains the desired data through other means, such as direct observation.

SELF-REPORT RESEARCH

Types of Self-Report Research

Survey Research

5. A survey is an attempt to collect data from members of a population in order to determine the current status of that population with respect to one or more variables.

6. In a sample survey, the researcher infers information about a population of interest based on the responses of a selected sample drawn from that population; preferably the sample is either a simple-random sample or stratified-random sample.

7. In a census survey, an attempt is made to acquire data from each and every member of a population; a census survey is usually conducted when a population is relatively small and readily accessible.

8. Sample surveys are sometimes referred to as cross-sectional since information is collected at some point in time from a sample that, it is hoped, represents all relevant subgroups in the population.

9. One type of survey that has gained popularity in business recently is the employee attitude, or morale, survey.

10. A more complex purpose of survey research is to assess parts of the overall corporate culture.

Follow-up Studies

11. A follow-up study is conducted to determine the status of a group of interest after some period of time.

12. In a large organizational development program intended to improve employee morale and overall effectiveness, follow-up studies should be built into the basic design of the program.

13. Follow-up studies may also be conducted solely for research purposes.

Sociometric Studies

14. Sociometry is the assessment and analysis of the interpersonal relationships within a group of individuals.

15. The basic sociometric process involves asking each member to indicate with which other members she or he would most like to engage in a particular activity.

16. The choices made by the group members are graphically depicted in a diagram called a sociogram.

Conducting Self-Report Research

17. Self-report research requires the collection of standardized, quantifiable information from all members of a population or sample.

Conducting a Questionnaire Study

18. In comparison to use of an interview procedure, a questionnaire is much more efficient in that it requires less time, is less expensive, and permits collection of data from a much larger sample.

19. Questionnaires may be administered to subjects but are usually mailed; they may also be presented on a computer terminal.

Statement of the Problem

20. The problem under investigation and the topic of the questionnaire must be of sufficient significance to motivate subjects to respond.

21. The problem must be defined in terms of specific objectives concerning the kind of information needed; specific hypotheses or questions must be formulated and every item on the questionnaire should directly relate to them.

Selection of Subjects

22. Subjects should be selected using an appropriate sampling technique (or an entire population may be used), and identified subjects must be persons who have the desired information and are likely to be willing to give it.

Construction of the Questionnaire

23. As a general guideline, the questionnaire should be as attractive, brief, and as easy to respond to as possible.

24. No item should be included that does not directly relate to the objectives of the study, and structured, or closed-form, items should be used if at all possible.

25. A structured item consists of a question and a list of alternative responses from which the responder selects.

26. In addition to facilitating response, structured items also facilitate data analysis; scoring is very objective and efficient.

27. An unstructured-item format, in which the responder has complete freedom of response (questions are asked with no possible responses indicated), is sometimes defended on the grounds that it permits greater depth of response and may permit insight into the reasons for responses.

28. With respect to item construction, the number one rule is that each question should deal with a single concept and be worded as clearly as possible; any term or concept that might mean different things to different people should be defined.

29. When necessary, questions should indicate a point of reference.

30. Avoid leading questions that suggest that one response may be more appropriate than another.

31. Do not ask a question that assumes a fact not necessarily in evidence.

32. Do not include a series of questions that will allow anyone to identify a specific responder.

33. To facilitate arranging items in your questionnaire, use separate note cards for each item; a computer program can also be used to edit and rearrange questionnaire material.

Validation of the Questionnaire

34. A too-often-neglected procedure is validation of the questionnaire in order to determine if it measures what it was developed to measure.

Preparation of a Cover Letter

35. Every mailed questionnaire must be accompanied by a cover letter that explains what is being asked of the responder, and why, and which, it is hoped, motivates the responder to fulfill the request.

36. The cover letter should be brief, neat, and addressed specifically to the potential responder.

37. The letter should explain the purpose of the study, emphasizing its importance and significance, and give the responder a good reason for cooperating.

38. It often helps if you can get the endorsement of a professional organization, institution, group, or manager with whom the responder is associated or whom the responder views with respect.

39. If the questions to be asked are at all threatening (such as items dealing with sex or attitudes toward management), anonymity or confidentiality of responses must be assured.

40. A specific deadline date by which the completed questionnaire is to be returned should be given.

41. The act of responding should be made as painless as possible. A stamped, addressed, return envelope should be included.

Pretesting the Questionnaire

42. The questionnaire should be tried out in a field test just as a research plan should be executed first as a pilot study and for essentially the same reasons.

43. Pretesting the questionnaire yields data concerning instrument deficiencies as well as suggestions for improvement.

Follow-up Activities

44. If your percentage of returns is not at *least* 70, the validity of your conclusions will be weak.

45. An initial follow-up strategy is simply to send out a reminder postcard.

46. Full-scale follow-up activities are usually begun shortly after the deadline for responding has passed.

Dealing with Nonresponse

47. If your response rate is below 70%, you have a problem with generalizability of results, since you do not know if the persons who did respond represent the population from which the sample was originally selected as well as the original sample.

48. The usual approach to dealing with excessive nonresponse is to try to determine if nonresponders are different from responders in some systematic manner by randomly selecting a small subsample of nonresponders and interviewing them, either in person or by phone.

Analysis of Results

49. The simplest way to present the results is to indicate the percentage of responders who selected each alternative for each item.

50. Relationships between variables can be investigated by comparing responses on one item with responses on other items.

Conducting an Interview Study

51. An interview is essentially the oral, in-person administration of a questionnaire to each member of a sample.

52. When well conducted it can produce in-depth data not possible with a questionnaire; it is expensive and time-consuming, however, and generally involves smaller samples.

53. The steps in conducting an interview study are basically the same as for a questionnaire study, with some unique differences.

Construction of the Interview Guide

54. The interviewer must have a written guide, which indicates what questions are to be asked and in what order, and what additional prompting or probing is permitted.

55. In order to obtain standardized, comparable data from each subject, all interviews must be conducted in essentially the same manner.

56. As with a questionnaire, each question in the interview should relate to a specific study objective.

57. Most interviews use a semi-structured approach involving the asking of structured questions followed by clarifying unstructured, or open-ended, questions.

58. Many of the guidelines for constructing a questionnaire apply to the construction of interview guides.

Communication During the Interview

59. Before the first formal question is asked, some time should be spent in establishing rapport and putting the interviewee at ease.

60. The interviewer should also be sensitive to the reactions of the subject and proceed accordingly.

Recording Responses

61. Responses made during an interview can be recorded manually by the interviewer or mechanically by a recording device.

62. In general, mechanical recording is more objective and efficient.

Pretesting the Interview Procedure

63. Feedback from a small pilot study can be used to revise questions in the guide that are apparently unclear, do not solicit the desired information, or produce negative reactions in subjects. Insights into better ways to handle certain questions can also be acquired.

64. The pilot study will determine whether the resulting data can be quantified and analyzed in the manner intended.

OBSERVATIONAL RESEARCH

Types of Observational Research

Nonparticipant Observation

65. In nonparticipant observation, the observer is not directly involved in the situation to be observed.

Naturalistic Observation

66. In naturalistic observation the observer purposely controls or manipulates nothing and in fact works very hard at not affecting the observed situation in any way.

Simulation Observation

67. In simulation observation the researcher creates the situation to be observed and tells subjects the activities in which they are to engage.

68. This technique allows the researcher to observe behavior that occurs infrequently in natural situations or not at all.

69. Three major types of simulation are individual role playing, group role playing, and game simulation.

The Case Study

70. A case study is the in-depth investigation of an individual, group, or institution.

71. The primary purpose of a case study is to determine the factors and relationships among the factors that have resulted in the current behavior or status of the subject of the study.

Content Analysis

72. Content analysis is the systematic, quantitative description of the composition of the object of the study.

73. Typical subjects for content analysis include reports, documents, and files.

Participant Observation

74. In participant observation, the observer actually becomes a part of, a participant in, the situation to be observed.

75. There are degrees of participation, and observation may be overt or covert.

76. Participant-observation studies vary in the degree of structure involved in the inquiry. Such studies may be designed to test hypotheses, to derive hypotheses, or both.

77. More typically, participant-observation studies are hypothesis generating. Thus, participant-observation research is characterized by the collection of large amounts of data that are difficult to analyze.

Ethnography

Definition

78. Ethnography involves intensive data collection on many variables over an extended period of time in a naturalistic setting.

79. The unit of observation in an ethnographic study is typically a business, or even an industry.

Method

80. Ethnographic research may involve nonparticipant observation, participant observation, or both.

81. Typically, ethnographic studies are characterized by some type of participant observation at an overt level.

82. Ethnography represents multi-instrument research, and the ethnographer uses a variety of data-collection strategies in conjunction with observation.

An Example

83. Having refined the research problem of interest, the ethnographic researcher makes informed decisions concerning the most appropriate environment to study and the most effective level of participation.

84. In ethnography, a tentative hypothesis or hypotheses guide the initial data-collection strategies. Initial data-collection efforts suggest other appropriate strategies, and so forth.

85. The major difference between ethnographic and traditional approaches is that the review of related literature, the study of previous research and theory, does not result in testable hypotheses, to be supported or not supported by the results of the study. Instead, the study of previous work results in tentative, working hypotheses and strategies only. The researcher analyzes the mass of data collected and attempts to derive specific, testable hypotheses that explain the observed behavior.

Ethnography in Summary

86. In an ethnographic study, results are difficult to analyze, findings are difficult to replicate, the process is costly, and we are usually dealing with an N of one.

87. When properly used, ethnography has the potential for providing insights not obtainable with other methods.

88. The approach needs to undergo constant refinement and adaptation in the direction of a more-structured ethnography.

Conducting Observational Research

89. The steps in conducting observational research are essentially the same as for other types of descriptive research.

Definition of Observational Variables

90. Once the behavior to be observed is determined, the researcher must clearly define what specific behaviors do and do not match the intended behavior.

91. Once a behavioral unit is defined, observations must be quantified so that all observers will count the same way.

92. Researchers typically divide observation sessions into a number of specific observation periods, that is, define a time unit. There should be correspondence between actual behavior frequency and recorded frequency.

93. Observation times may be randomly selected, so that different days and times of day are reflected in the observations, or all possibilities may be observed. The latter approach is only feasible for short periods of time and for a limited number of subjects.

Recording of Observations

94. Observers should have to observe and record only one behavior at a time.

95. It is a good idea to alternate observation periods and recording periods, especially if any inference is required on the part of the observers.

96. As a general rule, it is probably better to record observations as the behavior occurs.

97. Most observation studies facilitate recording by using an agreed-upon code, or set of symbols, and a recording instrument.

98. Probably the most often used type of recording form, and the most efficient, is a checklist that lists all behaviors to be observed so that the observer can simply check each behavior as it occurs. Rating scales are also sometimes used.

Assessing Observer Reliability

99. Determining observer reliability generally requires that at least two observers independently make observations; their recorded judgments as to what occurred can then be compared to see how well they agree.

100. One approach to increasing reliability is to use shorter observation periods and to base reliability calculations on both agreements and disagreements on occurrences and nonoccurrences of behavior. With this approach it is easier to determine whether observers are recording the same events at the same time.

101. Recording situations to be observed allows each observer to play back tapes at a time convenient for her or him, and to play them back as often as needed.

Training Observers

102. Observers need to be trained in order to have some assurance that all observers are observing and recording the same behaviors in the same way.

103. Observers must be instructed as to what behaviors to observe, how behaviors are to be coded, how behaviors are to be recorded, and how often.

104. Practice sessions using recordings of behaviors are most effective since segments with which observers have difficulty can be replayed for discussion and feedback purposes.

105. Training may be terminated when a satisfactory level of reliability is achieved (say 80%).

Monitoring Observers

106. The major way to ensure continued satisfactory levels of reliability is to monitor the recording activities of observers.

107. As a general rule, the more monitoring that can reasonably be managed, the better.

Reducing Observation Bias

108. *Observer bias* refers to invalid observations that result from the way in which the observer observes.

109. A *response set* is the tendency of an observer to rate the majority of observees as above average, average, or below average, regardless of the observees' actual behavior.

110. The *halo effect* refers to the phenomenon whereby initial impressions concerning an observee (positive or negative) affect subsequent observations.

111. Data recorded by untrained observers, such as incident reports or performance appraisals on employees made by supervisors, tend to be subjective and biased and are usually not useful for research purposes.

112. *Observee bias* refers to the phenomenon whereby persons being observed behave atypically simply because they are being observed.

113. The best way to handle the problem of observee bias is to make observers aware of it so that they can attempt to be as unobtrusive as possible.

114. Another approach to the problem of observee bias is to eliminate observees. If the same information can be determined by observing inanimate objects (referred to as unobtrusive measures), use them.

On the following pages is an example of descriptive research (Project III Reading 2). The article may be used as a study aid to assist you in more fully understanding the nature of descriptive research. Following the article, a Practice Self Test for reviewing the article is provided for you so that you can practice your review skills; Appendix C contains Suggested Responses so that you can check your responses from the self-test. Questions are also provided to allow you to evaluate the article from the standpoint of descriptive research.

Psychological Conditions of Personal Engagement and Disengagement at Work

William A. Kahn
Boston University

This study began with the premise that people can use varying degrees of their selves, physically, cognitively, and emotionally, in work role performances, which has implications for both their work and experiences. Two qualitative, theory-generating studies of summer camp counselors and members of an architecture firm were conducted to explore the conditions at work in which people personally engage, or express and employ their personal selves, and disengage, or withdraw and defend their personal selves. This article describes and illustrates three psychological conditions—meaningfulness, safety, and availability—and their individual and contextual sources. These psychological conditions are linked to existing theoretical concepts, and directions for future research are described.

People occupy roles at work; they are the occupants of the houses that roles provide. These events are relatively well understood; researchers have focused on "role sending" and "receiving" (Katz & Kahn, 1978), role sets (Merton, 1957), role taking and socialization (Van Maanen, 1976), and on how people and their roles shape each other (Graen, 1976). Researchers have given less attention to how people occupy roles to varying degrees—to how fully they are psycholog-

The guidance and support of David Berg, Richard Hackman, and Seymour Sarason in the research described here are gratefully acknowledged. I also greatly appreciated the personal engagements of this journal's two anonymous reviewers in their roles, as well as the comments on an earlier draft of Tim Hall, Kathy Kram, and Vicky Parker.

© *Academy of Management Journal* 1990. Vol. 33, No. 4, 692–724.

ically present during particular moments of role performances. People can use varying degrees of their selves, physically, cognitively, and emotionally, in the roles they perform, even as they maintain the integrity of the boundaries between who they are and the roles they occupy. Presumably, the more people draw on their selves to perform their roles within those boundaries, the more stirring are their performances and the more content they are with the fit of the costumes they don.

The research reported here was designed to generate a theoretical framework within which to understand these "self-in-role" processes and to suggest directions for future research. My specific concern was the moments in which people bring themselves into or remove themselves from particular task behaviors. My guiding assumption was that people are constantly bringing in and leaving out various depths of their selves during the course of their work days. They do so to respond to the momentary ebbs and flows of those days and to express their selves at some times and defend them at others. By focusing on moments of task performances, I sought to identify variables that explained the processes by which people adjust their selves-in-roles.

Existing organizational behavior concepts focusing on person-role relationships emphasize the generalized states that organization members occupy: people are to some degree job involved (Lawler & Hall, 1970; Lodahl & Kejner, 1965), committed to organizations (Mowday, Porter, & Steers, 1982; Porter, Steers, Mowday, & Boulian, 1974), or alienated at work in the form of self-estrangement (Blauner, 1964; Seeman, 1972). As previously conceptualized and measured, these concepts suggest that organization members strike and hold enduring stances (committed, involved, alienated), as if posing in still photographs. Such photographs would show people maintaining average levels of commitment and involvement over time. This perspective has offered some valuable lessons about the individual differences and situational factors that influence the psychological importance of work to people's identities or self-esteem (Jones, James, & Bruni, 1975; Lodahl, 1964), about the degree to which they consider a job central to their life (Dubin, 1956), about their willingness to exert effort for and remain part of their organizations (Mowday et al., 1982), and about the alienating effects of social systems (Blauner, 1964).

The cited research has yielded some understanding of what types of variables influence how organization members perceive themselves, their work, and the relation between the two. The understandings are general: they exist at some distance from the processes of people experiencing and behaving within particular work situations. For example, researchers have measured job involvement attitudinally with a paper-and-pencil scale asking people how much they intertwine their self-definition or self-esteem with work (e.g., "The most important things that happen to me involve my work"; Lodahl & Kejner, 1965). Often enough, employee absence from work gauges job involvement behaviorally (Blau & Boal, 1987). Both measures are broad, context-free sweeps at how present people are at work, yet neither goes to the core of what it means to be psychologically present in particular moments and situations. Doing so requires deeply probing people's experiences and situations during the discrete moments that make up their work lives. Such probing relies on studying both people's emotional reactions to conscious and unconscious phenomena, as clinical researchers do (e.g., Berg & Smith, 1985), and the objective properties of jobs, roles, and work contexts, as nonclinical researchers do (e.g., Lawler & Hall, 1970)—all within the same moments of task performances. Doing so focuses attention on the variance within the average stances of involvement and commitment that people strike over time.[1]

The specific, in-depth approach used here was designed to yield a grounded theoretical framework illustrating how psychological experiences of work and work contexts shape the processes of people presenting and absenting their selves during task performances. This conceptual framework was grounded in both empirical research and existing theoretical frameworks. Conceptually, my starting point was the work of Goffman (1961a), who suggested that people's attachment to and detachment from their roles varies. In the theatrical metaphor that Goffman employed, people act out momentary attachments and detachments in role performances. Behaviors signifying a lack of separation between people and their roles indicate role embracement, and behaviors pointedly separating them from disdained roles indicate role distance. Goffman's examples show his focus on nonverbal language: a traffic policeman at a rush hour intersection embraces his role, arms dancing and whistle blowing, and a father shepherding his son on a merry-go-round distances himself from his role, yawning and mock-grimacing (1961a: 108).

Goffman's work dealt with fleeting face-to-face encounters. A different concept was needed to fit organizational life, which is ongoing, emotionally charged, and psychologically complex (Diamond & Allcorn, 1985). Psychologists (Freud, 1922), sociologists (Goffman, 1961b; Merton, 1957), and group theorists (Bion, 1961; Slater, 1966; Smith & Berg, 1987) have documented the idea that people are inherently ambivalent about being members of ongoing groups and systems and seek to protect themselves from both isolation and engulfment by alternately pulling away from and moving toward their memberships. These pulls and pushes are people's calibrations of self-in-role, enabling them to cope with both internal ambivalences and external conditions.

The terms developed here to describe these calibrations of self-in-role are *personal engagement* and *personal disengagement.* They refer to the behaviors by which people bring in or leave out their personal selves during work role performances. I defined personal engagement as the harnessing of organization members' selves to their work roles; in engagement, people employ and express themselves physically, cognitively, and emotionally during role performances. I defined personal disengagement as the uncoupling of selves from work roles; in

---

[1]Hackett, Bycio, and Guion (1989) proposed and used "idiographic-longitudinal-analytical techniques" to achieve a similar focus.

disengagement, people withdraw and defend themselves physically, cognitively, or emotionally during role performances. The personal engagement and disengagement concepts developed here integrate the idea that people need both self-expression and self-employment in their work lives as a matter of course (Alderfer, 1972; Maslow, 1954).

Using these definitions to guide the research, I built on job-design research on relations between workers and the characteristics of their tasks (Hackman & Oldham, 1980). I combined that perspective with those focusing on the interpersonal (Bennis, Schein, Berlew, & Steele, 1964; Rogers, 1958), group (Bion, 1961; Smith & Berg, 1987), intergroup (Alderfer, 1985a), and organizational (Hochschild, 1983) contexts that enhance or undermine people's motivation and sense of meaning at work. The research premise was twofold: first, that the psychological experience of work drives people's attitudes and behaviors (Hackman & Oldham, 1980), and second, that individual, interpersonal, group, intergroup, and organizational factors simultaneously influence these experiences (Alderfer, 1985a).

Following these premises, I focused on delineating the psychological conditions in which people personally engage and disengage at work. These conditions are psychological experiences of the rational and unconscious elements of work contexts. I assumed that those work contexts, mediated by people's perceptions, create the conditions in which they personally engage and disengage. The research thus focused on people's experiences of themselves, their work, and its contexts. My aim was to map across individuals the general conditions of experience that influence degrees of personal engagement. I sought to identify psychological conditions powerful enough to survive the gamut of individual differences. This article describes and illustrates the nature of personal engagement and disengagement and the three psychological conditions found to influence those behaviors. I focus specifically on the nature of the conditions and their individual, social, and contextual sources.

METHODS

Generating a descriptive theory grounded in the behaviors, experiences, and perceptions of organization members required constant movement between theory and data: data suggested theoretical hypotheses and concepts, which suggested further data collection needs (Glaser & Strauss, 1967). I thus developed the theoretical framework in one organizational context and then redeveloped it in a different context. I entered the first setting armed with the sketchy definitions of personal engagement and disengagement outlined above, the desire to identify relevant psychological conditions, and the premise that those conditions would be created at the intersection of individual, interpersonal, group, intergroup, and organizational factors.

Different research stances were taken in the two studies. In the first context, a summer camp, I was both participant and observer. In the second context, an architecture firm, I was an outside researcher. Becoming an outsider constituted movement on my part from a relatively high degree of personal engagement to disengagement. I capitalized on the difference by using myself as a research tool, much as a clinician would (Alderfer, 1985b; Berg & Smith, 1985), reflecting on my experiences of conducting the research to inform both the process of generating the theory and its substance. The difficulty was in distinguishing the general properties of personal engagement and disengagement phenomena from the specific, biased ways in which I experienced and analyzed my roles (Berg & Smith, 1985). Consulting an outside supervisor familiar with the psychological issues involved in conducting such research enabled me to work through the personal issues that crop up in and influence clinical research and to manage the dynamics of the relationships with organizations (Berg, 1980).

The two organizations were selected because of their differences on a number of dimensions. To generate widely generalizable understandings about personal engagement and disengagement, I needed to identify conceptual commonalities in widely diverging settings. The camp, a temporary system dedicated to the education and enjoyment of adolescents, had little hierarchical structure and was a total system in which work and nonwork boundaries blurred. Working there was physically exhausting for counselors, who were cast in constant care-taking and disciplinary roles. The architecture firm, a permanent system dedicated to constructing buildings, had rigid hierarchical structures and project teams and an ebbing and flowing rhythm based on projects and negotiations. The contrasts in what it was for employees to express, employ, and defend themselves as members of these two settings seemed huge. Those contrasts suggested the second setting as a counterpoint to the first.

Camp Carrib

Setting

Camp Carrib[2] was a six-week summer camp in the West Indies, attended by 100 adolescents, 12–17 years old, from relatively wealthy U.S. and Western European backgrounds. A staff of 22 counselors ran the camp. Counselors taught particular athletic skills such as tennis, scuba diving, and waterskiing and lived with and supervised campers. A head counselor and camp director were responsible for the general welfare of the camp and subject to the authority of its elderly owners who participated sporadically in its daily operations. The camp director was the eldest son of the camp owners; he was preparing to assume increasing ownership and control during the coming years.

Participants

Data were collected on 16 counselors, 9 men and 7 women, ranging in age from 20 to 35 years, with an average age of 25.5 years. They had been at this camp an

---

[2]I have disguised the names of the two organizations and their members to protect confidentiality.

average of two and a half summers; some were newcomers and others, eight-year veterans. They represented each camp program, from the largest (scuba diving) to the smallest (drama). The counselors were all at camp partly because they had the free time to do so. That is, they were students or teachers between academic semesters, free-lance scuba-diving instructors, or people taking summer sabbaticals from their usual lives to work temporarily as counselors. All counselors were white Americans (with the exception of one Briton) from middle- or upper middle-class backgrounds.

Data Collection

I collected data using an assortment of qualitative methods: observation, document analysis, self-reflection, and in-depth interviewing. I was both a participant (the head tennis counselor) and an observer (the researcher). The camp's management agreed to my conducting the research before I joined the staff. I obtained the informed consent of the counselors at the end of the precamp orientation period, prior to the arrival of the campers; after a series of questions, clarifications, and guarantees of privacy, all counselors agreed to participate.

The first three weeks of camp involved observations and informal conversations meant to generate hypotheses and interview questions. I observed counselors in all types of situations, on-duty and off-duty, including task-related and social interactions with campers, other counselors, and camp management. Observations did not follow an explicit guide. I was looking for what I thought were examples of personal engagement and disengagement and for ways to explain those behaviors. I also sought clues in camp documents; the counselor handbook, the camp rules, and assorted camp brochures offered a sense of how the camp defined itself and the counselor role. During the second three weeks I interviewed the staff using questions based on the hypotheses I had developed. Interviews consisted of 24 open-ended questions designed to explore the counselors' perceptions of their experiences, involvements and lack thereof, roles, and the camp. The Appendix gives all questions. Probes that asked people to extend their analyses followed the questions. I taped the interviews, which lasted between 45 and 90 minutes (averaging 65 minutes).

E.S.B. and Associates

Setting

The second research site was a prestigious architecture firm in the northeastern United States. The firm, owned and operated by the principal architect (whose initials, E.S.B., gave the firm its name), was staffed by 45 employees working as registered architects, draftspersons, interior designers, administrators, and interns. The firm was highly regarded, had won a number of design competitions and awards, and was growing more or less steadily into a large corporation faced with more projects than it could comfortably handle. The firm was structured around the use of project teams that formed and reformed according to the demands of various projects in different stages of production. The firm's owner (also its president) was the principal designer for each project, and a senior architect, usually one of four vice presidents, was in charge of implementing his design concepts. As a project developed, the senior architect would form a team. At the time of the study, the firm was quite busy, working simultaneously on over 30 projects and negotiating contracts for others.

Participants

I collected data on 16 firm members, 10 men and 6 women, choosing them for the diversity of their experiences, demographic traits, and positions in the firm. The participants had an average age of 34.3 years: 7 were between 24 and 41, 5 were between 32 and 44, and 4 were between 48 and 54. They also averaged 5.8 years with the firm: 4 had been there for less than a year, 5 between 1 and 3 years, 4 between 5 and 11 years, and 3 between 12 and 23 years. These employees represented all levels and positions in the firm: I interviewed five senior architects, including the owner and the vice presidents; two designers; five draftspersons; two interns; and two support-staff members. All were white, American, and the products of middle-class or upper middle-class backgrounds. This group represented the larger population of the firm's employees in terms of age (averaging 31 years), gender (33 percent women), and positions in the firm.[3] Their average length of job tenure was higher than that of the larger population of the firm, which was sharply deflated by its high proportion of young, relatively inexperienced unregistered draftspersons.

Data Collection

The lengthy process of obtaining informed consent included attending a series of meeting with E.S.B. and the vice presidents, sending introductory letters to all employees, having telephone conversations with people who had questions or reservations about the project, distributing a contract letter cosigned by E.S.B. to all employees, and contacting members who agreed to be interviewed for the study. Data collection was structured around in-depth interviews. The interview format reflected the initial theory developed from the first study, translated into what I learned of the firm's language from the entry process (see the Appendix). After warm-up questions about an individual's job and work history and the firm, I asked participants to recall four different situations in which they had felt: (1) attentive, absorbed, or involved in their work, (2) uninvolved, detached, or distracted from their work, (3) differences between how they responded to a work situation and how they would have responded if they had not been at work,

---

[3]Occupational groups at the firm, in descending order of size, were: draftspersons, senior designers and licensed architects, model builders, administrative support people, vice presidents, associate vice presidents, interior designer, and president.

and (4) no differences from nonwork behavior in how they reacted to a work-related situation. I asked participants to describe and detail each situation, their behaviors and experiences, and how they understood or explained those experiences as best they could. The tactic of asking participants to in some sense relive particular situations reflected the phenomenological assumption that understanding psychological and emotional experience requires working from experienced realities to abstracted ideas (de Rivera, 1981; Kahn, 1984). Interviews were taped and lasted between 40 and 90 minutes (averaging 54 minutes).

Analysis

Data analysis occurred in three separate phases. The first phase occurred after the camp study. I transcribed and closely read interviews to identify what intuitively seemed to be moments in which people personally engaged or disengaged at work. I culled those experiences from the rest of the interviews as long quotations and analyzed them through an inductive process in which I articulated the characteristics that defined them as moments of personal engagement or disengagement. I then analyzed each experience to induce the psychological and contextual reasons why the counselors had personally engaged or disengaged. I was left with a set of categories of data, initial concepts to explain those data, and questions to guide the second study.

The second phase of data analysis, conducted after the study of the architecture firm, again involved transcribing interviews and identifying personal engagement and disengagement experiences. I sorted these data into the existing categories. The categories needed to change, however, to accommodate the new data and provide a base for a generalizable descriptive theory. The new categories reflected the greater complexity of both data and the concepts used to explain those data. With the greater complexity came sharper definition. The continuous movement between data and concepts ended when I had defined enough categories to explain what was recorded (Glaser & Strauss, 1967). The third phase of data analysis consisted of returning to the camp data and resorting and reanalyzing them in terms of the more complex categories and concepts.

In completing this cycle, I generated a collection of personal engagement and disengagement experiences. The examples were extended descriptions of moments in which people personally engaged or disengaged, pulled from the interviews and typed in their raw form on index cards. Each card included descriptions of behaviors, internal experiences, and contextual factors that described a specific moment of personal engagement or disengagement. I sorted experiences according to whether they clearly showed engagement or disengagement in terms of criteria given below. Examples that did not clearly fit either category were excluded. The collection finally included 86 personal engagement examples (40 from Camp Carrib, 46 from E.S.B. and Associates) and 100 personal disengagement examples (48 from Camp Carrib, 52 from E.S.B. and Associates). An independent coder similarly sorted a randomly selected sample of 60 experiences; there was 97 percent interrater agreement on the sortings.

These examples were used for statistical techniques that helped describe a model of personal engagement and disengagement. They did not serve to test the model; hypothesis testing relies on a stringent set of statistical assumptions that do not allow for generating and testing statistical assumptions from a single set of empirical observations (Hays, 1981). The descriptive statistics were based on my ratings of the extent to which the three psychological conditions described below were present in each of the 186 examples. Ratings were made on a nine-point format ranging from extremely absent to extremely present. An independent rater similarly rated a random sample of 36 examples, after hearing descriptions of the relevant psychological conditions and rating six practice situations. The rater was blind to whether those situations reflected personal engagement or disengagement. Correlations were calculated to determine the interrater reliability for each of the three scales. Correlations and statistics are presented below.

PERSONAL ENGAGEMENT AND PERSONAL DISENGAGEMENT

The conceptual framework presented here begins with defining and illustrating the concepts of personal engagement and disengagement that emerged from this research. Examples from the two studies and existing theoretical frameworks elucidate the concepts. I describe pure forms of personal engagement and disengagement separately; these represent the endpoints of a continuum. People's behaviors may show mixtures of personal engagement and disengagement; for the purposes of clarity, I do not discuss those mixtures.

Personal Engagement

Personal engagement is the simultaneous employment and expression of a person's "preferred self" in task behaviors that promote connections to work and to others, personal presence (physical, cognitive, and emotional), and active, full role performances. My premise is that people have dimensions of themselves that, given appropriate conditions, they prefer to use and express in the course of role performances. To employ such dimensions is to drive personal energies into physical, cognitive, and emotional labors. Such self-employment underlies what researchers have referred to as effort (Hackman & Oldham, 1980), involvement (Lawler & Hall, 1970), flow (Csikszentmihalyi, 1982), mindfulness (Langer, 1989), and intrinsic motivation (Deci, 1975). To express preferred dimensions is to display real identity, thoughts, and feelings. Self-expression underlies what researchers refer to as creativity (Perkins, 1981), the use of personal voice (Hirschman, 1970), emotional expression (Rafaeli & Sutton,

1987), authenticity (Baxter, 1982), nondefensive communication (Gibb, 1961), playfulness (Kahn, 1989), and ethical behavior (Toffler, 1986).

The combination of employing and expressing a person's preferred self yields behaviors that bring alive the relation of self to role. People who are personally engaged keep their selves within a role, without sacrificing one for the other. Miner's (1987) discussion of idiosyncratic jobs in formal systems offers further insight into this phenomenon. Self and role exist in some dynamic, negotiable relation in which a person both drives personal energies into role behaviors (self-employment) and displays the self within the role (self-expression). Personally engaging behaviors simultaneously convey and bring alive self and obligatory role. People become physically involved in tasks, whether alone or with others, cognitively vigilant, and empathically connected to others in the service of the work they are doing in ways that display what they think and feel, their creativity, their beliefs and values, and their personal connections to others.

For example, a scuba-diving instructor at the summer camp taught a special class to advanced divers. He spent a great deal of time with the students both in and out of class and worked to share with them his personal philosophy about the ocean and the need to take care of its resources. In doing so, he experienced moments of pure personal engagement. He described one diving expedition in which he employed his self physically, darting about checking gear and leading the dive; cognitively, in his vigilant awareness of divers, weather, and marine life; and emotionally, in empathizing with the fear and excitement of the young divers. He also expressed himself—the dimensions of himself that loved the ocean and wanted others to do so as well—during that expedition, talking about the wonders of the ocean, directing the boat drivers toward minimally destructive paths across the coral reef, showing his playfulness and joy underwater. The counselor was at once psychologically connecting with the campers and to a task that deeply tapped what he defined as important. In doing so, he was simultaneously fully discharging his role and expressing a preferred self.

At the architecture firm, a senior designer was involved in an important project during which such moments of personal engagement occurred. In one such moment, she employed herself physically ("I was just flying around the office"), cognitively (in working out the design-construction interfaces), and emotionally (she refused to give criticism publicly, empathizing with other people's feelings). At the same time, she expressed herself—the dimensions that hooked into the joy of creating designs both aesthetic and functional—by exhorting team members to think about how the clients would actually use the work, questioning the chief architect's assumptions about the design, providing criticism to others in ways both constructive and gentle, and working with the client as a collaborator rather than a "hired gun." At such moments, she behaved in ways that were both expressive of what she wanted to see acted out in the world and harnessed to the engine of task-oriented realities.

Personal Disengagement

Personal disengagement, conversely, is the simultaneous withdrawal and defense of a person's preferred self in behaviors that promote a lack of connections, physical, cognitive, and emotional absence, and passive, incomplete role performances. To withdraw preferred dimensions is to remove personal, internal energies from physical, cognitive, and emotional labors. Such unemployment of the self underlies task behaviors researchers have called automatic or robotic (Hochschild, 1983), burned out (Maslach, 1982), apathetic or detached (Goffman, 1961a), or effortless (Hackman & Oldham, 1980). To defend the self is to hide true identity, thoughts, and feelings during role performances. Such self-defense underlies what researchers have referred to as defensive (Argyris, 1982), impersonal or emotionally unexpressive (Hochschild, 1983; Rafaeli & Sutton, 1987), bureaucratic (Shorris, 1981), self-estranged (Seeman, 1972), and closed (Gibb, 1961) behaviors.

Personally disengaging means uncoupling self from role; people's behaviors display an evacuation or suppression of their expressive and energetic selves in discharging role obligations.[4] Role demands guide task behaviors without the interplay between internal thoughts and feelings and external requirements that characterize moments of personal engagement. People perform tasks at some distance from their preferred selves, which remain split off and hidden. They perform roles as external scripts indicate they should rather than internally interpret those roles; they act as custodians rather than innovators (Van Maanen & Schein, 1979). They become physically uninvolved in tasks, cognitively unvigilant, and emotionally disconnected from others in ways that hide what they think and feel, their creativity, their beliefs and values, and their personal connections to others.

Another senior designer at the architecture firm provided an example of disengagement, describing a moment in which he withdrew his energies physically, by farming out nonmanagement tasks to others: cognitively, by adopting an automatic, perfunctory approach marked by not questioning others' decisions, parameters, and design assumptions; and emotionally, by not empathizing with confused draftspersons and an upset client. He defended himself by displaying little of what he thought and felt within the conduct of the role. In working with the chief architect at that moment, he said little and waited to hear the other's responses; as he noted, "I exercised less than I probably could my own responses to something at that point, and had it be more how E.S.B. would respond." The designer suppressed what he himself thought and felt about the project. Anticipating and echoing the wishes of the president involved some presence of mind, but of a type that depended on disengaging his personal

---

[4]A different, related concept might be called "role disengagement"; this term refers to what occurs when people shed their roles as a way to uncouple self-in-role, avoid discharging role obligations, and simply be themselves.

thoughts from his tasks. He refrained from investing ideas, encouraging the creativity of other team members, or sharing his visions about the design and excitement about the process, all of which could have shaped the building profoundly and helped it reflect the images and principles he held.

At the camp, a counselor personally disengaged during moments of teaching a windsurfing class. She reported withdrawing herself physically ("sending them out and just laying around"), cognitively ("not telling them much or helping them out much"), and emotionally ("I was more bland, superficial, talking in flat, unemotional tones"). At that moment, she displayed little of who she preferred to be by not letting herself connect with and get close to the campers. As she noted, "I was really shut down, not letting loose or being funny or letting them get close to me by talking more about myself. I just didn't let them in, I guess." Her personal disengagement meant withdrawing and defending herself from the types of interpersonal connections that defined who she typically preferred to be in her counselor role.

PSYCHOLOGICAL CONDITIONS

Overview

The studies reported here focused on how people's experiences of themselves and their work contexts influenced moments of personal engagement and disengagement. My premise was that people employ and express or withdraw and defend their preferred selves on the basis of their psychological experiences of self-in-role. This premise is similar to Hackman and Oldham's (1980) notion that there are critical psychological states that influence people's internal work motivations. Here, the focus was on psychological conditions—the momentary rather than static circumstances of people's experiences that shape behaviors. These circumstances are like conditions in fleeting contracts; if certain conditions are met to some acceptable degree, people can personally engage in moments of task behaviors.

The three psychological conditions described and illustrated below were articulated through an inductive analysis that defined the experiential conditions whose presence influenced people to personally engage and whose absence influenced them to personally disengage. I analyzed each moment as if there were a contract between person and role (cf. Schein, 1970); the conditions of those contracts were induced, generalized across all moments, and connected to existing theoretical concepts. Three psychological conditions emerged: *meaningfulness, safety,* and *availability.* Together, the three conditions shaped how people inhabited their roles. Organization members seemed to unconsciously ask themselves three questions in each situation and to personally engage or disengage depending on the answers. The questions were: (1) How meaningful is it for me to bring myself into this performance? (2) How safe is it to do so? and (3) How available am I to do so?

The three conditions reflect the logic of actual contracts. People agree to contracts containing clear and desired benefits and protective guarantees when they believe themselves to possess the resources necessary to fulfill the obligations generated. That logic characterizes people's agreements to place increasing depths of themselves into role performances. People vary their personal engagements according to their perceptions of the benefits, or the meaningfulness, and the guarantees, or the safety, they perceive in situations. Engagement also varies according to the resources they perceive themselves to have—their availability. This contractual imagery helped make sense of the data on participants' experiences and offered a conceptual structure within which I could link the three pyschological conditions.

A look at the characteristics of situations that shaped participants' experiences of themselves, their roles, and the relations between the two will elucidate the three psychological conditions. Experiences—of benefits, guarantees, and resources—were generally associated with particular influences. Psychological meaningfulness was associated with work elements that created incentives or disincentives to personally engage. Psychological safety was associated with elements of social systems that created more or less nonthreatening, predictable, and consistent social situations in which to engage. Psychological availability was associated with individual distractions that preoccupied people to various degrees and left them more or fewer resources with which to engage in role performances. Table 1 summarizes the dimensions of the three focal conditions.

Psychological Meaningfulness

Psychological meaningfulness can be seen as a feeling that one is receiving a return on investments of one's self in a currency of physical, cognitive, or emotional energy. People experienced such meaningfulness when they felt worthwhile, useful, and valuable—as though they made a difference and were not taken for granted. They felt able to give to others and to the work itself in their roles and also able to receive. Lack of meaningfulness was connected to people's feeling that little was asked or expected of their selves and that there was little room for them to give or receive in work role performances. This formulation reflects concepts of how people invest themselves in tasks (Hackman & Oldham, 1980) and roles (Maehr & Braskamp, 1986) that satisfy personal (Alderfer, 1972; Maslow, 1954) and existential needs (May, Angel, & Ellenberger, 1958) for meaning in work and life.

The general link between personal engagement and psychological meaningfulness was explored with descriptive statistics calculated from the ratings of the 186 experiences I culled from the two studies. The statistics indicated that personal engagement was connected to higher levels of psychological meaningfulness ($\bar{x} = 7.8$, s.d. $= .84$) than personal disengagement ($\bar{x} = 3.24$, s.d. $= 1.75$; inter-rater reliability (r) $= .89$). These results suggest that people were personally engaging in situations characterized by more psychological meaningfulness than those in which they were disengaging.

TABLE 1
Dimensions of Psychological Conditions

Dimensions	Meaningfulness	Safety	Availability
Definition	Sense of return on investments of self in role performances.	Sense of being able to show and employ self without fear of negative consequences to self-image, status, or career.	Sense of possessing the physical, emotional, and psychological resources necessary for investing self in role performances.
Experiential components	Feel worthwhile, valued, valuable; feel able to give to and receive from work and others in course of work.	Feel situations are trustworthy, secure, predictable, and clear in terms of behavioral consequences.	Feel capable of driving physical, intellectual, and emotional energies into role performance.
Types of influence	Work elements that create incentives or disincentives for investments of self.	Elements of social systems that create situations that are more or less predictable, consistent, and nonthreatening.	Individual distractions that are more or less preoccupying in role performance situations.
Influences	Tasks: Jobs involving more or less challenge, variety, creativity, autonomy, and clear delineation of procedures and goals.	Interpersonal relationships: Ongoing relationships that offer more or less support, trust, openness, flexibility, and lack of threat.	Physical energies: Existing levels of physical resources available for investment into role performances.

The data indicated that three factors generally influenced psychological meaningfulness: task characteristics, role characteristics, and work interactions.

Task Characteristics

When organization members were doing work that was challenging, clearly delineated, varied, creative, and somewhat autonomous, they were more likely to experience psychological meaningfulness. I induced that finding from the two studies and from previous research (Hackman & Oldham, 1980) focusing on how job characteristics such as skill variety and autonomy are a source of meaning in work.

An ideal situation for psychological meaningfulness, for example, was working on a rich and complex project. Meaningful tasks demanded both routine and new skills, allowing people to experience a sense of both competence

TABLE 1
(continued)

Dimensions	Meaningfulness	Safety	Availability
Influences *cont.*	Roles: Formal positions that offer more or less attractive identities, through fit with a preferred self-image, and status and influence. Work interactions: Interpersonal interactions with more or less promotion of dignity, self-appreciation, sense of value, and the inclusion of personal as well as professional elements.	Group and intergroup dynamics: Informal, often unconscious roles that leave more or less room to safely express various parts of self; shaped by dynamics within and between groups in organizations. Management style and process: Leader behaviors that show more or less support, resilience, consistency, trust, and competence. Organizational norms: Shared system expectations about member behaviors and emotions that leave more or less room for investments of self during role performances.	Emotional energies: Existing levels of emotional resources available for investment into role performances. Insecurity: Levels of confidence in own abilities and status, self-consciousness, and ambivalence about fit with social systems that leave more or less room for investments of self in role performances. Outside life: Issues in people's outside lives that leave them more or less available for investments of self during role performances.

(from the routine) and growth and learning (from the new). As a draftsperson at the architecture firm noted,

> The project I'm working on includes the restoration of a historical building, reconstruction of a demolished historic room, and an addition of a new building to an old one. That's a lot of complexity, and difficult as far as projects go. It's also the one that gets me excited about coming into the office.

Similarly, a scuba counselor noted,

> That class was one of the more difficult and rewarding I've taught here. It was a tough dive, because of the weather, and dangerous. I had to be so aware all the time of everything: the kids and their air supplies, the compass work, the swells and currents. It was tough, but it felt great when it was over.

Meaningful tasks also allowed for some autonomy and the resulting sense of ownership over the work that previous research has noted (Hackman & Oldham, 1980). Such tasks were neither so tightly linked to nor so controlled by others that people performing them needed to constantly look for direction. Finally, the goals of potentially meaningful tasks were clear, allowing a good chance for success (cf. Locke, 1968). Clear goals were not always present in the architecture firm, where the ambiguity of the creative process was exacerbated by a president who would, in the words of one interviewee, offer "scribbles, bubbles, and waves" in design sketches and walk away, leaving behind more uncertainty than clarity.

Role Characteristics

The data indicated two components of work roles that influenced the experience of psychological meaningfulness. First, roles carried identities that organization members were implicitly required to assume. Organization members could like or dislike those identities and the stances toward others they required: they typically did so on the basis of how well the roles fit how they saw or wanted to see their selves (Goffman, 1961a; Hochschild, 1983). At the camp, counselors both taught the campers, which required trust, and policed them, which required distrust. Counselors usually found one or the other identity—teacher or policeman—more meaningful, although at times they were frustrated by the paradox of needing to be both and found neither meaningful. In the architecture firm, there were also various identities that members hooked into psychologically to different degrees: designer, decision maker, and with clients, collaborator or competitor. Comments from the firm's receptionist illustrated the unattractiveness of her work role:

> The role I'm required to perform, sitting up here in front and smiling and typing and being friendly . . . it's all bullshit, it's just a role, and there isn't any satisfaction in it for me. I'm more than that, and I want to be seen as a person apart from the work I do. This eight or nine hours is a waste, damaging, I think, to my own growth and what I think about myself.

Roles also carried status, or influence. When people were able to wield influence, occupy valuable positions in their systems, and gain desirable status, they experienced a sense of meaningfulness. The underlying dimension was power and what it bought: influence, and a sense of being valued, valuable, and needed. People search for ways to feel important and special, particularly since they generally feel powerless in the world as a whole (Lasch, 1984). In these organizations, roles that allowed people to have a sense of shaping the external world, whether in the form of kids' experiences or concrete buildings, offered a sense of meaningfulness. As one draftsperson put it, "It's amazing for me to walk through a building and see this front entry vestibule or this stairwell, and like see me, see that I had an impact." A scuba counselor measured his influence differently:

> I have a lot of kids who ask for me as their instructor, who come up and tell me that they don't like the other instructors and want to be with me. They feel open about separating us. It's not great that that happens, but it's very gratifying for me.

Role status was important partly as an indicator to people about how central to and needed in their organizations they were. Particular activities at both organizations were less central than others and widely perceived as such, and people performing those tasks were susceptible to feeling unimportant—particularly if others treated them as unimportant. A counselor in charge of an unpopular program remarked, "I don't have my special place; I'm just not special here to the kids." A support staff member at the firm noted that although his job was essential if others were to do their work, "It's treated as meaningless." Roles perceived as unimportant in an organizational constellation lacked the power to offer their occupants a sense of meaningfulness.

Work Interactions

People also experienced psychological meaningfulness when their task performances included rewarding interpersonal interactions with co-workers and clients. In the two studies, meaningful interactions promoted dignity, self-appreciation, and a sense of worthwhileness. They enabled relationships in which people wanted to give to and receive from others. As an architect noted,

> I would say that my involvement comes from individuals. It's an immediate, initial thing that happens, a connection that I make each time when I work with someone with whom I find some common ground, some shared ways of thinking about things. If I don't have that connection, it's tough for me to get going working with them.

Such connections are an invaluable source of meaning in people's lives because they meet relatedness needs (Alderfer, 1972): they allow people to feel known and appreciated and that they are sharing their existential journeys with others (May et al., 1958).

Meaningful interactions in the two settings often involved both personal and professional elements and a looseness of the boundaries separating the two. For the counselors, this meant interacting with other staff members not simply as co-workers but as cohorts. The image that some counselors invoked was of a platoon in which individuals thrown together under extraordinary circumstances develop emotional bonds transcending the relative superficiality of the connections between typical co-workers. At the architecture firm, meaningfulness also came from interpersonal connections that to some degree tapped people's emotional lives. That tapping occurred when people felt as if they fit in some way with those with whom they interacted and when people treated one another not as role occupants but as people who happened to occupy roles (Hochschild, 1983). The distinction was important to how much dignity and self-esteem people felt at work.

Interactions with clients, whether campers or builders, were sources of both gratification and frustration. Meaningful interactions allowed people to feel valuable and valued. They involved mutual appreciation, respect, and positive feedback. Client interactions reduced the sense of meaningfulness when they blocked the interpersonal connections allowing people to perform and enjoy their jobs. Camp counselors found meaningfulness diminished when the campers communicated a lack of care, respect, or appreciation for the counselors' work. As one counselor noted, "It's a question of whether they tap into me or not; you put the energy where it will be appreciated." Similarly, architectural clients who did not allow firm members to do the jobs for which they were trained or did not appreciate their efforts created relationships devoid of respect and meaningfulness. Organization members preferred to be psychologically absent in such relationships.

Psychological Safety

Psychological safety was experienced as feeling able to show and employ one's self without fear of negative consequences to self-image, status, or career. People felt safe in situations in which they trusted that they would not suffer for their personal engagement. This association reflects a tenet of clinical work stating that therapeutic relationships (Sandler, 1960), families (Minuchin, 1974), groups (Smith & Berg, 1987), and organizations (Schein, 1987) create contexts in which people feel more or less safe in taking the risks of self-expression and engaging the processes of change. In the two studies, situations promoting trust were predictable, consistent, clear, and nonthreatening; people were able to understand the boundaries between what was allowed and disallowed and the potential consequences of their behaviors. When situations were unclear, inconsistent, unpredictable, or threatening, personal engagement was deemed too risky or unsafe.

The general link between personal engagement and psychological safety was explored with descriptive statistics derived from the ratings of the group of 186 experiences. The statistics indicated that personal engagement was connected to higher levels of psychological safety ($\bar{x}$ = 7.7, s.d. = 1.21) than personal disengagement ($\bar{x}$ = 3.77, s.d. = 1.6; r = .83). These results suggest that people were personally engaging in situations characterized by more psychological safety than those in which they were personally disengaging.

The data indicated that four factors most directly influenced psychological safety: interpersonal relationships, group and intergroup dynamics, management style and process, and organizational norms.

Interpersonal Relationships

Interpersonal relationships promoted psychological safety when they were supportive and trusting. Such relationships had a flexibility that allowed people to try and perhaps to fail without fearing the consequences. At the architecture firm, such relations were those in which members shared ideas and concepts about designs without feeling that it was dangerous to do so; they felt that any criticism would be constructive rather than destructive. At the camp, safe relationships were those enabling counselors to teach, shepherd, and discipline campers as they thought best without needing to attend to other counselors' reactions. One counselor described that process:

> It's great to teach with John. Either one of us can make a mistake and back each other up and it's not an ego problem. If I make a mistake he'll come in and without saying you just made a mistake note that it can also be done another way. We play off one another that way instead of clashing, and it lets me teach my own way.

People felt safer in climates characterized by such openness (Jourard, 1968) and supportiveness (Gibb, 1961).

People did not feel such safety when they felt disconnected from others. A support staff member at the architecture firm noted of one designer that "with a glance he became a door; he put up this 'don't bother me' sign around him." Crossing such boundaries was perceived as unsafe. The staff member describing this relationship continued:

> When he puts up those walls, I know to stay away from him. But the problem is, I have to deal with him at some of those times. So we interact, but I keep it short, don't joke or anything. I did once and he went nuts. So I get monotonic, almost moronic, with him.

In such instances, threat reflects differences in position and power. Participants experienced relations among people representing different hierarchical echelons as potentially more stifling and threatening than relations with peers. Threats could be quite real. In the firm, superiors could deeply change or even end a subordinate's role. As one draftsperson noted,

> I'm pretty careful around Steve [a vice president], after he instilled a bit of fear in me. I'm minding my Ps and Qs. There's a testiness in his voice to me at times, and I have the sense that we're not communicating well. Because I'm in a very precarious position, I need to defer until I can figure out some better way of responding to him and working with him.

People were quicker to withdraw from potential conflict with members of higher echelons than they were to withdraw from conflicts with members of their own echelon.

Group and Intergroup Dynamics

The various unacknowledged characters, or unconscious roles, that individuals assumed also influenced psychological safety. Group dynamics were defined according to the unconscious plays that characterize the more conscious workings of organizations (Bion, 1961; Hirschhorn, 1988; Slater, 1966). Social systems have a mentality beyond the mentalities of individual members, connecting them by processes of unconscious alliance and collusion (Wells, 1980). In the context of a work group, members collude to act out plays that allay anxieties, conscious and unconscious. Such plays revolve, for example, around plots dealing with authority, competition, or sexuality and depend on organization members to play informal, unconscious roles. Once cast into these roles, people vary in how much room they have to safely bring their selves into work role performances (Minuchin, 1974). In the two settings studied, different implicit roles were more or less safe or unsafe havens from which people could personally engage depending on how much respect and authority those roles received.

In the architecture firm, for example, a group dynamic cast the firm's president as a father figure. Participating in the play that the image implied, other members took supporting roles whose status, power, and safety varied according to their proximity to the "father." The data revealed, for example, two firm members who occupied "mother" and "favored son" characters in their own and others' eyes, which created spaces in which they could safely personally engage. They referred to those roles in these comments:

> It's a family situation here, and I have a blind loyalty to him [E.S.B.]. I am a mother. I am the mother, here, which is hard sometimes, but it lets me interact with him and with others pretty much as I want to, within limits.

> I tend to be seen as the next generation of designers that he lays out. My designs aren't questioned as much as those of others, and I think it's because I'm seen as following his tradition but in my own way.

The firm's gofer emerged as the "bad son": he wore earrings, cracked jokes, dyed his hair red, and was seldom able to engage. He was frustrated with his inability to escape from the informal role in which he was cast—with his participation—and from which he found other parts of his self, such as the artist, excluded. In the same way, some counselors found themselves relegated to unattractive, supporting roles that reduced opportunities to safely engage.

The informal characters that people played partly reflected the identity and organizational groups they consciously and unconsciously represented to one another (Alderfer, 1985a). Members representing less powerful groups are often cast into unattractive, vulnerable roles, particularly in interactions with members representing more powerful groups (Miller, 1976; Smith, 1982). In both organizations, women spoke of situations in which it felt unsafe for them to personally engage because of what they experienced as men's undermining their role performances. One female counselor gave an example:

> There are times when I'm trying to get a girl camper to go to bed, and some male counselor starts flirting with the girl. It makes me look bad and undermines me incredibly. So I have to be 'the bitch.' If I didn't, and just dealt with the kids as I'd like to, they'd just hassle me and not listen to me.

Similar dynamics characterized relations between organizational subgroups. At the architecture firm, for example, people experienced differences along the dimension of tenure at the firm. New and old members tended to define situations involving members of the other category as less safe, as the remarks of one old member illustrated:

> I feel like there's a handful of us that are the old guard, and the rest are brand new. Those of us that have been here a long time have a different kind of relationship with each other than those that are just right off the street. We know each other so well, so we can be silly with one another. I am less likely to be as loose or candid with the new people as I am with the older ones.

A similar split occurred between counselors associated with the different activities. Counselors who taught different skills were accorded different status by the campers, the management, and even one another, and an informal hierarchy was established. Scuba instructors, for example, occupied the top of the hierarchy due to the perceived glamor and professionalization of their sport, and activities like drama and photography occupied the bottom, reflecting the campers' relative disinterest in them. The hierarchy influenced the psychological safety the counselors felt. A waterskiing counselor, for example, said she was interrupted and publicly corrected at a camp meeting by a scuba instructor as she described the internationally recognized distress signal:

> I felt like a total jerk out there in front of everyone, and angry at him for doing that. I was still right—but I backed down, assuming that he knew more about it because he was certified and all that. They're intimidating sometimes, so I just don't want to hassle with them.

The lack of psychological safety in such situations and the resulting suppression of individuals' voices reflects the distribution of authority and power among groups in organizations (Alderfer, 1985a).

Management Style and Process

Supportive, resilient, and clarifying management heightened psychological safety. Leaders translate system demands and reinforce members' behaviors in ways that may create different degrees of supportiveness and openness (Louis, 1986). Like supportive interpersonal relationships, supportive managerial environments allowed people to try and to fail without fear of the consequences. In practice, this meant opportunities to experiment with new design techniques in the firm or new teaching methods at the camp. People also felt safer when they had some control over their work. Managerial reluctance to loosen their control sent a message that their employees were not to be trusted and should fear overstepping their boundaries. That fear was compounded when managers were unpredictable, inconsistent, or hypocritical. An architect offered an example of such inconsistency,

> He [E.S.B.] goes over my head all the time. He'll tell me to do one thing, and I'll take care of it—like with a client or a design—and then he'll go and change it himself. It's like he goes over his own head—it's hilarious. Like if he had the time, he'd come over and redesign anything, even while it's being built. Crazy.

At such times, it was difficult for people in both organizations to trust the constancy of their task assignments or the control given them. It was hard to feel safe enough to invest their selves at work in any one direction. People need to feel that their authority figures are competent enough and secure enough in their own visions to create paths along which subordinates can safely travel (Kahn, 1990).

Members' perceived lack of safety also reflected their discomfort with the "tones" of management. In the architecture firm, some members had difficulty with how management dealt with firm members during office meetings:

> I've come away from those meetings feeling like I can ask a question as long as it's not threatening or it's a simple technical question about how the firm works. Impertinent questions will not be tolerated and are palmed off with a sarcastic response—even though they say we can ask anything.

The ambivalence with which the firm's management simultaneously welcomed and avoided openness sent mixed and thus distrusted messages to firm members.

At the camp, the tone the director set was at times similarly undermining. He occasionally took a cruel tone with the campers, and counselors observing such behavior could not help but learn the lesson taught the campers: that at times the camp was not a safe, supportive, caring system in which to be a member. One counselor directly expressed this when she said, "After seeing how Kurt rips into some of these kids, I'm pretty careful about not saying much when he's around. I just don't trust the guy." People's discomfort with the security of a managerial environment at times set limits on how safe they felt in employing and expressing their selves.

Organizational Norms

Finally, psychological safety corresponded to role performances that were clearly within the boundaries of organizational norms. Norms are shared expectations about the general behaviors of system members (Hackman, 1986). People that stayed within generally appropriate ways of working and behaving felt safer than those who strayed outside those protective boundaries. In this regard, safety meant not calling into question habitual patterns of thought and behavior that ensured predictability; questioning such patterns meant being treated as a deviant (Shorris, 1981). At the camp, safety was a matter of counselors' exerting appropriate amounts of energy in different activities and being appropriately trusting or mistrusting of campers. In the architecture firm, the important norms revolved around how much time and energy to give to certain projects, how candid or withholding to be in giving feedback and criticism, and how confrontational or reticent to be with clients.

Deviating from norms and the possibility of doing so were sources of anxiety and frustration, particularly for people with low status and leverage, as deviance is in most social systems. In the architecture firm, such norms were encoded into the design parameters the president set, which were known and reinforced throughout the firm. People reined themselves in or were reined in to conform with established parameters. A draftsperson described that process:

> How bold you're being creates a certain amount of anxiety. If you're doing something that is somewhat removed from the parameters that you think or suspect you're supposed to be working from, you get a little nervous. When that happens, I hunt around for someone to tell me what he [E.S.B.] would like. Or someone will come around and say no, he would never go for that. That's the bottom line.

In such moments, people focus almost exclusively on the external rules or cues governing the situation that will lead them through potentially dangerous thickets (Goffman, 1959). The analogous situation at the camp involved the extent to which counselors were encouraged to trust campers. A number of counselors described situations in which they were trying to, as one noted, "give the kids a break," but were countermanded by other staff members. Recalling such an incident, a counselor remarked that he "just stopped trying to trust the kids because it was more hassle than it was worth—it's easier to be the hardass, like the camp wants me to be." Norms regulate emotional as well as physical labor (Hochschild, 1983).

In the architecture firm, the physical office space starkly symbolized the ways that overstepping the boundaries of expected behavior felt unsafe. Wide open and without walls except for four-foot partitions, the office resembled an open-air maze of public work spaces. There was also a loft that looked like a balcony. The space suggested that people were at once actors and audience. Its openness symbolically placed them on a stage in which they were constantly exposed to the scrutiny of others. There was no backstage, no place in which they could doff all vestiges of role and use their own voices (Goffman, 1961b). The camp counselors similarly occupied a stage, playing to the camper audience. Openness came from the intimacy of a small, enclosed system in which there were no secrets. The implications for the use of personal voice were the same as in the architecture firm. As a counselor noted, "So many times you'd love to share something with another counselor, something you saw going on, but for whatever reason, you just can't say it because you know it'll get around." In contexts defined by a lack of protective boundaries, people chose to guard their selves by withdrawing when they felt unsafe. In the absence of external boundaries between self and others, people withdrew as a way of creating internal boundaries (Hirschhorn, 1988).

Psychological Availability

Psychological availability is the sense of having the physical, emotional, or psychological resources to personally engage at a particular moment. It measures how ready people are to engage, given the distractions they experience as members of social systems. In this study, people were more or less available to place their selves fully into role performances depending on how they coped with the various demands of both work and nonwork aspects of their lives. Research on stress (e.g., Pearlin, 1983) has often included a measure of self-assessment of ability to engage in coping strategies. Such components implicitly measure psychological availability.

The general link between personal engagement and psychological availability was explored with descriptive statistics performed on the ratings of the group of 186 experiences. The statistics indicated that personal engagement was connected to higher levels of psychological availability ($\bar{x} = 7.48$, s.d. = 1.04) than personal disengagement ($\bar{x} = 3.27$, s.d. = 1.56; $r = .81$). These results suggest that people were personally engaging in situations for which they were more psychologically available and disengaging in situations for which they were less available.[5]

The data from the two studies indicated that four types of distractions influenced psychological availability: depletion of physical energy, depletion of emotional energy, individual insecurity, and outside lives.

Physical Energy

Personal engagement demanded levels of physical energy, strength, and readiness that personal disengagement did not, as Goffman (1961a) suggested in his studies of nonverbal role performances. This requirement was clear in moments of personal disengagement in which people were simply depleted. The camp counselor role was physically demanding, given the strength of the sun on the island and the campers' unbounded energy. As one counselor said, "I'm not used to being out in the sun. For the first two weeks I took a nap every afternoon, but I was still physically blown away. I just couldn't be up with the kids the way I wanted because I was just too zonked." Physical incapacity was less common in the architecture firm, but it did occur after long hours at a drafting table. A draftsperson described such incapacity:

> Doing any of these tasks here means sitting down for eight hours. You're sitting down doing these very precise drawings. Your back is bent over, you're staring.

---

[5]The similarity of the patterns of rating scale results for the three psychological conditions raised questions about the extent to which they were conceptually distinguishable. I therefore examined the correlations among the three conditions using the ratings of the 186 examples of personal engagement and disengagement experiences. The correlations were: meaningfulness and safety, .32; meaningfulness and availability, .42; and safety and availability, .57.

Your back, your neck, your eyes—you feel physically awful and mentally exhausted, and all you think about is going home.

At such times, people were simply worn out and unavailable to engage.

Emotional Energy

Emotional ability to personally engage also influenced psychological availability. The premise is that employing and expressing the self in tasks requiring emotional labor takes a certain level of emotionality that personally disengaging does not (Hochschild, 1983). In the firm, the frustrations of trying to translate abstract design concepts into working drawings and building specifications were emotionally draining. An architect described such a situation:

It's a combination of not knowing what the answer is and trying different solutions and being totally frustrated and exhausted, so you just pull out of it. I spent a few days working out one design problem and was never satisfied with what I was coming up with. I just got worn down, got more and more distracted. I walked away from it, my mind was a mess. I just couldn't do it anymore.

At the camp, the unceasing demands of the campers for attention were emotionally draining. A counselor noted,

The kids just take it out of you after a while, and you've given them everything you have emotionally. Sometimes I just need to get away and have no demands on me to watch, to care, to give. I take walks then, down by the beach, and try to think and feel nothing.

At some point, people simply had nothing left to give and withdrew. People needed emotional resources to meet the demands of personal engagement.

Insecurity

Psychological availability also corresponded to how secure people felt about their work and their status. For individuals to express their selves in social systems, they must feel relatively secure about those selves (Gustafson & Cooper, 1985). Insecurity distracted members from bringing their selves into their work; it generated anxiety that occupied energies that would have otherwise been translated into personal engagements. One dimension of insecurity was lack of self-confidence, a particular issue for new, low-status members of both organizations. A new draftsperson voiced that insecurity:

I was somewhat anxious about how the speed and quality of my work was comparing to other people at my level in the office. Was I doing it fast enough, was I doing it right enough? I think about that, being here only three months. Are they going to keep me, or throw me back because I'm too small? So at times I tend to worry more about how my work is going to be received than about the work itself.

Counselors withdrew from performing their roles as they would have liked when they did not "want to step out of place," as one counselor said, or, as another said, they were "not sure about how much to put into the camp all the time." Being available was partly a matter of security in abilities and status and maintaining a focus on tasks rather than anxieties.

A second dimension of insecurity was heightened self-consciousness. When organization members focused on how others perceived and judged them—whether or not such judgment actually occurred—they were too distracted to personally engage. They would focus on external rather than internal cues (Goffman, 1959). This happened when people perceived themselves, consciously or not, as actors on stages, surrounded by audiences and critics, rather than as people simply doing their jobs. The self-consciousness preoccupied people, engaging them in the work of managing impressions rather than in the work itself. A designer offered an example of such preoccupation:

> I have to appear concerned and eager to work. I am a lot of times, but if you're not concentrating on showing that, people can get the wrong impression. Communicating with people means figuring out the best way to respond to certain situations. Just thinking: What are my communications like with this person now, who can I joke with and to what extent, and who shouldn't I joke with?

The stage-like quality of the two organizations exacerbated such self-consciousness. In the architecture firm, the physical space markedly resembled an open stage, complete with balcony; in the camp, the counselors were always performing for the camper audience.

A third dimension of insecurity was people's ambivalence about their fit with their organization and its purposes. This ambivalence could preoccupy people, leaving them little space, energy, or desire to employ or express themselves in moments of task performances. Their lack of commitment to the rather wealthy campers distracted some counselors at times. Firm members sometimes struggled with their commitment to the overall tenor of the design parameters and style set by the president, which one designer characterized as "blatant post-modernism." People struggling with their desires to contribute to the end goals of their systems became less able or willing—less available—to do so. It is difficult for people to engage personally in fulfilling work processes when organizational ends do not fit their own values, as research on organizational commitment has suggested (Mowday, Porter, & Steers, 1982). In dealing with such issues, people were already engaged in inner debates that spared little room for external engagements.

Outside Life

People's outside lives, which had the potential to take them psychologically away from their role performances, also influenced psychological availability. Members of both organizations were at times too preoccupied by events in their nonwork lives to invest energies in role performances; research on work-family boundaries has attested to such distraction (Hall & Richter, 1989). Counselors involved with other counselors were distracted by those relationships; a counselor who taught sailing and was in an intimate relationship with another counselor noted, "I've been coasting a lot with the kids—my energy is just in other places right now." A variety of personal distractions similarly incapacitated members of the architecture firm. A draftsperson applying to architecture schools noted, "I just don't concentrate as well because I'm thinking about that whole process."

People's outside lives could increase their availability. At times, events in their nonwork lives "charged" organization members. A camp counselor referred to how his "emotional high" from meeting a woman at an island casino gave him "amazing amounts of energy to spend with the kids." A draftsperson talked about feeling confident about making a presentation because of recent successes as a graphic artist. In such cases, the looseness of the boundaries separating work and nonwork let people draw on energies generated outside their formal roles.

DISCUSSION

The grounded theory described here cuts across a number of different existing conceptual frameworks to articulate the complex of influences on people's personal engagements and disengagements in particular moments of role performances. Besides its concern with specific moments of role performances, the resulting framework has a core focus different from others currently used to explain person-role relationships. This core has a number of key dimensions: a simultaneous concern with people's emotional reactions to conscious and unconscious phenomena and the objective properties of jobs, roles, and work contexts; the primacy of people's experiences of themselves and their contexts as the mediator of the depths to which they employ and express or withdraw and defend themselves during role performances; and the self-in-role as the unit of analysis, a focus on how both person and role are enlivened or deadened during role performances. The research described here articulated and defined these dimensions in the service of moving toward a theory of people's psychological presence and absence at work.

Directions for Future Research

The grounded theory described here carries with it implications for future research that will extend its conceptual dimensions and usefulness for practice. An immediate research agenda involves three arenas: the interplay of the three psychological conditions; individual differences; and the connections of personal engagement and disengagement to concepts currently used to explore person-role relationships.

Interplay of Psychological Conditions

A primary aim of future research might be to develop a dynamic process model explaining how the variables documented above combine to produce moments of personal engagement and disengagement. This exploratory research suggests that people tacitly deal with multiple levels of influences—individual, interpersonal, group, intergroup, and organizational—by examining them, at varying degrees of awareness, for what they imply about the meaningfulness, safety, and availability that characterize role performance situations. The question remains, How do the three conditions combine in particular situations to promote personal engagement or disengagement?

It seems likely that there are thresholds separating the levels of the three conditions that, taken together, promote personal engagement rather than disengagement. But how do those conditions coact to let people reach those thresholds? The coaction may be additive and compensatory: with the three conditions summed together, the strength of one may compensate for the weakness of others. Or it may involve a specific hierarchy: a person's experiencing a situation as extremely meaningful may compensate for a lack of personal availability, but the reverse may not be true. The coaction may also involve thresholds for each condition. People may have to feel minimal levels of meaningfulness, safety, and availability before their additive interplay can lead them across the threshold separating personal engagement from disengagement. Such questions, answered both qualitatively and quantitatively in future research, will offer a richer portrait of the processes by which personal engagements and disengagements are created.

Individual Differences

The focus of this research was identifying psychological conditions general enough to explain moments of personal engagement and disengagement across individuals. Yet presumably, individual differences shape people's dispositions toward personally engaging or disengaging in all or some types of role performances, just as they shape people's abilities and willingness to be involved or committed at work. Presumably, too, individual differences influence how people personally engage or disengage, given their experiences of psychological meaningfulness, safety, and availability in specific situations. Consider, for example, people who experience particular situations as unsafe. Although certain dispositional factors may lead someone to perceive a situation as unsafe, it is intriguing to think about the individual differences that shape what people do when they feel unsafe. Future research will focus on the courage that enables people to take the risk of employing and expressing their personal selves when it feels threatening to do so. Charting the role of courage is another dimension of developing a process model of personal engagement and disengagement.

Conceptual Connections

Another direction for future research involves connecting personal engagement and disengagement to existing concepts focusing on person-role relationships. Initially, this article suggested that although concepts such as involvement and commitment reflect average orientations over time as if in a still photograph, personal engagement and disengagement reveal the variance typically hidden in those averages. Regardless of levels of involvement and commitment, people still experience leaps (engagement) and falls (disengagement). Future research will focus on examining both quantitatively and qualitatively the connections between the relatively static levels of people's involvement and commitment and the constant fluctuations of self-in-role.

The variance that these new concepts reveal derives from the different depths of people's selves that they bring to or leave out of their role performances. In this article, I have emphasized people's expressions, employments, withdrawals, and defenses of their personal selves as the mechanisms by which they connect their depths to role performances. Future research might focus more closely on those depths and how they are plumbed in the course of role performances. Here, I have drawn little distinction between the physical, cognitive, and emotional paths along which people personally engage and disengage. It is likely, however, that a hierarchy relates increasing depths of engagement to the investment of self along physical, then cognitive, and finally emotional dimensions. Kelman (1958) postulated a similar hierarchy of dimensions regarding people's compliance with, identification with, and internalization of attitudes. Exploring that proposition further will help articulate distinguishable levels of personal engagement and disengagement and offer a way to understand the complexities of possible mixtures of personal engagement and disengagement. An individual might, for example, express and defend, or employ and withdraw simultaneously.

Conclusions

The conceptual model developed in this research has a number of components, some better developed than others. I deliberately included a wide range of factors in the model, taking seriously the multiple levels of influences— individual, interpersonal, group, intergroup, and organizational—that shape people's personal engagements and disengagements. It is at the swirling intersection of those influences that individuals make choices, at different levels of awareness, to employ and express or withdraw and defend themselves during role performances. The research approach taken here was to focus on the discrete moments of role performances that represent microcosms of the larger complexity; those moments are windows into the multiplicity of factors that are constantly relevant to person-role dynamics. Focusing on specific moments of work role performance is like using the zoom lens of a camera: a distant stationary image is brought close and revealed as a series of innumerable leaps of engagement and falls of disengagement.

REFERENCES

Alderfer, C. P. 1972. *Human needs in organizational settings.* New York: Free Press of Glencoe.

Alderfer, C. P. 1985a. An intergroup perspective on group dynamics. In J. Lorsch (Ed.), *Handbook of organizational behavior.* 190–222. Englewood Cliffs, N.J.: Prentice-Hall.

Alderfer, C. P. 1985b. Taking our selves seriously as researchers. In D. N. Berg & K. K. Smith (Eds.). *Exploring clinical methods for social research:* 35–70. Beverly Hills, Calif.: Sage Publications.

Argyris, C. 1982. *Reasoning, learning, and action: Individual and organizational.* San Francisco: Jossey-Bass.

Baxter, B. 1982. *Alienation and authenticity.* London: Tavistock Publications.

Bennis, W., Schein, E. H., Berlew, D. E., & Steele, F. I. 1964. *Interpersonal dynamics: Essays and readings on human interaction.* Homewood, Ill.: Dorsey Press.

Berg, D. N. 1980. Developing clinical field skills: An apprenticeship model. In C. P. Alderfer & C. L. Cooper (Eds.), *Advances in experiential social processes,* vol. 2: 143–163. New York: John Wiley & Sons.

Berg, D. N., & Smith, K. K. 1985. *Exploring clinical methods for social research.* Beverly Hills, Calif.: Sage Publications.

Bion, W. R. 1961. *Experiences in groups.* New York: Basic Books.

Blau, G. J., & Boal, K. B. 1987. Conceptualizing how job involvement and organizational commitment affect turnover and absenteeism. *Academy of Management Review,* 12: 288–300.

Blauner, R. 1964. *Alienation and freedom.* Chicago: University of Chicago Press.

Csikszentmihalyi, M. 1982. *Beyond boredom and anxiety.* San Francisco: Jossey-Bass.

Deci, E. L. 1975. *Intrinsic motivation.* New York: Plenum Press.

de Rivera, J. 1981. *Conceptual encounter: A method for the exploration of human experience.* Washington, D.C.: University Press of America.

Diamond, M. A., & Allcorn, S. 1985. Psychological dimensions of role use in bureaucratic organizations. *Organizational Dynamics,* 14(1): 35–59.

Dubin, R. 1956. Industrial workers' worlds: A study of the "central life interests" of industrial workers. *Social Problems,* 3: 131–142.

Freud, S. 1922. *Group psychology and the analysis of the ego.* London: International Psychoanalytic Press.

Gibb, J. R. 1961. Defensive communication. *Journal of Communication,* 11: 141–148.

Glaser, B. G., & Strauss, A. L. 1987. *The discovery of grounded theory.* Chicago: Aldine.

Goffman, E. 1959. *The presentation of self in everyday life.* New York: Doubleday Anchor.

Goffman, E. 1961a. *Encounters: Two studies in the sociology of interaction.* Indianapolis: Bobbs-Merrill Co.

Goffman, E. 1961b. *Asylums.* New York: Doubleday Anchor.

Graen, G. 1976. Role-making processes within complex interactions. In M. D. Dunnette (Ed.), *Handbook of industrial and organizational psychology:* 1201–1245. Chicago: Rand-McNally.

Gustafson, J. P., & Cooper, L. 1985. Collaboration in small groups. Theory and technique for the study of small-group processes. In A. D. Colman & M. H. Geller (Eds.). *Group relations reader,* vol. 2: 139–150. Washington, D.C.: A. K. Rice Institute Series.

Hackett, R. D., Bycio, P., & Guion, R. M. 1989. Absenteeism among hospital nurses: An idiographic-longitudinal analysis. *Academy of Management Journal,* 32: 424–453.

Hackman, J. R. 1986. The psychology of self-management in organizations. In M. S. Pallak & R. O. Perloff (Eds.), *Psychology and work: Productivity, change, and employment:* 89–136. Washington, D.C.: American Psychological Association.

Hackman, J. R., & Oldham, G. R. 1980. *Work redesign.* Reading, Mass.: Addison-Wesley.

Hall, D. T., & Richter, J. 1989. Balancing work life and home life: What can organizations do to help? *Academy of Management Executive,* 2: 212–223.

Hays, W. L. 1981. *Statistics* (3d. ed.) New York: Holt, Rinehart & Winston.

Hirschhorn, L. 1988. *The workplace within: Psychodynamics of organizational life.* Cambridge, Mass.: MIT Press.

Hirschman, A. O. 1970. *Exit, voice, and loyalty: Responses to decline in firms, organizations, and states.* Cambridge, Mass.: Harvard University Press.

Hochschild, A. R. 1983. *The managed heart: Commercialization of human feeling.* Berkeley: University of California Press.

Jones, A. P., James, L. R., & Bruni, J. R. 1975. Perceived leadership and employee confidence in the leader as moderated by job involvement. *Journal of Applied Psychology,* 60: 146–149.

Jourard, S. M. 1968. *Disclosing man to himself.* Princeton, N.J.: D. Van Nostrand Co.

Kahn, W. A. 1984. The structure of exaltation. *American Behavioral Scientist,* 27: 705–722.

Kahn, W. A. 1989. University athletic teams. In J. R. Hackman (Ed.), *Groups that work (and those that don't):* 250–264. San Francisco: Jossey-Bass.

Kahn, W. A. 1990. An exercise of authority. *Organizational Behavior Teaching Review,* 14(2): 28–42.

Katz, D., & Kahn, R. L. 1978. *The social psychology of organizations* (2d ed.). New York: Wiley.

Kelman, H. C. 1958. Compliance, identification and internalization: Three processes of attitude change. *Journal of Conflict Resolution,* 2: 51–60.

Langer, E. J. 1989. *Mindfulness.* Reading, Mass.: Addison-Wesley.

Lasch, C. 1984. *The minimal self.* New York: Norton.

Lawler, E. E., & Hall, D. T. 1970. Relationships of job characteristics to job involvement, satisfaction, and intrinsic motivation. *Journal of Applied Psychology,* 54: 305–312.

Locke, E. A. 1968. Toward a theory of task motivation and incentives. *Organizational Behavior and Human Performance,* 3: 157–189.

Lodahl, T. M. 1964. Patterns of job attitudes in two assembly technologies. *Administrative Science Quarterly,* 8: 482–519.

Lodahl, T., & Kejner, M. 1965. The definition and measurement of job involvement. *Journal of Applied Psychology,* 49: 24–33.

Louis, M. R. 1986. Putting executive action in context: An alternative view of power. In S. Srivastva & Associates (Eds.), *Executive power:* 111–131. San Francisco: Jossey-Bass.

Maehr, M. L., & Braskamp, L. A. 1986. *The motivation factor: A theory of personal investment.* Lexington, Mass.: D. C. Heath Co.

Maslach, C. 1982. *Burnout: The cost of caring.* Englewood Cliffs, N.J.: Prentice-Hall.

Maslow, A. 1954. *Motivation and personality.* New York: Harper & Row.

May, R., Angel, E., & Ellenberger, H. F. (Eds.). 1958. *Existence.* New York: Touchstone.

Merton, R. K. 1957. *Social theory and social structure.* New York: Free Press of Glencoe.

Miller, J. B. 1976. *Toward a new psychology of women.* Boston: Beacon Press.

Miner, A. S. 1987. Idiosyncratic jobs in formalized organizations. *Administrative Science Quarterly,* 32: 327–351.

Minuchin, S. 1974. *Families and family therapy.* Cambridge, Mass.: Harvard University Press.

Mowday, R. T., Porter, L. W., & Steers, R. M. 1982. *Employee-organization linkages: The psychology of commitment, absenteeism, and turnover.* New York: Academic Press.

Pearlin, L. I. 1983. Role strains and personal stress. In H. B. Kaplan (Ed.), *Psychological stress: Trends in theory and research:* 3–32. New York: Academic Press.

Perkins, D. N. 1981. *The mind's best work.* Cambridge, Mass.: Harvard University Press.

Porter, L., Steers, R., Mowday, R., & Boulian, P. 1974. Organizational commitment, job satisfaction, and turnover among psychiatric technicians. *Journal of Applied Psychology,* 59: 603–609.

Rafaeli, A., & Sutton, R. I. 1987. The expression of emotion as part of the work role. *Academy of Management Review,* 12: 23–37.

Rogers, C. R. 1958. The characteristics of a helping relationship. *Personnel and Guidance Journal,* 37: 6–16.

Sandler, J. 1960. The background of safety. *International Journal of Psychoanalysis,* 41: 352–356.

Schein, E. H. 1970. *Organizational psychology* (2d ed.). Englewood Cliffs, N.J.: Prentice-Hall.

Schein, E. H. 1987. *Process consultation,* vol. 2. Reading, Mass.: Addison-Wesley.

Seeman, M. 1972. Alienation and engagement. In A. Campbell & P.E. Converse (Eds.), *The human meaning of social change:* 467–527. New York: Russell Sage Foundation.

Shorris, E. 1981. *Scenes from corporate life: The politics of middle management.* Harmondsworth, England: Penguin.

Slater, P. E. 1966. *Microcosms.* New York: Wiley.

Smith, K. K. 1982. *Groups in conflict: Prisons in disguise.* Dubuque, Iowa: Kendall-Hunt.

Smith, K. K., & Berg, D. N. 1987. *Paradoxes of group life.* San Francisco: Jossey-Bass.

Toffler, B. L. 1986 *Tough choices: Managers talk ethics.* New York: John Wiley & Sons.

Van Maanen, J. 1976. Breaking in: Socialization to work. In R. Dubin (Ed.), *Handbook of work, organization, and society:* 67–130. Chicago: Rand McNally & Co.

Van Maanen, J., & Schein, E. H. 1979. Toward a theory of organizational socialization. In B. M. Staw (Ed.), *Research in organizational behavior,* vol. 1: 209–264. Greenwich, Conn.: JAI Press.

Wells, L., Jr. 1980. The group-as-a-whole: A systemic socio-analytic perspective on interpersonal and group relations. In C. P. Alderfer & C. L. Cooper (Eds.), *Advances in experiential social processes,* vol. 2: 165–199. New York: Wiley.

Appendix

Interview Schedules

Camp Carrib

1. Why did you choose to become a counselor?
2. Are you comfortable here on the island itself, and with the people?

3. Do you like being a member of a camp system as a counselor?
4. Do you enjoy being with kids generally and these kids in particular?
5. What do you like most about being a counselor here, and why?
6. What aspects of being a counselor here are personally and emotionally involving for you? What really grabs you, involves more of you than other roles you've held?
7. How would an observer like me be able to see your personal involvement? What does it look like?
8. What do you dislike most about being a counselor here, and why?
9. What aspects of being a counselor here are personally and emotionally uninvolving, that is, just turn you off so you're working automatically?
10. How would an observer like me be able to see that uninvolvement? What does it look like?
11. How do you find the demands of the counselor role?
12. How much control and autonomy do you have here?
13. How challenging do you find your role and its demands?
14. When can you coast through the work? When do you have to really stretch?
15. How do you like the way that your role is designed?
16. For what behaviors are you rewarded here, and what are those rewards?
17. How free are you to perform the role as you wish, at your own pace and style?
18. Where are you in the hierarchy? Do you feel in the center here?
19. How do you find working within your particular activity?
20. What is your relationship to the camp management, personally and professionally?
21. What emotional support systems do you have here at camp?
22. How much do you want to be personally and emotionally engaged here?
23. How is that involvement influenced by your physical and emotional energy?
24. How does the staff group influence your role performances?

E.S.B. and Associates
Warm-up

1. What is your job here?
2. How long have you worked here? What did you do before this job?
3. Who supervises you, and whom do you supervise?
4. What do you like most about working here?
5. What do you like least about your working here?

Situation 1
I'd like you to think about a time when you've been attentive and interested in what you're doing, felt absorbed and involved. A time when you didn't think about how you'd rather be doing something else, and you didn't feel bored. One example of this, outside of the workplace, is when we go to movies and get involved with them to the extent that we almost forget that we're just watching a movie: we don't think about ourselves, and the other things that we could be doing. This also happens when we're working, that we get so wrapped up in what we're doing that we forget about other things. This can be when we're doing something by ourselves, like writing or drafting, or when we're working with other people. Can you describe a particular time when you've felt like that here at work?

Situation 2

Now I'd like you to think about a time when you've felt uninvolved in what you were doing, a time when you were, say, bored, distracted, or feeling detached. We can use the movie example again, where we go to movies that just don't engage us and we are aware that it's just a movie or that we would rather be elsewhere. This too happens when we're at work, when we're doing something or working with someone, and we're not particularly involved in it for some reason or another. Can you describe a situation where this fits you?

Situation 3

Now I'd like you to think about a time when you did experience a difference between your response at work and the way in which you would have responded had you not been at work. This would be a time when you had to leave out more of who you are because you were at work. It's a time when you felt the difference between how you think you would have acted or reacted, based on your own personal experiences and feelings, and how you actually did act or react within the work situation. Can you describe a particular time when you've felt this?

Situation 4

Now I'd like you to think about a time when you felt like there wasn't much difference between your response at work and the way in which you would have responded had you not been at work. This would be a time at work when you left out less of who you are outside of work. It's a time when you didn't feel much difference between how you think you would have acted or reacted on the basis of your own personal experiences and feelings, and how you actually did act or react at work. Can you describe a particular time when you've felt this?

Closing

Is there anything that you want to add or stress that might help me understand the influences on when you do and don't feel involved or uninvolved here?

William Kahn earned his Ph.D. degree at Yale University. He is an assistant professor of organizational behavior at Boston University's School of Management. His research interests are personal engagement and disengagement at work, care-taking in organizations, and organizational diagnosis and change.

Practice Self-Test

The Problem

_____

_____

_____

The Procedures

_____

_____

_____

The Method of Analysis

_____

_____

_____

The Major Conclusion(s)

_____

_____

_____

Reasons for Classification as Descriptive Research

_____

_____

_____

Method-Specific Evaluation Criteria

Select the appropriate methodology (questionnaire, interview, or observation) listed below and use the article to answer the questions that apply to the methodology.

Questionnaire Studies

1. Are directions to questionnaire responders clear?
2. Does each item in the questionnaire relate to one of the objectives of the study?
3. Does each questionnaire item deal with a single concept?
4. When necessary, is a point of reference given for questionnaire items?
5. Are leading questions avoided in the questionnaire?
6. Are there sufficient alternatives for each questionnaire item?
7. Are questionnaire validation procedures described?
8. Was the questionnaire pretested?
9. Are pilot study procedures and results described?
10. Does the cover letter explain the purpose and importance of the study and give the potential responder a good reason for cooperating?
11. If appropriate, is confidentiality of responses assured in the cover letter?
12. Was the percentage of returns at least 70?
13. Are follow-up activities described?
14. If the response rate was low, was any attempt made to determine any major differences between responders and nonresponders?

Interview Studies

1. Does each item in the interview guide relate to a specific objective of the study?
2. When necessary, is a point of reference given in the guide for interview items?
3. Are leading questions avoided in the interview guide?
4. Does the interview guide indicate the type and amount of prompting and probing that was permitted?
5. Are the qualifications and special training of the interviewers described?
6. Is the method that was used to record responses described?
7. Did the researcher use the most reliable, unbiased method of recording responses that could have been used?
8. Were the interview procedures pretested?
9. Are pilot study procedures and results described?
10. Did the researcher specify how the responses to semi-structured and unstructured items were quantified and analyzed?

Observation Studies

1. Are the observational variables defined?
2. Were observers required to observe only one behavior at a time?
3. Was a coded recording instrument used?
4. Are the qualifications and special training of the observers described?
5. Is the level of observer reliability reported?
6. Is the level of observer reliability sufficiently high?
7. Were possible observer and observee biases discussed?
8. Was observation the best method to collect the data, i.e., observation was preferable to some unobtrusive measure that could have been used instead?

REFERENCES

AGNEW, N. M., & PYKE, S. W. (1978). *The science game: An introduction to research in the behavioral sciences.* Englewood Cliffs, NJ: Prentice-Hall.

ASSOCIATED PRESS WASHINGTON. (1990, February 16). Employees monitored by computer. *The Miami Herald,* p. 13A.

BARLOW, H., & HERSEN, M. (1984). *Single-case experimental designs* (2nd ed.). New York: Pergamon.

BECKER, H. S. (1958). Problems of inference and proof in participant observation. *American Sociological Review, 23*(6).

BENNE, K. D., & SHEATS, P. (1948). Functional roles of group members. *Journal of Social Issues, 2*, 42–47.

BIJOU, S. W., PETERSON, R. F., HARRIS, F. R., ALLEN, K. E., & JOHNSTON, M. S. (1969). Methodology for experimental studies of young children in natural settings. *Psychological Record, 19*, 177–210.

COOKE, R. A., & LAFFERTY, J. C. (1983). *Level V: Organizational cultural inventory-form I.* Plymouth, MI: Human Synergistics.

COOKE, R. A., & LAFFERTY, J. C. (1986). *Level V: Organizational cultural inventory-form III.* Plymouth, MI: Human Synergistics.

FOLTZ, K. (1990, January 11). Probing the shopper's psyche. *The Miami Herald,* p. 1F.

GERBER, B. (1989, June). Facts about customer satisfaction. *Training,* p. 86.

HACKMAN, J. R., & OLDHAM, G. (1980). *Work redesign.* Reading, MA: Addison-Wesley.

HOWELL, W., & DIPBOYE, R. (1986). *Essentials of industrial and organizational psychology* (3rd ed.). Chicago: Dorsey.

KANTER, R. M. (1983). *The change masters: Innovations for productivity in the American corporation.* New York: Simon and Schuster.

KREBS, A. (1974, September 11). Notes on people. *The New York Times.*

NAISBITT, J. (1982). *Megatrends: Ten new directions transforming our lives.* New York: Warner.

PELTO, P. J., & PELTO, G. H. (1978). *Anthropological research: The structure of inquiry* (2nd ed.). New York: Cambridge University Press.

PETERS, T.J., & WATERMAN, R.H. (1982). *In search of excellence: Lessons from America's best-run companies.* New York: Harper & Row.

REDDY, J. (1965, February 28). Heady thieves find Wheeling their Waterloo. *Chicago Sun Times,* pp. 18, 66.

REID, J. B., & DeMASTER, B. (1972). The efficiency of the spot-check in maintaining the reliability of data collected by observers in quasi-natural settings: Two pilot studies. *Oregon Research Bulletin,* 12 (8).

RICE, B. (1988, November). Work or perk? *Psychology Today,* pp. 26–29.

RUSSAKOFF, D. (1989, January 1). IRS tries to soften the flow. *The Miami Herald,* p. 31A.

SCHEIN, E. H. (1985). *Organizational culture and leadership.* San Francisco: Jossey-Bass.

SLIPY, D. M. (1990, October). Anthropologist uncovers real workplace attitudes. *HRMagazine,* pp. 76–79.

SMALHEISER, K. A. (1989, December). Communications & systems integration. *Fortune,* Special Advertising Section.

SUTTON, R. I., & RAFAELI, A. (1988). Untangling the relationship between displayed emotions and organizational sales: The case of convenience stores. *Academy of Management Journal,* 31(3), 461–487.

TAYLOR, F. W. (1911). *The principles of scientific management.* New York: Harper & Row.

TORNOW, W. W., & PINTO, P. R. (1976). The development of a managerial job taxonomy: A system for describing, classifying, and evaluating executive positions. *Journal of Applied Psychology,* 61, 410–418.

WEBB, E. J., CAMPBELL, D. T., SCHWARTZ, R. D., & SECHREST, L. (1966). *Unobtrusive measures: Non-reactive research in the social sciences.* Chicago: Rand McNally.

ZEMKE, R. (1989, April). Anthropologists in the corporate jungle. *Training,* pp. 49–59.

Correlational research involves collecting data in order to determine whether, and to what degree, a relationship exists . . . (page 318)

8

The Correlational Method

Objectives

After reading Chapter 8, you should be able to do the following:

1. Briefly state the purpose of correlational research.
2. List and briefly describe the major steps involved in the basic correlational research process.
3. Describe the range of numerical values associated with a correlational coefficient.
4. Describe how the size of the correlation coefficient affects its interpretation with respect to:
   a. statistical significance.
   b. its use in prediction.
   c. its use as an index of validity and reliability.
5. State two major purposes of relationship studies.
6. Identify and briefly describe the steps involved in conducting a relationship study.
7. Describe briefly two methods for computing correlation coefficients.
8. Describe the difference between a linear and a curvilinear relationship.
9. Identify and briefly describe two factors that may contribute to an inaccurate estimate of relationship.
10. Define briefly or describe predictor variables and criterion variables.
11. State three major purposes of prediction studies.
12. State the major difference between data-collection procedures in a prediction study and a relationship study.
13. Explain why cross-validation is an important procedure associated with multiple regression equations.

DEFINITION AND PURPOSE

Correlational research is sometimes treated as a type of descriptive research primarily because it describes an existing condition. The condition it describes, however, is distinctly different from the conditions typically described in self-report or observational studies; a correlational study describes in quantitative terms the degree to which variables are related. *Correlational research* involves collecting data in order to determine whether, and to what degree, a relationship exists between two or more quantifiable variables. Degree of relationship is expressed as a *correlation coefficient*. If a relationship exists between two variables, it means that scores within a certain range on one measure are associated with scores within a certain range on another measure. For example, there is a relationship between intelligence and academic achievement; persons who do well on intelligence tests tend to have higher grade point averages (GPA), and persons who do poorly on intelligence tests tend to have lower grade point averages. This does not mean, of course, that all persons with high intelligence get good grades; it means that overall there is a relationship between the two measures. The purpose of a correlational study may be simply to determine relationships between variables, or the purpose may be to use relationships in making predictions.

Relationship studies typically investigate a number of variables believed to be related to a major, complex variable such as productivity. Variables found not to be highly related are eliminated from further consideration; variables that are highly related may suggest causal-comparative or experimental studies to determine if the relationships are causal. As discussed in Chapter 1, the fact that there is a relationship between high consideration by the manager and high job satisfaction (Goodson, McGee, & Cashman, 1988) does not imply that consideration "causes" job satisfaction or that job satisfaction "causes" high consideration. Care must be taken in interpreting and using correlational studies to avoid suggesting that cause-effect relationships exist or do not exist based upon correlational results. For example, an article on stock options suggested a cause-effect relationship by saying, "Options are supposed to motivate an employee to make a company's stock more valuable, yet there's precious little evidence that they have that effect" (Stewart, 1990, p. 93). The evidence cited later in the article indicated that there was no "statistically significant correlation between performance and stock option compensation" (Stewart, 1990, p. 94); even if a statistically significant correlation had been found, it wouldn't necessarily support a cause-effect relationship. Regardless of whether a relationship is a cause-effect relationship, however, the existence of a strong relationship does permit prediction. For example, as discussed in Chapter 1, high school GPA and college GPA are highly related; students who have high GPAs in high school tend to have high GPAs in college, and students who have low GPAs in high school tend to have low GPAs in college. Therefore, high GPA can be, and is, used to predict college GPA. Also, as discussed in Chapter 5, correlational procedures are used to establish certain types of instrument validity and reliability.

Correlational studies provide an estimate of just how related two variables are. If two variables are strongly related, a correlation coefficient near $+1.00$ (or -1.00) will be obtained; if two variables are not related, a coefficient near .00 will be obtained. The more strongly related two variables are, the more accurate are predictions based on their relationship. While relationships are rarely perfect, a number of variables are sufficiently related to permit useful predictions.

THE BASIC
CORRELATIONAL RESEARCH PROCESS

While relationship studies and prediction studies have unique features that differentiate them, their basic processes are very similar. You should feel pretty familiar with most of these processes from your readings in Chapters 6 and 7.

Problem Selection

Correlational studies may be designed either to determine which variables of a list of likely candidates are related or to test hypotheses regarding expected relationships. Variables to be included should be selected on the basis of either a deductive or an inductive rationale. In other words, the relationships to be investigated should be suggested by theory or derived from experience. Correlational treasure hunts in which the researcher correlates all sorts of variables to see "what turns up" are to be strongly discouraged. This research strategy (appropriately referred to as the shotgun approach) does not involve hypothesis testing and is very inefficient. While it may lead to the discovery of an important relationship, it more often produces spurious correlation coefficients, that is, coefficients that do not accurately reflect the degree of relationship between two variables and that are not found if the variables are correlated again using another sample. The study reprinted at the end of this chapter contains the following warning regarding the selection of problems and variables:

> Thus, this study adds to the growing body of literature indicating that the choice of performance variables can have substantive implications for the results of research and that researchers must carefully choose performance measures that are appropriate to the particular research question they are investigating (McGuire, Sundgren, & Schneeweis, 1988, p. 869).

Sample and Instrument Selection

The sample for a correlational study is selected using an acceptable sampling method, and 30 subjects are generally considered to be a minimally acceptable sample size. As with any study, it is important to select or develop valid, reliable measures of the variables being studied. If inadequate data are collected, the resulting correlation coefficient will represent an inaccurate estimate of the degree of relationship. Further, if the measures used do not really measure the intended variables, the resulting coefficient will not indicate the intended relationships. Suppose, for example, you wanted to determine the relationship between skill in writing and secretarial skills. If you selected and administered a valid, reliable test of spelling skill and a valid, reliable test of secretarial skills, the resulting correlation coefficient would not be an accurate estimate of the intended relationship. Spelling skill is only one kind of writing skill; the resulting coefficient would indicate the relationship between secretarial skills and *one kind* of writing skill, spelling. Thus, care must be taken to select measures that are valid *for your purposes.* The importance of this is amply demonstrated by a series of legal decisions beginning with *Griggs v. Duke Power* (1971). In this landmark decision, Chief Justice Warren Burger in his unanimous Supreme Court opinion stated, "Nothing in the Act precludes the use of testing or measuring procedures; obviously they are useful. . . . What Congress has commanded is that any tests used must measure the person for the job and not the person in the abstract" (cited in Schuler, 1984, p. 203).

Design and Procedure

The basic correlational design is not complicated; two, or more, scores are obtained for each member of a selected sample, one score for each variable of interest, and the paired scores are then correlated. The resulting correlation coefficient indicates the degree of relationship between the two variables. Instead of using individuals as the unit being measured in the sample, a sample of groups such as companies or professional associations might be used. In this case, one score for each company on each variable of interest would be obtained and then the paired scores correlated. The study at the end of the chapter is an example of a correlational study in which companies rather than individuals are used. In the following discussion, whenever individuals are mentioned, you will usually be able to perform the same operation for companies or other units; to keep the illustrations as simple as possible, however, the examples used are generally for individuals. Different studies investigate different numbers of variables, and some use complex statistical procedures, but the basic design is similar in all correlational studies.

Data Analysis and Interpretation

When two variables are correlated the result is a correlation coefficient. A *correlation coefficient* is a decimal number, between .00 and +1.00, or .00 and −1.00, which indicates the degree to which two variables are related. If the coefficient is near +1.00, the variables are positively correlated. This means that a person with a high score on one variable is likely to have a high score on the other variable, and a person with a low score on one is likely to have a low score on the other; an increase in one variable is associated with an increase in the other variable. If the coefficient is near .00, the variables are not related. This means that a person's score on one variable is no indication of what the person's score is on the other variable. If the coefficient is near −1.00, the variables are inversely related. This means that a person with a high score on one variable is likely to have a low score on the other; an increase in one variable is associated with a decrease in the other variable, and vice versa (see Table 8.1). Table 8.1 presents four "scores" for each of eight management trainees: aptitude test scores, performance ratings, weight, and errors on a 20-item accounting test. As Table 8.1 illustrates, the aptitude test is positively related to performance rating, not related to weight, and negatively, or inversely, related to errors. The trainees with progressively higher aptitude test scores have progressively higher performance ratings. The trainees with higher aptitude test scores tend to make fewer errors (makes

Table 8.1

Hypothetical Sets of Data Illustrating a High Positive Relationship Between Two Variables, No Relationship, and a High Negative Relationship

	High Positive Relationship		No Relationship		High Negative Relationship	
	Test	*Rating*	*Test*	*Weight*	*Test*	*Errors*
1. Iggie	85	1.0	85	156	85	16
2. Hermie	90	1.2	90	140	90	10
3. Fifi	100	2.4	100	120	100	8
4. Teenie	110	2.2	110	116	110	5
5. Tiny	120	2.8	120	160	120	9
6. Tillie	130	3.4	130	110	130	3
7. Millie	135	3.2	135	140	135	2
8. Jane	140	3.8	140	166	140	1

sense!). The relationships are not perfect, and it would be very strange if they were. One's performance rating, for example, may be related to other variables besides aptitude, such as motivation. The data do indicate, however, that aptitude is one major variable related to both performance ratings and accounting examination errors. The data also illustrate an important concept often misunderstood by beginning researchers, namely that a high negative relationship is just as strong as a high positive relationship; −1.00 and +1.00 indicate equally perfect relationships. A coefficient near .00 indicates no relationship; the further away from .00 the coefficient is, in *either* direction (toward +1.00 or −1.00), the stronger the relationship. High positive and high negative relationships are equally useful for making predictions; knowing that Iggie has a low aptitude test score would enable you to predict both a low performance rating and a high number of errors. By the way, an aptitude test that performed this well would be a real blessing to a human resources person!

What a correlation coefficient *means* is difficult to explain. Some beginning researchers erroneously think that a correlation coefficient of .50 means that two variables are 50% related. Not true. In research talk, a correlation coefficient squared indicates the amount of common variance shared by the variables. Now, in English. Each of two variables will result in a range of scores; there will be score variance; that is, everyone will not get the same score. In Table 8.1, for example, aptitude test scores vary from 85 to 140 and performance ratings from 1.0 to 3.8. Common variance refers to the variation in one variable that is attributable to its tendency to vary with the other. If two variables are not related, then the variability of one set of scores has nothing to do with the variability of the other set; if two variables are perfectly related, then variability of one set of scores has everything to do with variability in the other set. Thus with no relationship the variables have no common variance, but with a perfect relationship all variance, or 100% of the variance, is shared, common variance. The percent of common variance is generally less than the numerical value of the correlation coefficient. In fact, to determine common variance you simply square the correlation coefficient. A correlation coefficient of .80 indicates $(.80)^2$, or .64, or 64% common variance. A correlation coefficient of .00 indicates $(.00)^2$, or .00, or 00% common variance, and a coefficient of 1.00 indicates $(1.00)^2$, or 1.00, or 100% common variance. Thus, a coefficient of .50 may look pretty good at first, but it actually means that the variables have 25% common variance.

Interpretation of a correlation coefficient depends upon how it is to be used. In other words, how large it needs to be in order to be useful depends upon the purpose for which it was computed. In a study designed to explore or test hypothesized relationships, a correlation coefficient is interpreted in terms of its statistical significance. In a prediction study, statistical significance is secondary to the value of the coefficient in facilitating accurate predictions. Statistical significance refers to whether the obtained coefficient is really different from zero and reflects a true relationship, not a chance relationship; the decision concerning statistical significance is made at a given level of probability. Although the concepts of statistical significance, level of significance, and degrees of freedom will be discussed further in Part IV, at this point you simply need to know that based on one sample of a given size, you cannot determine positively whether there is or is not a true relationship between the variables. You can, however, say there probably is or probably is not such a relationship. Relatedly, a hypothesis concerning relationship or lack of it (the null hypothesis) can be supported or not supported, not proven or disproven. To determine statistical significance, you only have to consult a table that tells you how large your coefficient needs to be in order to be significant at a given probability level, and given the size of your sample (see Table A.2 in the Appendix). For the same probability level, or significance level, a larger coefficient is required when smaller samples are involved. We can generally have a lot more confidence in a coefficient based on 100 subjects than one based on 10 subjects. Of course, you already know that you need at least 30 subjects for a correlation study to begin with! To illustrate the point, however, at the 95% confidence level, with 10 cases, you would need a coefficient of at least .6319 in order to conclude the existence of a relationship; with 102 cases you would need a coefficient of only .1946. How do we know this? We look it up on Table A.2 in the Appendix! If you are trying to read this table, the following information will help:

95% confidence level corresponds to $p = .05$,

10 cases corresponds to N, or number of cases, and

df is degrees of freedom.

Using the standard formula for determining degrees of freedom, $df = N - 2$, with $N = 10$ cases, df equals $10 - 2$, or 8; for 100 cases, df equals $100 - 2$, or 98. The whole concept of determining significance based on sample size makes more sense if you collected data on every member of a population, not just a sample. In this situation, no inference would be involved, and regardless of how small the actual correlation coefficient was, it would represent the true degree of relationship between the variables for that population. Even if the coefficient were only .11, for example, it would still indicate the existence of a relationship, a low one, but a relationship just the same. The larger the sample, the more closely it approximates the population and therefore the more probable it is that a given coefficient represent a true relationship.

You may also have noted another related concept: For a given sample size, the value of the correlation coefficient needed for significance increases as the level of confidence increases. As the level of confidence increases, the p value in the table gets smaller; the 95% confidence level corresponds to $p = .05$ and the 99% level to $p = .01$. Thus for 10 subjects ($df = 8$), and $p = .05$, a coefficient of at least .6319 is required; for 10 subjects and $p = .01$, however, a coefficient of at least .7646 is required. In other words, the more confident you wish to be that your decision concerning significance is the correct one, the larger the coefficient must be. Beware, however, of confusing significance with strength. No matter how high the level of significance is for a coefficient, a low coefficient still represents a weak relationship. The level of significance only indicates the probability that a given relationship is a true one, regardless of whether it is a weak relationship or a strong relationship.

Prediction is another story. The utility of a correlation coefficient goes beyond its statistical significance in a prediction study. With a sample of 102 subjects, for example, a coefficient of .1946 is significant at $p = .05$. This relationship would be of little value for most prediction purposes. Since the relationship is so low (the common variance is only $[.1946]^2$, or .0379, or 3.8%), knowing a person's score on one variable would be of little help in predicting her or his score on the other. A correlation coefficient much below .50 is generally useless for either group prediction or individual prediction, although a combination of several variables in this range may yield a reasonably satisfactory prediction. As you may recall from Chapter 5, the median correlation between GMAT scores and first-year grades for MBA students in 1982–83 was only .30; inclusion of other variables raised the median correlation to .38! Coefficients in the .60s and .70s are usually considered adequate for group prediction purposes and coefficients in the .80s and above for individual prediction purposes.

When correlation coefficients are used to estimate the validity or reliability of measuring instruments, the criterion of acceptability is even higher. A correlation coefficient of .40, for example, would be considered useful in a relationship study, not useful in a prediction study, and terrible in a reliability study; a coefficient of .60 would be considered useful in a prediction study but would still probably be considered unsatisfactory as an estimate of reliability. As discussed in Chapter 5, what does constitute an acceptable level of reliability is partly a function of the type of instrument. While all reliabilities in the .90s are acceptable, for certain kinds of instruments, such as personality measures, a reliability in the low .70s might be acceptable. The standards for acceptable observer reliability discussed in Chapter 7 are similar to those for test reliability. A researcher would be very happy with observer reliabilities in the .90s, satisfied with the .80s, minimally accepting of the .70s, and progressively more unhappy with the .60s, .50s, and so forth.

When interpreting a correlation coefficient you must always keep in mind that you are talking about a relationship only, not a cause-effect relationship. A significant correlation coefficient may *suggest* a cause-effect relationship but does not establish one. The only way to establish a cause-effect relationship is by conducting an experiment. When one finds a high relationship between two variables it is often very tempting to conclude that one "causes" the other. In fact, it may be that neither one is the cause of the other; there may be a third variable that "causes" both of them. To use the study reprinted at the end of this chapter as an example, the existence of a positive relationship between prior financial performance and corporate social responsibility could mean one of three things: (1) Better financial performance leads to more corporate social responsibility, (2) more corporate social responsibility leads to better financial performance, or (3) there is a variable that results in both better financial performance and more corporate social responsibility. It might be, for example, that some third variable, such as highly skilled CEOs with very high personal standards for social responsibility, is a major factor in both financial performance and corporate social responsibility. Which of the alternatives is in fact the true explanation cannot be determined through a correlational study, but you will want to read the results, discussion, and conclusions portions of that study for an example of the various ways relationships may be found and predictions may result from a correlation study.

RELATIONSHIP STUDIES

Relationship studies are conducted in an attempt to gain insight into the factors or variables that are related to complex variables such as productivity, motivation, and, as in the example at the end of the chapter, corporate social responsibility and financial performance. Variables found not to be related can be eliminated from further consideration. Identification of related variables serves several major purposes. First, such studies give direction to subsequent causal-comparative and experimental studies. Experimental studies are costly in more ways than one; correlational studies are an effective way of reducing unprofitable experimental studies and suggesting potentially productive ones. Also, in both causal-comparative and experimental research studies, the researcher is concerned with controlling for variables other than the independent variable that might be related to performance on the dependent variable. In other words, the researcher tries to identify variables that are correlated with the dependent variable and to remove their influence so that it will not be confused with that of the independent variable. Relationship studies help the researcher to identify such variables, to control for them, and therefore to investigate the effects of the intended variable. For example, the conclusions section of the corporate social responsibility study suggests that future studies investigate the influence of prior financial performance on subsequent financial performance and also the influence of financial performance on social responsibility rather than the reverse.

The relationship study strategy of attempting to understand a complex variable by identifying and analyzing variables related to it has been more productive for some complex variables than for others. For example, while a number of variables correlated with motivation have been identified, factors significantly related to leadership have not been as easy to pin down. Either some wholes are greater than the sum of their parts, or all the relevant parts have not yet been identified! If nothing else, however, relationship studies that have not uncovered useful relationships have at least identified variables that can be excluded from future studies, a necessary step in science.

Data Collection

In a relationship study the researcher first identifies, either inductively or deductively, variables potentially related to the complex variable under study. For example, if you were interested in factors related to success in a particular field, you might identify variables such as intelligence, past achievement, and aptitude. As pointed out previously, and reinforced by the courts, you should have some reason for including variables in the study. The shotgun approach, which involves checking all conceivable variables for possible relationships, is very inefficient and often misleading. The more correlation coefficients that are computed at one time, the more likely it is that the wrong conclusion will be reached for some of them concerning the existence of a relationship. On the one hand, if only one correlation coefficient is computed, the odds are greatly in our favor that we are making the correct decision. On the other hand, if 100 coefficients are computed, and if we are working at $p = .05$, the odds are working against us, since it is likely that we will erroneously conclude that a relationship exists 5 out of the 100 times. A smaller number of carefully selected variables is much to be preferred to a larger number of carelessly selected variables. We may find fewer significant correlation coefficients, but we can have more confidence that the ones we do find represent true relationships, not chance ones, which are not likely to be found again.

The next step in data collection is to identify an appropriate population of subjects from which to select a sample. The population must be one for which data on each of the identified variables can be collected, and one whose members are available to the researcher. Although data on some variables, such as years of experience, which can be found in personnel records, can be collected without direct access to subjects, many relationship studies require the administration of one or more instruments and in some situations, observation. Any of the types of instruments so far discussed, such as standardized tests, questionnaires, and observations may be used in a relationship study, and each must be selected with care. One advantage of a relationship study is that all the data may be collected within a relatively short period of time. Instruments may be administered at one session or several sessions in close succession. If employees are the subjects, as they often are, time demands on employees and supervisors are relatively small compared to those required for experimental studies; therefore, it is easier to obtain management approval.

Data Analysis and Interpretation

In a relationship study, the scores for each variable are in turn correlated with the scores for the complex variable of interest. Thus, there results one correlation coefficient for each variable; each coefficient represents the relationship between a particular variable and the complex variable under study. In the corporate social responsibility study, for example, you can see that Table 1 displays the correlations between the variable "1983 corporate social responsibility" and 12 other variables such as ROA, average assets, operating income growth, and so on. Since the end result in each case is a correlation coefficient, a number between -1.00 and $+1.00$, clearly each variable must be expressible in numerical form, that is, must be quantifiable. For the variable "corporate social responsibility," for example, simply classifying responsibility as positive, socially responsible, or negative would not work as well as assigning a numerical value to each company because simple classifications restrict the types of analysis available to the researcher.

There are a number of different methods of computing a correlation coefficient; which one is appropriate depends upon the type of data represented by each variable. Although we will discuss the actual computation of a correlation coefficient in Part IV, a brief overview is provided here to enable you to review correlation studies. The most commonly used technique for assessing correlation is the product moment correlation coefficient, usually referred to as the Pearson r, which is appropriate when both variables to be correlated are expressed as interval data or ratio data (a discussion of the different types of data was included in Chapter 5). Since many instruments used in business, such as personality measures and accounting data, are expressed in the form of interval data or ratio data, the Pearson r is usually the appropriate coefficient for determining relationship. Further, since the Pearson r results in the most reliable estimate of correlation, its use is preferred even when other methods may be applied.

If the data for one of the variables are expressed as ranks, the appropriate correlation coefficient is the rank difference correlation coefficient, usually referred to as the Spearman rho. Rank data are involved when, instead of using a score for each subject or variable, subjects are arranged in order of score and each subject is assigned a rank from one to however many subjects there are. The "Fortune 500" is a familiar example of rank-ordered data. For the group of 500 companies that "make the cut," for example, the company with the highest score in the variables used for assessment is assigned a rank of 1, the company with the second highest rating 2, and the company with the lowest rating 500. If only one of the variables to be correlated is in rank order, say Fortune 500 order, then the other variables to be correlated with it must also be expressed in terms of ranks in order to use the Spearman rho technique. Thus, if number of employees were to be correlated with Fortune 500 order, the actual number of employees per se would not be involved in the computation of the correlation coefficient; rather the number of employees would be set in rank order before the computation was done. Although it's highly unlikely, if two companies ever had the same number of employees, and therefore, the same highest rank, they would each be assigned the average of rank 1 and rank 2, namely 1.5; similarly, if two companies further down in the list were tied in number of employees, say at rank number 28, their ranks of 28 and 29 would be averaged at 28.5. Although the Pearson r is more precise than the Spearman rho, with a small number of subjects (less than 30) the Spearman rho is much easier to compute and results in a coefficient very close to the one that would have been obtained had a Pearson r been computed. When the number of subjects is large, however, the process of ranking becomes more time-consuming (although this could, of course, be handled by the trusty computer) and the Spearman rho loses its only advantage over the Pearson r.

There are also a number of other correlational techniques that are encountered less often but that should be used when appropriate. Some variables, for example, can only be expressed in terms of a dichotomy. Since an individual is usually either male or female, the variable of sex cannot be expressed on a scale from 1 to 30. Thus sex is typically expressed as a 1 or 0 (female versus male) or as a 1 or 2 (female versus male). A 2, however, does not mean more of something than a 1, and 1 does not mean more than 0; these numbers indicate difference only, not difference in amount. Other variables that may be expressed as a dichotomy include political affiliation (Democrat versus Republican), smoking status (smoker versus nonsmoker), and educational status (high school graduate versus high school dropout). The above examples illustrate "true" dichotomies in that a person is or is not a female, a Democrat, a smoker, or a high school dropout. Artificial dichotomies may also be created by operationally defining a midpoint and categorizing subjects as falling above it or below it. Subjects with aptitude tests of 50 or above might be classified as "high aptitude subjects," for example, and subjects with aptitude scores of 49 or below might be classified as "low aptitude subjects." Such classifications are also typically translated into a "score" of 1 or 0. For additional discussion concerning alternative techniques for calculating correlation coefficients, you will want to check Glass & Stanley (1984).

Most correlational techniques are based on the assumption that the relationship being investigated is a linear one. If a relationship is linear, then plotting the scores on the two variables will result in something resembling a straight line. If a relationship is perfect (+1.00 or −1.00), the line will be perfectly straight; if there is no relationship, the points will form no pattern but will instead be scattered in a random fashion. Figure 8.1, which plots the data presented in Table 8.1, illustrates the concept of a linear relationship. Not all relationships, however, are linear; some are curvilinear. If a relationship is curvilinear, an increase in one variable is associated with a corresponding increase in another variable *to a point,* at which point further increase in the first variable results in a corresponding decrease in the other variable (or vice versa). The relationship between age and agility, for example, is a curvilinear one. As Figure 8.2 illustrates, agility increasingly improves with age, peaks, or reaches its maximum, somewhere in the 20s, and then progressively decreases as age increases. Two other examples of curvilinear relationships are age of car and dollar value, and anxiety and achievement. A car decreases in value as soon as it leaves the lot and continues to do so over time until it becomes an antique (!), and then it increases in value as time goes by. In contrast, increases in anxiety are associated with increases in achievement (no anxiety at all is not very conducive to learning) to a point; at some point anxiety becomes counterproductive and interferes with learning in that as anxiety increases, achievement decreases. If a relationship is suspected of being curvilinear, then a correlational technique that results in an eta ratio is required. If you try to use a correlational technique that assumes a linear relationship when the relationship is in fact curvilinear, your estimate of the degree of relationship will be way off base. Since it will in no way resemble a straight line, the coefficient will generally indicate little or no relationship; the positive relationship and negative relationship that combine to

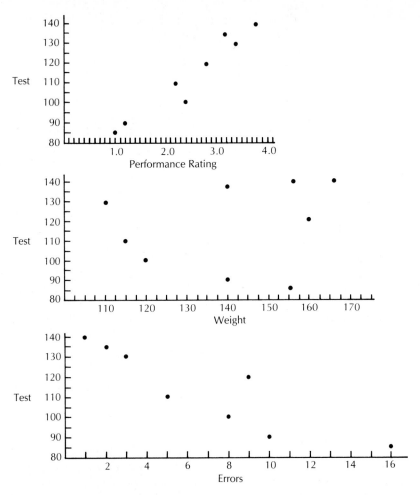

Figure 8.1. Data points for scores presented in Table 8.1 illustrating a strong positive relationship (Test and Performance Rating), no relationship (Test and Weight), and a strong negative relationship (Test and Errors).

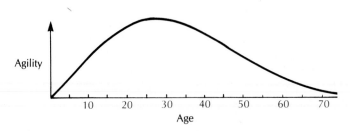

Figure 8.2. The curvilinear relationship between age and agility.

form a high curvilinear relationship will in a sense cancel each other out if a technique that assumes linearity (totally positive or totally negative) is applied (Nunnally, 1978).

In addition to computing correlation coefficients for a total sample group, it is sometimes profitable to examine relationships separately for certain defined sub-groups. The relationship between two variables may be different, for example, for females and males, college graduates and noncollege graduates, or high-ability trainees and low-ability trainees. When the subgroups are lumped together, such differential relationships may be obscured. There are also other factors that may contribute to an inaccurate estimate of relationship. *Attenuation,* for example, refers to the principle that correlation coefficients tend to be lowered owing to the fact that less-than-perfectly-reliable measures are used. In relationship studies a correction for attenuation can be applied that provides an estimate of what the coefficient would be if both measures were perfectly reliable. If such a correction is used, it must be kept in mind that the resulting coefficient does not represent what was actually found. Such a correction is not used in prediction studies, since predictions must be made based on existing measures, not hypothetical, perfectly reliable, instruments.

Another factor that may lead to a coefficient representing an underestimate of the true relationship between two variables is a restricted range of scores. The more variability there is in each set of scores, the higher the coefficient is likely to be. The correlation coefficient for age and success, for example, would probably tend to decrease as these variables were measured at higher management levels. Thus, the relationship would probably not be found to be as high for senior management as for first-line supervisors. The reason is that, although first-line supervisors may be any age, not many very young people are senior managers because they simply haven't the years of experience that typically are required for reaching a senior management level. In other words, the range of ages is much smaller, or more restricted, for senior managers, and a correlation coefficient based on such scores will tend to be reduced. There is also a correction for restriction in range that may be applied to obtain an estimate of what the coefficient would be if the range of scores were not restricted. It should be interpreted with the same caution as the correction for attenuation, since it does not represent what was actually found. Application of this correction, for example, in fully mature, large companies would be far more appropriate than using the correction formula with entrepreneurial Silicon Valley computer companies, which may have very young senior managers.

PREDICTION STUDIES

If two variables are strongly related, scores on one variable can be used to predict scores on the other variable. High school grades, for example, can be used to predict college grades. The variable upon which the prediction is made is referred to as the *predictor,* and the variable predicted is referred to as the *criterion.* Prediction studies are often conducted to facilitate decision making concerning individuals or to aid in the selection of individuals. Prediction studies are also conducted to test theoretical hypotheses concerning variables believed to be predictors of a criterion (how many "predictors" of stock market performance have you seen?) and to determine the predictive validity of individual measuring instruments. The results of prediction studies are used, for example, to predict an individual's likely level of success in a particular task, such as assembly-line work, to predict which of a number of individuals are likely to succeed in a job or vocational training program, and to predict in which area of work an individual is most likely to be successful. Thus, the results of prediction studies are used by a number of groups besides researchers, such as counselors and human resources professionals.

If several predictor variables each correlate well with a criterion, then a prediction based on a combination of those variables will be more accurate than a prediction based on any one of them. For example, an employment decision based on a combination of review and rating of the application form to determine how many of the stated criteria are met by the applicant, three reference checks in which the applicant is rated, test scores, and a series of interviews in which the interviewers are asked to rate the applicant, is likely to be more valid than a decision based only on one interview. Again, with regard to employment practices, the courts have entered the picture regarding predictions. In *Chrisner v. Complete Auto Transit,* a two-year experience requirement was upheld as an acceptable single predictor for a particular job (Schuler, 1984). In general, however, multiple predictors are required for employment because jobs usually involve a variety of skills, knowledge, and ability. The complexity of this issue with regard to legal issues requires the human resources practitioner not only to have a thorough understanding of the law but also an ability to use and interpret a variety of statistics, especially those indicating relationships. Although there are major differences between prediction studies and relationship studies, both involve determining the relationship between a number of identified variables and a complex variable.

Data Collection

As with a relationship study, subjects must be selected from whom the desired data can be collected and who are available to the researcher. Instruments selected must also be valid measures of the variables of interest. It is especially important that the measure of the criterion variable be a valid one. If the criterion were "success on the job," success would have to be carefully defined in quantifiable terms. Size of desk would probably not be a valid measure of success, whereas number of promotions or salary increases probably would be. The major difference in data-collection procedures for a relationship study and a prediction study is that in a relationship study data on all variables are collected within a relatively short period of time, whereas in a prediction study predictor variables are measured some period of time before the criterion variable is measured. In determining the predictive validity of a secretarial-aptitude test, for example, success in the secretarial job would probably be measured at the end of six months or a year, whereas the aptitude test would be administered some time prior to the beginning of the job. The corporate social responsibility study, for example, suggests that prior financial performance is a better predictor of social responsibility than subsequent financial performance.

Data Analysis and Interpretation

As with a relationship study, each predictor variable is correlated with the criterion variable. The correlation values will similarly range from $+1.00$ to -1.00; significance of the correlation will be determined by checking the correlation level on a chart of significance. Again, caution in interpretation must be observed, as the level of statistical significance should not be mistaken for a level of practical significance, which may be considerably higher. Thus a statistically significant relationship of .35 ($df = 30$, $p = .05$) may not be strong enough to satisfy the requirements of practical significance, which might well be $>.60$ for predictions. Since a combination of variables usually results in a more accurate prediction than any one variable, prediction studies often result in a prediction equation referred to as a multiple-regression equation.

MULTIPLE-REGRESSION EQUATIONS

A *multiple-regression equation* uses all variables that individually predict the criterion to make a more accurate prediction. You can see how this works if you review Table 4 in the corporate social responsibility study. In that example, variables such as prior and subsequent accounting performance, market performance, accounting risk, and market risk were all assessed to determine possible relationships to the dependent variable, social responsibility. Because of the complexity of analysis involved, multiple-regression analyses are almost always done by computer programs. Although the computer printout will provide you with information regarding the correlations between each predictor variable of possible interest and the dependent, or criterion, variable, the printout will also provide you with an F ratio indicating the relationship among all the predictor variables and the criterion variable. Most printouts will also indicate the probability level for you, but, if not, you can again look it up using a table such as the one in Appendix A. As a caveat, however, since relationships are rarely perfect, predictions made by a multiple-regression equation are not perfect. Thus, predicted scores are generally placed in a confidence interval.

As you may know, college admissions personnel use prediction equations that include a number of variables in order to predict college GPA. A predicted college GPA of 1.20 might be placed in an interval of 0.80 to 1.60. In other words, students with a predicted GPA of 1.20 would be predicted to earn a GPA somewhere in the range between 0.80 and 1.60. A college that does not accept all applicants will probably as a general rule fail to accept any applicants with such a projected GPA range even though it is very likely that some of those students would be successful if admitted. Although the predictions for any given individual might be way off (either too high or too low), for the total group of applicants, predictions are quite accurate on the whole; most applicants predicted to succeed, do so. Similarly, in an equation developed to predict success in a particular job, factors such as prior experience, aptitude tests, results of interviews, and the like may be combined as an aid in hiring. In this *multiple-predictor approach*, one of two strategies is usually used (Schuler,

1987). In the *multiple-cutoff* approach, a candidate must exceed a specified base rate on each of the predictors to continue in contention for the position; that is, the results of the predictors are not combined. Thus a very high score on the aptitude test will not compensate for a total lack of experience. In the *multiple-hurdle* approach, candidates must meet the criteria for each predictor before going on to the next predictor, or hurdle. A legal requirement applied to the multiple-predictor approach in hiring is the application of the 80%, or 4/5 rule. This rule specifies that the impact of the predictors must be such that for each predictor, if a company hires 50% of all white male applicants, it must also hire at least 40% of all minority applicants. Prior to 1982, this rule applied only to the final hiring decision; now it applies to each predictor in order to avoid disparate impact in hiring decisions (Schuler, 1987). Another application of multiple-regression analysis in human resource management is in the area of indirect compensation. As company costs for benefits increase, compensation managers need to assess carefully, and be able to predict the relative attractiveness, cost, and benefit of, the wide variety of benefits options open to companies and employees. As with relationship studies, and for similar reasons, prediction equations may be formulated for each of a number of subgroups as well as for a total group.

An interesting phenomenon characteristic of multiple-regression equations is referred to as shrinkage. Shrinkage is the tendency of a prediction equation to become less accurate when used with a different group, a group other than the one on which the equation was originally formulated. The reason for shrinkage is that an initial equation may be the result of chance relationships that will not be found again with another group of subjects. Thus, any prediction equation should be validated with at least one other group, and variables that are no longer found to be related to the criterion measure should be taken out of the equation; this procedure is referred to as cross-validation.

Summary/Chapter 8

DEFINITION AND PURPOSE

1. *Correlational research* involves collecting data in order to determine whether, and to what degree, a relationship exists between two or more quantifiable variables.

2. Degree of relationship is expressed as a *correlation coefficient.*

3. If a relationship exists between two variables, it means that scores within a certain range on one measure are associated with scores within a certain range on another measure.

4. The fact that there is a relationship between variables does not imply that one is the cause of the other.

5. Correlational studies provide an estimate of just how related two variables are. If two variables are highly related, a correlation coefficient near 1.00 (or −1.00) will be obtained; if two variables are not related, a coefficient near .00 will be obtained.

6. The more highly related two variables are, the more accurate are predictions based on their relationship.

THE BASIC CORRELATIONAL RESEARCH PROCESS

Problem Selection

7. Correlational studies may be designed either to determine which variables of a list of likely candidates are related or to test hypotheses regarding expected relationships.

Sample and Instrument Selection

8. The sample for a correlational study is selected using an acceptable sampling method, and 30 subjects are generally considered to be a minimally acceptable sample size.

9. It is important to select or develop valid, reliable measures of the variables being studied.

Design and Procedure

10. The basic correlational design is not complicated; two (or more) scores are obtained for all members of a selected sample, one score for each variable of interest, and the paired scores are then correlated.

Data Analysis and Interpretation

11. A *correlation coefficient* is a decimal number between .00 and +1.00, or .00 and −1.00, which indicates the degree to which the two variables are related.

12. If the coefficient is near +1.00, the variables are positively related. This means that a person with a high score on one variable is likely to have a high score on the other variable, and a person with a low score on one is likely to have a low score on the other; an increase in one variable is associated with an increase in the other.

13. If the coefficient is near .00, the variables are not related.

14. If the coefficient is near −1.00, the variables are inversely related. This means that a person with a high score on one variable is likely to have a low score on the other variable, and a person with a low score on one is likely to have a high score on the other; an increase in one variable is associated with a decrease in the other variable, and vice versa.

15. A correlation coefficient squared indicates the amount of common variance shared by the variables.

16. How large a correlation coefficient needs to be in order to be useful depends upon the purpose for which it was computed.

17. In a study designed to explore or test hypothesized relationships, a correlation coefficient is interpreted in terms of its statistical significance.

18. In a prediction study, statistical significance is secondary to the value of the coefficient in facilitating accurate predictions.

19. "Statistical significance" refers to whether the obtained coefficient is really different from zero and reflects a true relationship, not a chance relationship.

20. To determine statistical significance you only have to consult a table that tells you how large your coefficient needs to be in order to be significant at a given level of confidence and given the size of your sample.

21. For the same level of confidence, or significance level, a larger coefficient is required when smaller samples are involved.

22. For a given sample size, the value of the correlation coefficient needed for significance increases as the level of confidence increases.

23. No matter how significant a coefficient is, a low coefficient represents a low relationship.

24. A correlation coefficient much below .50 is generally useless for either group prediction or individual prediction, although a combination of several variables in this area may yield a reasonably satisfactory prediction.

25. Coefficients in the .60s and .70s are usually considered adequate for group prediction purposes, and coefficients in the .80s and above for individual prediction purposes.

26. While all reliabilities in the .90s are acceptable, for certain kinds of instruments, such as personality measures, a reliability in the low .70s might be acceptable.

27. When interpreting a correlation coefficient you must always keep in mind that you are talking about a relationship only, not a cause-effect relationship.

RELATIONSHIP STUDIES

28. Relationship studies are conducted in an attempt to gain insight into the factors, or variables, that are related to complex variables such as achievement, motivation, and corporate social responsibility.

29. Such studies give direction to subsequent causal-comparative and experimental studies. Also, in both causal-comparative and experimental studies, the researcher is concerned with controlling for variables other than the independent variable that might be related to performance on the dependent variable. Relationship studies help the researcher to identify such variables.

Data Collection

30. In a relationship study the researcher first identifies, either inductively or deductively, variables potentially related to the complex variable under study.

31. The shotgun approach, which involves checking all conceivable variables for possible relationships, is very inefficient and often misleading.

32. A smaller number of carefully selected variables is much to be preferred to a large number of carelessly selected variables.

33. The population must be one for which data on each of the identified variables can be collected, and one whose members are available to the researcher.

34. One advantage of a relationship study is that all the data may be collected within a relatively short period of time.

Data Analysis and Interpretation

35. In a relationship study, the scores for each variable are in turn correlated with the scores for the complex variable of interest.

36. Each variable must be expressible in numerical form, that is, must be quantifiable.

37. The most commonly used technique is the product moment correlation coefficient, usually referred to as the Pearson *r,* which is appropriate when both variables to be correlated are expressed as ratio data or interval data.

38. If data for one of the variables are expressed as ranks, the appropriate correlation coefficient is the rank difference correlation coefficient, usually referred to as the Spearman rho.

39. There are also a number of other correlational techniques that are encountered less often but that should be used when appropriate.

40. Most correlational techniques are based on the assumption that the relationship being investigated is a linear one.

41. If a relationship is curvilinear, an increase in one variable is associated with a corresponding increase in another variable *to a point,* at which point further increase in the first variable results in a corresponding decrease in the other variable (or vice versa).

42. In addition to computing correlation coefficients for a total sample group, it is sometimes profitable to examine relationships separately for certain defined subgroups.

43. Attenuation refers to the principle that correlation coefficients tend to be lowered owing to the fact that less-than-perfectly-reliable measures are used.

44. In relationship studies, a correction for attenuation can be applied that provides an estimate of what the coefficient would be if both measures were perfectly reliable.

45. Another factor that may lead to a coefficient representing an underestimate of the true relationship between two variables is a restricted range of scores.

46. There is a correction for restriction in range that may be applied to obtain an estimate of what the coefficient would be if the ranges of scores were not restricted.

PREDICTION STUDIES

47. If two variables are highly related, scores on one variable can be used to predict scores on the other variable.

48. The variable upon which the prediction is made is referred to as the *predictor,* and the variable predicted is referred to as the *criterion.*

49. Prediction studies are often conducted to facilitate decision making concerning individuals or to aid in the selection of individuals.

50. Prediction studies are also conducted to test theoretical hypotheses concerning variables believed to be predictors of the criterion and to determine the predictive validity of individual measuring instruments.

51. If several predictor variables each correlate well with a criterion, then a prediction based on a combination of those variables will be more accurate than a prediction based on any one of them.

Data Collection

52. As with a relationship study, subjects must be selected from whom the desired data can be collected and who are available to the researcher.

53. The major difference in data-collection procedures for a relationship study and a prediction study is that in a relationship study data on all variables are collected within a relatively short

period of time, whereas in a prediction study predictor variables are measured some period of time before the criterion variable is measured.

Data Analysis and Interpretation

54. As with a relationship study, each predictor variable is correlated with the criterion variable.

55. Since a combination of variables usually results in a more accurate prediction than any one variable, prediction studies often result in a prediction equation referred to as a multiple-regression equation.

MULTIPLE-REGRESSION EQUATIONS

56. A *multiple-regression equation* uses all variables that individually predict the criterion to make a more accurate prediction.

57. Because of the complexity of analysis involved, multiple-regression analyses are almost always done by computer programs.

58. Although the computer printout will provide you with information regarding the correlations between each predictor variable of possible interest and the dependent, or criterion, variable, the printout will also provide you with an F ratio indicating the relationship among all the predictor variables and the criterion variable.

59. Since relationships are not perfect, predictions made by a multiple-regression equation are not perfect.

60. Predicted scores are generally placed in a confidence interval.

61. As with relationship studies, and for similar reasons, prediction equations may be formulated for each of a number of subgroups as well as for the total group.

62. Shrinkage is the tendency of a prediction equation to become less accurate when used with a different group, a group other than the one on which the equation was originally formulated.

63. Any prediction equation should be validated with at least one other group, and variables that are no longer found to be related to the criterion measure should be taken out of the equation; this procedure is referred to as cross-validation.

On the following pages is an example of correlational research (Project III Reading 3). The article may be used as a study aid to assist you in more fully understanding the nature of correlational research. Following the article, Practice Self-Test for reviewing the article is provided for you so that you can practice your review skills; Appendix C contains Suggested Responses so that you can check your responses from the self-test. Questions are also provided to allow you to evaluate the article from the standpoint of correlational research.

Corporate Social Responsibility and Firm Financial Performance

Jean B. McGuire
Concordia University

Alison Sundgren

Thomas Schneeweis
University of Massachusetts

Using *Fortune* magazine's ratings of corporate reputations, we analyzed the relationships between perceptions of firms' corporate social responsibility and measures of their financial performance. Results show that a firm's prior performance, assessed by both stock-market returns and accounting-based measures, is more closely related to corporate social responsibility than is subsequent performance. Results also show that measures of risk are more closely associated with social responsibility than previous studies have suggested.

The management literature has acknowledged social responsibility as an important corporate duty (Quinn, Mintzberg, & James, 1987). Given the significance of corporate social responsibility in corporate decision making, the relationship between a firm's social and ethical policies or actions and its financial performance (Arlow & Gannon, 1982; Ullmann, 1985) is an important topic.

Various arguments have been made regarding the relationship between firms' social responsibility and their financial performance. One view is that firms face a trade-off between social responsibility and financial performance. Those holding this view propose that firms incur costs from socially responsible actions that put them at an economic disadvantage compared to other, less responsible, firms (Aupperle, Carroll, & Hatfield, 1985; Ullmann, 1985; Vance, 1975). A second, contrasting viewpoint is that the explicit costs of corporate social responsibility are minimal and that firms may actually benefit from socially responsible actions in terms of employee morale and productivity (Moskowitz, 1972; Parket & Eibert, 1975; Soloman & Hansen, 1985). A third perspective is that the costs of socially responsible actions are significant but are offset by a reduction in other firm costs. For instance, stakeholder theory (Cornell & Shapiro, 1987) suggests that a firm must satisfy not only stockholders and bondholders, but also those with less explicit, or implicit, claims. Stakeholder theory further suggests that implicit claims like product quality are less costly to

The cooperation of *Fortune* magazine in providing data from its annual survey is gratefully acknowledged. Bradford Knipes assisted in data analysis and commented or earlier drafts of this article. The authors gratefully acknowledge the reviewers' comments.

©*Academy of Management Journal* 1988, Vol. 31, No. 4, 854–872.

a firm than explicit claims like wage contracts or stockholder or bondholder demands. Low social responsibility however, may encourage some stakeholders to doubt the ability of a firm to honor implicit claims and may increase the number of a firm's more costly explicit claims.

In addition, Alexander and Bucholtz (1978) and Bowman and Haire (1975) have suggested that stakeholders and stock- and bondholders may see corporate social responsibility as indicating management skill. In short, a firm has an investment in reputation, including its reputation for being socially responsible. An increase in perceived social responsibility may improve the image of the firm's management and permit it to exchange costly explicit claims for less costly implicit charges. In contrast, a decline in the level of stakeholders' view of a firm's social responsibility may reduce its reputation and result in an increase in costly explicit claims.

In this study, we used data from the *Fortune* survey of corporate reputations to examine two aspects of the relationship between corporate social responsibility and firm financial performance that previous research has ignored. First, we not only measured performance in terms of accounting- and stock-market-based measures but also in terms of risk. Second, we examined not only the extent to which social responsibility predicted financial performance but also whether prior financial performance predicted social responsibility. This study also improved on the the methodology used in previous studies by using evaluations of social responsibility made by knowledgeable external sources.

THEORETICAL FRAMEWORK

Research into the relationship between corporate social responsibility and financial performance has been based on several theoretical arguments. Those who have suggested a negative relation between social responsibility and financial performance have argued that high responsibility results in additional costs that put a firm at an economic disadvantage compared to other, less socially responsible firms (Bragdon & Marlin, 1985; Vance, 1975). These added costs may result from actions like making extensive charitable contributions, promoting community development plans, maintaining plants in economically depressed locations, and establishing environmental protection procedures. In addition, concern for social responsibility may limit a firm's strategic alternatives. For example, a firm may forgo certain product lines, such as weapons or pesticides, and avoid plant relocations and investment opportunities in certain locations (e.g., South Africa).

In contrast, other scholars investigating corporate social responsibility and performance have argued for a positive association. Several authors have cited improved employee and customer goodwill as an important outcome of social responsibility (Davis, 1975; Soloman & Hansen, 1985). For example, a firm perceived as high in social responsibility may face relatively few labor problems, and customers may be favorably disposed to its products. Socially responsible activities may also improve a firm's standing with such important constituencies as bankers, investors, and government officials. Improved relationships with these constituencies may bring economic benefits (Moussavi & Evans, 1986). Indeed, banks and other institutional investors have reported social considerations to be a factor in their investment decisions (Spicer, 1978). High corporate social responsibility may therefore improve a firm's access to sources of capital.

Lastly, modern corporate stakeholder theory (Cornell & Shapiro, 1987) contends that the value of a firm depends on the cost not only of explicit claims but also of implicit claims. From this viewpoint, the set of claimants on a firm's resources goes beyond the stockholders and bondholders to include stakeholders who have explicit claims on the firm like wage contracts and others with whom the firm has made implicit contracts, involving, for instance, quality service and social responsibility. If a firm does not act in a socially responsible manner, parties to implicit contracts concerning the social responsibility of the firm may attempt to transform those implicit agreements into explicit agreements that will be more costly to it. For example, if a firm fails to meet promises to government officials in regard to actions that affect the environment (dumping, etc.), government agencies may find it necessary to pass more stringent regulations, constituting explicit contracts, to force the firm to act in a socially responsible manner. Moreover, socially, irresponsible actions may spill over to other implicit stakeholders, who may doubt whether the firm would honor their claims. Thus, firms with an image of high corporate social responsibility may find that they have more low-cost implicit claims than other firms and thus have higher financial performance (Cornell & Shapiro, 1987).

Although theory and research have focused primarily on the relationship between corporate social responsibility and measures of financial performance, an argument for a relationship between social responsibility and such measures of financial risk as variance in earnings and in stock returns can also be made (Spicer, 1978; Ullmann, 1985). First, low levels of social responsibility may increase a firm's financial risk. Investors may consider less socially responsible firms to be riskier investments because they see management skills at the firm as low (Alexander & Bucholtz, 1978; Spicer, 1978). Investors and other constituencies may also anticipate an increase in firm costs owing to lack of social responsibility. For example, the government may levy fines, and law suits, such as those recently filed against pharmaceutical, chemical, and asbestos firms, that may threaten a firm's very existence. Perceptions of low social responsibility may also decrease a firm's ability to obtain capital at consistent rates.

In contrast, a high degree of corporate social responsibility may permit a firm to have relatively low financial risk as the result of more stable relations with the government and the financial community. In addition, to the degree that a firm has high social responsibility, it may also have a low percentage of total debt to total assets. A low total debt ensures that a firm can easily continue to satisfy implicit claims. Thus, compared to other firms, firms with high social responsibility may have lower market- and accounting-based total risk because they are less sensitive to certain external events, like governmental actions, and have a lower debt. The impact of social responsibility on measures of a firm's systematic risk may, however, be minimal, since most events affecting a firm's level of social responsibility do not systematically affect all other firms in the marketplace (Cornell & Shapiro, 1987).

Most studies have related social responsibility and concurrent financial performance. We also explored the effects of prior and subsequent performance on subsequent and prior evaluations of corporate social responsibility. The theoretical arguments suggested regarding the concurrent relationship between corporate social responsibility and financial performance also apply to the relationship with subsequent financial performance. The benefits of social responsibility cited earlier (e.g., employee motivation, customer goodwill) may carry over into later periods. To the degree that a firm with relatively high social responsibility can implement implicit contracts, its financial performance may improve and variability in market- and accounting-based performance measures may decline.

Corporate social responsibility may also be linked to past firm performance. Its financial performance may influence a firm's evolving social policy and actions (Ullmann, 1985). Policies and expenditures, particularly in discretionary areas such as social programs, may be especially sensitive to the existence of slack resources (Cyert & March, 1963). If corporate social responsibility is viewed as a significant cost, firms with relatively high past financial performance may be more willing to absorb these costs in the future (Parket & Eibert, 1975; Ullmann, 1985). In contrast, less profitable firms may be less willing to undertake socially responsible actions.

PREVIOUS RESEARCH

Previous research has yielded mixed results regarding the relationships between corporate social responsibility and measures of firm performance. Reviews by Aupperle and colleagues (1985), Cochran and Wood (1984), and Ullmann (1985) have all found mixed results concerning the concurrent relationship between social responsibility and firm performance. Ullmann suggested that those conflicting results may derive, in part, from differences in research methodologies and measures of financial performance.

Studies using stock-market-based measures of return have reported mixed results regarding the relationship between social responsibility and performance. Moskowitz (1972) ranked 67 selected firms in terms of his evaluation of their level of social responsibility and reported higher than average stock returns for highly ranked firms. Vance (1975), however, found a subset of the firms rated by Moskowitz had lower stock-market performance than a comparison sample of firms listed in the New York Stock Exchange Composite Index, Dow Jones Industrials, and Standard and Poor's Industrials. The studies by Vance and Moskowitz, however, both failed to adjust for risk. Other studies that have attempted to adjust stock-return performance measures for risk have found little relationship between social responsibility and market performance. Alexander and Bucholtz (1978), using the firms listed in Moskowitz's study, found little association between social responsibility and risk-adjusted return on securities.[1]

Studies examining the relationship between social responsibility and accounting-based performance measures have generally found positive results. Bragdon and Marlin (1972), Bowman and Haire (1975), and Parket and Eibert (1975) found generally positive associations between corporate social responsibility and accounting-based measures of performance. However, those studies did not control for the possible effects of other variables. Later studies that have attempted to control for differences in risk have offered more cautious support for the relationship between social responsibility and accounting-based performance measures. Cochran and Wood (1984) found a positive correlation between social responsibility and accounting performance after controlling for the age of assets. In contrast, Aupperle and colleagues (1985) found no significant relationships between social responsibility and a firm's ROA adjusted by its ranking in the Value Line Safety Index. Since financial risk and performance vary with industry, Sturdivant and Ginter (1977) compared accounting-based measures of performance of a subsample of the firms rated by Moskowitz to industry averages. They categorized firms as best, honorably mentioned, and worst in terms of social responsibility. Firms given an honorable mention had higher accounting-based performance than the other firms.

Previous studies on the relationship between social responsibility and risk have also produced mixed results. Spicer (1978) found that firms rated high on social performance, as measured by pollution control activities, had lower total and systematic risk than less socially responsible firms. Aupperle and colleagues also (1985) found a negative association between corporate social responsibility and accounting-based risk but found that the association between market-based risk and social responsibility was insignificant.

Previous studies have also employed varying measures of corporate social responsibility. Three methods have commonly been used. The first uses expert evaluations of corporate policies. The validity of this methodology, of course, depends on the skill and qualifications of those making the assessments (Abbott & Monsen, 1979). Previous studies have used an index from the Council of Concerned Businessmen (Sturdivant & Ginter, 1977) and two rankings from *Business and Society* (Moskowitz, 1972, 1975). The validity of these indexes is subject to criticism. Moskowitz's ratings were based on his own evaluation. In the case of the ratings published in 1975, done on samples of businessmen and M.B.A. students, the expertise of the evaluators and the accuracy of the information are questionable (Bowman & Haire, 1975).

Other researchers have used content analysis of corporate annual reports or other corporate documents (Abbot & Monsen, 1979; Anderson & Frankel, 1980;

---

[1]Adjusting for beta adjusts for systematic or general market risk. Lubatkin and Shrieves (1986) and Aaker and Jacobson (1987) discuss the adjustment of market-based-performance measures for risk.

Bowman & Haire, 1975; Preston, 1978). Such measures, however, confuse social orientation with corporate actions (Arlow & Gannon, 1982; Ullmann, 1985). Moreover, such documents often have more public relations value than informational value. The relationship between such public statements and actual corporate actions is uncertain. Bowman and Haire found a positive association between emphasis on corporate social responsibility in annual reports and the Moskowitz ratings. Preston, however, found no relation between these variables. Parket and Eibert (1975) used a corporation's willingness to respond to a questionnaire on social responsibility as an indicator of the firm's concern with the issue.

The third method of measuring corporate social responsibility uses performance in controlling pollution as a proxy measure. The Council of Concerned Businessmen Pollution Performance Index is frequently used (Bragdon & Marlin, 1972; Folger & Nutt, 1975; Spicer, 1978). Pollution control, however, reflects only one aspect of social responsibility and is only valid for certain industries (Bragdon & Marlin, 1972).

The types of measures previous studies have used influence results because accounting- and stock-market-based performance measures focus on different aspects of performance, and each is subject to particular biases (McGuire, Schneeweis, & Hill, 1986). Accounting-based measures tap only historical aspects of firm performance (McGuire, Schneeweis, & Hill, 1986). Moreover, they are subject to bias from managerial manipulation and differences in accounting procedures (Branch, 1983; Brilloff, 1972, 1976). Accounting performance should also be adjusted for risk, industry characteristics, and other variables (Aaker & Jacobson, 1987; Arlow & Gannon, 1982; Davidson, Worrell, & Gilberton, 1986; Michel & Shaked, 1984; Ullmann, 1985).

To avoid the problems of accounting-based measures, some authors have used stock-market-based measures of performance. Market returns have several advantages over accounting-based measures: they are (1) less susceptible to differential accounting procedures and managerial manipulation and (2) represent investors' evaluations of a firm's ability to generate future economic earnings rather than past performance.

Problems also exist, however, with the use of stock-market-based measures of performance (McGuire, Schneeweis, & Branch, 1986). Ullmann (1985) suggested that the use of market measures implies that investors' valuation of firm performance is a proper performance measure. Since firms face multiple constituencies (Pfeffer & Salancik, 1978), sole concentration on investors' evaluations may not be sufficient.

Given the debate over the proper measure of financial performance, in this study we used both accounting- and stock-market-based measures to investigate the relationships between concurrently, previously, and subsequently measured firm performance and corporate social responsibility. We also improved upon the methodology used in previous studies by using evaluations of corporate social responsibility from knowledgeable external sources.

METHODS

Data

Data on corporate social responsibility were obtained from *Fortune* magazine's annual survey of corporate reputations. *Fortune* has conducted the survey each fall since 1982 and published summary results each January. The survey covers the largest firms in 20–23 industry groups (the number of industry groups varies from year to year). Over 8,000 executives, outside directors, and corporate analysts are asked to rate the ten largest companies in their industry on eight attributes: financial soundness, long-term investment value, use of corporate assets, quality of management, innovativeness, quality of products or services, use of corporate talent, and community and environmental responsibility. Ratings are on a scale of 0 (poor) to 10 (excellent). The response rate of those surveyed has averaged almost 50 percent for each year of the survey (*Fortune,* 1983, 1986), Chakravarthy (1986) and Wartick (1987) have also used this data set.

The *Fortune* magazine survey was chosen for several reasons. First, it provides comparable data over a extended period. Second, the number of respondents is comparable or superior to those of other ratings. Third, respondents rate only firms in an industry with which they are familiar. They have direct access to internal firm and industry information that is particularly critical in the area of corporate social responsibility, where annual reports and other official documents provide incomplete and inconsistent information (Bowman & Haire, 1979).[2]

Evidence for the validity of the evaluations comes from empirical studies using other dimensions of the *Fortune* survey (Chakravarthy, 1986; McGuire, Schneeweis, & Branch, 1987). Those studies have found that the *Fortune* evaluations of firms' financial performance are highly correlated with accounting- and stock-market-based performance measures. Major changes in a firm's ranking often correspond to specific events, such as product changes or lawsuits, or to changes in performance (*Fortune,* 1986). The *Fortune* ratings differ from those of other evaluators of social responsibility in that the respondents are selected for their knowledge of a particular industry rather than for their specific knowledge of or interest in corporate social responsibility. Thus, their interpretation and evaluation of social responsibility may differ from those of others who are specifically interested in the issue. Wartick (1987), however, found the *Fortune* ratings to be associated with membership in the Issues Management Association,

---

[2]Industry analysts follow firms in a particular industry and advise investment houses and other institutional investors. Their livelihood, and that of their employers and investors, depends on their knowledge of firms in an industry. Since corporate social responsibility is one consideration in analysts' investment decisions (Spicer, 1978), they would be knowledgeable in this aspect of firm performance.

which suggests that the ratings do indicate an orientation toward corporate social responsibility.[3]

To evaluate the reliability of the ratings, we checked for consistency between the 1985 and 1986 evaluations. Although some modification of the ratings could be expected because of changing conditions and firm actions, major modifications would suggest lack of reliability. It should also be noted that the respondents *Fortune* uses change slightly each year. The correlation between the two sets of evaluations was .899.

Measures of Financial Performance

Data on accounting- and stock-market-based measures of firm performance and risk were obtained from the COMPUSTAT data base. The Appendix defines the measures of firm performance and risk we used. Market performance was measured by risk-adjusted return, or alpha, and total return. Market risk measures were beta, a measure of systematic risk, and the standard deviation of total return. Accounting-based performance measures were return on assets (ROA), total assets, sales growth, asset growth, and operating income growth. The ratio of debt to assets, operating leverage, and the standard deviation of operating income were our accounting-based measures of risk.

Periods of Analysis

Two sets of ratings of corporate social responsibility were used in this analysis. First, we computed average rankings for the period 1983–85, including the 98 firms and industries that appeared in all the yearly surveys and for which financial performance data were available. Second, to permit analysis of the relationship between corporate social responsibility and previous and subsequent firm financial performance, we used ratings of social responsibility for one year, 1983. *Fortune* produced these ratings in late 1982 and published them in January 1983. All the 131 firms rated by *Fortune* and for which financial performance data were available were included in this analysis.[4]

---

[3]To further validate the ratings, we compared the *Fortune* ratings to a rating of corporate social responsibility produced by the Council on Economic Priorities (1987). The council evaluated consumer products firms on charitable contributions, representation of women and minorities on their boards of directors and in executive positions, social disclosure, South Africa involvement, and nuclear and nonnuclear arms productions. Ratings of the 58 firms by both sources were compared by summing the number of "positive" or "socially responsible" evaluations given by the Council of Economic Priorities. The correlation between the two sets of evaluations was .47. Although the correlation is not as strong as would have been hoped, it is of interest. The Council of Economic Priorities ratings covered only consumer products, thus excluding many of the industries surveyed by *Fortune*. Moreover, differing definitions of corporate social responsibility likely influenced the correlation. For example, the council considered holding contracts for arms production to indicate lack of corporate social responsibility and it is unlikely that the *Fortune* evaluators did so.

[4]The mean social responsibility rating for the 1983 survey was 6.01, with a standard deviation of .774. The mean 1982–85 rating was 6.31, with a standard deviation of .688. The means and standard deviations of the other variables are available from the authors.

Financial performance variables were averaged over two periods: 1982–84 and 1977–81. Tables 1 and 2 show correlations among the financial variables for the periods studied. The financial performance variables for 1982–84 are contemporaneous with the 1983–85 social responsibility ratings and subsequent to the 1983 ratings. Thus, by comparing the 1982–84 financial performance ratings to the average *Fortune* rating for 1983–85, we could examine the concurrent relationship between corporate social responsibility and financial performance. Analysis of 1983 ratings in relation to the 1977–81 and 1982–84 financial performance variables permitted us to evaluate the relation between prior financial performance and corporate social responsibility using the 1977–81 measures and to evaluate subsequent financial performance using the 1982–84 data.

RESULTS

Correlational Analysis

Concurrent Performance

Table 3 presents the correlations between contemporaneous evaluations of corporate social performance (1983–85) and accounting- and market-based performance measures (1982–84). Correlations between social responsibility and stock-market-based measures of performance are insignificant (.04 and −.07), suggesting that there is little contemporaneous association. Three of the accounting-based measures of performance, however, are significantly correlated with corporate social responsibility. ROA and total assets show positive relationships (.47 and .20, respectively), and operating income growth has a negative correlation (−.21). The positive association between ROA, an accounting-based measure of contemporaneous performance, and corporate social responsibility supports the view that, through its effects on stakeholders, social responsibility affects financial performance (Cornell & Shapiro, 1987). The negative association with operating income growth might be due to the high social responsibility ratings of several mature firms such as IBM (*Fortune,* 1983, 1986) that may tend to have more stable earnings than other firms. The other accounting measures have little association with corporate social responsibility.

The accounting- and stock-market-based risk measures tend to be negatively associated with social responsibility. Both beta and the standard deviation of total return show negative correlations (−.27 and −.45, respectively). One accounting-based risk measure, the ratio of debt to assets, has a significant negative association with corporate social responsibility. These results are also consistent with the view (Cornell & Shapiro, 1987) that firms with many implicit contracts with stakeholders may have lower debt than other firms.

TABLE 1

Correlations Among 1977–81 Financial Variables[a]

Variables	1	2	3	4	5	6	7	8	9	10	11	12
1. 1983 corporate social responsibility												
2. ROA	.51**											
3. Average assets	.15	−.05										
4. Operating income growth	.04	.16*	−.15									
5. Sales growth	.15	.17*	−.02	.81**								
6. Asset growth	.35**	.22*	.22*	−.15	−.02							
7. Alpha	.17*	−.17*	−.17*	.62**	.49**	.42**						
8. Total return	.08	.23**	−.23**	.66**	.53**	.46**	.96**					
9. Debt to assets	−.49**	−.68**	.20*	.05	.09	.01	.01	.05				
10. Operating leverage	.23**	.25**	.07	.24**	.12	.08	.21*	.17*	.11			
11. Standard deviation of operating income	.16*	.09	.84**	−.20*	.02	.03	−.16*	−.20*	.05	.02		
12. Beta	−.32**	−.12	−.27**	.21*	.27**	.23**	.10	.35**	.15	.09	−.16*	
13. Standard deviation of total return	−.44**	−.29**	−.27**	.18*	.15	−.14	.01	.24**	.28**	−.12	−.18*	.89**

[a] $N = 131$

* $p < .05$

** $p < .01$

TABLE 2
Correlations Among 1982–84 Financial Variables[a]

Variables	1	2	3	4	5	6	7	8	9	10	11	12
1. 1983 corporate social responsibility												
2. ROA	.41**											
3. Average assets	.15	.01										
4. Operating income growth	−.03	.02	.11									
5. Sales growth	.02	.16*	.10	−.68**								
6. Asset growth	.03	.11	.15	.43**	.71**							
7. Alpha	−.07	.29**	.12	.11	.42**	.14						
8. Total return	−.15	.22**	.16*	.51**	.54**	.38**	.93**					
9. Debt to assets	−.44**	−.47**	.32**	.15	.13	.14	.17*	.25**				
10. Operating leverage	−.06	−.03	.16*	−.08	−.08	−.04	−.04	−.06	.11			
11. Standard deviation of operating income	.09	.18*	.74**	.32**	.21*	.12	.22*	.24**	.13	.08		
12. Beta	−.32**	−.27**	.08	.11	.10	.13	−.53**	−.18*	.13	−.05	−.03	
13. Standard deviation of total return	−.44**	−.37**	.14	.09	−.05	−.14	−.45**	−.19*	.32**	.00	.32**	.77**

[a] $N = 131$
* $p < .05$
** $p < .01$

347

TABLE 3
Correlations Between Corporate Social Responsibility
and Firm Performance[a]

Performance Dimensions	1983–85 Social Responsibility and 1982–84 Performance	1983 Social Responsibility and 1977–81 Performance	1983 Social Responsibility and 1982–84 Performance
ROA	.47**	.52**	.41**
Total assets	.20	.15	.15
Operating income growth	−.21	.04	−.03
Sales growth	.04	.15	.02
Asset growth	.03	.35**	.03
Alpha	.04	.17*	−.07
Total return	−.07	.08	−.15
Debt/assets	−.49**	−.49**	−.44**
Operating leverage	−.05	.23**	−.06
Standard deviation of operating income	.11	.15	.09
Beta	−.27*	−.32**	−.32**
Standard deviation of total return	−.45**	−.44**	−.44**

[a] N = 98, 131, and 131 for columns 1, 2, and 3, respectively.
*$p < .05$
**$p < .01$

Pre- and Post-Survey Analysis

Analysis of the concurrently measured relationship between social responsibility and financial performance does not address the question of whether prior high financial performance allows a firm to engage in future socially responsible activities or if significant associations between current social responsibility and performance are artifacts of previous high performance. Table 3 presents results of the correlation analysis between prior firm financial performance and corporate social responsibility. The level of correlation for two measures of market return, total return and alpha, provides little support for the relationship between prior stock-market performance and subsequent social responsibility: the correlations are positive but significant only for alpha. Of the accounting-based performance measures, ROA, sales growth, and asset growth are associated with high perceived social responsibility (.52, .15, and .35), but correlations for the other accounting performance measures are insignificant. Corporate social responsibility is negatively associated with risk as measured by the ratio of debt to assets (−.49), beta (−.32), and the standard deviation of total return (−.44) and positively associated with operating leverage. These results suggest that low-risk firms and firms with a high return on assets will later have an image of high social responsibility.

Table 3 also shows the correlations between corporate social responsibility and performance measured at a later time. ROA is again highly correlated with social responsibility; measures of stock-market performance, however, show little association with it. However, both stock-market and accounting-based risk measures are negatively correlated with previous social responsibility (debt to assets $-.44$, beta, $-.32$; standard deviation of total return, $-.44$).

Regression Analysis

To test the multivariate relationship between corporate social responsibility and firm performance, we also conducted regression analyses. Since measures of financial performance tend to be correlated (McGuire, Schneeweis, & Branch, 1986), care must be taken in interpreting individual regression coefficients. Table 4 presents the results of stepwise regression analyses using perceived corporate social responsibility in 1983 as the independent variable.

Prior stock-market and accounting-based performance measures were used separately to predict social responsibility. Accounting-based performance had a higher explanatory value than stock-market performance ($R^2 = .294$ and .129, respectively.) Accounting risk variables also appeared to produce a better explanatory model than stock-market risk variables ($R^2 = .287$ and .211, respectively). One possible reason for these results is that two market-based measures, total return and beta, are related primarily to systematic movements among all firms. In contrast, accounting measures are more likely to capture unique, or unsystematic, firm attributes. Since actions leading to high or low perceived corporate social responsibility may be predominately unsystematic, accounting performance may better capture social responsibility.

Subsequently measured accounting-based performance appeared to be a better predictor of social responsibility than subsequent stock-market performance ($R^2 = .195$ and .052, respectively). In contrast, subsequent stock-market risk produced a better explanatory model than subsequent accounting risk ($R^2 = .193$ and .287).

A comparison of equations using performance measured before and after 1983 thus suggests that perceptions of social responsibility are more closely associated with prior financial performance than with subsequent financial performance. With only one exception, prior performance and risk were better predictors than were subsequent performance and risk. The results of regression equations in which both market- and accounting-based risk and return are used to explain social responsibility offer further support. In all cases, the equations using prior accounting- and stock-market-based measures of risk and return had a higher predictive value than those using subsequent measures.

DISCUSSION

The correlation and regression results presented in this study suggest several conclusions. First, although performance tended to predict corporate social responsibility better than risk, measures of risk also explained a significant

TABLE 4
Results of Regression Analysis Predicting 1983
Corporate Social Responsibility

Variables	Beta	F	Multiple R	R^2	Adjusted R^2	F
Prior accounting performance						
ROA	.669	44.07	.514	.265		
Average assets	.141	3.55	.543	.269		
Sales growth	.641	3.71	.548	.301		
Operating income growth	−.364	2.92	.563	.317		
Variables as a set					.294	13.73**
Prior market performance						
Alpha	1.121	19.28	.168	.028		
Total return	−.963	16.11	.378	.143		
Variables as a set					.129	10.04**
Prior accounting risk						
Debt/assets	.279	39.18	.493	.242		
Standard deviation of operating income	.357	5.46	.526	.276		
Operating leverage	.398	4.68	.551	.304		
Variables as a set					.287	17.34*
Prior market risk						
Standard deviation of total return	−.235	16.50	.437	.191		
Beta	.537	2.92	.459	.211		
Variables as a set					.211	16.02**
Subsequent accounting performance						
ROA	.590	24.59	.413	.171		
Average assets	.973	3.31	.437	.191		
Sales growth	−.148	0.12	.441	.195		
Operating income growth	−.496	0.63	.442	.195		
Variables as a set					.195	7.16**
Subsequent market performance						
Total return	−.346	5.85	.146	.021		
Alpha	.241	3.80	.227	.052		
Variables as a set					.052	3.26*
Subsequent accounting risk						
Debt/assets	−.253	30.37	.437	.191		
Standard deviation of operating income	.281	3.36	.461	.212		
Operating leverage	.494	0.49	.462	.213		
Variables as a set					.193	16.75**

TABLE 4
(continued)

Variables	Beta	F	Multiple R	R^2	Adjusted R^2	F
Subsequent market risk						
Standard deviation of						
total return	−.211	22.46	.361	.131		
Beta	.572	6.46	.148	.175		
Variables as a set					.287	17.34**
Prior accounting risk/return						
ROA	.317	4.66	.514	.265		
Debt/assets	−.215	11.17	.549	.301		
Average assets	.368	6.96	.594	.353		
Sales growth	.717	3.21	.613	.376		
Operating leverage	.288	2.34	.620	.384		
Operating income growth	−.342	2.26	.626	.392		
Standard deviation of						
operating income	−.419	2.04	.634	.402		
Asset growth	.869	0.71	.635	.403		
Variables as a set					.361	9.61**
Prior market risk/return						
Standard deviation of						
total return	−.217	13.85	.438	.192		
Total return	.117	3.40	.475	.226		
Beta	.347	1.11	.482	.232		
Variables as a set					.233	12.03**
Subsequent accounting risk/return						
Debt/assets	−.259	23.40	.437	.191		
Average assets	.323	16.43	.535	.286		
ROA	.327	6.37	.564	.318		
Standard deviation of						
operating income	−.519	4.88	.585	.342		
Operating income growth	.796	0.17	.588	.346		
Operating leverage	−.583	0.48	.591	.349		
Sales growth	.951	0.57	.591	.349		
Variables as a set					.309	8.82*
Subsequent market risk/return						
Standard deviation of						
return	−.220	25.43	.361	.131		
Alpha	−.125	6.62	.448	.201		
Beta	.380	2.69	.457	.219		
Variables as a set					.199	11.09**

*$p < .05$
**$p < .01$

portion of the variability in social responsibility across firms. We noted earlier that theoretical arguments can be made for a relationship between social responsibility and firm risk. Lack of social responsibility may expose a firm to significant additional risk from lawsuits and fines and may limit its strategic options. Rather than looking for increased profitability from socially responsible actions, managers and those interested in the financial impact of social responsibility might look toward reduced risk. Since high risk must be balanced by high returns, firms with low social responsibility should earn high returns to justify the increased risk. Our data, however, suggest that firms low in social responsibility also experience lower ROA and stock-market returns than do firms high in social responsibility.

Second, accounting-based measures, particularly ROA, proved to be better predictors of corporate social responsibility than market measures. There may be several reasons for this trend. If perceptions of social responsibility are firm-specific (unsystematic), accounting measures of return should be more sensitive to them than stock-market measures, which reflect systematic market trends. Moreover, indexes are subject to managerial manipulation (Branch, 1983: Briloff, 1972, 1976) and tend to be stable over time (McGuire, Schneeweis, & Hill, 1986). Stock-market returns are more variable over time since they primarily respond to unexpected changes in information.

Perhaps most interesting is that prior performance is generally a better predictor of corporate social responsibility than subsequent performance. Thus, associations found between concurrent social responsibility and performance may partially be artifacts of previous high financial performance. Firms with high performance and low risk may be better able to afford to act in a socially responsible manner. Links between responsibility and subsequent financial performance may also be artifacts of prior high performance and the stability of accounting return data. Subsequent studies should attempt to separate the effects of prior, current, and future firm performance on the relationship between financial performance and corporate social responsibility.

CONCLUSIONS

The results of this study suggest several conclusions and avenues for future research. First, rather than examining the relationship between corporate social responsibility and a firm's subsequent financial performance, future research should investigate the influence of prior firm performance. In essence, it may be more fruitful to consider financial performance as a variable influencing social responsibility than the reverse. Previous studies have emphasized management preferences, industry, and organizational characteristics as influencing social responsibility (Arlow & Gannon, 1982; Sturdivant & Ginter, 1977). Second, the results suggest reduction of firm risk as an important benefit of social responsibility, one that previous research focusing on firm profitability and stock-market return has overlooked. Investigation of those two areas would do more to move research on social responsibility into theoretically and empirically fruitful areas than does investigation of concurrent measures (Ullmann, 1985).

This study also suggests that researchers give increased attention to the measure of firm performance used in studies of corporate social responsibility. Davidson, Worrell, and Gilberton (1986) noted that researchers have viewed the choice of performance variables as relatively straightforward compared to the problems of measuring corporate social responsibility. They further suggested that social responsibility may influence various aspects of firm performance in different ways. The inconsistency of results obtained using various financial performance variables supports that suggestion. Thus, this study adds to the growing body of literature indicating that the choice of performance variable can have substantive implications for the results of research and that researchers must carefully choose performance measures that are appropriate to the particular research question they are investigating. The results reported here also support the importance of controlling for risk in studies of social responsibility because adjusting for risk affects performance measures.

Although the *Fortune* data have provided a measure of corporate social responsibility new to the literature, the validity and appropriateness of this measure require further examination. As do other measures of social responsibility, the *Fortune* ratings may reflect the biases of the evaluators, who may not have defined or evaluated corporate social responsibility as other, less financially oriented evaluators might have. In addition, the context and purposes of the *Fortune* evaluation, which differ from those of other evaluations, may have influenced results.

However, major shortcomings in current research in corporate social responsibility have been the difficulty of measuring that concept (Abbott & Monsen, 1979; Ullmann, 1985) and consequent reliance on a limited set of measures. The introduction of a new measure of social responsibility helps reduce the mono-measure bias that has plagued the current body of research.

REFERENCES

Aaker, D., & Jacobson, R. 1987. The role of risk in explaining differences in profitability. *Academy of Management Journal,* 30: 277–296.

Abbott, W. F., & Monsen, R. 1979. On the measurement of corporate social responsibility: Self-reported disclosure as a measure of corporate social involvement. *Academy of Management Journal,* 22: 501–515.

Alexander, G., & Bucholtz, R. 1978. Corporate social responsibility and stock market performance. *Academy of Management Journal,* 21: 479–486.

Anderson, J. C., & Frankel, A. W. 1980. Voluntary social reporting: An isobeta portfolio analysis. *Accounting Review,* 55: 467–479.

Arlow, O., & Gannon, M. 1982. Social responsiveness, corporate structure, and economic performance. *Academy of Management Review,* 7: 235–241.

Aupperle, K., Carroll, A., & Hatfield, J. 1985. An empirical examination of the relationship between corporate social responsibility and profitability. *Academy of Management Journal,* 28: 446–463.

Bowman, E., & Haire, M. 1975. A strategic posture towards CSR. *California Management Review,* 18(2): 49–58.

Bradgon, J. H., & Marlin, J. 1972. Is pollution profitable? *Risk Management,* 19(4): 9–18.

Branch, B. 1983. *Misleading accounting: The danger and the potential.* Working paper, University of Massachusetts, Amherst.

Briloff, R. 1972. *Unaccountable accounting.* New York: Harper & Row.

Briloff, R. 1976. *The truth about corporate accounting.* New York: Harper & Row.

Carroll, A. B. 1979. A three-dimensional conceptual model of corporate social responsibility. *Academy of Management Review,* 4: 497–505.

Chakravarthy, B. 1986. Measuring strategic performance. *Strategic Management Journal,* 7: 437–458.

Cochran, P., & Wood, R. 1984. Corporate social responsibility and financial performance. *Academy of Management Journal,* 27: 42–56.

Cornell, B., & Shapiro, A. 1987. Corporate stakeholders and corporate finance. *Financial Management,* 16: 5–14.

Council on Economic Priorities. 1987. *Rating American's corporate conscience.* Reading, Mass.: Addison-Wesley.

Cyert, R. M., & March, J. G. 1963. *A behavioral theory of the firm.* Englewood Cliffs, N.J.: Prentice-Hall.

Davidson, W. N., Worrell, D. L., & Gilberton, D. 1986. *The appropriateness of using accounting data in studies relating corporate social responsibility to firm financial performance.* Paper presented at the Academy of Management annual meeting, Chicago.

Folger, H., & Nutt, F. 1975. A note on social responsibility and stock valuation. *Academy of Management Journal,* 18: 155–159.

Fortune. 1983. Ranking America's corporations. 107(1): 34–44.

Fortune. 1986. America's most admired corporations. 113(1): 18–27.

Lubatkin, M., & Shrieves, R. 1986. Towards a reconciliation of market performance measures to strategic management research. *Academy of Management Review,* 11: 497–512.

McGuire, J., Schneeweis, T., & Branch, B. 1986. *A comparison of alternative measures of corporate performance.* Unpublished manuscript, University of Massachusetts, Amherst.

McGuire, J., Schneeweis, T., & Branch, B. 1987. *Perceptions of management quality and firm financial performance.* Unpublished manuscript, University of Massachusetts, Amherst.

McGuire, J., Schneeweis, T., & Hill, J. 1986. An analysis of alternative measures of strategic performance. In R. Lamb & P. Stravastava (Eds.), *Advances in strategic management,* vol. 4: 107–153. Greenwich, Conn.: JAI Press.

Michel, A., & Shaked, I. 1984. Does business diversification affect performance? *Financial Management,* 12(2): 18–25.

Moskowitz, M. 1972. Choosing socially responsible stocks. *Business and Society,* 1: 71–75.

Moskowitz, M. 1975. Profiles in corporate social responsibility. *Business and Society,* 13: 29–42.

Moussavi, F., & Evans, D. 1986. *An attributional approach to measuring corporate social performance.* Paper presented at the Academy of Management meetings, San Diego.

Parket, R., & Eibert, H. 1975. Social responsibility: The underlying factors. *Business Horizons*, 18: 5–10.

Pfeffer, J., & Salancik, G. 1978. *The external control of organizations*. New York: Harper & Row.

Preston, L. E. 1978. Analyzing corporate social performance: Methods and results. *Journal of Contemporary Business*, 7: 135–149.

Quinn, J., Mintzberg, H., & James, R. 1987. *The strategy process*. Englewood Cliffs, N.J.: Prentice-Hall.

Solomon, R., & Hansen, K. 1985. *It's good business*. New York: Atheneum.

Spicer, B. H. 1978. Investors, corporate social performance, and information disclosure. An empirical study. *Accounting Review*, 53: 94–111.

Sturdivant, F. D., & Ginter, J. L. 1977. Corporate social responsiveness. *California Management Review*, 19(3): 30–39.

Ullmann, A. 1985. Data in search of a theory: A critical examination of the relationships among social performance, social disclosure, and economic performance. *Academy of Management Review*, 10: 540–577.

Vance, S. 1975. Are socially responsible firms good investment risks? *Management Review*, 64: 18–24.

Wartick, S. 1987. *The contribution of issues management to corporate performance*. Paper presented at the Academy of Management meetings, New Orleans.

Appendix

Alpha (α) was defined as return in excess of that due to general market movements, derived from the following market model:

$$R_i = \hat{\alpha}_i + \hat{b}_i R_{mt},$$

where

R_{it} = return on firm i in period t,

R_{mt} = return on index M (Standard and Poor's 500 Industrials) in period t,

$\hat{\alpha} = R - \hat{b}\overline{R}_m$, and

$$\hat{b} = \frac{\text{Cov}(R_i, R_m)}{\text{Var}(R_m)}.$$

Assets growth was the percent change in total assets (change in total assets/total assets). **Average assets** were beginning assets less ending assets divided by 2. **Beta** (β) was the covariance of a firm's stock-market return relative to the return of the stock market, standardized by stock-market return variance derived from the market model equation. Systematic, nondiversifiable risk. **Ratio of debt to assets** was total debt divided by total assets. **Operating income growth** was the percent change in operating income. Operating income is net sales less cost of goods sold and operating expenses before deducting depreciation, amortization, and depletion. **Operating leverage** was the extent to which fixed costs were used in a firm's operation. We used break-even analysis to measure the extent to which operating leverage was employed. Operating leverage = (sales − variable costs)/(sales − variable costs − fixed costs). **Return on assets** (ROA) is a measure of operating performance of how well assets have been employed since being received by a firm. Measured as (net income + interest expense)/average total assets. **Sales growth** was the percent change in gross sales and other operating revenue less discounts, returns, and allowances (change in sales/sales). ***Standard deviation in operating income growth,*** a measure of the variability in operating income growth (*OIG*), was defined as

$$\sum_{i=1}^{n} (OIG - \overline{OIG})^2/n,$$

where n = number of years.

Standard deviation in total return (SDTR), a measure of the variability in stock-market return, was defined as

$$\sum_{i=1}^{n} (TR - \overline{TR})^2/n,$$

Total return was the percent change in stock-market valuation in year *t*, measured as $[(\text{price}_t + \text{dividend}_t) - \text{price}_{t-}]/\text{price}_{t-1}$.

Jean McGuire is an associate professor of management at Concordia University, Montreal, Canada. She received her Ph.D. degree form Cornell University. Her research interests include organizational conflict and power, and strategy implementation.

Alison Sundgren is a student at the University of Massachusetts. She received her B.A. degree from Smith College.

Thomas Schneeweis is a professor of finance at the University of Massachusetts, Amherst. He received his Ph.D. degree from the University of Iowa. His research interests include financial futures and performance measurement.

Practice Self-Test

The Problem

_____

_____

_____

The Procedures

_____

_____

_____

The Method of Analysis

_____

_____

_____

The Major Conclusion(s)

_____

_____

_____

Reasons for Classification as Correlational Research

_____

_____

_____

Method-Specific Evaluation Criteria

Select the appropriate methodology (Relationship Studies or Prediction Studies) that follows and use the article to answer the questions that apply to the methodology.

Relationship Studies

1. Were variables carefully selected or was a shotgun approach used?
2. Is the rationale for variable selection described?
3. Are conclusions and recommendations based on values of correlation coefficients corrected for attenuation or restriction in range?
4. Do the conclusions indicate causal relationships between the variables investigated?

Prediction Studies

1. Is a rationale given for selection of predictor variables?
2. Is the criterion variable well defined?
3. Was the resulting prediction equation validated with at least one other group?

REFERENCES

GLASS, G. V., & STANLEY, J. C. (1984). *Statistical methods in education and psychology* (2nd ed.). Englewood Cliffs, NJ: Prentice-Hall.

GOODSON, J. R., McGEE, G. W., & CASHMAN, J. F. (1988). Situational leadership theory. *Group & Organizational Studies, 14*(4), 446–461.

McGUIRE, J. B., SUNDGREN, A., & SCHNEEWEIS, T. (1988). Corporate social responsibility and firm financial performance. *Academy of Management Journal, 31*(4), 854–872.

NUNNALLY, J. C. (1978). *Psychometric theory* (2nd ed.). New York: McGraw-Hill.

SCHULER, R. W. (1984, 1987). *Personnel and human resource management* (2nd & 3rd eds.). St. Paul, MN: West.

STEWART, T. A. (1990, January 1). The trouble with stock options. *Fortune.* pp. 93–95.

*The problem becomes even more serious when the researcher attempts
to match simultaneously on two or more variables. (page 364)*

9

The Causal-Comparative Method

Objectives

After reading Chapter 9, you should be able to do the following:

1. Briefly state the purpose of causal-comparative research.

2. State the major differences between causal-comparative and correlational research.

3. State one major way in which causal-comparative and experimental research are the same and one major way in which they are different.

4. Diagram and describe the basic causal-comparative design.

5. Identify and describe three types of control procedures that can be used in a causal-comparative study.

6. Explain why the results of causal-comparative studies must be interpreted very cautiously.

DEFINITION AND PURPOSE

Like correlational research, causal-comparative research is sometimes treated as a type of descriptive research, since it too describes conditions that already exist. Causal-comparative research, however, also attempts to determine reasons, or causes, for the current status of the phenomenon under study. The causal-comparative method entails procedures distinctly different from those involved in self-report or observational research and qualifies as a separate method of research.

Causal-comparative, or ex post facto, research is that research in which the researcher attempts to determine the cause, or reason, for existing differences in the behavior or status of groups of individuals. In other words, it is observed that groups are different on some variable, and the researcher attempts to identify the major factor that has led to this difference. Such research is referred to as ex post facto (Latin for "after the fact") since both the effect and the alleged cause have already occurred and are studied by the researcher in retrospect. For example, as a possible explanation of apparent differences in career success of female MBAs, a researcher might hypothesize that participation in team sports between ages 7 and 21 was the major contributing factor. The researcher would then select a group of female MBAs who had participated in team sports and a group who had not and would compare the career success of the two groups. If the group that participated in team sports exhibited a higher level of career success than those who didn't participate, the researcher's hypothesis would be supported.

The basic causal-comparative approach, therefore, involves starting with an effect and seeking possible causes. A variation of the basic approach involves starting with a cause and investigating its effect on some variable. Such research is concerned with what-is-the-effect-of-X questions. For example, a researcher might wish to investigate what long-range effect previous work experience has on the academic success of graduate management students. The researcher might hypothesize that students who have previous supervisory experience are more successful at the end of graduate school than those who do not. At the time of graduation, the researcher would identify a group of graduate management students who had previous supervisory experience and a group of graduate management students who did not. The overall GPAs of the two groups would be compared. If the group with previous supervisory experience exhibited higher GPAs, the researcher's hypothesis would be supported.

Beginning researchers often confuse causal-comparative research with both correlational research and experimental research. Correlational and causal-comparative research are probably confused because of the lack of manipulation common to both and the similar cautions regarding interpretations of results. There are definite differences, however. Causal-comparative studies *attempt* to identify cause-effect relationships, and correlational studies do not. Causal-comparative studies typically involve two (or more) groups and one independent variable, whereas correlational studies typically involve two (or more) variables and one group. Also, causal-comparative studies involve comparison, whereas correlational studies involve correlation.

It is understandable that causal-comparative research and experimental research are at first difficult to distinguish; both attempt to establish cause-effect relationships and both involve group comparisons. In an experimental study, however, the researcher creates the "cause," deliberately makes the groups different, and then observes what effect that difference has on some dependent variable. In contrast, in a causal-comparative study the researcher first observes an effect and then tries to determine the cause; in other words, the researcher attempts to determine what difference between the groups has led to the observed difference on some dependent variable. To put it as simply as possible, the major difference between them is that in experimental research the independent variable, the alleged cause, is manipulated; in causal-comparative research it is not because it has already occurred. In experimental research, the researcher can randomly form groups and manipulate a variable. In other words, the researcher can determine "who" is going to get "what," with "what" being the independent variable. In causal-comparative research, the groups are already formed and already different on the independent variable. Causal-comparative groups are already different in that one group may have had an experience that the other did not have, or one group may possess a characteristic that the other group does not. In any event, the difference between the groups (the independent variable) was not brought about by the researcher. In the article reprinted at the end of this chapter, for example, the independent variables that are investigated include union membership and gender; obviously the researcher did not manipulate or control either of these variables.

Independent variables in causal-comparative studies are variables that cannot be manipulated (such as socioeconomic status), should not be manipulated (such as number of cigarettes smoked per day), or simply are not manipulated but could be (such as method of orienting new employees). There are a number of important business problems for which it is impossible or impractical to manipulate the independent variable. Ethical considerations often prevent manipulation of a variable that could be manipulated but should not be, such as number of cigarettes smoked. If the nature of the independent variable is such that it may cause physical or mental harm to subjects, it should not be manipulated. For example, if a researcher were interested in determining the effect of exposure to radiation in the workplace on the future health of employees, it would obviously not be ethical to expose workers to this risk for the sake of science. Thus, causal-comparative research permits investigation of a number of variables that cannot be studied experimentally. You will recall other examples of ethical considerations that were discussed in Chapter 3.

Causal-comparative studies also identify relationships that may lead to experimental studies. As mentioned previously, experimental studies are costly in more ways than one and should be conducted only when there is good reason to believe the effort will be fruitful. Like correlational studies, causal-comparative studies help to identify variables worthy of experimental investigation. In fact, causal-comparative studies are sometimes conducted solely for the purpose of determining the probable outcome of an experimental study. Suppose, for example, a factory manager is unable to find workers with sufficient basic skills (math, reading, writing) to employ in the factory. In reviewing the options for developing basic skills, the manager is considering the implementation of microcomputer-assisted, remedial, basic-skills instruction in his or her factory. The manager might consider trying it out on an experimental basis for a year in one plant before initiating total implementation. Even such limited adoption, however, would be costly in terms of equipment and training. Thus, as a preliminary measure, to facilitate his or her decision, the manager might have a causal-comparative study conducted comparing the effect of microcomputer-assisted, remedial, basic-skills training in factories similar to his or her own factory with the effect of some other type of remedial, basic-skills training in his or her own or another factory. Through a government grant or industry effort focused on literacy, it is possible that such information could be obtained. If no differences were found in the causal-comparative study, the manager would probably not go ahead with the experimental tryout and would thus not unnecessarily waste time, money, and effort.

Despite its many advantages, the causal-comparative method has some serious limitations, which must also be kept in mind. Since the independent variable has already occurred, the same kinds of controls cannot be exercised as in an experimental study. Extreme caution must be applied in interpreting results. An apparent cause-effect relationship may not be as it appears. As with a correlational study, only a relationship is established, not necessarily a causal one. The alleged cause of an observed effect may in fact be the effect, or there may be a third variable that has "caused" both the identified cause and effect. The study at the end of this chapter, for example, suggests that perceived job autonomy is lower in a unionized environment than in a nonunion environment. It might also be true that the low perception of job autonomy is what "caused" unionization to take place, or, as the authors of that study point out, additional factors such as time of unionization, gender, and job complexity may be important factors in perceptions of autonomy. If a measure of perceptions of autonomy had been taken before and after unionization, the results might have been the reverse of those obtained in this study. Thus, cause-effect relationships established through causal-comparative research are at best tenuous and tentative. Only experimental research, which guarantees that the alleged cause, or independent variable, came before the observed effect, or dependent variable, can truly establish cause-effect relationships. As discussed previously, however, causal-comparative studies have their place; they permit investigation of variables that cannot or should not be investigated experimentally, facilitate decision making, provide guidance for experimental studies, and are less costly on all dimensions. For many business purposes, therefore, the causal-comparative study will serve very nicely, and a practitioner skilled in this methodology can be quite productive in an "action research" environment.

CONDUCTING A CAUSAL-COMPARATIVE STUDY

The basic causal-comparative design is quite simple, and although the independent variable is not manipulated, there are control procedures that can be exercised. Causal-comparative studies also involve a wider variety of statistical techniques than the other methods of research thus far discussed.

Design and Procedure

The basic causal-comparative design involves selecting two groups differing on some independent variable and comparing them on some dependent variable. As Figure 9.1 indicates, the researcher selects two groups of subjects, loosely referred to as experimental and control groups, although it is probably more accurate to refer to them as comparison groups. The groups may differ in that one group possesses a characteristic that the other does not or has had an experience that the other has not (Case A). Or the groups may differ in degree; one group may have had different kinds of experiences (Case B). The example of Case A from our study would be two groups, one group holding jobs covered by collective bargaining agreements and thus considered unionized and one group considered nonunionized. An example of Case B would be two groups, one group that was newly unionized (less than 1 year) and a second group that had been unionized more than 15 years. In both cases, the groups are compared on some independent variable. The researcher may administer a test of the dependent variable (any of the types of instruments thus far discussed) or collect already available data, as was done with the study at the end of the chapter.

Case A

Group	Independent Variable	Dependent Variable
Experimental	X	0
Control	( )	0

OR

Case B

Group	Independent Variable	Dependent Variable
Experimental	X_1	0
Control	X_2	0

X = independent variable
( ) indicates no manipulation
0 = dependent variable

Figure 9.1. The basic causal-comparative design.

Definition and selection of the comparison groups is a very important part of the causal-comparative procedure. The characteristic or experience differentiating the groups must be clearly and operationally defined, as each group will represent a different population. The way in which the groups are defined will affect the generalizability of the results. If a researcher decided to compare a group of employees who are considered to be "emotionally disabled" with a group of employees classified as "emotionally able," the terms *emotionally disabled* and *emotionally able* would have to be operationally defined. Although "emotional disability" could refer to any number of things, in one study of this type, it was described as "hospitalized over the past two months due to a disabling mental illness . . . severe depression with suicidal tendencies, which are currently controlled by medication and weekly therapy" (Czajka & DeNisi, 1988, p. 397). If samples are to be selected from the defined population, random selection is generally the preferred method of selection. The important consideration is to select samples that are representative of their respective populations and similar with respect to critical variables other than the independent variable. You may want to refer to the "Sample" section of the study at the end of this chapter to see how this might be done. As with experimental studies, the goal is to have groups that are as similar as possible on all relevant variables except the independent variable. In order to determine the equality of groups, information on a number of background and current status variables may be collected. In order to promote equality, or to correct for identified inequalities, there are a number of control procedures available to the researcher.

Control Procedures

Lack of randomization, manipulation, and control are all sources of weakness in a causal-comparative design. Randomization of subjects to groups, for example, is probably the best single way to try to insure equality of groups. This is not possible in causal-comparative studies since the groups already exist and, furthermore, have already received the "treatment," or independent variable. A problem already discussed is the possibility that the groups are different on some other major variable besides the identified independent variable, and it is this other variable that is the real cause of the observed difference between the groups. For example, if a researcher simply compared a group of MBAs who had previous supervisory experience with a group that had not, she or he might conclude that previous supervisory experience significantly improved overall GPAs of the graduates. What if, however, all the students with previous supervisory experience were also involved in a tuition-reimbursement program at work that paid 100% for As, 50% for Bs, and nothing for lower grades. It might very well be that the researcher was inadvertently measuring something very different, such as an interest in getting one's tuition paid, instead of simply previous supervisory experience. If, however, the researcher was aware of the situation, she or he could control for this variable by only studying students using this type of tuition-reimbursement program. Thus, the two groups to be controlled, one of which had previous supervisory experience, would be equated with respect to their financially based motivation, which is basically an extraneous variable. The above example is but one illustration of a number of statistical and nonstatistical methods that can be applied in an attempt to control for extraneous variables. Although we will discuss several of these methods here, they will be discussed in more detail in regard to their use in experimental research.

Matching

Matching is a control technique that is sometimes used in experimental studies. You may remember that the research study at the end of Chapter 1 regarding quality circles used a matching technique. If a researcher has identified a variable believed to be related to performance on the dependent variable, as the quality circles researcher did, she or he may control for that variable by pair-wise matching of subjects. In other words, for each subject in one group, the researcher finds a subject in the second group with the same or a similar score on the control variable. If a subject in either group does not have a suitable match, the subject is eliminated from the study. You may recall that this was done in the quality circle study. Thus, the resulting matched groups are identical or very similar with respect to the identified extraneous variable or variables. As you may have deduced, a major problem with pair-wise matching is that there are invariably subjects who have no match and must therefore be eliminated from the study. The problem becomes even more serious when the researcher attempts to match simultaneously on two or more variables.

Comparing Homogeneous Groups or Subgroups

Another way of controlling an extraneous variable, which is also used in experimental research, is to compare groups that are homogeneous with respect to that variable. For example, if gender were an identified extraneous variable, the researcher might limit groups to contain only subjects who were male; this has been done in many of the older research studies in business. Of course, this procedure not only lowers the numbers of subjects in the study, but it additionally restricts the generalizability of the findings. If females have been excluded from the study for some reason, this seriously hampers the importance of the research in today's business environment.

A similar but more satisfactory approach is to form subgroups within each group that represent all levels of the control variable. For example, each group might be divided into male and female subgroups. The comparable subgroups in each group can be compared, as was done in the unionization study. In addition to controlling for the variable, this technique has the added advantage of permitting the researcher to see if the independent variable affects the dependent variable differently at different levels of the control variable. If this question is of interest, the best approach is not to do several separate analyses but to build the control variable right into the design and analyze the results with a statistical technique called factorial analysis of variance. *Factorial analysis of variance* allows the researcher to determine the effect of the independent variable and the control variable, both separately and in combination. In other words, it permits the researcher to determine if there is an interaction between the independent variable and the control variable such that the independent variable operates differently at different levels of the control variable. As was found in the study at the end of the chapter, males and females reacted very differently to perceptions of job autonomy.

Analysis of Covariance

The *analysis of covariance,* which is also used in experimental studies, is a statistical method that can be used to equate groups on one or more variables. In essence, analysis of covariance adjusts scores on a dependent variable for initial differences on some other variable (assuming that performance on the other variable is related to performance on the dependent variable, which is what control is all about anyway). For example, in a study on the effectiveness of two methods of training employees to input data using a computer, one could "covary" on typing speed, thus equating scores on data-input speed. Analysis of covariance entails application of a nasty little formula, but fortunately there are computer programs readily available that can do the calculations for you. The methods of analysis we are discussing—analysis of variance (see next page), factorial analysis of variance, and analysis of covariance—will be discussed further in Part IV.

Data Analysis and Interpretation

Analysis of data in causal-comparative studies involves a variety of descriptive and inferential statistics. All the statistics that may be used in a causal-comparative study may also be used in an experimental study; a number of them will be described in Part IV. Briefly, however, the most commonly used descriptive statistics are the *mean,* which indicates the average performance of a group on a measure of some variable, and the *standard deviation,* which indicates how spread out a set of scores is. If scores are relatively close together and clustered around the mean, the standard deviation will be small; if they are widely scattered covering a wide range of scores, the standard deviation will be larger. The most commonly used inferential statistics are the following:

1. The *t* test is used to see if there is a significant difference between the means of two groups.
2. Analysis of variance (ANOVA) is used to see if there is a significant difference among the means of two or more groups.
3. The chi square test (χ^2), is used to compare group frequencies to see if an event occurs more frequently in one group than another.

As is repeatedly pointed out, interpretation of the findings in a causal-comparative study requires considerable caution. Owing to lack of randomization, manipulation, and other types of control characteristic of experimental studies, it is difficult to establish cause-effect relationships with any great degree of confidence. The cause-effect relationship may in fact be the reverse of the one hypothesized (the alleged cause may be the effect and vice versa), or there may be a third factor, which is the "real" cause of both the alleged cause (independent variable) and effect (dependent variable). In some cases, reversed causality is not a reasonable alternative and need not be considered. For example, good typing skills may "cause" faster learning in computer data input, but speed in learning computer data input will not "cause" good typing skills. Similarly, one's sex may affect one's achievement in statistical analysis, but one's achievement in statistical analysis certainly does not affect one's sex! In other cases, however, reversed causality is more plausible and should be investigated. For example, it is equally plausible that motivation affects salary increases and that salary increases affect motivation. It is also equally plausible that excessive absenteeism causes, or leads to, involvement in substance abuse as well as that involvement in substance abuse causes, or leads to, excessive absenteeism. The way to determine the correct order of causality, which variable caused which, is to determine which one occurred first. If, in the above example, it could be demonstrated that a period of excessive absenteeism was frequently followed by an employee's being arrested for substance abuse, then it could more reasonably be concluded that excessive absenteeism leads to involvement in substance abuse. If, however, it were determined that prior to the employee's first involvement in substance abuse his or her attendance was good but following it, poor, then the hypothesis that involvement in substance abuse leads to excessive absenteeism would be more reasonable. Of course, we wouldn't draw such a conclusion based on our observation of one employee!

The possibility of a third, common cause is plausible in many situations. Suppose, for example, that math anxiety may affect both motivation and achievement in learning statistics. One way to control for a potential common cause is to equate groups on the suspected variable. In the above example, students in both a high-motivation group and a low-motivation group could be selected from among subjects with similar levels of math anxiety. It is clear that in order to investigate or control for alternative hypotheses, the researcher must be aware of them when they are plausible and must present evidence that they are not in fact the true explanation for the behavioral differences being investigated.

Summary/Chapter 9

DEFINITION AND PURPOSE

1. Causal-comparative, or ex post facto, research is that research in which the researcher attempts to determine the cause, or reason, for existing differences in the behavior or status of groups of individuals.

2. The basic causal-comparative approach involves starting with an effect and seeking possible causes.

3. A variation of the basic approach involves starting with a cause and investigating its effect on some variable.

4. Causal-comparative studies *attempt* to identify cause-effect relationships; correlational studies do not.

5. The major difference between experimental research and causal-comparative research is that in experimental research the independent variable, the alleged cause, is manipulated, and in causal-comparative research it is not because it has already occurred.

6. In experimental research the researcher can randomly form groups and manipulate a variable—can determine "who" is going to get "what," with "what" being the independent variable; in causal-comparative research the groups are already formed and already different on the independent variable.

7. Causal-comparative groups are already different in that one group may have had an experience that the other did not have, or one group may possess a characteristic that the other group does not; in any event, the difference between the groups (the independent variable) was not determined by the researcher.

8. Independent variables in causal-comparative studies are variables that cannot be manipulated (such as socioeconomic status), should not be manipulated (such as number of cigarettes smoked per day), or simply are not manipulated but could be (such as method of orienting new employees).

9. Causal-comparative studies identify relationships that may lead to experimental studies.

10. As with a correlational study, only a relationship is established, not necessarily a causal one.

11. The alleged cause of an observed effect may in fact be the effect, or there may be a third variable that has "caused" both the identified cause and the effect.

12. Cause-effect relationships established through causal-comparative research are at best tenuous and tentative.

13. Only experimental research, which guarantees that the alleged cause, or independent variable, came before the observed effect, or dependent variable, can truly establish cause-effect relationships.

CONDUCTING A CAUSAL-COMPARATIVE STUDY

Design and Procedure

14. The basic causal-comparative design involves selecting two groups differing on some independent variable and comparing them on some dependent variable.

15. The groups may differ in that one group possesses a characteristic that the other does not, *or* the groups may differ in degree; one group may possess more of a characteristic than the other or the two groups may have had different kinds of experiences.

16. The important consideration is to select samples that are representative of their respective populations and similar with respect to critical variables other than the independent variable.

17. In order to determine the equality of groups, information on a number of background and current status variables may be collected.

Control Procedures

18. Lack of randomization, manipulation, and control are all sources of weakness in a causal-comparative design.

19. A problem in control is the possibility that the groups are different on some other major variable besides the identified independent variable, and it is this other variable that is the real cause of the observed difference between the groups.

Matching

20. For each subject in one group the researcher finds a subject in the second group with the same or a similar score on the control variable.

21. A major problem with pair-wise matching is that there are invariably subjects who have no match and must therefore be eliminated from the study.

Comparing Homogeneous Groups or Subgroups

22. Another way of controlling an extraneous variable, which is also used in experimental research, is to compare groups that are as homogeneous as possible.

23. A similar but more satisfactory approach is to form subgroups within each group that represent all levels of the control variable. In addition to controlling for the variable, this technique has the added advantage of permitting the researcher to see if the independent variable affects the dependent variable differently at different levels of the control variable. If this question is of interest, the best approach is not to do several separate analyses but to build the control variable right into the design and analyze the results with a statistical technique called factorial analysis of variance.

Analysis of Covariance

24. The *analysis of covariance,* which is also used in experimental studies, is a statistical method that can be used to equate groups on one or more variables.

25. In essence, analysis of covariance adjusts scores on a dependent variable for initial differences on some other variable (assuming that performance on the other variable is related to performance on the dependent variable, which is what control is all about anyway).

Data Analysis and Interpretation

26. Analysis of data in causal-comparative studies involves a variety of descriptive and inferential statistics.

27. The most commonly used descriptive statistics are the *mean*, which indicates the average performance of the group on a measure of some variable, and the *standard deviation*, which indicates how spread out a set of scores is; standard deviation indicates whether the scores are relatively close together and clustered around the mean or spread out covering a wide range of scores.

28. The most commonly used inferential statistics are the *t* test, which is used to see if there is a significant difference between the means of two groups; analysis of variance, which is used to see if there is a significant difference among the means of three or more groups; and the chi square test, which is used to compare group frequencies. The chi square test is used to see if an event occurs more frequently in one group than another.

29. As repeatedly pointed out, interpretation of the findings in a causal-comparative study requires considerable caution.

30. The alleged cause-effect relationship may in fact be the reverse of the one hypothesized (the alleged cause may be the effect and vice versa).

31. There may be a third factor, which is the real "cause" of both the alleged cause (independent variable) and the effect (dependent variable).

32. The way to determine the correct order of causality, which variable caused which, is to determine which one occurred first.

33. One way to control for a potential common cause is to equate groups on the suspected variable.

On the following pages is an example of causal-comparative research (Project III Reading 4). The article may be used as a study aid to assist you in more fully understanding the nature of causal-comparative research. Following the article, a practice self-test for reviewing the article is provided for you so that you can practice your review skills. Appendix C contains Suggested Responses so that you can check your responses from the self-test. Questions are also provided to allow you to evaluate the article from the standpoint of causal-comparative research.

Perceived Job Autonomy in the Manufacturing Sector: Effects of Unions, Gender, and Substantive Complexity

Sandra L. Kirmeyer
University of Missouri

Arie Shirom
Tel-Aviv University

This study examined the relationship of unionization to employees' perceptions of the amount of freedom they have in deciding what to do on their jobs and how to do it. There are several reasons for believing that job autonomy, both perceived and actual discretion in making decisions, is lower for employees who work under union contracts than for those who do not. Both management practices and union priorities may be accountable. We did not assume—as has much previous research and theory—that the influence of unions is uniform for all employees. In particular, we hypothesized that the relationship between unionization and perceived job autonomy is stronger for men than for women.

Managerial policies and practices may diminish the perceived job autonomy of employees in unions, because management may resort to formalization of policies and practices (Kochan, 1980) to ensure uniform treatment of rank-and-file employees across jobs, often a key issue in collective bargaining. This results in narrower and more uniformly applied job descriptions (Slichter, Healy, & Livernash, 1960) and centrally coordinated work rules and disciplinary regulations (Dimick, 1978). Additionally, as Verma and Kochan (1985) noted, since the 1970s, some nonunion plants have adopted sophisticated strategies for human resource management that emphasize employees' involvement in decision making and broad-banded job classification as a means of avoiding unionization. Thus, we expect employees to experience lower job autonomy in unionized firms than in nonunionized firms either as a direct result of management decisions in the first, or as an indirect result of such decisions in the second.

Another reason to expect lower actual and perceived job autonomy among unionized employees is that union officials have traditionally emphasized bread-and-butter issues like wages, benefits, and employment security, and have regarded issues having to do with job enrichment, such as increases in discretion, task variety, feedback, as ranking at the bottom of their priorities (Holley, Field, & Crowley, 1981). Thus, union officials may not be predisposed to resist managerial adjustments that constrain employees' job autonomy.

We thank G. Hausfater and the anonymous reviewers for their helpful comments and suggestions on an earlier draft of this manuscript.

©*Academy of Management Journal* 1986, Vol. 29, No. 4, 832–840.

With regard to gender differences, previous research suggests several ways in which women may benefit less from union membership than do men: (1) the wage premium paid for union labor is substantially less for women than men, even when occupations, industries, and personal qualifications are comparable (Antos, Chandler, & Mellow, 1980);[1] (2) unions have been slow to address issues that particularly affect women, such as equal pay and the need for childcare (Dewey, 1971; Sutton, 1980); and (3) women have failed to achieve leadership positions in unions in proportion to their numbers (Dewey; Sutton). Further, women continue to be overrepresented at the low end of the job spectrum in positions having little decision making power or autonomy (Brown, 1975; Heilman, 1983). For women, unionization may therefore reduce job discretion in positions that involve very little discretion to begin with. Thus, we expected men to have greater perceived job autonomy than women even under union contracts and we expected that the difference in perceived autonomy that union status would account for to be smaller for women than men. In these ways we expected gender and union status to interact in determining perceived job autonomy.

For both women and men, unionization is only one of many factors related to job autonomy, which should in general be closely tied to the objective structure of employees' jobs. One facet of structure that has been shown to influence job autonomy is substantive complexity (Rousseau, 1982), or the degree to which "the work, in its very substance, requires initiative, thought, and independent judgment" (Kohn & Schooler, 1983: 22). Since union jobs may differ systematically from nonunion jobs in complexity, we controlled for substantive complexity before examining effects of unionization. Following the above rationale, we hypothesized that at any given level of substantive complexity, employees in union jobs have less perceived autonomy than their nonunion counterparts.

The present investigation differed from previous studies of unions' effects on job content in several important ways. We focused exclusively on job autonomy, rather than relying on a composite measure of job scope that combines a variety of dimensions along which jobs can vary (cf. Berger, Olson, & Boudreau 1983; Kochan & Helfman, 1981). Job autonomy is of particular interest because of its effects on employees' mental health. For instance, Karasek (1979) found that freedom in making decisions on the job was associated with relatively fewer symptoms of exhaustion, anxiety, and depression, even when job demands were heavy. In addition, we analyzed data collected for a homogeneous sample of employees in manufacturing industries, thereby eliminating variability in levels of union representation and bargaining strength due to differences in economic sectors.

---

[1]It is important to note, however, that the union wage premium paid to women is substantial, even though it does not equal that paid to men. Moreover, the recent national attention that the issue of pay equity has received is largely due to the efforts of unions, especially the American Federation of State, County, and Municipal Employees.

METHODS

Sample

Drawing from the 1977 Quality of Employment Survey (Quinn & Staines, 1979), a national, cross-sectional probability sample of 1,515 adults working 20 hours or more per week that represents all employed adults, occupations, and industries, we selected 290 employees. We restricted our selection to nonsupervisory personnel who worked 30 to 70 hours per week in manufacturing. The employing industries produced a broad range of durable and nondurable goods; the largest proportions were producers of transportation equipment, machinery, metals, and apparel. We restricted the sample thus because supervisors lay outside of the potential domain of collective bargaining, and their jobs may differ systematically from nonsupervisory positions in autonomy and substantive complexity. Using only data from employees in manufacturing reduced heterogeneity and assured adequate numbers of union members. The proportion of union membership in the manufacturing sector is large relative to the total labor force; it was 37 percent in 1978 (U.S. Department of Labor, 1980). Slightly less than one-half of the employees in our sample (n = 140) held jobs covered by collective bargaining agreements and were thus considered to be unionized.

Measures

Indices, constructed from items from existing surveys (Quinn & Staines, 1979), measured job autonomy as well as several control variables. Control variables included factors known to precede unionization (Block & Premack, 1983; Fiorito & Greer, 1982), including employees' levels of educational attainment, sizes of firms, and such direct outcomes of collective bargaining as wages.

Demographic information was available on gender, race, age, marital status, years of school completed, geographic location of residence, and size of city of residence for all employees. Information on conditions of employment included firms' sizes and employees' organizational tenure. The measure of actual income was derived from employees' reports of their hourly wages or salaries. The distribution of hourly wages deviated substantially from normality, and so we used a logarithmic transformation to reduce distributional skewness and kurtosis.

Employees' occupational titles taken from the *Dictionary of Occupational Titles* (DOT) (U.S. Employment Service, 1977) were used to derive scores for substantive job complexity. For each title,[2] the score was the sum of three 3-digit

---

[2]The 1977 Quality of Employment Survey used a shorter list of job titles than did the DOT; for example, the DOT differentiated four kinds of tailors, whereas the Quality of Employment Survey grouped all tailors into a single category. For manufacturing jobs, the error introduced by the use of broader job categories appears to have been small, since the 3-digit complexity codes assigned to titles within the broader job categories were usually identical.

codes for complexity of work with people (clients or co-workers), data (information or ideas), and things (equipment). The scale of complexity of dealing with things, for example, rose from handling equipment, through driving or operating equipment, to precision work or setting up equipment. We assigned scores for substantive complexity independently of employees' responses on the survey and based them solely on job title. Fine (1968) developed this scheme for scoring occupational complexity, which has been used extensively for occupational description and classification (Miller, Treiman, Cain, & Roos, 1980). Kohn and Schooler (1983) provided evidence of convergent validity; they found that the DOT appraisals for occupations as a whole were highly correlated (multiple $R = .78$) with ratings of the complexity of work with people, data, and things based on interviews with individual employees.

The scale that measured perceived job autonomy, taken from Quinn and Staines (1979), used a 4-point format with 1 for strongly disagree and 4 for strongly agree. It asked respondents to indicate the extent to which they agreed that as employees, they (1) had freedom to decide what to do, and (2) how to do their own work, (3) had responsibility for deciding how the job got done, (4) had a lot to say about what happened on the job, and (5) had latitude to decide when to take breaks, (6) with whom they worked, and (7) the speed at which they worked. Scores were based on the average of all items in the scale. The average interitem correlation was .37 ($\alpha = .80$).

RESULTS

Consistent with previous research (Block & Premack, 1983; Fiorito & Greer, 1982), employees who worked under union contract differed significantly ($p < .05$) from those who did not, both in their personal backgrounds and employment characteristics. Unionized employees were more likely to be male, nonwhite, and employed in large industrial firms outside of the South. They had less education, had been with their present employers longer, and received higher wages than their nonunion counterparts. Union and nonunion employees did not differ in age or marital status, nor did their cities of residence differ as to size of population.

Given the many significant differences between union and nonunion employees, we sought to determine which of them overlapped and which were most strongly related to union status. For this purpose, we used discriminant function analysis, identifying five variables—race, education, geographic region, firm's size, and wages—that contributed significantly to the optimal discrimination of union and nonunion employees (Wilks' $\lambda = .77$, $\chi^2_5 = 73.2$, $p < .001$). In subsequent regression analyses, these five variables served as controls.

To examine the contributions to perceived job autonomy of unionization and substantive complexity, we used hierarchical regression analysis, with control variables entered first. Next, we entered employee's gender, then substantive complexity, and lastly, union status. The regression equation accounted for 21 percent of the variance in perceived job autonomy ($F_{9,269} = 9.06$, $p < .0001$). In the final equation with all variables entered, gender added 6 percent to the variance in perceived autonomy accounted for by the control variables ($\beta = .28$, $t_{278} = 4.78$, $p < .0001$); substantive complexity contributed an additional 3 percent ($\beta = .16$, $t_{278} = 2.65$, $p < .01$), and union status added 5 percent ($\beta = -.26$, $t_{278} = -4.09$, $p < .0001$). Employees highest in perceived autonomy were men who held positions involving complex dealings with people, data, and things, and whose workplaces were not unionized. Conversely, those lowest in perceived autonomy were women whose work did not involve complex dealings with people, data, and things, and whose jobs were unionized.

However, gender qualified the contributions of substantive complexity and unionization. Table 1 presents the results of a split group analysis (Arnold, 1982, 1984) used to compare regression weights estimated separately for men and women. The significance of the difference of the two regression weights was tested with the t formula provided by Arnold (1982).

For women, the substantive complexity of their jobs significantly predicted perceived autonomy but union status did not. In both unionized and nonunionized firms, women with relatively high autonomy held positions that were more substantively complex. Although union status had no direct relationship to women's perceived autonomy, it appeared to be indirectly related to autonomy through its association with substantive complexity. On the average, women who worked under union contracts held jobs that were less substantively complex than those of their nonunionized counterparts ($t_{83} = 3.28$, $p < .002$). Within the union sector, women held less complex jobs than did men ($t_{138} = -3.01$, $p < .003$), despite comparable organizational tenure (for men, $\bar{x} = 5.6$ years; for women, $\bar{x} = 5.9$ years).

For men, the reverse pattern held: substantive complexity did not predict their perceptions of job autonomy, but unionization did. Regardless of the actual

TABLE 1
Results of Regression Equations of Perceived Job Autonomy
on Substantive Complexity and Union Status

Independent Variables	Women[b]			Men[b]		
	sr^2	Betas	t	sr^2	Betas	t
Control variables[a]	.04		.82	.03		1.06
Substantive complexity	.11	.37	2.97*	.02	.11	1.52
Union status	.00	−.03	−.21	.10	−.36	−4.64**
R^2	.15			.15		
F	1.92			4.70**		
df	(7,74)			(7,190)		

[a]Control variables were race, education, geographic region, firm's size, and hourly wages.
[b]The squared semipartial coefficient (sr^2) at each step is the increase in R^2 associated with the predictor variable entered when all previously entered variables have been partialled.
*$p > .01$.
**$p > .001$

complexity of their dealings with people, data, and things, men who saw their jobs as providing more freedom in deciding how to do their work were more likely to hold positions in nonunion firms. No difference was found in the substantive complexity of jobs held by men who worked under union contract and the jobs of those who did not.

Union status added nothing to the variance explained by other variables in women's perceived job autonomy, but it explained 10 percent of the variance for men (see Table 1). A significant difference between men and women was found in the standardized regression coefficients for union status ($t_{275} = 2.38, p < .02$), indicating that for women, union status made a smaller difference in scores for job autonomy than it did for men.

We also found that an employee's gender moderated the relationship between substantive complexity and perceived autonomy; however, the evidence was less conclusive. Substantive complexity added 11 percent to the variance in women's job autonomy explained by other variables, compared to 2 percent for men. A marginally significant difference was found between men and women in the standardized regression coefficients for substantive complexity ($t_{275} = 1.94, p < .06$).

Thus, for perceived job autonomy, the relative importance of union status and substantive complexity differed for men and women. It should be noted, however, that the overall regression equation was significant only for men (see Table 1), suggesting that the present model is less predictive of women's perceptions of job autonomy than men's. The evidence is not conclusive, since the lack of significance could also be due to the small number of women in the sample.

DISCUSSION

The purpose of our investigation was to examine the relationship of unionization and employees' freedom in deciding how to do their work. We found that employees who held union jobs in manufacturing perceived themselves to be less autonomous than their nonunion counterparts, a result consistent with previous research (Berger et al., 1983; Kochan & Helfman, 1981). Our findings, coupled with those of Berger and his colleagues and with Kochan and Helfman's, suggest that the negative effect of unions on job content persisted through 1977, despite a growing interest in union-management programs on work redesign and employee participation. Nonetheless, our findings must be evaluated with caution, since any negative effects that unions have on job autonomy may be more characteristic of older plants unionized between 1940 and the 1960s, than of newer, more recently unionized plants (Verma & Kochan, 1985).

The findings reported here expand on previous research by demonstrating that unions and substantive complexity do not have uniform relationships to perceived autonomy across employees; rather, gender qualifies these relationships. Gender differences in values and preferences concerning work are unlikely to account for these differential relationships. In recent analyses of national survey data, researchers have found few differences between women and men in work values (Lacy, Bokemeier, & Shepard, 1983; Walker, Tausky, & Oliver, 1982). Rather, the lower complexity of women's jobs in union firms, and the stronger relationship of complexity to perceived job autonomy for women than for men may be due to typing of jobs by gender. According to Heilman's (1983) fit model of occupational gender bias, women are expected by both others and themselves to be less active, competent, and independent than men. In keeping with these expectations, women are typically assigned, or choose, jobs demanding relatively less effort, skill, and judgment. Thus, women in manufacturing who held more substantively complex jobs were the exception rather than the rule; for them, complexity should have a pronounced effect on their evaluations of job autonomy.

Gender-typing is also one possible explanation of the finding that union status was a more important predictor of perceived autonomy for men than women. Following Kochan (1980), we conceptualized the effect of unionization on job autonomy as mediated primarily by managerial policies and practices. Managerial adjustments that reduce freedom in decision making in union firms, or increase discretion in nonunion firms, may result in greater absolute changes in men's job autonomy than in women's, because gender-typing may restrict women's access to jobs with discretion (Brown, 1975).

A second possible explanation is that unions raise members' expectations on quality-of-work-life issues or their willingness to voice existing dissatisfactions (cf. Kochan & Helfman, 1981). However, a union's influence on employees' expectations and behavior may often be greater for men than women. On the basis of investigations of group dynamics and attitude changes (e.g. Cartwright & Zander, 1968), we suggest that employees are more likely to identify with and be influenced by unions when they see them as instrumental to personal goals. Compared to men, women may perceive unions as having lower instrumental value, since the wage premium paid for union labor is less for women than for men, and unions have often failed to address the issues of equal pay and childcare (Antos et al., 1980; Dewey, 1971; Sutton, 1980). Empirical evidence consistent with the possibility that gender mediates union identification has been reported (Gordon, Philpot, Burt, Thompson, & Spiller, 1980); that study found important differences between men and women in union loyalty and willingness to act to protect the interests of the union.

Since our data are cross-sectional and do not include independent measures of actual administrative policies and procedures, we cannot choose between these alternative explanations. Moreover, given the small size of our sample, the generalizability of our findings must be evaluated cautiously. Thus, further research is required to address the issue of generality and provide a precise explanation of how unions affect job autonomy.

In addition, more research is needed on the implications for employees' well-being of managerial policies that reduce the substantive complexity of work, or lower autonomy. In a longitudinal analysis, Kohn and Schooler (1983) demonstrated that work's substantive complexity actually changes employees' intellectual flexibility. Thus, managerial policies and practices that reduce substantive complexity or constrain autonomy may have unanticipated, long-term consequences for employees' intellectual functioning and psychological well-being.

REFERENCES

Antos, J. R., Chandler, M., & Mellow, W. 1980. Sex differences in union membership. *Industrial and Labor Relations Review*, 33: 162–169.

Arnold, H. J. 1982. Moderator variables: A clarification of conceptual, analytic, and psychometric issues. *Organizational Behavior and Human Performance*, 29: 143–174.

Arnold, H. J. 1984. Testing moderator variable hypotheses: A reply to Stone and Hollenbeck. *Organizational Behavior and Human Performance*, 34: 214–224.

Berger, C. J., Olson, C. A., & Boudreau, J. W. 1983. Effects of unions on job satisfaction: The role of work-related values and perceived rewards. *Organizational Behavior and Human Performance*, 32: 289–324.

Block, R. N., & Premack, S. L. 1983. The unionization process: A review of the literature. In D. B. Lipsky & J. M. Douglas (Eds.), *Advances in industrial and labor relations*, vol. 1: 31–71. Greenwich, Conn.: JAI Press.

Brown, J. S. 1975. How many workers enjoy discretion on the job? *Industrial Relations*, 14: 196–202.

Cartwright, D., & Zander, A. 1968. *Group dynamics: Research and theory* (3rd ed.). New York: Harper & Row Publishers.

Dewey, L. 1971. Women in labor unions. *Monthly Labor Review*, 94(2): 42–48.

Dimick, D. E. 1978. Employee control and discipline. *Relations Industrielles*, 33(1): 23–37.

Fine, S. A. 1968. *The third edition of the dictionary of occupational titles—Content, contrasts, and critique*. Kalamazoo, Mich.: Upjohn Institute for Employment Research.

Fiorito, J., & Greer, C. R. 1982. Determinants of U.S. unionism: Past research and future needs. *Industrial Relations*, 21: 1–33.

Gordon, M. E., Philpot, J. W., Burt, R. E., Thompson, C. A., & Spiller, W. E. 1980. Commitment of the union: Development of a measure and an examination of its correlates. *Journal of Applied Psychology*, 65: 479–499.

Heilman, M. E. 1983. Sex bias in work settings: The lack of fit model. In B. M. Staw & L. L. Cummings (Eds.), *Research in organizational behavior*, vol. 5: 269–298. Greenwich, Conn.: JAI Press.

Holley, W. H., Field, H. S., & Crowley, J. C. 1981. Negotiating quality of worklife, productivity, and traditional issues: Union members preferred roles of their union. *Personnel Psychology*, 34: 309–328.

Karasek, R. S. 1979. Job demands, job decision latitude, and mental strain: Implications for job redesign. *Administrative Science Quarterly*, 24: 285–308.

Kochan, T. A. 1980a. Collective bargaining and organizational behavior research. In B. M. Staw & L. L. Cummings (Eds.), *Research in organizational behavior*, vol. 2: 129–176. Greenwich, Conn.: JAI Press.

Kochan, T. A., & Helfman, D. 1981. Effects of collective bargaining on economic and behavioral outcomes. In R. Ehrenberg (Ed.), *Research in labor economics*, vol. 4: 321–366. Greenwich, Conn.: JAI Press.

Kohn, M. L., & Schooler, C. 1983. *Work and personality: An inquiry into the impact of social stratification.* Norwood, N.J.: Ablex.

Lacy, W. B., Bokemeier, J. L., & Shepard, J. M. 1983. Job attribute preferences and work commitment of men and women in the United States. *Personnel Psychology,* 36: 315–329.

Miller, A. R., Treiman, D. J., Cain, P. S., & Roos, P. A. 1980. *Work, jobs, and occupations: A critical review of the Dictionary of Occupational Titles.* Washington, D. C.: National Academy Press.

Quinn, R. P., & Staines, G. L. 1979. *The 1977 quality of employment survey.* Ann Arbor, Mich.: Institute for Social Research.

Rousseau, D. M. 1982. Job perceptions when working with data, people, and things. *Journal of Occupational Psychology,* 55: 43–52.

Slichter, S. H., Healy, J. J., & Livernash, E. R. 1960. *The impact of collective bargaining on management.* Washington, D. C.: The Brookings Institution.

Sutton, J. R. 1980. Some determinants of women's trade union membership. *Pacific Sociological Review,* 23: 377–391.

U. S. Department of Labor. 1980. *Handbook of Labor Statistics* (BLS Bulletin No. 2070). Washington, D.C.: U.S. Government Printing Office.

U.S. Employment Service. 1977. *Dictionary of occupational titles* (4th ed.). Washington, D.C.: U. S. Department of Labor.

Verma, A., & Kochan, T. A. 1985. The growth and nature of the nonunion sector within a firm. In T. A. Kochan (Ed.), *Challenges and choices facing American labor:* 89–117. Cambridge, Mass.: The MIT Press.

Walker, J. E., Tausky, C., & Oliver, D. 1982. Men and women at work: Similarities and differences in work values within occupational groupings. *Journal of Vocational Behavior,* 21: 17–36.

Sandra L. Kirmeyer earned her Ph.D. degree at Claremont Graduate School, Claremont, California; she is an assistant professor of psychology and Director of the dual Ph.D.-M.B.A. Graduate Studies Program at the University of Missouri, Columbia. Her current research interests include work overload stress in the service sector, organizational communication, and behavior-setting analysis.

Arle Shirom earned his Ph.D. degree at the University of Wisconsin, Madison; he is an associate professor of organizational behavior in the graduate department of labor studies, Tel-Aviv University, Israel, and Director of the Institute for Labor and Social Research, Tel-Aviv University. His current research interests include work-related stress among teachers, nurses, policy-makers, and senior army officers.

Practice Self-Test

The Problem

The Procedures

_____

_____

_____

The Method of Analysis

_____

_____

_____

The Major Conclusion(s)

_____

_____

_____

Reasons for Classification as Causal-Comparative Research

_____

_____

_____

Method-Specific Evaluation Criteria

Use the questions listed below to evaluate the article with respect to the specific characteristics of a causal-comparative study:

1. Are the characteristics or experiences that differentiate the groups (the independent variable) clearly defined or described?
2. Are critical extraneous variables identified?
3. Were any control procedures applied to equate the groups on extraneous variables?
4. Are causal relationships found discussed with due caution?
5. Are plausible alternative hypotheses discussed?

REFERENCES

Czajka, J. M., & DeNisi, A. S. (1988). Effects of emotional disability and clear performance standards on performance ratings. *Academy of Management Journal, 31*(2), 394–404.

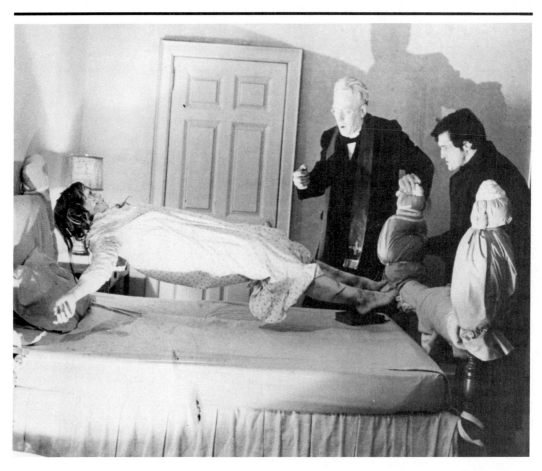

Single-subject experimental designs . . . are typically used to study the behavior change an individual exhibits as a result of some intervention . . . (page 418)

10

The Experimental Method

Objectives

After reading Chapter 10, you should be able to do the following:

1. Briefly state the purpose of experimental research.

2. List the basic steps involved in experimental research.

3. Describe three ways in which a variable can be manipulated.

4. Explain the purpose of control.

5. Define briefly or describe internal validity and external validity.

6. Identify and briefly describe eight major threats to the internal validity of an experiment.

7. Identify and briefly describe six major threats to the external validity of an experiment.

8. Discuss briefly the purpose of experimental design.

9. Identify and briefly describe five ways to control extraneous variables.

10. For each of the preexperimental, true experimental, and quasi-experimental group designs discussed in this chapter:
    a. Draw a diagram.
    b. List the steps involved in its application.
    c. Identify major problems (e.g., sources of invalidity) with which it is associated

11. Describe briefly the definition and purpose of a factorial design.

12. Explain briefly what is meant by the term *interaction*.

13. For each of the A-B-A single-subject designs discussed in this chapter:
    a. Draw a diagram.
    b. List the steps involved in its application.
    c. Identify major problems with which it is associated.

14. Describe briefly the procedures involved in using a multiple-baseline design.

15. Describe briefly an alternating-treatments design.

16. Describe briefly how data resulting from the application of a single-subject design are analyzed.

17. Describe briefly three types of replication involved in single-subject research.

DEFINITION AND PURPOSE

The experimental method is the only method of research that can truly test hypotheses concerning cause-effect relationships. It represents the most valid approach to the solution of business-and-management-related problems, both practical and theoretical, and to the advancement of management as a science. In an experimental study, the researcher manipulates at least one independent variable (IV), controls other relevant variables, and observes the effect on one or more dependent variables (DV). The researcher determines "who gets what," or, to state it differently, which group of subjects gets which treatment. This manipulation of the independent variable is the one characteristic that differentiates all experimental research from the other methods of research.

The *independent variable,* also referred to as the experimental variable, the cause, or the treatment, is that activity or characteristic believed to make a difference. In business research independent variables that typically are manipulated include method of training, type of reinforcement, frequency of reinforcement, arrangement of the working environment, type of work equipment, and, in market research, a wide variety of customer-related variables. This list is, of course, by no means exhaustive.

The *dependent variable,* also referred to as the criterion variable, effect, or posttest, is the outcome of the study, the change, or difference in groups that occurs as a result of manipulation of the independent variable. It is referred to as the dependent variable since it is "dependent" on the independent variable. The dependent variable may be measured by a test, but other measures are also options for the researcher. Since the independent variable is a variable that the researcher believes will make things "better," increase good things, or decrease bad things, the dependent variable may also be such factors as attendance, number of complaints or disciplinary actions, productivity, attitude, morale, or job satisfaction. The only restriction on the dependent variable is that it represents an outcome that is measurable. Obviously this restriction is more difficult for measures of morale and job satisfaction than for productivity or attendance!

The experimental method is both the most demanding and the most productive method of research. When well conducted, experimental studies produce the soundest evidence concerning hypothesized cause-effect relationships. The results of experimental research permit prediction but not the kind characteristic of correlational research. A correlational prediction is specific and predicts a particular score for a particular individual. Predictions based on experimental findings are more global and take the form, "If you use approach X_1, you will probably get better results than if you use approach X_2." Experimental research has repeatedly confirmed, for example, that systematically applied positive reinforcement leads to improved work behavior. Although there are a number of alternative designs from which a researcher can select, the basic experimental process is the same in all studies.

The Experimental Process

The steps in an experimental study are basically the same as for other types of research:

1. selection and definition of a problem
2. selection of subjects and measuring instruments
3. selection of a design
4. execution of procedures
5. analysis of data
6. formulation of conclusions

Ideally, an experimental study is guided by at least one hypothesis that states an expected causal relationship between two variables. The actual experiment is conducted in order to confirm (support) or disconfirm the experimental hypothesis. In an experimental study, the researcher is in on the action from the very beginning; the researcher forms or selects the groups, decides what is going to happen to each group, tries to control all relevant factors besides the change that she or he has introduced, and observes or measures the effect on the groups at the end of the study.

An experiment typically involves two groups, an experimental group and a control group (although as you will see later, there may be only one group, or there may be three or more groups). The experimental group typically receives a new treatment that is under investigation, while the control group usually receives either a different treatment or is treated as usual. The control group is needed for comparison purposes to see if the new treatment is more effective than the usual or traditional approach or to see if one approach is more effective than another. You remember the example of the use of control groups from the quality circle article at the end of Chapter 1.

A common misconception among beginning researchers is that a control group always receives nothing. As you remember from the discussion of ethics in research in Chapter 3, this would hardly be fair and might even create a jeopardy for the company and the researcher in terms of potential legal action. If in a study, for example, the independent variable was the type of employee training, the experimental group might be trained with a new method, while the control group was trained with a traditional method. The control group would still receive training; it would not sit in a closet while the study was being conducted. Otherwise you would not be evaluating the effectiveness of a new method as compared to the traditional method but rather the effectiveness of a new method as compared to no training at all! Any method of training is probably going to be more effective than no training at all. Thus, the control group also receives a form of the independent variable. The two groups that are to receive different treatments are equated on all other variables that might be related to performance on the dependent variable, for example, aptitude. In other words, the researcher makes every effort to ensure that the two groups are as equivalent as possible on all variables *except* the independent variable.

After the groups have been exposed to the treatment for some period of time, the researcher administers a test of the dependent variable (or measures it in some other way) and then determines whether there is a significant difference between the groups. In other words, the researcher determines whether the treatment made a difference. One problem associated with experimental studies in business is that subjects are often not exposed to the experimental treatment for a sufficient period of time. No matter how effective employee-assistance programs may be, they are not likely to reduce substance abuse, for example, if employees are exposed to treatment for only a few hours. Thus, to test adequately a hypothesis concerning the effectiveness of employee-assistance programs in correcting substance-abuse problems, the experimental group would need to be exposed to the program over a period of time. The experimental treatment should be given a chance to work.

Another problem associated with experimental research is that the treatments received by the groups are not sufficiently different to make a difference. For example, if your study were comparing employee-assistance programs using behavior modification with those using group therapy, it would be vital that both treatments be operationalized according to clearly stated definitions. If in your study behavior modification meant nothing more than a series of group discussions with occasional positive feedback, it would not be very different from the techniques that might be used in group therapy. Thus, you would be very unlikely to find a major difference between your experimental and control groups at the end of the study, even though you might have found a difference if behavior modification had been correctly operationalized to include such things as establishment of a baseline, a clear schedule of reinforcement, and use of appropriate rewards.

Manipulation and Control

Direct manipulation by the researcher of at least one independent variable is the single characteristic that differentiates all experimental research from other methods of research. Manipulation of an independent variable seems to be a difficult concept for some beginning researchers to grasp. Quite simply it means that the researcher decides what forms or values the independent variable (or cause) will take and which group will get which form. For example, if the independent variable was the number of informal performance appraisals, the researcher might decide that there should be three groups, one group receiving no informal performance appraisals, a second group receiving one informal appraisal, and a third group receiving two informal appraisals within a specified time period. There are many independent variables in business that can be manipulated (active variables), and many that cannot (assigned variables). You can manipulate such variables as method of training, supervision, and work conditions; you cannot manipulate such variables as personal factors (sex, age, and so on) or economic conditions and company profitability. In other words, you can require that employees receive one method of supervision or another, but you cannot require employees to be male or female; they already are male or female. In order to manipulate a variable, *you* have to decide who is going to be what or who is going to get what. Although the design of an experimental study may include assigned variables, *at least one* variable must be manipulated.

The different values or forms that the independent variable may take are basically presence versus absence (X versus no X), presence in varying degrees (a lot of X versus a little X), or presence of one kind versus presence of another kind (X_1 versus X_2). An example of "X versus no X" would be a study comparing the effectiveness of informal performance appraisal versus no informal performance appraisal on employee job satisfaction. An example of "a lot of X versus a little X" would be a study comparing the effectiveness of frequent versus infrequent informal performance appraisals; one group might receive informal appraisals on a weekly basis, and another group might receive appraisals on a monthly basis. An example of "X_1 versus X_2" would be a study to compare the effectiveness of frequent, informal performance appraisals versus quality circles in increasing employee job satisfaction. Experimental designs may get quite complex and involve simultaneous manipulation of several independent variables. At this stage of the game, however, you'd better stick to just one!

Control refers to efforts on the part of the researcher to remove the influence of any variable (other than the independent variable) that might affect performance on the dependent variable. In other words, the researcher wants the groups to be as similar as possible, so that the only major difference between them is the independent variable, which is the difference caused by the researcher. To illustrate the importance of control, suppose you conducted a study to compare the effectiveness of peer mentors versus senior-management mentors in helping management trainees adjust to the company. Peer mentors might be employees who had just completed the management-training program, and senior-management mentors might be volunteers from a variety of departments. Now suppose peer mentors met with each member of the management-trainee group for at least 1 hour per day for a month, while the senior-management mentors helped each member of a second group of management trainees for a maximum of 2 hours per week for a month. Would the comparison be fair? Certainly not (for any number of reasons!) Subjects with the peer mentors would have received at least two-and-one-half times as much help (at least 5 hours per week versus no more than 2 hours per week). Thus, at least one variable that would need to be controlled would be *time.* In order for the comparison even to begin to be fair, members of both groups of trainees would have to be met with for the same amount of time. Then the researcher could begin to compare the effectiveness of different *kinds* of help, not different *amounts.* That is just one example of the kinds of factors that must be considered in planning an experiment.

Some variables that need controlling may be relatively obvious; in the example just given, variables such as trainee skill level and aptitude would need to be considered. Other variables in need of control may not be as obvious; in this study, for example, the researcher would need to ensure that both groups discussed the same topics and that the peer mentors were adequately informed regarding things the trainees might question such as company policy and procedure. Thus, we see that there are really two different kinds of variables that need to be controlled:

1. *subject variables,* such as skill level and aptitude, on which subjects in the two groups might differ, and
2. *environmental variables,* such as discussion topics and information level of the mentors, that might cause unwanted differences between the groups.

The researcher strives to ensure that the characteristics and experiences of the groups are as equal as possible on all important variables except, of course, the independent variable. If at the end of some period of time the groups differ in performance on the dependent variable, the difference can be attributed to the independent variable, or treatment. Control is not easy in an experiment, especially in business where real live subjects are involved; it is a lot easier to control solids, liquids, and gases in a chemical laboratory. The task is not an impossible one, however, since the researcher can concentrate on identifying and controlling only those variables that might really affect the dependent variable. If two groups differed significantly with respect to shoe size, for example, the results of the study would probably not be affected. Also, there are a number of techniques at the researcher's disposal that can be used to control for extraneous variables, and we will discuss these later in the chapter.

THREATS TO EXPERIMENTAL VALIDITY

Any uncontrolled *extraneous variables* affecting performance on the dependent variable are threats to the validity of an experiment. An experiment is valid if results obtained are due only to the manipulated independent variable, and if they are generalizable to situations outside of the experimental setting. The two conditions that must be met are referred to as internal validity and external validity.

Internal validity refers to the condition that observed differences on the dependent variable are a direct result of manipulation of the independent variable, not some other variable. In other words, the outcome of the study is the result of what the researcher did, not something else. If someone can come up with an alternative explanation (a rival hypothesis) for your results, your study was not internally valid. To use a former example, if the peer mentors had worked with trainees (subjects) for 5 hours per week, and the management mentors only 2, and if the peer-mentored group out-performed the management-mentored group, then time, or amount of mentoring, would be a plausible alternative explanation for the results. The degree to which results are attributable to manipulation of the independent variable is the degree to which an experimental study is internally valid.

External validity refers to the condition that results are generalizable, or applicable, to groups and environments outside the experimental setting. In other words, the results of the study, the confirmed cause-effect relationship, can be expected to be reconfirmed with other groups, in other settings, at other times, as long as the conditions are similar to those of the study. If a study was conducted using groups of beginning bank tellers, for example, the results should be applicable to other groups of beginning bank tellers. As mentioned previously, if research results are not generalizable to any other situation outside the experimental setting, then no one can profit from anyone else's research, and each and every effort would have to be reestablished over and over and over. An experimental study can only contribute to business-and-management theory or practice if there is some assurance that confirmed relationships and observed effects are replicable and likely to occur at other times and places with other groups. The term *ecological validity* is sometimes used to refer to the degree to which results can be generalized to other environments. If results cannot be replicated in other environments by other researchers, the study has low ecological validity.

So all one has to do in order to conduct a valid experiment is to maximize internal validity and maximize external validity, right? Wrong. Unfortunately, there is a "catch-22" complicating the researcher's experimental life. Maximization of internal validity requires exercise of very rigid control over subjects and conditions in a laboratory-like environment. The more a situation is controlled, however, the less realistic it becomes, and the less generalizable to nonlaboratory settings the results become. In other words, laboratory findings are generalizable to other laboratories. A study can contribute little to management practice if there is no assurance that a technique found to be effective in a controlled laboratory setting will also be effective in a natural business setting. In contrast, the more natural the experimental setting is, the more difficult it is to control extraneous variables. It is very difficult, however, to conduct a well-controlled study in an actual business. Thus the researcher must strive for balance between control and realism. If a choice is involved, the researcher should err on the side of too much control rather than too little. A study that is not internally valid is worthless. In fact, one research strategy is first to demonstrate an effect in a highly controlled environment (for the sake of internal validity) and then to repeat the study in a more natural setting (for the sake of external validity).

Although lab-like settings are generally preferred for the investigation of theoretical problems, experimentation in natural, or field, settings has its advantages, especially for certain practical problems. In the final analysis, however, the researcher usually strives for a compromise, or an environment somewhere between a lab setting and a natural business setting. Many studies, for example, are conducted in simulated business settings that the researcher makes as much like a natural business setting as possible. You will see many studies using business students, rather than working managers, for example, and simulated settings such as a bank teller training room rather than the actual teller work stations on the banking floor. These approaches permit the researcher to exercise sufficient control to ensure adequate internal validity, while at the same time maintaining a degree of realism necessary for generalizability.

In the pages to come many threats to internal and external validity will be discussed. Some extraneous variables are definite threats to internal validity, some are definite threats to external validity, and some may be threats to both. How potential threats are classified, or labeled, is not the important thing; what is important is that you, as a researcher, be aware of their existence and make efforts to control for them. As you read, you may begin to feel that there are just too many of them for one little researcher to control all at the same time. The task is not as formidable as it may at first appear. As you will see later, there are a number of experimental designs that control many threats for you; all you have to do is select a "good" design and go from there. Also, each of the threats to be discussed is only a potential threat that may not be a problem in a particular study.

Threats to Internal Validity

Probably the most authoritative source regarding experimental design and threats to experimental validity is the work of Campbell and Stanley (1972). Campbell and Stanley identified eight major threats to internal validity, or to put it another way, sources of internal invalidity.

1. *History* refers to the occurrence of any event that is not part of the experimental treatment but that may affect performance on the dependent variable. The longer a study lasts, the more likely it is that history may be a problem. Happenings such as a bomb scare, an epidemic of influenza, or even current events are examples of history. For example, suppose you had conducted beginning investor classes designed to increase interest in investing in the stock market during the autumn of 1990. Suppose that between the time you began the classes and the time you administered some posttest measure of interest, the world crisis over Iraq's invasion of Kuwait occurred. Such an event could easily wipe out any effect the investor classes might have had; posttest scores might show considerably less interest when they might otherwise have shown increased interest. Thus, while the researcher has no control over the occurrence of such events, he or she can select a design that controls *for* their occurrence.

2. *Maturation* refers to physical or mental changes that may occur within the subjects over a period of time. These changes may affect the subjects' performance on the measure of the dependent variable. Especially in studies that last for any length of time, subjects may become, for example, older, more skilled in manipulating materials, unmotivated, anxious, or just plain bored. If you recall the quality circle study, the subjects experienced initial increases in involvement but after about 18 months, their responses returned to about the pre-study level. By testing at regular intervals over the duration of the study, the researcher was able to determine not only what was happening to the subjects but also when maturation began to occur. Maturation is more of a threat in some studies than in others. As with history, the researcher cannot control the occurrence of maturation but can control *for* its occurrence.

3. *Testing* refers to improved scores on a posttest resulting from subjects having taken a pretest. In other words, taking a pretest may improve performance on a posttest, regardless of whether there is any treatment or instruction in between. Testing is more likely to be a threat when the time between testings is short; a pretest taken in January is not likely to affect performance on a posttest taken the following December. This phenomenon is also more likely to occur in some studies than in others, for example, when the tests measure factual information that can be recalled. On the one hand, if you enrolled in a 1-day memory-improvement course and were given a pretest first thing in the morning and the same test at the end of the day, would your improvement be due to increased memory skills or simply the effect of testing? On the other hand, taking a pretest on economic principles is much less likely to improve performance on a similar posttest. One obvious way to control for testing is to use a design that does not involve a pretest. Another way to control for testing is to use alternate forms, one form for the pretest and another for the posttest. It is a factor that should at least be considered when selecting both the measuring instrument and the experimental design.

4. *Instrumentation* refers to unreliability, or lack of consistency, in measuring instruments, which may result in an invalid assessment of performance. Instrumentation may occur in several different ways. If two different tests are used for pretesting

and posttesting, and the tests are not of equal difficulty, invalidity due to instrumentation may occur. If the posttest is more difficult, it may fail to show improvement that is actually present; whereas if the posttest is less difficult, it may indicate an improvement that is not present. If data are collected through observation, observers may not be observing or evaluating behavior the same way at the end of the study as at the beginning. In fact, if they are aware of the nature of the study, they may unconsciously tend to see and record what they know the researcher is hypothesizing. If data are collected through the use of a mechanical device, such as a biofeedback device, there may be some malfunction resulting in inaccurate measurement. Thus, the researcher must take care in selecting tests, caution observers, and check mechanical devices. In addition, the researcher can select an experimental design that controls for this factor.

5. *Statistical regression* usually occurs when subjects are selected on the basis of their extreme scores. It refers to the tendency of subjects who score highest on a pretest to score lower on a posttest and the tendency of subjects who score lowest on a pretest to score higher on a posttest. The tendency is for scores to regress, or move toward, the mean (average) or expected score. For example, suppose a researcher wished to determine the effectiveness of a new method of instruction in research in improving the ability of graduate students to conduct research studies. The researcher might administer a 100-item, multiple-choice pretest, with 4 alternatives per item, on research concepts. Sample questions might read, "Which of the following factors is an example of a threat to Internal Validity?" The researcher might then select for the study the 30 students who scored lowest. Now suppose none of the pretested students knew *anything* about research methods and guessed on *every* single question. With 100 items, and 4 choices per item, a student would be expected to receive a score of 25 just by guessing. Some students, however, just because of rotten guessing, would receive scores much lower than 25, and other students, just by chance, would receive much higher scores than 25. If they were administered the test a second time, *without* any instruction intervening, their expected score would still be 25. Thus students who scored very low the first time would be expected to have a second score closer to 25, and students who scored very high the first time would also be expected to score closer to 25 the second time. In the above study, if students were selected because of their very low pretest scores, they would be expected to do better on the posttest, regardless of the treatment. The researcher might erroneously attribute their improved research ability to the new method of research instruction. The researcher must therefore be aware of statistical regression and, if at all possible, select a design that controls for this phenomenon. (Also, students should not count on statistical regression to get them through finals without studying!)

6. *Differential selection of subjects* usually occurs when already formed groups are used. It refers to the fact that the groups may be different before the study even begins, and this initial difference may at least partially account for posttest differences. Suppose, for example, you received permission to use two of Dr. Mean's graduate management classes in your study regarding the effect of simulated corporate profitability (independent variable) on motivation (dependent variable); there would

be no guarantee that the two classes were at all equivalent. If your luck was really bad, one class might be employed in the public sector and the other in the private sector. It would not be too surprising if the groups performed differently, with the class made up of private-sector employees, who are presumably much more sensitive to corporate profitability, doing much better! We might expect reverse results if the independent variable was a perception of service to the public, the dependent variable was motivation, and the same classes were used. Thus, using already formed groups should be avoided if possible. If they must be used, groups should be selected that are as similar as possible, and a pretest should be administered to check for initial equivalence.

7. *Mortality,* let us make perfectly clear, *does not* mean that the subjects die! Mortality, or attrition, which is more likely to occur in longer studies, refers to the fact that subjects who drop out of a group may share a characteristic such that their absence has a significant effect on the results of the study. In the quality circle study, for example, the subjects who left the company during the study may have been too discouraged before the beginning of quality circle groups to have their interest in the job renewed by *any* new factor. Mortality is especially a problem when volunteers are used. They rarely drop out of control groups because few or no demands are made on them, but they may drop out of an experimental group if too much effort is required for participation. The experimental group that remains at the end of the study may as a whole represent a more motivated group than the control group. In the quality circle study, the problem of mortality was addressed, since the researcher believed there was a good chance some workers would leave employment before the study was complete; in the research design that was used, the researcher could—and did—drop the other half of a matched pair when an employee dropped out of the study.

8. *Selection-maturation interaction* means that selection may also interact with factors such as history and testing, although selection-maturation interaction is more common. What this means is that if already formed groups are used, one group may profit more (or less) from a treatment or have an initial advantage (or disadvantage) because of maturation, history, or testing factors. Suppose, for example, that you received permission to use two of Dr. Mean's policy classes, and both classes were average classes and apparently equivalent on all relevant variables. Suppose, however, that one day Dr. Mean had to miss one of her classes but not the other (maybe she had a toothache), and Dr. Wonderful took over one—your experimental group—of Dr. Mean's classes. As luck would have it, Dr. Wonderful covered much of the material now included in your posttest (remember history?). Unbeknownst to you, your experimental group would have a definite advantage to begin with, and it might be this initial advantage that caused posttest differences, rather than your independent variable. Thus, the researcher must select a design that controls for this potential problem or make *every* effort to determine if it is operating in the study.

Threats to External Validity

There are also several major threats to external validity that limit, or make questionable, generalization to nonexperimental populations. Building on the work of

Campbell and Stanley (1972), Bracht and Glass (1968) refined and expanded the discussion of threats to external validity, or sources of external invalidity. Bracht and Glass classify threats to external validity into two categories:

1. Threats affecting "to whom," or to what persons; results can be generalized, which are referred to as problems of *population validity*.
2. Threats affecting "to what," or to what environments (settings, dependent variables, and so forth); results can be generalized, which are referred to as problems of *ecological validity*.

The discussion to follow incorporates the contributions of Bracht and Glass into Campbell and Stanley's original conceptualizations.

1. *Pretest-treatment interaction* occurs when subjects respond or react differently to a treatment because they have been pretested. A pretest may sensitize or alert subjects to the nature of the treatment. The treatment effect may be different from what it would have been had subjects not been pretested. Thus results are only generalizable to other pretested groups. The results are not even generalizable to the unpretested population from which the sample was selected. This potential problem is more or less serious depending upon the subjects, the nature of the tests, the nature of the treatment, and the duration of the study. Studies involving self-report measures of personality such as attitude scales are especially susceptible to this problem. Campbell and Stanley illustrate the effect by pointing out the probable lack of comparability of one group viewing the anti-prejudice film *Gentlemen's Agreement* right after taking a lengthy pretest dealing with anti-Semitism and another group viewing the film without a pretest. Individuals in the unpretested group could quite conceivably enjoy the movie as a good love story and be unaware that it deals with a social issue; pretested individuals would have to be pretty dense not to see a connection between the pretest and the message of the film. Taking a pretest on economic principles, however, would probably affect very little (if at all) a group's responsiveness to a new method of teaching economics.

The pretest-treatment interaction is likely to be heightened among employees who may see connections between *any* kind of test and the job situation because of a potential or perceived impact on their employment or career advancement. If a pretest is used, the effect can be minimized if there is a relatively long period of time between the pretest and posttest. Windle (1954), for example, reviewed 41 studies involving pretesting and posttesting with personality inventories and found a relationship between improved posttest scores and amount of time between pretesting and posttesting. Studies in which the interval between pretesting and posttesting was less than two months were more likely to find better adjustment scores on posttest measures. Thus, for some studies the potential interactive effect of a pretest is a more serious consideration. In such studies the researcher should select a design that either controls for the effect or allows the researcher to determine the magnitude of the effect.

A possible parallel, as yet undocumented, threat to validity proposed by Bracht and Glass is posttest sensitization. *Posttest sensitization* refers to the possibility that treatment effects may only occur *if* subjects are posttested. In other words, the very act of posttesting "jells" treatment influences such that effects are manifested and measured that would not have occurred if a posttest had not been given. Suppose, for example, we have a study in which one randomly formed group views *Gentlemen's Agreement* and another does not; both groups are then posttested with a self-report attitude scale dealing with anti-Semitism. Members of the experimental group, who saw the film, have time to process the film's message while completing the posttest. As with pretest-treatment interaction, it is possible that unposttested individuals could view the film and enjoy it as a good love story without being aware of the social issue being addressed. In studies in which there is a strong possibility that posttest sensitization may occur, unobtrusive measures are recommended, if feasible.

2. *Multiple-treatment interference* can occur when the same subjects receive more than one treatment in succession. It refers to the carryover effects from an earlier treatment that make it difficult to assess the effectiveness of a later treatment. Suppose you are interested in comparing two different approaches to increasing employee productivity—behavior modification and strict supervision (perhaps an extreme example used to make a point). Let us say that for 2 months behavior-modification techniques using praise and rewards are systematically applied to the subjects, and at the end of this period productivity is found to be significantly higher than before the study began. Now suppose that for the next two months the same subjects are supervised closely with verbal warnings and written records of disciplinary action over small infractions, and at the end of the 2 months behavior is equally as good as after the 2 months of behavior modification. Can you then conclude that behavior modification and strict supervision are equally effective methods of increasing productivity? Cer-tain-ly not. In fact, the goal of behavior modification is to produce behavior that is self-maintaining, which means that it continues after direct intervention is stopped. Thus, the higher productivity exhibited by the subjects at the end of the study could well be because of the effectiveness of the previous behavior modification and exist in spite of the strict supervision. If it is not possible to select a design in which each group receives but one treatment, the researcher should try to minimize potential multiple-treatment interference by allowing sufficient time to elapse between treatments and by investigating distinctly different types of independent variables.

Multiple-treatment interference may also occur when subjects who have already participated in a study are selected for inclusion in another, theoretically unrelated, study. Weitz (1967), for example, found that college psychology students, who had participated in a study of guilt, were so suspicious during a subsequent study of cognitive dissonance that their responses could not be used. Thus, if the accessible population for a study is one whose members are likely to have participated in other studies (psychology majors, for example), then information on previous participation should be collected and evaluated *before* subjects are selected for the current study. Some of the companies cited as "innovative" in the management-related literature of recent years would have to be viewed with caution by researchers simply because of the amount of study and scrutiny they have already received. If any members of the accessible population are eliminated from consideration because of previous research activities, note should be made of this limitation in the research report.

3. *Selection-treatment interaction* is similar to the differential-selection-of-subjects problem associated with internal invalidity. It also occurs when subjects are not randomly selected for treatment. Interaction effects aside, the very fact that subjects are not randomly selected from a population severely limits the researcher's ability to generalize since the representativeness of the sample is in question. Even if intact groups are randomly selected, the possibility exists that the experimental group is in some important way different from the control group and/or from the larger population. This nonrepresentativeness of groups may also result in a selection-treatment interaction such that the results of a study hold only for the groups involved and are not representative of the treatment effect in the intended population. Bracht and Glass (1968) discuss what they refer to as *interaction-of-personological-variables-and-treatment effects,* which they consider to be a population-validity problem. Such an interaction occurs when actual subjects at one level of a variable react differently to a treatment from the way other potential subjects in the population, at another level, would have reacted. As an example, a researcher might conduct a study on the effectiveness of computer-assisted financial analysis on the productivity of managers. Groups available to the researcher (the accessible population) may represent mostly first-line supervisors with minimal responsibility for policy decisions rather than the entire range of managers (the target population). If no effect is found, it may be that it would have been found if the subjects were truly representative of the target population. And similarly, if an *effect* is found, it might not have been. Thus, extra caution must be taken in stating conclusions and generalizations based on studies involving existing groups.

While selection-treatment interaction is a definite weakness associated with several less-than-wonderful designs, it is also an uncontrolled variable associated with the designs involving randomization. One's accessible population is often a far cry from one's target population, creating another population-validity problem. The way in which a given population becomes available to a researcher may make generalizability of findings questionable, no matter what the internal validity of an experiment may be. If a researcher is turned down by 9 companies and accepted by a 10th, the accepting system is bound to be different from the other 9, and from the population of companies to which the researcher would like to generalize. Management and personnel in this company may exhibit more openness, more introspection as a company, greater familiarity with research techniques and/or management consultants, or even a pride in being included in a study than management and personnel in an average company. It is therefore recommended that the researcher report problems involved in acquiring subjects, including the number of times he or she was turned down, so that the reader can judge the seriousness of a possible selection-treatment interaction.

4. *Specificity of variables,* like selection-treatment interaction, is a threat to generalizability regardless of the experimental design used. Specificity of variables refers to the fact that a given study is conducted according to the following terms:

a. with a specific kind of subject

b. based on a particular, operational definition of the independent variable

c. using specific measuring instruments

d. at a specific time

e. under a specific set of circumstances

For example, "Japanese management" might be found to be effective *with* college-educated employees and *when* productivity is measured using the Baloney Productivity Test.

We have already discussed the importance of carefully describing the population from which subjects are selected and the method of sample selection. Care must also be taken in terms of generalization of results. A researcher would definitely be overgeneralizing, for example, if based on a study involving computer analysts, the researcher concluded that a treatment was effective for employees in computer-related industries. We have also discussed the need to describe procedures in sufficient detail to permit another researcher to replicate the study. Of course, such detailed descriptions also permit interested readers to assess how applicable the findings are to their situation. Experimental procedures represent an operational definition of the independent variable. When a number of studies that supposedly manipulated the same independent variable get different results, it is often difficult to determine reasons for discrepancies because of inadequate descriptions of treatment procedures.

Relatedly, generalizability of results is tied to the definition of the dependent variable and to the actual instrument used to measure it. Many studies related to leadership have not clearly defined the dependent variable, i.e., leadership. This confusion of terminology finally led to an analysis of approximately 300 studies of leadership in an effort to find common results (Bass, 1981; Yukl, 1981; Stogdill, 1974). One of the researchers finally concluded, "Certain traits increase the likelihood that a leader will be effective, but they do not guarantee effectiveness, and the relative importance of different traits is dependent on the nature of the leadership situation" (Yukl, 1981, p. 70). Further, the actual instrument administered represents an operational definition of the intended dependent variable, and there are often a number from which to select.

Throughout this book, reference has been made to *productivity* as a dependent variable. Certainly this is a topic of great interest to business people, but there is no total agreement even within industries on the proper or best way to measure productivity, profitability, morale, or any of a number of issues of interest. One is reminded of the story of nameless airline officials who, as a cost-cutting strategy, informed the pilots that if fuel consumption was lower than expected in a given time period, the resulting savings would be divided among the pilots. One way to save fuel is to delay the warm-up period for one or more engines until the last possible minute. Unfortunately, this also causes engines to wear out more quickly. In this situation is *savings* to be defined in the short term based on gallons of fuel or in the long term based on overall operating costs? This raises the whole question of comparability of instruments that supposedly measure the same thing and may remind you of the discussion on reliability and validity in Chapter 5.

Generalizability of results may also be affected by short-term or long-term events that occur while the study is taking place. This potential threat is referred to as *interaction-of-history-and-treatment effects*. It describes the situation in which results are different from what they might have been if events extraneous to the study had not occurred right before or during the study. Short-term, emotion-packed events, such as the firing of a CEO or a hostile takeover, for example, might affect the behavior of subjects. Usually the researcher is aware of such happenings and can assess their possible impact on results. This may not always be true, however. Who would have anticipated, for example, that a Japanese car manufacturer would discontinue serving the customary strawberry jam in the company cafeteria as part of the mourning observation when Emperor Hirohita died (L. Kriska, personal communication, February 15, 1989)? Of course, accounts of such events—the emotion-packed event, not the absence of strawberry jam—should also be included in the research report. The impact of more long-term events, such as wars and depressions, however, is more subtle and tougher to evaluate. The effects of such influences can only be detected through replication of the basic study over time.

Another threat to external validity related to time is what Bracht and Glass (1968) refer to as the *interaction-of-time-of-measurement-and-treatment effect*. This threat results from the fact that posttesting may yield different results depending upon when it is done; a treatment effect that is found based on the administration of a posttest immediately following the treatment may not be found if a delayed posttest is given some time after treatment; conversely, a treatment may have a long-term but not a short-term effect. Recall the discussion of follow-up studies, which suggested that attitude changes, for example, tend to dissipate over time. Similarly, courtesy training may have an initial effect, which may or may not last, while career-development activities may have a stronger long-term effect than the immediate results would indicate. Thus, really the only way to assess the generalizability of findings over time is to measure the dependent variable at various times following treatment, as was done in the quality circle study in Chapter 1.

To deal with the threats associated with specificity, the researcher must (a) operationally define variables in a way that has meaning outside of the experimental setting and (b) be careful in stating conclusions and generalizations. Also, as we shall see, it may be possible to deal with at least some of these threats through revisions or extensions of basic experimental designs.

5. *Experimenter effects* suggests that researchers may represent potential threats to the external validity of their own studies. Rosenthal (1966) has identified a number of ways in which the experimenter may unintentionally affect execution of study procedures, the behavior of subjects, or the assessment of that behavior, and hence results. Possible biasing influences may be passive or active. Passive elements include characteristics or personality traits of the experimenter such as sex, age, race, anxiety level, and hostility level. Rosenthal refers to these influences collectively as the *"experimenter-personal-attributes effect."* Active bias results when the researcher's

expectations affect her or his behavior and hence outcomes. Such behavior on the part of the researcher is referred to as the *experimenter-bias effect.* In other words, the way an experimenter looks, feels, or acts may unintentionally affect study results, typically in the desired direction.

One form of experimenter bias occurs when the researcher affects subjects' behavior or is inaccurate in evaluating their behavior because of previous knowledge concerning the subjects. This problem is similar to the halo effect in that knowledge of a subject's behavior in one situation may color judgment concerning his or her behavior in another situation. Suppose a researcher hypothesizes that positive reinforcement increases employee motivation. If the researcher knows that Susie Shiningstar is in the experimental group and that Susie is an outstanding employee, he or she may give Susie's level of motivation a higher rating than it actually warrants. This example also illustrates another way in which a researcher's expectations concerning study outcomes may actually contribute to producing those outcomes; knowing which subjects are in which group may cause the researcher to be unintentionally biased in evaluating their performance.

Rosenthal has demonstrated the experimenter-bias effect in a number of interesting studies. In one study (Rosenthal & Fode, 1963), two groups of graduate students were each given rats and instructions to train the rats to perform a discrimination-learning task. One group of students was told that because of selective breeding their rats were "maze-bright" and would learn quickly and well; the other students were told that their rats were "maze-dull." In reality, both sets of rats were just average, run-of-the-mill rats, which had been randomly assigned to the two groups of students. Lo and behold, however, the "smart" rats significantly outperformed the "dumb" rats!

It should be noted that the studies of Rosenthal and his associates have been accused of being affected by experimenter bias! Seriously, some researchers have pointed out some methodological flaws, and others have suggested that the results would not have been obtained had properly trained observers been used. It is true that many of their findings have not been replicated, and some researchers have concluded that the experimenter-bias effect is apparently more difficult to demonstrate than one might believe based on Rosenthal's research (Barber, Forgione, Chaves, Calverley, McPeake, & Bowen, 1969; Barber & Silver, 1968). Of course, Rosenthal might claim that they are victims of experimenter bias and failed to find an effect because they did not expect to! H-m-m-m.

In any event, the message to the researcher is to be on the safe side and not be involved directly in conducting her or his own study, if at all possible. Further, the researcher should avoid communicating expectations to any personnel connected with the study.

6. *Reactive arrangement* refers to a number of factors associated with the way in which a study is conducted and the feelings and attitudes of the subjects involved. As discussed previously, in an effort to maintain a high degree of control for the sake of internal validity, a researcher may create an experimental environment that is highly artificial and hinders generalizability of findings to nonexperimental settings. Another

type of reactive arrangement results from the subjects' knowledge that they are involved in an experiment or their feeling that they are in some way receiving special attention. The effect that such knowledge or feelings can have on the behavior of subjects was demonstrated at the Hawthorne Plant of the Western Electric Company in Chicago many years ago (Roethlisberger & Dickson, 1939). As most students of management know, studies were conducted to investigate the relationship between various working conditions and productivity. As part of their studies, the researchers investigated the relationship between light intensity and worker output. When the researchers increased light intensity, production went up. They increased it some more, and production went up some more. The brighter the place became, the more production rose. As a check, the researchers decreased illumination, and guess what—production went up! The darker it got, the more the workers produced. The researchers soon concluded that it was the attention the workers were receiving, and not the illumination, that was affecting production. To this day, the term *Hawthorne effect* is used to describe any situation in which subjects' behavior is affected not by treatment per se but by their knowledge of participation in a study.

As with the experimenter-bias effect, some researchers have criticized the methodology used in these studies and have seriously questioned the validity of results. Some researchers point out that all the subjects were women, that experimental group sizes were small, and that there was apparently considerable variability in how the women reacted to treatments; additionally, attempts to replicate the effect have not been too successful (Cook & Campbell, 1979). Based on his own research and a comprehensive review of related literature, another researcher concluded that the Hawthorne effect probably does not affect the results of studies in which achievement is measured nearly as much as is generally believed (Cook, 1967). As always, however, it is best for the researcher to be on the safe side and to take appropriate precautions.

A related effect is known as the *John Henry effect.* Folk hero John Henry, you may recall, was a "steel drivin' man," who worked for a railroad. When he heard that a steam drill was going to replace him and his fellow steel drivers, he challenged, and set out to beat, the machine. Through tremendous effort he managed to win the ensuing contest, dropping dead at the finish line. This phenomenon has been shown to operate in research studies. If for any reason control groups or their managers feel threatened or challenged by being in competition with a new program or approach, they may outdo themselves and perform way beyond what would normally be expected—even if it "kills" them (Saretsky, 1972). When this effect occurs, the treatment under investigation does not appear to be very effective, since posttest performance of experimental subjects is not much (if at all) better than that of control subjects.

A similar phenomenon in medical research resulted in the *placebo effect,* which is sort of the antidote for the Hawthorne and John Henry effects. In medical research it was discovered that any "medication" could make subjects feel better, even sugar and water. To counteract this effect, the placebo approach was developed, in which half of the subjects receive the true medication and half receive a placebo (sugar and water, for example); this fact is, of course, not known to the subjects. The application of the placebo effect in business-and-management research is that all groups in an experiment should *appear* to be treated the same way. Subjects should not feel special if they are in the experimental group, nor should they they feel shortchanged if they are in the control group. Suppose, for example, you have four groups of truck drivers, two experimental and two control, and the treatment is a film designed to promote defensive driving. If the experimental subjects are to be excused from their routes for a couple of hours in order to view the film, then the control groups also should be excused and shown another film whose content is unrelated to the purpose of the study. As an added control you might have all the subjects told that there are two movies and that eventually all of them will see both movies. In other words, it should appear as if *all* the subjects are doing the same thing.

Another related effect is the *novelty effect*. The novelty effect, which is also called the *honeymoon effect* (Lawler & Mohrman, 1987), refers to increased interest, motivation, or participation on the part of subjects simply because they are doing something different. In other words, a treatment may be effective because it is different and not better per se. To counteract the novelty effect, the study should be conducted over a period of time sufficient to allow the newness to wear off. This is especially true if the treatment involves activities very different from the subjects' usual routine.

GROUP EXPERIMENTAL DESIGNS

The validity of an experiment is a direct function of the degree to which extraneous variables are controlled. If such variables are not controlled, it is difficult to evaluate the effects of an independent variable and the generalizability of effects. The term *confounding* is sometimes used to refer to the fact that the effects of the independent variable may be confused by or mixed up with extraneous variables such that it is difficult to determine the effects of each. The researcher might say, "The effects were confounded by the effects of the extraneous variable . . .," for example. Control of extraneous variables is what experimental design is all about; good designs control many sources of invalidity, while poor designs control only a few. If you recall, the two types of extraneous variables in need of control that were previously identified are subject variables and environmental variables. Subject variables include organismic variables and intervening variables. *Organismic variables* are characteristics of the subject or organism, such as sex, which cannot be directly controlled but the effects of which can be controlled. *Intervening variables* are variables that intervene between the independent variable and the dependent variable, such as anxiety or boredom, which cannot be directly observed or controlled but the effects of which also can be controlled.

Control of Extraneous Variables

Randomization is the best single way to attempt to control for many extraneous variables at the same time. The logical implication of this statement is that randomization should be used whenever possible; subjects should be randomly selected from a population whenever possible, subjects should be randomly assigned to groups whenever possible, treatments should be randomly assigned to groups whenever possible, and anything else you can think of (observers, time periods, mechanical devices) should also be randomly assigned if possible. Recall that *random selection* means selection by pure chance and is usually accomplished using a table of random numbers. *Random assignment* means assignment by pure chance and is usually accomplished by again using the table of random numbers or even by flipping a coin (heads—you're in the experimental group, tails—you're in the control group) if two groups are involved, or by rolling dice if more than two groups are involved. Randomization is effective in creating equivalent, representative groups that are essentially the same on all relevant variables the researcher identified and probably even a few that didn't occur to him or her. Randomly formed groups is a characteristic unique to experimental research; it is a control factor not possible with causal-comparative research. The rationale is that if subjects are assigned at random to groups, there is no reason to believe that the groups are greatly different in any systematic way. Thus, the groups would be expected to perform essentially the same way on the dependent variable *if* the independent variable makes no difference; therefore, if the groups perform differently at the end of the study, the difference can be attributed to the treatment, or independent variable. The larger the groups, the more confidence the researcher can have in the effectiveness of randomization; recall that 15 subjects per group is the smallest acceptable minimum. In addition to equating groups on subject variables such as intelligence, randomization also equalizes groups on environmental variables. Supervisors, for example, can be randomly assigned to groups so that the experimental groups will not have all the "Carmel Kandee" supervisors or all the "Homer Hartless" supervisors (and likewise the control groups). Clearly, the researcher should use as much randomization as possible. If subjects cannot be randomly selected, those available should at least be randomly assigned. If subjects cannot be randomly assigned to groups, then at least treatment condition should be randomly assigned to the existing groups.

In addition to randomization, there are other ways to control for extraneous variables. Certain environmental variables, for example, can be controlled by holding them constant for all groups. Recall the peer-mentor versus management-mentor study; "help time" was an important variable that had to be held constant, that is, be the same, for the two groups. Other such variables that might need to be held constant include (1) training materials, (2) meeting place and time (subjects might be more alert in the morning than in the afternoon), and (3) years of experience of participating supervisors. Controlling subject variables is critical. If the groups are not the same to start with, you haven't even given yourself a fighting chance. Regardless of whether groups can be randomly formed, there are a number of techniques at your disposal that can be used to try to equate groups.

Matching

Matching is a technique for equating groups on one or more variables the researcher has identified as being highly related to performance on the dependent variable. You will recall that the researcher in the quality circle study used matching as a control strategy. The most commonly used approach to matching involves random assignment of pair members, one member to each group. In other words, for each of the available subjects, the researcher attempts to find another subject with the same or a similar score on the control variable(s) on which the subjects are being matched. If the researcher is matching on sex, obviously the "match" must be of the same sex, not a similar sex. If the researcher is matching on variables such as pretest scores, aptitude test scores, or years of experience, however, the similar-score concept makes sense. Unless the available number of subjects is very large, it is unreasonable to try to make exact matches. Thus, the researcher might decide that on years of experience anything plus or minus six months constitutes an acceptable match. As the researcher identifies each matched pair, one member of the pair is randomly assigned to one group and the other member to the other group. If a subject does not have a suitable match, the subject is excluded from the study. The resulting matched groups are identical or very similar with respect to the identified extraneous variable.

A major problem with such matching is that there are invariably subjects who do not have a match and must be eliminated from the study. This factor may cost the researcher many subjects, especially if matching is attempted on two or more variables (imagine trying to find a match for a male with more than 10 years of experience and an extremely low skill level). One way to combat loss of subjects is to match less closely. The researcher might then decide that years of experience within one year plus or minus constitute an acceptable match. This procedure may increase subjects but it tends to defeat the purpose of matching. There's a major difference between 3 months' experience and 15 months,' for example. A related procedure is to rank all subjects from highest to lowest based on their scores on the control variable. The first two subjects (the subjects with the highest and next highest years of experience) are the first pair, no matter how far apart their scores are; one member is randomly assigned to one group, and one member to the other. The next two subjects (the subjects with the third and fourth highest scores) are the next pair, and so on. The major advantage of this approach is that no subjects are lost; the major disadvantage is that it is a lot less precise than pair-wise matching (see the quality circle study). Advanced statistical procedures, such as analysis of covariance (ANCOVA), and the availability of computer programs to compute such statistics have greatly reduced the research use of matching.

Comparing Homogeneous Groups or Subgroups

Another way of controlling an extraneous variable, which was discussed previously with respect to causal-comparative research, is to compare groups that are homogeneous with respect to that variable. For example, if years of experience were an identified extraneous variable, the researcher might select a group of subjects with between 2 and 10 years of experience (no beginners or "burnt out cases"!). The researcher would then randomly assign half of the selected subjects to the experimental group and half to the control group. Of course this procedure also lowers the number of subjects in the study and additionally restricts the generalizability of the findings. Further, if random assignment is possible, using only a homogeneous subgroup really makes sense only if one wants to have an additional guarantee concerning group equality on the control variable.

As with causal-comparative research, a similar but more satisfactory approach is to form subgroups representing all levels of the control variable. For example, the available subjects might be divided into highly experienced (over 10 years), very experienced (8–10 years), moderately experienced (5–7 years), somewhat experienced (2–4 years), and inexperienced (under 2 years) subgroups. Half the selected subjects from each of the subgroups could then be randomly assigned to the experimental group and half to the control group. The procedure just described should sound familiar since it describes stratified sampling (you knew that!). If the researcher is interested not just in controlling the variable but also in seeing if the independent variable affects the dependent variable differently at different levels of the control variable, the best approach is to build the control variable right into the design and to analyze the results with a statistical technique called factorial analysis of variance (Right, it's in Part IV, but it's too late to drop the course after all this work!).

Using Subjects as Their Own Controls

Using subjects as their own controls involves exposing the same group to the different treatments, one treatment at a time. This helps to control for subject differences since the same subjects get both treatments. Of course this approach is not always feasible; you cannot teach the same statistical procedures twice to the same group using two different methods of instruction (well, you could, but it might not make much sense). A problem with this approach in some studies is carryover effects of one treatment to the next. To use a previous example, it would be difficult to evaluate the effectiveness of strict supervision in increasing productivity if the group receiving strict supervision were the same group that had previously been exposed to behavior modification. If only one group is available, a better approach, if feasible, is randomly to divide the group into two smaller groups, each of which receives both treatments but in a different order. In this example, the researcher could at least get some idea of the effectiveness of strict supervision because there would be a group that received it before they experienced behavior modification.

Analysis of Covariance

The analysis of covariance is a statistical method for equating randomly formed groups on one or more variables. In essence, an analysis of covariance adjusts scores on a dependent variable for initial differences on some other variable, such as pretest scores, aptitude, years of experience, or age (assuming that performance on the other variable is related to performance on the dependent variable). In a study comparing the effectiveness of two methods of teaching computer data entry, the researcher could covary on typing speed, thus equating scores on a measure of achievement in data input. Although analysis of covariance can be used in studies when groups cannot be randomly formed, it is most appropriate when randomization is used. Despite randomization, for example, it might be found that two groups differ significantly in terms of pretest scores. Analysis of covariance can be used in such situations to correct, or adjust, posttest scores for initial pretest differences. Calculation of an analysis of covariance is quite a complex, lengthy procedure if you do it by hand, but there are many computer programs readily available that can do the work for you when you know how to use them.

Types of Group Designs

A selected experimental design dictates to a great extent the specific procedures of a study. Selection of a given design dictates such factors as whether there will be a control group, whether subjects will be randomly assigned to groups, whether each group will be pretested, and how resulting data will be analyzed. Depending upon the particular combination of such factors represented, different designs are appropriate for testing different types of hypotheses, and designs vary widely in the degree to which they control the various threats to internal and external validity. Of course there are certain threats to validity that no design can control for; experimenter bias, for example, is a potential threat with any design. Some designs, however, clearly do a better job than others. In selecting a design, you must first determine which designs are appropriate for your study and for testing your hypothesis. You then determine which of those that are appropriate are also feasible given any constraints under which you may be operating. If, for example, you must use existing groups, a number of designs will automatically be eliminated. From the designs that are appropriate and feasible, you select the one that controls the most sources of internal and external invalidity. In other words, you select the best design you possibly can that will yield the data you need to test your hypothesis or hypotheses.

There are two major classes of experimental designs:

1. Single-variable designs involve one independent variable that is manipulated.
2. Factorial designs involve two or more independent variables, at least one of which is manipulated.

Single-variable designs are classified as preexperimental, true experimental, or quasi-experimental, depending upon the control they provide for sources of internal and external invalidity. Preexperimental designs do not do a very good job of controlling threats to validity and should be avoided. In fact, the results of a study based on such a design are so questionable that they are practically worthless for all purposes except, perhaps, a preliminary investigation of a problem. The true experimental designs represent a very high degree of control and are always to be preferred. Quasi-experimental designs do not control as well as true experimental designs but do a much better job than the preexperimental designs. To take a lighter look at the subject, if we were to assign letter grades to experimental designs, all the true experimental designs would get an A, the quasi-experimental designs would get a B or a C (some are better than others), and preexperimental designs would get a D or an F (at least one is barely defensible for limited purposes). Thus, if you have a choice between a true experimental design and a quasi-experimental design, select the true design. If your choice is between a quasi-experimental design and a preexperimental design, select the quasi-experimental design. If your choice is between a preexperimental design or not doing the study at all, think the project through very thoroughly; if you can't arrange to do a follow-up study with an acceptable (C or better) design, you might really be better off not spending your time on it. The poor designs are discussed here primarily so that:

1. You will know what *not* to do.
2. You will be able to explain to others why these approaches won't work.
3. You will recognize them in case you come across one in a published form and will be appropriately critical of the "findings."

Factorial designs are basically elaborations of true experimental designs and permit investigation of two or more variables, individually and in interaction with each other. In business, as in life, variables do not operate in isolation. After an independent variable has been investigated using a single-variable design, it is often useful to study the variable in combination with one or more other variables. As stated previously, some variables work differently at different levels of another variable. Since a factorial design involves two or more variables, there is an almost infinite number of acceptable possibilities for such designs.

The designs to be discussed represent, therefore, the basic designs in each category. Campbell and Stanley (1972) and Cook and Campbell (1979) present a number of variations for those of you who are getting hooked on research.

Pre-experimental Designs

Here is a research riddle for you: Can you do an experiment with only one group? The answer is yes—but not a really good one. Two of the preexperimental designs involve only one group. As Figure 10.1 illustrates, none of the preexperimental designs does a very good job of controlling extraneous variables that jeopardize validity. Again, remember the preexperimental designs are presented so you know what to avoid. There are basically three preexperimental designs:

1. *The one-shot case study* involves one group, which is exposed to a treatment (X) and then posttested (O). All the sources of invalidity are not relevant; testing, for example, is not a concern as there is no pretest. As Figure 10.1 indicates, however, *none* of the threats to validity that are relevant are controlled. Even if the subjects score high on the posttest, you cannot attribute their performance to the treatment, since you do not even know what they knew before you administered the treatment (so much for claiming you learned something in most of your courses based on the final exam grades!). If you, as a researcher, have a choice between using this design and not doing a study, don't waste your time.

2. *The one-group pretest-posttest design* involves one group, which is pretested (O), exposed to a treatment (X), and posttested (O). The success of the treatment is

Designs	Sources of Invalidity									
	Internal								External	
	History	Maturation	Testing	Instrumentation	Regression	Selection	Mortality	Selection Interactions	Pretest-X Interaction	Multiple-X Interference
One-shot case study X O	−	−	(+)	(+)	(+)	(+)	−	(+)	(+)	(+)
One-group pretest-posttest design O X O	−	−	−	−	−	(+)	+	(+)	−	(+)
Static group comparison X_1O X_2O	+	−	(+)	(+)	(+)	−	−	−	(+)	(+)

Symbols:

X or X_1 = unusual treatment
  X_2 = control treatment
   O = test, pretest or
      test

  + = factor controlled for
(+) = factor controlled for
     because not relevant
 − = factor not controlled for

Each line of Xs and Os represents a group

Note: Figures 10.1 and 10.2 basically follow the format used by Campbell and Stanley and are presented with a similar note of caution: The figures are intended to be supplements to, not substitutes for, textual discussions. You should not totally accept or reject designs because of their +s and −s; you *should* also be aware that which design is most appropriate for a given study is determined not only by the controls provided by the various designs but also by the nature of the study and the setting in which it is to be conducted.

While the symbols used in these figures, and their placement, vary somewhat from Campbell and Stanley's format, the intent, interpretations, and textual discussions of the two presentations are in agreement (personal communication with Donald T. Campbell, April 22, 1975).

Figure 10.1. Sources of invalidity for pre-experimental designs

determined by comparing pretest and posttest scores. Although it controls invalidity not controlled by the one-shot case study, a number of additional factors are relevant to this design that are not controlled. If subjects do significantly better on the posttest, it cannot be assumed that the improvement is due to the treatment. History and maturation are not controlled; something may happen to the subjects or inside the subjects to make them perform better the second time. The longer the study is, the more likely this becomes. Testing and instrumentation are not controlled; the subjects may learn something on the first test that helps them on the second test, or unreliability of the measures may be responsible for the apparent improvement. Statistical regression is also not controlled. Even if subjects are not selected on the basis of extreme scores (high or low), it is possible that a group may do very poorly, just by poor luck, on the pretest; subjects may guess badly just by chance on a multiple-choice pretest, for example, and improve on a posttest simply because their score based on guessing is more in line with an expected score. The external-validity-factor pretest-treatment interaction is also not controlled. Pretest-treatment interaction may cause subjects to react differently to the treatment from the way they would have if they had not been pretested.

To illustrate the problems associated with this design, let us examine a hypothetical study. Suppose a professor teaches a very demanding statistics course and is concerned that the high anxiety of the students interferes with their learning. The kindly professor therefore prepares a 100-page booklet that explains the course, and she tries to convince students that they will have no problems and will receive all the help they need to complete successfully the course, even if they have a poor math background and cannot add 2 and 2. The professor wants to see if the booklet works (to justify copying costs, if nothing else), so at the beginning of the term she administers an anxiety scale and then gives each student a copy of the booklet with instructions to read it as soon as possible. Two weeks later, she administers the anxiety scale again, and, sure enough, the students indicate much less anxiety than at the beginning of the term. The professor is well satisfied with the booklet and its effectiveness in reducing anxiety. Is the satisfaction warranted? If you think about it, you will see that there are a number of alternative factors that could explain the decreased anxiety. Students, for example, are typically more anxious at the beginning of a course because they do not know what is coming; most of us fear the unknown. After being in a course for a couple of weeks, students usually find that it is not as bad as they had imagined (right?), or they have dropped it (remember mortality?). Besides, the professor doesn't even know if the students read the masterpiece! Unlike this example, the only situations for which the one-group pretest-posttest design is even remotely appropriate is when the behavior to be measured is not likely to change all by itself. Certain prejudices, for example, are not likely to change unless a concerted effort is made.

3. *The static-group comparison* involves at least two groups. One group receives a new, or unusual treatment; the other receives a traditional, or usual treatment, and both groups are posttested. The first group is usually referred to as the experimental group and the second group as the control group. It is probably more accurate to call both groups comparison groups, since each really serves as the control for the other; each group receives some form of the independent variable. So, for example, if the independent variable is type of orientation, the "experimental" group (X_1) may receive the new, whoop-de-do company orientation complete with slide show, and the "control" group may receive the routine orientation with somebody from the human resources department telling them about the benefit package. Occasionally, but not often, the experimental group may receive something while the control group receives nothing parallel. In this case, X_1 = orientation program and X_2 = no orientation program ("There's your desk—get to work!"). The whole purpose of a control group is to indicate what the performance of the experimental group would have been if it had not received the experimental treatment. Of course, this purpose is fulfilled only to the degree that the control group is equivalent to the experimental group on other variables.

This design can be expanded to deal with any number of groups. For three groups, for example, the design would take the following form:

$$X_1 \quad O$$
$$X_2 \quad O$$
$$X_3 \quad O$$

Which group is the control group? Basically, each group serves as a control, or comparison, group for the other two. For example, if the independent variable were number of performance appraisals, then X_1 might represent two appraisals, X_2 might represent one appraisal, and X_3 no appraisal. Thus X_3 (no appraisal) would help us to assess the impact of X_2 (one appraisal), and X_2 would help us to asses the impact of X_1 (two appraisals). As previously stated, the degree to which the groups are equivalent is the degree to which their comparison is reasonable. Since subjects are not randomly assigned to groups, and since there are no pretest data, however, it is difficult to determine just how equivalent they are. It is always possible that the posttest differences are due to group differences, not just treatment effects (maturation, selection, and selection interactions). Mortality is also a problem, since if you lose subjects from the study you have no information concerning what you have lost (no pretest data). On the positive side, the presence of a control group controls for history, since it is assumed that events occurring outside of the experimental setting will equally affect both groups. Of course the existence of a control group (in this and other designs) permits the occurrence of events that are group-specific, events such as a power failure or a violent storm. These events, referred to as within-group, or intrasession, history, are more likely to occur when groups are "treated" at different times. If not controlled for in some way, their occurrence should be described fully in the research report.

Earlier it was suggested that at least one of the preexperimental designs was "barely defensible." The static-group comparison design is occasionally employed in a preliminary, or exploratory, study. For example (*True Confessions* time here!), early in a semester, one of the authors of this text wondered if the kind of test items given to research students affects their retention of course concepts. For the rest of the term, students in one section of the introductory research course were given multiple-choice tests, and students in another section were given short-answer tests. At the end of the term, group performance was informally compared. The short-answer test section had higher total scores for the course. Therefore, in a subsequent semester, a formal study was executed with randomly formed groups and everything. Thus, an exploratory study, based on a static-group comparison design (two sections, treated differently, and then posttested), led to a formal study, which employed a true experimental design (Gay, 1980).

True Experimental Designs

The true experimental designs control for nearly all sources of internal and external invalidity. As Figure 10.2 indicates, all of the true experimental designs have one characteristic in common that none of the other designs has—random assignment of subjects to groups. Ideally subjects should be randomly selected and randomly

Designs	Sources of Invalidity									
	Internal								External	
	History	Maturation	Testing	Instrumentation	Regression	Selection	Mortality	Selection Interactions	Pretest-X Interaction	Multiple-X Interference
TRUE EXPERIMENTAL DESIGNS										
1. Pretest-Posttest Control-Group Design R O X_1 O R O X_2 O	+	+	+	+	+	+	+	+	−	(+)
2. Posttest-Only Control-Group Design R X_1 O R X_2 O	+	+	(+)	(+)	(+)	+	−	+	(+)	(+)
3. Solomon Four-Group Design R O X_1 O R O X_2 O R X_1 O R X_2 O	+	+	+	+	+	+	+	+	+	(+)
QUASI-EXPERIMENTAL DESIGNS										
4. Nonequivalent Control-Group Design O X_1 O O X_2 O	+	+	+	+	−	+	+	−	−	(+)
5. Time Series Design O O O O X O O O O	−	+	+	−	+	(+)	+	(+)	−	(+)
6. Counterbalanced Designs X_1 O X_2 O X_3 O X_3 O X_1 O X_2 O X_2 O X_3 O X_1 O	+	+	+	+	+	+	+	−	−	−

New Symbol:
R = random assignment of subjects to groups

Figure 10.2 Sources of invalidity for true experimental designs and quasi-experimental designs

assigned; however, to qualify as a true design, at least random assignment must be involved. Note too that all the true designs involve a control group. Also, while the posttest-only control-group design may *look* like the static-group-comparison design, random assignment makes them very different in terms of control. There are three basic experimental designs:

1. *The pretest-posttest control-group design* involves at least two groups, both of which are formed by random assignment; both groups are administered a pretest of the dependent variable, one group receives a new, or unusual, treatment, and both groups are posttested. By the way, although a number of measures may be administered before a study begins, for stratified-random-sampling purposes, for example, the term *pretest* usually refers to a test of the dependent variable. Posttest scores are compared to determine the effectiveness of the treatment. The pretest-posttest control group design may also be expanded to include any number of treatment groups. For three groups, for example, this design would take the following form:

$$R \quad O \quad X_1 \quad O$$
$$R \quad O \quad X_2 \quad O$$
$$R \quad O \quad X_3 \quad O$$

The combination of random assignment and the presence of a pretest and a control group serves to control for all sources of internal invalidity. Random assignment controls for regression and selection factors; the pretest controls for mortality; randomization and the control group control for maturation; and the control group controls for history, testing, and instrumentation. Testing, for example, is controlled because if pretesting leads to higher posttest scores, the advantage should be equal for both the experimental and control groups. The only definite weakness with this design is a possible interaction between the pretest and the treatment, which may make the results generalizable only to other pretested groups. As discussed before, the seriousness of this potential weakness depends upon such factors as the nature of the pretest, the nature of the treatment, and the length of the study. It is more likely to occur with reactive measures such as attitude scales and in short studies. When this design is used, the researcher should assess and report the probability of its occurrence. A researcher might indicate, for example, that possible pretest interaction was believed to be minimized by the nonreactive nature of the pretest (accounting procedures) and by the length of the study (nine months).

There are three basic ways in which the data can be analyzed in order to determine the effectiveness of the treatment and to test the research hypothesis; one of them is clearly inappropriate, one is not very appropriate, and one is clearly most appropriate.

One approach is to compare the pretest and posttest scores of each group; if the experimental group improves significantly but not the control group, it is concluded that the treatment is effective. This approach is inappropriate because the real question is whether the experimental group is better than the control group; thus the appropriate comparison is the posttest scores of each group. If the researcher finds that both groups have improved significantly (e.g., each group's average posttest, accounting-procedures score is significantly higher than its pretest, accounting-procedures score after nine months of different instruction), this still does not indicate whether one group is significantly better than the other; we would expect both groups to improve their accounting procedures in 9 months, no matter what method of instruction was used, so the question involves which treatment has done a better job.

A second approach is to compute gain, or difference, scores for each subject (posttest score minus pretest score) and then to compare the average gain of the experimental group with the average gain of the control group. Gain scores entail problems, however. For one thing, all subjects do not have the same "room" to gain. On a 100-item test, who is better, the trainee who goes from a pretest score of 80 to a posttest score of 99 (a gain of 19), or a trainee who goes from a pretest score of 20 to a posttest score of 70 (a gain of 50)?

The third approach, and the one usually recommended, is simply to compare the posttest scores of the two groups. (Surprise! the simplest approach is recommended!) The pretest is only used to see if the groups are essentially the same on the dependent variable. If they are, posttest scores can be directly compared using a t test; if they are not (random assignment does not *guarantee* equality); posttest scores can be analyzed using analysis of covariance. Recall that covariance adjusts posttest scores for initial differences on any variable, including pretest scores. The researcher may choose to use analysis of covariance *even if* the pretest scores are essentially the same because this procedure may be used to increase the power of the statistical test, but we'll come back to this later.

A variation of the pretest-posttest control-group design involves random assignment of members of matched pairs to the groups, one member to each group in order to control more closely for one or more extraneous variables. Some researchers would argue, however, that there is really no advantage to this technique, since any variable that can be controlled through matching can be better controlled using other procedures such as analysis of covariance.

Another variation of this design involves one or more additional posttests. For example:

$$R \quad O \quad X_1 \quad O \quad O$$
$$R \quad O \quad X_2 \quad O \quad O$$

This variation has the advantage of providing information on the effect of the independent variable both immediately following treatment and also at a later date. Recall that *interaction-of-time-of-measurement-and-treatment effects* was discussed as a threat to external validity. It is a potential threat to generalizability because posttesting may yield different results depending upon when it is done; a treatment effect (or lack of same) that is found based on the administration of a posttest immediately following the treatment may not be found if a delayed posttest is given sometime after treatment. While this variation does not completely solve the problem, it does minimize it. This variation may also give the researcher some idea about effects that are of great importance from a practical standpoint. For example, if new supervisors are given a week-long, concentrated program of supervisory training, they may do very well on a posttest administered on Friday afternoon; the real question for management, however, is more likely to be how well they do six weeks to three months after the course is over. Of course, how many additional posttests should be given, and when, depends upon the variables being investigated.

2. *The posttest-only control-group design* is exactly the same as the pretest-posttest control-group design except there is no pretest; subjects are randomly assigned to groups, exposed to the independent variable, and posttested. Posttest scores are then compared to determine the effectiveness of the treatment. As with the pretest-posttest control-group design, the posttest-only control-group design can be expanded to include more than two groups.

The combination of random assignment and the presence of a control group serve to control for all sources of internal invalidity except mortality and all external sources of invalidity. Mortality is not controlled for because of the absence of pretest data on subjects. Mortality may or may not be a problem, however, depending upon the study. If the study is relatively short in duration, for example, no subjects may be lost. In this case the researcher may report that while mortality is a potential threat to validity with this design, it did not prove to be a threat in his or her particular study, since the group sizes remained constant throughout the duration of the study. Thus, if the probability of differential mortality is low, the posttest-only design can be a very effective design. Of course if there is any chance that the groups may be different with respect to initial knowledge related to the dependent variable (despite random assignment), the pretest-posttest control-group design should be used. Which design is best depends upon the study. If the study is to be lengthy (good chance of mortality), or if there is a chance that the two groups differ on initial knowledge related to the dependent variable, then the pretest-posttest control-group design may be the best.

A variation of the posttest-only control-group design involves random assignment of matched pairs to the groups, one member to each group, in order to control more closely for one or more extraneous variables. As with the pretest-posttest control-group design, however, there is really no advantage to this technique; any variable that can be controlled through matching can be better controlled using other procedures.

What if, however, you face the following dilemma:

1. The study is going to last two months.
2. Assessment of initial knowledge is essential.
3. The pretest is an attitude scale.
4. The treatment is designed to change attitudes.

Here we have a classic situation where pretest-treatment interaction is probable. Do we throw up our hands in despair? Of course not. One solution is to select the lesser of the two evils, perhaps taking our chances with mortality. Another solution, if sufficient subjects are available, is to use the Solomon four-group design, to be discussed next. If you look at Figure 10.2 you will see that the Solomon four-group design is simply a combination of the pretest-posttest control-group design (the top two lines) and the posttest-only control-group design (the third and fourth lines).

3. *The Solomon four-group design* involves random assignment of subjects to one of four groups. Two of the groups are pretested and two are not; one of the pretested groups and one of the unpretested groups receive the experimental treatment. All four groups are posttested. As Figure 10.2 indicates, this design is a combination of the pretest-posttest control-group design and the posttest-only control-group design, each of which has its own major source of invalidity (pretest-treatment interaction and mortality, respectively). The combination of these two designs results in a design that controls for pretest-treatment interaction and also for mortality. The correct way to analyze data resulting from application of this design is to use a 2×2 factorial analysis of variance. The two independent variables are the treatment variable and the pretest variable; in other words, whether a group is pretested or not is an independent variable, just as the experimental variable is. The factorial analysis tells the researcher whether the treatment is effective and also whether there is an interaction between the treatment and the pretest. To put it as simply as possible, if the pretested experimental group performs differently on the posttest from the way the unpretested experimental group did, there is probably a pretest-treatment interaction. If no interaction is found, then the researcher can have more confidence in the generalizability of treatment differences.

A common misconception among beginning researchers is that since the Solomon four-group design controls for so many sources of invalidity, it is the best design. This is not true. For one thing, this design requires twice as many subjects as either of the other true experimental designs, and subjects are often hard to come by. Further, if mortality is not likely to be a problem, and pretest data are not needed, then the posttest-only design may be best; if pretest-treatment interaction is unlikely, and testing is a normal part of the subjects' environment (school, for example), then the pretest-posttest control-group design may be the best. Which design is the best depends upon the nature of the study and the conditions under which it is to be conducted. A general rule of thumb, however, may be to keep studies as simple as possible; as in art, there may be a value to the simple and elegant solution rather than a complicated procedure designed primarily to dazzle the observer.

Quasi-experimental Designs

Sometimes it's just not possible to assign subjects randomly to groups. In order to receive permission to use employees in a study, for example, a researcher often has to agree to use existing work groups. When this occurs, however, there are still a number of designs available to the researcher that provide adequate control of sources of invalidity; these designs are referred to as quasi-experimental designs. Keep in mind that designs such as these are *only* to be used when it is not feasible to use a true experimental design. Although Campbell and Stanley (1971) discuss a number of such designs, only three of the major ones will be discussed here.

1. *The nonequivalent control-group design* should be familiar to you since it looks very much like the pretest-posttest control-group design; the only difference is that the nonequivalent control-group design does not involve random assignment of subjects to groups (although treatment should be randomly assigned to groups, if possible). Two existing groups are pretested, administered a treatment, and posttested. The lack

of random assignment adds sources of invalidity not associated with the pretest-posttest control-group design—possible regression and interaction between selection and variables such as maturation, history, and testing. The more similar the groups are, the better; the researcher should make every effort to use groups that are as equivalent as possible. Comparing a group of experienced insurance claims processors with a group of trainees, for example, would not do. If differences between the groups on any major extraneous variable are identified, analysis of covariance can be used to equate the groups statistically. An advantage of this design is that since work groups are used "as is," possible effects from reactive arrangements are minimized. Subjects may not even be aware that they are involved in a study, although you'll want to think through the ethics of that pretty clearly. As with the pretest-posttest control-group design, the nonequivalent control-group design may be extended to include more than two groups.

2. *The time-series design* is actually an elaboration of the one-group pretest-posttest design. One group is repeatedly pretested, exposed to a treatment, and then repeatedly posttested. If a group scores essentially the same on a number of pretests and then significantly improves following a treatment, the researcher has more confidence in the effectiveness of the treatment than if just one pretest and one posttest are administered. To use a former example, if our statistics professor measured anxiety several times before giving the students the booklet, he would be able to see if anxiety was declining naturally. History is still a problem with this design, however, since something might happen between the last pretest and the first posttest, the effect of which might be confused with the treatment. Instrumentation may also be a problem but not an expected problem, unless for some reason the researcher changes measuring instruments during the study. Pretest-treatment interaction is also a validity problem. It should be clear that if one pretest can interact with a treatment, more than one pretest can only make matters worse! An excellent application of this design is in a production area in which the pretest and posttest can be an unobtrusive measure. The number of widgets produced during a week can be counted over a number of weeks before and after the treatment, for example, without the employees being aware that pretest and posttest measures are being taken. Number of absences or accidents might be unobtrusive measures for stress-management or accident-prevention programs using a time-series design.

While statistical analyses appropriate for this design are rather advanced, determining the effectiveness of the treatment basically involves analysis of the pattern of the test scores. Figure 10.3 illustrates several possible patterns that might be found; Campbell and Stanley (1971) discuss a number of other possibilities. In Figure 10.3 the vertical line between O_4 and O_5 indicates the point at which the treatment was introduced. Pattern A does not indicate a treatment effect; performance was increasing before the treatment was introduced, and it continued to increase at the same rate following introduction of the treatment. In fact pattern A represents the reverse situation to that encountered by our statistics professor and the anxiety-reducing booklet. Patterns B and C do indicate a treatment effect; the effect appears to be more permanent in pattern C than in pattern B. Pattern D does not indicate a treatment

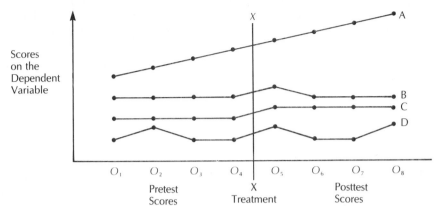

Figure 10.3. Possible patterns for the results of a study based on a time-series design.

effect even though subject scores are higher on O_5 than O_4. The pattern is too erratic. Scores appear to be fluctuating up and down; the O_4 to O_5 fluctuation cannot be attributed to the treatment. The four patterns shown illustrate that just comparing O_4 to O_5 is not sufficient; in all four cases O_5 indicates a higher score than O_4, but only in two of the patterns does it appear that the difference is due to a treatment effect.

A variation of the time-series design, which is referred to as the multiple time-series design, involves the addition of a control group to the basic design as follows:

$$O \ O \ O \ O \ X_1 \ O \ O \ O \ O$$
$$O \ O \ O \ O \ X_2 \ O \ O \ O \ O$$

This variation eliminates history and instrumentation as threats to validity and thus represents a design with no probable sources of internal invalidity. The design can be more effectively used in situations where testing is a naturally occuring event not likely to be noticed. As previously noted, however, if unobtrusive measures can be used, this variation may also be applied.

3. *Counterbalanced designs* have all groups receive all the treatments but in a different order. Although Figure 10.2 represents the design for three groups and three treatments, any number of groups may be involved (two or more); the only restriction is that the number of groups equals the number of treatments. The order in which the groups receive the treatments is randomly determined. While subjects may be pretested, this design is usually employed when intact groups must be used and when administration of a pretest is not possible or feasible. The static-group comparison also can be used in such situations, but the counterbalanced design controls several additional sources of invalidity.

In the situation shown in Figure 10.2, there are three groups and three treatments (or two treatments and a control group). The first horizontal line indicates that group A receives treatment 1 and is posttested, then receives treatment 2 and is posttested, and then treatment 3 and is posttested. The second line indicates that group B receives treatment 3, then treatment 1, and then treatment 2, and is posttested after each treatment. The third line indicates that group C receives treatment 2, then treatment 3, then treatment 1, and is posttested after each treatment. To put it another way, the first column indicates that at time 1, while group A is receiving treatment 1, group B is receiving treatment 3 and group C is receiving treatment 2. All three groups are posttested and the treatments are shifted to produce the second column. The second column indicates that at time 2, while group A is receiving treatment 2, group B is receiving treatment 1, and group C is receiving treatment 3. The groups are then posttested again, and the treatments are again shifted to produce the third column. The third column indicates that now, at time 3, group A is receiving treatment 3, group B is receiving treatment 2, and group C is receiving treatment 1. All groups are posttested again. (This is *not*, by the way, a research variation of the old comedy routine "Who's on First?") Thus, each row represents a replication of the study. In order to determine the effectiveness of the treatments, the average performance of the groups for each treatment can be compared. In other words, the posttest scores for all the groups for the first treatment can be compared to the posttest scores of all the groups for the second treatment, and so forth, depending upon the number of groups and treatments.

A unique weakness of this design is potential multiple-treatment interference, which can result when the same group receives more than one treatment. Thus, a counterbalanced design should really only be used when the treatments are such that exposure to one will not affect evaluation of the effectiveness of another. Of course, there are not too many situations in business where this condition can be met. You cannot, for example, teach the same procedure for processing complaints to the same group using several different methods of training. A possible example of a counterbalanced design would be to test the effectiveness of three supervisors by having them rotate from work group to work group and measure production with each supervisor. If you find that you need to use this design, there are sophisticated analysis procedures that can be applied to determine both the effects of treatments and the effects of the order of those treatments.

Factorial Designs

Factorial designs involve two or more independent variables, at least one of which is manipulated by the researcher. They are basically elaborations of true experimental designs and permit investigation of two or more variables, individually and in interaction with each other. In business, variables do not operate in isolation. After an independent variable has been investigated using a single-variable design, it is often useful then to study the variable in combination with one or more other variables. Some variables work differently at different levels of another variable; some management theorists believe, for example, that one method of supervision may be more effective for workers with a high level of readiness (a mixture of ability, technical skills, and self-confidence) while another method may be more effective with workers with a lower level of readiness (Hersey & Blanchard, 1988). The term *factorial* refers to the fact that the design involves more than one independent variable, or factor. In this example, supervision is a factor and experience is a factor. Each factor has two or more levels; the factor "method of supervision" has at least two levels since there are more than two ways to supervise employees (task behavior vs. relationship behavior, for example), and the factor of readiness has at least two levels, ranging from very ready to very unready. Thus, a 2 × 2 factorial design has two factors and each factor has two levels. The 2 × 2 is the simplest factorial design. As another example, a 2 × 3 factorial design has two factors; one factor has two levels and the second factor has three levels (such as very ready, moderately ready, and very unready). Suppose we have three independent variables, or factors: supervision (high task, combination task-relationship, and high relationship); experience (very ready, moderately ready, and very unready); and classification of job (professional, clerical). How would you symbolize this study? Right, it is a 3 × 3 × 2 factorial design. Since we've mentioned Hersey & Blanchard, those of you familiar with their work know that they use four levels of leadership (S_1–S_4) and four levels of readiness of workers (R_1–R_4); a design to test this theory would require at least a 4 × 4 factorial design, right? If you are interested in pursuing studies dealing with this theory, you may want to review a study by Goodson, McGee, and Cashman (1989) dealing with the interaction of leader behavior and follower readiness.

The simplest factorial design, the 2 × 2, requires four groups, as Figure 10.4 illustrates. In Figure 10.4 there are two factors: one factor, type of sales, has two levels, large appliances and small electronics, and the other factor, type of compensation, has two levels, salary and commission. Each of the groups represents a combination of one level of one factor and one level of the other factor. Thus, group 1 is composed of salespeople in large appliances receiving salaries, group 2 is composed of salespeople in large appliances receiving commissions, group 3 is composed of salespeople in small electronics receiving salaries, and group 4 is composed of salespeople in small electronics receiving commissions. If this design were used, a number of salespeople in large appliances would be randomly assigned to either group 1 or group 2, and an equal number of salespeople in small electronics would be randomly assigned to either group 3 or group 4. This should sound familiar since it represents stratified random sampling. In such a design both variables may be manipulated, but the 2 × 2 design usually involves one manipulated, or experimental, variable, and one nonmanipulated

| | | Type of Sales | |
		Large Appliances	Small Electronics
Type of Compensation	Salary	Group 1	Group 2
	Commission	Group 3	Group 4

Figure 10.4. An example of the basic 2 × 2 factorial design.

variable; the nonmanipulated variable is often referred to as a control variable. *Control variables* are usually physical or mental characteristics of the subjects such as sex, age, or aptitude. In the above example, either variable could be manipulated, but we would probably designate type of sales as the control variable; we would select salespeople with equivalent amounts of experience in sales and product knowledge, for example, so that the other variable, type of compensation, becomes the manipulated variable or treatment. When symbolizing such designs, the manipulated variable is traditionally placed first. Thus, a study with two independent variables, type of supervision (three types, manipulated), and experience of workers (very experienced, very inexperienced), would be symbolized 3×2, not 2×3.

The purpose of a factorial design is to determine whether the effects of an experimental variable are generalizable across all levels of a control variable or whether the effects are specific to specific levels of the control variable. Also, a factorial design can demonstrate relationships that a single-variable experiment cannot. For example, a variable found not to be effective in a single-variable experiment may be found to interact significantly with another variable. The second example in Figure 10.5 illustrates this possibility.

Figure 10.5 represents two possible outcomes for an experiment involving a 2×2 factorial design. The number in each box, or cell, represents the average posttest measurement of that group. Thus, in the top example, the experienced workers under

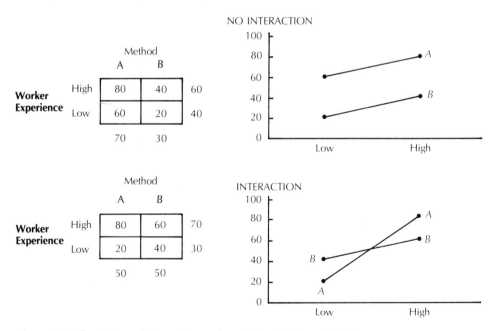

Figure 10.5 Illustration of interaction and no interaction in a 2×2 factorial design.

method A had an average production rate (posttest score) of 80. The marginal row and column numbers outside of the boxes represent average production rates across boxes, or cells. In the top example, the average production rate for method A was 70 (found by averaging the scores of all the subjects under method A regardless of experience level), and for subjects under method B, 30. By examining the cell averages, we see that method A was better than method B for experienced workers (80 versus 40), and method A was also better for inexperienced workers (60 versus 20). Thus, method A was better, regardless of experience level; there was *no interaction* between method and experience. The experienced workers in each method outperformed the inexperienced workers in each method (no big surprise), and the subjects in method A outperformed the subjects in method B at each level of experience. The graph to the right of the results illustrates the lack of interaction.

In the bottom example, which method was better, A or B? The answer is, it depends! Depends on what? Depends on which experience level we are talking about. For experienced workers, method A was better (80 versus 60); for inexperienced workers, method B was better (20 versus 40). Even though experienced workers did better than inexperienced workers regardless of method, how well they did *depended* upon which method they were under. It cannot be said that either method was better in general; which method was better depended upon the experience level. Perhaps experienced workers found it quite difficult to change from an old method (method A), or inexperienced workers found it easier to learn the new method (method B); given time, perhaps the difference would disappear, but at the time of the experiment, at least, there was a difference. Now suppose the study had not used a factorial design but had simply compared two groups of subjects, one group receiving method A and one group receiving method B; each group would have been composed of both experienced and inexperienced workers. The researcher would have concluded that method A and method B were equally effective, since the overall average score, or productivity, for method A was 50 and the overall average score for method B was 50! By using a factorial design it was determined that an *interaction* appears to exist between the variables such that each of the methods is differentially effective depending upon the experience level of the subjects. The graph to the right of the results illustrates the interaction.

There are a lot of possible factorial designs depending upon the nature and the number of independent variables. Theoretically, a researcher could simultaneously investigate 10 factors in a $2 \times 2 \times 2 \times 2 \times 2 \times 3 \times 3 \times 3 \times 4 \times 4$ design, for example. In reality, however, more than 3 factors are rarely used. For one thing, each additional factor increases the number of subjects that are required. In Chapter 4, it was stated that the minimum number of subjects per group for an experimental study is 15. Thus, a pretest-posttest control-group design with two groups requires at least 30 subjects (2×15). Since a 2×2 design involves 4 groups, 60 subjects (4×15) are required. Similarly, a $3 \times 3 \times 2$ design, which involves 18 groups, requires 270 subjects. It is easy to see that things quickly get out of hand. This is not to say that studies are not done with smaller group sizes—they are. But such situations are usually the result of the lack of an adequate number of subjects being available, or mortality during the study, not intentional planning. The results of such studies require cautious interpretation. For another thing, when too many factors are involved, resulting interactions become difficult, if not impossible, to interpret. Interpretation of a two-way interaction, such as the one illustrated in Figure 10.5, is relatively straightforward. But how, for example, would you interpret a five-way interaction between supervision method, experience, sex, aptitude, and morale? Such interpretations tend to have no meaning. Besides, it's not easy to graph a five-way interaction! A better way of handling this sort of problem would probably be to isolate the two most important factors, using a statistical method called a multiple-regression analysis (see Chapter 8 for a brief discussion of this method) and then devise a design to test the effect of the two selected variables. When used correctly and reasonably, however, factorial designs are very effective for testing certain research hypotheses that cannot be tested with a single-variable design.

SINGLE-SUBJECT EXPERIMENTAL DESIGNS

As you would probably guess, single-subject experimental designs (also commonly referred to as single-case experimental designs) are designs that can be applied when the sample size is one. They can also be applied when a number of individuals are considered as one group. They are typically used to study the behavior change an individual exhibits as a result of some intervention, or treatment. In single-subject designs each subject serves as his or her own control in variations on a time-series design. Basically, the subject is alternately exposed to a nontreatment and a treatment condition, or phase, and performance is repeatedly measured during each phase. The nontreatment condition is symbolized as A and the treatment condition is symbolized as B. For example, we might do the following:

1. Observe and record excessive time at lunch on five occasions.
2. Apply a behavior-modification procedure (such as immediate verbal counseling for tardiness, praise for returning on time) and observe five more occasions.
3. Stop the behavior modification procedure and observe five more times.

Our design would be symbolized as A-B-A. While single-subject designs have their roots in clinical psychology and psychiatry, they are also used in many educational settings and have a definite place in business, particularly for supervisors.

The use of single-subject designs has increased steadily since about the mid-1960s, paralleling the increased application of behavior modification techniques. Publication of the first issue of the *Journal of Applied Behavior Analysis* in 1968 by the Society for the Experimental Analysis of Behavior signaled a new acceptance for single-subject research, an acceptance based on an improved methodology. Whereas previously single-subject research was generally equated with a descriptive, case-study approach, it now has become associated with a more controlled, experimental approach.

Single-Subject Versus Group Designs

As single-subject designs have become progressively more refined and capable of dealing with threats to experimental validity, they have come to be viewed as acceptable substitutes for traditional group designs in a number of situations. At the very least they are considered to be valuable complements to such designs.

Most experimental-research problems require traditional group designs for their investigation. This is mainly because the results are intended to be applied to groups. As an example, if we were investigating the comparative effectiveness of two approaches to marketing a product, we would be interested in which approach, in general, produces better results. Except in very specialized applications, businesses do not approach potential customers on an individual basis, and therefore they seek strategies that are relatively effective with groups of potential consumers. Large marketing efforts require the application of strategies associated with descriptive research or involving a group-comparison design. In addition to being inappropriate, a single-subject design would be very impractical for such a research problem because single-subject designs require multiple measurements during each phase (e.g., no treatment, treatment, no treatment) of the study. Recall that in the previous example on excessive lunch break, 15 separate observation periods were involved (5 per phase). It would be highly impractical to try to observe a large group in such detail.

There are, however, a number of research questions for which traditional group designs are not appropriate for two major reasons. First, group-comparison designs are frequently opposed on ethical, philosophical, or legal grounds (recall Chapter 3). By definition, group-comparison designs involve a control group that does not receive the experimental treatment. Withholding a program from employees with a demonstrated need for the potentially beneficial program, or intervention, may be opposed or actually prohibited, as it is in many employment and training issues. The fact that the effectiveness of the treatment has not yet been demonstrated and the fact that the purpose of the research is to assess its effectiveness are irrelevant. That the treatment is potentially effective is sufficient to raise objections if an attempt is made to prevent any eligible subjects from receiving it. In early 1990, residents of a southern state became aware that the a state agency had contracted for a study on the effectiveness of a job-training program for welfare recipients; the control group, some 5,500 people, would cease receiving job-training benefits for 3 years while the researchers evaluated their success compared to the success of the individuals who continued receiving job-training benefits! On a smaller scale, how would you like to explain to the control-group employees that they would not be attending the career-development seminar or the stress-management workshop? In these situations, the comparison aspect of group-comparison designs is the issue.

A second reason why the application of a group-comparison design may not be appropriate has probably already occurred to you. The size of the population of interest and consequent sample size may be so small that it is impossible to form two equivalent groups. If the treatment, for example, is aimed at improving the skills of beginning bank tellers, the number of trainees available at any one locale may be quite small. If there are, say, 10 such trainees, application of a single-subject design is clearly preferable to the formulation of two more-or-less equivalent groups of 5 trainees each.

Further, single-subject designs are most frequently applied in action-research settings where the primary emphasis is on immediate improvement in a very specific setting and not on making a contribution to a research base. In such settings, the overriding objective is the identification of intervention strategies that will change the behavior of specific individuals or groups. This is especially important when individuals are engaging in behavior that is clearly detrimental to productivity, such as substance abuse, high accident rates, doing low-quality work, or spending excessive time away from the job. Of course it is hoped that a treatment found to be effective in changing a particular behavior of a particular subject in a particular setting (action research, in other words), will be found over time to be effective for other behaviors and subjects in various settings.

External Validity

A major criticism leveled at single-subject research studies is that they suffer from low external validity; that is, the results cannot be generalized to the population of interest as they can with group designs. While this allegation is basically true, it is also true that the results of a study using a group design cannot be generalized to any individual within the group. If we randomly select subjects and randomly assign them to groups, the result is two relatively heterogeneous groups. The average posttest performance of the treatment group may not adequately reflect the performance of any individual within the group. Thus, group designs and single-subject designs each have their own generalizability problems. If your concern is with improving the functioning of an individual, a group design is not going to be appropriate.

Usually, however, we are interested in generalizing the results of our research to persons other than those directly involved in the study. For single-subject designs, the key to generalizability is replication. If a researcher applies the same treatment using the same single-subject design to a number of subjects and gets essentially the same results in *every* case (or even in *most* cases), our confidence in the findings is increased; there is evidence for the generalizability of the results for other subjects. If other researchers in other settings apply the same treatment to other subjects and get essentially the same results, the case for the efficacy of the treatment becomes stronger. The more diverse the replications are (i.e., different kinds of subjects, different behaviors, different settings), the more generalizable the results are.

One generalizability problem associated with many single-subject designs is the possible effect of the baseline condition (phase one) on the subsequent effects of the treatment condition. If your tardy employee sees you watching the clock each time he or she returns from lunch, it may change the behavior before you *begin* your planned intervention! We can never be entirely sure that the treatment effects are the same as they would have been if the treatment phase had been the first and not the second phase. This problem, of course, parallels the pretest-treatment interaction problem associated with a number of group designs.

Internal Validity

If proper controls are exercised in connection with the application of a single-subject design, the internal validity of the resulting study may be quite good. For an in-depth discussion of the topics to follow, you may want to consult Barlow & Hersen (1984).

Repeated and Reliable Measurement

As with a time-series design, pretest performance is measured a number of times prior to implementation of the treatment or intervention. In single-subject designs these sequential measures of pretest performance are referred to as baseline measures. As a result of these measures taken over some period of time, sources of invalidity such as maturation are controlled for in the same way as for the time-series design. Unlike the time-series design, however, performance is also measured at various times while the treatment is being applied. This added dimension greatly reduces the potential threat to validity from history, a threat to internal validity associated with the time-series design.

One very real threat to the internal validity of most single-subject designs is instrumentation. Recall that "instrumentation" refers to unreliability, or inconsistency, in measuring instruments that may result in an invalid assessment of performance. Since repeated measurement is a characteristic of all single-subject designs, it is especially important that measurement of the target behavior, or performance, be done in exactly the same way every time or as nearly the same as is humanly possible. Thus, every effort should be made to promote observer reliability by clearly, and in sufficient detail, defining the target behavior, e.g. tardiness. Typically, as previously suggested, studies using single-subject designs are concerned with some type of behavior requiring observation as the major data-collection strategy. In such studies it is critical that the observation conditions (e.g., location, time of day) be standardized. If one observer makes all the observations, then intraobserver reliability should be estimated. If more than one observer is involved, then interobserver reliability should be estimated. Consistency of measurement is especially crucial as we move from phase to phase. If an event of history occurs at the same time we move from a baseline to a treatment phase, the result will be an invalid assessment of the effect of the treatment. Suppose, for example, that the tardy employee is your secretary. After observing him returning late from lunch every day for a week and recording the times, you are ready to begin the treatment phase. If, however, the secretary at the next desk is going on vacation this week and your secretary is expected to cover for her, the conditions will be altered sufficiently to invalidate your treatment.

Relatedly, the nature and conditions of the treatment should be specified in sufficient detail to permit replication. Some single-subject designs involve reinstatement of the treatment phase following measurement of posttest performance. For example, with an A-B-A-B design, we have a baseline phase, a treatment phase, a return to baseline conditions (withdrawal of the treatment), and a second treatment phase. If its effects are to be validly assessed, the treatment must involve precisely the same procedures every time it is introduced. Also, since the key to generalizability for single-subject designs is replication, it is clearly a necessity for the treatment to be sufficiently standardized to permit other researchers to apply it as it was originally applied and as it was intended to be applied.

Baseline Stability

Another factor related to the internal validity of single-subject designs is the length of the baseline and treatment phases. A major question is, How many measurements of behavior should be taken before treatment is introduced? There is no easy answer. The purpose of the baseline measurements is to provide a description of the target behavior as it naturally occurs *without* the treatment. Thus, the baseline serves as the basis of comparisons for assessing the effectiveness of the treatment.

If most behaviors were very stable, there would be no problem. But human behavior is variable and, in some situations, very variable. With the tardy secretary, for example, we would not expect him to return from lunch with exactly the same minutes of tardiness each day. There would be fluctuations, and he will be later at some times than at others. Such fluctuations, however, usually fall within some consistent range. Therefore, a sufficient number of baseline measurements are usually taken to establish a pattern. The establishment of a pattern is referred to as baseline stability. We might observe, for example, that the secretary is normally between 5 and 25 minutes late each day. These figures then become our basis of comparison for assessing the effectiveness of the treatment. If during the treatment phase the minutes of lateness range from 0 to 2 or steadily decrease until they reach 0, and if the minutes of lateness increase when the treatment is withdrawn, the effectiveness of the treatment is demonstrated.

In the absence of baseline stability, the existence of an apparent trend affects the number of baseline data points. If the target behavior is found to be getting progressively worse, there are progressively more minutes of tardiness, for example, fewer measurements are required to establish the baseline pattern. If, however, the behavior is getting progressively better, at an acceptable rate, there is no point in introducing the treatment until, or unless, the behavior stabilizes and ceases to improve. In general, however, three data points are usually considered the minimum number of measurements necessary to establish baseline stability.

Normally, the length of the treatment phase and the number of measurements taken during the treatment phase parallel the length and measurement of the baseline phase. If, for example, baseline stability is established after 3 consecutive days of tardiness, then the treatment phase could consist of 3 days. There are reasons for varying phase length, however. In a study involving daily observations, for example, it might take several weeks to establish baseline (secretary is late two to three times each week) but well over a month to bring behavior to a criterion level. (If you are losing patience with this example and thinking, ''Why not just fire him?'' consider the fact that if you *do* need to terminate the employee after all this effort, your human resources department will love your data!)

The Single-Variable Rule

An important principle of single-subject research is that only one variable at a time should be manipulated. In other words, as we move from phase to phase (any phase), only one variable should be changed, i.e., added or withdrawn. This means that even though you're excited because your treatment appears to be working on the tardiness, it's not the right time to work on the secretary's spelling errors in your letters! (Maybe you should just fire him.) Seriously though, sometimes an attempt is made to manipulate two variables simultaneously in order to assess their interactive effects. This practice is not sound and prevents us from assessing adequately the effects of either variable.

Types of Single-Subject Designs

Single-subject designs can be classified into three major categories:A-B-A withdrawal, multiple-baseline, and alternating treatments. A-B-A designs basically involve alternating phases of baseline (A) and treatment (B). Multiple-baseline designs entail the systematic addition of behaviors, subjects, or settings targeted for intervention. They are used mainly for situations in which the baseline cannot be recovered once treatment is introduced and for situations in which treatment cannot or should not be withdrawn once it is applied. An alternating-treatments design involves the relatively rapid alternating of treatments for a single subject. Its purpose is to assess the relative effectiveness of two (or more) treatment conditions.

This section will describe the basic designs in each category and will present some common variations. The literature on design contains many variations in addition to these:

A-B-A Withdrawal Designs

A-B-A withdrawal designs have a number of variations, the least complex of which is the A-B design. Since "withdrawal" refers to withdrawal of treatment and return to baseline, the A-B design is essentially a prewithdrawal design, in the same sense that the one-shot case-study (X O) group design is a preexperimental design. Variations of the basic A-B-A withdrawal design not discussed in this section are used infrequently in research studies.

1. *The A-B design* is an improvement over the simple case-study approach, although its internal validity is suspect. When this design is used, baseline measurements are repeatedly made until stability is presumably established; treatment is then introduced and an appropriate number of measurements are made during treatment. If behavior improves during the treatment phase, the effectiveness of the treatment is allegedly demonstrated. We could symbolize this design as follows:

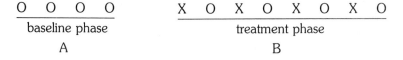

O O O O	X O X O X O X O
baseline phase	treatment phase
A	B

Of course, the specific number of measurements (O) involved in each phase will vary from experiment to experiment. The problem is that we don't know if behavior improved *because of* the treatment or for some other reason. It is always possible that the observed behavior change occurred as a result of the influence of some other, unknown variable or that the behavior would have improved naturally, without the treatment.

2. *Additive designs,* variations of the A-B design, involve the addition of another phase (or phases) in which the experimental treatment is supplemented with another treatment. An A-B-BC design, for example, might represent baseline (A), positive verbal reinforcement (B), and positive verbal reinforcement plus group recognition or some other reward (BC). Such designs are commonly used when an initial treatment is not satisfactory in terms of desired effects, and they suffer from the same validity problems as the basic A-B design.

3. *The A-B-A design,* in which we simply add a second baseline phase to the A-B design, gives us a much improved design. If the behavior is better during the treatment phase than during either baseline phase, the effectiveness of the treatment has presumably been demonstrated. Using familiar symbolism, we could represent this design in the following way:

O O O O	X O X O X O X O	O O O O
baseline phase	treatment phase	baseline phase
A	B	A

Suppose, for example, that you were supervising an employee processing orders from a home office via a computer hookup. During an initial baseline phase you might observe the number of orders processed during 4 working sessions. You might then introduce reinforcement in the form of a friendly greeting flashed on the worker's computer screen at the beginning of the work session and observe the number of orders processed during 4 observation periods in the treatment phase. Lastly, you might stop the friendly greetings and observe the number of orders processed during an additional 4 sessions. If the number of orders processed was greater during the treatment phase (assuming all other variables were equal), we would conclude that the friendly greeting was the probable cause.

4. *The reversal design,* in which the treatment is reversed during the second baseline phase, is useful in some situations if it is feasible and ethical to use it. In a reversal design the treatment phase is not followed by a control, baseline phase but rather by a treatment-reversal phase. In other words, a condition that is essentially the opposite of the treatment condition is implemented (think of it as an A-B-ᗺ-A design!). To use a former example, if the treatment phase (B) involved friendly greetings used as a reinforcement of on-task behavior (processing orders), and a reversal design was used, then the treatment phase would be followed by a phase involving reinforcement for *off-task* behavior ("Hi! Please call me as soon as you turn the computer on so we can chat.") On-task behaviors would probably be dramatically reduced during this phase.

It should be noted that there is some terminology confusion in the literature concerning A-B-A designs. The A-B-A withdrawal designs are frequently referred to as reversal designs, which they are not, since treatment is generally withdrawn following baseline assessment, not reversed. A reversal design is but one kind of withdrawal design, representing a special kind of withdrawal (Leitenberg, 1973). When applicable, a reversal design typically produces more dramatic results than a nonreversal design. The major problem with this design is that its application is not very often feasible or desirable. If we are trying to increase order processing, for example, encouraging off-task behavior for the sake of treatment reversal would not be advisable for obvious reasons.

The internal validity of the A-B-A design is superior to that of the A-B design. With the A-B design it is possible that behaviors would have improved without treatment intervention. It is very unlikely, however, that behavior would coincidentally improve during the treatment phase and also coincidentally deteriorate during the subsequent baseline phase. The major problem with this design is an ethical one, since the experiment ends with the subject not receiving the treatment. Of course if the treatment has not been shown to be effective, there is no problem. But if it has been found to be beneficial, the desirability of removing it is questionable.

A variation of the A-B-A design that eliminates this problem is the B-A-B design. As you have probably gathered, this design involves a treatment phase (B), a withdrawal phase (A), and a return-to-treatment phase (B). Although this design yields an experiment that ends with the subject receiving treatment, the lack of an initial baseline phase makes it very difficult to assess the effectiveness of the treatment; in other words, we have no systematic data concerning the frequency of target behaviors prior to treatment. Some studies have involved a short baseline phase prior to application of the B-A-B design. Such a strategy, however, only approximates a better solution, which is application of an A-B-A-B design.

Before moving on to the A-B-A-B design, there is one other variation of the A-B-A design that should at least be mentioned, namely, the *changing-criterion design*. In this design, a baseline phase is followed by successive treatment phases, each of which has a more stringent criterion for acceptable behavior level. Thus, each treatment phase becomes the baseline phase for the next treatment phase. This process continues until the final desired level of behavior is being achieved consistently. This design is useful for behaviors that involve step-by-step increases or decreases in frequency. It is particularly useful for training situations involving complex operations in which the trainee is rewarded for successively getting more of the operation correct until he or she is able consistently to perform the entire operation correctly.

5. *The A-B-A-B design* is basically the A-B-A design with the addition of a second treatment phase. Not only does this design overcome the ethical objection to the A-B-A design, by ending the experiment during a treatment phase; it also greatly strengthens the conclusions of the study by demonstrating the effects of the treatment *twice*. The second treatment phase can be extended as long as desired beyond the termination of the actual study. If treatment effects are essentially the same during both B phases, the possibility that the effects are a result of extraneous variables that

just happened to be operating during the treatment phase is greatly reduced. The A-B-A-B design can be symbolized in the following manner:

O O O O	X O X O X O X	O O O O O	X O X O X O X O
baseline	treatment	baseline	treatment
A	B	A	B

When application of this design is feasible, it provides very convincing evidence of treatment effectiveness.

An interesting variation of the A-B-A-B design, which is used mainly when treatment involves reinforcement techniques, is the A-B-C-B design. The purpose of this design is to control for improvements in behavior that might result because the subject is receiving special attention (remember the Hawthorne effect?). For example, suppose the treatment, B, was reinforcement in the form of commissions, awarded contingent upon the completion of sales. With the A-B-A-B design, the experiment would involve baseline, contingent reinforcement, baseline, and contingent reinforcement. With the A-B-C-B design, the C phase would involve an amount of noncontingent reinforcement equal to the amount of contingent reinforcement received during B phases. In the example, the salesperson might receive a 10% commission on all sales during the B phase; during the C phase, the salesperson would receive a special bonus equal to the amount of commission he or she received during the initial B phase. In other words, the subject would receive an equal amount of money but not specifically for exhibiting the desired behavior.

Multiple-Baseline Designs

Multiple-baseline designs are used when the only alternative would be an A-B design. This is the situation when the treatment is such that it is not possible to withdraw it and return to baseline or when it would not be ethical to withdraw it or reverse it. In the most extreme situation, the treatment might be some kind of surgical procedure. Multiple-baseline designs are also used when treatment can be withdrawn but the effects of the treatment carry over into the second baseline phase and a return to baseline conditions is difficult or impossible. The effects of many treatments do not disappear when treatment is removed (See Figure 10.3, pattern C): actually, in many situations it is highly desirable if they do not. Reinforcement techniques, for example, are designed to produce improved behavior that will be maintained when external reinforcements are withdrawn.

There are three basic types of multiple-baseline design:

1. across behaviors
2. across subjects
3. across settings designs

With a multiple-baseline design, instead of collecting baseline data for one target behavior for one subject in one setting, we collect data on several behaviors for one subject, one behavior for several subjects, or one behavior and one subject in several settings. As an example, suppose you were trying to improve the courtesy of taxicab drivers (you live in a resort area and work for the Chamber of Commerce!). You might decide that the courteous driver: (a) greets the passenger, (b) puts luggage in the cab *gently*, (c) consults the passenger with regard to the radio, and (d) adjusts the air conditioning to suit the passenger. To establish our baseline we could take a number of taxi rides with one driver and see if the driver did these four things (one subject, several behaviors), *or* we could approach 20 taxicab drivers and see if they greet us (one behavior, several subjects), *or* we could ride with the same taxicab driver from the airport, from an office building, and from a private home and see if he or she offered to adjust the air conditioning for us each time (one subject, one behavior, several settings). After establishing our baseline, we then systematically, over a period of time, apply the treatment to each behavior (or subject or setting) one at a time until all behaviors (or subjects or settings) are under treatment. In the nontreatment, A phase, on greeting the passenger, for example, we would simply observe whether or not the driver did this on our first group of rides. On the second group of rides, the treatment, B phase, if the driver greeted us, we would respond positively to the greeting and mention it when presenting the tip ("I appreciated your friendly greeting at the airport; it made my ride more pleasant"). If the driver did not greet us during the treatment rides, the rider-experimentor might greet him or her pleasantly before giving the destination and mention the importance of the greeting when presenting the tip. If measured performance improves in each case only after treatment is introduced, then the treatment is judged to be effective. There are, of course, variations that can be applied. We might, for example, collect data on one target behavior for several subjects in several settings. In this situation, performance for the group of subjects in each setting would be summed or averaged, and results would be presented for the group as well as for each individual.

When applying treatments across behaviors, it is important that the behaviors be able to be treated independently. If we apply treatment to behavior one, for example, the other target behaviors should remain at baseline levels. If other behaviors change when behavior one is treated, the design is not valid for assessing treatment effectiveness. When applying treatment across subjects, the subjects should be as similar as possible (matched on key variables such as age and sex), and the experimental setting should be as identical as possible for each subject. When applying treatment across settings, it is preferable that the settings be natural, although that is not always possible. We might, for example, systematically apply treatment (e.g., tangible reinforcement) to successive work periods. Or, as with the taxidriver, we might apply treatment first from the airport, then from an office building, and then from a private home. In case you're wondering, these might qualify as "different settings" based on what the driver experiences before you ride with him or her—waiting in line at the airport, negotiating city traffic around the office building, and locating a private home in a suburban area. Sometimes it is necessary, owing to the nature of the target behavior, to evaluate the treatment in a contrived, or simulated, setting. The target behavior, for example, may be an important one but one that does not occur naturally very often (recall the discussion in Chapter 7 on simulation observation). If we are teaching a rookie police officer to decide whether or not to shoot in various emergency situations, simulated settings are obviously the only feasible approach.

Application of the multiple-baseline designs might be symbolized as follows:

Case 1	Case 2	Case 3
Behavior 1 A-B-B-B-B	Subject 1 A-B-B-B-B	Setting 1 A-B-B-B-B
Behavior 2 A-A-B-B-B	Subject 2 A-A-B-B-B	Setting 2 A-A-B-B-B
Behavior 3 A-A-A-B-B	Subject 3 A-A-A-B-B	Setting 3 A-A-A-B-B

This arrangement would represent the situation in which the treatment, once applied, would not be withdrawn. We could also symbolize case 1 as follows:

Behavior 1   O O OXOXOXOXOXOXOXOXOXOXOXOXOXO

Behavior 2   O O O O O XOXOXOXOXOXOXOXOXOXOXO

Behavior 3   O O O O O O O OXOXOXOXOXOXOXOXOXO

In this example, treatment was applied to behavior 1 first and then behavior 2 and then behavior 3 until all three behaviors were under treatment. If measured performance improved in each case only after treatment was introduced, then the treatment would be judged to be effective. We could symbolize cases 2 and 3 in the same manner. In all cases, the more behaviors, subjects, or settings involved, the more convincing the evidence is for the effectiveness of the treatment. What constitutes a sufficient *minimum* number of replications, however, is another issue (similar to the minimum-number-of-subjects-per-group issue discussed in Chapter 4). Although some investigators believe that four or more are necessary, three replications are generally accepted to be an adequate minimum.

In an interesting study by Bates (1980), a multiple-baseline design was applied to an experimental group ($N = 8$) whose performance was also compared to that of a control group ($N = 8$). The purpose of the study was to investigate the effectiveness of an interpersonal-skill training package (i.e., verbal instruction, modeling, rehearsal, feedback, incentives, and homework) on the social-skill performance of moderately and mildly retarded adults. Following initial assessments, the training package was systematically applied to four social behaviors: introductions and small talk; asking for help; differing with others; and handling criticism. In two experiments, the targeted behaviors were approached in a different order. As the group means presented in Figure 10.6 show, behavior improved in each case only after treatment. Some statistically significant differences were also found in favor of the experimental group. Although results support the effectiveness of the treatment package, it should be noted that the study would have been strengthened if the baseline phase for introductions

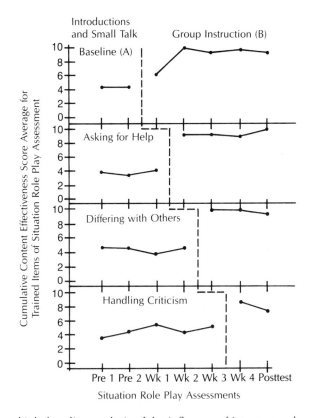

Figure 10.6. A multiple-baseline analysis of the influence of interpersonal skills training on Exp. 1's cumulative content effectiveness score across four social skill areas. (Bates, 1980, Figure 1. Copyright 1980 by the Society for the Experimental Analysis of Behavior, Inc. Reproduced by permission.)

and small talk and the treatment phase for handling criticism had included at least three data points (especially given the downward trend of the latter). Also, as mentioned previously, results for individuals are expected to be presented in addition to group results. In the actual publication reporting the research, the author did indicate that individual multiple-baseline graphic displays for all experimental subjects were available upon request.

Although multiple-baseline designs are generally used when there is a problem with returning to baseline conditions, that is, baseline levels are not recoverable, they can be used very effectively for situations in which baseline is recoverable. If the target behaviors for the taxi drivers were greeting the passenger, consulting regarding the radio, and adjusting the air conditioning, it is perfectly possible to return to baseline conditions with these behaviors. If we applied an A-B-A design within a multiple-baseline framework, the result could be symbolized as follows:

Greets the passenger	A-B-A-A-A
Consults about radio	A-A-B-A-A
Adjusts air conditioning	A-A-A-B-A

OR

Greets the passenger	O O OXOXOXO O O O O O O O O O
Consults about radio	O O O O O OXOXOXO O O O O O O
Adjusts air conditioning	O O O O O O O O OXOXOXO O O O

Such a design would combine the basic features of an A-B-A design and a multiple-baseline design and would provide very convincing evidence regarding treatment effects. In essence it would represent three replications of an A-B-A experiment. Whenever baseline is recoverable and there are no carryover effects, any of the A-B-A designs can be applied within a multiple-baseline framework.

Alternating-Treatments Designs

Alternating-treatments-design experiments have been steadily increasing since the late 1970s. The main reason for this increase is the fact that the design currently represents the only valid approach to assessing the relative effectiveness of two (or more) treatments, within a single-subject context. Traditionally, comparative effectiveness has been studied using a group-comparison design, such as the pretest-posttest control-group design. The fact that a particular treatment is more effective for an identified group (or groups), however, tells us nothing concerning its effectiveness for any individual; the alternating-treatments design serves this purpose.

In the literature, the alternating-treatments design is referred to by a number of different terms: multiple-schedule design, multi-element-baseline design, multi-element-manipulation design, randomization design; and simultaneous-treatment design. There is some consensus, however, that "alternating-treatments" most accurately describes the nature of the design. The alternating-treatments design involves the relatively rapid alternation of treatments for a single subject. The qualifier "relatively" is attached to "rapid" because alternation does not necessarily occur within fixed intervals of time such as an hour or even a day. If an employee with some work-related problems were to meet with the boss every Tuesday, for example, then on some Tuesdays he or she would receive one treatment (e.g., verbal reinforcement) and on other Tuesdays another treatment (e.g., more interesting work). As this example suggests, the treatments (let's refer to them as T_1 and T_2) are not typically alternated in a T_1-T_2-T_1-T_2 . . . fashion (to the great relief of the boss who doesn't have to think up "interesting work" every other week!). Rather, to avoid potential validity threats such as ordering effects, treatments are alternated on a random basis, e.g., T_1-T_2-T_2-T_1-T_2-T_2-T_1-T_1-T_2.

This design has several pluses that make it attractive to investigators. First, no withdrawal is necessary; thus, if one treatment is found to be more effective, it may be continued beyond the termination of the experiment. Incidentally, this design may also be used to alternate treatment and no-treatment conditions, also with the advantage of not having to withdraw an effective treatment. Second, no baseline phase is necessary since we are usually attempting to determine which treatment is more effective, not whether a treatment is better than no treatment. For the situation where we are alternating treatment and no-treatment, baseline (no-treatment) phases are incorporated into the design on a random basis. These advantages contribute to another major advantage, namely, that a number of treatments can be studied more quickly and efficiently than with other designs. One potential problem with this design, multiple-treatment interference (carryover effects from one treatment to the other), is believed by many investigators to be minimal; researchers have consistently observed such effects to be short-lived and to occur mainly when subjects have difficulty discriminating between treatments, which does not happen often (Blough, 1983).

Data Analysis and Interpretation

Data analysis in single-subject research typically involves visual inspection and analysis of a graphic presentation of results. First, an evaluation is made concerning the adequacy of the design, e.g., were there a sufficient number of data points within each phase? Second, assuming a sufficiently valid design, an assessment of treatment effectiveness is made. The primary criterion is typically the practical *significance* of the results, rather than the statistical significance. Effects that are small but statistically significant may not be large enough to make a sufficient difference in the behavior of a subject (Kazdin, 1977). As an example, suppose the subject is a 28-year-old employee who exhibits dangerous, aggressive behavior toward other employees. A 5% reduction in such behavior, as a result of treatment, may be statistically significant, but it is clearly not good enough.

Kazdin (1984), who has published extensively in behavioral-change journals, believes that statistical analysis may provide a valuable supplement to visual analysis. It may be useful, for example, in identifying promising approaches in need of further refinement and study. There are a number of statistical analyses available to the single-subject researcher, including t and F tests (to be discussed in Part IV). Each design involves two or more phases that can be compared statistically. For example, if we apply an A-B-A-B design, behavior in the two A phases combined can be compared to performance in the two B phases combined using a t-test.

Whether statistical tests should be used in single-subject research is currently a controversial issue. To date they have not been used much, and their future application in single-subject research is uncertain. As Kazdin emphasizes, however, the key to sound data evaluation is judgment, and the use of statistical analysis does not remove this responsibility from the researcher. This principle is as important for group-oriented research, which regularly applies statistical techniques, as it is for single-subject research, which rarely does.

Replication

Replication is a vital part of all research and especially single-subject research since initial findings are generally based on one subject or a small number of subjects. The more results are replicated, the more confidence we have in the procedures that produced those results. Also, replication serves to delimit the generalizability of findings; i.e., it provides data concerning the subjects, behaviors, and settings to which results are applicable. There are three basic types of replication of single-subject experiments:

1. *Direct replication* refers to replication by the same investigator, with the same subject or with different subjects, in a specific setting (e.g., an office). Generalizability is promoted when replication is done with other subjects, matched as closely as possible on relevant variables, who share the same problem. When replication is done on a number of subjects with the same problem at the same location at the same time, the process is referred to as *simultaneous replication*. When intervention involves a small group, results are presented separately for each subject (Fisher, 1979). When an effective approach is subsequently directly replicated at least three times, the next step is systematic replication.

2. *Systematic replication* refers to replication that follows direct replication and that involves different investigators, behaviors, or settings. Over an extended period of time, techniques are identified that are consistently effective in a variety of situations. We know, for example, that supervisor attention can be a powerful factor in behavior change. At some point, enough data are amassed to permit the third stage of replication, clinical replication.

3. *Clinical replication* involves the development of treatment packages, composed of two or more interventions that have been found to be effective individually, originally designed for persons with complex behavior disorders. Although it does not involve a "complex behavior disorder," an example of a situation in which this process might be used would involve potential employees who, because of a lack of training, education, and experience, may have difficulty obtaining employment. The treatment package might involve such diverse interventions as skill training in word processing, educational training in spelling and punctuation, and training in awareness in areas as diverse as business apparel and manners. Clinical replication, in this situation probably called "program evaluation," would be an appropriate methodology for testing such a complex group of interventions.

Summary/Chapter 10

DEFINITION AND PURPOSE

1. In an experimental study, the researcher manipulates at least one independent variable (IV), controls other relevant variables, and observes the effect on one or more dependent variables (DV).

2. The *independent variable,* also referred to as the experimental variable, the cause, or the treatment, is that activity or characteristic believed to make a difference.

3. The *dependent variable,* also referred to as the criterion variable, effect, or posttest, is the outcome of the study, the change or difference in groups that occurs as a result of manipulation of the independent variable.

4. When they are well conducted, experimental studies produce the soundest evidence concerning hypothesized cause-effect relationships.

5. Predictions based on experimental findings are more global and take the form, "If you use approach X_1 you will probably get better results than if you use approach X_2."

The Experimental Process

6. The steps in an experimental study are basically the same as for other types of research: (a) selection and definition of a problem, (b) selection of subjects and measuring instruments, (c) selection of a design, (d) execution of procedures, (e) analysis of data, and (f) formulation of conclusions.

7. An experimental study is guided by at least one hypothesis that states an expected causal relationship between two variables.

8. In an experimental study, the researcher is in on the action from the very beginning; the researcher forms or selects the groups, decides what is going to happen to each group, tries to control all relevant factors besides the change that she or he has introduced, and observes or measures the effect on the groups at the end of the study.

9. An experiment typically involves two groups, an experimental group and a control group (although there may be only one group, or there may be three or more groups).

10. The experimental group typically receives a new treatment that is under investigation, while the control group usually receives either a different treatment or is treated as usual.

11. The two groups that are to receive different treatments are equated on all other variables that might be related to performance on the dependent variable.

12. After the groups have been exposed to the treatment for some period of time, the researcher administers a test of the dependent variable (or measures it in some way) and then determines whether there is a significant difference between the groups.

Manipulation and Control

13. Direct manipulation by the researcher of at least one independent variable is the single characteristic that differentiates all experimental research from other methods of research.

14. The different values or forms that the independent variable may take are basically presence versus absence (X versus no X), presence in varying degrees (a lot of X versus a little X), or presence of one kind versus presence of another kind (X_1 versus X_2).

15. *Control* refers to efforts on the part of the researcher to remove the influence of any variable (other than the independent variable) that might affect performance on the dependent variable.

16. There are two different kinds of variables that need to be controlled: *subject variables,* such as skill level and aptitude, on which subjects in the two groups might differ, and *environmental variables,* such as discussion topics and information level of the mentors, that might cause unwanted differences between the groups.

THREATS TO EXPERIMENTAL VALIDITY

17. Any uncontrolled, extraneous variables affecting performance on the dependent variable are threats to the validity of an experiment.

18. An experiment is valid if results obtained are due only to the manipulated independent variable, and if they are generalizable to situations outside of the experimental setting.

19. *Internal validity* refers to the condition that observed differences on the dependent variable are a direct result of manipulation of the independent variable, not some other variable.

20. *External validity* refers to the condition that results are generalizable, or applicable, to groups and environments outside of the experimental setting.

21. The term *ecological validity* is sometimes used to refer to the degree to which results can be generalized to other environments.

22. The researcher must strive for balance between control and realism. If a choice is involved, the researcher should err on the side of too much control rather than too little.

23. Although lab-like settings are generally preferred for the investigation of theoretical problems, experimentation in natural, or field, settings has its advantages, especially for certain practical problems.

Threats to Internal Validity

24. *History* refers to the occurrence of any event that is not part of the experimental treatment but that may affect performance on the dependent variable.

25. *Maturation* refers to physical or mental changes that may occur within the subjects over a period of time. These changes may affect the subjects' performance on the measure of the dependent variable.

26. *Testing* refers to improved scores on a posttest resulting from subjects having taken a pretest.

27. *Instrumentation* refers to unreliability, or lack of consistency, in measuring instruments, which may result in an invalid assessment of performance.

28. *Statistical regression* usually occurs when subjects are selected on the basis of their extreme scores. It refers to the tendency of subjects who score highest on a pretest to score lower on a posttest and of subjects who score lowest on a pretest to score higher on a posttest.

29. *Differential selection of subjects* usually occurs when already formed groups are used. It refers to the fact that the groups may be different before the study even begins, and this initial difference may at least partially account for posttest differences.

30. *Mortality,* or attrition, is more likely to occur in longer studies. It refers to the fact that subjects who drop out of a group may share a characteristic such that their absence has a significant effect on the results of the study.

31. *Selection-maturation interaction* means that selection may also interact with factors such as history and testing, although selection-maturation interaction is more common. This means that if already formed groups are used, one group may profit more (or less) from a treatment or may have an initial advantage (or disadvantage) because of maturation, history, or testing factors.

Threats to External Validity

32. Threats affecting "to whom" or to what persons that results can be generalized are referred to as problems of *population validity*.

33. Threats affecting "to what" or to what environments (settings, dependent variables, and so forth) results can be generalized are referred to as problems of *ecological validity*.

34. *Pretest-treatment interaction* occurs when subjects respond or react differently to a treatment because they have been pretested. The treatment effect may be different from what it would have been had subjects not been pretested.

35. *Posttest sensitization* refers to the possibility that treatment effects may occur only *if* subjects are posttested. In other words, the very act of posttesting "jells" treatment influences such that effects are manifested and measured that would not have occurred if a posttest had not been given.

36. *Multiple-treatment interference* can occur when the same subjects receive more than one treatment in succession; it refers to the carryover effects from an earlier treatment, which make it difficult to assess the effectiveness of a later treatment.

37. *Multiple-treatment interference* may also occur when subjects who have already participated in a study are selected for inclusion in another, theoretically unrelated, study.

38. *Selection-treatment interaction* is similar to the differential-selection-of-subjects problem associated with internal invalidity. It also occurs when subjects are not randomly selected for treatment.

39. Interaction effects aside, the very fact that subjects are not randomly selected from a population severely limits the researcher's ability to generalize, since representativeness of the sample is in question.

40. This nonrepresentativeness of groups may also result in a selection-treatment interaction such that the results of a study hold only for the groups involved and are not representative of the treatment effect in the intended population.

41. *Interaction-of-personological-variables-and-treatment effect* occurs when actual subjects at one level of a variable react differently to a treatment from the way other potential subjects in the population, at another level, would have reacted.

42. Although selection-treatment interaction is a definite weakness associated with several of the poorer designs, it is also an uncontrolled variable associated with the designs involving randomization. One's accessible population is often a far cry from one's target population, creating another population-validity problem.

43. *Specificity of variables* is a threat to generalizability regardless of the experimental design used.

44. *Specificity of variables* refers to the fact that a given study is conducted (a) with a specific kind of subject, (b) based on a particular, operational definition of the independent variable, (c) using specific measuring instruments, (d) at a specific time, and (e) under a specific set of circumstances.

45. Generalizability of results may also be affected by short-term or long-term events that occur while the study is taking place. This potential threat is referred to as *interaction-of-history-and-treatment-effects*.

46. *Interaction-of-time-of-measurement-and-treatment effect* results from the fact that post-testing may yield different results depending upon when it is done.

47. To deal with the threats associated with specificity, the researcher must (a) operationally define variables in a way that has meaning outside of the experimental setting and (b) be careful in stating conclusions and generalizations.

48. Among other factors, *experimenter effects* include characteristics or personality traits of the experimenter such as sex, age, race, anxiety level, and hostility level (experimenter-personal-attributes effect.).

49. Active bias results when the researcher's expectations affect her or his behavior and hence outcomes (experimenter-bias effect).

50. One form of experimenter bias occurs when the researcher affects subjects' behavior or is inaccurate in evaluating their behavior, because of previous knowledge concerning the subjects.

51. Knowing which subjects are in which group may cause the researcher to be unintentionally biased in evaluating their performance.

52. *Reactive arrangements* refers to a number of factors associated with the way in which a study is conducted and the feelings and attitudes of the subjects involved.

53. In an effort to maintain a high degree of control for the sake of internal validity, a researcher may create an experimental environment that is highly artificial and hinders generalizability of findings to nonexperimental settings.

54. Another type of reactive arrangement results from the subjects' knowledge that they are involved in an experiment or their feeling that they are in some way receiving special attention *(Hawthorne effect)*.

55. If for any reason control groups or their managers feel threatened or challenged by being in competition with a new program or approach, they may outdo themselves and perform way beyond what would normally be expected *(John Henry effect)*.

56. The *placebo effect* is a kind of antidote for the Hawthorne and John Henry effects. The application of the placebo effect in business-and-management research is that all groups in an experiment should *appear* to be treated the same.

57. The *novelty effect*, which is also called the *honeymoon effect*, refers to increased interest, motivation, or participation on the part of subjects simply because they are doing something different.

GROUP EXPERIMENTAL DESIGNS

58. The validity of an experiment is a direct function of the degree to which extraneous variables are controlled.

59. Control of extraneous variables is what experimental design is all about; good designs control many sources of invalidity, while poor designs control only a few.

60. Subject variables include organismic variables and intervening variables.

61. *Organismic variables* are characteristics of the subject or organism, such as sex, which cannot be directly controlled but for which the effects can be controlled.

62. *Intervening variables* are variables that intervene between the independent variable and the dependent variable, such as anxiety or boredom, which cannot be directly observed or controlled but for which the effects also can be controlled.

Control of Extraneous Variables

63. Randomization is the best single way to attempt to control for many extraneous variables at the same time.

64. Randomization should be used whenever possible; subjects should be randomly selected from a population whenever possible, subjects should be randomly assigned to groups whenever possible, treatments should be randomly assigned to groups whenever possible, and anything else you can think of (observers, time periods, mechanical devices) should also be randomly assigned if possible.

65. Randomization is effective in creating equivalent, representative groups that are essentially the same on all relevant variables the researcher has identified and probably even a few that didn't occur to him or her.

66. Randomly formed groups is a characteristic unique to experimental research; it is a control factor not possible with causal-comparative research.

67. Certain environmental variables, for example, can be controlled by holding them constant for all groups.

68. Controlling subject variables is critical.

Matching

69. *Matching* is a technique for equating groups on one or more variables that the researcher has identified as being highly related to performance on the dependent variable.

70. The most commonly used approach to matching involves random assignment of pair members, one member to each group.

71. A major problem with such matching is that there are invariably subjects who do not have a match and must be eliminated from the study.

72. One way to combat loss of subjects is to match less closely.

73. A related procedure is to rank all subjects from highest to lowest based on their scores on the control variable; each two adjacent scores constitute a pair.

Comparing Homogeneous Groups or Subgroups

74. Another way of controlling an extraneous variable is to compare groups that are homogeneous with respect to that variable.

75. As with causal-comparative research, a similar but more satisfactory approach is to form subgroups representing all levels of the control variable.

76. If the researcher is interested not just in controlling the variable but also in seeing if the independent variable affects the dependent variable differently at different levels of the control variable, the best approach is to build the control variable right into the design and to analyze the results with a statistical technique called *factorial analysis of variance*.

Using Subjects as Their Own Controls

77. Using subjects as their own controls involves exposing the same group to the different treatments, one treatment at a time.

Analysis of Covariance

78. The *analysis of covariance* is a statistical method for equating randomly formed groups on one or more variables.

79. In essence, analysis of covariance adjusts scores on a dependent variable for initial differences on some other variable, such as pretest scores, aptitude, years of experience, age (assuming that performance on the "other variable" is related to performance on the dependent variable).

Types of Group Designs

80. A selected experimental design dictates to a great extent the specific procedures of a study.

81. Selection of a given design dictates such factors as whether there will be a control group, whether subjects will be randomly assigned to groups, whether each group will be pretested, and how resulting data will be analyzed.

82. Depending upon the particular combination of such factors represented, different designs are appropriate for testing different types of hypotheses, and designs vary widely in the degree to which they control the various threats to internal and external validity.

83. From the designs that are appropriate and feasible, you select the one that controls the most sources of internal and external invalidity.

84. There are two major classes of experimental designs: *single-variable designs,* which involve one independent variable that is manipulated, and *factorial designs,* which involve two or more independent variables, at least one of which is manipulated.

85. Single-variable designs are classified as preexperimental, true experimental, or quasi-experimental, depending upon the control they provide for sources of internal and external invalidity.

86. Preexperimental designs do not do a very good job of controlling threats to validity and should be avoided.

87. The true experimental designs represent a very high degree of control and are always to be preferred.

88. Quasi-experimental designs do not control as well as true experimental designs but do a much better job than the preexperimental designs.

89. Factorial designs are basically elaborations of true experimental designs and permit investigation of two or more variables, individually and in interaction with each other.

Pre-experimental Designs

90. *The one-shot case study* involves one group, which is exposed to a treatment (X) and then posttested (O).

91. None of the threats to validity that are relevant are controlled.

92. *The one-group pretest-posttest design* involves one group, which is pretested (O), exposed to a treatment (X), and posttested (O).

93. Although it controls invalidity not controlled by the one-shot case study, a number of additional factors are relevant to this design that are not controlled.

94. *The static-group comparison* involves at least two groups; one group receives a new, or unusual, treatment, the other receives a traditional, or usual, treatment, and both groups are posttested.

95. Since subjects are not randomly assigned to groups, and since there are no pretest data, however, it is difficult to determine just how equivalent they are.

True Experimental Designs

96. The true experimental designs control for nearly all sources of internal and external invalidity.

97. All of the true experimental designs have one characteristic in common that none of the other designs have—random assignment of subjects to groups.

98. Ideally subjects should be randomly selected and randomly assigned; however, to qualify as a true design, at least random assignment must be involved.

99. All the true designs involve a control group.

100. *The pretest-posttest control-group design* involves at least two groups, both of which are formed by random assignment. Both groups are administered a pretest of the dependent variable; one group receives a new, or unusual, treatment; and both groups are posttested.

101. The combination of random assignment and the presence of a pretest and a control group serves to control for all sources of internal invalidity.

102. The only definite weakness with this design is a possible interaction between the pretest and the treatment, which may make the results generalizable only to other pretested groups.

103. The best approach to data analysis is simply to compare the posttest scores of the two groups. The pretest is only used to see if the groups are essentially the same on the dependent variable. If they are, posttest scores can be directly compared using a *t* test; if they are not (random assignment does not *guarantee* equality), posttest scores can be analyzed using analysis of covariance.

104. A variation of the pretest-posttest control-group design involves random assignment of members of matched pairs to the groups, one member to each group in order, to control more closely for one or more extraneous variables.

105. *The posttest-only control-group design* is exactly the same as the pretest-posttest control-group design *except* there is no pretest. Subjects are randomly assigned to groups, exposed to the independent variable, and posttested. Posttest scores are then compared to determine the effectiveness of the treatment.

106. The combination of random assignment and the presence of a control group serves to control for all sources of internal invalidity except mortality. Mortality is not controlled for because of the absence of pretest data on subjects.

107. A variation of the posttest-only control-group design involves random assignment of matched pairs to the groups, one member to each group, in order to control more closely for one or more extraneous variables.

108. *The Solomon four-group design* involves random assignment of subjects to one of four groups. Two of the groups are pretested and two are not; one of the pretested groups and one of the unpretested groups receive the experimental treatment. All four groups are posttested.

109. This design is a combination of the pretest-posttest control-group design and the posttest-only control-group design, each of which has its own major source of invalidity (pretest-treatment interaction and mortality, respectively). The combination of these two designs results in a design that controls for pretest-treatment interaction *and* for mortality.

110. The correct way to analyze data resulting from application of this design is to use a 2 × 2 factorial analysis of variance. The factorial analysis tells the researcher whether there is an interaction between the treatment and the pretest.

111. Which design is best depends upon the nature of the study.

Quasi-experimental Designs

112. Sometimes it's just not possible to assign subjects randomly to groups. When this occurs, however, quasi-experimental designs are available to the researcher. They provide adequate control of sources of invalidity.

113. *The nonequivalent control-group design* looks very much like the pretest-posttest control-group design; the only difference is that the nonequivalent control-group design does not involve random assignment of subjects to groups.

114. The lack of random assignment adds sources of invalidity not associated with the pretest-posttest control-group design—possible regression and interaction between selection and variables such as maturation, history, and testing.

115. The researcher should make every effort to use groups that are as equivalent as possible.

116. If differences between the groups on any major extraneous variable are identified, analysis of covariance can be used to statistically equate the groups.

117. An advantage of this design is that since work groups are used "as is," possible effects from reactive arrangement are minimized.

118. *The time-series design* is actually an elaboration of the one-group pretest-posttest design. One group is repeatedly pretested, exposed to a treatment, and then repeatedly posttested.

119. If a group scores essentially the same on a number of pretests and then significantly improves following a treatment, the researcher has more confidence in the effectiveness of the treatment than if just one pretest and one posttest are administered.

120. History is still a problem with this design, however, since something might happen between the last pretest and the first posttest, the effect of which might be confused with the treatment. Pretest-treatment interaction is also a validity problem.

121. Although statistical analyses appropriate for this design are rather advanced, determining the effectiveness of the treatment basically involves analysis of the pattern of the test scores.

122. A variation of the time-series design, which is referred to as the multiple time-series design, involves the addition of a control group to the basic design. This variation eliminates history and instrumentation as threats to validity and thus represents a design with no probable sources of internal validity.

123. In a *counterbalanced design,* all groups receive all the treatments but in a different order.

124. The only restriction is that the number of groups equals the number of treatments.

125. While subjects may be pretested, this design is usually employed when intact groups must be used and when administration of a pretest is not possible or feasible.

126. In order to determine the effectiveness of the treatments, the average performance of the groups for each treatment can be compared.

127. A unique weakness of this design is potential multiple-treatment interference, which can result when the same group receives more than one treatment.

128. A counterbalanced design should really only be used when the treatments are such that exposure to one will not affect evaluation of the effectiveness of another.

Factorial Designs

129. Factorial designs involve two or more independent variables, at least one of which is manipulated by the researcher.

130. They are basically elaborations of true experimental designs and permit investigation of two or more variables, individually and in interaction with each other.

131. In business, variables do not operate in isolation.

132. The term *factorial* refers to the fact that the design involves several factors. Each factor has two or more levels.

133. The 2×2 is the simplest factorial design.

134. Both variables may be manipulated, but the 2×2 design usually involves one manipulated, or experimental, variable, and one nonmanipulated variable; the nonmanipulated variable is often referred to as a control variable.

135. *Control variables* are usually physical or mental characteristics of the subjects such as sex, age, or aptitude.

136. The purpose of a factorial design is to determine whether the effects of an experimental variable are generalizable across all levels of a control variable or whether the effects are specific to specific levels of the control variable. Also, a factorial design can demonstrate relationships that a single-variable experiment cannot.

137. If one value of the independent variable is more effective regardless of the level of the control variable, there is no interaction.

138. If an interaction exists between the variables, different values of the independent variable are differentially effective depending upon the level of the control variable.

139. Theoretically, a researcher could simultaneously investigate 10 factors in a $2 \times 2 \times 2 \times 2 \times 2 \times 3 \times 3 \times 3 \times 4 \times 4$ design, for example.

140. In reality, however, more than three factors are rarely used.

SINGLE-SUBJECT EXPERIMENTAL DESIGNS

141. Single-subject experimental designs (also commonly referred to as single-case experimental designs) are designs that can be applied when the sample size is one.

142. They can also be applied when a number of individuals are considered as one group.

143. Single-subject designs are typically used to study the behavior change an individual exhibits as a result of some intervention, or treatment.

144. Basically, the subject is alternately exposed to a nontreatment and a treatment condition, or phase, and performance is repeatedly measured during each phase.

145. The nontreatment condition is symbolized as A and the treatment condition is symbolized as B.

Single-Subject Versus Group Designs

146. At the very least single-subject designs are considered to be valuable complements to group designs.

147. Most experimental-research problems require traditional group designs for their investigation. This is mainly because the results are intended to be applied to groups.

148. There are, however, a number of research questions for which traditional group designs are not appropriate for two major reasons. First, group-comparison designs are frequently opposed on ethical, philosophical, or legal grounds, since by definition group-comparison designs involve a control group that does not receive the experimental treatment. Second, the size of the population of interest and consequent sample size may be so small that it is impossible to form two equivalent groups. Further, single-subject designs are most frequently applied in action-research settings where the primary emphasis is on immediate improvement in a very specific setting, not contribution to a research base.

External Validity

149. Results of single-subject research cannot be generalized to the population of interest as they can with group designs.

150. It is also true that the results of a study using a group design cannot be generalized to any individual within the group.

151. For single-subject designs, the key to generalizability is replication.

152. One generalizability problem associated with many single-subject designs is the possible effect of the baseline condition (phase one) on the subsequent effects of the treatment condition.

Internal Validity

Repeated and Reliable Measurement

153. As with a time-series design, pretest performance is measured a number of times prior to implementation of the treatment or intervention. In single-subject designs these sequential measures of pretest performance are referred to as baseline measures.

154. As a result of these measures taken over some period of time, sources of invalidity such as maturation are controlled for in the same way as for the time-series design.

155. Unlike the time-series design, however, performance is also measured at various points in time while the treatment is being applied. This added dimension greatly reduces the potential threat to validity from history, a threat to internal validity associated with the time-series design.

156. One very real threat to the internal validity of most single-subject designs is instrumentation. Since repeated measurement is a characteristic of all single-subject designs, it is especially important that measurement of the target behavior, or performance, be done in exactly the same way every time, or as nearly the same as is humanly possible.

157. In single-subject studies it is critical that the observation conditions (e.g., location, time of day) be standardized.

158. If one observer makes all the observations, then intraobserver reliability should be estimated. If more than one observer is involved, then interobserver reliability should be estimated.

159. The nature and conditions of the treatment should be specified in sufficient detail to permit replication. If its effects are to be validly assessed, the treatment must involve precisely the

same procedures *every* time it is introduced, either in the same study or in another study by another researcher.

Baseline Stability

160. The purpose of the baseline measurements is to provide a description of the target behavior as it naturally occurs *without* the treatment. The baseline serves as the basis of comparisons for assessing the effectiveness of the treatment.

161. A sufficient number of baseline measurements are usually taken to establish a pattern. The establishment of a pattern is referred to as baseline stability.

162. Normally, the length of the treatment phase and the number of measurements taken during the treatment phase parallel the length and measurement of the baseline phase.

The Single-Variable Rule

163. An important principle of single-subject research is that only one variable at a time should be manipulated.

Types of Single-Subject Designs
A-B-A Withdrawal Designs

164. *The A-B design* is used when baseline measurements are repeatedly made until stability is presumably established; treatment is then introduced and an appropriate number of measurements are made during treatment. If behavior improves during the treatment phase, the effectiveness of the treatment is allegedly demonstrated.

165. The problem is that we don't know if behavior improved *because of* the treatment or for some other reason.

166. *Additive designs,* variations of the A-B design, involve the addition of another phase (or phases) in which the experimental treatment is supplemented with another treatment.

167. By simply adding a second baseline phase to the A-B design we get a much improved design, the *A-B-A design.*

168. In some situations, when it is feasible and ethical to do so, the treatment may actually be reversed during the second baseline phase. In such situations, we refer to the design as a *reversal design,* and a condition that is essentially the opposite of the treatment condition is implemented.

169. The internal validity of the A-B-A design is superior to that of the A-B design. With the A-B design it is possible that behaviors would have improved without treatment intervention. It is very unlikely, however, that behavior would coincidentally improve during the treatment phase *and* coincidentally deteriorate during the subsequent baseline phase.

170. The major problem with this design is an ethical one, since the experiment ends with the subject *not* receiving the treatment.

171. The B-A-B design involves a treatment phase (B), a withdrawal phase (A), and a return to treatment phase (B).

172. Although this design yields an experiment that ends with the subject receiving treatment, the lack of an initial baseline phase makes it very difficult to assess the effectiveness of the treatment.

173. In the *changing-criterion design*, a baseline phase is followed by successive treatment phases, each of which has a more stringent criterion for an acceptable behavior level.

174. The *A-B-A-B design* is basically the A-B-A design with the addition of a second treatment phase.

175. Not only does this design overcome the ethical objection to the A-B-A design by ending the experiment during a treatment phase, it also greatly strengthens the conclusions of the study by demonstrating the effects of the treatment *twice*.

176. The second treatment phase can be extended as long as desired beyond the termination of the actual study.

177. When application of the A-B-A-B design is feasible, it provides very convincing evidence of treatment effectiveness.

178. An interesting variation of the A-B-A-B design, which is used mainly when treatment involves reinforcement techniques, is the A-B-C-B design.

179. With the A-B-C-B design, the C phase would involve an amount of noncontingent reinforcement equal to the amount of contingent reinforcement received during B phases.

180. *Multiple-baseline designs* are used when the only alternative would be an A-B design. This is the situation when the treatment is such that it is not possible to withdraw it and return to baseline or when it would not be ethical to withdraw it or reverse it.

181. Multiple-baseline designs are also used when treatment can be withdrawn but the effects of the treatment carry over into the second baseline phase and a return to baseline conditions is difficult or impossible.

182. There are three basic types of multiple-baseline design: (a) across behaviors, (b) across subjects, and (c) across settings.

183. With a multiple-baseline design, instead of collecting baseline data for one target behavior for one subject in one setting, we collect data on several behaviors for one subject, one behavior for several subjects, or one behavior and one subject in several settings. After establishing our baseline, we then systematically, over a period of time, apply the treatment to each behavior (or subject or setting) one at a time until all behaviors (or subjects or settings) are under treatment. If measured performance improves in each case only after treatment is introduced, then the treatment is judged to be effective.

184. When applying treatments across behaviors, it is important that the behaviors be able to be treated independently.

185. When applying treatment across subjects, the subjects should be as similar as possible (matched on key variables such as age and sex), and the experimental setting should be as identical as possible for each subject.

186. When applying treatment across settings, it is preferable that the settings be natural, although that is not always possible.

187. In all cases, the more behaviors, subjects, or settings involved, the more convincing the evidence is for the effectiveness of the treatment. Three replications are generally accepted to be an adequate minimum.

188. Whenever the baseline is recoverable and there are no carryover effects, any of the A-B-A designs can be applied within a multiple-baseline framework.

Alternating Treatments Design

189. The *alternating-treatments design* currently represents the only valid approach to

assessing the relative effectiveness of two (or more) treatments, within a single-subject context.

190. The alternating-treatments design involves the relatively rapid alternation of treatments for a single subject.

191. To avoid potential validity threats such as ordering effects, treatments are alternated on a random basis, e.g., T_1-T_2-T_2-T_1-T_2-T_2-T_1-T_1-T_2.

192. This design has several pluses that make it attractive to investigators. First, no withdrawal is necessary. Second, no baseline phase is necessary. Third, a number of treatments can be studied more quickly and efficiently than with other designs.

193. One potential problem with this design, multiple-treatment interference (carryover effects from one treatment to the other), is believed by many investigators to be minimal.

Data Analysis and Interpretation

194. Data analysis in single-subject research typically involves visual inspection and analysis of a graphic presentation of results. First, an evaluation is made concerning the adequacy of the design. Second, assuming a sufficiently valid design, an assessment of treatment effectiveness is made.

195. The primary criterion is typically the *practical significance* of the results, rather than the statistical significance. Effects that are small but statistically significant may not be large enough to make a sufficient difference in the behavior of a subject.

196. Statistical analysis may provide a valuable supplement to visual analysis.

197. There are a number of statistical analyses available to the single-subject researcher, including t and F tests.

198. The key to sound data evaluation is judgment, and the use of statistical analysis does not remove this responsibility from the researcher.

Replication

199. The more results are replicated, the more confidence we have in the procedures that produced those results.

200. Also, replication serves to delimit the generalizability of findings.

201. *Direct replication* refers to replication by the same investigator, with the same subject or with different subjects, in a specific setting (e.g., an office).

202. When replication is done on a number of subjects with the same problem at the same location at the same time, the process is referred to as *simultaneous replication*. When intervention involves a small group, results are presented separately for each subject.

203. *Systematic replication* refers to replication that follows direct replication and that involves different investigators, behaviors, or settings.

204. *Clinical replication* involves the development of a treatment package, composed of two or more interventions that have been found to be effective individually, originally designed for persons with complex behavior disorders.

Practice Self-Test

At the end of Chapter 1, you reviewed an example of experimental research. As a study aid, you may want to review the analysis you made of that article when you finished reading Chapter 1. Further to practice your review skills, answer the following specific questions related to experimental research. Suggested responses to these questions are found in Appendix C. Project Reading: **Consequences of Quality Circles in an Industrial Setting: A Longitudinal Assessment**

Method-Specific Review Questions

1. Was an appropriate experimental design selected?
2. Is a rationale for design selection given?
3. Are sources of invalidity associated with the design identified and discussed?
4. Is the method of group formation described?
5. Was the experimental group formed in the same way as the control group?
6. Were existing groups used or were groups randomly formed?
7. Were treatments randomly assigned to groups?
8. Were critical extraneous variables identified?
9. Were any control procedures applied to equate groups on extraneous variables?
10. Is there any evidence to suggest reactive arrangements (for example, the Hawthorne effect)?

Project III Performance Criteria

To review:

The description of Samples-Subjects (see Chapter 4) should describe the population from which the sample was selected (allegedly, of course), including its size and major characteristics.

The description of the Instrument(s) (see Chapter 5) should describe the purpose of the instrument (what it is intended to measure) and available validity and reliability coefficients.

Now you are ready to add the description of the Design to these previous subsections. It should indicate why the design was selected, potential threats to validity associated with the design, and aspects of the study that are believed to have minimized these threats. A figure should be included illustrating how the selected design was applied in the study. For example, you might say:

Since random assignment of subjects to groups was possible, and since administration of a pretest was not advisable owing to the reactive nature of the dependent variable (morale), the posttest-only control-group design was selected for this study (see Figure 1).

Group	Assignment	N	Treatment	Posttest
1	Random	15	Reinforcement	So-so Morale Scale
2	Random	15	No Reinforcement	So-so Morale Scale

Figure 1. Experimental design.

The description of Procedures should also be added. It should describe in detail all steps that were executed in conducting the study. The description should include the following:

1. how the groups were formed
2. how and when pretest data were collected
3. the ways in which the groups were different (the independent variable, or treatment)
4. aspects of the study that were the same or similar for all groups
5. how and when posttest data were collected

Note. If the dependent variable was measured with a test (collection of pretest and/or posttest data), the specific test or tests administered should be named. If a test was administered strictly for selection-of-subjects purposes, that is, not as a pretest of the dependent variable, it too should be described.

A student example of a complete Project III on Method is included in the next few pages so that you can see the level of expertise you should have at this point.

Method

Subjects

The sample group was selected from the employee population of Rapare Corporation's North Plant. Rapare Corporation is located in a large metropolitan area and is a provider of consumer goods. The corporation includes a centrally located administrative office and two production facilities (North and South). The North facility has 300 employees, including a plant manager, 10 division supervisors, and 289 workers. The work force of the corporation is made up of primarily non-Hispanic white males (55%), and smaller percentages of Hispanic males (13%), Afro-American males (9%), non-Hispanic white females (8%), Hispanic females (8%), and Afro-American females (7%). The age distribution reflects the following percentages: 20-30 (years of age), 10%; 30-40, 35%; 40-50, 50%; 50-60, 4%; and 60-70, 1%.

Forty subjects were randomly selected from the work force, excluding the plant manager and division supervisors. The 40 were then randomly assigned to two groups of 20 each. The sample selected appropriately reflected the employee work group in regard to ethnicity, sex, and age.

Instruments

Two instruments were administered in the study: Milani's (1975) Attitude Toward Job scale (MAT-J) and his Attitude Toward Company scale (MAT-C). The MAT-J contains 16 items, which measure predispositions, feelings, and/or opinions about one's present job. The MAT-C contains 10 items, which measure predispositions, feelings, and/or opinions about one's present employer. Both are standard attitude scales based on the Thurstone successive-intervals scaling technique. Subjects are given a list of statements and are instructed to place an ''X'' in front of the statements with which they agree. For each scale, a subject's attitude score is the average of the scale values of the statements selected. In the present study, each subject's score for overall attitude was the sum of the attitude scores for the two measures.

1

Although the instruments were originally developed for administration to supervisors, they were judged to be appropriate for nonsupervisory personnel. The items are very general and applicable to virtually all employees, e.g., "This job is disliked by everyone," and "I am made to feel that I am really a part of this organization." Internal-consistency reliability was computed for the subjects in the study using the KR-21 formula and was found to be $\underline{r} = .86$.

Design

The design used in this study was the posttest-only control-group design (see Figure 1). This design was selected because of the feasibility of random assignment to groups and the control provided for sources of internal and external validity. The pretest-posttest control group design was not used because of the potentially reactive nature of the dependent variable, attitudes toward job and company. The only major threat to validity associated with the design used is mortality, i.e., employee turnover. A normal turnover rate of 5% (1 employee per group) was anticipated but did not occur. Thus, the sample sizes remained constant throughout the duration of the study.

Group	Assignment	n	Treatment	Posttest
1	Random	20	Participatory Budget Planning Team	MAT-J[a] + MAT-C[b]
2	Random	20	Nonparticipatory Budget Planning	MAT-J + MAT-C

[a]Milani's Attitude Toward Job scale.
[b]Milani's Attitude Toward Company scale.

Figure 1. Experimental design.

2

Procedure

Prior to the beginning of the fiscal year, the plant manager and supervisors were informed that a study was to take place. The content of the study was not disclosed, but the manager and supervisors did know that the study would involve inclusion of workers in budgetary planning for the following fiscal year. They were asked to assist by releasing the selected workers in their respective areas for participation and to cooperate by providing information and assistance as needed by the planning group. All supervisory personnel agreed to assist with this portion of the study.

The 40 randomly selected workers were notified, and all agreed to participate in the study. They were then randomly assigned to two groups of 20 each; one group was randomly designated to be the experimental group.

During the next week, the workers in the experimental group received a letter from the training department, which explained a program in which they would be involved over the next 6 months; workers in the control group received a letter explaining that they would be scheduled for the program during the second half of the year. The letter explained a three-phase workshop program, which included the following topics: understanding fiscal management, prioritizing the fiscal plan, and developing a fiscal plan. These workshops were taught on a weekly basis, one half day a week, during the employees' scheduled work time. Each workshop lasted 8 weeks, for a total of 24 weeks. In order not to disrupt the work schedule more than necessary and to provide for discussion, employees were asked to attend either the morning or afternoon workshop; half the supervisors attended the morning workshops and the other half attended the afternoon workshops. The plant manager attended the workshops as it was appropriate.

During the first workshop (understanding fiscal management), the fiscal limitations of the corporation, fiscal needs and wants, and goal identification and goal setting were discussed. Over the third and fourth months, the participants in the workshops prioritized, through consensus decision making, the fiscal plan. This was done by reviewing and ranking the corporation's goals and its fiscal needs and wants. During the final 2

3

months, the workshop participants determined the fiscal plan that would be implemented for the upcoming fiscal year.

 After completion of the final workshop, the sample groups were administered the MAT-J and MAT-C. To avoid problems with distribution and return of the instruments, a secretary from the training department met with the experimental and control groups. The workers received the instruments, completed them, and returned them to the secretary.

4

Reference

Milani, K. (1975). The relationship of participation in budget-setting to industrial supervisor performance and attitudes: A field study. The Accounting Review, 50, 274-284.

5

(Note: References is a new page.)

REFERENCES

BARBER, T. X., FORGIONE, A., CHAVES, J. F., CALVERLEY, D. S., McPEAKE, J. D., & BOWEN, B. (1969). Five attempts to replicate the experimenter bias effect. *Journal of Consulting and Clinical Psychology, 33,* 1–6.

BARBER, T. X., & SILVER, M. J. (1968). Fact, fiction, and the experimenter bias effect. *Psychological Bulletin Monograph, 70*(6, Pt. 2), 1–29.

BARLOW, D. W., & HERSEN, M. (1984). *Single-case experimental designs: Strategies for studying behavior change* (2nd ed.). New York: Pergamon Press.

BASS, B. M. (1981). *Stogdill's handbook of leadership.* New York: Free Press.

BATES, P. (1980). Effectiveness of interpersonal skills training on the social skill acquisition of moderately and mildly retarded adults. *Journal of Applied Behavior Analysis, 13,* 237–248.

BLOUGH, P. M. (1983). Local contrast in multiple schedules: The effect of stimulus discriminability. *Journal of Experimental Analysis of Behavior, 39,* 427–437.

BRACHT, G. H., & GLASS, G. V. (1968). The external validity of experiments. *American Educational Research Journal, 5,* 437–474.

CAMPBELL, D. T., & STANLEY, J. C. (1972). *Experimental and quasi-experimental designs for research.* Chicago: Rand McNally.

COOK, D. L. (1967). *The impact of the Hawthorne effect in experimental designs in educational research* (Cooperative Research Project No. 1757). Washington, D.C.: U.S. Office of Education.

COOK, T. D., & CAMPBELL, D. T. (1979). *Quasi-experimentation: Design & analysis issues for field settings.* Boston: Houghton Mifflin.

FISHER, E. B., JR. (1979). Overjustification effects in token economies. *Journal of Applied Behavior Analysis, 12,* 407–415.

GAY, L. R. (1980). The comparative effects of multiple-choice versus short-answer tests on retention. *Journal of Educational Measurement, 17,* 45–50.

GOODSON, J. R., McGEE, G. W., & CASHMAN, J. F. (1989). Situational leadership theory: A test of leadership prescriptions. *Group & Organizational Studies, 14*(4), 446–461.

HERSEY, P., & BLANCHARD, K. H. (1988). *Management of organizational behavior: Utilizing human resources* (5th ed.). Englewood Cliffs, NJ: Prentice-Hall.

KAZDIN, A. E. (1977). Assessing the clinical or applied importance of behavior change through social validation. *Behavior Modification, 1,* 427–452.

KAZDIN, A. E. (1984). Statistical analysis for single-case experimental designs. In D. H. Barlow & M. Hersen, *Single-case experimental designs: Strategies for studying behavior change* (2nd ed., pp. 285–324). New York: Pergamon Press.

LAWLER, E. E., III, & MOHRMAN, S. A. (1987). Quality circles: After the honeymoon. *Organizational Dynamics, 15*(4), 42–54.

LEITENBERG, H. (1973). The use of single-case methodology in psychotherapy research. *Journal of Abnormal Psychology, 82,* 87–101.

MELVIN, L. R. (1987). The effects of test item format upon the achievement of college level students in an actual classroom setting. *Dissertation Abstracts International.* (University Microfilms No. 88-05, 675.)

ROETHLISBERGER, F. S., & DICKSON, W. J. (1939). *Management and the worker.* Cambridge, MA: Harvard University Press.

ROSENTHAL, R. (1966). *Experimenter effects in behavioral research.* New York: Appleton-Century-Crofts.

Rosenthal, R., & Fode, K. L. (1963). The effect of experimenter bias on the performance of the albino rat. *Behavioral Science, 8*, 183–189.

Saretsky, G. (1972). The OEO P.C. experiment and the John Henry effect. *Phi Delta Kappan, 53*, 579–581.

Stogdill, R. M. (1974). *Handbook of leadership.* New York: Free Press.

Weitz, J. (1967). Tiny theories. *American Psychologist, 22*, 157.

Windle, C. (1954). Test-retest effects in personality questionnaires. *Educational and Psychological Measurement, 14*, 617–633.

Yukl, G. A. (1981). *Leadership in organizations.* Englewood Cliffs, NJ: Prentice-Hall.

PART FOUR

Data Analysis and Interpretation
Or the Word Is "Statistics,"
Not "Sadistics"

Statistics is a set of procedures for describing, synthesizing, analyzing, and interpreting quantitative data. One thousand pieces of data, for example, can be represented by a single number. You would not expect two groups to perform in exactly the same way on a posttest, even if they were essentially equal; application of the appropriate statistic helps you to decide if the difference between groups is big enough to represent a true difference as distinct from a difference attributable only to chance.

Choice of appropriate statistical techniques is determined to a great extent by the design of the study and by the kind of data to be collected. The posttest-only control-group design and the Solomon four-group design discussed in Chapter 10 each suggest different statistical analyses for investigating group differences. As with the design, statistical procedures and techniques are identified and described in detail in the research plan. Analysis of the data is as important as any other component of the research process. Regardless of how well the study is conducted, inappropriate analyses can lead to inappropriate conclusions. Although certain statistical techniques seem to enjoy an almost faddish popularity from time to time, the complexity of the analysis is not an indication of its quality; a simple statistic is often more appropriate than a more complicated one. In the final analysis, the choice of statistical techniques is largely determined by the research hypothesis to be tested.

There are a wide variety of statistics available to the researcher. Part Four will describe and explain only those most commonly used in behavioral science and management research. The intent is that you be able to apply and interpret these statistics, not that you necessarily understand their theoretical rationale and mathematical derivation. Despite what you have heard, statistics is easy. In order to calculate the statistics to be described, you need to know only how to add, subtract, multiply, and divide. That is all there is. All formulas, no matter how gross they may look, turn into arithmetic problems when applied to your data. The arithmetic problems involve only the operations of addition, subtraction, multiplication, and division; the formulas tell you how often and in what order to perform those operations. Now, if you are a smarty, you are probably thinking, "Sure, but what about square roots?" While it is true that many of the formulas involve square roots, you do not have to know how to find the square root of anything because the square root of any reasonable number can be found simply by using the square root button on your calculator.

Even if you have a hangup about math and have not had a math course since junior high school, you will be able to calculate statistics; no calculus is required. The very hardest formula still requires arithmetic, maybe sixth-grade arithmetic if you have to divide by a big number, but arithmetic just the same. In fact, you do not have to divide big numbers if you don't want to—calculators are definitely allowed! All you have to do is follow the steps as presented, and you can't go wrong. You are going to be pleasantly surprised to see just how easy statistics is. Trust us!

The goal of Part Four is that you be able to select, apply, and correctly interpret analyses appropriate for a given study. After you have read Part Four, you should be able to perform the following project.

Project IV Guidelines

Based on Projects II and III, which you have already completed, you will now prepare to write the *Results* section of a research report. Project IV involves the following steps:

1. Generate data for each of the subjects in your study.
2. Summarize and describe the data using descriptive statistics.
3. Statistically analyze the data using inferential statistics.
4. Interpret the results in terms of your original research hypothesis.
5. Present the results of your data analysis in a summary table.

If STATPAK, the microcomputer program that accompanies this text, is available to you through your instructor, use it to check your work. If you want to use any of the other statistical packages available for the computer, feel free to do so.
(See Performance Criteria, p. 550)

Looks bad, right? (page 482)

11

Descriptive Statistics

Objectives

After reading Chapter 11, you should be able to do the following:

1. Describe the process of coding data, giving three examples of variables that would require coding.

2. List the steps involved in graphing data using a:
   a. line chart.
   b. bar graph.
   c. pie chart.

3. Define or describe three measures of central tendency.

4. Define or describe three measures of variability.

5. List four characteristics of normal distributions.

6. List two characteristics of:
   a. positively skewed distributions.
   b. negatively skewed distributions.

7. Define or describe two measures of relationship.

8. Calculate the following statistics:
   a. mean.
   b. standard deviation.
   c. Spearman rho.
   d. Pearson r.
   e. Spearman-Brown correction formula.
   f. Kuder-Richardson formula (KR-21).
   g. Standard error of measurement.

If STATPAK, the microcomputer program that accompanies this text, is available to you, use it to check your work. Isn't this fun?

TABULATION AND CODING PROCEDURES

In Chapter 5 we discussed the selection or development of instruments or methodologies for collecting data. Just as we recommended in Chapter 2 that you be extremely careful with your notes for your literature review, we will again recommend

457

extreme care in handling the raw data you collected using whatever instrument or methodology you selected. This is definitely not the time to imitate the "shoebox" approach to income tax preparation!

After the instruments have been scored or other measurement data recorded, the results are transferred to summary data sheets and/or data cards. Recording the data in a systematic manner facilitates its examination as well as data analysis. If analysis is to consist of a simple comparison of the posttest scores or data of one, two, or more groups, data are generally placed in columns, one for each group, in ascending or descending order (see Table 11.1, column X). If pretest measures are involved, similar, additional columns are formed. For example, Table 11.1 presents a pretraining rating (column X), a posttraining score (column Y), a posttraining rating (column Y^1), a combination pretraining rating and posttraining score (column X + Y), and a follow-up rating (column Z) for a group of 20 trainees. When planned analyses involve subgroup comparisons, data will be tabulated separately for each subgroup. The same is true for questionnaires. If the research hypotheses or questions are concerned with subgroup comparisons, responses to each should be tallied by subgroup. To use a former example, a police chief might be interested in comparing the attitude toward gun control of patrol officers with the attitude of detectives. Thus,

Table 11.1

Raw Data for Trainees for Pretraining Rating (X), Posttraining Scores and Rating (Y and Y^1), and Follow-up Rating (Z)

Subject	X	Y	Posttraining Y^1	X + Y	Z
S 1	19	53	18	72	20
S 2	19	48	16	67	20
S 3	18	36	12	54	19
S 4	17	46	15	63	20
S 5	17	44	15	61	17
S 6	16	48	16	64	15
S 7	16	37	12	53	18
S 8	15	39	13	54	20
S 9	14	42	14	56	11
S10	12	28	9	40	16
S11	11	45	15	46	19
S12	11	47	16	58	18
S13	10	49	16	59	11
S14	10	40	13	50	11
S15	9	38	13	47	20
S16	8	39	13	47	15
S17	8	50	17	58	17
S18	8	30	10	38	17
S19	6	33	11	39	11
S20	6	38	13	44	16

for a question such as, Do you favor legislation implementing gun control? the chief would tally the number of yes, no, and undecided responses separately for patrol officers and detectives.

When a number of different kinds of data are collected for each subject, such as several test scores and biographical information, data are sometimes recorded on data cards, one card for each subject. The card for each subject follows the same format, and both the variable names and the actual data are frequently coded. The variable "pretest data entry scores," for example, may be coded as PDE, and the sex of the subject may be recorded as "1" or "2" (male versus female). When a number of different analyses are to be performed, data cards facilitate analysis, since they can be easily sorted and resorted to form the piles, or subgroups, required for each analysis.

An alternative, and more attractive strategy, is to use a computerized data base management program such as dBase IV (Ashton-Tate, 1989), R:Base (Microrim, 1989), or Double Helix (Odesta, 1989). Use of the computer is highly recommended if complex or multiple analyses are to be performed, or if a large number of subjects are involved. Some of the software programs, such as Lotus 1-2-3 (Lotus, 1989) and dBase, have the capacity to load data directly into statistical programs on mainframe or personal computers such as SPSS^x or SPSS/PC (Statistical Package for the Social Sciences) (SPSS Inc., 1985). Of course, you can also load the data directly into the statistical program you intend to use. For example, Figure 11.1 shows the data presented as Table 11.1 using SPSS/PC+; Figure 11.2 shows the same data using another personal computer statistical program called Statview™512+. If you are using any computer program to analyze your raw data, coding of the data is especially important and, some users contend, the most difficult part of the process because of the need for caution and planning. With most of these programs, data for all variables and subjects are converted to numerical values following the directions in the manual for the particular program you are using. This coding is done because long entries take up considerable space and contribute to typographical and spelling errors that mess up subsequent manipulations. It's important, therefore, to be sure you keep accurate written records of which pieces of data you recorded as X, Y, or Z, for example, or whether males or females are coded as 0 or 1. Also, once the data are entered, you should make a paper copy ("hard copy" in computereze) both as a record and also to check your work for accuracy. The major advantage of computer programs is the capacity of the computer to select different variables to examine in different ways, to rearrange data by subgroups, and to extract information without reentering all your data. The major disadvantages are the initial time it takes to learn to use the program and the unfortunate fact that some students rely on the computer to handle their data appropriately without the student's full understanding what is happening—or should happen!

In general, the first step in coding data is to give each subject an identification (ID) number. If there are 50 subjects, for example, they may be numbered from 01 to 50. As this example illustrates, if the highest value for a variable is two digits (e.g., 50), then all represented values must be two digits. Thus, the first subject is 01, not 1. (Remember "007"? Based on this coding, how many agents may there be in "Her

```
data list file = 'a:regdata'
/id 1–3(a) x 5–6 y 8–9 y1 11–12 xy 14–15 z 17–18 xyz 20–21.
list id x y y1 xy z xyz.
The raw data or transformation pass is proceeding
        20 cases are written to the uncompressed active file.
```

Page 2   SPSS/PC+

ID	X	Y	Y1	XY	Z	XYZ
s1	19	53	18	72	20	92
s2	19	48	16	67	20	87
s3	18	36	12	54	19	73
s4	17	46	15	63	20	83
s5	17	44	15	61	17	78
s6	16	48	16	64	15	79
s7	16	37	12	53	18	71
s8	15	39	13	54	20	64
s9	14	42	14	56	11	57
s10	12	28	9	40	16	56
s11	11	45	15	46	19	65
s12	11	47	16	58	18	74
s13	10	49	16	59	11	70
s14	10	40	13	50	11	61
s15	9	38	13	47	20	67
s16	8	39	13	47	15	62
s17	8	50	17	58	17	75
s18	8	30	10	38	17	55
s19	6	33	11	39	11	50
s20	6	38	13	44	16	60

Number of cases read =   20   Number of cases listed =   20

Figure 11.1. Example of commands and data printout for Table 11.1 data using SPSS/PC+.

Majesty's Secret Service"?) Similarly, scores or values that range from, say, $75 to $135, are coded 075 to 135. The next step is to make decisions as to how nonnumeric, or categorical, data will be coded. Categorical data include such variables as sex, group membership, and employment level (e.g., salaried employee versus hourly employee). Thus, if the study involves 50 subjects, 2 groups of 25, then group membership may be coded "1" or "2," for "experimental group" and "control group" respectively. Categorical data also refer to the situation where subjects choose

	X	Y	Y1	XY	Z
1	19	53	18	72	20
2	19	48	16	67	20
3	18	36	12	54	19
4	17	46	15	63	20
5	17	44	15	61	17
6	16	48	16	64	15
7	16	37	12	53	18
8	15	39	13	54	20
9	14	42	14	56	11
10	12	28	9	40	16
11	11	45	15	46	19
12	11	47	16	58	18
13	10	49	16	59	11
14	10	40	13	50	11
15	9	38	13	47	20
16	8	39	13	47	15
17	8	50	17	58	17
18	8	30	10	38	17
19	6	33	11	39	11
20	6	38	13	44	16

Figure 11.2. Example of data printout for Table 11.1 data using Statview™512+.

from a small number of alternatives representing a wider range of values; they are most often associated with survey instruments. For example, secretaries might be asked the following question:

12. How many hours do you spend per week in duplicating materials?
  a. 0–5 hours
  b. 6–10 hours
  c. 11–15 hours
  d. 16–20 hours

Responses might be coded (a) = 1, (b) = 2, (c) = 3, (d) = 4. (By the way, what's wrong with the question above as a survey question? If you said, among other things, that there was no option for "more than 20 hours," award yourself a gold star!)

Once the data have been prepared for analysis, the choice of statistical procedures to be applied is determined not only by the research hypothesis and design but also by the type of measurement scale represented by the data. Again, in Chapter 5 we discussed the different types of measurement scales: nominal, ordinal, interval, and ratio. Each scale allows for different types of statistical manipulation.

TYPES OF DESCRIPTIVE STATISTICS

The first step in data analysis is to describe, or summarize, the data using descriptive statistics. In some studies, such as certain questionnaire surveys, the entire analysis procedure may consist solely of calculating and interpreting descriptive statistics. Descriptive statistics permit the researcher to describe meaningfully a set of data consisting of many, many figures with a small number of indices. If such indices are calculated for a sample drawn from a population, the resulting values are referred to as *statistics;* if they are calculated for an entire population, they are referred to as *parameters.*

The major types of descriptive statistics are measures of central tendency, measures of variability, measures of relationship, and measures of relative position. *Measures of central tendency* are used to determine the typical or average score of a group of figures; *measures of variability* indicate how spread out a group of figures are; *measures of relationship* indicate to what degree two sets of figures are related; and *measures of relative position* describe a subject's performance compared to the performance of all other subjects. Before you actually calculate any of these measures, it is often useful to present the data in graphic form.

Graphing Data

As discussed previously, data are often recorded on summary sheets in columns and are placed in ascending or descending order. Data in this form are easily graphed. Graphing data permits the researcher to see what the distribution of figures looks like. The shape of the distribution may not be self-evident, especially if it involves a large number of figures. As we shall see later, the shape of the distribution may influence our choice of certain descriptive statistics. In Chapter 8 when we were discussing relationships between different sets of data, the scattergram was used to demonstrate the different kinds of relationships (see Figure 8.1). In addition to scattergrams, the most commonly used methods of graphing data in business research include the following:

1. *Line charts,* in which dotted or solid lines are used to graph data, are frequently used to display business data. The most common example of a line chart is the *time-series line chart.* This chart displays the changes in data over a period of time. Sales information, for example, might be collected over a period of months as shown in Table 11.2. A chart is then constructed listing the highest to the lowest sales on the vertical axis (also called the Y-axis); on the horizontal axis (or X-axis) the months in which the data were collected are listed. A dot is then placed on the chart at the intersection of sales and months, and the dots are connected to provide a graphic depiction of the sales for the time period of interest (see Figure 11.3). By means of different colors or shadings, combinations of data may be displayed on the same line chart. Thus, the data shown in Figure 11.3 might also include a second line that represented inventory or some other information of interest. This kind of line chart is called a *component-part line chart.*

Another common method of graphing research data using a line chart is to construct a *frequency polygon.* The first step in constructing a frequency polygon is to list all

Table 11.2
Hypothetical Monthly Sales

Month	Sales in Thousands of Dollars
January	670
February	750
March	580
April	600
May	550
June	700

"scores" and to tabulate how many subjects received each score. If the sales figures for 85 sales associates were collected, the results might be as shown in Table 11.3.

Once the scores are tallied, the steps are as follows:

1. Place all the scores on a horizontal axis, at equal intervals, from lowest score to highest.
2. Place the frequencies of scores at equal intervals on the vertical axis, starting with zero.
3. For each score, find the point where the score intersects with its frequency of occurrence and make a dot.
4. Connect all the dots with straight lines (see Figure 11.4).

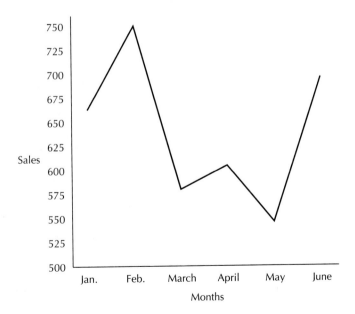

Figure 11.3. Line chart of hypothetical monthly sales.

Table 11.3
Frequency Distribution Based on 85 Hypothetical Sales Records

Sales in Dollars	Frequency of Sales Records
78	1
79	4
80	5
81	7
82	7
83	9
84	9
85	12
86	10
87	7
88	6
89	3
90	4
91	1

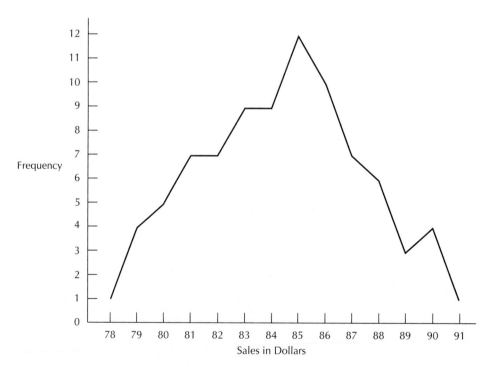

Figure 11.4. Frequency polygon based on 85 hypothetical sales records.

From Figure 11.4 we can see that most of the sales associates achieved at or near $850 in sales, with progressively fewer sales associates achieving higher or lower sales. In other words, the sales records appear to form a relatively normal distribution, a concept to be discussed a little later. This knowledge would be helpful in selecting an appropriate measure of central tendency.

2. *Bar graphs,* a second way of graphing data, may be used in most instances in which a line chart is used. Figure 11.5 shows the same information depicted in Figure 11.4 but uses a bar graph instead of a line chart.

Bar graphs may be vertical, as in Figure 11.5, or they may be horizontal. In addition, *duo-directional bar graphs* may be used to illustrate positive and negative numbers on a single chart. *Component bar charts,* in which each bar is divided into segments to represent the different elements that make up each bar, may be used. In this case, for example, the bars might be broken down by different types of sales (see Figure 11.6). As seen in this illustration, comparisons may be made of percentages of sales or actual dollar amounts. Another variation, *grouped bar charts,* break down the component parts and group them together so that comparisons may be made.

3. *Pie charts* are also used to display business data graphically. The information shown on a component bar chart might also be displayed on a pie chart (see Figure 11.7). Pie charts may be placed side by side, as in Figure 11.7, so that comparisons can easily be made.

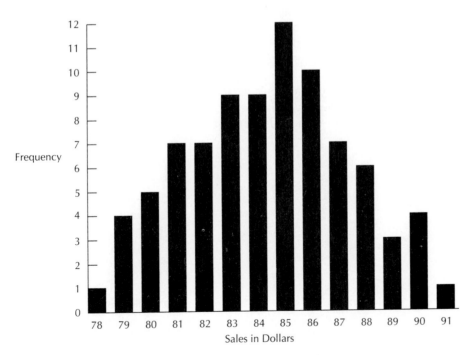

Figure 11.5. Bar graph based on 85 hypothetical sales records.

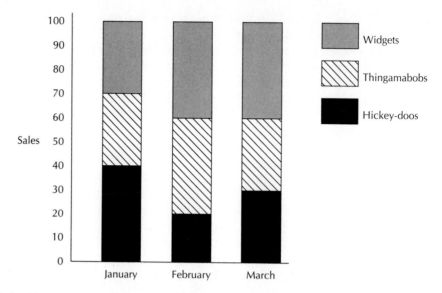

Figure 11.6. Component bar chart using hypothetical sales data.

If you want more detailed information on graphing data using line charts, bar charts, or pie charts, most business statistics books will be of assistance. In addition, graphics programs and statistical software programs such as Lotus 1-2-3 (Lotus, 1989), and Double Helix (Odesta, 1989) designed for use with personal computers can graph your data for you. In presenting graphed data, it is wise to remember that the purpose of this method of presentation is to clarify and present information in an attractive, easy-to-grasp way. It is very easy, however, to mislead the consumer of graphed data. In Figure 11.7, for example, it would appear to the casual observer that "widgets" did much better in February than in January because their percentage of total sales

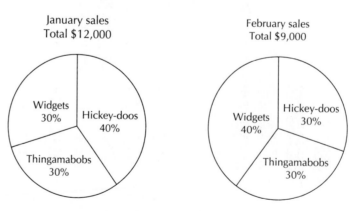

Figure 11.7. Pie chart using hypothetical sales data.

increased from 30 to 40. In actuality, widget sales remained steady at $3,600, while hickey-doo sales dropped from $4,800 to $2,700, and thingamabob sales dropped from $3,600 to $2,700. The apparent change in widget sales is the result of total sales decreasing overall from $12,000 to $9,000. It is also very easy to mislead the consumer of graphed data by changing the horizontal and/or vertical axis of line charts and bar graphs. Descriptive statistics such as measures of central tendency and variability still provide the most precise way of presenting data.

Measures of Central Tendency

Measures of central tendency give the researcher a convenient way of describing a set of data with a single number. The number resulting from computation of a measure of central tendency represents the average or typical "score" or figure attained by a group of subjects. The three most frequently encountered indices of central tendency are the mode, the median, and the mean. Each of these indices is appropriate for a different scale of measurement:

1. The *mode,* which is appropriate for nominal data, is the figure that appears more frequently in the distribution than any other figure. For the data presented in Table 11.3 and graphed in Figure 11.4, for example, the mode is $85 since 12 subjects achieved that level of sales. The mode is not established through calculation; it is determined by looking at a set of figures or at a graph of figures and seeing which figure occurs most frequently. There are several problems associated with the mode, and it is therefore of limited value and seldom used. For one thing, a set of figures may have two (or more) modes, in which case it is referred to as bimodal. For the sales figures $75, $80, $80, $82, $83, and $83, for example, there are two modes—$80 and $83. Another problem with the mode is that it is an unstable measure of central tendency; equal-size samples randomly selected from the same accessible population are likely to have different modes. When nominal data are involved, however, the mode is the only appropriate measure of central tendency.

2. The *median,* which is appropriate with ordinal data, is that point in a distribution above and below which are 50% of the figures; in other words, the median is the midpoint. If there are an odd number of figures, the median is the middle figure (assuming the figures are arranged in order). For example, for the sales figures $75, $80, $82, $83, $87, the median is $82, the middle figure. If there are an even number of figures, the median is the point halfway between the two middle figures. For example, for sales figures of $21, $23, $24, $25, $26, $30, the median is $24.50; for the figures $50, $52, $55, $57, $59, $61, the median is $56. Thus, the median is not necessarily the same as one of the figures in the set.

The median is only the midpoint of the figures and does not take into account each and every figure in the set; it ignores, for example, extremely high figures and extremely low figures. Two quite different sets of figures may have the same median. For example, for the figures $60, $62, $65, $67, $72, the median is $65; for the figures $60, $62, $65, $67, $89, the median is also $65. As we shall see shortly, this apparent lack of precision may be advantageous at times.

As mentioned, the median is the appropriate measure of central tendency when the data represent an ordinal scale. It is the measure of central tendency mentioned, for example, any time the *Fortune* 500 is used. For certain other distributions, the median may be selected as the most appropriate measure of central tendency even though the data represent an interval scale or a ratio scale; it is often used, for example, in discussing median income or the median cost of housing. While the median appears to be a rather simple index to determine, it cannot always be arrived at simply by looking at the set of figures; it does not always fall neatly between two different figures. With 500 companies listed in the *Fortune* 500, the median for 1989 (*Fortune*, 1990) would fall at $1,617.2 million in sales, with company 250 above at $1,618.0 million in sales and company 251 below the median at $1,616.5 million in sales ($1618.0 − $1616.5)/2) + $1,616.5 = $1,617.2). By contrast, determining the median for the figures $80, 82, 84, 84, 84, 88 is not so easy and requires the application of a relatively complex formula; this is an excellent application of a computer statistics package, as a matter of fact!

3. The *mean*, which is appropriate with interval or with ratio data, is the arithmetic average of the figures in a distribution; it is the most frequently used measure of central tendency. The symbol for the mean is $\overline{X}$ when the scores are labeled as Xs, or any other symbol with a bar over it. Thus $\overline{Y}$ would indicate the mean of the Y scores. The mean is calculated by adding up all the figures in the set and dividing that total by the number of figures. Therefore the formula for finding the mean of the X scores or set of figures would be:

$$\overline{X} = \frac{\Sigma X}{N}.$$

In the formula above, Σ is the symbol used to mean "sum of" so ΣX means "add up the Xs"; N indicates the number of figures. You would read the above formula, "the mean $(\overline{X})$ is equal to the sum of the scores (ΣX) divided by the number of subjects (N)." In order to find $\overline{X}$, we would first need to find ΣX and N.

X Scores	
Iggie	1
Hermie	2
Fifi	3
Teenie	4
Tiny	5
ΣX =	15

Clearly, $\Sigma X = 1 + 2 + 3 + 4 + 5 = 15$
N = 5. (There are 5 subjects, right?)

Now we have everything we need to find the mean and all we have to do is substitute the correct number for each symbol.

$$\overline{X} = \frac{\Sigma X}{N} = \frac{15}{5} = 3$$

Although this looked like a simple arithmetic problem, you have just learned how to calculate a statistic! Was it hard? Cer-tain-ly not! Are they all going to be that easy? Of course! You have also learned some statistical notation such as $\overline{X}$, N, and Σ. You will find a list of these symbols in the Glossary.

As you have seen, by the very nature of the way in which the mean is computed, it takes into account, or is based on, each and every one of the figures in the set. Unlike the median, the mean is definitely affected by extreme figures in the set. Thus, in certain cases, the median may actually give a more accurate estimate of the "typical" figure than the mean does.

In general, however, the mean is the preferred measure of central tendency. As mentioned, it is appropriate when the data represent either an interval or a ratio scale; it is a more precise, stable index than either the median or the mode. If equal-size samples are randomly selected from the same population, the means of those samples will be more similar to each other than either the medians or the modes. While the mode is almost never the most appropriate measure of central tendency when the data represent an interval or a ratio scale, the median may be. In the situation described previously, in which there are one or more extreme scores or figures, the median will not be the most "accurate" representation of the performance of the total group, but it will be the best index of "typical" performance. As an example of this concept, suppose you wanted to set production goals for a group of workers doing piecework. For the previous week you had the following production figures for nine workers in the number of units produced: 96, 96, 97, 99, 100, 101, 102, 104, 155. For these figures, the measures of central tendency are as follows:

mode   =   96   (most frequent figure)
median = 100   (middle figure)
mean   = 105.6 (arithmetic average)

In this case, the median clearly represents the "typical" performance best. The mode is too low, and the mean is higher than all of the production figures except one. The mean is "pulled up" in the direction of the 155 production figure, whereas the median essentially ignores it. Obviously production goals set using the mode in this case would be too low, while goals set using the mean would be too high, even though you could say that the "average" worker completed 105.6 units in the week. The different pictures presented by the different measures are part of the reason for the phrase "lying with statistics." In fact, by selecting one index of central tendency over another, one may present a particular point of view in a stronger light. In a labor-management dispute over pay, for example, very different estimates of the pay received by a "typical" employee will be obtained depending upon which index of central tendency is used. Let us say that the following figures represent annual employee pay in a particular department: $12,000, $13,000, $13,000, $15,000, $16,000, $18,000, $45,000. For these earnings, the measures of central tendency are as follows:

mode   = $13,000 (most frequent)
median = $15,000 (middle)
mean   = $18,857 (arithmetic average)

Both labor and management could overstate their argument, labor by using the mode and management by using the mean. The mean is higher than every annual payment except one, $45,000, which in all likelihood would be the salary of the manager. Thus, in this case, the most appropriate index of typical annual pay would be the median.

Unlike labor-management disputes, in research, we are not interested in arguing a point of view but rather in describing the data in the most appropriate way. For the majority of sets of data, the mean is the most appropriate measure of central tendency.

Measures of Variability

Although measures of central tendency are very useful statistics for describing a set of data, they are not sufficient. Two sets of data that are very different can have identical means or medians. As an example, consider the following sets of data:

Set A: 79   79   79   80   81   81   81
Set B: 50   60   70   80   90   100   110

The mean of both sets of data is 80 and the median of both is 80, but set A is very different from set B. In set A the figures are all very close together and clustered around the mean. In set B the figures are much more spread out; in other words, there is much more variation, or variability, in set B. Thus, there is a need for a measure that indicates how spread out the figures are or, in other words, how much variability there is. There are a number of descriptive statistics that serve this purpose, and they are referred to as *measures of variability.*

1. The *range,* which is the only appropriate measure of variability for nominal data, is simply the difference between the highest score or figure in a set and the lowest figure. The range is determined by subtraction. As an example, the range for the figures presented as Set A, 79, 79, 79, 80, 81, 81, 81, is 2 (81 − 79 = 2), while the range for Set B, 50, 60, 70, 80, 90, 100, 110, is 60 (110 − 50 = 60). Thus, if the range is small the figures in the distribution are close together, whereas if the range is large, the figures are more spread out. Like the mode, the range is not a very stable measure of variability, and its chief advantage is that it gives a quick, rough estimate of variability.

2. The *quartile deviation,* which is the appropriate measure of variability for ordinal data, is one half of the difference between the upper quartile and the lower quartile in a distribution. To put it more simply, the upper quartile is the 75th percentile, or that

point below which are 75% of the scores or figures in a distribution; the lower quartile, correspondingly, is the 25th percentile, or that point below which are 25% of the scores or figures in the distribution. To apply this to our favorite example of ordinal data, the *Fortune* 500, this means that the upper quartile includes the sales of companies 1 through 125, the second quartile includes the sales of companies 126 through 250, the third quartile includes the sales of companies 251 through 375, and the lower quartile includes the sales of companies 376 through 500. By subtracting the lower quartile from the upper quartile and then dividing the result by two, we get a measure of variability. If the quartile deviation is small, the figures are close together; conversely, if the quartile deviation is large, the figures are more spread out. The quartile deviation is a more stable measure of variability than the range and is appropriate whenever the median is appropriate. Calculation of the quartile deviation involves a process very similar to that used to calculate the median, which just happens to be the second quartile. (Remember?)

3. The *standard deviation,* which is appropriate when the data represent an interval scale or ratio scale, is by far the most frequently used index of variability; it is represented in statistical notation as *SD*. Like the mean, its counterpart measure of central tendency, the standard deviation is the most stable measure of variability and takes into account each and every score. In fact, the first step in calculating the standard deviation involves finding out how far each score or figure in the distribution is from the mean, that is, subtracting the mean from each of the figures in the distribution. Now (concentrate!), if we square each difference, add up all the squares, and divide by the number of scores or figures, we have a measure of variability called the *variance.* If the variance is small, the scores are close together; if the variance is large, the scores are more spread out. The square root of the variance is called the *standard deviation,* and like the variance, a small standard deviation indicates that the scores are close together, and a large standard deviation indicates that the scores are more spread out. Fortunately, to calculate the standard deviation we do not have to calculate deviation scores; we can use a raw score formula, which gives us the same answer with less grief. Before you look at the formula, remember that no matter how bad it looks it is going to turn into an easy arithmetic problem, just as the formula for the mean did. Ready?

$$SD = \sqrt{\frac{SS}{N-1}} \quad \text{where } SS = \Sigma X^2 - \frac{(\Sigma X)^2}{N}.$$

$$OR$$

$$SD = \sqrt{\frac{\Sigma X^2 - \frac{(\Sigma X)^2}{N}}{N-1}}.$$

In other words, the *SD* is equal to the square root of the sum of squares *(SS)* divided by $N - 1$.

If the standard deviation of a population is being calculated, the formula is exactly the same, except we divide *SS* by *N*, instead of $N - 1$. The reason is that a sample standard deviation is considered to be a biased estimate of the population standard deviation. When we select a sample, especially a small sample, the probability is that subjects will come from the middle of the distribution and that extreme figures will not be represented (because there are so few of them). Thus, the range of sample figures will be smaller than the population range, as will be the sample standard deviation. As the sample size increases, so do the chances of getting extreme figures; thus, the smaller the sample, the more important it is to correct for the downward bias. By dividing by $N - 1$ instead of N, we make the denominator (the bottom part) smaller, and thus $SS/N - 1$ is larger, closer to the population standard deviation and SS/N. For example, if $SS = 18$ and $N = 10$, then

$$\frac{SS}{N-1} = \frac{18}{9} = 2; \quad \frac{SS}{N} = \frac{18}{10} = 1.8$$

Now just relax and look at each piece of the formula for SD; you already know what each piece means. Starting with the easy one, N refers to what? Right—the number of subjects. How about (ΣX)? Right—the sum of the figures. And $(\Sigma X)^2$? Right—the square of the sum of the figures. That leaves ΣX^2, which means the sum of what?—Fantastic! The sum of the X^2s. Okay, let's use the same figures we used to calculate the mean. The first thing we need to do is square each figure and then add up those squares—while we are at it we can also go ahead and add up all the figures:

	X	X^2	
Iggie	1	1	
Hermie	2	4	$\Sigma X = 15$
Fifi	3	9	$\Sigma X^2 = 55$
Teenie	4	16	$N = 5$
Tiny	5	25	$N - 1 = 4$
	$\Sigma X = 15$	$\Sigma X^2 = 55$	

Do we have everything we need? Does the formula ask for anything else? We are in business. Substituting each symbol with its numerical equivalent we get

$$SS = \Sigma X^2 - \frac{(\Sigma X)^2}{N} = 55 - \frac{(15)^2}{5}$$

Another statistic? No, just another arithmetic problem! A hard arithmetic problem? No! Well, yes, it's harder than 15/5 but it is not *hard*. If we just do what the formula tells us to do we will have no problem at all. The first thing it tells us to do is to square 15:

$$SS = \Sigma X^2 - \frac{(\Sigma X)^2}{N} = 55 - \frac{(15)^2}{5} = 55 - \frac{225}{5}$$

So far so good? The next thing the formula tells you to do is divide 225 by 5:

$$= 55 - 45$$

It is looking a lot better; now it is *really* an easy arithmetic problem. Okay, the next step is to subtract 45 from 55:

$$SS = 10$$

Mere child's play. Think you can figure out the next step? Terrific! Now that we have SS, we simply substitute it into the standard deviation formula as follows:

$$SD = \sqrt{\frac{SS}{N - 1}} = \sqrt{\frac{10}{4}} = \sqrt{2.5}$$

To determine the square root of 2.5, simply punch in 2.5 on your calculator and hit the square root symbol: voilà—square root is 1.58. Now you know how to do two statistics—the mean and standard deviation. Were they hard? No! Just keep remembering that when you look at the next formula, no matter how bad it looks, it is really just an arithmetic problem.

As we've stated before, however, using a personal computer or mainframe statistical program to do some of the calculations for you will simplify things considerably, as long as you understand what you're doing. Using the data in column X from Table 11.1, for example, and the software program Statview™512+, you will get a display or printout that gives you the mean, standard deviation, count, range, and other information you might find useful in computing various statistics (see Figure 11.8).

The importance of knowing the mean and standard deviation of a set of figures is that the two statistics will give you a pretty good picture of what the distribution looks like. An interesting phenomenon associated with the standard deviation is the fact that if the distribution is relatively normal (about which we will have more to say shortly), then the mean plus 3 SD and the mean minus 3 SD encompasses over 99%, or just about all, the figures in the distribution. If you're curious, the number 3 is a constant when working with standard deviations. Each distribution has its own mean and its own standard deviation, which are calculated based on the figures in the distribution.

$X_1 : X$

Mean:	Std. Dev.:	Std. Error:	Variance:	Coef. Var.:	Count:
12.5	4.371	.977	19.105	34.968	20

Minimum:	Maximum:	Range:	Sum:	Sum Squared:	# Missing:
6	19	13	250	3488	0

Figure 11.8. Descriptive statistics for raw data in Column X, Table 11.1.

Once these are computed, 3 times the standard deviation added to the mean and 3 times the standard deviation subtracted from the mean includes just about all the scores. The above concept can be expressed as follows:

$$\overline{X} \pm 3\ SD = 99 + \% \text{ of the scores.}$$

As an example, suppose that for a set of scores the mean is calculated to be 80 and the standard deviation to be 1. In this case, the mean plus 3 SD is equal to 80 + 3(1) = 80 + 3 = 83. The mean minus 3 SD is equal to 80 − 3(1) = 80 − 3 = 77. Thus, almost all the scores fall between 77 and 83. This makes sense since, as we mentioned before, a small standard deviation (in this case SD = 1) indicates that the scores are close together, not very spread out.

As another example, suppose that for another set of scores the mean is again calculated to be 80, but this time the standard deviation is calculated to be 4. In this case, the mean plus 3 SD is equal to 80 + 3(4) = 80 + 12 = 92. To put it another way:

$$80 \text{ plus } 1\ SD = 80 + 4 = 84$$
$$80 \text{ plus } 2\ SD = 80 + 4 +\ \ 4 = 88$$
$$80 \text{ plus } 3\ SD = 80 + 4 +\ \ 4 +\ \ 4 = 92$$

Now, the mean minus 3 SD is equal to 80 − 3(4) = 80 − 12 = 68.
To illustrate further:

$$80 \text{ minus } 1\ SD = 80 - 4 = 76$$
$$80 \text{ minus } 2\ SD = 80 - 4 -\ \ 4 = 72$$
$$80 \text{ minus } 3\ SD = 80 - 4 -\ \ 4 -\ \ 4 = 68$$

Thus, more than 99% of the scores fall between 68 and 92. This makes sense since a larger standard deviation (in this case SD = 4) indicates that the scores are more spread out. Clearly, if you know the mean and standard deviation of a set of scores you have a pretty good idea of what the scores look like. You know the average score and you know how spread out, or how variable, the scores are. Thus, together the mean and standard deviation describe a set of data quite well.

The Normal Curve

The +3 concept is valid only when the scores are normally distributed, that is, form a normal, or bell-shaped, curve. Most of you, as students, are probably familiar with the concept of grading "on the normal curve." When this is done, a certain percentage of students receive a grade of C, a smaller percentage receive Bs and Ds, and an even smaller percentage receive As and Fs. Such grading is based on the assumption (which may or may not be true in a given situation) that the students' scores do indeed form a normal curve. Many, many variables, such as height, weight, IQ scores, production and sales figures, manufacturing defects, and delivery times, do yield a normal curve if a sufficient number of subjects are measured.

Normal Distributions

If a variable is normally distributed, that is, forms a normal curve, then several things are true:

1. 50% of the figures in the distribution are above the mean and 50% of the figures are below the mean.
2. The mean, median, and mode are the same.
3. Most of the figures in the distribution are near the mean, and the farther from the mean a figure is, the fewer the number of subjects who attain that figure.
4. The same number, or percentage, of the figures in the distribution is between the mean and plus one standard deviation ($\overline{X} + 1\ SD$) as is between the mean and minus one standard deviation ($\overline{X} - 1\ SD$), and similarly for $\overline{X} \pm 2\ SD$ and $\overline{X} \pm 3$ SD (see Figure 11.9).

In Figure 11.9, the symbol σ (the Greek letter sigma) is used to represent the standard deviation of a population, that is, $1\ \sigma = 1\ SD$, and the mean $(\overline{X})$ is designated as 0. The vertical lines at each of the standard deviation (σ) points delineate a certain percentage of the total area under the curve. As Figure 11.9 indicates, if a set of scores or figures forms a normal distribution, the $\overline{X} + 1\ SD$ includes 34.13% of the figures, and the $\overline{X} - 1\ SD$ includes 34.13% of the figures. Each succeeding standard deviation encompasses a constant percentage of the cases. Since the $\overline{X} \pm 2.58\ SD$ (approximately 2½ SDs) includes 95% of the cases, we see that $\overline{X} \pm 3\ SD$ includes almost all the scores, as pointed out previously.

Below the row of standard deviations in Figure 11.9 is a row of percentages. As you move from left to right, from point to point, the cumulative percentage of figures that fall below each point is indicated. Thus, at the point that corresponds to $-3\ SD$, we see that only 0.1% of the figures fall below this point. The numerical value corresponding to $+1\ SD$, by contrast, is 84.1% (rounded to 84%) on the next row of figures). Relatedly, the next row, percentile equivalents, also involves cumulative percentages. The figure 20 in this row, for example, indicates that 20% of the figures fall below this point. Near the bottom of Figure 11.9, under Wechsler Scales, is a row labeled Deviation IQs. This row indicates that the mean IQ for the Wechsler Scale is 100 and the standard deviation is 15 (115 is in the column corresponding to $+1\ SD$ $(+1\sigma)$ and since the mean is 100, 115 represents $\overline{X} + 1\ SD = 100 + 15 = 115$. An IQ of 145 represents a score 3 SDs above the mean (average) IQ. If your IQ is in this neighborhood you are certainly a candidate for MENSA! An IQ of 145 corresponds to a percentile of 99.9. On the other side of the curve, we see that an IQ of 85 corresponds to a score one standard deviation below the mean ($\overline{X} - 1\ SD = 100 - 15 = 85$) and to the 16th percentile. Note that the mean always corresponds to the 50th percentile. In other words, the average score is always that point above which are 50% of the cases and below which are 50% of the cases.

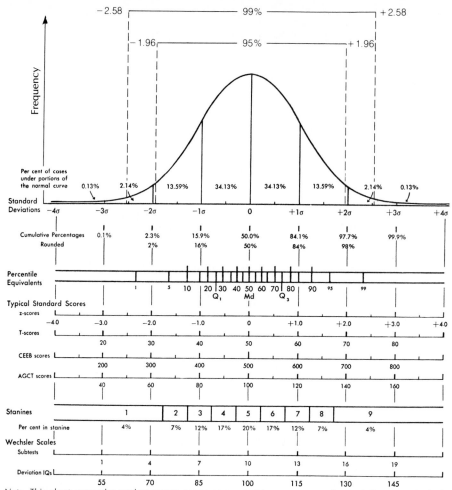

Note. This chart cannot be used to equate scores on one test to scores on another test. For example, both 600 on the CEEB and 120 on the AGCT are one standard deviation above their respective means, but they do not represent "equal" standings because the scores were obtained from different groups.

Figure 11.9. Characteristics of the normal curve. *Source:* Courtesy of the Psychological Corporation.

Thus, if the scores or figures are normally distributed, the following statements are true:

$$\overline{X} \pm 1.0\ SD = \text{approximately 68\% of the figures.}$$
$$\overline{X} \pm 2.0\ SD = \text{approximately 95\% of the figures}$$
$$(1.96\ SD \text{ is exactly 95\%}).$$
$$\overline{X} \pm 2.5\ SD = \text{approximately 99\% of the figures.}$$
$$(2.58\ SD \text{ is exactly 99\%}).$$
$$\overline{X} \pm 3.0\ SD = \text{approximately 99+\% of the figures.}$$

And similarly, the following are always true:

$$\overline{X} - 3.0 \; SD = \text{approximately the 0.1 percentile.}$$
$$\overline{X} - 2.0 \; SD = \text{approximately the 2nd percentile.}$$
$$\overline{X} - 1.0 \; SD = \text{approximately the 16th percentile.}$$
$$\overline{X} \qquad\qquad = \text{the 50th percentile.}$$
$$\overline{X} + 1.0 \; SD = \text{approximately the 84th percentile.}$$
$$\overline{X} + 2.0 \; SD = \text{approximately the 98th percentile.}$$
$$\overline{X} + 3.0 \; SD = \text{approximately the 99th percentile.}$$

You may have noticed that the ends of the curve never touch the baseline and that there is no definite number of standard deviations that corresponds to 100%. This is because the curve allows for the existence of unexpected extremes at either end and because each additional standard deviation includes only a tiny fraction of a percent of the scores or figures. As an example, for the IQ test the mean plus 5 SDs would be $100 + 5(15) = 100 + 75 = 175$. Surely 5 SDs would include everyone. Wrong! There has been a very small number of persons who have scored near 200, which corresponds to +6.67 SDs. Thus, while $\pm$ 3 SDs includes just about everyone, the exact number of standard deviations required to include every figure in a distribution varies from variable to variable.

As mentioned earlier, many variables form a normal distribution, including physical measures, such as height and weight, and psychological measures, such as intelligence and aptitude. Many measures in business such as sales, delivery schedules, and production times form normal distributions if enough cases are measured. In other words, a variable that is normally distributed in a population may not be normally distributed in a small sample. Thus production times for an excellent company (a small sample) will not necessarily represent production times for the industry overall (the population). In Figure 11.9, the standard deviation is symbolized as σ, instead of SD, to indicate that the curve represents the scores of a population, not a sample. Depending upon the size and nature of a particular sample, as mentioned above, the assumption of a normal curve may or may not be a valid one. Since research studies deal with a finite number of subjects, and often a not very large number, research data only more or less approximate a normal curve; correspondingly all of the equivalencies (standard deviation, percentage of cases, and percentiles) are also only approximations. This is an important point, since most of the statistics used in behavioral science research, including business and management, are based on the assumption that the variable is normally distributed. If this assumption is badly violated in a given sample, then certain statistics should not be used. In general, however, the fact that most variables are normally distributed allows us quickly to determine many useful pieces of information concerning a set of data.

Skewed Distributions

When a distribution is not normal, it is said to be skewed. A normal distribution is symmetrical, and the values of the mean, the median, and the mode are the same. A distribution that is skewed is not symmetrical, and the values of the mean, the median, and the mode are different. In a symmetrical distribution, there are approximately the same number of extreme figures (very high and very low) at each end of the distribution. In a skewed distribution there are more extreme figures at one end than the other. If the extreme figures are at the lower end of the distribution, the distribution is said to be negatively skewed; if the extreme figures are at the upper, or higher, end, the distribution is said to be positively skewed (see Figure 11.10).

As we can see by looking at the negatively skewed distribution, most of the subjects or cases performed well, but a few did poorly. Conversely, for the positively skewed distribution, more of the subjects did poorly, but a few did very well. In both cases, the mean is "pulled" in the direction of the extreme figures in the distribution. Since the mean is affected by these extremes and the median is not, the mean is always closer to the extremes than the median. Thus, for a negatively skewed distribution the mean $(\overline{X})$ is always lower, or smaller, than the median (labeled md); for a positively skewed distribution the mean is always higher, or greater, than the median. Since the mode is not affected by extreme scores, no "always" statements can be made concerning its relationship to the mean and the median in a skewed distribution. Usually, however, as Figure 11.10 indicates, in a negatively skewed distribution the mean and the median are lower, or smaller, than the mode, whereas in a positively skewed distribution the mean and the median are higher, or greater, than the mode. To summarize:

negatively skewed: mean < median < mode
positively skewed: mean > median > mode

Since the relationship between the mean and the median is constant, the skewedness of a distribution can be determined without constructing a frequency polygon or line chart. If the mean is less than the median, the distribution is negatively skewed; if the mean and the median are the same, or very close, the distribution is symmetrical; if the mean is greater than the median, the distribution is positively

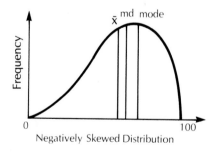

Negatively Skewed Distribution

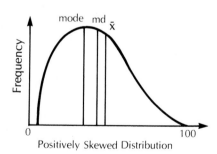

Positively Skewed Distribution

Figure 11.10. A positively skewed distribution and a negatively skewed distribution, each resulting from the administration of a 100-item instrument.

skewed. The farther apart the mean and the median are, the more skewed is the distribution. If the distribution is very skewed, then the assumption of normality required for many statistics is violated.

Measures of Relationship

Correlational research was discussed in detail in Chapter 8. You will recall that correlational research involves collecting data in order to determine whether and to what degree a relationship exists between two or more quantifiable variables—not a causal relationship, just a relationship. Degree of relationship is expressed as a correlation coefficient, which is computed based on the two sets of scores. The correlation coefficient provides an estimate of just how related two variables are. If two variables are highly related, a correlation coefficient near $+1.00$ (or -1.00) will be obtained; if two variables are not related, a coefficient near .00 will be obtained. There are a number of different methods of computing a correlation coefficient; which one is appropriate depends upon the scale of measurement represented by the data. The two most frequently used correlational analyses are the rank-difference correlation coefficient, usually referred to as the Spearman rho (a Greek letter pronounced like "row, row, row your boat"), and the product-moment correlation coefficient, usually referred to as the Pearson r (an English letter pronounced—well, as "r"). Let's discuss these two measures in greater detail:

1. The *Spearman rho* is the appropriate measure of correlation when the data for one of the variables are expressed as ranks instead of scores or intervals. It is thus appropriate when the data represent an ordinal scale (although it may be used with interval data) and is used when the median and quartile deviation are used. The statistics appropriate for ordinal data are referred to as nonparametric statistics, which will be further discussed in the next chapter. Notice that we said if *one* of the variables to be correlated is in rank order, for example, the *Fortune* 500, then the other variable to be correlated with it must also be expressed in terms of ranks in order to use the Spearman rho technique. Thus, if number of employees were to be correlated with *Fortune* 500 standing, a rank order of companies by number of employees would have to be developed, and the actual numbers would not be involved in the computation of the correlation coefficient.

To compute a Spearman rho, the following formula is used:

$$r_s = 1 - \frac{6\Sigma d^2}{N(N^2 - 1)}.$$

In this statistic, r_s simply refers to the Spearman rho, d is the difference in the ranks of the two sets of rankings, and N is the number of pairs of ranks. Now, suppose we have six candidates for a data-entry clerk position with a particular company. The manager who interviewed the candidates gives you a ranking indicating her first, second, third, fourth, fifth, and sixth choices. If, in addition, you have the results of an aptitude test taken by each candidate, you could correlate the two sets of information about the candidates to determine if there is a correlation between the manager's ranking and the aptitude test. Suppose the scores on the aptitude test are as follows:

	X (Aptitude)
George	51
Maria	49
Casey	68
Beatrice	55
Francisco	55
Daniel	48

To use these scores, we must first do what? Right, rank them so we can correlate them with the manager's rankings (if one variable is in rank order, the other must be also, remember?). The highest score is Casey at 68, so he or she ranks #1. Beatrice and Francisco are next best at 55, so which is ranked next? Both have to be #2 in order to be fair, but that would make the next candidate #3, when actually she or he is the 4th best-qualified candidate based on aptitude. To resolve this difference, we split the difference and rank Beatrice and Francisco both at #2.5 and George at #4. Maria and Daniel rank #5 and #6. Now our ranking looks like this:

	X (Aptitude)
Casey	1
Beatrice	2.5
Francisco	2.5
George	4
Maria	5
Daniel	6

Now let's construct a table to show us the two rankings, our calculations of the differences (d), and the differences squared (d^2):

Aptitude (X)	Manager's rank (Y)	$d = x - y$	d^2
1	2	−1	1
2.5	1	+1.5	2.25
2.5	3	−0.5	0.25
4	5	−1	1
5	4	+1	1
6	6	0	0
			$\Sigma d^2 = 5.50$

Now let's plug that into our statistic:

$$r_s = 1 - \frac{6\Sigma d^2}{N(N^2 - 1)}$$

$$= 1 - \frac{6(5.5)}{6(36 - 1)} = 1 - \frac{33}{210} = 1 - .157 = .843 = .84$$

So? If you recall the discussion in Chapter 8, you will remember that we need a table to determine whether .84 is good or not. Table A.3 in the Appendix is used in the following way: First find N in the left-hand column, in our case $N = 6$; then locate the designated level of α (α is the Greek letter alpha and indicates the level of significance; more about it later), in the row across the top, in our case $\alpha = .05$. Now find the intersection between N and the level of α on the table. With an $N = 6$, at $\alpha = .05$, a significant correlation, according to the table in Appendix A, would be .886; therefore, our .84, which is smaller than the required .886, does not indicate a significant correlation between the aptitude test ranks and the manager's rankings. You might have noticed when you were looking up the level of significance, if we had selected $\alpha = .10$, the required number for a significant relationship with $N = 6$ is .829; therefore, our correlation would be significant at $\alpha = .10$ (.84 > .829). It is not acceptable, however, to shift α levels "after the fact."

Although the Spearman rho is interpreted in the same way as the Pearson r and produces a coefficient somewhere between -1.00 and $+1.00$ (if a group of subjects achieve identical ranks on two variables the coefficient will be $+1.00$), there is one difference between the techniques that should be mentioned. The Pearson r permits several subjects to have the same score on a given variable, but as you saw with our example, the Spearman rho does not permit several subjects to have the same rank. If more than one subject receives the same score, then their ranks are averaged as was done in the example.

2. The *Pearson r* is the most appropriate measure of correlation when the sets of data to be correlated represent either interval or ratio scales. Like the mean and the standard deviation, the Pearson r takes into account each and every score or figure in both distributions; it is also the most stable measure of correlation. Since most of the measures used in business and management represent interval scales, the Pearson r is usually the appropriate coefficient for determining relationship. An assumption associated with the application of the Pearson r is that the relationship between the variables being correlated is a linear one. If this is not so, the Pearson r will not yield a valid indication of relationship. If there is any question concerning the linearity of the relationship, the two sets of data should be plotted as previously shown in Figure 8.1 and Figure 8.2.

The formula for the Pearson r looks very complicated, but it is not (have we lied to you so far?). It looks bad because it has a lot of pieces, but each piece is quite simple to calculate. Now, to calculate a Pearson r we need two sets of scores or figures. Using our job candidates from the previous illustration, let's assume that instead of ranking the candidates, the manager who interviewed them assigned points for each quality she was interested in. Her final "scores" for each candidate are listed below in column "Y":

	X (Aptitude)	Y (Interview)
Casey	68	8
Beatrice	55	9
Francisco	55	7
George	51	3
Maria	49	5
Daniel	48	2

The question is, Are these two variables related? Positively? Negatively? Not at all?

In order to answer those questions we apply the formula for the Pearson r to the data. Looks bad, right?

$$r = \frac{\Sigma XY - \frac{(\Sigma X)(\Sigma Y)}{N}}{\sqrt{\left[\Sigma X^2 - \frac{(\Sigma X)^2}{N}\right]\left[\Sigma Y^2 - \frac{(\Sigma Y)^2}{N}\right]}}.$$

Now, if you look at each piece you will see that you already know how to calculate all of them except one. You should have no problem with ΣX, ΣY, ΣX^2, ΣY^2. And even though there are 10 scores in our example, there are only 5 subjects, so $N = 5$. What is left? The only new symbol in the formula is ΣXY. To get that we'll simply multiply each X score by the subject's Y score and add up the results. Now let's determine each value we need to complete the formula:

	X	Y	X²	Y²	XY
Casey	68	8	4624	64	544
Beatrice	55	9	3025	81	495
Francisco	55	7	3025	49	385
George	51	3	2601	9	153
Maria	49	5	2401	25	245
Daniel	48	2	2304	4	96
	326	34	17,980	232	1,918
	ΣX	ΣY	ΣX^2	ΣY^2	ΣXY

Now guess what we're going to do. We're going to turn that horrible-looking statistic into a horrible-looking arithmetic problem. Of course it will really be an easy arithmetic problem if we do it one step at a time.

$$r = \frac{\Sigma XY - \frac{(\Sigma X)(\Sigma Y)}{N}}{\sqrt{\left[\Sigma X^2 - \frac{(\Sigma X)^2}{N}\right]\left[\Sigma Y^2 - \frac{(\Sigma Y)^2}{N}\right]}}.$$

$$= \frac{1{,}918 - \frac{(326)(34)}{6}}{\sqrt{\left[17{,}980 - \frac{(326)^2}{6}\right]\left[232 - \frac{(34)^2}{6}\right]}}.$$

It still doesn't look good, but you have to admit it looks better. Let's start with the numerator (the top part). The first thing the formula tells you to do is to multiply 326 by 34:

$$= \frac{1{,}918 - \frac{11{,}084}{6}}{\sqrt{\left[17{,}980 - \frac{(326)^2}{6}\right]\left[232 - \frac{(34)^2}{6}\right]}}.$$

The next step is to divide 11,084 by 6:

$$= \frac{1{,}918 - 1{,}847.33}{\sqrt{\left[17{,}980 - \frac{(326)^2}{6}\right]\left[232 - \frac{(34)^2}{6}\right]}}.$$

The next step is a real snap. Don't let the decimals scare you; using your calculator, all you have to do is subtract 1,847.33 from 1,918:

$$= \frac{70.67}{\sqrt{\left[17{,}980 - \frac{(326)^2}{6}\right]\left[232 - \frac{(34)^2}{6}\right]}}.$$

So much for the numerator. Was that hard? No! It was very easy. Right? Right. Now for the denominator (the bottom part). If you think hard you will realize that you have seen the formula for the denominator before. Hint: It was not in connection with the mean! Since you've seen it before, let's do two steps at once. We'll square both 326 and 34:

$$= \frac{70.67}{\sqrt{\left[17{,}980 - \frac{106{,}276}{6}\right]\left[232 - \frac{1{,}156}{6}\right]}}.$$

And next? Divide 106,276 by 6 and divide 1,156 by 6:

$$= \frac{70.67}{\sqrt{[17,980 - 17,712.67]\,[232 - 192.67]}}.$$

Now subtract:

$$= \frac{70.67}{\sqrt{[267.33]\,[39.33]}}.$$

And multiply:

$$= \frac{70.67}{\sqrt{10514.09}}.$$

Find the square root using your calculator:

$$= \frac{70.67}{\sqrt{10514.09}} = \frac{70.67}{102.54} = .69$$

Fanfare! Ta-ta-ta-ta! We're through! In case you got lost in the action, .69 is the correlation coefficient, the Pearson r. In other words, $r = +.69$.

Is .69 good? Does it represent a true relationship? Is .69 significantly different from .00? If you recall the discussion in Chapter 8 and with regard to the Spearman rho, you know that to determine whether .69 represents a true relationship we need a table. Specifically, we need a table that indicates how large our r needs to be in order to be significant, given the number of subjects we have and the level of significance at which we are working (see Table A.2 in the Appendix). The number of subjects affects the degrees of freedom, which for the Pearson r are always computed by the formula $N - 2$. Thus, for our example, degrees of freedom $(df) = N - 2 = 6 - 2 = 4$. If we select $\alpha = .05$ as our level of significance, we are now ready to use Table A.2. (If the degrees of freedom and level of significance (α) discussion lost you, we'll discuss them at length in the next chapter.) Look at Table A.2 and find the column labeled df and run your left index finger down the column until you hit 4, the df associated with our r; keep your left finger right there for the time being. Locate .05 ($\alpha = .05$) in the row across the top with your right index finger. Now run your right index finger straight down the table until they meet. If you follow directions well, you should have ended up at .8114, which rounds off to .81. Now we compare our coefficient to the table value. Is $.69 \geq .81$? No, .69 is not greater than or equal to .81. Therefore, our coefficient does not indicate a true relationship between X and Y. Even though it *looks* big, it is not big enough given that we only have six subjects. We are not positive that there is no relationship, but the odds are against it. The same table could have been used if the r had been a negative number, $-.69$. The table does not know or care whether the r is positive or negative. It only tells you how large r must be in order to indicate a relationship significantly different from .00, a true relationship.

Table 11.4
Data for Aptitude and Interview Correlation using Statview™512+

	Aptitude X_1	Interview Y_1
1	68	8
2	55	9
3	55	7
4	51	3
5	49	5
6	48	2

Although we firmly believe that you should calculate at least one example of each statistic that it is feasible to do by hand before using computer software to do your calculations, you might be interested in seeing how this same process would be simplified by using a statistical program on a personal computer. Using Statview™512+ (BrainPower, 1986) on a MacIntosh computer, we first identify our columns "Aptitude" and "Interview" and enter the data (see Table 11.4), select our variables and the statistical procedure, note correlation, and then view the results (see Figure 11.11).

As you have seen, the arithmetic involved in calculating a correlation coefficient for a few numbers is not all that complicated. For larger numbers and many more cases, you will, of course, want to use the computer. Suppose, for example, that you wanted to know if the pretraining ratings of the trainees whose data are presented in Table 11.1 would be a good predictor of the their follow-up ratings. In other words, you would want to calculate the correlation between column X, pretraining ratings, and column Z, follow-up ratings. Since you already have the data recorded in your computer program, you could determine this correlation coefficient with ease. Figure 11.12 shows us that the coefficient is .471. Using Appendix A.2, we can determine that .471, with 18 *df* ($N - 2$ or $20-2=18$), is significant at $\alpha = .05$.

Corr. Coeff. X_1 : Aptitude Y_1 : Interview			
Count:	Covariance:	Correlation:	R-squared:
6	14.133	.689	.475

Figure 11.11. Example of printout showing correlation coefficient for aptitude and interview data using Statview™512+.

Corr. Coeff. X₁ : X Y₁ : Z			
Count:	Covariance:	Correlation:	R-squared:
20	6.763	.471	.222

Figure 11.12. Example of printout showing the correlation coefficient for pretraining ratings (X) and follow-up ratings (Z) using data from Table 11.1.

It might be interesting to look back at the Spearman rho correlation that we calculated using the data in Table 11.4 so you can see the difference between the Spearman rho correlation and the Pearson *r* for the same data. In that calculation, we used the same aptitude tests, but rather than numerical ratings from the manager, we used rank order ratings and had to convert our aptitude test results to rank order also. The resulting correlation coefficient was .84. Although .84 *looks* a lot better than .69, which of the two would you have more confidence in? Remember that the Pearson *r* is the more stable of the indices than the Spearman rho. Anytime you have to convert data to a lower-level scale, you lose important information.

Do not forget, however, that even if a correlation coefficient is statistically significant, it does not necessarily mean that the coefficient has any practical significance. Whether the coefficient is useful depends upon the use to which it will be put; a coefficient to be used in a prediction study needs to be much higher than a coefficient to be used in a relationship study. Suppose, for example, that we wanted to use our aptitude scores to predict whether the manager would prefer specific candidates, or, conversely, wanted to use the manager's ratings to predict aptitude scores. If we had obtained a statistically significant .89 correlation coefficient, it would most likely be sufficient to indicate a practically useful relationship; in some situations, however, it might not be. With the .69 coefficient between aptitude and interview rating, which indicates no significant relationship, however, we'll want to keep using both the aptitude test and the manager's ratings in our hiring. In the second example, with the correlation coefficient of .471 presented in Figure 11.12, we did find a significant relationship between pretraining ratings and follow-up ratings of our trainees from Table 11.1. We might not feel very comfortable with that low a relationship even though it was statistically significant. In the next chapter we'll look at some ways you might find a better way to predict success for the trainees. However, now that you know how to compute the mean, standard deviation, Spearman rho, and Pearson *r*, you have the necessary tools to compute some other formulas referred to in Chapter 5.

Spearman-Brown Correction Formula

In Chapter 5, you will remember that we talked about reliability. Briefly, there were several ways to determine reliability using correlations, which included test-retest, equivalent forms, and split-half reliabilities. Each of these is usually determined through application of the Pearson *r* formula. In our discussion of split-half reliability, however, we mentioned that because the test in question is shorter than the actual test, since we are correlating odds and evens, the Pearson r will tend to underestimate the actual reliability of a test. To counteract this phenomenon, the Spearman-Brown Correction formula is applied to Pearson r statistics in split-half computations. Using the Pearson r, the Spearman-Brown Correction formula is simply this:

$$r_{\text{total test}} = \frac{2r_{\text{split-half}}}{1 + r_{\text{split-half}}}.$$

In other words, to determine the reliability, multiply the split-half r by 2, and divide that figure by 1 + the split-half r. If we determine that the split-half reliability of an instrument is .88, using the formula, we multiply 2 by .88 to get 1.76 (the numerator); add 1 to .88 = 1.88 (the denominator), and then divide 1.76 by 1.88 to get .94; therefore, a more accurate reliability estimate for our instrument would be .94.

Rationale Equivalence Reliability

Another method of determining reliability discussed in Chapter 5 is rationale equivalence reliability, which is determined through application of one of the Kuder-Richardson formulas, usually formula 20 or 21 (KR-20 or KR-21). Now that you can calculate means and standard deviations, you can use the following formula for KR-21:

$$r_{\text{total test}} = \frac{(K)(SD^2) - \overline{X}(K - \overline{X})}{(SD^2)(K - 1)}.$$

In this formula, the only thing you haven't used so far is K, which simply stands for the number of items in the instrument. Therefore, to read the formula, you would say: "The reliability of the total test is equal to the number of items on the test (K) times the standard deviation squared (SD^2), minus the mean $(\overline{X})$ times the number of items on the test minus the mean $(K - \overline{X})$, divided by the standard deviation squared (SD^2) times the number of items on the test minus 1 $(K - 1)$. Well, it's not cocktail party talk, but . . . . So, to use this formula for a 25-item test with a mean of 15 $(\overline{X} = 15)$, and a standard deviation of 5 $(SD = 5)$, we would set it up as follows:

$$
\begin{aligned}
r_{\text{total test}} &= \frac{(K)(SD^2) - \overline{X}(K - \overline{X})}{(SD^2)(K - 1)} \\
&= \frac{(25)(5^2) - 15(25 - 15)}{(5^2)(25 - 1)} \\
&= \frac{(25)(25) - 15(10)}{(25)(24)} \\
&= \frac{625 - 150}{600} \\
&= \frac{475}{600} = .79
\end{aligned}
$$

Standard Error of Measurement

Before we end all this fun, there is one more calculation that we promised you we'd work with. If you recall in Chapter 5, when we discussed reliability, we indicated that the standard error of measurement (SE_m) was a measure of the variability of test scores based on the reliability coefficient of the test and the standard deviation of the test scores. This measure is used to estimate the difference between an individual's obtained score on a test and his or her true score. The formula for determining the SE_m is going to look pretty simple to you now:

$$SE_m = SD\sqrt{1 - r}.$$

Piece of cake, right? To use this formula for a 25-item test, suppose we calculated the standard deviation of a set of scores to be 5 ($SD = 5$) and the split-half reliability (using the Pearson r) to be .84 ($r = .84$). In this case the standard error of measurement would be calculated as follows:

$$SE_m = SD\sqrt{1 - r} = 5\sqrt{1 - .84}$$
$$= 5\sqrt{.16}$$
$$= 5(.4)$$
$$= 2.0$$

Thus an individual who scored 23 on the test might have a true score of 23 ± 2, or somewhere between 21 and 25.

Application of Descriptive Statistics

Almost always in a research study, descriptive statistics such as the mean and standard deviation are computed and reported separately for each group in the study. If ordinal data are used, of course, the median and quartile deviation would be reported. A correlation coefficient is usually computed only in a correlational study; if the reliability of an instrument used in a causal-comparative or experimental study is computed, however, it should be reported. In order to test our hypothesis, we almost always need more than descriptive statistics; application of one or more inferential statistics is usually required.

Summary/Chapter 11

TABULATION AND CODING PROCEDURES

1. After instruments have been scored, the results are transferred to summary data sheets and/or data cards.

2. If planned analyses involve subgroup comparisons, data will be tabulated separately for each subgroup.

3. When a number of different kinds of data are collected for each subject, such as several test scores and biographical information, data are frequently recorded on data cards, one card for each subject.

4. The card for each subject follows the same format, and both the variable names and the actual data are frequently coded.

5. An alternative and more attractive strategy is to use a computerized data-base management program; data for all variables and subjects are usually converted to numerical values as the data are entered into the data-base-management program, since long entries take up considerable space and contribute to typographical and spelling errors that mess up subsequent manipulations.

TYPES OF DESCRIPTIVE STATISTICS

6. The first step in data analysis is to describe, or summarize, the data using descriptive statistics.

7. Descriptive statistics permit the researcher to describe meaningfully many, many scores with a small number of indices.

8. If such indices are calculated for a sample drawn from a population, the resulting values are referred to as *statistics;* if they are calculated for an entire population, they are referred to as *parameters.*

Graphing Data

9. Graphing data permits the researcher to see what the distribution of "scores" looks like.

10. The shape of the distribution may not be self-evident, especially if a large number of scores are involved.

11. The shape of the distribution may influence our choice of certain descriptive statistics.

12. The most commonly used methods of graphing data in business research are the following:

   a. Line charts, in which dotted or solid lines are used to graph data, are frequently used to display business data. The most common example of a line chart is the *time-series line chart.* Other examples include *component-line charts* and *frequency polygons.*

   b. Bar graphs, a second way of graphing data, may be used in most instances in which a line chart is used. Bar graphs may be vertical or they may be horizontal. *Duo-directional bar graphs, component bar graphs,* and *grouped bar graphs* are useful variations of the bar graph.

   c. Pie charts are also used to display business data graphically. Pie charts may be placed side by side so that comparisons can easily be made.

13. In presenting graphed data, it is wise to remember that the purpose of this method of presentation is to clarify and present information in an attractive, easy-to-grasp way. It is very easy, however, to mislead the consumer by graphed data.

Measures of Central Tendency

14. Measures of central tendency give the researcher a convenient way of describing a set of data with a single number.

15. The number resulting from computation of a measure of central tendency represents the average or typical "score" or figure attained by a group of subjects. The three most frequently encountered indices of central tendency are the *mode,* the *median,* and the *mean.* Each of these indices is appropriate for a different scale of measurement:

   a. The *mode,* which is appropriate for nominal data, is the score that is attained by more subjects than any other score. The mode is not established through calculation; it is determined by looking at a set of figures or at a graph of figures and seeing which figure occurs most frequently. There are several problems associated with the mode, and it is therefore of limited value and seldom used.

   b. The *median,* which is appropriate with ordinal data, is that point in a distribution above and below which are 50% of the scores or figures; in other words, the median is the midpoint. It does not take into account each and every figure in the set and ignores extremely high figures and extremely low figures.

   c. The *mean,* which is appropriate with interval or ratio data, is the arithmetic average of the scores or figures; it is the most frequently used measure of central tendency. By the very nature of the way in which the mean is computed, it takes into account, or is based on, each and every one of the scores or figures in the set. The formula for the mean is:

$$\overline{X} = \frac{\Sigma X}{N}$$

16. In situations in which there are one or more extreme scores or figures, the median will be the best index of "typical" performance.

Measures of Variability

17. Two sets of data that are very different can have identical means or medians. Thus, there is a need for a measure that indicates how spread out the figures are or, in other words, how much variability there is.

18. There are a number of descriptive statistics that serve this purpose, and they are referred to as measures of variability:

   a. The *range,* which is the only appropriate measure of variability for nominal data, is simply the difference between the highest score or figure in a set and the lowest figure. The range is determined by subtraction. Like the mode, the range is not a very stable measure of variability, and its chief advantage is that it gives a quick, rough estimate of variability.

   b. The *quartile deviation,* which is the appropriate measure of variability for ordinal data, is one half of the difference between the upper quartile and the lower quartile in a distribution. The quartile deviation is a more stable measure of variability than the range and is appropriate whenever the median is appropriate.

   c. The *standard deviation,* which is appropriate when the data represent an interval scale or ratio scale, is by far the most frequently used index of variability; it is represented in statistical notation as *SD.* Like the mean, its counterpart measure of central tendency, the standard deviation is the most stable measure of variability and takes into account each and every score. The formula for the standard deviation is:

$$SD = \sqrt{\frac{SS}{N-1}}.$$

where

$$SS = \Sigma X^2 - \frac{(\Sigma X)^2}{N}.$$

OR

$$SD = \sqrt{\frac{\Sigma X^2 - \frac{(\Sigma X)^2}{N}}{N-1}}.$$

19. The importance of knowing the mean and standard deviation of a set of figures is that the two statistics will give you a pretty good picture of what the distribution looks like.

20. If the distribution is relatively normal, then the mean plus 3 SD and the mean minus 3 SD encompasses over 99%, or just about all, the scores or figures in the distribution.

The Normal Curve

21. Many variables yield a normal curve if a sufficient number of subjects are measured.

Normal Distributions

22. If a variable is normally distributed, that is, forms a normal curve, then several things are true:

   a. 50% of the figures in the distribution are above the mean and 50% of the figures are below the mean.

   b. The mean, median, and mode are the same.

   c. Most of the figures in the distribution are near the mean, and the farther from the mean a figure is, the fewer the number of subjects who attain that figure.

   d. The same number, or percentage, of the figures in the distribution is between the mean and plus one standard deviation $(\overline{X} + 1\ SD)$ as is between the mean and minus one standard deviation $(\overline{X} - 1\ SD)$, and similarly for $\overline{X} \pm 2\ SD$ and $\overline{X} \pm 3\ SD$.

23. If the scores or figures are normally distributed, the following statements are true:
   $\overline{X} \pm 1.0\ SD$ = approximately 68% of the figures
   $\overline{X} \pm 2.0\ SD$ = approximately 95% of the figures (1.96 SD is exactly 95%)
   $\overline{X} \pm 2.5\ SD$ = approximately 99% of the figures (2.58 SD is exactly 99%)
   $\overline{X} \pm 3.0\ SD$ = approximately 99$^+$% of the figures
   And similarly, the following are always true:
   $\overline{X} - 3.0\ SD$ = approximately the 0.1 percentile
   $\overline{X} - 2.0\ SD$ = approximately the 2nd percentile
   $\overline{X} - 1.0\ SD$ = approximately the 16th percentile
   $\overline{X}$ $\qquad$ = the 50th percentile
   $\overline{X} + 1.0\ SD$ = approximately the 84th percentile
   $\overline{X} + 2.0\ SD$ = approximately the 98th percentile
   $\overline{X} + 3.0\ SD$ = approximately the 99th percentile

24. Many variables form a normal distribution, including physical measures, such as height and

weight, and psychological measures, such as intelligence and aptitude; many measures in business such as sales, delivery schedules, and production times form normal distributions if enough cases are measured.

25. Since research studies deal with a finite number of subjects, and often a not very large number, research data only more or less approximate a normal curve.

Skewed Distributions

26. When a distribution is not normal, it is said to be skewed.

27. A distribution that is skewed is not symmetrical, and the values of the mean, the median, and the mode are different.

28. In a skewed distribution there are more extreme figures at one end than the other. If the extreme figures are at the lower end of the distribution, the distribution is said to be negatively skewed; if the extreme figures are at the upper, or higher, end of the distribution, the distribution is said to be positively skewed.

29. In both cases, the mean is "pulled" in the direction of the extreme scores or figures in the distribution.

30. For a negatively skewed distribution the mean $(\overline{X})$ is always lower, or smaller, than the median (labeled md); for a positively skewed distribution the mean is always higher, or greater, than the median. Usually in a negatively skewed distribution the mean and the median are lower, or smaller, than the mode, whereas in a positively skewed distribution the mean and the median are higher, or greater, than the mode.

Measures of Relationship

31. Degree of relationship is expressed as a correlation coefficient, which is computed based on the two sets of scores.

32. If two variables are highly related, a correlation coefficient near $+1.00$ (or -1.00) will be obtained; if two variables are not related, a coefficient near .00 will be obtained.

33. There are a number of different methods of computing a correlation coefficient; which one is appropriate depends upon the scale of measurement represented by the data:

   a. The *Spearman rho* is the appropriate measure of correlation when the data for one of the variables are expressed as ranks instead of scores or intervals. It is thus appropriate when the data represent an ordinal scale (although it may be used with interval data) and is used when the median and quartile deviation are used. If *one* of the variables to be correlated is in rank order, for example, the *Fortune* 500, then the other variable to be correlated with it must also be expressed in terms of ranks in order to use the Spearman rho technique. The formula to compute the Spearman rho is:

$$r_s = 1 - \frac{6\Sigma d^2}{N(N^2 - 1)}.$$

   b. The Pearson *r* is the most appropriate measure of correlation when the sets of data to be correlated represent either interval scales or ratio scales. Like the mean and the standard deviation, the Pearson *r* takes into account each and every score or figure in both distributions; it is also the most stable measure of correlation. Since most of the measures used in business and management represent interval scales, the Pearson *r* is usually the appropriate coefficient for determining relationship. An assumption associated with the application of the Pearson r is that the relationship between the variables being correlated is a linear one. The formula for the Pearson r is:

$$r = \frac{\Sigma XY - \frac{(\Sigma X)(\Sigma Y)}{N}}{\sqrt{\left[\Sigma X^2 - \frac{(\Sigma X)^2}{N}\right]\left[\Sigma Y^2 - \frac{(\Sigma Y)^2}{N}\right]}}.$$

Spearman-Brown Correction Formula

34. To counteract the tendency to underestimate reliability, the Spearman-Brown Correction formula is applied to Pearson r statistics in split-half reliability computations. Using the Pearson r, the Spearman-Brown Correction formula is:

$$r_{\text{total test}} = \frac{2r_{\text{split-half}}}{1 + r_{\text{split-half}}}.$$

Rationale Equivalence Reliability

35. Another method of determining reliability is rationale equivalence reliability, which is determined through application of one of the Kuder-Richardson formulas, usually formula 20 or 21 (KR-20 or KR-21). The formula for KR-21 is:

$$r_{\text{total test}} = \frac{(K)(SD^2) - \overline{X}\,(K - \overline{X})}{(SD^2)(K - 1)}.$$

Standard Error of Measurement

36. The standard error of measurement (SE_m) is a measure of the variability of test scores based on the reliability coefficient of the test and the standard deviation of the test scores. The formula for determining the SE_m is:

$$SE_m = SD\sqrt{1 - r}.$$

REFERENCES

ASHTON-TATE. (1989). *dBase* [computer program]. Torrance, CA: Ashton-Tate.

BRAINPOWER. (1986). *Statview*™512+ [computer program]. Calabasas, CA: Abacus Concepts.

FORTUNE. (1990, April). The *Fortune* 500 largest U.S. industrial corporations. *Fortune*, pp. 354–356.

LOTUS. (1989). *Lotus 1-2-3* [computer program]. Cambridge, MA: Lotus Development.

MICRORIM. (1989). *R:Base for DOS* [computer program]. Redmond, WA: Microrim.

ODESTA. (1989). *Double Helix* [computer program]. Northbrook, IL: Odesta Corporation.

SPSS INC. (1985). *SPSS*ˣ [computer program]. Chicago: SPSS Inc.

Are we having fun yet? (page 512)

12

Inferential Statistics

Objectives:

After reading Chapter 12, you should be able to do the following:

1. Explain the concept of standard error.
2. Describe how sample size affects standard error.
3. Define or describe the null hypothesis.
4. State the purpose of a test of significance.
5. Define or describe Type I and Type II errors.
6. Define or describe the concept of significance level (probability level).
7. Describe one-tailed and two-tailed tests.
8. Explain the difference between parametric tests and nonparametric tests.
9. State the purpose and explain the strategy of the t test.
10. Define or describe independent and nonindependent samples.
11. State the purpose of the t test for independent samples (when it is used).
12. State the purpose of the t test for nonindependent samples.
13. Describe one major problem associated with analyzing gain scores (difference scores).
14. State the purpose of the simple analysis of variance.
15. State the purpose of multiple-comparison procedures.
16. State the purpose of a factorial analysis of variance.
17. State the major purpose of analysis of covariance.
18. State two uses of multiple regression.
19. State the purpose of chi square.
20. Generate three columns of five one-digit numbers, compute each of the following statistics, giving the formula and showing your work, state whether each result is statistically significant at $\alpha = .05$, and interpret each result:
    a. t test for independent samples using columns 1 and 2.
    b. t test for nonindependent samples using columns 2 and 3.
    c. Simple analysis of variance using all three columns.
    d. Scheffé test based on "c" above.

    e. chi square in which you sum the numbers in each column and treat them as if they were the total number of people responding yes, no, and undecided, in a survey.

If Statpak, the microcomputer program that accompanies this text, is available to you, use it to check your work.

CONCEPTS UNDERLYING APPLICATION

Inferential statistics deal with, of all things, inferences. Inferences about what? Inferences about populations based on the behavior of samples. Most business-and-management research studies deal with samples. You will recall that the "goodness" of the various sampling techniques is a function of their effectiveness in producing representative samples; the more representative a sample is, the more generalizable the results will be to the population from which the sample was selected. Results that hold only for the sample upon which they are based are of very limited value. Consequently, random samples are required since they seem to produce the most representative samples. Inferential statistics are concerned with determining how likely it is that results based on a sample or samples are the same results that would have been obtained for the entire population.

As you recall from Chapter 11, sample values, such as the mean, are referred to as *statistics;* the corresponding values in the population are referred to as *parameters.* Inferential statistics are used to make inferences concerning parameters, based on sample statistics. Suppose, for example, that you wanted to know whether the widgets provided by vendor A were better than the widgets provided by vendor B. If you examined a sample of vendor A's widgets and a sample of vendor B's widgets and found a difference in the mean number of defective widgets between the two vendors' widgets, the question of real interest is whether a similar difference exists in the population from which the samples were selected. It could be that no real difference exists in the population and that the difference found for the samples was a chance one; if two different samples had been used, it is likely that no difference would have been found. And now we get to the heart of inferential statistics, the concept of "how likely is it"; if you find a difference between two sample means and conclude that the difference is large enough to infer that a true difference exists in the population, how likely is it that you are wrong? In other words, inferences concerning populations are only probability statements; the researcher is only "probably" correct when making an inference and concluding that there is a true difference in the population.

There are a number of concepts underlying the application of inferential statistics with which you should be familiar. Before the various types of inferential statistics are described and the major ones calculated, these concepts will be discussed.

Standard Error

Inferences concerning populations are based on the behavior of samples. The chances of the composition of a sample being identical to that of its parent population, however, are virtually nil. If we randomly select a number of samples from the same population and compute the mean for each, it is very likely that each mean will be somewhat different from *every* other mean and that none of the means will be identical to the population mean. Your first sample of vendor A's widgets might have an average of two defects, and a subsequent sample might have more or less. This expected, chance variation among the means (as well as chance variation in any other statistic) is referred to as *sampling error*. Recall that in Chapter 4 we discussed the fact that unlike sampling bias, sampling error is not the researcher's fault. Sampling error just happens and is as inevitable as death and taxes (at least for us poor folks). Thus, if a difference is found between sample means, the question of interest is whether the difference is a result of sampling error or a reflection of a true difference.

An interesting characteristic of sampling errors is that they are normally distributed. Errors vary in size (from small errors to large errors), and these errors form a normal curve. Although sampling errors are random fluctuations, they actually behave in a very orderly manner. Thus, if a sufficiently large number of equal-size large samples are randomly selected from a population, all samples will not have the same mean on the variable measured, *but* the means of those samples will be approximately normally distributed around the population mean. The mean of all the sample means (simply add up the means of each sample and divide by the number of samples) will yield a good estimate of the population mean. Because the sample means will approximate a normal distribution, most will be very close to the population mean; the number of means that are considerably different from the population mean (as estimated by the mean of the sample means) will decrease as the size of the difference increases. In other words, very few means will be much higher or much lower than the population mean. An example may help to clarify this concept.

Let us suppose that we know that the average number of jelly beans in a pound is 100. Suppose further that we randomly selected a sample of $N = 100$ bags of jelly beans to check. We might get the following results:

64	82	87	94	98	100	104	108	114	121
67	83	88	95	98	101	104	109	115	122
68	83	88	96	98	101	105	109	116	123
70	84	89	96	98	101	105	110	116	124
71	84	90	96	98	102	105	110	117	125
72	84	90	97	99	102	106	111	117	127
74	84	91	97	99	102	106	111	118	130
75	85	92	97	99	103	107	112	119	131
75	86	93	97	100	103	107	112	119	136
78	86	94	97	100	103	108	113	120	142

If we compute the mean, we get $\frac{10038}{100} = 100.38$, which is a good estimate of the population mean for a pound of jelly beans, which we know is 100. Further, if you check the scores, you will discover that 71% of the packages contain between 84 and

116 jelly beans, and 96% of the packages contain between 68 and 142 jelly beans. If we calculated the standard deviation, we would discover it to be 16, so our distribution approximates a normal curve quite well; the percentage of cases falling within each successive standard deviation is very close to the percentage characteristic of a normal curve (71% as compared to 68%, and 96% as compared to 95%). The concept illustrated by this example is a comforting one. It tells us, in essence, that most of the sample means we obtain will be close to the population mean and only a few will be very far away. In other words, once in a while, just by chance, we will get a sample that is quite different from the population but not very often.

As with any normally distributed set of figures, a distribution of sample means has not only its own mean but also its own standard deviation. The standard deviation of the sample means (the standard deviation of sampling errors, in other words) is usually referred to as the *standard error of the mean*. The standard error of the mean $(SE_{\overline{X}})$ tells us by how much we would expect our sample means to differ if we used other samples from the same population. According to normal curve percentages, we can say that approximately 68% of the sample means will fall between plus and minus one standard error of the mean (remember, the standard error of the mean is a standard deviation), 95% will fall between plus and minus two standard errors, and 99+ % will fall between plus and minus three standard errors. In other words, if the mean is 60, and the standard error of the mean is 10, we can expect 95% of the sample means to fall between 40 and 80 [60 ± 2 (10)]. A sample mean might very well be 65, but a sample mean of 95 is highly unlikely. Thus, given a number of large, randomly selected samples, we can estimate quite well population parameters by computing the mean and standard deviation of the sample means.

It is not necessary, however, to select a large number of samples in order to estimate standard error. If we know the standard deviation of the population, we can estimate the standard error of the mean by dividing the standard deviation by the square root of our sample size ($\sqrt{N}$). In most cases, however, we do not know the mean or standard deviation of the population. In these cases, we estimate the standard error by dividing the standard deviation of the sample by the square root of the sample size minus one:

$$SE_{\overline{X}} = \frac{SD}{\sqrt{N-1}}.$$

Using this estimate of the $SE_{\overline{X}}$, the sample mean, $\overline{X}$, and characteristics of the normal curve, we can estimate probable limits within which the population mean falls. These limits are referred to as confidence limits. Thus, if a sample $\overline{X}$ is 80, and $SE_{\overline{X}}$ is 1.00, if we say that the population mean falls between 79 and 81 $(\overline{X} \pm 1\ SE_{\overline{X}})$, we have approximately a 68% chance of being correct; if we say that the population mean falls between 78 and 82 $(\overline{X} \pm 2\ SE_{\overline{X}})$, we have approximately a 95% chance of being correct; if we say the population mean falls between 77 and 83 $(\overline{X} \pm 3\ SE_{\overline{X}})$, we have approximately a 99+ % chance of being correct. In other words, the probability of the population mean being less than 78 or greater than 82 is only $\frac{5}{100}$, or 5%. Note that as our degree of confidence increases, the limits get farther apart. This makes sense since we are 100% confident that the population mean is somewhere between our sample mean $\pm \infty$ (infinity)!

You have probably come to the realization by now that the smaller the standard error of the mean is, the better; a smaller standard error indicates less sampling error. The major factor affecting the standard error of the mean is sample size. As the size of the sample increases, the standard error of the mean decreases. This makes sense, since if we used the whole population there would be no sampling error at all. A large sample is more likely to represent a population than a small sample. This discussion should help you to understand why samples should be as large as possible; smaller samples entail more error than large samples. Another factor affecting the standard error of the mean is the size of the population standard deviation. If it is large, members of the population are very spread out on the variable of interest, and sample means will also be very spread out. Our jelly beans, for example, must have lacked uniformity if our one-pound sample bags contained anywhere from 64 to 142 jelly beans! "Designer" beans, no doubt. Of course the researcher has no control over the size of the population standard deviation, but he or she can control sample size to some extent. Thus, the researcher should make every effort to acquire as many subjects as possible so that inferences about the population of interest will be as correct as possible.

All of this discussion has been in reference to the standard error of the mean. An estimate of standard error, however, can also be computed for other measures of central tendency as well as measures of variability, relationship, and relative position. Further, an estimate of standard error can also be determined for the difference between means. In other words, at the conclusion of an experimental study we may have two sample means, one mean for the experimental group and one for the control group. In order to determine whether or not the difference between those means probably represents a true population difference, we need an estimate of the standard error of the difference between two means. Differences between two sample means are normally distributed around the mean difference in the population. Most differences will be close to the true difference, and a few will be way off. In order to determine whether a difference found between sample means probably represents a true difference or a chance difference, tests of significance are applied to the data. Tests of significance allow us to determine whether or not there is a significant difference between the means. Many tests of significance are based upon an estimate of standard error; they typically test a null hypothesis.

The Null Hypothesis

When we talk about the difference between two sample means being a true difference we mean that the difference was caused by the treatment (independent variable) and not by chance. In other words, the difference is either caused by the treatment, as stated in the research hypothesis, or is the result of chance, random sampling error. The chance explanation for the difference is called the *null hypothesis*. The null hypothesis says in essence that there is no true difference or relationship between parameters in the populations and that any difference or relationship found for the samples is the result of sampling error. A null hypothesis might state the following:

> There is no significant difference in the mean productivity of data-entry personnel who receive incentive pay and data entry personnel who receive straight salaries.

Similarly, another null hypothesis might state:

> There is no significant difference in mean defects of widgets provided by vendor A and widgets provided by vendor B.

The hypothesis says that there really is not any difference between the two methods or sources, and if you find one in your study, it is not a true difference but a chance difference resulting from sampling error.

The null hypothesis for a study is usually (although not necessarily) different from the research hypothesis. The research hypothesis usually states that one method is expected to be more effective than another. Why have both? It is difficult to explain simply, but essentially the reason is that rejection of a null hypothesis is more conclusive support for a positive research hypothesis. In other words, if the results of your study support your research hypothesis, you only have one piece of evidence based upon one situation. If you reject a null hypothesis, your argument is stronger. As an analogy, suppose you hypothesize that all research textbooks contain a chapter on sampling. If you examine one research textbook, and it does contain such a chapter, you haven't proven your hypothesis; you have just found one little piece of evidence to support your hypothesis. If, on the other hand, the textbook you examine does not contain a chapter on sampling, your hypothesis is disproven. In other words, 1 book is enough to disprove your hypothesis, but 1,000 books are not enough to prove it; there may always be a book somewhere that does not contain a chapter on sampling. In a research study, the test of significance selected to determine whether a difference between means is a true difference provides a test of the null hypothesis. As a result, the null hypothesis is either rejected, as being probably false, or not rejected, being probably true. Notice the word *probably*. We never know for sure whether we are making the correct decision; what we can do is estimate the probability of our being wrong. After we make the decision to reject or not reject the null hypothesis, we make an inference back to our research hypothesis. If, for example, our research hypothesis states that A is better than B, and if we reject the null hypothesis that A = B, and if the mean for A is greater than the mean for B (and not vice versa), then we conclude that our research hypothesis was supported. If we do not reject the null hypothesis A = B, then we conclude that our research hypothesis was not supported. Let's try it in pictures:

We hypothesize:

$$A = B \text{ (null hypothesis: there is NO difference)}$$

We find:

$A > B$

Therefore:

$A \neq B$ (null hypothesis is rejected: there IS a difference)

So, we reject the null hypothesis and support the research hypothesis:

$A > B$

It goes back to the analogy: 1 case is sufficient to reject a statement, but 1,000 may not be enough to prove it because there might always be a case "out there" that disproves it.

At this point you might be saying, "But if it was true 1000 times, that's true enough for me!" That brings us to the next point: In order to test a null hypothesis we need a test of significance, and we need to select a probability level that indicates how much risk we are willing to take that the decision we make is wrong.

Tests of Significance

At the end of an experimental research study the researcher typically has two or more means. These means are very likely to be at least a little different. The researcher must then decide whether the means are significantly different, different enough to conclude that they represent a true difference. In other words, the researcher must make the decision whether or not to reject the null hypothesis. The researcher does not make this decision based on her or his own best guess. Instead, the researcher selects and applies an appropriate test of significance. The test of significance helps us to decide whether we can reject the null hypothesis and infer that the difference is significantly greater than a chance difference. If the difference is too large to attribute to chance, we reject the null hypothesis; if not, we do not reject it.

The test of significance is made at a preselected probability level, indicated by our old friend α (alpha), which allows us to state that we have rejected the null hypothesis because we would expect to find a difference as large as we have found by chance in only 5 out of every 100 studies ($\alpha = .05$), or in only 1 in every 100 studies ($\alpha = .01$), or whatever; therefore, we conclude that the null hypothesis is *probably* false and reject it. Obviously, if we can say we would expect such a difference by chance in only 1 in 100 studies, we are more confident in our decision than if we say we would expect such a chance difference in 5 in 100. How confident we are depends upon the level of significance, or probability level, at which we perform our test of significance.

There are a number of different tests of significance that can be applied in research studies, some of which are more appropriate than the others in a given situation. Factors such as the research question, the scale of measurement represented by the data (nominal, ordinal, interval, or ratio), the method of subject assignment to groups (random or not), the size and number of the groups, and the number of dependent and independent variables determine which test of significance should be selected for a given experiment. Before we get to the specific tests of significance, however, we need to discuss the factors involved in specifying our acceptable level of probability in advance.

Decision Making: Levels of Significance and Type I and Type II Errors

As we have said, based on a test of significance the researcher will either reject or not reject the null hypothesis as a probable explanation for results. In other words, the researcher will make the decision that the difference between the means is, or is not, too large to attribute to chance. The researcher never knows for sure whether he or she is right or wrong, only whether he or she is probably correct. Rather than two possibilities, right or wrong, there are actually four possibilities:

1. Null hypothesis is true (A = B); researcher says it's true = Correct!
2. Null hypothesis is false (A ≠ B); researcher says it's false = Correct!
3. Null hypothesis is true (A = B); researcher says it's false = Oops!
4. Null hypothesis is false (A ≠ B); researcher says it's true = Ooooops!

These wrong decisions that can be made by researchers have names. If the researcher rejects a null hypothesis that is really true (option 3), the researcher makes a Type I error; if the researcher fails to reject a null hypothesis that is really false (option 4), the researcher makes a Type II error.

When the researcher makes a decision to reject or not reject the null hypothesis, she or he does so with a given probability of being correct. This probability of being correct is referred to as the significance level, or probability level, of the test of significance. If the decision is made to reject the null hypothesis, the means are concluded to be significantly different—too different to be the result of chance error. If the null hypothesis is not rejected, the means are determined to be not significantly different. The level of significance, or probability level, selected determines how large the difference between the means must be in order to be declared significantly different. The most commonly used probability level (symbolized as α) is the .05 level. Some studies use $\alpha = .01$ and occasionally an exploratory study will use $\alpha = .10$.

The probability level selected determines the probability of committing a Type I error, that is, of rejecting a null hypothesis that is really true (A = B). Thus, if you select $\alpha = .05$ you have a 5% probability of making a Type I error, whereas if you select $\alpha = .01$ you have only a 1% probability of committing a Type I error. The less chance of being wrong you are willing to take, the greater the difference between the means must be. As an example, examine the six possible outcomes presented here and decide whether you think the means are significantly different. Assume that the means indicate the mean performance in terms of successful resolution of 100 customer problems of two groups of 20 customer-service representatives:

	Group A	Group B			Group A	Group B
1.	70.0	70.4	4.		70.0	75.0
2.	70.0	71.0	5.		70.0	80.0
3.	70.0	72.0	6.		70.0	90.0

How about outcome 1? Is 70.0 significantly different from 70.4? Probably not. How about outcome 2, 70.0 versus 71.0? Probably not significantly different. How about outcome 6, 70.0 versus 90.0? That difference is probably significant. How about outcome 5, 70.0 versus 80.0? Probably significant. But what about outcome 4, 70.0 versus 75.0? H-m-m-m. Is a difference of 5 calls a big enough difference? Up to a certain point the difference is probably too small to represent a true difference. Beyond a certain point the difference becomes large enough that it probably is a true difference. Where is the magic point? At what point does a difference stop being "too small" and become "big enough?" The answer to these questions depends upon the probability level at which we perform our selected test of significance. The smaller our probability level is, the larger the difference must be. In the above example, if we are working at $\alpha = .05$, then a difference of 5 (say 70.0 versus 75.0) might be big enough. If we are working at $\alpha = .01$ (a smaller chance of being wrong), a difference of at least 10 might be required (say 70.0 versus 80.). Got the idea?

Thus, if you are working at $\alpha = .05$, and as a result of your test of significance you reject the null hypothesis, you are saying in essence that you do not believe the null hypothesis is true because the chances are only 5 out of 100 (.05) that a difference as large as (or larger than) the one you found would occur just by chance as a result of sampling error. In other words, there is a 95% chance that the difference resulted from manipulation of the independent variable, not chance. Similarly, if you are working at $\alpha = .01$ and reject the null hypothesis, you are saying that a difference as large as the one you have found would be expected to occur by chance only once for every 100 studies (1 out of 100, or .01). So why not set α at .000000001 and hardly ever be wrong? Good question: we're glad you asked it. If you select α to be very, very small, you definitely decrease your chances of committing a Type I error; you will hardly ever reject a true null hypothesis. *But,* guess what happens to your chances of committing a Type II error? Right. As you decrease the probability of committing a Type I error, you increase the probability of committing a Type II error (not rejecting a null hypothesis when you should). For example, you might conduct a study for which a mean difference of 9.5 represents a true difference in the population. If you set α at .0001, however, you might require a mean difference of 20.0. If the difference actually found was 11.0, you would not reject the null hypothesis (11.0 < 20.0), although there really is a difference (11.0 > 9.5). How do you select an α level, and when do you decide?

The choice of a probability level, α, is made prior to execution of the study. The researcher considers the relative seriousness of committing a Type I versus a Type II error and selects α accordingly. In other words, the researcher compares the consequences of making the two possible wrong decisions. As an example, suppose you work in an insurance company and one day your boss comes up to you and she says,

I understand you have research training, and I want you to do a study for me. I am considering implementing the Whoopee Claims Processing System in the office next year.

This system is very costly, however; if implemented, we will have to spend a great deal of money on machinery and training. I don't want to do that unless it *really* works. I want you to conduct a pilot study this year with several groups in the office and then tell me if the Whoopee System really results in more efficient claims processing. I know you got an A in your research course, so you'll have my complete support in setting up the groups the way you want and in implementing the study.

In this case, which would be more serious, a Type I error or a Type II? On the one hand, suppose you conclude that the groups are significantly different and Whoopee really works. Suppose it really does not (you made a Type I error). Guess who's going to be *really upset* if a large investment was based on your decision, and at year's end there's no difference in efficiency. On the other hand, suppose you conclude that Whoopee doesn't really make a difference. Suppose it really does (you made a Type II error). What will happen? Nothing. You will tell the boss the system doesn't work well enough, you will get a memo for your effort, the system will not be implemented, and life will go on as usual. No one will know you made a wrong decision (until the hotshot who got an A+ comes along). For this situation, however, would you rather commit a Type I or a Type II error? Type II, obviously. In fact, you want to be very sure you do not commit a Type I error. Therefore you would select a very small α, perhaps $\alpha = .01$, or even $\alpha = .001$. You want to be pretty darn sure there is a difference before you say there is.

As another example, suppose you have a hunch about a new way to process insurance claims. Before you make a formal proposal to try out your method, you'd like to conduct a pilot or exploratory study. If you conclude it makes a difference, you'll propose a trial study of the method (and risk being a hero!). If you conclude it doesn't make a difference, you'll scratch that idea and work on something else. Now which would be more serious? A Type I or Type II error? If, on the one hand, you conclude there is a difference, and there really is not (Type I error), no real harm will be done; further research may be done that disconfirms your original findings, but you'll probably be considered innovative. If, on the other hand, you conclude that the technique makes no difference and it really does (Type II error), a technique may be prematurely abandoned; with a little refinement, probably during the proposal stage, this new technique might make a real difference. In this case, you would probably rather commit a Type I error than a Type II error. Therefore, you might select an α level as low as .10.

Other than the situations we've just discussed, $\alpha = .05$ is a reasonable probability level for most studies. The consequences of committing a Type I error are usually not too serious. A big DON'T in selecting a probability level is to compute a test of significance, such as a t test, and then see "how significant it is." If the results just happen to be significant at $\alpha = .01$, you do not say "oh goodie" and report that the t was significant at the .01 level. You "pays your money, and takes your choice!" Similarly, you do not state that "results were pretty significant," or, conversely, "not quite significant."

A common misconception among beginning researchers is the notion that if you reject a null hypothesis you have "proven" your research hypothesis. Rejecting a null hypothesis or not rejecting a null hypothesis only supports or does not support a research hypothesis. If you reject a null hypothesis and conclude that the groups are really different, it does not mean that they are different for the reason you hypothesized. They may be different for some other reason. If you fail to reject the null hypothesis, it does not necessarily mean that your research hypothesis is wrong. The study, for example, may not have represented a fair test of your hypothesis. To use a former example, if you were investigating your new method of processing claims and your experimental group had only one day to use your new method, you probably would not find any differences between the groups (although the experimental group might be even slower!) This would not mean that the new method doesn't work; if your study were conducted over a month-long period it might very well make a difference.

Two-Tailed and One-Tailed Tests

Tests of significance are usually two-tailed. The null hypothesis states that there is no difference between the groups (A = B), and a two-tailed test allows for the possibility that a difference may occur in either direction: Either group mean may be higher than the other (A > B or B > A). Your new method of processing claims might be more OR less efficient than the old method. A one-tailed test assumes that a difference can occur in only one direction ("things CAN'T get any worse!). In this case, the null hypothesis states that one group is not better than another (A $\not>$ B), and the one-tailed test assumes that if a difference occurs it will be in favor of that particular group (A > B). As an example, suppose a null hypothesis states the following:

There is no difference in productivity between pieceworkers who receive daily feedback and those who receive weekly feedback.

For a two-tailed test, the research hypothesis might state this:

There is a difference in productivity between pieceworkers who receive daily feedback and those who receive weekly feedback.

A two-tailed test of significance would allow for the possibility that either the group that received daily feedback or the group that received weekly feedback might be more productive. For a one-tailed test, the research hypothesis might state this:

Pieceworkers who receive daily feedback are more productive than pieceworkers who receive weekly feedback.

In this case, the assumption would be that if a difference were found between the groups, it would be in favor of the group that received daily feedback. In other words, the researcher would consider it highly unlikely that receiving weekly feedback could result in better productivity than receiving daily feedback.

As mentioned before, tests of significance are usually two-tailed. To select a one-tailed test of significance the researcher has to be pretty sure that a difference can occur in only one direction; this is not very often true. When appropriate, however, a one-tailed test has one major advantage: The value resulting from application of the test of significance required for significance is smaller. In other words, it is "easier" to find a significant difference. It is difficult to explain simply why this is so, but it has to do with α. Suppose you are computing a t test of significance at $\alpha = .05$. If your test is two-tailed, you are allowing for the possibility of a positive t or a negative t; in other words, you are allowing that the mean of the first group may be higher than the mean of the second group ($\overline{X}_1 - \overline{X}_2 =$ a positive number), or that the mean of the second group may be higher than the mean of the first group ($\overline{X}_1 - \overline{X}_2 =$ a negative number). Thus, our α value, say, .05, has to be divided in half with half for each possibility (.025 and .025 = .05). For a one-tailed test, the entire α value, again .05, is concentrated on one possible outcome, a positive t. Since .025 is a smaller probability of committing a Type I error than .05, a larger t value is required. This explanation applies to any α value and to other tests of significance besides the t test. While this is definitely not the most scientific explanation of two-tailed and one-tailed tests, it should give you some conceptual understanding.

Degrees of Freedom

After you have determined whether the test will be two-tailed or one-tailed, selected a probability level, and computed a test of significance, you are ready to consult the appropriate table in order to determine the significance of your results. As you may recall from our discussion of the significance of r in Chapters 8 and 11, the appropriate table is usually entered at the intersection of your probability level and your degrees of freedom, df. Degrees of freedom are a function of such factors as the number of subjects and the number of groups. Recall that for the Pearson r correlation coefficient, the appropriate degrees of freedom were determined by the formula $N - 2$, number of subjects minus 2. It's difficult to explain in plain English what the concept of degrees of freedom means but an illustration may help. Suppose we ask you to name any five numbers. You agree and say, "25, 44, 62, 82, and 2." In this case $N = 5$; you had five choices or five degrees of freedom. Now suppose we tell you to name five more and you say, "1, 2, 3, 4, . . . ," and we say, "Wait! The mean of the five numbers must be 4." Now you have no choice—the last number must be 10 ($1 + 2 + 3 + 4 + 10 = 20$; $20 \div 5 = 4$). You lost one degree of freedom because of that one restriction that the mean must be 4. Instead of having $N = 5$ degrees of freedom, you had only $N = 4$ ($5 - 1$) degrees of freedom. Each test of significance has its own formula for determining degrees of freedom. For the Pearson r correlation coefficient, the formula is $N - 2$ with 2 as a constant. Each of the inferential statistics we are about to discuss also has its own formula for degrees of freedom.

TESTS OF SIGNIFICANCE: TYPES

Different tests of significance are appropriate for different sets of data. It is important that the researcher select an appropriate test; an incorrect test can lead to incorrect conclusions. After considering the research question, the first decision in selecting an appropriate test of significance is whether a parametric test may be used or whether a nonparametric test must be selected. Parametric tests are usually more powerful and generally to be preferred. By "more powerful" is meant "more likely to reject a null hypothesis that is false;" in other words, the researcher is less likely to commit a Type II error.

Parametric tests, however, require that certain assumptions be met in order for them to be valid:

1. The variable being measured is normally distributed in the population (or at least that the form of the distribution is known). Since most of the variables studied in business and management are normally distributed, this assumption is usually met.

2. The data represent an interval scale or a ratio scale of measurement. Again, since most measures in business and management represent interval data, this assumption is usually met (with the exception of certain ranked data that we have mentioned previously). One of the major advantages of using an interval scale or a ratio scale is that it permits application of a parametric test of the data.

3. The subjects are selected independently for the study; in other words, the selection of one subject in no way affects the selection of any other subject. Recall that the definition of random sampling is sampling in which *every* member of the population has an equal and *independent* chance of being selected for the sample. Thus, if randomization is involved in subject selection, the assumption of independence is met.

4. The variances of the population comparison groups are equal (or at least that the ratio of the variances is known). Recall that the variance of a group of figures is nothing more than the standard deviation squared.

With the exception of independence, some violation of one or more of these assumptions usually does not make too much difference so that the same decision is made concerning the statistical significance of the results. If one or more assumptions are greatly violated, however, such as if the distribution is extremely skewed, parametric statistics should not be used. In such cases, a nonparametric test should be used. Nonparametric tests make no assumptions about the shape of the distribution. They are usually used when the data represent an ordinal or a nominal scale, when a parametric assumption has been greatly violated, or when the nature of the distribution is not known.

If the data represent an interval scale or a ratio scale, a parametric test should be used unless another of the assumptions is greatly violated. As mentioned before, parametric tests are more powerful. It is more difficult with a nonparametric test to reject a null hypothesis at a given level of significance; it usually takes a large sample size to reach the same level of significance. Another advantage of parametric statistics is that they permit tests of a number of hypotheses that cannot be tested with a nonparametric test; there are a number of parametric statistics that have no counterpart among nonparametric statistics. Since parametric statistics seem to be relatively hearty, that is, do their job even with moderate assumption violations, they will usually be selected for analysis of research data.

With one exception, all the statistics to be discussed are parametric statistics. Of course, we are not going to discuss each and every statistical test available to the researcher; a number of additional courses and graduate programs will help you explore statistics if you want to pursue the subject. Basically some of the useful, commonly used statistics will be described, and a smaller number of frequently used statistics will be calculated. Although the statistics to be calculated are considered to be basic-level statistics, they will be sufficient not only to allow you to feel more comfortable with the subject but also to understand many of the research articles in your field.

The *t* Test

The *t* test is used to determine whether two means are significantly different at a selected probability level. In other words, for a given sample size the *t* indicates how often a difference $(\overline{X}_1 - \overline{X}_2)$ as large or larger would be found when there is no true population difference. The *t* test makes adjustments for the fact that the distribution of scores for small samples becomes increasingly different from a normal distribution as sample sizes become increasingly smaller. Distributions for smaller samples, for example, tend to be higher at both the mean and the ends. For a given α level, the values of *t* required to reject a null hypothesis are progressively higher for progressively smaller samples; as the size of the samples becomes larger (approaches infinity), the score distribution approaches normality.

The strategy of the *t* test is to compare the *actual* mean difference observed with the difference *expected* by chance. The *t* test involves forming the ratio of these two values. In other words, the numerator for a *t* test is the difference between the sample means $(\overline{X}_1 - \overline{X}_2)$, and the denominator is the chance difference that would be expected if the null hypothesis were true, in other words, the standard error of the difference between the means. The denominator, or error term, is a function of both sample size and group variance. Smaller sample sizes and greater variation within groups are associated with an expectation of greater random differences between groups. To explain it one more way, even if the null hypothesis is true, you do not expect two sample means to be identical; there is going to be some chance variation. The *t* ratio determines whether the observed difference is sufficiently larger than a difference that would be expected by chance. After the numerator is divided by the denominator, the resulting *t* value is compared to the appropriate *t* table value, again using the probability level and the degrees of freedom; if the calculated t value is equal to or greater than the table value, then the null hypothesis is rejected. There are two different types of *t* tests, one for independent samples and one for nonindependent samples:

1. *The* t *test for independent samples* is used when samples are randomly formed, that is, formed without any type of matching. The members of or items in one group are not related to members of or items in the other group in any systematic way other than that they are selected from the same population. If two groups are randomly formed, the expectation is that they are essentially the same at the beginning of the study with respect to performance on the dependent variable. Therefore, if they are

essentially the same at the end of the study, the null hypothesis is probably true; if they are different at the end of the study, the null hypothesis is probably false, that is, the treatment or variable does make a difference. The key word here is *essentially*. We do not expect them to be identical at the end since they are bound to be somewhat different; the question is whether they are significantly different. Thus, the *t* test for independent samples is used to determine whether there is a significant difference between the means of two independent samples at a preselected α level.

To calculate the *t* test for independent samples, use the following formula:

$$t = \frac{\overline{X}_1 - \overline{X}_2}{\sqrt{\left(\frac{SS_1 + SS_2}{n_1 + n_2 - 2}\right)\left(\frac{1}{n_1} + \frac{1}{n_2}\right)}}.$$

Quit whimpering! You are already familiar with each of the pieces! The numerator is simply the difference between the two means $(\overline{X}_1 - \overline{X}_2)$. Each of the *n*s refers to the number of subjects in each group. What about the *SS*s? We calculate them the same way as we did for the standard deviation, so to calculate the SS_1:

$$SS_1 = \Sigma X_1^2 - \frac{(\Sigma X_1)^2}{n_1}.$$

Remember the insurance claims processors? Suppose for your pilot test you had five processors use the old method $(n_1 = 5)$ and five your new method $(n_2 = 5)$. The number of errors you found were as follows:

Group 1	Group 2
3	2
4	3
5	3
6	3
7	4

Are these two sets of errors significantly different? Sure they're different, but are they *significantly* different? Let's enter them into our *t* test formula and find out. First we'll calculate the means, sums, and sums of squares *(SS)*, and, while we're at it, we'll label group 1 as X_1 and group 2 as X_2:

X_1	X_1^2	X_2	X_2^2
3	9	2	4
4	16	3	9
5	25	3	9
6	36	3	9
7	49	4	16
$\Sigma X_1 = 25$	$\Sigma X_1^2 = 135$	$\Sigma X_2 = 15$	$\Sigma X_2^2 = 47$

$$\overline{X}_1 = \frac{25}{5} = 5 \qquad \overline{X}_2 = \frac{15}{5} = 3$$

Now we need the SSs:

$$SS_1 = \Sigma X_1^2 - \frac{(\Sigma X_1)^2}{n_1} \qquad SS_2 = \Sigma X_2^2 - \frac{(\Sigma X_2)^2}{n_2}$$

$$= 135 - \frac{(25)^2}{5} \qquad\qquad = 47 - \frac{(15)^2}{5}$$

$$= 135 - 125 \qquad\qquad\quad = 47 - 45$$

$$= 10 \qquad\qquad\qquad\qquad = 2$$

OK, let's enter our figures into the formula:

$$t = \frac{\overline{X}_1 - \overline{X}_2}{\sqrt{\left(\dfrac{SS_1 + SS_2}{n_1 + n_2 - 2}\right)\left(\dfrac{1}{n_1} + \dfrac{1}{n_2}\right)}} = \frac{5 - 3}{\sqrt{\left(\dfrac{10 + 2}{5 + 5 - 2}\right)\left(\dfrac{1}{5} + \dfrac{1}{5}\right)}}.$$

Now let's do all the simple addition and subtraction:

$$= \frac{2}{\sqrt{\left(\dfrac{12}{8}\right)\left(\dfrac{2}{5}\right)}}.$$

If we convert the fractions to decimals (divide the numerator by the denominator):

$$= \frac{2}{\sqrt{(1.5)(.4)}} = \frac{2}{\sqrt{.60}}.$$

Find the square root of .60 by using your calculator:

$$= \frac{2}{.78} = 2.56$$

So, t equals 2.56. Assuming we selected $\alpha = .05$, the only thing we need before we go to the t table is the appropriate degrees of freedom. For the t test for independent samples, the formula for degrees of freedom is $n_1 + n_2 - 2$; for our example, $df = n_1 + n_2 - 2 = 5 + 5 - 2 = 8$. Therefore, $t = 2.56$, $\alpha = .05$, $df = 8$. Using Table A.4 in the Appendix, the p values in the table are the probabilities associated with various α levels. In our case, we are really asking the question: Given $\alpha = .05$, and $df = 8$, what is the probability of getting $t \geq 2.56$ if there really is no difference? Find the intersection of 8 df and .05 p, and what do you have? The value 2.306 is the t value required to reject the null hypothesis with $\alpha = .05$, and $df = 8$. Is our value 2.56 > 2.306? Yes, and therefore we reject the null hypothesis. Are the means different? Yes. Are they significantly different? Yes. Was that hard? Of course not. Are all tests of significance going to be that easy? Of course.

Suppose our t value had been 2.29. What would we have concluded? We would have concluded that there is no significant difference between the groups. How about if we concluded that our t was *almost* significant? Boooo! A t is not *almost* significant or *really* significant; it is or it is not significant. You will never, ever see a research report that says "aw shucks, almost made it" or "pret-ty close!" So what about our little test for improving claims processing? Guess what? It may not be faster, but now you can tell the boss that your new method significantly reduces errors (of course, if you do, based on a sample of 5 in each group, you may be wa-a-a-y out on a limb!).

What if our t value had been -2.56? (Table A.4 has no negative values.) We would have done exactly what we did; we would have looked up 2.56. The only thing that determines whether the t is positive or negative is the order of the means; the denominator is always positive. In our example we had a mean difference of $5 - 3$, or 2. If we had reversed the means, we would have had $3 - 5$, or -2. As long as we know which mean goes with which group, the order is unimportant. The only thing that matters is the size of the difference. So, if you do not like negative numbers, put the larger mean first. Remember, the table is two-tailed; it is prepared to deal with a difference in favor of either group.

2. *The t test for nonindependent samples* is used when samples are formed by some type of matching. The ultimate matching, of course, is when the two samples are really the same sample group at two different times, such as one group that receives two different treatments at two different times or that is pretested before a treatment and then posttested. When samples are not independent, the members of one group are systematically related to the members of a second group (especially if it is the same group at two different times). If samples are nonindependent, measures on the dependent variable are expected to be correlated, and a special t test for correlated, or nonindependent, means must be used. When samples are nonindependent, the error term of the t test tends to be smaller, and therefore there is a higher probability that the null hypothesis will be rejected. Thus, the t test for nonindependent samples is used to determine whether there is probably a significant difference between the means of two matched, or nonindependent, samples or between the means for one sample at two different times.

In order to calculate the t test for nonindependent samples, use the following formula:

$$t = \frac{\bar{D}}{\sqrt{\dfrac{\Sigma D^2 - \dfrac{\Sigma D^2}{N}}{N(N-1)}}}.$$

You probably remember from our discussion of Spearman rho correlations in Chapter 11, that D stands for difference. In this case, D represents the difference between the matched pairs, or $\bar{X}_2 - \bar{X}_1$. To use this formula, let's assume that we have a set of measurements for two matched groups. For the sake of argument, let's say that we're comparing the number of days absent from work for a group of day shift workers (X_1) and a matched group of night shift workers (X_2). To speed things up a little, we'll calculate the Ds and D^2s in the example below, continued on the next page:

X_1	X_2	D	D^2
2	4	+2	4
3	5	+2	4

X_1	X_2	D	D^2
4	4	0	0
5	7	+2	4
6	10	+4	16
		$\Sigma D = \overline{10}$	$\Sigma D^2 = \overline{28}$

$$\overline{D} = \frac{\Sigma D}{N} = \frac{10}{5} = 2$$

Now we have everything we need, so let's substitute our numbers in the formula:

$$t = \frac{\overline{D}}{\sqrt{\dfrac{\Sigma D^2 - \dfrac{(\Sigma D)^2}{N}}{N(N-1)}}} = \frac{2}{\sqrt{\dfrac{28 - \dfrac{(10)^2}{5}}{5(5-1)}}}.$$

Now, squaring the 10 and doing our subtraction in the denominator:

$$= \frac{2}{\sqrt{\dfrac{28 - \dfrac{100}{5}}{5(4)}}}$$

$$= \frac{2}{\sqrt{\dfrac{28 - 20}{20}}}$$

$$= \frac{2}{\sqrt{\dfrac{8}{20}}}$$

$$= \frac{2}{\sqrt{.4}}$$

$$= \frac{2}{.63} = 3.17$$

Thus, $t = 3.17$. Assuming $\alpha = .05$, the only thing we need before we go to the t table is the appropriate degrees of freedom. For the t test for nonindependent samples, the formula for degrees of freedom is $N - 1$, or the number of pairs minus 1; in our example, $N - 1 = 5 - 1 = 4$. Therefore, $t = 3.17$, $\alpha = .05$, $df = 4$. Now go to Table A.4 again (the t table doesn't know or care whether our t test is for independent or nonindependent samples). Using the t table we find that for $p = .05$ and $df = 4$, the table value for t required for rejection of the null hypothesis is 2.776. Is our value 3.17 > 2.776? Yes, and therefore we reject the null hypothesis (absence rates of our day workers are *not* the same as absence rates of our night workers). Are the groups different? Yes. Are they significantly different? Yes. Are we having fun yet? Definitely!

Analysis of Gain or Difference Scores

When two groups are pretested, administered a treatment, and then posttested, the t test may or may not be the appropriate analysis technique. Many beginning researchers (and some not-so-beginning researchers) assume that the logical procedure is as follows:

1. Subtract each subject's pretest scores from his or her posttest score (resulting in a gain, or difference, score).
2. Compute the mean gain, or difference, score for each group.
3. Calculate a t value for the difference between the two average mean differences.

There are a number of problems associated with this approach, the major one being a lack of equal opportunity to grow. Every subject does not have the same room to gain. A subject who scores very low on a pretest has a lot of room, and a subject who scores very high has only a little room (referred to as the ceiling effect). With our example of absenteeism rates for our night workers, suppose we institute an incentive program to reduce absences; who has improved, or gained, more—the subject who improved from 10 absences to 2 or the subject who went from 2 to 0 (a difference of only 2 but it represents no absences over the whole year)?

The correct analysis of posttest measures or scores for two groups depends upon the performance of the two groups on the pretest. If both groups are essentially the same on the pretest, for example, both groups have the same rate of absences, then posttest scores or measures can be directly compared using a t test. If, however, there is a difference between the groups on the pretest, as we saw in our t test for independent samples between day and night workers, then the preferred posttest analysis is analysis of covariance. Recall that analysis of covariance adjusts posttest scores for initial differences on some variable (in this case the pretest) related to performance on the dependent variable. Thus, in order to determine whether analysis of covariance is necessary, a Pearson r can be calculated to determine if there is a significant relationship between pretest scores and posttest scores or measures. If not, a simple t test can be computed on posttest scores or measures (or, as we shall see shortly, analysis of covariance may be computed anyway, but for a different reason).

Analysis of Variance

A method of statistical analysis that is useful for studies involving two or more groups is analysis of variance. Essentially the analysis of variance is used to determine whether the normal variance that is found is occurring primarily within the sample groups (in which case there may be no significant difference between the groups) or primarily between the groups (in which case there may very well be a significant difference between the groups). The major types of analysis of variance that are used include the following:

1. *Simple analysis of variance* (ANOVA) is used to determine whether there is a significant difference between two or more means at a selected probability level. This technique is also called one-way analysis of variance or simple linear analysis of variance. In a study involving three groups and ratio or interval data, for example, the ANOVA is an appropriate analysis technique. Three (or more) posttest means are bound to be different; the question is whether the differences represent true

differences or chance differences resulting from sampling error. To answer this question at a given probability level the ANOVA is applied to the data and an F ratio is computed. You may be wondering why you cannot just compute a lot of t tests, one for each pair of means. Aside from some statistical problems concerning resulting distortion of your probability level, it is more convenient to perform one ANOVA than several ts. For four means, for example, six separate t tests would be required:

$$\bar{X}_1 - \bar{X}_2, \bar{X}_1 - \bar{X}_3, \bar{X}_1 - \bar{X}_4,$$
$$\bar{X}_2 - \bar{X}_3, \bar{X}_2 - \bar{X}_4,$$
$$\bar{X}_3 - \bar{X}_4.$$

The concept underlying ANOVA is that the total variation, or variance, of scores can be attributed to two sources—variance between groups (variance caused by the treatment) and variance within groups (error variance). As with the t test, a ratio is formed (the F ratio) with group differences as the numerator (variance between groups) and an error term as the denominator (variance within groups). Randomly formed groups are assumed to be essentially the same at the beginning of a study on a measure of the dependent variable. At the end of the study, after administration of the independent variable (treatment), we determine whether the between groups (treatment) variance differs from the within groups (error) variance by more than what would be expected by chance. In other words, if, on the one hand, the treatment variance is enough larger than the error variance, a significant F ratio results, the null hypothesis is rejected, and it is concluded that the treatment had a significant effect on the dependent variable. If, on the other hand, the treatment variance and error variance are essentially the same (do not differ by more than what would be expected by chance), the resulting F ratio is not significant, and the null hypothesis is not rejected. The greater the difference, the larger the F ratio. To determine whether or not the F ratio is significant, an F table is entered at the place corresponding to the selected probability level and the appropriate degrees of freedom. The degrees of freedom for the F ratio are a function of the number of groups and the number of subjects.

As an example, let us suppose that instead of a day and night shift, we had three shifts—7 A.M. to 3 P.M. (X_1), 3 P.M. to 11 P.M. (X_2), and 11 P.M. to 7 A.M. (X_3). Randomly selected subjects from each shift had the following numbers of absences during the previous year:

X_1	X_2	X_3
1	2	4
2	3	4
2	4	4
2	5	5
3	6	7

These sets of data are different, but are they significantly different? The appropriate test of significance to use in order to answer this question is the simple, or one-way, analysis of variance. Recall that the total variation, or variance, is a combination of between group variance and within group variance. In other words:

total sum of squares = between sum of squares + within sum of squares, or

$$SS_{total} \quad = \quad SS_{between} \quad + \quad SS_{within}$$

In order to compute an ANOVA we need each term, *but,* since C = A + B, or C (SS_{total}) = A ($SS_{between}$) + B (SS_{within}), we only have to compute any two terms and we can easily get the third. Since we have to calculate only two, we might as well do the two easiest, SS_{total} and $SS_{between}$. Once we have these, we can get SS_{within} by subtraction. The formula for $SS_{between}$ is as follows:

$$SS_{between} = \frac{(\Sigma X_1)^2}{n_1} + \frac{(\Sigma X_2)^2}{n_2} + \frac{(\Sigma X_3)^2}{n_3} - \frac{(\Sigma X)^2}{N}.$$

The formula for SS_{total} is even easier:

$$SS_{total} = \Sigma X^2 - \frac{(\Sigma X)^2}{N}.$$

Returning to absence data for the three shifts, let's compute the squares and sums we need for these formulas:

X_1	X_1^2	X_2	X_2^2	X_3	X_3^2
1	1	2	4	4	16
2	4	3	9	4	16
2	4	4	16	4	16
2	4	5	25	5	25
3	9	6	36	7	49
$\Sigma X_1 = 10$	$\Sigma X_1^2 = 22$	$\Sigma X_2 = 20$	$\Sigma X_2^2 = 90$	$\Sigma X_3 = 24$	$\Sigma X_3^2 = 122$

$$\Sigma X = \Sigma X_1 + \Sigma X_2 + \Sigma X_3 \ = 10 + 20 + 24 = 54$$
$$\Sigma X^2 = \Sigma X_1^2 + \Sigma X_2^2 + \Sigma X_3^2 = 22 + 90 + 122 = 234$$
$$N = n_1 + n_2 + n_3 \qquad = 5 + 5 + 5 = 15$$

Solving for SS_{total} first:

$$SS_{total} = \Sigma X^2 - \frac{(\Sigma X)^2}{N} = 234 - \frac{(54)^2}{15}$$

$$= 234 - \frac{2916}{15} = 234 - 194.4 = 39.6$$

So, $SS_{total} = 39.6$. Now let's do $SS_{between}$:

$$SS_{between} = \frac{(\Sigma X_1)^2}{n_1} + \frac{(\Sigma X_2)^2}{n_2} + \frac{(\Sigma X_3)^2}{n_3} - \frac{(\Sigma X)^2}{N}$$

$$= \frac{(10)^2}{5} + \frac{(20)^2}{5} + \frac{(24)^2}{5} - 194.4 \text{ (We just did that!)}$$

$$= \frac{100}{5} + \frac{400}{5} + \frac{576}{5} - 194.4$$

$$= 20 + 80 + 115.2 - 194.4 = 20.8$$

So, $SS_{between} = 20.8$. Now, to determine SS_{within}, we subtract $SS_{between}$ (20.8) from SS_{total} (39.6), $39.6 - 20.8 = 18.8$; so $SS_{within} = 18.8$. To summarize what we know so far, let's complete a summary table:

Source of Variation	Sum of Squares	df	Mean Square	F
Between	20.8	$(K-1)$		
Within	18.8	$(N-K)$		
Total	39.6	$(N-1)$		

The first thing you probably noticed is that each term has its own formula for degrees of freedom. The formula for the between term is $K - 1$, where K is the number of treatment groups; thus, for our example the degrees of freedom are $K - 1 = 3 - 1 = 2$. The formula for the within term is $N - K$, where N is the total sample size and K is still the number of treatment groups; thus, for our example the degrees of freedom for the within term $N - K = 15 - 3 = 12$. We don't really need them, but for the total term $df = N - 1 = 15 - 1 = 14$. Now we need the mean squares, which are determined by dividing each sum of squares by its appropriate degrees of freedom:

$$\text{mean square} = \frac{\text{sum of squares}}{\text{degrees of freedom}} \quad \text{or} \quad MS = \frac{SS}{df}.$$

Finally, the F ratio is the ratio of the mean square between (MS_B) and the mean square within (MS_W):

$$F = \frac{MS_B}{MS_W}.$$

Filling in the rest of our summary table we have:

Source of Variation	Sum of Squares	df		Mean Square	F
Between	20.8	$(K-1)$	2	10.40	6.62
Within	18.8	$(N-K)$	12	1.57	
Total	39.6	$(N-1)$	14		

Thus, $F = 6.62$ with 2 and 12 degrees of freedom. Assuming $\alpha = .05$, we are now ready to go to the F table, Table A.5 in the Appendix. Across the top of Table A.5, the row labeled n_1 refers to the degrees of freedom for the between term, in our case, 2. Down the extreme left-hand side of the table, in the column labeled n_2, are the degrees of freedom for the within term, in our case, 12. Now, where the values intersect we find 3.88, the value of F required for significance (to reject the null hypothesis) if $\alpha = .05$. The question is whether our F value $6.62 > 3.88$, and of course it is; therefore, there is a significant difference among the group means.

   If the F ratio is determined to be nonsignificant, the party is over. But what if it is significant? What do you know? With our example, all we know is that there is at least one significant difference somewhere, but we do not know where that difference is; we do not know which means are significantly different from which other means. It might be, for example, that in a study with four groups three of the means are equal but all are greater than the fourth mean ($\bar{X}_1 = \bar{X}_2 = \bar{X}_3$ and each mean $> \bar{X}_4$). It might mean, however, that $\bar{X}_1 = \bar{X}_2$ and $\bar{X}_3 = \bar{X}_4$ but, however, $\bar{X}_1$ and $\bar{X}_2$ are both greater than $\bar{X}_3$ and $\bar{X}_4$. When the F ratio is significant, and more than two means are involved, multiple-comparison procedures are used to determine which means are significantly different from which other means. There are a number of different multiple-comparison techniques available to the researcher. In essence, they involve calculation of a special form of the t test, a form for which the error term is based on the combined variance of all the groups, not just the groups being compared. This special t adjusts for the fact that many tests are being executed. What happens is that when many tests are performed, the probability level, α, tends to increase; if α is supposed to be .05, it will actually end up being greater, maybe .90, if many tests are performed. Thus, the chance of finding a significant difference is increased but so is the chance of committing a Type I error. Which mean comparisons are to be made should generally be decided upon before the study is conducted, not after, and should be based upon the research hypothesis. In other words, application of a multiple-comparison technique should not be essentially a "fishing expedition" in which the researcher looks for any difference she or he can find. It is possible to obtain a nonsignificant F ratio and yet to find a significant difference between two or more means. Some statisticians believe that it is legitimate to investigate this possibility if the F ratio is nonsignificant (most do not). All statisticians and researchers, however, agree that multiple-comparison techniques should not be applied with abandon in the hopes that something will turn up.

Of the many multiple-comparison techniques available, probably the most often used is the *Scheffé test*. The Scheffé test is appropriate for making any and all possible comparisons involving a set of means. The calculations for this approach are quite simple, and sample sizes do not have to be equal, as they do with some multiple-comparison techniques. The Scheffé test is very conservative, which is good new and bad news. The good news is that the probability of committing a Type I error for any comparison of means is never greater than the α level selected for the original analysis of variance. The bad news is that it is entirely possible, given the comparisons selected for investigation, to find no significant differences, even though the F for the analysis of variance was significant. In general, however, the flexibility of the Scheffé test and its ease of application make it useful for a wide variety of situations.

In the example we used for the analysis of variance, we determined that there was a difference in absenteeism among the three shifts. In order to find out *where,* we will apply the Scheffé test. As you study the following formula, you will notice that we already have almost all the information we need to apply the Scheffé test:

$$F = \frac{(\overline{X}_1 - \overline{X}_2)^2}{MS_W \left(\dfrac{1}{n_1} + \dfrac{1}{n_2}\right)(K-1)} \text{ with } df = (K-1),(N-K).$$

The MS_W was calculated at the time we did the ANOVA and is equal to 1.57. We also calculated the degrees of freedom, 2 and 12; therefore, all we need is $\overline{X}_1$ and $\overline{X}_2$. To compare any other two means, we would simply change the $\overline{X}$s and ns. Looking back at the ANOVA example, we see that the sums for each group were 10, 20, and 24, respectively. Thus the three means are as follows:

$$\overline{X}_1 = \frac{\Sigma X_1}{n_1} = \frac{10}{5} = 2.00$$

$$\overline{X}_2 = \frac{\Sigma X_2}{n_2} = \frac{20}{5} = 4.00$$

$$\overline{X}_3 = \frac{\Sigma X_3}{n_3} = \frac{24}{5} = 4.80$$

Applying the Scheffé test to $\overline{X}_1$ and $\overline{X}_2$ we get this:

$$F = \frac{(\overline{X}_1 - \overline{X}_2)^2}{MS_W \left(\dfrac{1}{n_1} + \dfrac{1}{n_2}\right)(K-1)} = \frac{(2.00-4.00)^2}{1.57\left(\dfrac{1}{5} + \dfrac{1}{5}\right)2}$$

$$= \frac{(-2.00)^2}{1.57 \left(\frac{2}{5}\right) 2}$$

$$= \frac{4}{1.57 \, (.4) \, 2}$$

$$= \frac{4}{1.256} = 3.18$$

Since the value of F required for significance is 3.88 if $\alpha = .05$ and $df = 2$ and 12, and since $3.18 < 3.88$, we conclude that there is no significant difference between $\overline{X}_1$ and $\overline{X}_2$. Therefore, we would conclude that the absence rate between the 7 A.M.-to-3 P.M. shift and the 3 P.M.-to-11 P.M. shift is not significantly different. If we apply the same formula to $\overline{X}_1$ and $\overline{X}_3$, however, we find the value of F is 6.24. Since $6.24 > 3.88$, we conclude that there is a significant difference between $\overline{X}_1$ and $\overline{X}_3$. Similarly, applying the Scheffé test to $\overline{X}_2$ and $\overline{X}_3$, we find the F value is .51; since $.51 < 3.88$, there is no significant difference between $\overline{X}_2$ and $\overline{X}_3$. To summarize:

For $\overline{X}_1$ and $\overline{X}_2$, there is no significant difference.
For $\overline{X}_1$ and $\overline{X}_3$, there is a significant difference.
For $\overline{X}_2$ and $\overline{X}_3$, there is no significant difference.

Although there is a difference between $\overline{X}_1$ and $\overline{X}_2$, and between $\overline{X}_2$ and $\overline{X}_3$, the difference is not significant; therefore, we can only state that the night shift (11 P.M. to 7 A.M.) has a significantly greater number of absences than the day shift (7 A.M. to 3 P.M.), but that there is no significant difference in absences between the day and afternoon shifts (7 A.M. to 3 P.M. and 3 P.M. to 11 P.M.) or between the afternoon and night shifts (3 P.M. to 11 P.M. and 11 P.M. to 7 A.M.) How can this be? Well, there is a difference, but it's just not significant.

The Scheffé test can also be used to compare combinations of means. Suppose, for example, that group 1 was a control group and we wanted to compare the mean of group 1 to the mean of groups 2 and 3 combined. First we would have to combine the means for groups 2 and 3 as follows:

$$\overline{X}_{2+3} = \frac{n_2 \overline{X}_2 + n_3 \overline{X}_3}{n_2 + n_3} = \frac{5(4.00) + 5(4.80)}{5 + 5}$$

$$= \frac{20 + 24}{10} = \frac{44}{10} = 4.40$$

Next we simply calculate the F ratio using $\overline{X}_1 = 2.00$ and the combined mean for $\overline{X}_{2+3} = 4.40$ using the following formula:

$$F = \frac{(\overline{X}_1 - \overline{X}_{2+3})^2}{MS_W \left(\dfrac{1}{n_1} + \dfrac{1}{n_2 + n_3}\right)(K - 1)}.$$

If you worked out that formula for our example, you would discover that $F = 6.13$; since $6.13 > 3.88$, we would conclude that there is a significant difference between $\overline{X}_1$ and $\overline{X}_{2+3}$. In other words, the experimental groups performed significantly better than the control group.

If you're sitting there saying, "Oh, dear, there must be a better way!" of course there is, now that you have some idea what you're doing. The answer is to use a computer statistical program to handle the whole thing for you. As an example, we used the data we entered for Table 11.1 with regard to trainees in the SPSS/PC+ program, except this time we pretended that columns X, Y^1, and Z were ratings for three different groups instead of three sets of ratings on one group at different times. The directions and printout from the ANOVA based on this data are presented as Figure 12.1. As you can see, the printout gives us essentially the same chart—source of variance, *df*, sum of squares, mean squares, and *F* ratio—that we completed on our sample ANOVA in this chapter. In addition, the printout also provided the *F* probability, .0016, so we didn't even need to look that up. And, as if that weren't enough, because we told the program to give us "all statistics" (/statistics = all., in the program directions), it also provided the descriptive statistics we would probably like to have—the mean, standard deviation, and so on. If your instructor wants you to use SPSS, he or she will probably ask you to review the manuals (Nie, Hull, Jenkins, Steinbrenner, & Bent, 1975; SPSS Inc., 1986) related to this software program; in addition, you will probably want to undertake some instruction through your campus computer center.

2. *Factorial analysis of variance* is used if a research study is based upon a factorial design and investigates one dependent variable, two or more independent variables, and the interactions between them. Such an analysis yields a separate *F* ratio for each independent variable and one for each interaction. Analysis of the data presented in Figure 10.5, for example, would yield three *F*s—one for the manipulated independent variable, method, one for the control variable, worker experience, and one for the interaction between method and worker experience. For the no interaction example, the *F* for method would probably be significant since method A appears to be significantly more effective than method B (70 versus 30); the *F* for worker experience would also probably be significant, since experienced workers appear to have performed significantly better than inexperienced workers (60 versus 40); the *F* for the interaction between method and worker experience would not be significant, since method A is more effective than method B for both worker experience groups, not differentially effective for one level of worker experience or another ($80 > 40$, $60 > 20$).

By contrast, for the interaction example, the *F* for method would not be significant, since method A is equally as effective as method B overall ($50 = 50$); the *F* for worker

```
set more=off/include=off/length=79/eject=on/listing= 'a:out12'.
data list free file='a:anovadata' /t avg.
list t avg.
oneway avg by t (1,3)
/statistics = all./
anova avg by t (1,3)
/statistics = all.
```

Page   4   SPSS/PC+   1/14/91
              ─ ─ ─ ─ ─ ─ ─ ─ ─ ─ O N E W A Y ─ ─ ─ ─ ─ ─ ─ ─ ─ ─

      Variable AVG
By Variable T

                              Analysis of Variance
                                 Sum of   Mean   F   F
      Source   D.F.   Squares   Squares   Ratio   Prob.
Between Groups   2   170.1000   85.0500   7.1873   .0016
Within Groups   57   674.5000   11.8333
Total   59   844.6000

                                Standard   Standard
Group   Count   Mean   Deviation   Error   95 Pct Conf Int for Mean
Grp 1   20   12.5000   4.3710   .9774   10.4543 to   14.54
Grp 2   20   13.8500   2.3681   .5295   12.7417 to   14.95
Grp 3   20   16.5500   3.2843   .7344   15.0129 to   18.08
Total   60   14.3000   3.7836   .4885   13.3226 to   15.27
```

**Figure 12.1.** Examples of SPSS/PC+ directions and printout for ANOVA and descriptive statistics.

experience would probably be significant, since more experienced workers still appear to have performed significantly better than less experienced workers (70 versus 30). The *F* for interaction between method and worker experience, however, would probably be significant, since the methods appear to be differentially effective depending on worker experience; method A is better for more experienced subjects (80 versus 60), and method B is better for less experienced subjects (20 versus 40). Another way of looking at it is to see that for the no interaction example (80 + 20) = (60 + 40); for the interaction example (80 + 40) + (20 + 60).

A factorial analysis of variance is not as difficult to calculate as you may think. If no more than two variables are involved, you can calculate a factorial analysis of variance using a calculator, although use of a computer is probably preferable . If more than two variables are involved, it is better to use a computer. Many statistics software programs for personal computers will allow you to calculate this statistic; in addition, you may also want to use a mainframe computer program at your university.
```

3. *Analysis of covariance* (ANCOVA) is another variation of the analysis of variance. It is used in two major ways: (a) as a technique for controlling the effects of extraneous variables on the dependent variable and (b) as a means of increasing power. Basically, ANCOVA is a statistical, rather than an experimental, method that can be used to equate groups on one or more variables. Use of the ANCOVA is essentially equivalent to matching groups on the variable or variables to be controlled (Roscoe, 1975). In a number of situations, covariance is the preferred approach to control. As pointed out previously, for example, analysis of pretest-posttest gain scores or measures has several disadvantages. Thus, for a study based on a pretest-posttest control-group design, ANCOVA is a superior method for controlling for pretest differences.

Essentially, ANCOVA adjusts posttest scores for initial differences on some variable and compares adjusted scores. In other words, the groups are equalized with respect to the control variable and then compared. It's sort of like handicapping in bowling; in an attempt to equalize teams, high scorers are given little or no handicap, low scorers are given big handicaps, and so forth. Any variable that is correlated with the dependent variable can be controlled for using covariance. Pretest performance, work experience, skill level, and specific aptitude are variables that might be controlled through the use of analysis of covariance. If the variance to be controlled is a variable (such as years of experience) that is not affected by manipulation of the independent variable under study, then it doesn't really matter when such data are collected—prior to, during, or following the experiment. Otherwise, as in the case of a pretest of the dependent variable, or aptitude for the skill to be taught, the covariate data must be collected prior to the initiation of treatments. By using ANCOVA we are attempting to reduce variation in posttest scores that is attributable to another variable. Ideally, we would like *all* posttest variance to be attributable to the treatment conditions.

Analysis of covariance is a control technique used in both causal-comparative studies in which already formed, not necessarily equal groups are involved and in experimental studies in which either existing groups or randomly formed groups are involved; randomization does not guarantee that groups will be equated on all variables. Unfortunately, the situation for which ANCOVA is least appropriate is the situation for which it is most often used. ANCOVA is based on the assumption that subjects have been randomly assigned to experimental groups. If existing, or intact, groups are involved but treatments are assigned to groups randomly, covariance may still be used, but results must be interpreted with due caution. If ANCOVA is used with existing groups and nonmanipulated independent variables, as in causal-comparative studies, the results are likely to be misleading at best. There is evidence, for example, that improper use of ANCOVA tends to give an artificial advantage to whichever group scores higher initially on the variable to be controlled. Thus, for example, if an experimental group has a higher pretest score than a control group, it is difficult to interpret the results if the experimental group scores significantly higher than the control group on the posttest (Campbell & Boruch, 1975). There are other assumptions associated with the use of analysis of covariance. Violation of these assumptions is not as serious, however, if subjects have been randomly assigned to treatment groups (Elasoff, 1969; Evans & Anastasio, 1968; Winer, 1971).

A second, not previously discussed, function of ANCOVA is that it increases the power of a statistical test by reducing within-group (error) variance. Although increasing sample size also increases power, the researcher is often limited to samples of a given size because of financial and practical reasons. The power-increasing function of ANCOVA is directly related to the degree of randomization involved in formation of the groups; the results of ANCOVA are least likely to be valid when already formed groups to which treatments have not been randomly assigned are used. Further, since randomization increases the validity of ANCOVA, and since randomization can generally be counted on to equate groups on relevant variables, Huck (1972) and others urge that researchers consider the primary value of analysis of covariance to be its ability to increase power rather than its ability to equate groups on extraneous variables.

Application of the analysis of covariance technique is quite a complex, lengthy procedure which is hardly ever hand calculated. Almost all researchers use computer programs to calculate this statistic for reasons both of accuracy and sanity!

4. *Multivariate analysis of variance* (MANOVA) is a statistical technique that can be used when the study involves more than one dependent variable and one or more independent variables. In instances in which covariates are involved, a *multivariate analysis of covariance* (MANCOVA) may be applied. Again, a computer should probably be used to calculate this statistic.

Multiple Regression

As discussed in Chapter 8, since a combination of variables usually results in a more accurate prediction than any one variable, prediction studies often result in a prediction equation, referred to as a multiple-regression equation. A multiple-regression equation uses variables that are known to predict the criterion individually to make a more accurate prediction; as much as possible, the variables selected should not correlate with each other so that each makes a unique contribution. Thus, for example, we might use aptitude test results, interview-based rankings, previous work experience, and educational level to predict worker performance after one year on the job. Use of multiple regression is increasing, primarily because of its versatility and precision. It can be used with data representing any scale of measurement, and it can be used to analyze the results of experimental and causal-comparative, as well as correlational, studies. It determines not only whether variables are related but also the degree to which they are related.

To see how multiple regression works, let's go back to our trainees in Chapter 11. When we tried to determine whether the pretraining rating (column X from Table 11.1) was a good predictor of the follow-up rating (column Z), we calculated a correlation coefficient of $r = .47$ (18 *df*, $p < .05$). We could keep calculating correlation coefficients between the variables that we have to see, which gives us the

```
This procedure was completed at 17:15:39
regression variables = x y y1 xy z xyz
 /dependent = z
 /method= enter x
 /dependent = z
 /method= enter y
 /dependent = z
 /method= stepwise
 /dependent = z
 /enter = x y y1 xy .
```

**** M U L T I P L E   R E G R E S S I O N ****

Equation Number 4   Dependent Variable..   Z

Beginning Block Number 1. Method: Enter
   X   Y   Y1   XY

Variable(s) Entered on Step Number
  1..   XY
  2..   X
  3..   Y1
  4..   Y

Multiple R	.68335
R Square	.46696
Adjusted R Square	.32482
Standard Error	2.69871

Analysis of Variance

	DF	Sum of Squares	Mean Square
Regression	4	95.70423	23.92606
Residual	15	109.24577	7.28305

F =   3.28517   Signif F = .0402

---------------------- Variables in the Equation ----------------------

Variable	B	SE B	Beta	T	Sig T
XY	-.39024	.28274	-1.13543	-1.380	.1877
X	.87481	.34584	1.16424	2.529	.0231
Y1	6.23364	2.65439	4.49464	2.348	.0330
Y	-1.80951	.94182	-3.77291	-1.921	.0739
(Constant)	15.25173	3.97102		3.841	.0016

Figure 12.2. Example of directions and printout of stepwise regression using data from Table 11.1 and SPSS/PC.

best prediction formula, or we could have the computer calculate a *stepwise regression*. Using this procedure, the computer compares each factor to our criterion variable, Z, to determine what the relationships are. Finally, it will provide us with a formula we might use for future predictions (Figure 12.2). As you can see, the variables that were entered were XY, X, Y_1, and Y. As the F ratio is 3.28, with a significant F of .0402, we might conclude that we'd developed a great formula, but think about it. Do you remember what we said XY (really X + Y) was? A combination score—which means that two of the factors were used twice in the formula. If you're saying that doesn't make sense, you're right. The point is, if you don't know what you're doing with the computer, fooling around with the figures can give you very misleading—wrong, in other words—results. The same data manipulated in the same way but using Statview^{TM}512+ gives us the following printout (Figure 12.3). As you can see, the information is essentially the same, although the terminology may differ.

Stepwise Regression Y_1:Z   4 H variables

(Last Step) STEP NO. 4   VARIABLE ENTERED: H_4 : HY

R:	R-squared:	Adj. R-squared:	Std. Error:
.683	.467	.325	2.699

Analysis of Variance Table

Source:	DF:	Sum Squares:	Mean Square:	F-test:
REGRESSION	4	95.704	23.926	3.285
RESIDUAL	15	109.246	7.283	
TOTAL	19	204.95		

8

STEP NO. 4 Stepwise Regression Y_1 :Z   4 H variables

Variables in Equation

Parameter:	Value:	Std. Err.:	Std. Value:	F to Remove:
INTERCEPT	15.252			
• H	.875	.346	1.164	6.398
• Y	-1.81	.942	-3.773	3.691
• Y1	6.234	2.654	4.495	5.515
• HY	-.39	.283	-1.135	1.905

Figure 12.3. Example of printout of stepwise regression using data from Table 11.1 and StatView^{TM}512+.

For example, SPSS/PC uses the term *constant,* whereas the other program uses *intercept* to label the same value. Once again, you need to have some familiarity with the program you are using or you'll wind up like a recent cartoon character saying, "*F* = 2 WHAT ?" In addition to the purely technical problems related to this procedure, it is also somewhat controversial because it is overly dependent on chance; researchers are urged to verify their findings using a second sample when stepwise regression analysis (otherwise called statistical regression) is used (Tabachnick & Fidell, 1989).

As a better example of regression analysis, suppose we use the earlier example concerning worker performance. Suppose that, after 1 year's performance on the job, 30 workers have performance appraisals in which each is given a rating between 20 (high) and 5 (low) (see Table 12.1, column 1). In order to determine the best predictor or predictors of high performance, data are collected regarding each of the workers' aptitude tests results (column 2), interview ratings (column 3), years of previous experience (column 4), and years of education (column 5). This information is entered into a computer program using column 1, the performance appraisal, as the criterion variable Y, and the other variables as predictors X_1, X_2, X_3, and X_4 respectively. The results of the multiple-regression analysis (see Figure 12.4) indicates that using these variables, we could predict performance with a high level of confidence as $R = .976$ (29 *df, p* = .0001). The best predictor turns out to be the aptitude test (t = 13.3, p = .0001), with the interview as the next best predictor (t = 3.66, p = .001). Experience and education are not good predictors in this position, so we might want to disregard these variables in future hiring decisions. A study involving more variables works exactly the same way; at each step it is determined which variable adds the most to the prediction and how much it adds. As with the MANOVA, ANCOVA, and MANCOVA, computer analysis is almost always used to calculate multiple regression.

It should be noted that the sign, positive or negative, of the relationship between a predictor and the criterion has nothing to do with how good a predictor the variable is. Recall that $r = -1.00$ represents a relationship just as strong as $r = +1.00$; the only difference indicated is the nature of the relationship. It should also be noted that the number of predictor variables is related to the needed sample size; the greater the number of variables, the larger the sample size needs to be. The larger the sample size is in relation to the number of variables, the greater the probability is that the prediction equation will work with groups other than those involved in creating the equation. A problem with regression analysis for the beginning researcher is the temptation to try out all sorts of combinations in order to hit on a significant relationship; as we have cautioned previously, statistics used in shotgun fashion may result in finding "significant" relationships, but often these prove to be spurious. A much more acceptable procedure is to use a logical, hypothesis-based approach to the data.

With increasing frequency, multiple regression is being used as an alternative to the various analysis-of-variance techniques. When this is so, the dependent variable (perhaps posttest scores or measures) becomes the criterion variable, and the predictors include group membership (experimental versus control) and any other

Table 12.1

*Data for Multiple Regression Analysis with Performance as the Criterion
Variable and Aptitude, Interview Rating, Experience, and Education as
Predictor Variables using StatView™512+*

	Performance Y_1	Aptitude X_1	Interview X_2	Experience X_3	Education X_4
1	20	68	8	2	14
2	19	67	9	1	13
3	19	65	8	1	12
4	19	67	9	2	12
5	18	66	8	1	12
6	18	67	6	1	14
7	17	66	7	2	12
8	17	65	8	1	12
9	17	62	9	2	12
10	15	63	7	1	12
11	14	61	7	2	13
12	13	60	6	1	12
13	13	59	7	2	13
14	11	55	6	1	12
15	11	53	6	2	14
16	10	50	6	1	12
17	10	54	5	1	12
18	10	53	7	2	13
19	10	55	6	1	12
20	9	50	7	2	12
21	9	45	7	1	14
22	9	46	5	1	12
23	8	40	7	2	13
24	8	44	6	2	12
25	8	45	5	1	13
26	7	40	5	2	14
27	7	42	5	2	13
28	7	40	6	1	12
29	6	38	7	2	14
30	6	37	5	1	12

Multiple Regression Y1 :Performance   4 X variables

DF:	R:	R-squared:	Adj. R-squared:	Std. Error:
29	.976	.952	.944	1.088

Analysis of Variance Table

Source:	DF:	Sum Squares:	Mean Square:	F-test:
REGRESSION	4	582.551	145.638	122.941
RESIDUAL	25	29.615	1.185	p=.0001
TOTAL	29	612.167		

Residual Information Table

SS[e(i)-e(i-1)]:	e ≥ 0:	e < 0:	DW test:
26.896	15	15	.908

1

Multiple Regression Y1 :Performance   4 X variables
Beta Coefficient Table

Parameter:	Value:	Std. Err.:	Std. Value:	t-Value:	Probability:
INTERCEPT	-17.191				
Aptitude	.361	.027	.816	13.324	.0001
Interview	.844	.231	.228	3.66	.0012
Experience	-.515	.454	-.057	1.135	.2673
Education	.391	.27	.069	1.452	.1591

2

Figure 12.4. Example of printout of multiple regression analysis result with performance as the criterion variable and aptitude, interview rating, experience, and education as predictor variables using Statview™512+.

appropriate variables, such as pretest scores. The results indicate not only whether group membership is significantly related to posttest performance but also the magnitude of the relationship. Notice that we have said "relationship"; regression analysis may reveal relationships among variables but not necessarily causality. A strong relationship between variables may stem from many sources, including some that are not currently under investigation. Causality can be demonstrated only by showing that manipulation of the independent variable(s) is always followed by a change in the dependent variable(s), assuming that all the extraneous variables are controlled (Tabachnick & Fidell, 1989, p. 127).

Chi Square

Chi square, symbolized as χ^2 and pronounced "keye" as rhyming with "eye," is a nonparametric test of significance appropriate when the data are in the form of frequency counts occurring in two or more mutually exclusive categories. Chi square also may be used when the original data are in the form of interval data or ratio data and are transformed into nominal data, but it is not usually appropriate because precision is lost in the transformation. A chi square test compares proportions actually observed in a study with the proportions expected if the groups are not significantly different. Expected proportions are usually the frequencies that would be expected if the groups were equal; however, they may be based on past data. The chi square value increases as the difference between observed and expected frequencies increases. Whether the chi square value is significant is determined by consulting a chi square table just as was done with r, t, and F values.

The chi square can be used to compare frequencies occurring in different categories, or the categories may be groups, so that the chi square is comparing groups with respect to the frequency of occurrence of different events. As an example, suppose you stopped 90 shoppers in a supermarket and asked them to taste three different brands of peanut butter (unidentified to the shoppers, of course) and tell you which one tasted better. Suppose that 40 shoppers chose brand X, 30 chose brand Y, and 20 chose brand Z. If the null hypothesis were true (X = Y = Z), you would expect an equal number of shoppers to select each brand: 30, 30, and 30. To determine whether the frequencies observed (fo = 40, 30, and 20) were significantly different from the frequencies expected (fe = 30, 30, and 30), a chi square test could be applied. If the chi square were significant, the null hypothesis would be rejected, and it would be concluded that the brands do taste different.

As another example, you might wish to compare the effectiveness of two different types of reimbursement, commissioned and salaried, to see which is more effective in increasing sales of new cars. At the end of a 6-month study you might collect the sales figures for the two groups. Tabulation might reveal that the commissioned group sold 100 new cars and the salaried group sold 80. Would this represent a true difference or a chance difference? In this case, the total number of cars sold was 180 (100 + 80); if the groups were essentially the same, you would expect each group to sell the same number of cars, namely 180 ÷ 2 = 90. In order to determine whether the groups were significantly different, you would compare the frequencies observed (fo = 100, 80) with the frequencies expected (fe = 90, 90) using a chi square test of significance.

The chi square may also be used when frequencies are categorized along more than one dimension, sort of a factorial chi square. In the just-cited study, for example, sales could be classified by type of reimbursement and experience level of the salesperson, a two-way classification, in order to determine if effectiveness of reimbursement is independent of the experience level of the sales person. When a two-way classification is used, determination of expected frequencies is a little more complex but still not difficult.

To calculate the chi square statistic, let's use our peanut butter example. As you recall, we asked 90 shoppers to indicate which of three peanut butters they thought tasted better; 40 picked brand X, 30 picked brand Y, and 20 picked brand Z. If there were no difference among the brands we would expect the same number (90 ÷ 3 = 30) to choose each brand. Therefore, we would have the following table:

Brand

	X	Y	Z	
Observed	40	30	20	Total = 90
Expected	30	30	30	

In order to determine whether the observed frequencies are significantly different from the expected frequencies, we apply the following (easiest of all) formula:

$$\chi^2 = \sum \left[\frac{(fo - fe)^2}{fe} \right].$$

All this formula says is that for each category, X, Y, and Z, we subtract the expected frequency (fe) from the observed frequency (fo), square the difference $(fo - fe)^2$, and then divide by the expected frequency, fe. The Σ says that after we do the above for each term we add up the resulting values. Thus, substituting our table's values into the formula we get the following:

$$
\begin{array}{cccccc}
 & \overset{\text{X}}{\overset{fo \quad fe}{}} & & \overset{\text{Y}}{\overset{fo \quad fe}{}} & & \overset{\text{Z}}{\overset{fo \quad fe}{}} \\
\chi^2 = & \dfrac{(40 - 30)^2}{30} & + & \dfrac{(30 - 30)^2}{30} & + & \dfrac{(20 - 30)^2}{30} \\
= & \dfrac{(10)^2}{30} & + & \dfrac{(0)^2}{30} & + & \dfrac{(10)^2}{30} \\
= & \dfrac{100}{30} & + & 0 & + & \dfrac{100}{30} \\
= & 3.33 & + & 0 & + & 3.33 \\
= & 6.66 & & & &
\end{array}
$$

Thus $\chi^2 = 6.66$. The degrees of freedom for a one-dimensional chi square are determined by the formula $(K - 1)$ where K equals the number of categories, in this case, 3. Thus $df = K - 1 = 3 - 1 = 2$. Therefore, we have $\chi^2 = 6.66$, $\alpha = .05$, $df = 2$.

To determine whether the differences between observed and expected frequencies are significant, we compare our chi square value to the appropriate value in Table A.6 in the Appendix. Using a predetermined α level of .05, move your finger along the top of the chart labeled p until you find .05; then find 2 under the df column on the extreme left hand side. You will find that they intersect at 5.991. Is our value 6.66 > 5.991? Yes. Therefore, we reject the null hypothesis. There is a significant difference between observed and expected proportions; the brands of peanut butter compared don't taste the same! Suppose we had selected $\alpha = .01$. The chi square value required for significance would be 9.210. Is our value of 6.66 > 9.210? No. Therefore, at $\alpha = .01$, we would not reject the null hypothesis, and we would conclude that there is no significant difference between observed and expected frequencies; the three brands of peanut butter taste the same.

Thus, you can see that selection of an α level is important; different conclusions may very well be drawn with different α levels.

We have discussed a number of different inferential statistics and calculated some of the major ones. Figure 12.5 summarizes the conditions for which each of the statistics discussed in this section are appropriate.

Statistic	Number of Groups	Number of Independent Variables	Type of Data	Related Designs[a]
t test for independent samples	2	1	interval or ratio	1, 2, 4[b]
t test for nondependent samples	2	1	interval or ratio	4 (if groups are matched)
simple ANOVA	≥ 2	1	interval, ratio	1, 2, 4
Scheffé test	≥ 2	1	interval, ratio	1, 2, 4
MANOVA (factorial)	≥ 2	≥ 2	interval, ratio	3
ANCOVA (covariance)	≥ 2	≥ 2	interval, ratio	1, 2, 3, 4
multiple regression	≥ 1	≥ 1	all	1, 2, 3, 4
chi square	≥ 2	≥ 1	nominal	1, 2, 3, 4

[a]See Figure 10.2
[b]The t test for independent samples is appropriate for designs 1 and 4 if there is no relationship between pretest scores and posttest scores. If there is, analysis of covariance is required.

Figure 12.5. Summary of conditions for which selected statistics are appropriate.

Summary/Chapter 12

CONCEPTS UNDERLYING APPLICATION

1. Inferential statistics deal with inferences about populations based on the behavior of samples.

2. Inferential statistics are concerned with determining how likely it is that results based on a sample or samples are the same results that would have been obtained for the entire population.

3. Sample values, such as the mean, are referred to as *statistics;* the corresponding values in the population are referred to as *parameters.*

4. Inferential statistics are used to make inferences concerning parameters, based on sample statistics.

5. If a difference between means is found for two groups at the end of a study, the question of interest is whether a similar difference exists in the population from which the samples were selected.

6. Inferences concerning populations are only probability statements; the researcher is only "probably" correct when making an inference and concluding that there is a true difference or a true relationship in the population.

Standard Error

7. Expected, chance variation among the means is referred to as *sampling error.*

8. If a difference is found between sample means, the question of interest is whether the difference is a result of sampling error or a reflection of a true difference.

9. An interesting characteristic of sampling errors is that they are normally distributed.

10. If a sufficiently large number of equal-size large samples are randomly selected from a population, all samples will not have the same mean on the variable measured, *but* the means of those samples will be normally distributed around the population mean. The mean of all the sample means will yield a good estimate of the population mean.

11. As with any normally distributed set of figures, a distribution of sample means has not only its own mean but also its own standard deviation. The standard deviation of the sample means (the standard deviation of sampling errors, in other words) is usually referred to as the *standard error of the mean.*

12. The standard error of the mean ($SE_{\bar{x}}$) tells us by how much we would expect our sample means to differ if we used other samples from the same population.

13. According to normal curve percentages, we can say that approximately 68% of the sample means will fall between plus and minus one standard error of the mean (remember, the standard error of the mean is a standard deviation), 95% will fall between plus and minus two standard errors, and 99+ % will fall between plus and minus three standard errors.

14. If we know the standard deviation of the population, we can estimate the standard error of the mean by dividing the standard deviation by the square root of our sample size ($\sqrt{N}$).

15. In most cases, however, we do not know the mean or standard deviation of the population. In these cases, we estimate the standard error by dividing the standard deviation of the sample by the square root of the sample size minus one:

$$SE_{\overline{X}} = \frac{SD}{\sqrt{N-1}}.$$

16. The smaller the standard error of the mean is, the better; a smaller standard error indicates less sampling error.

17. The major factor affecting the standard error of the mean is sample size. As the size of the sample increases, the standard error of the mean decreases.

18. The researcher should make every effort to acquire as many subjects as possible so that inferences about the population of interest will be as correct as possible.

19. An estimate of standard error can also be computed for other measures of central tendency as well as measures of variability, relationship, and relative position. Further, an estimate of standard error can also be determined for the difference between means.

20. Differences between two sample means are normally distributed around the mean difference in the population.

The Null Hypothesis

21. When we talk about the difference between two sample means being a true difference we mean that the difference was caused by the treatment (independent variable), not by chance.

22. The *null hypothesis* says in essence that there is no true difference or relationship between parameters in the populations and that any difference or relationship found for the samples is the result of sampling error.

23. The null hypothesis for a study is usually (although not necessarily) different from the research hypothesis.

24. Rejection of a null hypothesis is more conclusive support for a positive research hypothesis.

25. In a research study, the test of significance selected to determine whether a difference between means is a true difference provides a test of the null hypothesis. As a result, the null hypothesis is either rejected, as being probably false, or not rejected, as being probably true.

26. After we make the decision to reject or not reject the null hypothesis, we make an inference back to our research hypothesis.

27. In order to test a null hypothesis we need a test of significance, and we need to select a probability level that indicates how much risk we are willing to take that the decision we make is wrong.

Tests of Significance

28. The test of significance helps us to decide whether we can reject the null hypothesis and infer that the difference is significantly greater than a chance difference.

29. The test of significance is made at a preselected probability level, indicated by α (alpha), which allows us to state that we have rejected the null hypothesis because we would expect to find a difference as large as we have found by chance in only 5 out of every 100 studies ($\alpha = .05$), or in only 1 in every 100 studies ($\alpha = .01$), or whatever; therefore, we conclude that the null hypothesis is *probably* false and reject it.

30. There are a number of different tests of significance that can be applied in research studies, one of which is more appropriate than the others in a given situation.

31. Factors such as the scale of measurement represented by the data (nominal, ordinal, interval, or ratio), the method of subject selection (random or not), size and number of the groups, and the number of independent variables determine which test of significance should be selected for a given experiment.

Decision Making: Levels of Significance and Type I and Type II Errors

32. The researcher makes a decision that the difference between the means is, or is not, too large to attribute to chance. The researcher never knows for sure whether he or she is right or wrong, only whether he or she is probably correct.

33. There are four possibilities:

   a. Null hypothesis is true (A = B); researcher says it's true = Correct.
   b. Null hypothesis is false (A ≠ B); researcher says it's false = Correct.
   c. Null hypothesis is true (A = B); researcher says it's false = Incorrect.
   d. Null hypothesis is false (A ≠ B); researcher says it's true = Incorrect.

   If the researcher rejects a null hypothesis that is really true (option c), the researcher makes a Type I error; if the researcher fails to reject a null hypothesis that is really false (option d), the researcher makes a Type II error.

34. When the researcher makes a decision to reject or not reject the null hypothesis, she or he does so with a given probability of being correct. This probability of being correct is referred to as the significance level, or probability level, of the test of significance.

35. If the decision is made to reject the null hypothesis, the means are concluded to be significantly different (A ≠ B); that difference is too great to be the result of chance error. If the null hypothesis is not rejected, the means are determined to be not significantly different (A ≠ B but not significantly).

36. The level of significance, or probability level, selected determines how large the difference between the means must be in order to be declared significantly different.

37. The most commonly used probability level (α) is the .05 level. Some studies use $\alpha = .01$ or .001, and occasionally an exploratory study will use $\alpha = .10$.

38. The probability level selected determines the probability of committing a Type I error, that is, of rejecting a null hypothesis that is really true (A = B).

39. The smaller our probability level is, the larger the mean difference must be in order to be a significant difference.

40. As you decrease the probability of committing a Type I error, you increase the probability of committing a Type II error (not rejecting a null hypothesis when you should).

41. The choice of a probability level, α, is made prior to execution of the study. The researcher considers the relative seriousness of committing a Type I versus a Type II error and selects α accordingly.

42. Rejection of a null hypothesis or lack of rejection only supports or does not support a research hypothesis; it does not "prove" anything.

Two-Tailed and One-Tailed Tests

43. Tests of significance are usually two-tailed.

44. The null hypothesis states that there is no difference between the groups (A = B), and a two-tailed test allows for the possibility that a difference may occur in either direction: Either group mean may be higher than the other (A > B or B > A).

45. A one-tailed test assumes that a difference can occur in only one direction; the null hypothesis states that one group is not better than another (A ≯ B), and the one-tailed test assumes that if a difference occurs it will be in favor of that particular group (A > B).

46. To select a one-tailed test of significance the researcher has to be very sure that a difference can occur in only one direction; this is not very often the case.

47. When appropriate, a one-tailed test has one major advantage: The value resulting from application of the test of significance required for significance is smaller. In other words, it is "easier" to find a significant difference.

Degrees of Freedom

48. After you have determined whether the test will be two-tailed or one-tailed, selected a probability level, and computed a test of significance, you are ready to consult the appropriate table in order to determine the significance of your results.

49. The appropriate table is usually entered at the intersection of your probability level and your degrees of freedom, *df*.

50. Degrees of freedom are a function of such factors as the number of subjects and the number of groups.

51. Each test of significance has its own formula for determining degrees of freedom.

TESTS OF SIGNIFICANCE: TYPES

52. Different tests of significance are appropriate for different sets of data.

53. It is important that the researcher select an appropriate test; an incorrect test can lead to incorrect conclusions.

54. The first decision in selecting an appropriate test of significance is whether a parametric test may be used or whether a nonparametric test must be selected.

55. Parametric tests are usually more powerful and generally to be preferred. By "more powerful" is meant more likely to reject a null hypothesis that is false; in other words, the researcher is less likely to commit a Type II error.

56. Parametric tests require that certain assumptions be met in order for them to be valid:

   a. The variable being measured is normally distributed in the population (or at least the form of the distribution is known).

    b. The data represent an interval scale or a ratio scale of measurement.

    c. The subjects are selected independently for the study; in other words, the selection of one subject in no way affects the selection of any other subject. Every member of the population has an equal and *independent* chance of being selected for the sample.

    d. The variances of the population comparison groups are equal (or at least the ratio of the variances is known).

57. With the exception of independence, some violation of one or more of these assumptions usually does not make too much difference so that the same decision is made concerning the statistical significance of the results.

58. If one or more assumptions are greatly violated, such as if the distribution is extremely skewed, parametric statistics should not be used. In such cases, a nonparametric test should be used. Nonparametric tests make no assumptions about the shape of the distribution.

59. Nonparametric tests are usually used when the data represent an ordinal or nominal scale, when a parametric assumption has been greatly violated, or when the nature of the distribution is not known.

60. If the data represent an interval scale or a ratio scale, a parametric test should be used unless another of the assumptions is greatly violated.

61. Besides being more powerful, parametric tests also have the advantage that they permit tests of a number of hypotheses that cannot be tested with a nonparametric test; there are a number of parametric statistics that have no counterpart among nonparametric statistics.

The *t* Test

62. The *t* test is used to determine whether two means are significantly different at a selected probability level.

63. For a given sample size the *t* indicates how often a difference $(\overline{X}_1 - \overline{X}_2)$ as large or larger would be found when there is no true population difference.

64. The strategy of the *t* test is to compare the *actual* mean difference observed with the difference *expected* by chance. The *t* test involves forming the ratio of these two values. In other words, the numerator for a *t* test is the difference between the sample means $(\overline{X}_1 - \overline{X}_2)$, and the denominator is the chance difference that would be expected if the null hypothesis were true, in other words, the standard error of the difference between the means.

65. The denominator, or error term, is a function of both sample size and group variance.

66. Smaller sample sizes and greater variation within groups are associated with an expectation of greater random differences between groups.

67. The *t* ratio determines whether the observed difference is sufficiently larger than a difference that would be expected by chance.

68. After the numerator is divided by the denominator, the resulting *t* value is compared to the appropriate *t* table value, again using the probability level and the degrees of freedom; if the calculated *t* value is equal to or greater than the table value, then the null hypothesis is rejected.

69. There are two different types of t tests, one for independent samples and one for dependent samples:

   a. *The* t *test for independent samples* is used when samples are randomly formed, that is, formed without any type of matching. If two groups are randomly formed, the expectation is that they are essentially the same at the beginning of the study with respect to performance on the dependent variable. Therefore, if they are essentially the same at the end of the study, the null hypothesis is probably true; if they are different at the end of the study, the null hypothesis is probably false, that is, the treatment or variable probably does make a difference. Thus, the t test for independent samples is used to determine whether there is probably a significant difference between the means of two independent samples. To calculate the t test for independent samples, use the following formula:

$$t = \frac{\overline{X}_1 - \overline{X}_2}{\sqrt{\left(\dfrac{SS_1 + SS_2}{n_1 + n_2 - 2}\right)\left(\dfrac{1}{n_1} + \dfrac{1}{n_2}\right)}}.$$

   For the t test for independent samples, the formula for degrees of freedom is:

$$n_1 + n_2 - 2.$$

   If your t value is equal to or greater than the t table value, you reject the null hypothesis; the means are significantly different at α selected a level.

   b. *The* t *test for nonindependent samples* is used when samples are formed by some type of matching. The ultimate matching, of course, is when the two samples are really the same sample group at two different times, such as one group that receives two different treatments at two different times or that is pretested before a treatment and then posttested. When samples are not independent, the members of one group are systematically related to the members of a second group (especially if it is the same group at two different times). If samples are nonindependent, measures on the dependent variable are expected to be correlated, and a special t test for correlated, or nonindependent, means must be used. The t test for nonindependent samples is used to determine whether there is probably a significant difference between the means of two matched, or nonindependent, samples or between the means for one sample at two different times. In order to calculate the t test for nonindependent samples, use the following formula:

$$t = \frac{\overline{D}}{\sqrt{\dfrac{\Sigma D^2 - \dfrac{(\Sigma D)^2}{N}}{N(N-1)}}}.$$

   For the t test for nonindependent samples, the formula for degrees of freedom is the following:

$$N - 1, \text{ the number of pairs minus 1.}$$

Analysis of Gain or Difference Scores

70. There are a number of problems associated with using gain or difference scores, the major one being a lack of equal opportunity to grow. Every subject does not have the same room to gain.

71. If both groups are essentially the same on the pretest, then posttest scores or measures can be directly compared using a t test.

72. If there is a difference between the groups on the pretest, then the preferred posttest analysis is analysis of covariance.

Analysis of Variance

73. A method of statistical analysis that is useful for studies involving two or more groups is analysis of variance.

74. Essentially the analysis of variance is used to determine whether the normal variance that is seen among subjects is occurring primarily within the sample groups (in which case there may be no significant difference between the groups) or primarily between the groups (in which case there may very well be a significant difference between the groups).

75. The major types of analysis of variance that are used include the following:

a. *Simple analysis of variance* (ANOVA) is used to determine whether there is a significant difference between two or more means at a selected probability level. This technique is also called one-way analysis of variance or simple linear analysis of variance. The concept underlying ANOVA is that the total variation, or variance, of scores can be attributed to two sources—variance between groups (variance caused by the treatment) and variance within groups (error variance). As with the t test, a ratio is formed (the F ratio) with group differences as the numerator (variance between groups) and an error term as the denominator (variance within groups). At the end of the study, after administration of the independent variable (treatment), we determine whether the between groups (treatment) variance differs from the within groups (error) variance by more than what would be expected by chance. ANOVA is based on the fact that

$$SS_{total} = SS_{between} + SS_{within}$$

The formula for $SS_{between}$ is:

$$SS_{between} = \frac{(\Sigma X_1)^2}{n_1} + \frac{(\Sigma X_2)^2}{n_2} + \frac{(\Sigma X_3)^2}{n_3} - \frac{(\Sigma X)^2}{N}.$$

The formula for SS_{total} is:

$$SS_{total} = \Sigma X^2 - \frac{(\Sigma X)^2}{N}.$$

The formula for the between term is $K - 1$, where K is the number of treatment groups. The formula for the within term is $N - K$, where N is the total sample size and K is still the number of treatment groups.

The mean square is determined by dividing each sum of squares by its appropriate degrees of freedom:

$$\text{mean square} = \frac{\text{sum of squares}}{\text{degrees of freedom}} \quad \text{or} \quad MS = \frac{SS}{df}.$$

The F ratio is the ratio of the mean square between (MS_B) and the mean square within (MS_W):

$$F = \frac{MS_B}{MS_W}.$$

If the F ratio is greater than the F table value, you reject the null hypothesis; there is a significant difference among the means. If the F ratio is significant, a multiple-comparison test is applied to determine the relationship between the means; the Scheffé test is most commonly used and is appropriate for making any and all possible comparisons involving a set of means. To calculate the Scheffé test:

$$F = \frac{(\bar{X}_1 - \bar{X}_2)^2}{MS_W\left(\frac{1}{n_1} + \frac{1}{n_2}\right)(K - 1)} \quad \text{with } df = (K - 1), (N - K).$$

The MS_W is the same as that calculated for the ANOVA. The significance of each F is determined using the degrees of freedom from the analysis of variance.

b. *Factorial analysis of variance* is used if a research study is based upon a factorial design and investigates one dependent variable, two or more independent variables, and the interactions between them. Such an analysis yields a separate F ratio for each independent variable and one for each interaction. If more than two variables are involved, it is usually better to use a computer.

c. *Analysis of covariance* (ANCOVA) is another variation of the analysis of variance; it is used in two major ways, as a technique for controlling extraneous variables and as a means of increasing power. Basically ANCOVA is a statistical, rather than an experimental, method that can be used to equate groups on one or more variables. Essentially, ANCOVA adjusts posttest scores for initial differences on some variable and compares adjusted scores. ANCOVA is based on the assumption that subjects have been randomly assigned to treatment groups. It is best used in conjunction with true experimental designs. If existing, or intact, groups are involved but treatments are assigned to groups randomly, ANCOVA may still be used, but results must be interpreted with caution. ANCOVA increases the power of a statistical test by reducing within-group (error) variance. ANCOVAs are usually calculated on the computer because the formula is complex.

d. *Multivariate analysis of variance* (MANOVA) is a statistical technique that may be used when the study involves more than one dependent variable and one or more independent variables. In instances in which covariates are involved, a *multivariate analysis of covariance* (MANCOVA) may be applied.

Multiple Regression

76. A multiple-regression equation uses variables that are known to predict the criterion individually to make a more accurate prediction.

77. Use of multiple regression is increasing, primarily because of its versatility and precision. It can be used with data representing any scale of measurement, and it can be used to analyze the results of experimental and causal-comparative, as well as correlational, studies.

78. It determines not only whether variables are related but also the degree to which they are related.

79. The first step in multiple regression is to identify the variable that *best* predicts the criterion, that is, is most highly correlated with it.

80. The next step is to identify the variable that most improves the prediction, which is based on the first variable only.

81. With increasing frequency, multiple regression is being used as an alternative to the various analysis-of-variance techniques. When this is the case, the dependent variable (perhaps posttest scores or measures) becomes the criterion variable, and the predictors include group membership (experimental versus control) and any other appropriate variables, such as pretest scores.

82. Variations of multiple-regression analysis that are frequently seen in business-and-management research include *stepwise regression analysis*.

83. Computer analysis is almost always used to calculate multiple regression.

Chi Square

84. Chi square, symbolized as χ^2, is a nonparametric test of significance appropriate when the data are in the form of frequency counts occurring in two or more mutually exclusive categories.

85. Chi square compares proportions actually observed in a study with the proportions expected to be seen if they are significantly different.

86. Expected proportions are usually the frequencies that would be expected if the groups were equal; however, they may be based on past data.

87. The chi square can be used to compare frequencies occurring in different categories, or the categories may be groups, so that the chi square is comparing groups with respect to the frequency of occurrence of different events.

88. The chi square may also be used when frequencies are categorized along more than one dimension, sort of a factorial chi square.

89. To calculate chi square, use the following formula:

$$\chi^2 = \sum \left[\frac{(fo - fe)^2}{fe} \right].$$

90. The degrees of freedom for a one-dimensional chi square are determined by the formula $(K - 1)$ where K equals the number of categories.

91. If the chi square value is equal to or greater than the chi square table value, you reject the null hypothesis; there is a significant difference between observed and expected frequencies.

REFERENCES

BrainPower. (1986). *Statview™512+* [computer program]. Calabasas, CA: Abacus Concepts.

Campbell, D. T., & Boruch, R. F. (1975). Making the case for randomized assignment to treatment by considering the alternatives: Six ways in which quasi-experimental evaluations in compensatory education tend to underestimate effects. In C. A. Bennett and A. A. Lumsdaine (Eds.), *Evaluation and experiment: Some critical issues in assessing social programs.* Seattle, WA: Academic Press.

Elasoff, J. D. (1969). Analysis of covariance: A delicate instrument. *American Educational Research Journal, 6,* 383–401.

Evans, S. H., & Anastasio, E. J. (1968). Misuse of analysis of covariance when treatment effect and covariate are confounded. *Psychological Bulletin, 69,* 225–234.

Huck, S. W. (1972). The analysis of covariance: Increased power through reduced variability. *Journal of Experimental Education, 41*(1), 42–46.

Nie, N. H., Hull, C. H., Jenkins, J. G., Steinbrenner, K., & Bent, D. H. (1975). *Statistical package for the social sciences* (2nd ed.). New York: McGraw-Hill.

Roscoe, J. T. (1975). *Fundamental statistics for the behavioral sciences* (2nd ed.). New York: Holt, Rinehart and Winston.

SPSS Inc. (1986). *SPSS^x user's guide* (2nd ed.). New York: McGraw-Hill.

Tabachnick, B. G., & Fidell, L. S. (1989). *Using multivariate statistics* (2nd ed.). New York: Harper & Row.

Winer, B. J. (1971). *Statistical principles in experimental design* (2nd ed.). New York: McGraw-Hill.

. . . all subsequent records have been given a royal escort whenever similar journeys have been called for. (page 545)

13

Postanalysis Procedures

Objectives:

After reading Chapter 13, you should be able to do the following:

1. List at least six guidelines to be followed in verifying and storing data.

2. Explain how a rejected null hypothesis relates to a research hypothesis.

3. Explain how a null hypothesis that is not rejected relates to a research hypothesis.

4. Identify the major use of significant unhypothesized relationships.

5. Explain the difference between statistical and practical significance.

6. Define or describe replication.

VERIFICATION AND STORAGE OF DATA

After you have completed all the statistical analyses necessary to describe your data and test your hypothesis, you do not say, "Thank goodness, I'm done!" and happily throw away all your data and work sheets. Whether you do your statistical analysis by hand, with the aid of a calculator, or with the aid of a computer, all data must be thoroughly checked and stored in an organized manner.

Verification

Verification involves double-checking the input and evaluating the output. Double-checking input may seem a bit excessive, but output is only valid to the degree that input is accurate. There is an old but apt expression, GIGO—Garbage In, Garbage Out. Thus, original scores or measures should be rechecked (or some percentage of them), as well as data sheets. Coded data should be compared with uncoded data to make sure all data were coded properly. If a computer was used and data files created, they should be printed out in "hard copy" (on paper) and compared with data sheets. Considering that the entire study is worthless if inaccurate data are analyzed and considering all the effort expended at this point on the entire study, the time involved in rechecking input is time well spent.

When statistical analyses are done by hand or with a calculator, both the accuracy of computations and the reasonableness of the results need to be checked. You may have noticed that we applied each statistic step by step, leaving no steps to the imagination. This was probably helpful to some and annoying to others. Math superstars seem to derive great satisfaction from doing several steps in a row "in their heads" and writing down the results instead of separately recording the result of each step. This may save time in the short run but not necessarily in the long run. If you end up with a result that just doesn't look right, it's a lot easier to spot an error if every step is in front of you.

Simply checking the steps you followed in arithmetic may not help you spot the problem; you often have to check every value you substituted into the formula to make it an arithmetic problem. A very frustrated student came to one of us with the sad tale that he had been up all night, had rechecked his work over and over and over, and still kept getting a negative sum of squares in his ANOVA. He was at the point where he could easily have been convinced that squares can be negative! A review of his work revealed very quickly that the problem was not in his execution of ANOVA but in the numbers he was using to do the ANOVA. Early in the game he had added ΣX_1^2, ΣX_2^2, and ΣX_3^2, and obtained a number much, much larger than their actual sum. From that point on, he was doomed. The moral of the story is that if you have checked a set of figures several times and they are still correct, do not check them 50 more times; look elsewhere instead. Make sure you are using the correct formula and make sure you have substituted the correct numbers. The anecdote also illustrates that the results should make sense. If your scores range from 20 to 94, and you get a standard deviation of 1.2, you have probably made a mistake somewhere because 1.2 doesn't look reasonable. Similarly, if your means are 24.2 and 26.1 and you get a t ratio of 44.82, you had better recheck everything very carefully.

When analyses are done by computer, output must be carefully checked. Some people are under the mistaken impression that if a result was produced by a computer, it is automatically correct. (These people evidently don't have charge accounts!) Computers may not make mistakes, but people do, and people write the software programs and input the data. A student once came to his instructor excitedly waving a printout. It had run! No error messages! Finis! The problem was that the printout indicated mean IQs for the groups that were numbers like 10.42. The student had obviously given the computer an incorrect instruction concerning the placement of decimal points. Hating to kill the mood but being obligated to say something, the instructor casually asked the student if the results looked OK to him. The instructor's hopes that the student would find his own error were dashed when the student replied, "They *must* be right; the *computer* did them!"

The "blind faith" problem just illustrated is compounded by the number of persons who use the computer to perform analyses they do not understand. Computer usage has been made almost too easy. A person with little or no knowledge of analysis of covariance (ANCOVA), for example, can, by following directions, have a computer perform the analysis. Such a person could not possibly know whether the results make sense. You may now be beginning to see the wisdom of the advice never to use the computer to apply a statistic that you haven't previously done by hand at least once. Also, although you can usually be pretty safe in assuming that the computer will accurately execute each analysis, it is a good idea to spot check. The computer only does what it has been programmed to do, and programming errors do occur. Thus, if the computer gives you six F ratios, calculate at least one yourself; if it agrees with the one the computer gave you, the rest are most probably correct. If this all seems extreme to you, one of our former students did, indeed, use a statistics software program that did just fine—until it got to computing six F ratios—*all* of which were done incorrectly!

Storage

When you are convinced that your work is accurate, all data sheets or cards, work sheets, records of calculations, printouts, and computer disks should be labeled, organized, and filed in a safe place. You never know when you might need your data again. Sometimes an additional analysis is desired either by the original researcher or by another researcher who wishes to analyze the data using a different statistical technique. Also, it is not highly unusual to use data from one study in a later study. Therefore, all of the data should be carefully labeled with as many means of identification as possible, such as the dates of the study, the nature of the treatment group, and whether data are pretest data, posttest data, or data for a control variable (such as years of experience). All work sheets should also be clearly labeled to indicate the identity of the group(s), the analysis, and the scores, for example "claims processing simplification group/standard deviation/posttest." If the same analysis covers more than one page, fully label each page and indicate "page 1 of 4, page 2 of 4, ... " A convenient, practical way to store printed data is in loose-leaf ring binders or notebooks. Notebooks can be labeled on the binding, for example, "Work Simplification Study, Spring, 1992," and pages are not likely to slip out and become lost as they do from manila file folders. Lastly, find a safe place for all and guard it very carefully. Years ago, one of us learned a lesson the hard way. In the process of being moved from one location to another, the box containing all the data for a major study was lost, never to be seen again (you know, like socks in the dryer). Naturally, since that time several requests for the data have been received. Also, since that tragic event, all subsequent records have been given a royal escort whenever similar journeys have been made.

INTERPRETATION OF RESULTS

The result of the application of a test of significance is a number and only a number, a value that is statistically significant or not statistically significant. What it actually *means* requires interpretation by the researcher. The results of statistical analyses need to be interpreted in terms of the purpose of the study, the original research hypothesis, with respect to other studies that have been conducted in the same area of research, and also in terms of practical implications.

Hypothesized Results

The researcher must discuss whether the results support the research hypothesis and why or why not. Minimally this means, for example, that you will state that hypotheses one and two were supported and that hypothesis three was not. The hypotheses that were supported are quite simple to deal with; hypotheses that are not supported require some explanation from the researcher as to suspected reasons why your "educated guess" didn't turn out to be so. Changing your hypothesis, like changing your α, after the fact to fit the findings is absolutely, positively not acceptable — ever!

Similarly, if your results are not in agreement with other research, reasons for the discrepancy must be discussed. There may have been validity problems in your study, or you may have discovered a relationship previously not uncovered. The work of Yvonne Brackbill is a good example of the latter; the results of her studies suggested that contrary to previous evidence derived from animal studies, immediate feedback is not necessarily superior to delayed feedback when human beings are involved, especially with respect to delayed retention (Brackbill & Kappy, 1962). Subsequent studies have confirmed her findings. If, however, you reject a null hypothesis, your research hypothesis may be supported, but it is not proven. One study doesn't "prove" anything; it only shows that in one instance the hypothesis was supported. A supported research hypothesis doesn't necessarily mean that your treatment would "work" with different populations, different materials, and different dependent variables. As an example, if an employee assistance program (EAP) is found to be effective for alcohol abusers, it doesn't necessarily mean that the EAP will be effective for other substance abusers. In other words, do not overgeneralize your findings.

If you do not reject the null hypothesis and your research hypothesis is not supported, you do not apologize. The natural reaction to this situation for beginning researchers is to be very disappointed. In the first place, failure to reject a null hypothesis does not necessarily mean that your research hypothesis is false, but even if it is, it is just as important to know what doesn't work as it is to know what does work; similarly, it is as important to know which variables aren't related as to know which are. This fact is reinforced by the comments of Sutton and Rafaeli (1988, p. 484) who state:

> Finally, we learned much about the role of expressed emotion in organizational life from this research because it entailed two complete cycles of induction and deduction. Unfortunately, however, it is not normative in the organizational studies literature, nor in other scholarly areas, to report unsuccessful efforts at induction or deduction. Studies that find no significant relationships are usually not published. Moreover, we occasionally hear of studies in which the findings contradict initial hypotheses but that are written as if the unexpected results were predicted at the outset of the investigation. The tendency to report only successful predictions persists even though failed predictions offer important lessons about the research process and about organizational life (Mirvis & Berg, 1977). We hope that, in some small way, this research is a step toward changing those norms.

Of course, if there were some serious validity problems with your study, you should describe them in detail. Also, if for some reason you lost a lot of subjects, you should discuss why you lost them, and how the study may have been affected. Recall, for example, that an insufficient number of subjects affects the power of a study and that power refers to statistical ability to reject a false null hypothesis. In other words, if your sample size is too small, you may lack the power to reject the null hypothesis even if it is false. Power is also affected by the type of statistic used (parametric tests are more powerful than nonparametric tests) and by group variance on the dependent variable. In any case, do not rationalize. If your study was well planned and well conducted, and no unforeseen mishaps occurred, don't try to come up with *some* reason why your study didn't "come out right." It may very well have "come out right"; the null hypothesis might be true. But you don't know that. All you know is that it wasn't rejected in your study. In other words, there is no evidence either way concerning the truth or falsity of the hypothesized relationship.

Unhypothesized Results

Unhypothesized results should be interpreted with great care. Often during a study an apparent relationship will be noticed that was not hypothesized. You might notice, for example, that experimental subjects appear to require less time to learn a new method of doing something, an unhypothesized relationship. As stated previously, you don't change your original hypothesis, nor do you slip in a new one; hypotheses must be formulated a priori based on deductions from theory and/or experience. A true test of a hypothesis comes from its ability to explain and predict what *will* happen, not what *is* happening. You can and should, however, collect and analyze data on these unforeseen relationships and present your results as such. These findings may then form the basis for a later study, conducted by yourself or another investigator, specifically designed to test a hypothesis related to your findings. Don't fall into the trap, however, of searching frantically for something—anything!—that might be significant if your study doesn't appear to be going as hypothesized. Fishing expeditions in experimental studies are just as bad as fishing expeditions in correlational studies.

Statistical Versus Practical Significance

We're going to talk about common sense now. The fact that results are statistically significant doesn't automatically mean that they are of any business value. Statistical significance only means that your results would be likely to occur by chance a certain percentage of the time, say 5%. All this means is that the observed relationship or difference is probably a real one, not necessarily an important one. With very large samples, for example, a very small correlation coefficient may be statistically significant but of no real practical use to anybody. Similarly, the error term of the *t* test is affected by the sample size; as the sample size increases, the error term (denominator) tends to decrease, and the *t* ratio increases. Thus, with very large samples a very small mean difference may yield a significant *t*. A mean difference of two points might be statistically significant but probably not worth the effort or expenditure of installing new machinery or a new method of processing materials.

Thus, in a way, the smaller sample sizes typically used in management research actually have a redeeming feature. Given that smaller sample sizes mean less power, and given that a greater mean difference is probably required for rejection of the null hypothesis, more observed relationships are probably significant than if larger samples were involved. Of course, by the same token, this same lack of power may keep the researcher from finding some important relationships. In any event, care (i.e., common sense) should always be taken in interpreting results; before excitedly announcing your results, try to think how your boss's boss will view them from a "big picture" perspective. The fact that method A is significantly more effective than method B *statistically* doesn't mean that the whole world should immediately adopt method A!

Replication of Results

Perhaps the strongest support for a research hypothesis comes from replication of results, i.e., the study is done again. The second (third, etc.) study may be a repetition of the original study, using the same or different subjects, or it may represent an alternative approach to testing the same hypothesis. Although repeating the study with the same subjects (which is feasible only in certain types of research, such as those involving single-subject designs) supports the reliability of results, repeating the study with different subjects in the same or different settings increases the generalizability of the findings (Sidman, 1960). Brackbill's hypothesis concerning the effectiveness of delayed feedback, for example, was increasingly supported as other researchers repeatedly demonstrated the effect with other types of subjects and other learning tasks. The need for replication is especially great when an unusual or new relationship is found in a study or when the results have practical significance and the treatment investigated might really make a difference. Interpretation and discussion of a replicated finding will invariably be less hedgy than a first-time-ever finding, and rightly so.

The significance of a relationship may also be enhanced if it is replicated in a more natural setting. A highly controlled study, for example, might find that method A is more effective than method B in a laboratory-like environment. Interpretation and discussion of the results in terms of practical significance and implications for the real world would have to be stated with due caution. Supporting the effectiveness of method A in the training center is one issue; what happens during the night shift on the factory floor may be entirely different. If the same results can be obtained in a real situation, however, the researcher may be less tentative concerning their generalizability.

Summary/Chapter 13

VERIFICATION AND STORAGE OF DATA

1. Whether you do your analysis by hand, with the aid of a calculator, or with the aid of a computer, all data must be thoroughly checked and stored in an organized manner.

Verification

2. Verification involves double-checking the input and evaluating the output. Double-checking input may seem a bit excessive, but output is only valid to the degree that input is accurate.

3. Original scores or measures should be rechecked (or some percentage of them), as well as data sheets.

4. Coded data should be compared with uncoded data to make sure all data were coded properly.

5. If the computer was used and data files created, they should be printed out in "hard copy" (on paper) and compared with data sheets.

6. When analyses are done by hand or with a calculator, both the accuracy of computations and the reasonableness of the results need to be checked.

7. Simply checking the steps you followed in arithmetic may not help you spot the problem; you often have to check every value you substituted into the formula to make it an arithmetic problem.

8. When analyses are done by computer, output must be checked very carefully.

9. Although you can usually be pretty safe in assuming that the computer will accurately execute each analysis, it is a good idea to spot check.

Storage

10. When you are convinced that your work is accurate, all data sheets or cards, work sheets, records of calculations, printouts, and computer disks should be labeled, organized, and filed in a safe place.

11. All of the data should be carefully labeled with as many means of identification as possible, such as the dates of the study, the nature of the treatment group, and whether data are pretest data, posttest data, or data for a control variable (such as years of experience).

12. All work sheets should also be clearly labeled to indicate the identity of the group(s), the analysis, and the scores, for example "claims processing simplification group/standard deviation/posttest."

INTERPRETATION OF RESULTS

13. The results of statistical analyses need to be interpreted in terms of the purpose of the study, the original research hypothesis, with respect to other studies that have been conducted in the same area of research, and also in terms of practical implications.

Hypothesized Results

14. The researcher must discuss whether the results support the research hypothesis and why or why not.

15. Similarly, if your results are not in agreement with other research, reasons for the discrepancy must be discussed.

16. If you reject a null hypothesis, your research hypothesis may be supported, but it is not proven.

17. A supported research hypothesis doesn't necessarily mean that your treatment would work with different populations, different materials, and different dependent variables.

18. Failure to reject a null hypothesis does not necessarily mean that your research hypothesis is false, but even if it is, it is just as important to know what doesn't work as it is to know what does work; similarly, it is as important to know which variables aren't related as to know which are.

19. In other words, there is no evidence either way concerning the truth or falsity of the hypothesized relationship.

Unhypothesized Results

20. Unhypothesized results should be interpreted with great care.

21. Often during a study an apparent relationship will be noticed that was not hypothesized.

22. A true test of a hypothesis comes from its ability to explain and predict what *will* happen, not what *is* happening.

23. You can and should, however, collect and analyze data on these unforeseen relationships and present your results as such.

24. These findings may then form the basis for a later study, conducted by yourself or another investigator, specifically designed to test a hypothesis related to your findings.

Statistical Versus Practical Significance

25. The fact that results are statistically significant doesn't automatically mean that they are of any business value.

26. With very large samples a very small correlation coefficient may be statistically significant but of no real practical use to anybody; a mean difference of two points might be statistically significant but probably not worth the effort or expenditure of installing new machinery or a new method of processing materials.

Replication of Results

27. Perhaps the strongest support for a research hypothesis comes from replication of results; i.e., the study is done again.

28. The second (third, etc.) study may be a repetition of the original study, using the same or different subjects, or it may represent an alternative approach to testing the same hypothesis.

29. The need for replication is especially great when an unusual or new relationship is found in a study, or when the results have practical significance and the treatment investigated might really make a difference.

30. The significance of a relationship may also be enhanced if it is replicated in a more natural setting.

Project IV Performance Criteria

You are now ready to organize a project on *Results*.

If you are doing a simulated study, the data that you generate (scores or measures you make up for each subject) should make sense. If your dependent variable is number of days absent, for example, don't generate figures such as 225, 275, and 300; generate figures such as 2, 5, and 15. OK? Unlike a real study, you can make this one turn out any way you want!

Table 1

Means, Standard Deviations, and t *for the Daily Feedback and Weekly Feedback Groups on Claims Processing Productivity*

	Group		t
	Daily Feedback	Weekly Feedback	
M	52.68	44.82	2.56[a]
SD	6.00	5.12	

[a]$df = 38$, $p < .05$.

Depending upon the scale of measurement represented by your data, select and compute the appropriate descriptive statistics.

Depending upon the scale of measurement represented by your data, your research hypothesis, and your research design, select and compute the appropriate test of significance. Determine the statistical significance of your results for a selected probability level. Present your results in a summary statement and in a summary table, and relate how the significance or nonsignificance of your results supports or does not support your original research hypothesis. For example, you might say the following:

> Computation of a *t* test for independent samples indicated that the group that received daily feedback produced significantly more ($t = 2.56$, $df = 38$, $p < .05$) than the group that received weekly feedback (see Table 1). Therefore, the original hypothesis that "claims processors who receive daily feedback will process more claims than claims processors who receive weekly feedback" was supported.

Project IV should look like the *Results* sections of a research report. Although your actual calculations should not be part of Project IV, they should be attached to it when you submit it to your instructor.

On the following pages, an example is presented that illustrates the performance called for by Project IV.

Results

A t test for independent samples (α = .05) was used to compare the attitude scores of the experimental and control groups. Random assignment of the employees to the two groups made the t test for independent samples the appropriate test of significance. Results showed that the means for the two groups differed significantly (see Table 1).

Table 1

Means, Standard Deviations, and t Test for the Participatory and Nonparticipatory Groups for Attitude Scores

Attitude Scores	Group		t
	Participatory	Nonparticipatory	
M	13.50	10.98	2.60[a]
SD	2.75	3.38	

[a]df = 38, p < .05

Therefore, the original hypothesis that "employees at companies using participatory budget–planning teams have more positive attitudes toward their jobs and company than employees of companies using traditional, nonparticipatory budget planning" was supported.

1

Worksheet

S	Experimental		Control	
	X_1	$X_1{}^2$	X_2	$X_2{}^2$
1	17.87	319.34	17.82	317.55
2	17.22	296.53	16.50	272.25
3	16.37	267.98	15.42	237.78
4	16.14	260.50	14.10	198.81
5	15.76	248.38	12.39	153.51
6	15.11	228.31	12.26	150.31
7	14.94	223.20	12.02	144.48
8	14.73	216.97	11.75	138.06
9	14.59	212.87	11.61	134.79
10	14.45	208.80	10.93	119.46
11	13.68	187.14	10.46	109.41
12	13.27	176.09	10.43	108.78
13	12.90	166.41	10.27	105.47
14	12.36	152.77	9.54	91.01
15	11.64	135.49	9.48	89.87
16	10.92	119.25	9.16	83.90
17	10.47	109.62	8.71	75.86
18	10.13	102.62	7.02	49.28
19	9.84	96.82	5.27	27.77
20	7.51	56.40	4.42	19.54
	269.90	3,785.49	219.56	2,627.89
	ΣX_1	$\Sigma X_1{}^2$	ΣX_2	$\Sigma X_2{}^2$

$$\bar{X}_1 = \frac{269.90}{20}$$

$$= 13.50$$

$$\bar{X}_2 = \frac{219.56}{20}$$

$$= 10.98$$

$$SS_1 = \Sigma X_1{}^2 - \frac{(\Sigma X_1)^2}{n_1}$$

$$= 3,785.49 - \frac{(269.90)^2}{20}$$

$$= 3,785.49 - \frac{72,846.01}{20}$$

$$= 3,785.49 - 3,642.30$$

$$= 143.19$$

$$SD_1 = \sqrt{\frac{SS_1}{n_1 - 1}} = \sqrt{\frac{143.19}{19}}$$

$$= \sqrt{7.54}$$

$$= 2.75.$$

$$SS_2 = \Sigma X_2{}^2 - \frac{(\Sigma X_2)^2}{n_2}$$

$$= 2,627.89 - \frac{(219.56)^2}{20}$$

$$= 2,627.89 - \frac{48,206.59}{20}$$

$$= 2,627.89 - 2,410.33$$

$$= 217.56$$

$$SD_2 = \sqrt{\frac{SS_2}{n_2 - 1}} = \sqrt{\frac{217.56}{19}}$$

$$= \sqrt{11.45}$$

$$= 3.38$$

2

$$t = \dfrac{\overline{X}_1 - \overline{X}_2}{\sqrt{\left(\dfrac{SS_1 + SS_2}{n_1 + n_2 - 2}\right)\left(\dfrac{1}{n_1} + \dfrac{1}{n_2}\right)}}$$

$$= \dfrac{13.50 - 10.98}{\sqrt{\left(\dfrac{143.19 + 217.56}{20 + 20 - 2}\right)\left(\dfrac{1}{20} + \dfrac{1}{20}\right)}}$$

$$= \dfrac{2.52}{\sqrt{\left(\dfrac{360.75}{38}\right)\left(\dfrac{2}{20}\right)}}$$

$$= \dfrac{2.52}{\sqrt{(9.49)(.10)}}$$

$$= \dfrac{2.52}{\sqrt{.95}}$$

$$= \dfrac{2.52}{.97}.$$

$$\underline{t} = 2.60, \ \underline{df} = 38, \underline{p} < .05$$

Note: The $\underline{t}$ table does not have $\underline{df} = 38$.

To be conservative, I used $\underline{df} = 30$.

3

Experimental Group

STANDARD DEVIATION FOR SAMPLES AND POPULATIONS

STATISTIC	VALUE
NO. OF SCORES (N)	20
SUM OF SCORES (EX)	269.90
MEAN ($\bar{X}$)	13.49
SUM OF SQUARED SCORES (EX^2)	3785.49
SUM OF SQUARES (SS)	143.19
STANDARD DEVIATION FOR A POPULATION	2.68
STANDARD DEVIATION FOR A SAMPLE	2.75

Control Group

STANDARD DEVIATION FOR SAMPLES AND POPULATIONS

STATISTIC	VALUE
NO. OF SCORES (N)	20
SUM OF SCORES (EX)	219.56
MEAN ($\bar{X}$)	10.98
SUM OF SQUARED SCORES (EX^2)	2627.92
SUM OF SQUARES (SS)	217.59
STANDARD DEVIATION FOR A POPULATION	3.30
STANDARD DEVIATION FOR A SAMPLE	3.38

4

```
═══════════════════════════════════════════
         t-TEST FOR INDEPENDENT SAMPLES
═══════════════════════════════════════════

STATISTIC                               VALUE
───────────────────────────────────────────
NO. OF SCORES IN GROUP ONE                 20
SUM OF SCORES IN GROUP ONE             269.90
MEAN OF GROUP ONE                       13.49
SUM OF SQUARED SCORES IN GROUP ONE    3785.49
SS OF GROUP ONE                        143.19
NO. OF SCORES IN GROUP TWO                 20
SUM OF SCORES IN GROUP TWO             219.56
MEAN OF GROUP TWO                       10.98
SUM OF SQUARED SCORES IN GROUP TWO    2627.92
SS OF GROUP TWO                        217.59
t-VALUE                                  2.58
DEGREES OF FREEDOM                         38
═══════════════════════════════════════════

                   END
```

5

REFERENCES

BRACKBILL, Y., & KAPPY, M. S. (1962). Delay of reinforcement and retention. *Journal of Comparative and Physiological Psychology, 55*(1), 14–18.

MIRVIS, P., & BERG, P. (1977). *Failures in organizational development.* New York: Wiley.

SIDMAN, M. (1960). *Tactics of scientific research: Evaluating experimental data in psychology.* New York: Basic Books.

SUTTON, R. I., & RAFAELI, A. (1988). Untangling the relationship between displayed emotions and organizational sales: The case of convenience stores. *Academy of Management Journal, 31*(3), 461–487.

PART FIVE

Research Reports

There are a variety of reasons for which people conduct research. The motivation for doing a research project may be no more than that such a project is a degree requirement, it may stem from a need to improve specific business practices, or it may come from a strong desire to contribute to management theory. Whatever the reason for their execution, most research studies culminate with the production of a research report.

A number of manuals are available that describe various formats and styles for writing research reports, although there are a number of elements that are common to most reports regardless of the format followed. Virtually all research reports, for example, contain a statement of the problem, a description of the procedures, and a presentation of results. Further, all research reports have a common purpose, namely, to communicate as clearly as possible the purpose, procedures, and findings of the study. A well-written report describes a study in sufficient detail to permit replication by another researcher.

You have already written many of the components of a research report through your work in Parts Two, Three, and Four. In Part Five you will integrate all your previous efforts to produce a complete report.

The goal of Part Five is for you, having conducted a study, to be able to produce a complete report. After you have read Part Five, you should be able to perform the following project:

Project V Guidelines

Based on Projects II, III, and IV, prepare a research report that follows the general format for a thesis or dissertation.

See Performance Criteria, p. 580

The research report should . . . reflect scholarship. (page 562)

14

Preparation of a Research Report

Objectives

After reading Chapter 14, you should be able to do the following:

1. List 10 general rules for writing and preparing a research report.

2. Identify and briefly describe the major sections and subsections of a research report.

3. List four major differences between a research report prepared as a thesis or dissertation and a research report prepared as a manuscript for publication.

4. List two guidelines for presenting a paper at a professional meeting.

5. Discuss the two major ways of presenting research material within a company.

6. Discuss the differences between academic reports such as theses and dissertations and in-house reports such as the executive summary.

GENERAL GUIDELINES

If you carefully prepare a research plan before you conduct your study, you have a good head start on writing your research report, especially the introduction section. While you are conducting your study, you can profitably use any free time you have by revising and refining the introduction and method sections of the report, which is one of the reasons we urged you to use word processing in all of your work. The study may not be executed exactly as planned, but the procedures should not diverge drastically from the original plan. When the study is completed, the final draft of the method section can incorporate any final changes in procedures. After all the data are analyzed, you are ready to write the final sections of the report. The major guideline previously described for analyzing, organizing, and reporting related literature is applicable to this task—make an outline. The chances of your results and conclusions being presented in an organized, logical manner are greatly increased if the sequence is thought through before anything is actually written. Formulation of an outline greatly facilitates the thinking-through process. To review briefly, development of an outline involves identification and ordering of major topics followed by differentiation of each major heading and logical subheadings. The time spent in working on an outline is well worth it, since it is much easier to reorganize an outline that is not quite right than to reorganize a document written in paragraph form. Any of the outlining programs discussed in Chapter 2 may be used at this point. Your first report draft will almost never be your last; two or three revisions of each section are to be expected, because each time you read a section you will see ways to improve its organization or clarity. Also, other people who review your report for you, such as your instructor or boss, will see areas in need of rethinking or rewording that you have not noticed.

While the research plan may have been written in the future tense ("subjects *will* be randomly selected . . ."), by the time you get to the research report the party is over and each section is written in the past tense ("subjects *were* randomly selected"). Further, in addition to conscientiously following a selected style and format, there are several general rules of good report writing that the researcher should know and follow.

General Rules for Writing and Typing

Probably the foremost rule of research report writing is that the writer must be as objective as possible. A research report is a scientific document, not a novel or treatise. In other words, the report should not contain subjective statements ("*clearly* strict supervision is no good"), overstatements ("*excellent* results!"), or emotional statements ("every year downtrodden airline workers suffer from the unethical practices of greedy employers"). Further, the report should not be written as if it were a legal brief intended to present arguments in favor of a position ("the purpose of this study was to *prove* . . ."). The research report should contain an objective, factual description of past research and the study upon which the report is based. In discussing the implications of the study and making recommendations for future research or action, a little more latitude is permitted. Even so, in very formal writing, personal pronouns such as *I, my, we,* and *our* should be avoided where possible. In cases where this is required, impersonal pronouns and the passive voice may be substituted for personal pronouns; "I determined . . . " may be stated "It was determined . . . ," for example, or "We randomly selected subjects . . . " may be written "Subjects were randomly selected."

The research report should be written in a clear, simple, straightforward style; you don't have to be boring, just concise. Say what you have to say in the fewest number of words using the simplest language. Instead of saying, "The population comprised all exempt human resources currently endeavoring at Mucky Muck Industries," just say, "The population was all salaried employees at Mucky Muck Industries." This is not the time to try to be cited for doublespeak as when workers who are fired are described as "initating a career-enhancement program," or hospitalized patients who die are characterized as suffering from "diagnostic misadventure of a high magnitude," or farm animals are referred to as "grain-consuming animal units" that are kept in "single-purpose agricultural structures," i.e., pig pens or chicken coops (Elgood, 1990). The research report should also reflect scholarship; correct spelling, grammar, and punctuation are not too much to expect of a scientific report—or of you! Do not say you are the world's worst speller; even if you don't have a spelling program on your computer, you do have access to a dictionary. Some computer programs will check grammar, but if you are in doubt, a number of books may be consulted including *Webster's Dictionary of English Usage* (1989), *Harbrace College Handbook* (Hodges, Whitten, Horner, Webb, & Miller, 1990), and *The Elements of Style* (Strunk & White, 1979). It is also a good idea to have someone you know, someone who is perhaps stronger in these areas, review your manuscript for you and indicate errors. Another little trick that may work is simply to read your manuscript aloud (lock yourself in the bathroom); it's amazing what you "hear" that you weren't able to "see."

While different style manuals suggest different rules of writing, there are several rules that are common to most manuals. Use of abbreviations and contractions, for instance, is generally discouraged. Rather than saying "American Bankers Ass'n", or "ABA", say "American Bankers Association." Exceptions to the abbreviation rule include commonly used and understood abbreviations, such as IQ, and abbreviations defined by the researcher to promote clarity, simplify presentation, or reduce repetition. If the same sequence of words is going to be used repeatedly, the researcher will often define an abbreviation in parentheses the first time the sequence is used and thereafter use only the abbreviation, for example, "the American Bankers Association (ABA)" and subsequently, "the ABA . . . " In formal writing, contractions such as *shouldn't, isn't,* and *won't* should be avoided as well. Authors are usually cited by last name only in the main body of the report; first names, initials, and titles are not given. Instead of saying, "Professor Dudley Q. McStrudle (1990) concluded . . . ," you would say, "McStrudle (1990) concluded . . . " These guidelines hold only for the main body of the report. Tables, figures, footnotes, and references may include abbreviations, while footnotes and references usually give at least the author's initials. With regard to numbers, most style manuals suggest that if the first word of the sentence is a number ("Twenty-five employees were tested") or if the number is nine or less ("a total of three surveys"), numbers are usually expressed as words. Otherwise, numbers are generally expressed as Arabic numerals ("a total of 500 questionnaires were sent"); if one number in a sentence is expressed as an Arabic numeral, all numbers pertaining to the same category are (not "Of 500 surveys only six were returned," but rather, "Of 500 surveys only 6 were returned.").

The same standards of scholarship applied to writing the report also apply to the typing. Reports that are full of typos lead readers to wonder if the study was done as carelessly as the typing. If you have someone else do your typing, you are still responsible for the appearance of the paper. As one style manual states,

> The author is responsible for the quality of presentation of all aspects of the paper: correct spelling and punctuation, accurate quotations with page numbers, complete and accurate references, relevant content, coherent organization, legible appearance, and so forth. . . . The typist is responsible only for accurate transcription of the manuscript [and] should type only what appears in the author's draft except for minor technical errors, such as an occasional misspelled word (American Psychological Association, 1983, p. 136).

If you have any special instructions such as not to split words at the end of a line, share them with your typist and be sure they are understood. You may want to give your typist a copy of the style manual you are following to ensure that required guidelines (such as size of margins, placement of page numbers, and formats for cover pages) are followed. In the final analysis, however, the responsibility for proofreading is yours; reading the report aloud again may help you find errors that are easily overlooked during silent reading.

We cannot say enough about the benefits of computer word processing in writing your report. So many features such as the ability to edit, check spelling and grammar, alphabetize, and arrange items such as references in standard formats are available with word processing that the old electric typewriter is truly an endangered species. Review Chapter 2 for specific suggestions of word processing programs that will enable you to accomplish many of these purposes. In addition, high-quality printing, including laser printing, allows you to produce results that are virtually identical to excellent typed or even printed quality.

Format and Style

Most research reports consistently follow a selected system for format and style. While many such systems are available, a given report usually strictly follows one of them. Format refers to the general pattern of organization and arrangement of the report. The number and types of headings and subheadings to be included in the report are determined by the format used. Style refers to the rules of spelling, capitalization, punctuation, and typing followed in preparing the report. While specific formats may vary in terms of specific headings included, all research reports follow a similar format that parallels not only the steps involved in conducting the study but also the sections of this textbook. One format may call for a discussion section, for example, while another may require a summary, conclusions, and recommendations section (or both), but all formats for a research report entail a section in which the results of the study are discussed and interpreted. All research reports should also include a condensed description of the study, whether it be a summary of a dissertation or an abstract of a journal article.

Most colleges, universities, and professional journals either have developed their own, required style manual or have selected one that must be followed. One such manual, which is increasingly being adopted as the required guide for theses and dissertations, as well as professional journals in business and management, is the *Publication Manual* (American Psychological Association, 1983). This format is becoming increasingly popular, primarily because it eliminates the need for formal footnotes at the bottom of the page; it has been used throughout this book and in the student examples. If you are not bound by any particular format and style system, this manual, usually referred to as the APA manual, is recommended.

TYPES OF RESEARCH REPORTS

Research reports usually take the form of a thesis, dissertation, journal article, paper read at a professional meeting, or executive summary and report in a particular business. In fact, the same report may take several forms; dissertation studies frequently are described at professional meetings and prepared for publication. Similarly, a research report in business might be presented at a meeting as well as written up as an executive summary. As mentioned previously, and as you probably noticed when you reviewed the literature related to your problem, the components of all research reports are very similar. Depending upon its form, the report may be divided into sections or chapters, but these divisions are similar in content. We will begin with the longest type of report, the dissertation, and conclude with the briefest, the executive summary.

Dissertations

While specifics will vary considerably, most research reports prepared for a degree requirement follow the same general format. Figure 14.1 presents an outline of the typical contents of such a report. As Figure 14.1 indicates, theses and dissertations include a set of fairly standard preliminary pages, components that directly parallel the research process, and supplementary information, which is included in appendixes.

PRELIMINARY PAGES
     Title page
     Approval page
     Acknowledgment page
     Abstract
     Table of contents
     List of tables
     List of figures
MAIN BODY OF THE REPORT
     Introduction
          Statement of the problem
          Review of related literature
          Statement of the hypothesis
     Method
          Subjects
          Instruments
          Design
          Procedure
     Results
     Discussion (conclusions and recommendations)
     References (bibliography)
APPENDIXES
     Author's vita

Figure 14.1. Common components of a research report submitted for a degree requirement

Preliminary Pages

The preliminary pages set the stage for the report to follow and indicate where in the report each component, table, and figure may be found:

1. The *title page* usually indicates the title of the report, the author's name, the degree requirement being fulfilled, the name and location of the college or university awarding the degree, the date of the submission of the report, and signatures of approving committee members (although approvals may be listed on a separate page). The title should be brief (15 words or less, as a rule of thumb), and at the same time it should describe the purpose of the study as clearly as possible. Unnecessary words such as "A study of" or "An investigation of" may be omitted, but the title should at least indicate the major independent and dependent variables, and sometimes it names the population studied. For example, review the following titles from an issue of the *Academy of Management Journal:*

"Strategic change: The effects of founding and history" (Boeker, 1989)

"Work-related consequences of smoking cessation" (Manning, Osland & Osland, 1989)

"Inertia and creeping rationality in strategic decision processes" (Frederickson & Iaquinto, 1989)

Each of these titles specifies the relationship that was investigated. A good title clearly communicates what the study is about. Recall that when you reviewed the literature and looked under key words in the various indexes, you made decisions based on titles listed concerning whether the articles were probably related or not related to your problem. When the titles were well constructed it was fairly easy to determine the probable relationship or lack of relationship to your problem; when they were vaguely worded it was difficult to determine without examining the report of the study. After you write your title, apply the communication test: Would *you* know what the study was about if you read the title in an index?

2. The *acknowledgment page* permits the writer to express appreciation to persons who have contributed significantly to the completion of the report. Notice the word *significant.* Everyone who had anything to do with the study or the report cannot (and should not) be mentioned. It is appropriate to thank your major professor for her or his guidance and assistance as well as your boss or company contact person; it is not appropriate to thank your third-grade teacher for giving you confidence in your ability.

3. The *abstract* is required by some colleges and universities, while others require a summary; the current trend is in favor of abstracts. The content of abstracts and summaries is identical; only the positioning differs. Whereas an abstract precedes the main body of the report, a summary follows the discussion section. The size of the abstract will determine the amount of detail permitted and its emphasis. Abstracts are often required to be no more than a given maximum number of words, usually between 100 and 500. Shorter abstracts usually concentrate more on the problem and on the results than on the method. Since the abstract of a report is often the only part read (remember when you did your review of the literature?) it should describe

the most important aspects of the study, including the problem investigated, the type of subjects and instruments involved, the design, the procedures, and the major results and conclusions. A reader should be able to tell from an abstract exactly what a study was about and what it found. You will probably want to review the research articles printed at the end of Chapters 1, 6, 7, 8, and 9 for examples of abstracts.

4. The *table of contents* is basically an outline of your report, which indicates on which page each major section (or chapter) and subsection begins. Entries listed in the table of contents should be identical to the headings and subheadings in the report.

5. The *list of tables* is presented on a separate page and gives the number and title of each table and the page on which it can be found. Table titles should be exactly as they are given for the actual tables. As an example:

List of Tables

Table   Page

1. Means and standard deviations for all tests by group and experiment....................22
2. Analysis of variance of production figures for traditional and
   work-simplification subjects for experiment 1 25

---

6. The *list of figures* is also presented on a separate page and gives the number and exact title of each figure and the page on which it can be found:

List of Figures

Figure   Page

1. Experimental designs for experiment 1 and experiment 2 14
2. Plot of production figures for all groups before and after
   each training and practice session 23

It might be noted, however, that if only one table and one figure are presented in the report, it would probably make sense to combine these as a list of tables and figures and present them on one page. If you take this option, however, be sure to list tables before figures. This is called *parallel construction* and indicates that whatever you list first should continue to be discussed first, and so on.

The Main Body of the Report

With the exception of the section for discussion, you are already quite familiar with the major components of a research report. Therefore, we will review each of these components briefly and will discuss the discussion section in more depth. The major components include the following:

1. The *introduction* is already written and in pretty good shape if the researcher carefully developed a research plan prior to conducting the study. The introduction section includes these elements:

a. statement of the problem

b. review of related literature

c. statement of the hypothesis or hypotheses

d. definition of terms

A well-written statement of a problem generally indicates the variables, and the specific relationship between those variables, investigated in the study. The statement should be accompanied by a presentation of the background of the problem, including a justification for the study in terms of the significance of the problem.

The review of related literature describes and analyzes what has already been done related to the problem. The review of related literature is not a series of abstracts or annotations but rather an analysis of the relationships and differences among related studies and reports. The review should flow in such a way that the least-related references are discussed first and the most-related references are discussed last, just prior to the statement of the hypothesis. The review should conclude with a brief summary of the literature and its implications.

A good hypothesis states as clearly and concisely as possible the expected relationship (or difference) between two variables and defines those variables in operational, measurable terms. The hypothesis (or hypotheses) logically follows the review of related literature; it is based upon the implications of previous research. A well-developed hypothesis is testable; that is, it can be confirmed or disconfirmed through the collection and analysis of data.

The introduction also includes the operational definition of terms used in the study that do not have a commonly known meaning or for which several meanings may be used. Some institutions require that one section of the introduction be devoted to defining all the terms in one place. Usually, however, it is better to define each term the first time it appears in the report.

2. The *method* section, like the introduction, is already written and included in the research plan. The procedure portion may require some revision, but even it should be in reasonably good shape. The method section includes these elements:

a. description of the subjects

b. description of the instrument(s)

c. description of the design

d. description of the procedure

e. important assumptions and limitations

The description of subjects includes demographics regarding the subjects and also a specific description of the way they were selected. In addition, this section provides a definition and description of the population from which the sample was selected. The description of the population should indicate its size and major characteristics such as age, experience level, educational level, and any other variable that might be related to performance on the dependent variable. A good description of the population enables the reader of the report to determine how similar the study subjects were to the population with which the reader is involved and thus how applicable the results might be; readers interested in applying study results to a small factory in the Midwest need to know that the study was done with office workers in a multiethnic Eastern city.

The description of instruments should identify and describe all instruments used to collect data pertinent to the study, be they tests, questionnaires, interview or observation forms, or unobtrusive data such as absenteeism reports or productivity figures. The description of each instrument or means of measurement should relate the function of the instrument in the study (for example, selection of subjects or measurement of the dependent variable), what the instrument is intended to measure, and data related to reliability and validity. If an instrument such as a questionnaire has been developed by the researcher, the description needs to be more detailed and should relate the manner in which it was developed. It should also state pretesting and validation efforts, subsequent instrument revisions, steps involved in scoring and determining reliability, and guidelines for interpretation. A copy of the instrument itself, accompanying scoring keys, and other pertinent data related to a newly developed test are generally placed in the appendix of the thesis or dissertation.

The description of the design, including a diagram, is especially important in an experimental study. In other types of research the description of the design may be combined with the procedure. In an experimental study, the description of the basic design (or variation of a basic design) applied in the study should include a rationale for selection and a discussion of sources of invalidity associated with the design, and why and how they may have been minimized in the study being reported.

The procedure portion should describe each step followed in conducting the study, in chronological order, in sufficient detail to permit the study to be replicated by another researcher. In the physical sciences it is not unusual for procedures to be 5 to 10 pages in length to accommodate the need for replication. It should make clear exactly how subjects and also treatments were assigned to groups. The time and conditions of any pretest administrations should be described, followed by a detailed explanation of the study itself. The ways in which groups were different (the treatment or independent variable) should be clearly delineated as well as ways in which they were similar (the control procedures). Any unforeseen events that occurred that might have affected the results should be discussed in terms of their seriousness and probable consequences. Also, any insights regarding ways to improve procedures should be shared so that other researchers may profit from the investigator's experiences.

3. The *results* section describes the statistical techniques that were applied to the data and the results of each analysis. For each hypothesis, the statistical test of significance selected and applied to the data is described, followed by a statement indicating whether the hypothesis was supported or not supported. Tables and figures are used to present findings in summary or graph form and add clarity to the presentation. Tables present numerical data in rows and columns and usually include descriptive statistics, such as means and standard deviations, and the results of tests of significance, such as t and F ratios. While a figure may be any nontabular presentation of information (such as a diagram or chart), figures in the results section are usually graphical presentations of data. Figures can often be used to show relationships not

evident in tabular presentations of data. Interactions, for example, are clearer when illustrated in a figure. If figures are based on numerical data, that data should be presented in a table or in the figure itself. Good tables and figures are uncluttered and self-explanatory; it is better to use two tables or figures than one that is crowded. They should stand alone, that is, be interpretable without the aid of related textual material. Tables and figures follow their related textual discussion and are referred to by number, not name or location. In other words, the text should say "see Table 1," not "see the table with the means" or "see the table on the next page."

Figure 14.2 illustrates appropriate use and format of tables and figures. The authors (Kesner, Victor, & Lamont, 1986) investigated the relationship between inclusion of outside board members on corporation boards and the commission of illegal acts by the corporation in an effort to evaluate the effectiveness of the trend toward including outsiders as a means of reducing questionable practices. No significant relationship was found between the proportion of outsiders and the number of illegal acts; further, firms with a majority of outsiders did not differ significantly from those with a majority of insiders with regard to illegal acts. In order to determine whether prosecution for illegal acts caused firms to change the structure of their boards, data were divided into 2-year periods, shown in Figure 14.2, and regression analyses based on this causal model are presented as Table 14.1. This analysis led to the conclusions that (a) illegal acts are not related to changes in board structure, and (b) there is no evidence that board structure is related to the commission of illegal acts.

4. The *discussion* section is included in every research report; it allows for the discussion and interpretation of results, conclusions, implications, and recommenda-

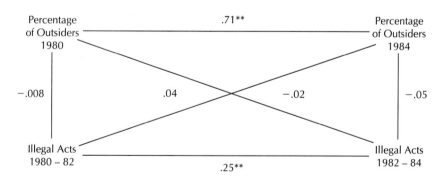

Illegal acts 1980–82 refers to the number of illegal acts between the first quarter of 1980 and the second quarter of 1982. Illegal acts 1982–84 refers to the number of illegal acts between the third quarter of 1982 and the fourth quarter of 1984. Values on paths are standardized coefficients (β's).

**$p < .01$

Source: Adapted from "Board Composition and the Commission of Illegal Acts: An Investigation of *Fortune* 500 Companies" by I. F. Kesner, B. Victor, and B. T. Lamont, 1986, *Academy of Management Journal*, 4, p. 797. Copyright 1986 by *Academy of Management Journal*. Adapted by permission.

Figure 14.2. Board composition and illegal acts, cross-lagged panel analysis.

Table 14.1

Results of Regression Analysis of Determinants of Illegal Acts and Board Composition

Independent Variables	Percentage of Outsiders, 1984		Numbers of Illegal Acts			
			1980		1984	
	β	t	β	t	β	t
Percentages of outsiders						
1980	.680	19.80**	−.006	−.16	.13	.21
1984					−.49	−.75
Numbers of illegal acts						
1980	.003	.97			.19	5.10**
1984	.003	−.75				
R^2		.51		.0001		.06
F		131.18		.03		8.67

**$p < .01$

Source: Adapted from Board Composition and the Commission of Illegal Acts: An Investigation of *Fortune* 500 Companies by I. F. Kesner, B. Victor, and B. T. Lamont, 1986, *Academy of Management Journal, 4*, p. 797. Copyright 1986 by *Academy of Management Journal*. Adapted by permission.

tions. Interpretation of results may be presented in a separate section titled "Discussion," or it may be included in the same section as the other analysis of results items. If only one hypothesis was tested and/or if the discussion is brief, it may be included in the results section. What this section is called is unimportant; what is important is how well it is done. Each result is discussed in terms of the original hypothesis to which it relates and in terms of its agreement or disagreement with previous results obtained by other researchers in other studies. Two common errors committed by beginning researchers are (a) to confuse results and conclusions and (b) to overgeneralize results. A result is the outcome of a test of significance, for example, the mean of group 1 is found to be significantly larger than the mean of group 2. The corresponding conclusion is that the original hypothesis was supported and that method A was more effective than method B. Overgeneralization refers to the statement of conclusions that are not warranted by the results. For example, if a group of bank-management trainees receiving individual mentoring were found to receive higher first-year performance evaluations than a group of trainees without formal mentoring, it would be an overgeneralization to conclude that mentoring is critical to career advancement for management employees.

The researcher should also discuss the theoretical and practical implications of the findings and make recommendations for future research or future action. In this portion of the report the researcher is permitted more freedom in expressing opinions that are not necessarily direct outcomes of data analysis. He or she is free to discuss any possible revisions or additions to existing theory and to encourage studies designed to test hypotheses suggested by the results. The researcher may also discuss implications of the findings for business or management practice and suggest studies designed to replicate the study in other settings and with other subjects in order to increase the generalizability of the findings. The researcher may also suggest next-step studies designed to investigate another dimension of the problem. For example, a study finding the type of mentoring to be a factor in career advancement might suggest that the amount of mentoring may also be a factor and recommend future research in that area.

5. The *references* section, or bibliography, lists all the sources, alphabetically by authors' last names, that were directly used in writing the report. Most of the references will, of course, appear in the introduction section of the report. Every source cited in the paper must be included in the references, and every entry listed in the references must appear in the paper; in other words, the sources in the paper and the sources in the references must correspond exactly. The style manual, such as the APA manual, will give you the correct procedure for all in-text and reference citations. For thesis and dissertation studies, if sources were consulted that were not directly cited in the main body of the report, these may be included in an appendix; also, when reference lists are quite lengthy, they may be subdivided into sections such as "Books," "Articles," and "Unpublished." Again, the style manual will determine the form. This form is usually different for books, journal articles, and magazine articles.

Appendixes

Appendixes are usually necessary in thesis and dissertation reports. Appendixes include information and data pertinent to the study that either are not important enough to be included in the main body of the report or are too lengthy. Appendixes contain such entries as materials especially developed for the study (tests, questionnaires, and cover letters, for example), raw data, and data-analysis sheets. Infrequently, an index may be required. An index alphabetically lists all items of importance or interest in the report and the page on which each can be found. The longer the document, the more useful an index will be. Also, a number of universities ask that a vita be included. The vita is a short autobiography describing professionally related activities and experiences of the author. Information typically included in a vita describes educational training and degrees earned, professional work experience, memberships in professional organizations, and publications, if any. Often your résumé will suffice.

Journal Articles

Preparation of a research report for publication in a professional journal serves the interest of the professional community as well as that of the researcher. Progress in research requires that researchers share their efforts so that others may profit from and build upon them. Dissertations and theses are not read nearly as often as professional journals; thus, publication in a frequently read journal permits the largest possible audience to read about and use the findings of a research study. From a personal point of view, it is definitely to the researcher's advantage, especially the new graduate, to have work published. When you are applying for a position, for example, most of what a prospective employer knows about you is what he or she reads about you in your résumé. Since a newly graduated individual is likely to be short on professional experience, having a published work will make you stand out.

Based on your review of related literature and your references, you should be able to identify two or three journals that publish studies in the area of research represented by your study. Examination of a recent issue should give you some guidance concerning the format, style, and length that are acceptable to the selected journal. In addition, most journals include a section giving instructions for submitting manuscripts.

If your formal report is quite lengthy, you may want to make it into two articles, especially if there is more than one hypothesis. To shorten a report in another way, you can edit the introduction and method sections to include only the critical information; the results and conclusions are of greater potential interest to readers and, therefore, are left pretty much as they stand. It's probably a good idea to ask someone at your college or university to review your article before you submit it; once it is sent off, it will usually be subject to a *blind review,* meaning that the information identifying you or your institution is not known to the reviewers. If your article is not accepted, you will often be given the reviewers' comments and can use them for revision before you submit the article to another journal. Although it is considered unethical to submit an article to more than one journal at a time, it is perfectly OK to revise it and submit it to another journal if you are rejected by the first.

Results Presented at Professional Meetings

Essentially there are two types of professional meetings that may be interested in your research—those that emphasize research and those that emphasize good practice. If you choose the first, you should be prepared to be somewhat more scholarly in your presentation. In fact, your presentation will be similar to the material included in a journal article, and although it may have been submitted for publication, it should not have been published before the meeting. In this sort of meeting, you will want to present the highlights of your research and have copies of your paper available for those who are interested.

In the "good practice" sort of professional meeting, the emphasis will be less on your research and very much more on the practical implications of your study. Often the participants in this sort of meeting will have little or no idea, for example, of what you're talking about if you refer to a *t* test or an *F* ratio—remember yourself just a few months ago? They will have a keen interest, however, in finding out exactly what you did and how it worked out. The key, in both instances, is to gear your presentation to your audience. It is wise to attend one of these meetings before you present your study so you can assess the type of presentation that is successful. In fact, most professional associations have student chapters or will give student rates for attendance so that you can get a preview of what to expect. Either way, determine the length of time you will have and what the expectations are. Most important of all, don't read your report to the audience; any nervousness you may experience can be covered fairly well by some good graphics (e.g., slides or overhead projections) that can be seen by everyone. The trick is to get the audience more interested in your fascinating study than they are in you. All of which brings us to presenting your findings in the actual work setting. This may happen through a meeting, a written report, or both.

In-House Reports

If you do your study within a company, undoubtedly it's a good idea to determine beforehand what the format for reporting will be. If the report is to be presented at a meeting, try to attend a similar meeting first or at least get someone who goes to such meetings fairly often to fill you in on what to expect. Again, remember that most of your audience will not know—and may very well be turned off by—research jargon, so it's a good idea to tone down the technical research terminology while still getting your point across. Figures and tables are extremely helpful—but not necessarily the ones that list means, standard deviations, F ratios, and so on. This is your backup ammunition that allows you to speak with confidence about your findings and recommendations. Again, graphics that present your conclusions clearly and concisely are a terrific support. Slides and overhead projections are not difficult to make and are well worth the effort. Remember to keep the presentations clear and simple; one idea or concept per graphic is acceptable. A rehearsal for such events is always in order, and it's particularly helpful to find an audience (spouse or best friend) who doesn't know anything about research to listen to you and tell you if you make sense. This is *not* the time to allow your feelings to be hurt!

Similarly, if your report is to be made in writing, a simple rule of thumb is to remember that most executives don't want to read more than one page. Yes, one! And not your abstract, which probably has too much jargon in it. One of the authors had a professor once whose midterm exam was to present all the material from the first half of the course in two typed pages; it took a *lot* of editing to get that down, with several well-thought-out graphics as support! The key here is edit, edit, edit. Each word has to be worth its weight in gold and really work for you. Your written report will usually include at least the following:

1. *Title page,* including report title, organization, your name, the organization, and the date.
2. *Executive summary,* giving a very brief review of the method, more emphasis on the results, and clearly stated recommendations.
3. *Table of contents* listing each heading and subheading and the page on which each may be found.
4. *Introduction,* in which the background of the problem may be found. Also, your review of the literature may be summarized primarily with an eye toward what others in the industry or related industries are doing or have tried to do.
5. *Method,* which includes a brief review of your subjects, instruments, and procedures.

6. *Conclusions and recommendations,* which will contain your findings, in both written and graphic form, and your specific recommendations for future action.

7. *Appendix,* which contains any other information needed to understand your report, including copies of any questionnaires or other instruments you may have used. If large or complicated tables or figures are included in your report and you think they will distract the reader, these may also be placed in the appendix.

All of our recommendations regarding typing and attractiveness of your report apply even more to the report presented to a company. Just as you want your résumé to reflect your professionalism, you will want your research report to represent you as a professional. One of the authors recalls seeing a copy of an executive summary containing misspellings, errors in grammar, and amateurish graphics and charts that had been presented to a company; the only printable comment was, "Don't you have word processing? Spelling programs? Computer-generated graphics?" You went to a lot of effort to obtain professional training in your field; let it show.

Summary/Chapter 14

GENERAL GUIDELINES

1. If you carefully prepare a research plan before you conduct your study, you have a good head start on writing your research report.

2. The major guideline previously described for analyzing, organizing, and reporting related literature is applicable to this task—make an outline.

3. Development of an outline involves identification and ordering of major topics followed by differentiation of each major heading and logical subheadings.

4. The research report is written in the past tense.

General Rules for Writing and Typing

5. Probably the foremost rule of research report writing is that the writer must be as objective as possible.

6. A research report is a scientific document, so it should not contain subjective statements, overstatements, or emotional statements.

7. The report should not be written as if it were a legal brief intended to present arguments in favor of a position.

8. The report should contain an objective, factual description of past research and the study upon which the report is based.

9. In discussing the implications of the study and making recommendations for future research or action, a little more latitude is permitted.

10. In very formal writing, personal pronouns such as *I, my, we,* and *our* should be avoided where possible.

11. The research report should be written in a clear, simple, straightforward style; you don't have to be boring, just concise.

12. Say what you have to say in the fewest number of words using the simplest language.

13. The research report should also reflect scholarship; correct spelling, grammar, and punctuation are not too much to expect of a scientific report.

14. While different style manuals suggest different rules of writing, there are several rules that are common to most manuals. Use of abbreviations and contractions, for instance, is generally discouraged.

15. Authors are usually cited by last name only in the main body of the report; first names, initials, and titles are not given.

16. Tables, figures, footnotes, and references may include abbreviations, while footnotes and references usually give at least the author's initials.

17. With regard to numbers, most style manuals suggest that if the first word of the sentence is a number or if the number is nine or less, numbers are usually expressed as words. Otherwise, numbers are generally expressed as Arabic numerals; if one number in a sentence is expressed as an Arabic numeral, all numbers pertaining to the same category are.

18. The same standards of scholarship applied to writing the report also apply to the typing. If you have someone else do your typing, you are still responsible for the appearance of the paper.

Format and Style

19. Most research reports consistently follow a selected system for format and style.

20. Format refers to the general pattern of organization and arrangement of the report.

21. Style refers to the rules of spelling, capitalization, punctuation, and typing followed in preparing the report.

22. While specific formats may vary in terms of specific headings included, all research reports follow a similar format that parallels the steps involved in conducting the study.

23. Most colleges, universities, and professional journals either have developed their own, required style manual or have selected one that must be followed.

TYPES OF RESEARCH REPORTS

24. Research reports usually take the form of a dissertation, journal article, paper read at a professional meeting, or executive summary and report in a particular business.

25. Depending upon its form, the report may be divided into sections or chapters but these divisions are similar in content.

Dissertations

26. Preliminary Pages
The preliminary pages set the stage for the report to follow and indicate where in the report each component, table, and figure may be found:

   a. The *title page* usually indicates the title of the report, the author's name, the degree requirement being fulfilled, the name and location of the college or university awarding the degree, the date of the submission of the report, and signatures of approving committee members. The title should be brief but should at least indicate the major independent and dependent variables.

b. The *acknowledgment page* permits the writer to express appreciation to persons who have contributed significantly to the completion of the report.

c. The *abstract* is required by some colleges and universities, while others require a summary; the current trend is in favor of abstracts. The content of abstracts and summaries is identical; only the positioning differs. Whereas an abstract precedes the main body of the report, a summary follows the discussion section. Abstracts are often required to be no more than a given maximum number of words, usually between 100 and 500. It should describe the most important aspects of the study, including the problem investigated, the type of subjects and instruments involved, the design, the procedures, and the major results and conclusions.

d. The *table of contents* is basically an outline of your report, which indicates on which page each major section (or chapter) and subsection begins. Entries listed in the table of contents should be identical to the headings and subheadings in the report.

e. The *list of tables* is presented on a separate page and gives the number and title of each table and the page on which it can be found. Table titles should be exactly as they are given for the actual tables.

f. The *list of figures* is also presented on a separate page and gives the number and exact title of each figure and the page on which it can be found.

27. The Main Body of the Report

a. The *introduction* includes a description of the problem, a review of related literature, a statement of the hypothesis, and definition of terms. A well-written statement of a problem generally indicates the variables, and the specific relationship between those variables, investigated in the study. The review of related literature describes and analyzes what has already been done related to the problem. The review should conclude with a brief summary of the literature and its implications. The hypothesis (or hypotheses) logically follows the review of related literature; it is based upon the implications of previous research. A well-developed hypothesis is testable; that is, it can be confirmed or disconfirmed through the collection and analysis of data. The introduction also includes the operational definition of terms used in the study that do not have a commonly known meaning or for which several meanings may be used.

b. The *method* section includes a description of the subjects, instruments, design, procedure, assumptions, and limitations. The description of subjects includes not only statistics regarding the subjects but also a definition and description of the population from which the sample was selected; it may describe the method used in selecting the sample or samples. The description of instruments should identify and describe all instruments used to collect data pertinent to the study, be they tests, questionnaires, interview or observation forms, or unobtrusive data such as absenteeism reports or productivity figures. The description of the design, including a diagram, is especially important in an experimental study. The procedure portion should describe each step followed in conducting the study, in chronological order, in sufficient detail to permit the study to be replicated by another researcher. Any unforeseen events that occurred that might have affected the results should be discussed in terms of their seriousness and probable consequences. Also, any insights regarding ways to improve procedures should be shared so that other researchers may profit from the investigator's experiences.

c. The *results* section describes the statistical techniques that were applied to the data and the results of each analysis. For each hypothesis, the statistical test of significance selected and applied to the data is described, followed by a statement indicating whether the hypothesis was supported or not supported. Tables and figures are used to present findings in summary or graph form and add clarity to the presentation. Good tables and figures are uncluttered and self-explanatory; it is better to use two tables or figures than one that is crowded.

d. The *discussion* section is included in every research report; it allows for the discussion and interpretation of results, conclusions, implications, and recommendations. Each result is discussed in terms of the original hypothesis to which it relates and in terms of its agreement or disagreement with previous results obtained by other researchers in other studies. Two common errors committed by beginning researchers are to confuse results and conclusions and to overgeneralize results. A result is the outcome of a test of significance; the corresponding conclusion is that the original hypothesis was supported. Overgeneralization refers to the statement of conclusions that are not warranted by the results. The researcher should also discuss the theoretical and practical implications of the findings and make recommendations for future research or future action. In this portion of the report the researcher is permitted more freedom in expressing opinions that are not necessarily direct outcomes of data analysis.

e. The *references* section, or bibliography, lists all the sources, alphabetically by authors' last names, that were directly used in writing the report. Every source cited in the paper must be included in the references, and every entry listed in the references must appear in the paper. The style manual, such as the APA manual, will give you the correct procedure for all in-text and reference citations. This form is usually different for books, journal articles, and magazine articles. It is important that whatever form is used be followed consistently, and it is recommended that you determine the form during your review of the literature and use it from the very beginning.

Appendixes

28. Appendixes include information and data pertinent to the study that either are not important enough to be included in the main body of the report or are too lengthy. Appendixes contain such entries as materials especially developed for the study (tests, questionnaires, and cover letters, for example), raw data, and data-analysis sheets. Infrequently, an index may be required. Also, a number of universities ask that a vita be included.

Journal Articles

29. Preparation of a research report for publication in a professional journal serves the interest of the professional community as well as that of the researcher.

30. Progress in research requires that researchers share their efforts so that others may profit from and build upon them.

31. From a personal point of view, it is definitely to the researcher's advantage, especially the new graduate, to have work published.

32. Based on your review of related literature and your references, you should be able to identify two or three journals that publish studies in the area of research represented by your study.

33. Examination of a recent issue should give you some guidance concerning the format, style, and length that are acceptable to the selected journal. In addition, most journals include a section giving instructions for submitting manuscripts.

34. If your formal report is quite lengthy, you may want to make it into two articles, especially if there is more than one hypothesis.

35. To shorten a report in another way, you can edit the introduction and method sections to include only the critical information; the results and conclusions are of greater potential interest to readers and, therefore, are left pretty much as they stand.

Results Presented at Professional Meetings

36. Essentially there are two types of professional meetings that may have interest in your research, those that emphasize research and those that emphasize good practice.

37. If you choose the first, you should be prepared to be somewhat more scholarly in your presentation.

38. In the "good practice" sort of professional meeting, the emphasis will be less on your research and much more on the practical implications of your study. Participants will have a keen interest in finding out exactly what you did and how it worked out.

39. The key, in both instances, is to gear your presentation to your audience.

40. Most important of all, don't read your report to the audience; any nervousness you may experience can be covered fairly well by some good graphics (e.g., slides, or overhead presentations) that can be seen by everyone. The trick is to get the audience more interested in your fascinating study than they are in you.

In-House Reports

41. If you do your study within a company, undoubtedly it's a good idea to determine beforehand what the format for reporting will be.

42. Remember that most of your audience will not know—and may very well be turned off by—research jargon, so it's a good idea to tone down the technical research terminology while still getting your point across.

43. Figures and tables that get your meaning across are extremely helpful—but not necessarily the ones that list mean, standard deviation, F ratios, and so on.

44. A rehearsal for such events is always in order, and it's particularly helpful to find an audience (spouse or best friend) who doesn't know anything about research to listen to you and tell you if you make sense. This is *not* the time to allow your feelings to be hurt!

45. If your report is to be made in writing, a simple rule of thumb is to remember that most executives don't want to read more than one page.

46. The key here is edit, edit, edit. Each word has to be worth its weight in gold and really work for you. Your written report will usually include at least the following:

   a. *Title page,* including report title, organization, your name and organization, and the date.

   b. *Executive summary,* with a very brief review of the method, emphasis on the results, and clearly stated recommendations.

    c. *Table of contents* listing each heading and subheading and the page on which each may be found.

    d. *Introduction,* in which the background of the problem may be found. Also, your review of the literature may be summarized primarily with an *eye* toward what others in the industry or related industries are doing or have tried to do.

    e. *Method,* which includes a brief review of your subjects, instruments, and procedures.

    f. *Conclusions and recommendations,* which will contain your findings, in both written and graphic form, and your specific recommendations for future action.

    g. *Appendix,* which contains any other information needed to understand your report, including copies of any questionnaires or other instruments you may have used. If large or complicated tables or figures are included in your report and you think they will distract the reader, these may also be placed in the appendix.

47. All the recommendations regarding typing and attractiveness of your report apply even more so to the report presented to a company. Just as you want your résumé to reflect your professionalism, you will want your research report to represent you as a professional.

Project V Performance Criteria

Your research report should include all the components presented in Figure 14.1 with the possible exceptions of omitting an acknowledgment page and appendixes. Development of Project V basically involves combining Projects II, III, and IV, writing a *Discussion* section, and preparing the appropriate preliminary pages (including an abstract) and references. In other words, you have already written most of Project V.

    As an alternative, your instructor may want you to prepare a one-page executive summary and the supporting sections described in Chapter 14.

On the following pages, a student example is presented that illustrates the performance called for by Project V. This example represents a synthesis of the previously presented projects that are printed following Chapters 2, 10, and 13.

Effects of Involvement in a Participatory
Budget Planning Team on Employee Attitudes
Toward Their Job and Company

Richard D. Prentiss
St. Thomas University

Submitted in partial fulfillment of
the requirements of MAN 503
September 1989

Table of Contents

i

List of Tables and Figures

ii

Abstract

The purpose of this study was to compare the attitudes toward job
and company of employees involved in participatory budget–planning
teams with those of employees involved in traditional,
nonparticipatory budget planning. By means of a posttest–only control–group
design and a $\underline{t}$ test for independent samples, it was found that the
employees ($\underline{n}$ = 20) who participated in budget planning had
significantly higher attitude scores on Milani's (1975) Attitude
Toward Job and Attitude Toward Company scales than the employees
($\underline{n}$ = 20) who did not participate [$\underline{t}$ (38) – 2.60, $\underline{p}$ < .05]. It was
concluded that participation in budget planning resulted in more
positive attitudes.

iii

Policy development and decision making traditionally have been handled at the highest levels of management. In areas such as budget planning, most employees have had little or no opportunity to participate in decision making; the extent of their involvement has been to implement the decisions made by senior managers. Over time, however, some managers have become aware that employee involvement is beneficial to the operation of the organization, and that, in order for businesses to excel, managers must solicit employee participation at all levels (Bookman, 1987). In the management literature, the terms <u>participatory</u> <u>management</u> and <u>teamwork</u> have come into common use. Webster (1984) defines <u>participate</u> as "to have or take a share with others" (p. 436) and <u>teamwork</u> as "joint action by a group of people" (p. 613). In a business context, these definitions can be further refined to suggest a process involving multidisciplinary, collaborative sharing of information and coordination and goal setting by a group (Fiorelli, 1983). In organizations that have implemented the teamwork process, reactions have been favorable, and a number of benefits have been experienced (Barmore, 1987; Hoerr, 1988). Indeed, in the minds of many, team work proves beneficial to any organization, regardless of the product or service provided. Thus the concept of employee involvement has now become as complex as the formation of participatory management teams (Hoerr, 1989a; Reynolds, 1988).

<u>Statement</u> <u>of</u> <u>the</u> <u>Problem</u>

The purpose of this study was to compare the attitudes toward job and company of employees involved in participatory budget—

1

planning teams with those of employees who experienced traditional, nonparticipatory budget planning. <u>Participatory</u> <u>budget</u> <u>planning</u> was defined as the use of employee teams in the planning, implementing, and reviewing of the annual budget. <u>Traditional, nonparticipatory</u> <u>budget</u> <u>planning</u> was defined as the use of senior management in the planning, implementing, and reviewing of the annual budget.

<u>Review</u> <u>of</u> <u>Related</u> <u>Literature</u>

In the past, businesses have been primarily concerned with the distribution of goods and services with the primary emphasis being on low cost and high profit margin. Employees have had little input regarding the operation of these organizations. Management thought that as long as employees remained somewhat motivated, the production and distribution of goods and services would be accomplished (Steers & Porter, 1975). Occasionally, however, management would solicit suggestions from employees regarding policies and procedures, and at some point it began to be recognized that employee suggestions often proved to be beneficial to the organization. Managers in some organizations began to capitalize on this by incorporating employee participation into their business. Over time, the process became more formalized and came to be referred to as participatory management. Eventually, team formation was found to be an effective strategy for implementation of the participatory management concept, and it was realized that the responsibilities of such teams could range from specific problem solving to overall operation of the company (Bunting, 1988; Gallagher, 1987).

2

As the incidence of participatory management teams has increased, the need for careful planning and monitoring has become evident (Vogt & Hunt, 1988). For successful implementation, it is imperative that key employees and managers who can assist in facilitating teamwork be identified (Booth, 1988; Reynolds, 1988). Further, after teams have been formed, both the role of the employees and the role of management must be clearly defined, group identity established, and plans developed (Belzer, 1989; Porco, 1985). And, in order to be effective, it is critical that the team concept be a continuous process that facilitates open communication and trust between employees and management (Bookman, 1987).

Overall, it appears that implementation of participatory management teams has proven to be beneficial both to employees and to the organizations that have used them. Employees and managers are experiencing a new form of enhanced communication. Employees have demonstrated a feeling of ownership of their workplace and a willingness to participate (Hardaker & Ward, 1987). For the organizations involved, the outcome has been increased productivity and cost-effective distribution of goods and services resulting from the development and application of more effective procedures (Barmore, 1987; Hoerr, 1988; Hoerr, 1989b).

As participatory management teams have evolved and become more proficient, their scope of responsibility has increased. Currently, such teams are becoming increasingly involved in budgetary matters, and there is some research evidence that such participation benefits both employees and organizations. Brownell

3

and Hirst (1986), for example, found an inverse relationship between employee participation in budget processes and job-related tension; high budgetary participation was associated with low job-related tension. In addition, Mia (1988) reported a direct relationship between employee participation and the effectiveness of the budgetary process; if employees are motivated and effective, communication improved, and an improved budgetary process was demonstrated.

Despite its apparent effectiveness, however, the participatory management team concept currently has only a superficial acceptance in the majority of business organizations. The reasons for this remain unclear, although some think that management and/or organized labor are the major adversaries of this concept (Hardaker & Ward, 1987). It is likely, however, that as the research base supporting its effectiveness grows, so will its implementation.

Statement of the Hypothesis

Implementation of participatory management teams in an organization has reportedly resulted in a variety of benefits, including enhanced employee-management communication and improved institutional efficiency and productivity. No research has been done, however, related to the effects on employees' attitudes toward their jobs and company. This variable is critical, as it affects both employees, in terms of job satisfaction, for example, and organizations, in terms of factors such as absenteeism. Based on the research reporting feelings of employee ownership and decreased

4

tension, it was hypothesized that employees at companies using
participatory budget-planning teams have more positive attitudes
toward their jobs and company than employees of companies using
traditional, nonparticipatory budget planning.

Method

<u>Subjects</u>

The sample group was selected from the employee population of
Rapare Corporation's North Plant. Rapare Corporation is located in a
large metropolitan area and is a provider of consumer goods. The
corporation includes a centrally located administrative office and
two production facilities (North and South). The North facility has
300 employees, including a plant manager, 10 division supervisors,
and 289 workers. The work force of the corporation is made up of
primarily non-Hispanic white males (55%) and smaller percentages
of Hispanic males (13%), Afro-American males (9%), non-Hispanic white
females (8%), Hispanic females (8%), and Afro-American females (7%). The age
distribution reflects the following percentages: 20-30 (years of age),
10%; 31-40, 35%; 41-50, 50%; 51-60, 4%; and 61-70, 1%.

Forty subjects were randomly selected from the work force,
excluding the plant manager and division supervisors. The 40 were
then randomly assigned to two groups of 20 each. The sample selected
appropriately reflected the employee work group in regard to
ethnicity, sex, and age.

5

Instruments

Two instruments were administered in the study: Milani's (1975) Attitude Toward Job scale (MAT–J) and his Attitude Toward Company scale (MAT–C). The MAT–J contains 16 items, which measure predispositions, feelings, and/or opinions about one's present job. The MAT–C contains 10 items and measures predispositions, feelings, and/or opinions about one's present employer. Both are standard attitude scales based on the Thurstone successive-intervals scaling technique. Subjects are given a list of statements and are instructed to place an "X" in front of the statements with which they agree. For each scale, a subject's attitude score is the average of the scale values of the statements selected. In the present study, each subject's score for overall attitude was the sum of the attitude scores for the two measures.

Although the instruments were originally developed for administration to supervisors, they were judged to be appropriate for nonsupervisory personnel. The items are very general and applicable to virtually all employees, e.g., "This job is disliked by everyone," and "I am made to feel that I am really a part of this organization." Internal consistency reliability was computed for the subjects in the study using the KR–21 formula and was found to be $r = .86$.

Design

The design used in this study was the posttest–only control–group design (see Figure 1). It was selected because of the feasibility of random assignment to groups and the control provided for sources of internal and external validity. The pretest–posttest control–group design was not used because of the potentially reactive nature of the dependent variable, attitudes toward job and company.

6

The only major threat to validity associated with the design used is mortality, i.e., employee turnover. A normal turnover rate of 5% (1 employee per group) was anticipated but did not occur. Thus, the sample sizes remained constant throughout the duration of the study.

Procedure

    Prior to the beginning of the fiscal year, the plant manager and supervisors were informed that a study was to take place. The content of the study was not disclosed, but the manager and supervisors did know that the study would involve inclusion of workers in budgetary planning for the following fiscal year. They were asked to cooperate by releasing the selected workers in their respective areas for participation and by providing information and assistance as needed by the planning group. All supervisory personnel agreed.

Group	Assignment	n	Treatment	Posttest
1	Random	20	Participatory Budget Planning Team	MAT-J[a] + Mat C[b]
2	Random	20	Nonparticipatory Budget Planning	MAT-J + MAT-C

[a]Milani's Attitude Toward Job scale. [b]Milani's Attitude Toward Company scale.

Figure 1. Experimental design.

7

The 40 randomly selected workers were notified and all agreed to participate in the study. They were then randomly assigned to two groups of 20 each; one group was randomly designated to be the experimental group.

During the next week, the workers in the experimental group received a letter from the training department that explained a program in which they would be involved over the next six months. Workers in the control group received a letter explaining that they would be scheduled for the program during the second half of the year. The letter explained a three-phase workshop program that included the following topics: understanding fiscal management, prioritizing the fiscal plan, and developing a fiscal plan. These workshops were taught on a weekly basis, one half day a week, during the employees' scheduled work time. Each workshop lasted 8 weeks, for a total of 24 weeks. In order not to disrupt the work schedule more than necessary and to provide for discussion, employees were asked to attend either the morning or afternoon workshop; half of the supervisors attended in the morning and the other half in the afternoon. The plant manager attended the workshops as it was appropriate.

During the first workshop (understanding fiscal management), the fiscal limitations of the corporation, fiscal needs and wants, and goal identification and goal setting were discussed. Over the third and fourth months, the participants in the workshops prioritized, through consensus decision making, the fiscal plan. This was done by reviewing and ranking the corporation's goals and its fiscal needs and wants. During the final two months, the workshop participants determined the fiscal plan that would be implemented for the coming fiscal year.

After completion of the final workshop, the sample groups were administered the MAT–J and MAT–C. To avoid problems with distribution and return of the instruments, a secretary from the training department met with the experimental and control groups. The workers received the instruments, completed them, and returned them to the secretary.

Results

A t test for independent samples (α = .05) was used to compare the attitude scores of the experimental and control groups. Random assignment of the employees to the two groups made the t test for independent samples the appropriate test of significance. Results showed that the means for the two groups differed significantly (see Table 1).

Table 1

Means, Standard Deviations and t Test for the Participatory and Nonparticipatory Groups for Attitude Scores

Attitude Scores	Group		t
	Participatory	Nonparticipatory	
M	13.50	10.98	2.60[a]
SD	2.75	3.38	

[a]df = 34, p < .05

9

Therefore, the original hypothesis that ''employees at companies using participatory budget-planning teams have more positive attitudes toward their jobs and company than employees of companies using traditional, nonparticipatory budget planning'' was supported.

Discussion

The results of this study support the research hypothesis: employees involved in participatory budget planning have more positive attitudes toward their jobs and company than employees involved in traditional, nonparticipatory budget planning. These results are consistent with those of Brownell and Hirst (1986) and Mia (1988).

Nevertheless, since the study used a small population in a consumer-product-oriented industry, results cannot be generalized to all forms of organizations. Additionally, the results must be evaluated with the knowledge that there may be some reactive effect resulting from the employees' participation in the workshops as a change from their daily routines prior to the study. It may be of great benefit to industry, however, to continue to study the effectiveness of similar employee-participation programs. In addition to employee attitude, variables such as productivity and cost containment should be investigated. Further, the attitudes of supervisors whose employees participate in budgetary planning should continue to be reviewed. By continuing research in this area, the full potential that may be achieved through employee participation can be evaluated.

10

References

Barmore, G. T. (1987). Teamwork: Charting a course for success. Mortgage Banking, 47(11), 90–96.

Belzer, E. J. (1989, August). 12 ways to better team building. Working Woman, pp. 12–14.

Bookman, B. (1987). Year round teamwork: Cooperation is not for Christmas only. Management World, 16, 37.

Booth, P. (1988). Employee involvement and corporate performance. Canadian Business Review, 15, 14.

Brownell, P., & Hirst, M. (1986). Reliance on accounting information, budgetary participation, and task uncertainty: Tests of a three-way interaction. Journal of Accounting Research, 24, 241–249.

Bunting, C. (1988, February). 'Group initiatives' make a game out of problem–solving. Camping Magazine, pp. 26–29.

Fiorelli, J. S. (1983). Power, decision making, and participation in interdisciplinary treatment teams. Dissertation Abstracts International, 44, 351B. (University Microfilms No. DA8311597).

Gallagher, M. (1987). Productive problem solving. Chilton's Distribution, 86(11), 70.

Guralnik, D. B. (Ed.) (1984). Webster's new world dictionary. New York: Warner.

Hardaker, M., & Ward, B. K. (1987). How to make a team work. Harvard Business Review, 65, 112–120.

11

Hoerr, J. P. (1988, November 28). Work teams can rev up paper-
pushers, too. Business Week, pp. 64–72.

Hoerr, J. P. (1989, February 20). Is teamwork a management plot?
Mostly not. Business Week, p. 70.

Hoerr, J. P. (1989, July 10). The payoff from teamwork. Business
Week, pp. 56–62.

Mia, L. (1988). Managerial attitude, motivation and the effectiveness
of budget participation. Accounting Organizations and Society,
13, 465–475.

Milani, K. (1975). The relationship of participation in budget setting
to industrial supervisor performance and attitudes: A field
study. The Accounting Review, 50, 274–284.

Porco, C. (1985). Developing a proactive communication style in
employees. Supervisory Management, 30(4), 23–28.

Reynolds, M. (1988, Spring). Building teams that work. Electric
Perspectives, 28–35.

Steers, R., & Porter, L. (1975). Motivation and work behavior.
New York: McGraw-Hill.

Vogt, J. F., & Hunt, B. D. (1988). What really goes wrong with
participatory work groups? Training & Development Journal,
42(5), 96–100.

12

REFERENCES

AMERICAN PSYCHOLOGICAL ASSOCIATION. (1983). *Publication manual* (3rd ed.). Washington, DC: Author.

BOEKER, W. (1989). Strategic change: The effects of founding and history. *Academy of Management Journal, 32*(3).

ELGOOD, G. (1990, February 4). Reader, this is a printed news vehicle. *The Miami Herald,* p. 9G.

FREDERICKSON, J. W., & IAQUINTO, A. L. (1989). Inertia and creeping rationality in strategic decision processes. *Academy of Management Journal, 32*(3).

HODGES, J. C., WHITTEN, M. E., HORNER, W. B., WEBB, S. S., & MILLER, R. K. (EDS.). (1990). *Harbrace college handbook* (11th ed.). New York: Harcourt Brace Jovanovich.

KESNER, I. F., VICTOR, B., & LAMONT, B. T. (1986). Board composition and the commission of illegal acts: An investigation of *Fortune* 500 companies. *Academy of Management Journal, 29*(4), 789–799.

MANNING, M. R., OSLAND, J. S., & OSLAND, A. (1989). Work-related consequences of smoking cessation. *Academy of Management Journal, 32*(3).

STRUNK, W., JR., & WHITE, E. B. (1979). *The elements of style* (3rd ed.). New York: Macmillan.

WEBSTER'S DICTIONARY OF ENGLISH USAGE. (1989). Springfield, MA: Merriam-Webster.

PART SIX
Research Critiques

Anyone who reads newspapers and magazines, listens to the radio, or watches TV is a consumer of research. We are constantly bombarded with the latest research findings concerning cholesterol and diet, the wrinkle-reducing powers of Retin-A, and all sorts of things that should make us look better and live longer. Many people tend to accept and act on such findings uncritically if they are labeled the results of "scientific research" or if they are transmitted by anyone in a white lab coat. Very few people question—or even know how to determine—the control procedures that were used or the generalizability of findings based on rats to human beings. You, as a professional consumer of research, are required to possess critical evaluation skills. In addition to being critical of data transmitted by the media, you have a responsibility to be informed concerning the latest findings in your professional area and to be able to differentiate good research from poor research. Decisions made based on invalid research are likely to be bad ones and may result in the adoption of unproductive practices.

Just because a study is reported in a journal doesn't necessarily mean that it was a good study; results are frequently published that are based on research involving one or more serious flaws. When you reviewed the literature related to your problem, you simply determined whether or not each study was related to your problem and, if so, in what way. Normally a researcher critically evaluates each reference and does not consider the results of poorly executed research. At the time you reviewed the literature you didn't possess the competence required to make quality discriminations. Competent evaluation of a research study requires knowledge of each of the components of the research process. Your work in previous chapters has given you that knowledge.

The goal of Part Six is for you to be able critically to analyze and evaluate research reports. After you have read Part Six, you should be able to perform the following task.

Project VI and/or Final Examination

Given a reprint of a research report and an evaluation form, evaluate the components of the report.

See Performance Criteria, p. 609

Normally a researcher critically evaluates each reference and does not consider the results of poorly executed research. (page 599)

15

Evaluation of a Research Report

Objectives

After reading Chapter 15, you should be able to do the following:

1. List at least three questions that should be asked to determine the adequacy of each of the major sections and subsections of a research report.

2. List at least three questions that should be asked to determine the adequacy of a study representing each of the following types of research:
   a. historical research.
   b. descriptive research, including
      questionnaire studies.
      interview studies.
      observation studies.
   c. correlational research, including
      relationship studies.
      prediction studies.
   d. causal-comparative research.
   e. experimental research.

GENERAL EVALUATION CRITERIA

At your current level of expertise you won't be able to evaluate every component of every study. You won't be able to determine, for example, whether the appropriate degrees of freedom were used in the calculation of an analysis of covariance (ANCOVA). There are, however, a number of basic errors or weaknesses that you should be able to detect. You should, for example, be able to identify the sources of invalidity associated with a study based on a one-group pretest-posttest design. You should also be able to detect obvious indications of experimenter bias that may have affected the results. A statement in a research report that "the purpose of this study was to prove . . ." should alert you to a probable bias effect.

As you read a research report, either as a consumer of research keeping up with the latest findings in your professional area or as a producer of research reviewing literature related to a defined problem, there are a number of questions you should ask yourself concerning the adequacy of execution of the various components. The answers to some of these questions are more critical than the answers to others. An

601

inadequate title is not a critical flaw; an inadequate design is. Some questions are difficult to answer if the study is not directly in your area of expertise. If your area is retailing, for example, you are probably not in a position to judge the adequacy of a review of the literature related to productivity in manufacturing. And, admittedly, the answers to some questions are more subjective than objective. Whether or not a good design was used is pretty objective; almost everyone would agree that the randomized posttest-only control-group design is a good design. Whether or not the most appropriate design was used, given the problem under study, involves a degree of subjective judgment; the need for inclusion of a pretest, for example, might be a debatable point. Despite the lack of complete precision, however, evaluation of a research report is a worthwhile process. Major problems and shortcomings are usually readily identifiable, and by mentally responding to a number of questions one formulates an overall impression concerning the validity of the study. For each component of a research report a number of evaluation questions are listed herewith for your consideration. This list is by no means exhaustive, and, as you read it, you may very well think of additional questions that might be asked. You may also be familiar with these questions, as some instructors use them as guidelines for evaluating their students' work on the projects you have completed.

Introduction

Problem (Chapter 2)
1. Is there a statement of the problem?
2. Is the problem "researchable," that is, can it be investigated through the collection and analysis of data?
3. Is background information on the problem presented?
4. Is the business significance of the problem discussed?
5. Does the problem statement indicate the variables of interest and the specific relationship between those variables that were investigated?
6. When necessary, are the variables directly or operationally defined?

Review of Related Literature (Chapter 2)
7. Is the review comprehensive?
8. Are all the references cited relevant to the problem under investigation?
9. Are the sources mostly primary, with only a few or no secondary sources?
10. Have the references been critically analyzed and the results of various studies compared and contrasted; i.e., is the review more than a series of abstracts or annotations?
11. Is the review well organized? Does it logically flow in such a way that the least-related references to the problem are discussed first and the most-related references are discussed last?

12. Does the review conclude with a brief summary of the literature and its implications for the problem investigated?

13. Do the implications discussed form an empirical or theoretical rationale for the hypotheses that follow?

Hypotheses (Chapter 2)

14. Are specific questions to be answered listed or specific hypotheses to be tested stated?

15. Does each hypothesis state an expected relationship or difference between two variables? If necessary, are the variables directly or operationally defined?

16. Is each hypothesis testable?

Method

Subjects (Chapter 4)

1. Are the size and major characteristics of the population studied described?

2. If a sample was selected, is the method of selecting the sample clearly described?

3. Is the method of sample selection described one that is likely to result in a representative, unbiased sample?

4. Did the researcher avoid the use of volunteers?

5. Are the size and major characteristics of the sample described?

6. Does the sample size meet the suggested guideline for minimum sample size appropriate for the method of research represented?

Instruments (Chapter 5)

7. Is a rationale given for the selection of instruments or measurements used?

8. Is each instrument or measurement described in terms of purpose and content?

9. Are the instruments or measurements appropriate for measuring the intended variables?

10. Is evidence presented that indicates that each instrument or measurement is appropriate for the sample under study?

11. Is instrument validity discussed and coefficients given if appropriate?

12. Is reliability discussed in terms of type and size of reliability coefficients?

13. If appropriate, are subtest reliabilities given?

14. If an instrument or measurement was developed specifically for the study, are the procedures involved in its development and validation described?

15. If an instrument or measurement was developed specifically for the study, are administration, scoring or tabulating, and interpretation procedures fully described?

Design and Procedure (Chapters 6, 7, 8, 9, 10, and 14)

16. Is the design appropriate for testing the hypotheses of the study?

17. Are the procedures described in sufficient detail to permit them to be replicated by another researcher?

18. If a pilot study was conducted, are its execution and results described as well as its impact on the subsequent study?

19. Are control procedures described?

20. Did the researcher discuss or account for any potentially confounding variables that he or she was unable to control?

Results (Chapters 11, 12, and 13)

1. Are appropriate descriptive statistics presented?

2. Was the probability level, α, at which the results of the tests of significance were evaluated specified in advance of the data analysis?

3. If parametric tests were used, is there evidence that the researcher avoided violating the required assumptions for parametric tests?

4. Are the tests of significance described appropriate, given the hypothesis and design of the study?

5. Was every hypothesis tested?

6. Are the tests of significance interpreted using the appropriate degrees of freedom?

7. Are the results clearly presented?

8. Are the tables and figures (if any) well organized and easy to understand?

9. Is there agreement between the tables and figures and the text, i.e., is each table and figure cited in the text?

Discussion, Conclusions, and Recommendations (Chapter 14)

1. Is each result discussed in terms of the original hypothesis to which it relates?

2. Is each result discussed in terms of its agreement or disagreement with previous results obtained by other researchers in other studies?

3. Are generalizations that are made warranted by the results?

4. Are the possible effects of uncontrolled variables on the results discussed?

5. Are theoretical and practical implications of the findings discussed?

6. Are recommendations for future action made?

7. Are the suggestions for future action based on practical significance or on statistical significance only; i.e., has the author avoided confusing practical and statistical significance?

8. Are recommendations for future research made?

Abstract or Summary (Chapter 14)

Note: You are asked to evaluate the abstract last because you are in a better position to evaluate it after you have evaluated the complete report.

1. Is the problem stated?
2. Are the number and type of subjects and instruments or measurements described?
3. Is the design used identified?
4. Are the procedures described?
5. Are the major results and conclusions stated?

METHOD-SPECIFIC EVALUATION CRITERIA

In addition to general criteria that can be applied to almost any study, there are specific questions that should be asked depending upon the method of research represented by the study. In other words, there are concerns that are specific to historical studies and likewise to descriptive, correlational, causal-comparative, and experimental studies. These should look familiar to you as they were first stated at the end of the chapters relating to each specific type of research. They are reprinted here as a summary and handy reference for you.

Historical Research (Chapter 6)

1. Were the sources of data related to the problem mostly primary?
2. Was each piece of data subjected to external criticism?
3. Was each piece of data subjected to internal criticism?

Descriptive Research (Chapter 7)

Questionnaire Studies
1. Are directions to questionnaire responders clear?
2. Does each item in the questionnaire relate to one of the objectives of the study?
3. Does each questionnaire item deal with a single concept?
4. When necessary, is a point of reference given for questionnaire items?
5. Are leading questions avoided in the questionnaire?
6. Are there sufficient alternatives for each questionnaire item?
7. Are questionnaire-validation procedures described?
8. Was the questionnaire pretested?
9. Are pilot study procedures and results described?
10. Does the cover letter explain the purpose and importance of the study and give the potential responder a good reason for cooperating?

11. If appropriate, is confidentiality of responses assured in the cover letter?
12. Was the percentage of returns approximately 70?
13. Are follow-up activities described?
14. If the response rate was low, was any attempt made to determine any major differences between responders and nonresponders?

Interview Studies

1. Does each item in the interview guide relate to a specific objective of the study?
2. When necessary, is a point of reference given in the guide for interview items?
3. Are leading questions avoided in the interview guide?
4. Does the interview guide indicate the type and amount of prompting and probing that was permitted?
5. Are the qualifications and special training of the interviewers described?
6. Is the method that was used to record responses described?
7. Did the researcher use the most reliable, unbiased method of recording responses that could have been used?
8. Were the interview procedures pretested?
9. Are pilot study procedures and results described?
10. Did the researcher specify how the responses to semistructured and unstructured items were quantified and analyzed?

Observation Studies

1. Are the observational variables defined?
2. Were observers required to observe only one behavior at a time?
3. Was a coded recording instrument used?
4. Are the qualifications and special training of the observers described?
5. Is the level of observer reliability reported?
6. Is the level of observer reliability sufficiently high?
7. Were possible observer and observee biases discussed?
8. Was observation the best method to collect the data, i.e., was observation preferable to some unobtrusive measure that could have been used instead?

Correlational Research (Chapter 8)

Relationship Studies

1. Were variables carefully selected; i.e., was a shotgun approach avoided?
2. Is the rationale for variable selection described?
3. Are conclusions and recommendations based on values of correlation coefficients corrected for attenuation or restriction in range?

4. Do the conclusions avoid indicating causal relationships between the variables investigated?

Prediction Studies

1. Is a rationale given for selection of predictor variables?
2. Is the criterion variable well defined?
3. Was the resulting prediction equation validated with at least one other group?

Causal-Comparative Research (Chapter 9)

1. Are the characteristics or experiences that differentiate the groups (the independent variable) clearly defined or described?
2. Are critical extraneous variables identified?
3. Were any control procedures applied to equate the groups on extraneous variables?
4. Are causal relationships found discussed with due caution?
5. Are plausible alternative hypotheses discussed?

Experimental Research (Chapter 10)

1. Was an appropriate experimental design selected?
2. Is a rationale for design selection given?
3. Are sources of invalidity associated with the design identified and discussed?
4. Is the method of group formation described?
5. Was the experimental group formed in the same way as the control group?
6. Were groups randomly formed and the use of existing groups avoided?
7. Were treatments randomly assigned to groups?
8. Were critical extraneous variables identified?
9. Were any control procedures applied to equate groups on extraneous variables?
10. Is there any evidence to suggest the researcher was able to avoid reactive arrangements (for example, the Hawthorne effect)?

Summary/Chapter 15

GENERAL EVALUATION CRITERIA

1. There are a number of basic errors or weaknesses that the beginning researcher should be able to detect in a research study.

2. You should also be able to detect obvious indications of experimenter bias that may have affected the results.

3. As you read a research report, either as a consumer of research keeping up with the latest findings in your professional area or as a producer of research reviewing literature related to a defined problem, there are a number of questions you should ask yourself concerning the adequacy of execution of the various components.

4. The answers to some of these questions are more critical than the answers to others.

5. Major problems and shortcomings are usually readily identifiable, and by mentally responding to a number of questions you can formulate an overall impression concerning the validity of the study.

Introduction

Method

Results

Discussion, Conclusions, and Recommendations

Abstract or Summary

METHOD-SPECIFIC EVALUATION CRITERIA

12. In addition to general criteria that can be applied to almost any study, there are specific questions that should be asked depending upon the method of research represented by the study.

Historical Research

Descriptive Research

Correlational Research

Causal-Comparative Research   See page 607

Experimental Research   See page 607

Project VI Performance Criteria

The evaluation form will list a series of questions about a study to which you must indicate a yes or no response. For example, you might be asked if there is a statement of hypotheses. If the answer is yes, you should indicate where the asked-for component is located in the study, such as a statement of a hypothesis on page 4, paragraph 3, lines 2 to 6.

In addition, if the study is experimental, you will be asked to identify and diagram the experimental design that was applied.

On the following pages a research report is reprinted. Following the report, a Self-Test is provided for you to use in evaluating the report. In answering the questions, use the following code:

Y   = Yes
N   = No
?   = Cannot tell (it cannot be determined from the information given)
NA = Question not applicable (pilot study wasn't used, for example)
X   = Given your current level of competence, you are not in a position to make a judgment

When appropriate as you answer the questions of the Self-Test, underline the components of the project that correspond to the questions to which you have responded Y. For example, if you decide there is a statement of the problem, underline it in the report. Since the study that you are going to evaluate is experimental, you are also asked to identify and diagram the experimental design used. If your responses match reasonably well with those given in the "Suggested Responses" (see Appendix C), you are probably ready for Project VI. Make sure that you understand the reason for any discrepancies, especially on questions for which responses are less judgmental and more objective; adequacy of the literature review is more judgmental whereas the presence or absence of a hypothesis can be objectively determined. In addition, you will probably want to review the analysis of the research articles following Chapters 1, 6, 7, 8, and 9.

As stated previously, many instructors use Project VI as a final examination for this course. If so, your instructor will provide you with further details regarding her or his requirements.

Page 1

Developing Strategic Management Goal-Setting Skills

Walter J. Wheatley
University of West Florida

Robert W. Hornaday
University of North Carolina, Charlotte

Tammy G. Hunt
Baylor University

¶ A   1   Although the use of management simulations in business policy courses has lost much of its luster, gaming is still a popular 3   method of instruction (Markulis and Strang, 1985). Estimates of the percentage of Academy of Management members currently 5   using games range from 32.7% (Alexander et al., 1984) to about 50% (Keeffe and Cozan, 1985; Eldredge and Galloway, 1983). 7   The popularity that business games once enjoyed (Twelker, 1972) seems to have leveled off (Norris, 1985).

¶ B   9   Two major reasons for the diminished glamour of gaming stand out in the literature. Some instructors quit using games 11   because of mainframe problems. It simply wasn't worth the time and effort to fight the technical, political, and budgetary battles 13   that had to be won to properly administer mainframe simulations. The expanding use of microcomputers for gaming (Cosenza et 15   al., 1985; Dennis, 1985) is rapidly eliminating most problems associated with mainframes (Fritzsche and Cotter, 1985; Goosen, 17   1985).

¶ C   The other reason for the decline in prestige of gaming is more 19   serious. Many are skeptical about the instructional value of games (Keeffe and Cozan, 1985). While gaming zealots are convinced 21   gaming is a beneficial method of instruction they have been unsuccessful in empirically demonstrating the advantages of 23   simulations to the satisfaction of the skeptics. The debate over the instructional value of gaming rages unabated.

SIMULATION & GAMES, Vol. 19 No. 2, June 1988 173–185
© 1988 Sage Publications, Inc.
Reprinted by permission of Sage Publications, Inc.

¶ D 25   The purpose of this article is to present both sides of this debate
           and to offer some empirical evidence on the effect of gaming on
     27   goal-setting.

BUSINESS GAMING EFFECTIVENESS RESEARCH

¶ E   A review of the literature on the benefits of business simulation
     29   offers conflicting results. On the positive side, there is evidence
           that gaming appears to support the objectives of strategy making,
     31   goal setting, and decision making (Wolfe, 1975) while enhancing
           student learning, interest, and motivation (Raia, 1966). Other
     33   evidence suggests that gaming is beneficial under conditions
           requiring high organizational learning and adaptation (Wolfe,
     35   1976) and is fulfilling the "capstone" purpose of undergraduate
           policy courses by providing a "worthwhile learning environment
     37   capable of teaching many of the policy decision-making elements
           of a Business Policy course" (Wolfe and Guth, 1975: 363).
     39   Business games are effective learning mediums for international
           business concepts (Klein, 1980) and can be successfully used to
     41   create varied learning environments (Thompson and Keon,
           1981).
¶ F 43   On the negative side, Neuhauser (1976: 124) states that there
           "is little evidence that games are in any sense efficient or effective
     45   methodological devices." Gaming has no positive effect on
           decision effectiveness (Newgren: 1981) or on student exam scores
     47   (Estes, 1979; Boseman and Schellenberger, 1974; Rowland and
           Gardner, 1973). Finally, of major importance, Norris and Snyder
     49   (1981) could not find a relationship between game performance
           and subsequent career success.
¶ G 51   In sum, the literature on the use of business simulations in
           business policy courses seems to show that students enjoy gaming
     53   and that games are good for teaching complex concepts. But
           student performance both in the classroom and in later life is not
     55   enhanced by participating in management simulations.
¶ H   Faulty research design seems to plague those who try to
     57   evaluate the effectiveness of business policy gaming. Butler et al.
           (1985) criticized existing gaming research for not following
     59   generally accepted research design guidelines. Their review of
           eight years of annual ABSEL Proceedings concluded that only
     61   70% of the articles used all three characteristics of good research
           design (control groups, randomization, and experimenter control
     63   of the treatment variable).
¶ I   Another major criticism of efforts to demonstrate the benefits
     65   of business policy gaming is the lack of empirically verifiable

Page 3

<table>
<tr><td></td><td>67</td><td>performance variables (Snow, 1976). The few studies that have attempted to investigate the effectiveness of simulations usually use purely academic performance measures such as the student's</td></tr>
</table>

¶ J   71

performance variables (Snow, 1976). The few studies that have
67 attempted to investigate the effectiveness of simulations usually
use purely academic performance measures such as the student's
69 mastery of policy principles and fail to control for the resulting
experimenter bias (Wolfe, 1975; Wolfe and Guth, 1975).
71 This study used a pretest-posttest research design that meets
the three standards established by Butler et al. (1985), and
73 employed an important performance variable (goal-setting) that
is measurable.

RESEARCH DESIGN

Randomization

¶ K   75   Data were collected from 230 business policy students (all
seniors) at a large southeastern university. All students who
77 registered for seven policy sections during the spring semester of
1985 took part in the testing.

Control Group

¶ L   79   Four sections (treatment group) taught by one instructor
participated in a simulation as the major focus of their business
81 policy studies. No case analyses were used in these four sections.
Another instructor taught the remaining three sections (the
83 control group) using the case-method approach. Demographic
data collected from all students showed little difference be-
85 tween the backgrounds and capabilities of the 134 students in
the treatment group and the 96 students in the control group
87 (Table 1).

Control of Treatment Variable

¶ M   The design provided clear control of the treatment variable by
89 the researchers. The treatment group participated in a simulation
and did not analyze cases. The control group did the reverse.

Performance Variable

¶ N   91   Goal-setting is a critical skill for top-level managers. In a 1983
survey, Boyd and Summers reported that goal-setting tied for
93 first place with strategic planning as items that should be included
in business policy courses. In this study, goal-setting was used as
95 the performance variable to evaluate performance between the

TABLE 1

Demographic and Performance Data Treatment Group Versus Control Group

	Treatment Group	Control Group	Entire Sample
Gender			
Male	70	57	127
Female	63	40	103
Chi Square = 0.760			
p. = 1.000[a]			
Major			
Management	14	8	22
Accounting	31	18	49
Finance	36	25	61
Marketing	12	10	22
Hospitality Admin.	12	10	22
Management Science	14	10	24
Other	14	16	30
Chi Square = 6.923			
p. = .954[a]			
Mean Age	22.45	22.76	22.56
F Ratio = 0.570			
p. = .451[a]			
Overall Grade Point Average	3.04	2.92	2.99
F Ratio = 1.438			
p. = .232[a]			

[a]Probabilities (p.) indicate the likelihood of no difference between treatment and control groups.

97 treatment group (simulation) and the control group (case method).

¶ O

99 Specifically, goal-setting ability was measured by counting the number of organizational goals each student could generate. The

101 number of items generated (ideational fluency) is an accepted outcome variable used in the evaluation of divergent thinking and creativity (Hershey and Kearnes, 1979; Khatana, 1976). Further-

103 more, Hargraves and Bolton (1972) and Parnes and Meadows (1959) found that when using this measure (ideational fluency),

105 there is a high positive correlation between the number of items generated and the quality of these items. In a study of goal

107 generation, Wheatley (1985) also found a strong correlation (.989) between the quantity and quality of goals generated. Thus,

109 there is evidence that subjects who generate a large number of goals also generate a large number of *quality* goals. Both

Page 5

111   theoretical and empirical support exists for counting goals generated to measure goal-setting performance.

¶ P   113   To motivate student performance, students were told that 20% percent of their course grade depended upon the number of

115   goals they could generate on both the pretest and the posttest (10% for each).

Control for the Demand Characteristic

¶ Q   117   In this type of research, a common cause of serious bias comes from respondents telling researchers the things the researchers

119   seem to want to hear (Rosenthal, 1977). This "demand characteristic" poses a special threat when using student subjects. Students

121   love to play games, and will try to "win" if they can figure out the objective of the exercise. To minimize the effects of demand, the

123   students in this study did not know the true purpose of the two goal-setting tests, except that the more goals they generated the

125   higher their course grade. In addition, the administration of other questionnaires during the semester served as a "bogus

127   pipeline" to eliminate any demand-compliant responses (Rosnow and Davis, 1977).

The Simulation

¶ R   129   The simulation used was developed by Carl Gooding (1976), presently at Georgia Southern, and further modified by Dan

131   Voich at Florida State University. Called ENSIM (Environmental Simulation), the game is a highly competitive general manage-

133   ment simulation with dynamic environmental constraints. ENSIM offers a realistic simulation of a manufacturing firm producing

135   two products in competition with up to 19 other firms. Student groups select pricing, marketing, inventory, and purchasing

137   strategies, and establish debt, equity, and dividend policies. Students make 29 decisions each monthly operating cycle.

139   ENSIM has been used for intercollegiate MBA competition in the southeast on several occasions. In the present study, students in

141   the treatment group were randomly assigned to two-member firms for the ENSIM competition.

Case Analysis

¶ S   143   The text used by the control group was Wheelan and Hunger's (1983) *Strategic Management and Business Policy*. This book is one of

145   the most popular business policy texts (Alexander et al., 1984).
The text contains a mix of high quality cases that illustrate

147   important strategy and policy issues. In the control group, cases
were analyzed on both an individual and group basis. In every

149   analysis, the students analyzed external and internal issues,
defined problems, and made recommendations concerning vari-

151   ous strategic management issues. Individual cases were analyzed
with the assistance of the instructor. The instructor intervened in

153   group cases only after the group had presented its analysis to the
class.

¶ T   155   In summary, the pretest-posttest research design provided for
randomization, a control group, control of the treatment variable,

157   a measurable performance variable, and demand-characteristic
control.

DATA COLLECTION

¶ U   159   At the beginning of the semester, shortly after the drop/add
period, all of the students received identical instruction on the

161   importance of goal-setting as a major component of the strategic
management process and on how to prepare quality goals. The

163   students were then asked to generate as many goals as they could
that they felt necessary for a business to attain in order to survive

165   and prosper. The criteria for quality goals (Steiner et al., 1982)
that they were instructed to follow were:

167   (1) concrete and specific, with the ability to lead and motivate
      (2) attainable, but requiring competitiveness, imagination, and

169   hard work to achieve
      (3) understood by those who are to develop means to achieve

171   them
      (4) conforming to ethical and social codes accepted by society

173   (5) mutually supportive to all other goals

175   This initial goal-generation task constituted the pretest, with the
number of goals generated by each individual student represent-

177   ing the measure of this variable. To avoid clues as to how many
goals a student was expected to generate, the students wrote each

179   goal separately on an unlimited number of three-by-five cards.
Throughout the semester class materials were examined in detail

181   by both instructors to ensure that all classes received equal
amounts of similar training on goal-setting skills. At the conclu-

183   sion of the semester the goal-generation task was repeated as a
posttest.

Page 7

RESULTS

Analysis

¶ V   185   Results of statistical analyses are shown in Table 2. In both
pretest and posttest the treatment group outperformed the
187   control group, 25.16 versus 21.89 and 38.77 versus 28.01,
respectively. In comparing differences in goal-setting ability
189   recorded by students participating in a simulation and those using
the case method, *improvement*, between the pretest and posttest is
191   the important measure. Table 2 shows that the mean improvement in goal generation is 13.60 for the treatment group,
193   compared to a 6.12 improvement for the control group. This
difference generated an *F*-ratio of 25.487 and a corresponding
195   *p*-value of less than .001. This is significant evidence that in this
research project the use of simulation provided greater improve-
197   ment in goal-setting than did the case-analysis method.

TABLE 2
Analysis of Variance

	n	mean	df	F	p.
Criterion: Number of Goals Generated					
Pretest	230	23.79	228	5.963	.015[a]
Treatment Group	134	25.16			
Control Group	96	21.89			
Post-test	230	34.25	228	51.369	.000[b]
Treatment Group	134	38.77			
Control Group	96	28.01			

	n	mean	df	F	p.
Criterion: Post-test/Pretest Improvement in Goals Generated					
Improvement	230	10.46	228	25.487	.000[b]
Treatment Group		134	13.60		
Control Group		96	6.12		

Criterion: Post-test/Pretest Improvement in Goals Generated with Pretest Score as Covariate			
Source of Variation	df	F	p.
Covariate			
Pretest (Regression Coefficient = −.414)	1	40.694	.000[b]
Main Effects (Improvement)			
Treatment Group	134	13.60	
Control Group	96	6.12	
Residual	227		

a. Probability of no difference .05.
b. Probability of no difference .001.

¶ W   199   Any pretest can be expected to be a major influence on the results of a posttest, and in this case there was a difference in the pretest scores of treatment and control groups (Table 2). To

201   control for the effects of the pretest scores, another ANOVA was performed on the data treating the results of the pretest as a

203   covariate. After adjusting for retest scores, the posttest-pretest improvement was more significant, yielding an F-ratio of 40.694,

205   with a corresponding p-value of less than .001. Note that the raw regression coefficient of the pretest covariate was negative,

207   indicating that scores on the pretest were negatively correlated with improvement scores.

Discussion

¶ X   209   The utilization of a pretest-posttest design by this research project coupled with the balanced representation existing be-

211   tween the treatment group and the control group offers strong assurance against threats to the integrity of this study. The large

213   sample size employed in the testing of goal-setting, an important strategic management skill, along with the efforts to control for

215   the effects of demand characteristics, adds to the rigor of the study. The significant statistical findings strongly suggest the

217   superiority of gaming over case analysis in enhancing the goal-setting ability of business policy students.

¶ Y   219   Any time experiments are conducted using students as subjects, the possibility of self-selection becomes prevalent. Students will

221   always have timing and instructor preferences. Hopefully, the fact that the course sections involved in this study, both treatment

223   and control, were distributed reasonably evenly throughout the week precluded the possibility of a timing bias. Instructor

225   preference should not have been a problem because course assignments were not finalized until after registration, and

227   because of limited course offerings students rarely drop or add courses.

¶ Z   229   Another possible weakness of the study is the significant difference in pretest scores between the treatment and control

231   groups. It is possible, of course, that the instructor of the treatment-group sections was unconsciously "teaching" goal-

233   setting techniques, while the instructor of the control-group sections was not. All that can be said to address this issue is that

235   both instructors took part in the research design, received their training from the same university concurrently, and had the same

237   amount of experience at teaching business policy. Their purpose in participating in the study was not to "prove" or "disprove" the

Page 9

239   superiority of either method of instruction, but to better understand the effectiveness of two different pedagogies.

¶   AA   241   In any case, the limitations to this study indicated by the pretest difference between treatment and control groups may be more

243   apparent than real. The important measure was improvement between pretest and posttest. Due to the nature of the goal-setting

245   tests, a student who listed, say, 25 goals on the pretest, would have to list 40 goals on the posttest to improve by 15 goals, whereas a

247   student who listed only 5 goals on the pretest would show equal improvement by generating only 20 goals on the posttest. Thus

249   the higher scores of the treatment group on the pretest may have made it harder for them to show improvement. The negative

251   coefficient of the pretest covariate (Table 2) indicates that this is likely.

CONCLUSIONS

¶   BB   253   Two major conclusions emerge from this study.

255   (1) Participation in a management simulation better enhances the goal setting abilities of business policy students than

257   does the case method of instruction without gaming.

(2) Rigorous research methods can be used in evaluating the

259   effectiveness of gaming in business policy instruction.

¶   CC   One caveat should be noted in relation to the first conclusion.

261   The authors do not suggest that this study proves that the use of simulation is more effective than the case analysis method in all

263   aspects of business policy instruction. The results of this study suggest *only* that participation in a simulation does a better job of

265   enhancing the goal-setting skills of business policy students. There are, of course, many other areas of business policy

267   instruction that must be addressed. The authors personally believe that the business policy educational framewrok developed

269   by Lang and Dittrick (1982) combining simulations and case analysis is probably the best approach.

¶   DD   271   In addition to replicating this goal-setting study, future research efforts should operationalize other performance variables

273   such as scenario building and environmental analysis. Emphasis should be upon comparative studies of different instructional

275   methods to provide a broader base of good research from which to argue the efficacy of gaming in business policy pedagogy.

REFERENCES

Alexander, L. E., H. O'Neil, N. Snyder, and J. Townsend (1984) "How academy members teach the business policy course." Proceedings, 44th Annual Meeting of the Academy of Management.

Boseman, F. F., and R. F. Schellenberger (1974) "Business gaming, an empirical approach." Simulation & Games 5: 383–402.

Boyd, C. W., and I. Summers (1983) "Business policy course content and the distinct disciple issue: a survey of professors," pp. 1–3 in Proceedings of the Southern Management Association Meeting.

Butler, R. J., P. M. Markulis, and D. R. Strang (1985) "Learning theory and research design: how has ABSEL fared?" Proceedings, Twelfth ABSEL Conference.

Cosenza, R. M., L. E. Boone, and D. L. Kurtz (1985) "Integrating microcomputers through the use of marketing COMPUPROBS," pp. 54–55 in Proceedings, Twelfth ABSEL Conference.

Dennis, T. L. (1985) "Painless computer simulation," pp. 157–158 in Proceedings, Twelfth ABSEL Conference.

Eldredge, D. L., and R. F. Galloway (1983) "Study of the undergraduate business policy course at AACSB-accredited universities." Strategic Management J. 4: 85–90.

Estes, J. E. (1979) "Research on the effectiveness of using a computerized simulation in the basic management course," pp. 225–228 in Proceedings, Sixth ABSEL Conference.

Fritzsche, D. J., and R. V. Cotter (1985) "A guide to writing microcomputer simulations," pp. 69–73 in Proceedings, Twelfth ABSEL Conference.

Gooding, C. (1976) "Decision making under environmental constraints: a management simulation game." Doctoral dissertation, University of Georgia.

Goosen, K. R. (1985) "From the Editor." ABSEL News & Views: 5–7.

Hargraves, D., and P. K. Bolton (1972) "Selected creativity tests for use in research," British J. of Psychology 63: 451–462.

Hershey, M., and P. Kearnes (1979) "The effect of guided fantasy on the creative thinking and writing ability of gifted students." Gifted Child Q. 23: 71–77.

Keeffe, M. J., and C. J. Cozan (1985) "Popular management simulations: why some simulations succeed and others fail." ABSEL News & Views 5: 6–7.

Khatana, J. (1976) "Major directions in creativity research." Gifted Child Q. 20: 216–228.

Klein, R. D. (1980) "Can business games effectively teach business concepts?" pp. 128–131 in Proceedings, Seventh ABSEL Conference.

Lang, J. R., and J. E. Dittrich (1982) "Information skill building and the development of competence: an educational framework for teaching business policy." Academy of Management Rev. 7: 269–279.

Markulis, P. M., and D. R. Strang (1985) "Techniques to enhance the learning of students participating in computerized simulations," pp. 30–34 in Proceedings, Twelfth ABSEL Conference.

Neuhauser, J. J. (1976) "Business games have failed." Academy of Management Rev. 1: 124–129.

Newgren, K. E., R. M. Stair, and R. R. Kuehn (1981) "Decision efficiency and effectiveness in a business simulation," pp. 263–265 in Proceedings, Eighth ABSEL Conference.

Page 11

Norris, D. R. (1985) "Management gaming: a longitudinal analysis of two decades of use in collegiate schools of business," p. 378 in Proceedings, 45th Annual Meeting of the Academy of Management.

Norris, D. R., and C. A. Snyder (1981) "External validation: an experimental approach to determining the worth of simulation games," pp. 247–250 in Proceedings, Eighth ABSEL Conference.

Parnes, S., and A. Meadows (1959) "Effects of brainstorming." J. of Educ. Psychology 50: 171–176.

Raia, A. P. (1966) "A study of the educational value of management games." J. of Business 39: 339–352.

Rosenthal, R. (1977) "Biasing effects of experimenters." Et Cetera: 253–264.

Rosnow, R. L., and D. J. Davis (1977) "Demand characteristics and the psychological experiment." Et Cetera: 361–313.

Rowland, K., and D. M. Gardner (1973) "The uses of business gaming in education and laboratory research." Decision Sciences 4: 268–283.

Snow, C. C. (1976) "A comment on business policy teaching research." Academy of Management Rev. 1: 133–135.

Steiner, G. A., J. B. Miner, and E. R. Gray (1982) "Management policy and strategy," New York: Macmillan.

Thompson, K. R., and T. L. Keon (1981) "Manipulating environments of a management simulation: a pedagogy and test," pp. 86–90 in Proceedings, Eighth ABSEL Conference.

Twelker, P. A. (1972) "Some reflections on instructional simulation and gaming." Simulation & Games 3: 147–153.

Wheatley, W. J. (1985) "Enhancing strategic planning through the use of guided imagery." Doctoral dissertation, Florida State University.

Wheelan, D. L., and J. D. Hunger (1983) "Strategic management and business policy." Reading, MA: Addison-Wesley.

Wolfe, J. (1975) "Effective performance behavior in a simulated policy and decision-making environment." Management Science 21: 872–882.

Wolfe, J. (1976) "The effects and effectiveness of simulation in business policy teaching applications." Academy of Managemtn Rev. 1: 47–56.

Wolfe, J., and G. R. Guth (1975) "The case approach vs. gaming in the teaching of business policy." J. of Business 48: 349–364.

Practice Self-Test

Directions: Use the code below to indicate your response to each question:

Y = Yes
N = No
NA = Question not applicable (pilot study wasn't used, for example)
?/X = Cannot tell from information given, or given your current level of competence, you are not in a position to make a judgment.

Page numbers for the research report may be found in the upper left or right corner of the page. Each paragraph in the report is identified with a letter, A, B, C, and so on; additionally, lines are numbered 1 through 276. For each item in which the information is requested, indicate on the answer sheet where the location of the item is by page, paragraph, and line number.

General Evaluation Criteria

Code: **Y** = Yes; **N** = No; **NA** = Not Applicable; **?/X** = Can't tell or no judgment

Problem

_____ 1. Is there a statement of the problem?
         Page _____, paragraph _____, line(s) _____.
_____ 2. Is the problem "researchable"; that is, can it be investigated through the collection and analysis of data?
_____ 3. Is background information on the problem presented?
         Page _____, paragraph _____, line(s) _____.
_____ 4. Is the significance of the problem discussed?
         Page _____, paragraph _____, line(s) _____.
_____ 5. Does the problem statement indicate the variables of interest and the specific relationship between those variables that were investigated?
_____ 6. When necessary, are the variables directly or operationally defined?
         Page _____, paragraph _____, line(s) _____.

Review of Related Literature

_____ 7. Is the review comprehensive?
_____ 8. Are all the references cited relevant to the problem under investigation?
_____ 9. Are the sources mostly primary, with only a few or no secondary sources?
_____ 10. Have the references been critically analyzed and the results of various studies compared and contrasted; i.e., is the review more than a series of abstracts or annotations?
_____ 11. Is the review well organized? Does it logically flow in such a way that the least-related references to the problem are discussed first and the most-related references are discussed last?

Code: **Y** = Yes; **N** = No; **NA** = Not Applicable; **?/X** = Can't tell or no judgment

_____ 12. Does the review conclude with a brief summary of the literature and its implications for the problem investigated?
Page _____, paragraph _____, line(s) _____.

_____ 13. Do the implications discussed form an empirical or theoretical rationale for the hypotheses, either stated or implied, that follow?

Hypotheses

_____ 14. Are specific questions to be answered listed or specific hypotheses to be tested stated?
Page _____, paragraph _____, line(s) _____.

_____ 15. Does each hypothesis/problem statement state an expected relationship or difference between two variables? If necessary, are the variables directly or operationally defined?

_____ 16. Is each hypothesis/problem statement testable?

Method

Subjects

_____ 17. Are the major characteristics, including size, of the population studied described?
Page _____, paragraph _____, line(s) _____.

_____ 18. If a sample was selected, is the method of selection clearly described?
Page _____, paragraph _____, line(s) _____.

_____ 19. Is the method of sample selection described one that is likely to result in a representative, unbiased sample?

_____ 20. Did the researcher avoid the use of volunteers?

_____ 21. Are the size and major characteristics of the sample described?
Page _____, paragraph _____, line(s) _____.

_____ 22. Does the population/sample size meet the suggested guideline for minimum sample size appropriate for the method of research represented?

Instruments

_____ 23. Is a rationale given for the selection of instruments or measurements used?
Page _____, paragraph _____, line(s) _____.

_____ 24. Is each instrument or measurement described in terms of purpose and content?
Page _____, paragraph _____, line(s) _____.

_____ 25. Are the instruments or measurements appropriate for measuring the intended variables?

_____ 26. If an instrument or measurement was developed specifically for the study, are the procedures involved in its development and validation described?
Page _____, Paragraph _____, line(s) _____.

Code: **Y** = Yes; **N** = No; **NA** = Not Applicable; **?/X** = Can't tell or no judgment

_____ 27. Is evidence presented that indicates that each instrument or measurement
is appropriate for the population/sample under study?
Page _____, Paragraph _____, line(s) _____.

_____ 28. Is instrument validity discussed and coefficients given if appropriate?
Page _____, Paragraph _____, line(s) _____.

_____ 29. Is reliability discussed in terms of type and size of reliability coefficients?
Page _____, Paragraph _____, line(s) _____.

_____ 30. If appropriate, are subtest reliabilities given?
Page _____, Paragraph _____, line(s) _____.

_____ 31. If an instrument or measurement was developed specifically for the
study, are administration, scoring or tabulating, and interpretation procedures fully described?
Page _____, Paragraph _____, line(s) _____.

Design and Procedure

_____ 32. Is the design appropriate for testing the hypotheses/problem of the study?

_____ 33. Are the procedures described in sufficient detail to permit them to be
replicated by another researcher?
Page _____, Paragraph _____, line(s) _____.

_____ 34. If a pilot study was conducted, are its execution and results described as
well as its impact on the subsequent study?
Page _____, Paragraph _____, line(s) _____.

_____ 35. Are control procedures described?
Page _____, Paragraph _____, line(s) _____.

_____ 36. Did the researcher discuss or account for any potentially confounding
variables that he or she was unable to control?
Page _____, Paragraph _____, line(s) _____.

Results

_____ 37. Are appropriate descriptive statistics presented?
Page _____, Paragraph _____, line(s) _____.

_____ 38. Was the probability level, α, at which the results of the tests of significance were evaluated specified in advance of the data analysis?
Page _____, Paragraph _____, line(s) _____.

_____ 39. If parametric tests were used, is there evidence that the researcher
avoided violating the required assumptions for parametric tests?
Page _____, Paragraph _____, line(s) _____.

_____ 40. Are the tests of significance described appropriate, given the hypothesis/
problem and design of the study?

_____ 41. Was every hypothesis tested?
Page _____, Paragraph _____, line(s) _____.

_____ 42. Are the tests of significance interpreted using the appropriate degrees of
freedom?

_____ 43. Are the results clearly presented?

_____ 44. Are the tables and figures (if any) well organized and easy to understand?

Code: **Y** = Yes; **N** = No; **NA** = Not Applicable; **?/X** = Can't tell or no judgment

_____ 45. Are the data in each table and figure referred to in the text?
Page _____, Paragraph _____, line(s) _____.

Discussion (Conclusions and Recommendations)

_____ 46. Is each result discussed in terms of the original hypothesis/problem to which it relates?
Page _____, Paragraph _____, line(s) _____.
_____ 47. Is each result discussed in terms of its agreement or disagreement with previous results obtained by other researchers in other studies?
Page _____, Paragraph _____, line(s) _____.
_____ 48. Are generalizations that are made warranted by the results?
_____ 49. Are the possible effects of uncontrolled variables on the results discussed?
Page _____, Paragraph _____, line(s) _____.
_____ 50. Are theoretical and practical implications of the findings discussed?
Page _____, Paragraph _____, line(s) _____.
_____ 51. Are recommendations for future action made?
Page _____, Paragraph _____, line(s) _____.
_____ 52. Are the suggestions for future action based on practical significance or on statistical significance only, i.e., has the author avoided confusing practical and statistical significance?
_____ 53. Are recommendations for future research made?
Page _____, Paragraph _____, line(s) _____.

Abstract or Summary

_____ 54. Is the problem stated?
Page _____, Paragraph _____, line(s) _____.
_____ 55. Are the number and type of subjects and instruments or measurements described?
Page _____, Paragraph _____, line(s) _____.
_____ 56. Is the design used identified?
Page _____, Paragraph _____, line(s) _____.
_____ 57. Are the procedures described?
Page _____, Paragraph _____, line(s) _____.
_____ 58. Are the major results and conclusions stated?
Page _____, Paragraph _____, line(s) _____.

Method-Specific Evaluation Criteria

59. Identify the experimental design used in this study _____

_____

60. On a separate sheet of paper, diagram the experimental design used in this study:
_____ 61. Was an appropriate experimental design selected?
_____ 62. Is a rationale for design selection given?
Page _____, Paragraph _____, line(s) _____.

Code: **Y** = Yes; **N** = No; **NA** = Not Applicable; **?/X** = Can't tell or no judgment

_____ 63. Are sources of invalidity associated with the design identified and discussed?
Page _____, Paragraph _____, line(s) _____.
_____ 64. Is the method of group formation described?
Page _____, Paragraph _____, line(s) _____.
_____ 65. Was the experimental group formed in the same way as the control
group?
_____ 66. Were groups randomly formed and the use of existing groups avoided?
_____ 67. Were treatments randomly assigned to groups?
_____ 68. Were critical extraneous variables identified?
Page _____, Paragraph _____, line(s) _____.
_____ 69. Were any control procedures applied to equate groups on extraneous
variables?
_____ 70. Is there any evidence to suggest the researcher was able to avoid reactive
arrangements (for example, the Hawthorne effect)?
Page _____, Paragraph _____, line(s) _____.

Reference Tables

Table A.1

Ten Thousand Random Numbers

	00-04	05-09	10-14	15-19	20-24	25-29	30-34	35-39	40-44	45-49
00	54463	22662	65905	70639	79365	67382	29085	69831	47058	08186
01	15389	85205	18850	39226	42249	90669	96325	23248	60933	26927
02	85941	40756	82414	02015	13858	78030	16269	65978	01385	15345
03	61149	69440	11268	88218	58925	03638	52862	62733	33451	77455
04	05219	81619	81619	10651	67079	92511	59888	72095	83463	75577
05	41417	98326	87719	92294	46614	50948	64886	20002	97365	30976
06	28357	94070	20652	35774	16249	75019	21145	15217	47286	76305
07	17783	00015	10806	83091	91530	36466	39981	62481	49177	75779
08	40950	84820	29881	85966	62800	70326	84740	62660	77379	90279
09	82995	64157	66164	41180	10089	41757	78258	96488	88629	37231
10	96754	17676	55659	44105	47361	34833	86679	23930	53249	27083
11	34357	88040	53364	71726	45690	66334	60332	22554	90600	71113
12	06318	37403	49927	57715	50423	67372	63116	48888	21505	80182
13	62111	52820	07243	79931	89292	84767	85693	73947	22278	11551
14	47534	09243	67879	00544	23410	12740	02540	54440	32949	13491
15	98614	75993	84460	62846	59844	14922	49730	73443	48167	34770
16	24856	03648	44898	09351	98795	18644	39765	71058	90368	44104
17	96887	12479	80621	66223	86085	78285	02432	53342	42846	94771
18	90801	21472	42815	77408	37390	76766	52615	32141	30268	18106
19	55165	77312	83666	36028	28420	70219	81369	41943	47366	41067
20	75884	12952	84318	95108	72305	64620	91318	89872	45375	85436
21	16777	37116	58550	42958	21460	43910	01175	87894	81378	10620
22	46230	43877	80207	88877	89380	32992	91380	03164	98656	59337
23	42902	66892	46134	01432	94710	23474	20523	60137	60609	13119
24	81007	00333	39693	28039	10154	95425	39220	19774	31782	49037
25	68089	01122	51111	72373	06902	74373	96199	97017	41273	21546
26	20411	67081	89950	16944	93054	87687	96693	87236	77054	33848
27	58212	13160	06468	15718	82627	76999	05999	58680	96739	63700
28	70577	42866	24969	61210	76046	67699	42054	12696	93758	03283
29	94522	74358	71659	62038	79643	79169	44741	05437	39038	13163
30	42626	86819	85651	88678	17401	03252	99547	32404	17918	62880
31	16051	33763	57194	16752	54450	19031	58580	47629	54132	60631
32	08244	27647	33851	44705	94211	46716	11738	55784	95374	72655
33	59497	04392	09419	89964	51211	04894	72882	17805	21896	83864
34	97155	13428	40293	09985	58434	01412	69124	82171	59058	82859

Reprinted by permission from *Statistical Methods* by George W. Snedecor and William G. Cochran, sixth edition © 1967 by Iowa State Univeristy Press, pp. 543–46.

Table A.1 (continued)

	50–54	55–59	60–64	65–69	70–74	75–79	80–84	85–89	90–94	95–99
00	59391	58030	52098	82718	87024	82848	04190	96574	90464	29065
01	99567	76364	77204	04615	27062	96621	43918	01896	83991	51141
02	10363	97518	51400	25670	98342	61891	27101	37855	06235	33316
03	96859	19558	64432	16706	99612	59798	32803	67708	15297	28612
04	11258	24591	36863	55368	31721	94335	34936	02566	80972	08188
05	95068	88628	35911	14530	33020	80428	33936	31855	34334	64865
06	54463	47237	73800	91017	36239	71824	83671	39892	60518	37092
07	16874	62677	57412	13215	31389	62233	80827	73917	82802	84420
08	92494	63157	76593	91316	03505	72389	96363	52887	01087	66091
09	15669	56689	35682	40844	53256	81872	35213	09840	34471	74441
10	99116	75486	84989	23476	52967	67104	39495	39100	17217	74073
11	15696	10703	65178	90637	63110	17622	53988	71087	84148	11670
12	97720	15369	51269	69620	03388	13699	33423	67453	43269	56720
13	11666	13841	71681	98000	35979	39719	81899	07449	47985	46967
14	71628	73130	78783	75691	41632	09847	61547	18707	85489	69944
15	40501	51089	99943	91843	41995	88931	73631	69361	05375	15417
16	22518	55576	98215	82068	10798	86211	36584	67466	69373	40054
17	75112	30485	62173	02132	14878	92879	22281	16783	86352	00077
18	80327	02671	98191	84342	90813	49268	94551	15496	20168	09271
19	60251	45548	02146	05597	48228	81366	34598	72856	66762	17002
20	57430	82270	10421	00540	43648	75888	66049	21511	47676	33444
21	73528	39559	34434	88586	54086	71693	43132	14414	79949	85193
22	25991	65959	70769	64721	86413	33475	42740	06175	82758	66248
23	78388	16638	09134	59980	63806	48472	39318	35434	24057	74739
24	12477	09965	96657	57994	59439	76330	24596	77515	09577	91871
25	83266	32883	42451	15579	38155	29793	40914	65990	16255	17777
26	76970	80876	10237	39515	79152	74798	39357	09054	73579	92359
27	37074	65198	44785	68624	98336	84481	97610	78735	46703	98265
28	83712	06514	30101	78295	54656	85417	43189	60048	72781	72606
29	20287	56862	69727	94443	64936	08366	27227	05158	50326	59566
30	74261	32592	86538	27041	65172	85532	07571	80609	39285	65340
31	64081	49863	08478	96001	18888	14810	70545	89755	59064	07210
32	05617	75818	47750	67814	29575	10526	66192	44464	27058	40467
33	26793	74951	95466	74307	13330	42664	85515	20632	05497	33625
34	65988	72850	48737	54719	52056	01596	03845	35067	03134	70322

Table A.1 (continued)

	00−04	05−09	10−14	15−19	20−24	25−29	30−34	35−39	40−44	45−49
35	98409	66162	95763	47420	20792	61527	20441	39435	11859	41567
36	45476	84882	65109	96597	25930	66790	65706	61203	53634	22557
37	89300	69700	50741	30329	11658	23166	05400	66669	48708	03887
38	50051	95137	91631	66315	91428	12275	24816	68091	71710	33258
39	31753	85178	31310	89642	98364	02306	24617	09609	83942	22716
40	79152	53829	77250	20190	56535	18760	69942	77448	33278	48805
41	44560	38750	83635	56540	64900	42912	13953	79149	18710	68618
42	68328	83378	63369	71381	39564	05615	42451	64559	97501	65747
43	46939	38689	58625	08342	30459	85863	20781	09284	26333	91777
44	83544	86141	15707	96256	23068	13782	08467	89469	93842	55349
45	91621	00881	04900	54224	46177	55309	17852	27491	89415	23466
46	91896	67126	04151	03795	59077	11848	12630	98375	53068	60142
47	55751	62515	22108	80830	02263	29303	37204	96926	30506	09808
48	85156	87689	95493	88842	00664	55017	55539	17771	69448	87530
49	07521	56898	12236	60277	39102	62315	12239	07105	11844	01117
50	64249	63664	39652	40646	97306	31741	07294	84149	46797	82487
51	26538	44249	04050	48174	65570	44072	40192	51153	11397	58212
52	05845	00512	78630	55328	18116	69296	91705	86224	29503	57071
53	74897	68373	67359	51014	33510	83048	17056	72506	82949	54600
54	20872	54570	35017	88132	25730	22626	86723	91691	13191	77212
55	31432	96156	89177	75541	81355	24480	77243	76690	42507	84362
56	66890	61505	01240	00660	05873	13568	76082	79172	57913	93448
57	41894	57790	79970	33106	86904	48119	52503	24130	72824	21627
58	11303	87118	81471	52936	08555	28420	49416	44448	04269	27029
59	54374	57325	16947	45356	78371	10563	97191	53798	12693	27928
60	64852	34421	61046	90849	13966	39810	42699	21753	76192	10508
61	16309	20384	09491	91588	97720	89846	30376	76970	23063	35894
62	42587	37065	24526	72602	57589	98131	37292	05967	26002	51945
63	40177	98590	97161	41682	84533	67588	62036	49967	01990	72308
64	82309	76128	93965	26743	24141	04838	40254	26065	07938	76236
65	79788	68243	59732	04257	27084	14743	17520	94501	55811	76099
66	40538	79000	89559	25026	42274	23489	34502	75508	06059	86682
67	64016	73598	18609	73150	62463	33102	45205	87440	96767	67042
68	49767	12691	17903	93871	99721	79109	09425	26904	07419	76013
69	76974	55108	29795	08404	82684	00497	51126	79935	57450	55671

Table A.1 (continued)

	50–54	55–59	60–64	65–69	70–74	75–79	80–84	85–89	90–94	95–99
35	27366	42271	44300	73399	21105	03280	73457	43093	05192	48657
36	56760	10909	98147	34736	33863	95256	12731	66598	50771	83665
37	72880	43338	93643	58904	59543	23943	11231	83268	65938	81581
38	77888	38100	03062	58103	47961	83841	25878	23746	55903	44115
39	28440	07819	21580	51459	47971	29882	13990	29226	23608	15873
40	63525	94441	77033	12147	51054	49955	58312	76923	96071	05813
41	47606	93410	16359	89033	89696	47231	64498	31776	05383	39902
42	52669	45030	96279	14709	52372	87832	02735	50803	72744	88208
43	16738	60159	07425	62369	07515	82721	37875	71153	21315	00132
44	59348	11695	45751	15865	74739	05572	32688	20271	65128	14551
45	12900	71775	29845	60774	94924	21810	38636	33717	67598	82521
46	75086	23537	49939	33595	13484	97588	28617	17979	70749	35234
47	99495	51534	29181	09993	38190	42553	68922	52125	91077	40197
48	26075	31671	45386	36583	93459	48599	52022	41330	60651	91321
49	13636	93596	23377	51133	95126	61496	42474	45141	46660	42338
50	32847	31282	03345	89593	69214	70381	78285	20054	91018	16742
51	16916	00041	30236	55023	14253	76582	12092	86533	92426	37655
52	66176	34037	21005	27137	03193	48970	64625	22394	39622	79085
53	46299	13335	12180	16861	38043	59292	62675	63631	37020	78195
54	22847	47839	45385	23289	47526	54098	45683	55849	51575	64689
55	41851	54160	92320	69936	34803	92479	33399	71160	64777	83378
56	28444	59497	91586	95917	68553	28639	06455	34174	11130	91994
57	47520	62378	98855	83174	13088	16561	68559	26679	06238	51254
58	34978	63271	13142	82681	05271	08822	06490	44984	49307	61617
59	37404	80416	69035	92980	49486	74378	75610	74976	70056	15478
60	32400	65482	52099	53676	74648	94148	65095	69597	52771	71551
61	89262	86332	51718	70663	11623	29834	79820	73002	84886	03591
62	86866	09127	98021	03871	27789	58444	44832	36505	40672	30180
63	90814	14833	08759	74645	05046	94056	99094	65091	32663	73040
64	19192	82756	20553	58446	55376	88914	75096	26119	83898	43816
65	77585	52593	56612	95766	10019	29531	73064	20953	53523	58136
66	23757	16364	05096	03192	62386	45389	85332	18877	55710	96459
67	45989	96257	23850	26216	23309	21526	07425	50254	19455	29315
68	92970	94243	07316	41467	64837	52406	25225	51553	31220	14032
69	74346	59596	40088	98176	17896	86900	20249	77753	19099	48885

Table A.1 (continued)

	00–04	05–09	10–14	15–19	20–24	25–29	30–34	35–39	40–44	45–49
70	23854	08480	85983	96025	50117	64610	99425	62291	86943	21541
71	68973	70551	25098	78033	98573	79848	31778	29555	61446	23037
72	36444	93600	65350	14971	25325	00427	52073	64280	18847	24768
73	03003	87800	07391	11594	21196	00781	32550	57158	58887	73041
74	17540	26188	36647	78386	04558	61463	57842	90382	77019	24210
75	38916	55809	47982	41968	69760	79422	80154	91486	19180	15100
76	64288	19843	69122	42502	48508	28820	59933	72998	99942	10515
77	86809	51564	38040	39418	49915	19000	58050	16899	79952	57849
78	99800	99566	14742	05028	30033	94889	55381	23656	75787	59223
79	92345	31890	95712	08279	91794	94068	49337	88674	35355	12267
80	90363	65162	32245	82279	79256	80834	06088	99462	56705	06118
81	64437	32242	48431	04835	39070	59702	31508	60935	22390	52246
82	91714	53662	28373	34333	55791	74758	51144	18827	10704	76803
83	20902	17646	31391	31459	33315	03444	55743	74701	58851	27427
84	12217	86007	70371	52281	14510	76094	96579	54853	78339	20839
85	45177	02863	42307	53571	22532	74921	17735	42201	80540	54721
86	28325	90814	08804	52746	47913	54577	47525	77705	95330	21866
87	29019	28776	56116	54791	64604	08815	46049	71186	34650	14994
88	84979	81353	56219	67062	26146	82567	33122	14124	46240	92973
89	50371	26347	48513	63915	11158	25563	91915	18431	92978	11591
90	53422	06825	69711	67950	64716	18003	49581	45378	99878	61130
91	67453	35651	89316	41620	32048	70225	47597	33137	31443	51445
92	07294	85353	74819	23445	68237	07202	99515	62282	53809	26685
93	79544	00302	45338	16015	66613	88968	14595	63836	77716	79596
94	64144	85442	82060	46471	24162	39500	87351	36637	42833	71875
95	90919	11883	58318	00042	52402	28210	34075	33272	00840	73268
96	06670	57353	86275	92276	77591	46924	60839	55437	03183	13191
97	36634	93976	52062	83678	41256	60948	18685	48992	19462	96062
98	75101	72891	85745	67106	26010	62107	60885	37503	55461	71213
99	05112	71222	72654	51583	05228	62056	57390	42746	39272	96659

Table A.1 (continued)

	50–54	55–59	60–64	65–69	70–74	75–79	80–84	85–89	90–94	95–99
70	87646	41309	27636	45153	29988	94770	07255	70908	05340	99751
71	50099	71038	45146	06146	55211	99429	43169	66259	99786	59180
72	10127	46900	64984	75348	04115	33624	68774	60013	35515	62556
73	67995	81977	18984	64091	02785	27762	42529	97144	80407	64524
74	26304	80217	84934	82657	69291	35397	98714	35104	08187	48109
75	81994	41070	56642	64091	31229	02595	13513	45148	78722	30144
76	59337	34662	79631	89403	65212	09975	06118	86197	58208	16162
77	51228	10937	62396	81460	47331	91403	95007	06047	16846	64809
78	31089	37995	29577	07828	42272	54016	21950	86192	99046	84864
79	38207	97938	93459	75174	79460	55436	57206	87644	21296	43393
80	88666	31142	09474	89712	63153	62333	42212	06140	42594	43671
81	53365	56134	67582	92557	89520	33452	05134	70628	27612	33738
82	89807	74530	38004	90102	11693	90257	05500	79920	62700	43325
83	18682	81038	85662	90915	91631	22223	91588	80774	07716	12548
84	63571	32579	63942	25371	09234	94592	98475	76884	37635	33608
85	68927	56492	67799	95398	77642	54913	91583	08421	81450	76229
86	56401	63186	39389	88798	31356	89235	97036	32341	33292	73757
87	24333	95603	02359	72942	46287	95382	08452	62862	97869	71775
88	17025	84202	95199	62272	06366	16175	97577	99304	41587	03686
89	02804	08253	52133	20224	68034	50865	57868	22343	55111	03607
90	08298	03879	20995	19850	73090	13191	18963	82244	78479	99121
91	59883	01785	82403	96062	03785	03488	12970	64896	38336	30030
92	46982	06682	62864	91837	74021	89094	39952	64158	79614	78235
93	31121	47266	07661	02051	67599	24471	69843	83696	71402	76287
94	97867	56641	63416	17577	30161	87320	37752	73276	48969	41915
95	57364	86746	08415	14621	49430	22311	15836	72492	49372	44103
96	09559	26263	69511	28064	75999	44540	13337	10918	79846	54809
97	53873	55571	00608	42661	91332	63956	74087	59008	47493	99581
98	35531	19162	86406	05299	77511	24311	57257	22826	77555	05941
99	28229	88629	25695	94932	30721	16197	78742	34974	97528	45447

Table A.2

Values of the Correlation Coefficient for Different Levels of Significance

df	p			
	.10	.05	.01	.001
1	.98769	.99692	.99988	.99999
2	.90000	.95000	.99000	.99900
3	.8054	.8783	.95873	.99116
4	.7293	.8114	.91720	.97406
5	.6694	.7545	.8745	.95074
6	.6215	.7067	.8343	.92493
7	.5822	.6664	.7977	.8982
8	.5494	.6319	.7646	.8721
9	.5214	.6021	.7348	.8471
10	.4973	.5760	.7079	.8233
11	.4762	.5529	.6835	.8010
12	.4575	.5324	.6614	.7800
13	.4409	.5139	.6411	.7603
14	.4259	.4973	.6226	.7420
15	.4124	.4821	.6055	.7246
16	.4000	.4683	.5897	.7084
17	.3887	.4555	.5751	.6932
18	.3783	.4438	.5614	.6787
19	.3687	.4329	.5487	.6652
20	.3598	.4227	.5368	.6524
25	.3233	.3809	.4869	.5974
30	.2960	.3494	.4487	.5541
35	.2746	.3246	.4182	.5189
40	.2573	.3044	.3932	.4896
45	.2428	.2875	.3721	.4648
50	.2306	.2732	.3541	.4433
60	.2108	.2500	.3248	.4078
70	.1954	.2319	.3017	.3799
80	.1829	.2172	.2830	.3568
90	.1726	.2050	.2673	.3375
100	.1638	.1946	.2540	.3211

Table A.2 is taken from Table VII of Fisher and Yates: *Statistical Tables for Biological, Agricultural and Medical Research*, published by Longman Group Ltd., London (previously published by Oliver and Boyd, Edinburgh), and by permission of the authors and publishers.

Table A.3

Critical Values of Spearman's Rank Correlation Coefficient with a Two-tailed Test

ABSOLUTE VALUES OF THE CRITICAL VALUES OF SPEARMAN'S RANK CORRELATION COEFFICIENT, r_s, FOR TESTING THE NULL HYPOTHESIS OF NO CORRELATION WITH A TWO-TAILED TEST*

n	$\alpha = .10$	$\alpha = .05$	$\alpha = .02$	$\alpha = .01$
5	0.900	—	—	—
6	0.829	0.886	0.943	—
7	0.714	0.786	0.893	—
8	0.643	0.738	0.833	0.881
9	0.600	0.683	0.783	0.833
10	0.564	0.648	0.745	0.818
11	0.523	0.623	0.736	0.794
12	0.497	0.591	0.703	0.780
13	0.475	0.566	0.673	0.745
14	0.457	0.545	0.646	0.716
15	0.441	0.525	0.623	0.689
16	0.425	0.507	0.601	0.666
17	0.412	0.490	0.582	0.645
18	0.399	0.476	0.564	0.625
19	0.388	0.462	0.549	0.608
20	0.377	0.450	0.534	0.591
21	0.368	0.438	0.521	0.576
22	0.359	0.428	0.508	0.562
23	0.351	0.418	0.496	0.549
24	0.343	0.409	0.485	0.537
25	0.336	0.400	0.475	0.526
26	0.329	0.392	0.465	0.515
27	0.323	0.385	0.456	0.505
28	0.317	0.377	0.448	0.496
29	0.311	0.370	0.440	0.487
30	0.305	0.364	0.432	0.478

Adapted from E. G. Olds, "Distributions of sums of squares of rank differences for small numbers of individuals," *Annals of Mathematical Statistics*, 9 (1938), 133–48, and "The 5% significance levels for sums of squares of rank differences and a correction," *Annals of Mathematical Statistics*, 20 (1949), 117–18, by permission of The Institute of Mathematical Statistics.

*The tabled values are *absolute values* of the critical values for *two-tailed tests*. For example, the critical values of r_s for $n = 10$ and $\alpha = .10$ are +0.564 and −0.564.

Table A.4

Distribution of t

df	.10	.05	.01	.001
			p	
1	6.314	12.706	63.657	636.619
2	2.920	4.303	9.925	31.598
3	2.353	3.182	5.841	12.924
4	2.132	2.776	4.604	8.610
5	2.015	2.571	4.032	6.869
6	1.943	2.447	3.707	5.959
7	1.895	2.365	3.499	5.408
8	1.860	2.306	3.355	5.041
9	1.833	2.262	3.250	4.781
10	1.812	2.228	3.169	4.587
11	1.796	2.201	3.106	4.437
12	1.782	2.179	3.055	4.318
13	1.771	2.160	3.012	4.221
14	1.761	2.145	2.977	4.140
15	1.753	2.131	2.947	4.073
16	1.746	2.120	2.921	4.015
17	1.740	2.110	2.898	3.965
18	1.734	2.101	2.878	3.922
19	1.729	2.093	2.861	3.883
20	1.725	2.086	2.845	3.850
21	1.721	2.080	2.831	3.819
22	1.717	2.074	2.819	3.792
23	1.714	2.069	2.807	3.767
24	1.711	2.064	2.797	3.745
25	1.708	2.060	2.787	3.725
26	1.706	2.056	2.779	3.707
27	1.703	2.052	2.771	3.690
28	1.701	2.048	2.763	3.674
29	1.699	2.045	2.756	3.659
30	1.697	2.042	2.750	3.646
40	1.684	2.021	2.704	3.551
60	1.671	2.000	2.660	3.460
120	1.658	1.980	2.617	3.373
∞	1.645	1.960	2.576	3.291

Table A.4 is taken from Table III of Fisher and Yates: *Statistical Tables for Biological, Agricultural and Medical Research,* published by Longman Group Ltd., London (previously published by Oliver and Boyd, Edinburgh), and by permission of the authors and publishers.

Table A.5

Distribution of F

			$p = .10$			
			n_1*			
n_2**	1	2	3	4	5	6
4	4.54	4.32	4.19	4.11	4.05	4.01
5	4.06	3.78	3.62	3.52	3.45	3.40
6	3.78	3.46	3.29	3.18	3.11	3.05
7	3.59	3.26	3.07	2.96	2.88	2.83
8	3.46	3.11	2.92	2.81	2.73	2.67
9	3.36	3.01	2.81	2.69	2.61	2.55
10	3.28	2.92	2.73	2.61	2.52	2.46
11	3.23	2.86	2.66	2.54	2.45	2.39
12	3.18	2.81	2.61	2.48	2.39	2.33
13	3.14	2.76	2.56	2.43	2.35	2.28
14	3.10	2.73	2.52	2.39	2.31	2.24
15	3.07	2.70	2.49	2.36	2.27	2.21
16	3.05	2.67	2.46	2.33	2.24	2.18
17	3.03	2.64	2.44	2.31	2.22	2.15
18	3.01	2.62	2.42	2.29	2.20	2.13
19	2.99	2.61	2.40	2.27	2.18	2.11
20	2.97	2.59	2.38	2.25	2.16	2.09
21	2.96	2.57	2.36	2.23	2.14	2.08
22	2.95	2.56	2.35	2.22	2.13	2.06
23	2.94	2.55	2.34	2.21	2.11	2.05
24	2.93	2.54	2.33	2.19	2.10	2.04
25	2.92	2.53	2.32	2.18	2.09	2.02
26	2.91	2.52	2.31	2.17	2.08	2.01
27	2.90	2.51	2.30	2.17	2.07	2.00
28	2.89	2.50	2.29	2.16	2.06	2.00
29	2.89	2.50	2.28	2.15	2.06	1.99
30	2.88	2.49	2.28	2.14	2.05	1.98
40	2.84	2.44	2.23	2.09	2.00	1.93
60	2.79	2.39	2.18	2.04	1.95	1.87
120	2.75	2.35	2.13	1.99	1.90	1.82
∞	2.71	2.30	2.08	1.94	1.85	1.77

*n_1 = degrees of freedom for the mean square between

**n_2 = degrees of freedom for the mean square within

Table A.5 is taken from Table V of Fisher and Yates: *Statistical Tables for Biological, Agricultural and Medical Research,* published by Longman Group Ltd., London (previously published by Oliver and Boyd, Edinburgh), and by permission of the authors and publishers.

Table A.5 (continued)

				$p = .05$		
				n_1*		
n_2**	1	2	3	4	5	6
4	7.71	6.94	6.59	6.39	6.26	6.16
5	6.61	5.79	5.41	5.19	5.05	4.95
6	5.99	5.14	4.76	4.53	4.39	4.28
7	5.59	4.74	4.35	4.12	3.97	3.87
8	5.32	4.46	4.07	3.84	3.69	3.58
9	5.12	4.26	3.86	3.63	3.48	3.37
10	4.96	4.10	3.71	3.48	3.33	3.22
11	4.84	3.98	3.59	3.36	3.20	3.09
12	4.75	3.88	3.49	3.26	3.11	3.00
13	4.67	3.80	3.41	3.18	3.02	2.92
14	4.60	3.74	3.34	3.11	2.96	2.85
15	4.54	3.68	3.29	3.06	2.90	2.79
16	4.49	3.63	3.24	3.01	2.85	2.74
17	4.45	3.59	3.20	2.96	2.81	2.70
18	4.41	3.55	3.16	2.93	2.77	2.66
19	4.38	3.52	3.13	2.90	2.74	2.63
20	4.35	3.49	3.10	2.87	2.71	2.60
21	4.32	4.47	3.07	2.84	2.68	2.57
22	4.30	3.44	3.05	2.82	2.66	2.55
23	4.28	3.42	3.03	2.80	2.64	2.53
24	4.26	3.40	3.01	2.78	2.62	2.51
25	4.24	3.38	2.99	2.76	2.60	2.49
26	4.22	3.37	2.98	2.74	2.59	2.47
27	4.21	3.35	2.96	2.73	2.57	2.46
28	4.20	3.34	2.95	2.71	2.56	2.44
29	4.18	3.33	2.93	2.70	2.54	2.43
30	4.17	3.32	2.92	2.69	2.53	2.42
40	4.08	3.23	2.84	2.61	2.45	2.34
60	4.00	3.15	2.76	2.52	2.37	2.25
120	3.92	3.07	2.68	2.45	2.29	2.17
∞	3.84	2.99	2.60	2.37	2.21	2.10

n_1 = degrees of freedom for the mean square between
**n_2 = degrees of freedom for the mean square within

Table A.5 (continued)

	$p = .01$					
	n_1*					
n_2**	1	2	3	4	5	6
4	21.20	18.00	16.69	15.98	15.52	15.21
5	16.26	13.27	12.06	11.39	10.97	10.67
6	13.74	10.92	9.78	9.15	8.75	8.47
7	12.25	9.55	8.45	7.85	7.46	7.19
8	11.26	8.65	7.59	7.01	6.63	6.37
9	10.56	8.02	6.99	6.42	6.06	5.80
10	10.04	7.56	6.55	5.99	5.64	5.39
11	9.65	7.20	6.22	5.67	5.32	5.07
12	9.33	6.93	5.95	5.41	5.06	4.82
13	9.07	6.70	5.74	5.20	4.86	4.62
14	8.86	6.51	5.56	5.03	4.69	4.46
15	8.68	6.36	5.42	4.89	4.56	4.32
16	8.53	6.23	5.29	4.77	4.44	4.20
17	8.40	6.11	5.18	4.67	4.34	4.10
18	8.28	6.01	5.09	4.58	4.25	4.01
19	8.18	5.93	5.01	4.50	4.17	3.94
20	8.10	5.85	4.94	4.43	4.10	3.87
21	8.02	5.78	4.87	4.37	4.04	3.81
22	7.94	5.72	4.82	4.31	3.99	3.76
23	7.88	5.66	4.76	4.26	3.94	3.71
24	7.82	5.61	4.72	4.22	3.90	3.67
25	7.77	5.57	4.68	4.18	3.86	3.63
26	7.72	5.53	4.64	4.14	3.82	3.59
27	7.68	5.49	4.60	4.11	3.78	3.56
28	7.64	5.45	4.57	4.07	3.75	3.53
29	7.60	5.42	4.54	4.04	3.73	3.50
30	7.56	5.39	4.51	4.02	3.70	3.47
40	7.31	5.18	4.31	3.83	3.51	3.29
60	7.08	4.98	4.13	3.65	3.34	3.12
120	6.85	4.79	3.95	3.48	3.17	2.96
∞	6.64	4.60	3.78	3.32	3.02	2.80

*n_1 = degrees of freedom for the mean square between
**n_2 = degrees of freedom for the mean square within

Table A.5 (continued)

	$p = .001$					
	n_1**					
n_2**	1	2	3	4	5	6
4	74.14	61.25	56.18	53.44	51.71	50.53
5	47.18	37.12	33.20	31.09	29.75	28.84
6	35.51	27.00	23.70	21.92	20.81	20.03
7	29.25	21.69	18.77	17.19	16.21	15.52
8	25.42	18.49	15.83	14.39	13.49	12.86
9	22.86	16.39	13.90	12.56	11.71	11.13
10	21.04	14.91	12.55	11.28	10.48	9.92
11	19.69	13.81	11.56	10.35	9.58	9.05
12	18.64	12.97	10.80	9.63	8.89	8.38
13	17.81	12.31	10.21	9.07	8.35	7.86
14	17.14	11.78	9.73	8.62	7.92	7.43
15	16.59	11.34	9.34	8.25	7.57	7.09
16	16.12	10.97	9.00	7.94	7.27	6.81
17	15.72	10.66	8.73	7.68	7.02	6.56
18	15.38	10.39	8.49	7.46	6.81	6.35
19	15.08	10.16	8.28	7.26	6.62	6.18
20	14.82	9.95	8.10	7.10	6.46	6.02
21	14.59	9.77	7.94	6.95	6.32	5.88
22	14.38	9.61	7.80	6.81	6.19	5.76
23	14.19	9.47	7.67	6.69	6.08	5.65
24	14.03	9.34	7.55	6.59	5.98	5.55
25	13.88	9.22	7.45	6.49	5.88	5.46
26	13.74	9.12	7.36	6.41	5.80	5.38
27	13.61	9.02	7.27	6.33	5.73	5.31
28	13.50	8.93	7.19	6.25	5.66	5.24
29	13.39	8.85	7.12	6.19	5.59	5.18
30	13.29	8.77	7.05	6.12	5.53	5.12
40	12.61	8.25	6.60	5.70	5.13	4.73
60	11.97	7.76	6.17	5.31	4.76	4.37
120	11.38	7.32	5.79	4.95	4.42	4.04
∞	10.83	6.91	5.42	4.62	4.10	3.74

*n_1 = degrees of freedom for the mean square between
**n_2 = degrees of freedom for the mean square within

Table A.6 Distribution of χ^2

df	.10	.05	.01	.001
			p	
1	2.706	3.841	6.635	10.827
2	4.605	5.991	9.210	13.815
3	6.251	7.815	11.345	16.266
4	7.779	9.488	13.277	18.467
5	9.236	11.070	15.086	20.515
6	10.645	12.592	16.812	22.457
7	12.017	14.067	18.475	24.322
8	13.362	15.507	20.090	26.125
9	14.684	16.919	21.666	27.877
10	15.987	18.307	23.209	29.588
11	17.275	19.675	24.725	31.264
12	18.549	21.026	26.217	32.909
13	19.812	22.362	27.688	34.528
14	21.064	23.685	29.141	36.123
15	22.307	24.996	30.578	37.697
16	23.542	26.296	32.000	39.252
17	24.769	27.587	33.409	40.790
18	25.989	28.869	34.805	42.312
19	27.204	30.144	36.191	43.820
20	28.412	31.410	37.566	45.315
21	29.615	32.671	38.932	46.797
22	30.813	33.924	40.289	48.268
23	32.007	35.172	41.638	49.728
24	33.196	36.415	42.980	51.179
25	34.382	37.652	44.314	52.620
26	35.563	38.885	45.642	54.052
27	36.741	40.113	46.963	55.476
28	37.916	41.337	48.278	56.893
29	39.087	42.557	49.588	58.302
30	40.256	43.773	50.892	59.703
32	42.585	46.194	53.486	62.487
34	44.903	48.602	56.061	65.247
36	47.212	50.999	58.619	67.985
38	49.513	53.384	61.162	70.703
40	51.805	55.759	63.691	73.402
42	54.090	58.124	66.206	76.084
44	56.369	60.481	68.710	78.750
46	58.641	62.830	71.201	81.400
48	60.907	65.171	73.683	84.037
50	63.167	67.505	76.154	86.661

Table A.6 is taken from Table IV of Fisher and Yates: *Statistical Tables for Biological, Agricultural and Medical Research*, published by Longman Group Ltd., London (previously published by Oliver and Boyd, Edinburgh), and by permission of the authors and publishers.

Glossary

The numbers in parentheses following each entry indicate the chapter in which the term is introduced or most completely discussed.

A-B design   A single-subject design in which baseline measurements are repeatedly made until stability is presumably established, treatment is introduced, and an appropriate number of measurements are made during treatment. **(10)**

A-B-A design   A single-subject design in which baseline measurements are repeatedly made until stability is presumably established, treatment is introduced, and an appropriate number of measurements are made, and the treatment phase is followed by a second baseline phase. **(10)**

A-B-A-B design   A single-subject design in which baseline measurements are repeatedly made until stability is presumably established, treatment is introduced, and an appropriate number of measurements are made, and the treatment phase is followed by a second baseline phase, which is followed by a second treatment phase. **(10)**

abstract   A summary of a study, which appears at the beginning of the report and describes the most important aspects of the study, including major results and conclusions. **(14)**

accessible population   The population from which the researcher can realistically select subjects. **(4)**

achievement test   An instrument that measures the current status of individuals with respect to proficiency in given areas of knowledge or skill. **(5)**

action research   A form of applied research commonly used in business to find immediate solutions to local problems. **(1)**

additive designs   Variations of the A-B design that involve the addition of another phase or phases in which the experimental treatment is supplemented with another treatment. **(10)**

alpha   (α) The level of probability preselected by the researcher to indicate significance. **(12)**

alternating-treatments design   A variation of a multiple-baseline design that involves the relatively rapid alternation of treatments for a single subject. **(10)**

analysis of covariance   A statistical method for equating groups on one or more variables and for increasing the power of a statistical test; adjusts scores on a dependent variable for initial differences on some variable such as pretest performance or experience. **(12)**

applied research   Research conducted for the purpose of applying, or testing, theory and evaluating its usefulness in solving problems. **(1)**

aptitude test   A measure of potential used to predict how well someone is likely to perform in a future situation. **(5)**

assumption   Any important "fact" presumed to be true but not actually verified; assumptions should be described in the procedures section of a research plan or report. **(14)**

attenuation   The principle that correlation coefficients tend to be lowered because less-than-perfectly reliable measures are used. **(8)**

basic research   Research conducted for the purpose of theory development or refinement. **(1)**

business research   The formal, systematic application of the scientific method to the study of problems in business and management. **(1)**

case study   An in-depth investigation of an individual, group, or company to determine the factors, and relationship among the factors, that have resulted in the current behavior or status of the subject of the study. **(7)**

causal-comparative research   Research that attempts to determine the cause, or reason, for existing differences in the behavior or status of groups of individuals; also referred to as *ex post facto research*. **(9)**

CD-ROM (compact disk, read-only memory)   A method of storing information such as the data bases used in literature reviews. **(2)**

census survey   Descriptive research that attempts to acquire data from each and every member of the population. **(7)**

changing-criterion design   A variation of the A-B-A design in which the baseline phase is followed by successive treatment phases, each of which has a more stringent criterion for the level of acceptable behavior. **(10)**

chi square   (χ^2) A nonparametric test of significance appropriate when the data are in the form of frequency counts; it compares proportions actually observed in a study with proportions expected to see if they are significantly different. **(12)**

clinical replication   The development and application of a treatment package, composed of two or more interventions that have been found to be effective individually, originally designed for persons with complex behavior disorders. **(10)**

cluster sampling   Sampling in which intact groups, not individuals, are randomly selected. **(4)**

common variance   The variation in one variable that is attributable to its tendency to vary with another variable. **(11)**

concurrent validity   The degree to which the scores on one test are related to the scores on another, already established test administered at the same time, or to some other valid criterion available at the same time. **(5)**

construct validity   The degree to which a test measures an intended hypothetical construct or nonobservable trait that explains behavior. **(5)**

contamination   The situation that exists when the researcher's familiarity with the subjects affects the outcome of the study. **(10)**

content analysis   The systematic, quantitative description of the composition of the object of the study. **(7)**

content validity   The degree to which a test measures an intended content area; it is determined by expert judgment and requires both item validity and sampling validity. **(5)**

control   Efforts on the part of the researcher to remove the influence of any variable other than the independent variable that might affect performance on a dependent variable. **(10)**

control group   The group in a research study that either receives a different treatment from the one the experimental group receives or is treated as usual. **(10)**

control variable   A nonmanipulated variable, usually a physical or mental characteristic of the subjects (such as sex). **(10)**

convenience sampling   The use of existing groups in research. **(4)**

correlational research   Research that involves collecting data in order to determine whether, and to what degree, a relationship exists between two or more quantifiable variables. **(8)**

correlation coefficient   A decimal number between .00 and ± 1.00 that indicates the degree to which two variables are related. **(8)**

counterbalanced design   A quasi-experimental design in which all groups receive all treatments, with each group receiving the treatments in a different order, the number of groups equaling the number of treatments, and all groups being posttested after each treatment. **(10)**

criterion   In a prediction study, the variable that is predicted. **(8)**

criterion-related validity   Validity that is determined by relating performance on a test to performance on another criterion; includes concurrent and predictive validity. **(5)**

cross-validation   Validation of a prediction equation with at least one group other than the group on which it was based; variables that are no longer found to be related to the criterion measure are removed from the equation. **(8)**

curvilinear relationship   A relationship in which increase in one variable is associated with a corresponding increase in another variable to a point at which further increase in the first variable is associated with a corresponding decrease in the other variable (or vice versa). **(8)**

deductive hypothesis   A hypothesis derived from theory that proves evidence supporting, expanding, or contradicting the theory. **(2)**

dependent variable   The change or difference in behavior that occurs as a result of the independent variable; also referred to as the criterion variable, the effect, the outcome, or the posttest. **(1)**

descriptive research   Research, normally conducted through survey or observation, that attempts to describe an existing condition. **(7)**

descriptive statistics   Data-analysis techniques enabling the researcher to describe meaningfully many scores with a small number of indices. **(11)**

developmental studies   Studies concerned with behavior variables that differentiate individuals at different levels of age, experience, or maturation. **(7)**

diagnostic test   A type of achievement test yielding multiple scores for each area of achievement measured that facilitates identification of specific areas of deficiency. **(5)**

differential selection of subjects   The fact that groups may be different before a study even begins, and this initial difference may at least partially account for posttest differences. **(10)**

direct replication   The replication of a study by the same investigator, with the same subjects or with different subjects, in a specific setting. **(10)**

ecological validity   The degree to which results can be generalized to environments outside the experimental setting. **(14)**

environmental variable   A variable in the setting in which a study is conducted that might cause unwanted differences between groups (e.g., training materials). **(10)**

equivalent forms   Two tests identical in every way except for the actual items included. **(5)**

equivalent-forms reliability   Indication of score variation that occurs from form to form of a test; also referred to as alternate-forms reliability. **(5)**

ethnography   The collection of data on many variables using a variety of methods over an extended period of time in a naturalistic setting. **(7)**

evaluation research   The systematic process of collecting and analyzing data in order to make decisions regarding the relative worth of two or more alternative actions. **(1)**

experimental group   The group in a research study that typically receives a new treatment, a treatment under investigation. **(10)**

experimental research   Research in which at least one independent variable is manipulated, other relevant variables are controlled, and the effect on one or more dependent variables is observed. **(10)**

experimenter bias   A situation in which the researcher's expectations concerning the outcomes of the study actually contribute to producing various outcomes. **(10)**

ex post facto research   See causal-comparative research. **(9)**

external criticism   The scientific analysis of data to determine their authenticity. **(6)**

external validity   The degree to which results are generalizable, or applicable, to groups and environments outside the experimental setting. **(14)**

F **ratio**   The results of an analysis of variance. **(12)**

factorial analysis of variance   The appropriate statistical analysis if a study is based on a factorial design and investigates two or more independent variables and the interactions between them; yields a separate *F* ratio for each independent variable and one for each interaction. **(12)**

factorial design   An experimental design that involves two or more independent variables (at least one of which is manipulated) in order to study the effects of the variables individually and in interaction with each other. **(10)**

follow-up study   A study conducted to determine the status of a group of interest after some period of time. **(7)**

Gantt chart   A method of diagramming a project useful in planning research. **(3)**

generosity error   The tendency to give an individual the benefit of the doubt whenever there is insufficient knowledge to make an objective judgment. **(10)**

halo effect   The phenomenon whereby initial impressions concerning an individual (positive or negative) affect subsequent measurements. **(10)**

Hawthorne effect   A type of reactive arrangement resulting from the subjects' knowledge that they are involved in an experiment or their feeling that they are in some way receiving "special" attention. **(10)**

historical research   The systematic collection and objective evaluation of data related to past occurrences in order to test hypotheses concerning causes, effects, or trends of those events that may help to explain present events and anticipate future events. **(6)**

history   Any event that is not part of the experimental treatment but that may affect performance on the dependent variable. **(10)**

Honeymoon effect   See novelty effect. **(10)**

hypothesis   A tentative, reasonable, testable explanation for the occurrence of certain behaviors, phenomena, or events. **(2)**

independent variable An activity or characteristic believed to make a difference with respect to some behavior; also referred to as the experimental variable, the cause, and the treatment. **(2)**

inductive hypothesis A generalization based on observation. **(2)**

inferential statistics Data-analysis techniques for determining how likely it is that results based on a sample or samples are the same results that would have been obtained for an entire population. **(12)**

instrumentation Unreliability in measuring instruments that may result in invalid assessment of subjects' performance. **(10)**

interaction The situation in which different values of the independent variable are differentially effective depending upon the level of the control variable. **(10)**

interjudge reliability The consistency of two (or more) independent scorers, raters, or observers. **(5)**

internal criticism The scientific analysis of data to determine their accuracy that takes into consideration the knowledge and competence of the author, the time delay between the occurrence and recording of events, biased motives of the author, and consistency of data. **(6)**

internal validity The degree to which observed differences on the dependent variable are a direct result of manipulation of the independent variable, not some other variable. **(10)**

interval scale A measurement scale that classifies and ranks subjects, is based upon predetermined equal intervals, but does not have a true zero point. **(5)**

intervening variable A variable that intervenes between, or alters the relationship between, an independent variable and a dependent variable, which cannot be directly observed or controlled (e.g., anxiety) but which can be controlled for. **(10)**

intrajudge reliability The consistency of the scoring, rating, or observing of an individual. **(5)**

item validity The degree to which test items represent measurement in the intended content area. **(5)**

John Henry effect The phenomenon whereby if for any reason members of a control group feel threatened or challenged by being in competition with an experimental group, they may outdo themselves and perform way beyond what would normally be expected. **(10)**

judgment sampling Selecting a sample believed to be representative of a given population based on the researcher's expert judgment, also referred to as purposive sampling. **(4)**

Likert scale An instrument that asks an individual to respond to a series of statements indicating, for example, whether she or he strongly agrees (SA), agrees (A), is undecided (U), disagrees (D), or strongly disagrees (SD), with each statement. **(5)**

limitation An aspect of a study that the researcher knows may negatively affect the results or generalizability of the results but over which he or she has no control. **(14)**

linear relationship The situation in which an increase (or decrease) in one variable is associated with a corresponding increase (or decrease) in another variable. **(8)**

logical validity Validity that is determined primarily through judgment; includes content validity. **(5)**

matching A technique for equating groups on one or more variables, resulting in each member of one group having a direct counterpart in another group. **(9)**

mean ($\bar{X}$)   The arithmetic average of a set of scores. **(11)**

measures of central tendency   Indices, such as mode, median, and mean, representing the average or typical score attained by a group of subjects. **(11)**

median   That point in distribution above and below which are 50% of the scores. **(11)**

mode   The score that is attained by more subjects in a group than any other scores. **(11)**

mortality   The fact that subjects who drop out of a study may share a characteristic such that their absence has a significant effect on the results of the study. **(10)**

multiple-baseline design   A single-subject design in which baseline data are collected on several behaviors for one subject or one behavior for several subjects and treatment is applied systematically over a period of time to each behavior (or each subject) one at a time until all behaviors (or subjects) are under treatment. **(10)**

multiple comparisons   Procedures used following application of analysis of variance to determine which means are significantly different from which other means. **(12)**

multiple-regression equations   A prediction equation using two or more variables that individually predict a criterion to make a more accurate prediction. **(12)**

multiple time-series design   A variation of the time-series design that involves the addition of a control group to the basic design. **(10)**

multiple-treatment interference   The carryover effects from an earlier treatment that make it difficult to assess the effectiveness of a later treatment. **(10)**

naturalistic observation   Observation in which the observer purposely controls or manipulates nothing and in fact works very hard at not affecting the observed situation in any way. **(7)**

negatively skewed distribution   A distribution in which there are more extreme scores at the lower end than at the upper, or higher, end. **(11)**

nominal scale   The lowest level of measurement that classifies persons or objects into two or more categories; a person can be in only one category, and members of a category have a common set of characteristics. **(5)**

nonequivalent control-group design   A quasi-experimental design involving at least two groups, both of which are pretested; one group receives the experimental treatment, and both groups are posttested. **(10)**

nonparametric test   A test of significance, such as χ^2, appropriate when the data represent an ordinal or nominal scale, when a parametric assumption has been greatly violated, or when the nature of the distribution is not known. **(12)**

nonparticipant observation   Observation in which the observer is not directly involved in the situation to be observed; i.e., the observer does not intentionally have an interest in or affect the object of the observation. **(7)**

nonprobability sampling   A technique in which it is not possible to specify the probabilty, or chance, that each member of a population has of being selected for the sample; a major source of bias, including convenience, judgment, and quota sampling. **(4)**

novelty effect   A type of reactive arrangement resulting from increased interest, motivation, or participation on the part of subjects simply because they are doing something different. **(10)**

null hypothesis   Statement that there is no relationship (or difference) between variables and that any relationship found will be a chance relationship, the result of sampling error, not a true one. **(2)**

observation research   Descriptive research in which the desired data are obtained not by asking individuals for it but through such means as direct observation. **(7)**

observee bias   The phenomenon whereby persons being observed behave atypically simply because they are being observed, thus producing invalid observations. **(7)**

observer bias   The phenomenon whereby an observer does not observe objectively and accurately, thus producing invalid observations. **(7)**

one-group pretest-posttest design   A preexperimental design involving one group that is pretested, exposed to a treatment, and posttested. **(10)**

one-shot case study   A preexperimental design involving one group that is exposed to a treatment and then posttested. **(10)**

operational definition   A definition of a concept in terms of processes , or operations. **(2)**

ordinal scale   A measurement scale that classifies subjects and ranks them in terms of the degree to which they possess a characteristic of interest. **(5)**

organismic variable   A characteristic of a subject, or organisim (e.g., sex), that cannot be directly controlled but that can be controlled for. **(10)**

parameter   A numerical index describing the behavior of a population. **(11)**

parametric test   A test of significance, such as t test or ANOVA, appropriate when the data represent an interval scale or ratio scale of measurement and other assumptions have been met. **(12)**

participant observation   Observation in which the observer actually becomes a part of, a participant in, the situation to be observed. **(7)**

Pearson _r_   A measure of correlation appropriate when the data represent either interval scales or ratio scales; takes into account each and every score and produces a coefficient between .00 and $\pm$ 1.00. **(12)**

percentile rank   A measure of relative position indicating the percentage of scores that fall at or below a given score. **(11)**

PERT/CPM (Program Evaluation and Review Technique/Critical Path Methodology)   An elaborate planning and control device that specifies events and relationships in planning a large study. **(3)**

pilot study   A small-scale study conducted prior to the conducting of the actual study; the entire study is conducted, every procedure is followed, and the resulting data are analyzed—all according to the research plan. **(3)**

placebo effect   The discovery in medical research that any "medication" could make subjects feel better, even sugar and water. **(10)**

population   The group to which the researcher would like the results of a study to be generalizable. **(4)**

positively skewed distribution   A distribution in which there are more extreme scores at the upper, or higher, end than at the lower end. **(11)**

posttest-only control-group design   A true experimental design involving at least two randomly formed groups; one group receives a new or unusual treatment, and both groups are posttested. **(10)**

prediction study   An attempt to determine which of a number of variables are most highly related to a criterion variable, a complex variable to be predicted. **(8)**

predictive validity   The degree to which a test is able to predict how well an individual will do in a future situation. **(5)**

predictor   In a prediction study, the variable upon which the prediction is based. **(8)**

pretest-posttest control-group design   A true experimental design that involves at least two randomly formed groups; both groups are pretested, one group receives a new or unusual treatment, and both groups are posttested. **(10)**

pretest-treatment interaction   The fact that subjects may respond or react differently to a treatment because they have been pretested. **(10)**

primary source   Firsthand information such as the testimony of an eyewitness, an original document, a relic, or a description of a study written by the person who conducted it. **(6)**

problem statement   A statement that indicates the variables of interest to the researcher and the specific relationship between those variables that is to be, or was, investigated. **(2)**

quartile deviation   One half the difference between the upper quartile (the 75th percentile) and the lower quartile (the 25th percentile) in a distribution. **(11)**

questionnaire   A written methodology for collecting information and/or opinions regarding the current state of a population. **(7)**

quota sampling   A type of nonprobability sampling in which the interviewers are given exact numbers, or quotas, of persons of varying characteristics who are to be interviewed; a source of bias in sampling. **(4)**

random sampling   The process of selecting a sample in such a way that all individuals in the defined population have an equal and independent chance of being selected for the sample. **(4)**

range   The difference between the highest and lowest score in a distribution. **(11)**

rationale-equivalence reliability   An estimate of internal consistency based on a determination of how all items on a test relate to all other items and to the total test. **(5)**

ratio scale   The highest level of measurement that classifies subjects, ranks subjects, is based upon predetermined equal intervals, and has a true zero point. **(5)**

reactive arrangements   Threats to the external validity of a study associated with the way in which a study is conducted and the feelings and attitudes of the subjects involved. **(10)**

relationship study   An attempt to gain insight into the variables, or factors, that are related to a complex variable such as achievement, leadership, productivity, or motivation. **(8)**

reliability   The degree to which a test consistently measures whatever it measures. **(5)**

replication   The fact that when a study is done again, the second study may be a repetition of the original study, using different subjects, or it may represent an alternative approach to testing the same hypothesis. **(10)**

research   The formal, systematic application of the scientific method to the study of problems. **(1)**

research and development (R & D)   A study that is directed at the development of effective products that can be used in the marketplace; a type of applied research. **(1)**

research hypothesis   A statement of the expected relationship (or difference) between two variables. **(2)**

research plan   A detailed description of a proposed study designed to investigate a given problem. **(3)**

response set   The tendency of an observer to rate the majority of observees the same regardless of the observees' actual behavior. **(5)**

review of literature   The systematic identification, location, and analysis of documents containing information related to a research problem. **(2)**

sample   A number of individuals selected from a population for a study, preferably in such a way that they represent the larger group from which they were selected. **(4)**

sample survey   Research in which information about a population is inferred based on the responses of a sample selected from that population. **(7)**

sampling   The process of selecting a number of individuals (a sample) from a population, preferably in such a way that the individuals represent the larger group from which they were selected. **(4)**

sampling bias   Systematic sampling error; three major sources of sampling bias are nonprobability sampling, the use of volunteers, and the use of available groups. **(4)**

sampling error   Expected, chance variation in variables that occurs when a sample is selected from a population. **(4)**

sampling validity   The degree to which a test samples the total intended content area. **(5)**

Scheffé test   A conservative multiple-comparison technique appropriate for making any and all possible comparisons involving a set of means. **(12)**

secondary source   Secondhand information, such as a brief description of a study written by someone other than the person who conducted it. **(6)**

selection-maturation interaction   The fact that if already formed groups are used in a study, one group may profit more (or less) from treatment or have an initial advantage (or disadvantage) because of maturation factors; selection may also interact with factors such as history and testing. **(10)**

selection-treatment interaction   The fact that if nonrepresentative groups are used in a study the results of the study may hold only for the groups involved and may not be representative of the treatment effect in the population. **(10)**

self-report research   Descriptive research in which information is solicited from individuals using, for example, questionnaires or interviews. **(7)**

semantic-differential scale   An instrument that asks an individual to give a quantitative rating to the subject of an attitude scale on a number of bipolar adjectives such as good-bad, friendly-unfriendly, positive-negative. **(5)**

shrinkage   The tendency of a prediction equation to become less accurate when used with a different group, a group other than the one on which the equation was originally formulated. **(8)**

simple analysis of variance (ANOVA)   A parametric test of significance used to determine whether there is a significant difference between or among two or more means at a selected probability level. **(12)**

simulation observation   Observation in which the resarcher creates the situation to be observed and tells the subjects what activities they are to engage in, for example, role playing; often used in assessment centers. **(7)**

simultaneous replication   Replication done on a number of subjects with the same problem, at the same location, at the same time. **(10)**

single-subject experimental designs   Designs applied when the sample size is one; used to study the behavior change that an individual exhibits as a result of some intervention, or treatment. **(10)**

single-variable design   A class of experimental designs involving only one independent variable (which is manipulated). **(10)**

single variable rule   An important principle of single-subject research that states that only one variable should be manipulated at a time. **(10)**

skewed distribution   A nonsymmetrical distribution in which there are more extreme scores at one end of the distribution than the other. **(11)**

sociometric study   A study that assesses and analyzes the interpersonal relationships within a group of individuals. **(7)**

Solomon four-group design   A true experimental design that involves random assignment of subjects to one of four groups; two groups are pretested, two are not; one of the pretested groups and one of the unpretested groups receive the experimental treatment, and all four groups are posttested. **(10)**

Spearman-Brown correction formula   A method of adjusting the results of a split-half reliability procedure to approximate other methods of estimating reliability of an instrument. **(11)**

Spearman rho   A measure of correlation appropriate when the data for at least one of the variables are expressed as ranks; it produces a coefficient between .00 and ± 1.00. **(11)**

specificity of variables   The fact that a given study is conducted with a specific kind of subject, using specific measuring instruments, at a specific time, under a specific set of circumstances—factors that affect the generalizability of the results. **(14)**

split-half reliability   A type of reliability that is based on the internal consistency of a test and is estimated by dividing a test into two equivalent halves and correlating the scores on the two halves. **(5)**

standard deviation   The most stable measure of variability, which takes into account each and every score in a distribution. **(11)**

standard error of the mean   The standard deviation of sample means, which indicates by how much the sample means can be expected to differ if other samples from the same population are used. **(12)**

standard error of measurement   An estimate of how often one can expect errors of a given size in an individual's test score. **(5)**

static group comparison   A preexperimental design that involves at least two nonrandomly formed groups; one receives a new or unusual treatment, and both are posttested. **(10)**

statistic   A numerical index describing the behavior of a sample or samples. **(11)**

statistical regression   The tendency of subjects who score highest on a pretest to score lower on a posttest, and of subjects who score lowest on a pretest to score higher on a posttest. **(10)**

statistical significance   The conclusion that results are unlikely to have occurred by chance; the observed relationship or difference is probably a real one. **(12)**

stratified random sampling   The process of selecting a sample in such a way that identified subgroups in the population are represented in the sample in the same proportion that they exist in the population or in equal proportion. **(4)**

structured item   A question and a list of alternative responses from which the responder selects; also referred to as a closed-form item. **(5)**

subject variable   A variable on which subjects in different groups in a study might differ, e.g., intelligence. **(4)**

survey   An attempt to collect data from members of a population in order to determine the current status of that population with respect to one or more variables. **(7)**

systematic replication   Replication that follows direct replication and that involves different investigators, behaviors, or settings. **(10)**

systematic sampling   Sampling in which individuals are selected from a list by taking every Kth name, where K equals the number of individuals on the list divided by the number of subjects desired for the sample. **(4)**

***t* test for independent samples**   A parametric test of significance used to determine whether there is a significant difference between the means of two independent samples at a selected probability level. **(12)**

***t* test for nonindependent samples**   A parametric test of significance used to determine whether there is a significant difference between the means of two matched, or nonindependent, samples at a selected probability level. **(12)**

target population   The population to which the researcher would ideally like to generalize results. **(4)**

test   A means of measuring the knowledge, skill, feelings, intelligence, or aptitude of an individual or group. **(5)**

testing   A threat to experimental validity that refers to improved scores on a posttest that are a result of subjects having taken a pretest. **(10)**

test objectivity   A situation in which an individual's score is the same, or essentially the same, regardless of who is doing the scoring. **(5)**

test-retest reliability   The degree to which scores on a test are consistent, or stable, over time. **(5)**

test of significance   A statistical test used to determine whether or not there is a significant difference between or among two or more means at a selected probability level. **(12)**

time-series design   A quasi-experimental design involving one group that is repeatedly pretested, exposed to an experimental treatment, and repeatedly posttested. **(10)**

Type I error   The rejection by the researcher of a null hypothesis that is actually true. **(12)**

Type II error   The failure of a researcher to reject a null hypothesis that is really false. **(12)**

unobtrusive measures   Inanimate objects (such as personnel files) that can be observed in order to obtain desired information. **(5)**

unstructured item   A question giving the responder complete freedom of response. **(5)**

validity   The degree to which a test measures what it is intended to measure; a test is valid for a particular purpose and for a particular group. **(5)**

variable   A concept that can assume any one of a range of values, e.g., aptitude, experience, speed. **(2)**

Suggested Responses to Self-Tests

PRACTICE SELF-TEST FOR CHAPTER 1

CONSEQUENCES OF QUALITY CIRCLES IN AN INDUSTRIAL SETTING: A LONGITUDINAL ASSESSMENT

Self-Test for Project 1

The Problem

The purpose of this study was to determine whether quality circles result in improved attitudes and behaviors for individual employees and whether they result in improved financial performance for the organization as a whole. (If you listed the hypotheses, that's OK.)

The Procedures

Experimental subjects were 73 employees of a moderate-size electronics company who volunteered to participate. The control group was a matched-pairs group from a similar plant. After a 2-day training period, the experimental group was organized into eight quality circles meeting once a week for 1 to 2 hours over a period of 36 months. Affective and behavioral data were measured before the initiation of the program, at 6 months, 18 months, and 36 months. Managerial assessment was conducted at the same times using a three-item scale. Limited interviews were conducted at 18 months and 48 months.

The Method of Analysis

For each instrument, differences were compared using a MANOVA; Duncan's multiple-range tests were also used. (At this point, you aren't expected to understand what either of these procedures indicates.)

The Major Conclusion(s)

In this organization, quality circles were successful from the standpoints of both the participants and the organization for around 2 years but then began to decline.

Method and Reasons

The method was experimental because a cause-effect relationship was investigated. The independent variable, quality circles, was manipulated (the researcher determined which employees were included in the experimental and control groups). The effect, on employee job satisfaction, organizational commitment, and performance were measured; management assessment of the impact on the bottom line was measured.

PRACTICE SELF-TEST FOR CHAPTER 6

MANAGEMENT TURNOVER THROUGH DEATHS OF KEY EXECUTIVES: EFFECTS ON INVESTOR WEALTH

The Problem

The purpose of this study was to examine the reaction of the securities' market to the deaths of certain key executives.

The Procedures

Stock performances of companies who had the death of their CEO reported in the *Wall Street Journal* were compared with predicted performance for 30 days following the death.

The Method of Analysis

Regression and *t* tests using standard-event methodology were used.

The Major Conclusion(s)

Market reaction to announced deaths of corporate chairmen was significantly positive (perhaps owing to the advanced age of the individuals involved); reactions to deaths of CEOs were not statistically significant, although sudden deaths of CEOs produced significant negative reactions, and deaths of CEOs with high name recognition appeared to produce somewhat negative reactions.

Reasons for Classification as Historical Research

The study is classified as historical research because it involves events occurring during the 15-year period from 1967 to 1981. The use of statistical analysis, however, would suggest that this study might also be classified as a correlational study, whereas its name might imply that the authors intended it as a causal-comparative study.

Method-Specific Evaluation Criteria

1. Were the sources of data related to the problem mostly primary or mostly secondary? **Mostly secondary.**
2. Was each piece of data subjected to external criticism? **Yes.**
3. Was each piece of data subjected to internal criticism? **Yes.**

PRACTICE SELF-TEST FOR CHAPTER 7

PSYCHOLOGICAL CONDITIONS OF PERSONAL ENGAGEMENT AND DISENGAGEMENT AT WORK

The Problem

The purpose of the study was to develop a theoretical framework for understanding "self-in-role" processes, i.e., the level of psychological presence, physically, cognitively, and emotionally, at specific times.

The Procedures

As participant-observer, the researcher studied 16 camp counselors using observation, document analysis, and in-depth interviews. As an observer, the researcher studied 16 employees of an architectural firm using in-depth interviews.

The Method of Analysis

Descriptive statistics (means and standard deviations) based on researcher's ratings, subsequently correlated with a blind rater's evaluation.

The Major Conclusion(s)

Three major factors—meaningfulness (including task and role characteristics and work interactions), safety (including interpersonal relationships, group and intergroup dynamics, management style and process, and organizational norms), and availability (including depletion of physical and emotional energy, individual insecurity, and outside lives)—emerged as conditions of engagement.

Reasons for Classification as Descriptive Research

The study used observation and interview techniques to collect data; no hypothesis testing was conducted. A theory suitable as a basis for future research was generated.

Method-Specific Evaluation Criteria

Select the appropriate methodology (questionnaire, interview, or observation) listed subsequently and use the study to answer the questions that apply to the methodology.
Interview Studies
E.S.B. and Associates interviews only:
  1. Does each item in the interview guide relate to a specific objective of the study? **Yes.**
  2. When necessary, is a point of reference given in the guide for interview items? **Yes.**
  3. Are leading questions avoided in the interview guide? **Yes.**
  4. Does the interview guide indicate the type and amount of prompting and probing that was permitted? **NA, researcher did interviews.**
  5. Are the qualifications and special training of the interviewers described? **NA.**
  6. Is the method that was used to record responses described? **Yes.**
  7. Did the researcher use the most reliable, unbiased method of recording responses that could have been used? **Yes.**
  8. Were the interview procedures pretested? **Not clear.**

9. Are pilot study procedures and results described? **NA, unless Camp Caribe is considered as a pilot study.**
10. Did the researcher specify how the responses to semistructured and unstructured items were quantified and analyzed? **Yes.**

PRACTICE SELF-TEST FOR CHAPTER 8

CORPORATE SOCIAL RESPONSIBILITY AND FIRM FINANCIAL PERFORMANCE

The Problem

The purpose of the study was to determine whether there was a relationship between perceptions of a firm's corporate social responsibility and its financial performance.

The Procedures

Using the 1983 *Fortune* rating of firms exhibiting corporate social responsibility and a variaty of measures of financial performance, the researchers looked for relationships.

The Method of Analysis

Pearson r and stepwise regression analysis were used.

The Major Conclusion(s)

Prior financial performance was more closely related to corporate social responsibility than subsequent financial performance on both stock market and accounting-based measures; measures of risk were also closely related.

Reasons for Classification as Correlational Research

The study sought to find relationships; no cause-effect relationships were intended.

Method-Specific Evaluation Criteria

Select the appropriate methodology (relationship studies or prediction studies) listed below and use the study to answer the questions that apply to the methodology.
Relationship Studies **Study was a relationship study.**
1. Were variables carefully selected or was a shotgun approach used? **They were selected.**
2. Is the rationale for variable selection described? **Yes.**
3. Are conclusions and recommendations based on values of correlation coefficients corrected for attenuation or restriction in range? **Not applicable.**
4. Do the conclusions indicate causal relationships between the variables investigated? **No.**
Prediction Studies **Not applicable.**

PRACTICE SELF-TEST FOR CHAPTER 9

PERCEIVED JOB AUTONOMY IN THE MANUFACTURING SECTOR: EFFECTS OF UNIONS, GENDER, AND SUBSTANTIVE COMPLEXITY

The Problem

The problem investigated in this study was whether union membership, gender, and substantive job compexity affect perceptions of job autonomy in the manufacturing sector.

The Procedures

Using data from a national, cross-sectional probability survey, the researchers derived a number of measures that were subjected to statistical analysis to determine possible effects.

The Method of Analysis

Discriminant function analysis was used as to determine controls with regard to group similarities; hierarchical regression analysis was used to determine causal-comparative relationships.

The Major Conclusion(s)

For women, the substantive complexity of their jobs significantly predicted perceived autonomy but, union status did not. For men, the reverse pattern held: Substantive complexity did not predict their perceptions of job autonomy, but unionization did.

Reasons for Classification as Causal-Comparative Research

Although predictions were mentioned, the researchers sought to find cause-effect relationships; as the data had been collected prior to the research study, the researchers were not able to control as in an experimental design.

Method-Specific Evaluation Criteria

Use the questions listed below to evaluate the study with respect to the specific characteristics of a causal-comparative study:
1. Are the characteristics or experiences that differentiate the groups (the independent variable) clearly defined or described? **Yes.**
2. Are critical extraneous variables identified? **Yes.**
3. Were any control procedures applied to equate the groups on extraneous variables? **Yes.**
4. Are causal relationships found discussed with due caution? **Yes.**
5. Are plausible alternative hypotheses discussed? **Yes.**

PRACTICE SELF-TEST FOR CHAPTER 10

CONSEQUENCES OF QUALITY CIRCLES IN AN INDUSTRIAL SETTING: A LONGITUDINAL ASSESSMENT

Method-Specific Review Questions

1. Was an appropriate experimental design selected? **Yes.**
2. Is a rationale for design selection given? **Yes.**
3. Are sources of invalidity associated with the design identified and discussed? **Yes.**
4. Is the method of group formation described? **Yes.**
5. Was the experimental group formed in the same way as the control group? **Yes.**
6. Were existing groups used or were groups randomly formed? **Existing groups.**
7. Were treatments randomly assigned to groups? **No.**
8. Were critical extraneous variables identified? **Yes.**
9. Were any control procedures applied to equate groups on extraneous variables? **Yes.**
10. Is there any evidence to suggest reactive arrangements (for example, the Hawthorne effect)? **No.**

PRACTICE SELF-TEST FOR CHAPTER 15

DEVELOPING STRATEGIC MANAGEMENT GOAL-SETTING SKILLS

Self-Test for Project VI

Code: **Y** = Yes; **N** = No; **NA** = Not Applicable; **?/X** = Can't tell or no judgment

Page numbers for Project VI may be found in the upper left or right corner of the page. Each paragraph in the report is identified with a letter—A, B, C, and so on; additionally, every other line is numbered 1 through 276. For each item on which information is requested, indicate on the answer sheet the location of the item by page, paragraph, and line.

General Evaluation Criteria

Code: **Y** = Yes; **N** = No; **NA** = Not Applicable; **?/X** = Can't tell or no judgment

Problem

__Y__ 1. Is there a statement of the problem?

Page ___2___ , paragraph ___D___ , line(s) ___25–27___ .

__Y__ 2. Is the problem "researchable"; that is, can it be investigated through the collection and analysis of data?

__Y__ 3. Is background information on the problem presented?

Page ___1___ , paragraph ___A—C___ .

__Y__ 4. Is the significance of the problem discussed?

Page ___1___ , paragraph ___C___ , line(s) ___18–24___

Code: **Y** = Yes; **N** = No; **NA** = Not Applicable; **?/X** = Can't tell or no judgment

___**Y**___ 5. Does the problem statement indicate the variables of interest and the specific relationship between those variables that were investigated?

___**N**___ 6. When necessary, are the variables directly or operationally defined?

Review of Related Literature

___**Y**___ 7. Is the review comprehensive?

___**Y**___ 8. Are all the references cited relevant to the problem under investigation?

___**Y**___ 9. Are the sources mostly primary, with only a few or no secondary sources?

___**Y**___ 10. Have the references been critically analyzed and the results of various studies compared and contrasted, i.e., is the review more than a series of abstracts or annotations?

___**Y**___ 11. Is the review well organized? Does it logically flow in such a way that the least-related references to the problem are discussed first and the most-related references are discussed last?

___**Y**___ 12. Does the review conclude with a brief summary of the literature and its implications for the problem investigated?

Page ___**2**___ , paragraph ___**G**___ , line(s) ___**51–55**___ .

___**Y**___ 13. Do the implications discussed form an empirical or theoretical rationale for the hypotheses, either stated or implied, that follow?

Hypotheses

___**N**___ 14. Are specific questions to be answered listed or specific hypotheses to be tested stated?

Note: Because no hypothesis is stated, the answers to questions 15 and 16 are NA. In the absence of a stated hypothesis, the implied hypothesis contained in the problem statement, page 2, paragraph D, lines 25–27, are used throughout the rest of the analysis when reference is made to hypothesis/problem statement.

___**NA**___ 15. Does each hypothesis/problem statement state an expected relationship or difference between two variables? If necessary, are the variables directly or operationally defined?

___**NA**___ 16. Is each hypothesis/problem statement testable?

Method

Subjects

___**Y**___ 17. Are the major characteristics, including size, of the population studied described?

Page ___**4**___ , paragraph ___**Table 1**___ .

___**NA**___ 18. If a sample was selected, is the method of selecting the sample clearly described?

Note: It appears that the entire accessible population of senior business-policy students was used; therefore further references to the sample are NA.

___**NA**___ 19. Is the method of sample selection described one that is likely to result in a representative, unbiased sample?

Code: **Y** = Yes; **N** = No; **NA** = Not Applicable; **?/X** = Can't tell or no judgment

__Y__ 20. Did the researcher avoid the use of volunteers?
Note: Although the researchers did not use volunteers, some issues of generalizability are raised by the awarding of points "to motivate" students, page 175, paragraph P, lines 113–116.

__NA__ 21. Are the size and major characteristics of the sample described?
__Y__ 22. Does the population/sample size meet the suggested guideline for minimum sample size appropriate for the method of research represented?

Instruments

__Y__ 23. Is a rationale given for the selection of instruments or measurements used?
Page __3–4__ , paragraph __N and O__ , line(s) __91–97, 106–112__ .
Note: Paragraph N contains justification for goal-setting in general; the more critical rationale for selection of the measurement methodology is contained in paragraph O.

__Y__ 24. Is each instrument or measurement described in terms of purpose and content?

Page __4__ , paragraph __O__ , line(s) __98–107__ .
__Y__ 25. Are the instruments or measurements appropriate for measuring the intended variables?
__Y__ 26. If an instrument or measurement was developed specifically for the study, are the procedures involved in its development and validation described?

Page __6__ , paragraph __U__ , line(s) __175–184__ .
__?/X__ 27. Is evidence presented that indicates that each instrument or measurement is appropriate for the population/sample under study?
Note: Although evidence is not presented, the measurement methodology is probably appropriate for the student population.

__Y__ 28. Is instrument validity discussed and coefficients given if appropriate?

Page __4__ , paragraph __O__ , line(s) __98–112__ .
__N__ 29. Is reliability discussed in terms of type and size of reliability coefficients?
__NA__ 30. If appropriate, are subtest reliabilities given?
__Y__ 31. If an instrument or measurement was developed specifically for the study, are administration, scoring or tabulating, and interpretation procedures fully described?

Page __6__ , paragraph __U__ , line(s) __159–177__ .
Note: Evidently goals were simply counted; no indication is made as to the quality of the goals generated, although students were given criteria for goals, page 6, paragraph U, lines 165–173.

Design and Procedure

__Y__ 32. Is the design appropriate for testing the hypotheses/problem of the study?
Note: As no specific hypothesis was stated, it would appear that this design was appropriate for studying the problem indicated.

Code: **Y** = Yes; **N** = No; **NA** = Not Applicable; **?/X** = Can't tell or no judgment

__Y__ 33. Are the procedures described in sufficient detail to permit them to be replicated by another researcher?

Page __3–6__ , paragraph __J–U__ , line(s) __71–183__ .

__NA__ 34. If a pilot study was conducted, are its execution and results described as well as its impact on the subsequent study?

__Y__ 35. Are control procedures described?

Page __5–6, 8–9__ , paragraph __Q, U, Y–AA__ , line(s) __117–128, 175–184, 219–252__ .

__N__ 36. Did the researcher discuss or account for any potentially confounding variables that he or she was unable to control?

Results

__N__ 37. Are appropriate descriptive statistics presented?

Note: Measure of central tendency, the mean, is given on page 187, Table 2; no measure of variability is stated. An interesting consideration, however, is whether the data are nominal or interval. The authors have evidently concluded that the data are interval, but frequency counts are usually treated as nominal data, in which case means are an inappropriate measure of central tendency.

__N__ 38. Was the alpha level, α, at which the results of the tests of significance were evaluated specified in advance of the data analysis?

__N__ 39. If parametric tests were used, is there evidence that the researcher avoided violating the required assumptions for parametric tests?

Note: Again, it is not clear that the data used in this study are interval. Additionally, it is not clear whether students represent a random sample or whether they were randomly assigned to groups.

__N__ 40. Are the tests of significance described appropriate, given the hypothesis/problem and design of the study?

Note: If the data are nominal, chi square rather than ANOVA would be the appropriate test. Another question is the use of gain scores as the basis for analysis; the researchers address the question, page 187, paragraph V, lines 188–197; in our judgment use of gain scores is inappropriate.

__NA__ 41. Was every hypothesis tested?

__?/X__ 42. Are the tests of significance interpreted using the appropriate degrees of freedom?

Note: As the test of significance is in question, it is unreasonable for the student to evaluate whether the degree of freedom used is appropriate.

__Y__ 43. Are the results clearly presented?

__N__ 44. Are the tables and figures (if any) well organized and easy to understand?

Note: Use of multiple tables would have added clarity to the presentation.

__Y__ 45. Are the data in each table and figure referred to in the text?

Page __3, 7–8__ , paragraph __L, V, W,__ , line(s) __87, 185, 200__ .

Code: **Y** = Yes; **N** = No; **NA** = Not Applicable; **?/X** = Can't tell or no judgment

Discussion (Conclusions and Recommendations)

__Y__46. Is each result discussed in terms of the original hypothesis/problem to which it relates?

      Page _____7_____ , paragraph _____V_____ , line(s) __185–197__ .

Note: The rest of paragraph V refers to improvement, which is not part of the original problem statement.

__N__ 47. Is each result discussed in terms of its agreement or disagreement with previous results obtained by other researchers in other studies?

__?/X__ 48. Are generalizations that are made warranted by the results?

Note: Conclusion 2 appears to be too broad.

__Y__49. Are the possible effects of uncontrolled variables on the results discussed?

      Page _____8_____ , paragraph _____Z_____ .

__Y__50. Are theoretical and practical implications of the findings discussed?

      Page _____9_____ , paragraph _____CC_____ , line(s) __260–270__ .

__Y__51. Are recommendations for future action made?

      Page _____9_____ , paragraph _____CC_____ , line(s) __260–270__ .

__?/X__ 52. Are the suggestions for future action based on practical significance or on statistical significance only; i.e., has the author avoided confusing practical and statistical significance?

Note: Although the raw data appear promising, the statistics used present a problem as indicated previously.

__Y__53. Are recommendations for future research made?

      Page _____9_____ , paragraph _____DD_____ , line(s) __271–276__ .

Abstract or Summary

Note: As there is no abstract or summary, the answer to questions 54 through 58 is NA.

__NA__54. Is the problem stated?

__NA__55. Are the number and type of subjects and instruments or measurements described?

__NA__56. Is the design used identified?

__NA__57. Are the procedures described?

__NA__58. Are the major results and conclusions stated?

Method-Specific Evaluation Criteria

59. Identify the experimental design used in this study.

                            Nonequivalent Control Group

Note: Although the design stated suggests pretest/posttest control-group design, in the absence of a clear statement regarding random assignment of subjects to groups, we must conclude that the design was quasi-experimental rather than a clear experimental design.

Code: **Y** = Yes; **N** = No; **NA** = Not Applicable; **?/X** = Can't tell or no judgment

60. Diagram the experimental design used in this study:

$$O \qquad X_1 \qquad O$$
$$O \qquad X_2 \qquad O$$

Where **O** = observation
X_1 = experimental treatment, simulation
X_2 = control group, case study

See previous note.

__Y___61. Was an appropriate experimental design selected?

Note: Although we would have preferred a clear experimental design, given the restrictions imposed by a real situation, this design is appropriate.

__Y___62. Is a rationale for design selection given?

Page ____2, 3____ , paragraph ____H, M___ .

__N___63. Are sources of invalidity associated with the design identified and discussed?

__N___64. Is the method of group formation described?

__Y___65. Was the experimental group formed in the same way as the control group?

__N___66. Were groups randomly formed and the use of existing groups avoided?

Note: Each of the answers just given is based on the information provided in the report; if students were in actuality randomly assigned to groups, the answers might be different.

__?/X__67. Were treatments randomly assigned to groups?

Note: Again, the answer is not clear from the research report.

__Y___68. Were critical extraneous variables identified?

Page ____5____ . paragraph ____Q___ .

__Y___69. Were any control procedures applied to equate groups on extraneous variables?

Note: Table 1 indicates a variety of tests to establish equivalence. Table 2, however, uses analysis of variance to control for initial differences; as discussed previously, this method of analysis may be inappropriate for the type of data collected.

__Y___70. Is there any evidence to suggest the researcher was able to avoid reactive arrangements (for example, the Hawthorne effect)?

Page ____5____ , paragraph ____Q___ .

Note: The major questions regarding this study focus on whether or not the groups were randomly assigned. If they were, then many of these answers would be different. Additionally, the type of data collected represents a problem with regard to the selection of the tests of significance.

Author Index

Subject Index